CONFLICT OF LAWS
SECOND EDITION

Other Books in the *Essentials of Canadian Law* Series

- International Trade Law
- Family Law
- Copyright Law
- The Law of Sentencing
- Administrative Law
- Securities Law
- Computer Law 2/e
- International Human Rights Law
- Franchise Law
- Legal Ethics and Professional Responsibility 2/e
- Refugee Law
- National Security Law: Canadian Practice in International Perspective
- Public International Law 2/e
- Individual Employment Law 2/e
- The Law of Partnerships and Corporations 3/e
- Civil Litigation
- Religious Institutions and the Law in Canada 3/e
- Detention and Arrest
- Canadian Telecommunications Law
- Intellectual Property Law 2/e
- Animals and the Law
- Income Tax Law 2/e
- Fundamental Justice
- Mergers, Acquisitions, and Other Changes of Corporate Control 2/e
- Personal Property Security Law 2/e
- The Law of Contracts 2/e
- Youth Criminal Justice Law 3/e
- Constitutional Law 4/e
- Bank and Customer Law in Canada 2/e
- The Law of Equitable Remedies 2/e
- The Charter of Rights and Freedoms 5/e
- Environmental Law 4/e
- Pension Law 2/e
- International and Transnational Criminal Law 2/e
- Remedies: The Law of Damages 3/e
- Freedom of Conscience and Religion
- The Law of Trusts 3/e
- The Law of Evidence 7/e
- Ethics and Criminal Law 2/e
- Insurance Law 2/e
- Immigration Law 2/e
- Criminal Law 6/e
- The Law of Torts 5/e
- Bankruptcy and Insolvency Law 2/e
- Legal Research and Writing 4/e
- Criminal Procedure 3/e
- Canadian Maritime Law 2/e
- Public Lands and Resources in Canada
- Statutory Interpretation 3/e

ESSENTIALS OF CANADIAN LAW

CONFLICT OF LAWS

SECOND EDITION

STEPHEN G A PITEL
Faculty of Law, Western University

NICHOLAS S RAFFERTY
Faculty of Law, University of Calgary

Conflict of Laws, second edition
© Irwin Law Inc., 2016

All rights reserved. No part of this publication may be reproduced, stored in a retrieval system, or transmitted, in any form or by any means, without the prior written permission of the publisher or, in the case of photocopying or other reprographic copying, a licence from Access Copyright (Canadian Copyright Licensing Agency), 1 Yonge Street, Suite 800, Toronto, ON, M5E 1E5.

Published in 2016 by

Irwin Law Inc.
14 Duncan Street
Suite 206
Toronto, ON
M5H 3G8

www.irwinlaw.com

ISBN: 978-1-55221-436-7
e-book ISBN: 978-1-55221-437-4

Library and Archives Canada Cataloguing in Publication

Pitel, Stephen G.A., author
    Conflict of laws / Stephen G.A. Pitel, Faculty of Law, Western University, Nicholas S. Rafferty, Faculty of Law, University of Calgary. — Second edition.

(Essentials of Canadian law)
Includes bibliographical references and index.
Issued in print and electronic formats.
ISBN 978-1-55221-436-7 (paperback).—ISBN 978-1-55221-437-4 (pdf)

    1. Conflict of laws—Canada. I. Rafferty, Nicholas, 1952–, author II. Title. III. Series: Essentials of Canadian law

| KE470 P58 2016 | 340.90971 | C2016-904934-5 |
| KF411 P58 2016 | | C2016-904935-3 |

Printed and bound in Canada.

1 2 3 4 5 20 19 18 17 16

SUMMARY TABLE OF CONTENTS

PREFACE xxi

CHAPTER 1:   Introduction 1

CHAPTER 2:   Domicile and Residence 9

CHAPTER 3:   Exclusion of Foreign Law 29

CHAPTER 4:   Foreign Currency Obligations 45

CHAPTER 5   Jurisdiction *In Personam* 53

CHAPTER 6:   *Forum Non Conveniens* 114

CHAPTER 7:   Anti-Suit Injunctions 145

CHAPTER 8:   Recognition and Enforcement of Foreign Judgments 162

CHAPTER 9:   Recognition and Enforcement of Foreign Arbitral Awards 207

CHAPTER 10: The Choice of Law Process 217

CHAPTER 11: Substance and Procedure 236

CHAPTER 12: Pleading and Proof of Foreign Law 249

CHAPTER 13: Tort 261

CHAPTER 14: Contract 285

CHAPTER 15: Unjust Enrichment 305

CHAPTER 16: Nature and *Situs* of Property 324

CHAPTER 17: Immovable Property 330

CHAPTER 18: Movable Property 347

CHAPTER 19: Succession 359

CHAPTER 20: Trusts 390

CHAPTER 21: Marriage 401

CHAPTER 22: Divorce 425

CHAPTER 23: Nullity 451

CHAPTER 24: Children 464

CHAPTER 25: Support Obligations 487

CHAPTER 26: Matrimonial Property 501

TABLE OF CASES 511

INDEX 549

ABOUT THE AUTHORS 559

DETAILED TABLE OF CONTENTS

PREFACE xxi

CHAPTER 1:
INTRODUCTION 1

A. Introduction 1
B. Terminology 2
C. The Three Central Questions 4
D. Types of Disputes 6
E. Sources of Rules and Key Resources 7

Further Readings 7

CHAPTER 2:
DOMICILE AND RESIDENCE 9

A. Introduction 9
B. Domicile 10
    1) Domicile of Origin 10
    2) Domicile of Choice 13
        a) Intention 13
        b) Residence 15
        c) Loss of Domicile of Choice 16
    3) Domicile of Dependency 17

       a) Minors 17
       b) Married Women 18
       c) The Mentally Incapable 19
   4) Choice of Law 20

C. **Residence** 20

   1) Citizenship Cases 21
   2) Ordinary Residence 23
   3) Habitual Residence 25
   4) Future Directions 26

D. **Corporations** 26

Further Readings 27

CHAPTER 3:
EXCLUSION OF FOREIGN LAW 29

A. **Introduction** 29

B. **Public Policy** 30

C. **Penal Law** 33

D. **Revenue Law** 37

E. **Other Public Law** 39

F. **Blocking Statutes** 41

Further Readings 43

CHAPTER 4:
FOREIGN CURRENCY OBLIGATIONS 45

A. **Introduction** 45

B. **Currency of Judgment** 46

C. **Currency of Loss** 50

Further Readings 52

CHAPTER 5:
JURISDICTION *IN PERSONAM* 53

A. **Introduction** 53

   1) Constitutional Considerations 55
   2) Existence and Exercise of Jurisdiction 56
   3) Statutory Reform 58
   4) Organization of the Topic 59

B. Presence-Based Jurisdiction 59
  1) Corporations 62
  2) Partnerships 66
C. Consent-Based Jurisdiction 66
D. Assumed Jurisdiction 71
  1) The *Morguard* Principle 71
  2) Application of the *Morguard* Principle 73
    a) *Muscutt*: Eight Factors 73
    b) The *CJPTA*: Some Presumptions 77
    c) *Club Resorts*: Presumptive Connecting Factors 78
  3) Presumptive Connecting Factors 80
    a) Property 82
      i) Property in the Jurisdiction 82
      ii) Trusts and Administration of Estates 83
    b) Contracts 83
    c) Restitutionary Obligations Arising in the Jurisdiction 86
    d) Torts Committed in the Jurisdiction 86
      i) Contract Connected with the Tort Made in the Jurisdiction 90
    e) Injunctions 91
    f) Enforcement of Foreign Judgments 92
    g) Defendant's Domicile, Ordinary Residence, or Carrying on Business in the Jurisdiction 93
    h) Family Law 94
    i) Other Factors 96
  4) Rebutting a Presumption 96
  5) Concurrent Claims 99
  6) Process and Manner of Service *Ex Juris* 101
E. Class Actions 103
  1) Jurisdiction over Defendants 103
  2) Jurisdiction over Non-resident Plaintiffs 105
F. Forum of Necessity 109

Further Readings 111

CHAPTER 6:
FORUM NON CONVENIENS 114

A. Introduction 114
B. Evolution of the Doctrine 115
C. Rationale for the Doctrine 117
D. Process Issues 119

1) Relationship to Taking Jurisdiction *119*
2) Onus of Proof *121*
3) Statutory and Regulatory Provisions *122*

E. **The Analysis** *123*

1) Physical Connections *125*
2) Applicable Law *126*
3) Specialized Expertise *126*
4) Jurisdiction Clauses *127*
5) *Lis Alibi Pendens* *132*
6) Juridical Advantages *135*
7) Other Factors *137*

F. **Conditions and Undertakings** *138*

G. **The Doctrine in Practice: An Example** *139*

H. **Statutory Transfer Scheme** *141*

I. **Stay of Proceedings in Favour of Arbitration** *141*

Further Readings *143*

CHAPTER 7:
ANTI-SUIT INJUNCTIONS *145*

A. **Introduction** *145*

B. **The English Approach** *147*

C. **The Canadian Approach** *148*

1) Assessing the Foreign Court's Analysis *152*
2) Need to Seek Stay of Foreign Proceedings *154*
3) Inappropriate Domestic Jurisdiction *155*
4) Interprovincial Anti-Suit Injunctions *157*

D. **Anti-Suit Injunctions in Furtherance of Exclusive Jurisdiction and Arbitration Clauses** *158*

Further Readings *161*

CHAPTER 8:
RECOGNITION AND ENFORCEMENT OF FOREIGN JUDGMENTS *162*

A. **Introduction** *162*

B. **The Test for Recognition and Enforcement** *164*

1) Jurisdiction *165*

2) Final Judgment 167
  3) Jurisdictional Competence of the Foreign Court 168
     a) Presence 170
     b) Submission 171
     c) Real and Substantial Connection 173
     d) Criticisms of the Real and Substantial Connection Test 177
     e) A Note about New Brunswick and Saskatchewan 178
  4) Monetary Judgments 179
  5) Non-monetary Judgments 181
     a) The Test for Enforcement 182
     b) Contempt Orders 184
     c) Making Extraterritorial Non-monetary Orders 186

C. Defences to Recognition and Enforcement 186
  1) The Scope of the Defences 187
  2) Fraud 188
  3) Denial of Natural Justice 189
  4) Public Policy 191
     a) Punitive Damages 192
     b) Multiple Damages 194
  5) Other Defences 195
  6) Foreign Negative Declarations 195
  7) Limitation Periods 196

D. Class Actions 198

E. Statutory Registration 201
  1) Scope 201
  2) Process 202
  3) Defences 203
  4) Bilateral Agreements 204

Further Readings 205

CHAPTER 9:

RECOGNITION AND ENFORCEMENT OF FOREIGN ARBITRAL AWARDS 207

A. Introduction 207

B. The *New York Convention* 208

C. The Model Law 210

D. The Common Law 213

E. Limitation Period Issues 214

Further Readings 215

CHAPTER 10:
THE CHOICE OF LAW PROCESS 217

A. Introduction 217

B. The Rationale for Choice of Law 217

C. The Choice of Law Process 221

D. Characterization 222

    1) What Is Characterized 223
    2) The Approach to Characterization 226

E. Ambiguities in Applying the Choice of Law Rule 229

    1) *Renvoi* 229
    2) The Incidental Question 230
    3) Time 231

F. Challenges to the Choice of Law Process 231

Further Readings 235

CHAPTER 11:
SUBSTANCE AND PROCEDURE 236

A. Introduction 236

B. Remedies 237

C. Limitation Periods 241

    1) Transitional Issues 242
    2) Statutory Developments 243
    3) Related Issues 244

D. Parties 245

Further Readings 247

CHAPTER 12:
PLEADING AND PROOF OF FOREIGN LAW 249

A. Introduction 249

B. The Voluntary Nature of Choice of Law 249

C. Foreign Law as Fact 251

D. Pleading of Foreign Law 252

E. Proof of Foreign Law 253

    1) Methods 253

2) Validity of Foreign Law 255
3) Failure of Proof 256

Further Readings 259

CHAPTER 13:
TORT 261

A. **Introduction** 261

B. **Historical Development** 261

C. **The Modern Canadian Rule** 264
   1) Interpreting the Rule and the Exception 267
   2) Maritime and Airborne Torts 271
   3) Interplay with Statutory Accident Legislation 272

D. **Recent Developments in Other Countries** 273
   1) The United Kingdom 273
   2) Australia 277

E. **Interplay between Tort and Contract** 278

F. **Internet Defamation** 279

G. **Constitutional Issues** 282

Further Readings 283

CHAPTER 14:
CONTRACT 285

A. **Introduction** 285

B. **The Proper Law Rule** 285
   1) Express Choice 287
   2) Implied Choice 290
   3) Absence of Choice 291

C. **Scope of the Applicable Law** 293
   1) Essential Validity 294
   2) Formation 294
   3) Formal Validity 296
   4) Capacity 297

D. **Mandatory Rules** 298

E. **Illegality** 300

F. **The Rome I Regulation** 302

Further Readings 303

CHAPTER 15:
UNJUST ENRICHMENT 305

A. Introduction *305*

B. English Common Law *307*

C. Canadian Law *311*

D. Options for Formulating a Rule *314*

   1) The Law of a Related Contract *315*
   2) The Law of the Place of Enrichment *318*
   3) The Proper Law *319*

E. Comparative Law Sources *320*

   1) European Union *321*
   2) American Law Institute *322*

Further Readings *323*

CHAPTER 16:
NATURE AND *SITUS* OF PROPERTY 324

A. Distinction between Movable Property and Immovable Property *324*

B. *Situs* of Property *327*

Further Readings *329*

CHAPTER 17:
IMMOVABLE PROPERTY 330

A. Jurisdiction over Foreign Immovable Property *330*

   1) The General Rule *330*
   2) Tortious Damage to Foreign Immovable Property *332*
   3) Exception Based on a Contract or Equity between the Parties *336*

B. Recognition of Foreign Judgments Affecting Land in the Forum *340*

C. Choice of Law *344*

Further Readings *345*

CHAPTER 18:
MOVABLE PROPERTY 347

A. Introduction *347*

B. Tangible Movable Property *348*

1) Retention of Title Clauses *349*
   2) Exceptions *351*
   3) A Role for *Renvoi*? *352*

C. **Intangible Movable Property** *353*
   1) Determining the Location *354*
   2) Priorities *356*

Further Readings *357*

CHAPTER 19:
SUCCESSION *359*

A. **Introduction** *359*

B. **Administration of Estates** *360*
   1) Local Grants of Representation *360*
   2) The Law Governing the Administration of an Estate *361*
   3) Foreign Personal Representatives *366*
      a) Actions by Foreign Personal Representatives *366*
      b) Actions against Foreign Personal Representatives *367*

C. **Succession (Beneficial Distribution)** *369*
   1) Jurisdiction *369*
   2) Recognition of Foreign Decisions *370*
   3) Choice of Law *371*
      a) Intestate Succession *372*
      b) Testamentary Succession *375*
         i)   Formal Validity of a Will *375*
         ii) Essential or Intrinsic Validity of a Will *377*
         iii) Personal Capacity to Make and to Take under a Will *379*
         iv) Construction of a Will *380*
         v)   Revocation of a Will *382*
         vi) Doctrine of Election *385*
      c) Dependants' Relief Legislation *386*
      d) Claims of Foreign Countries *387*

Further Readings *388*

CHAPTER 20:
TRUSTS *390*

A. **Introduction** *390*

B. **The *Hague Convention*** *391*
   1) Provincial Implementation *391*
   2) Scope *392*

3) Choice of Law Rules 393
4) Recognition 395

C. Provincial Statutes 396

D. Common Law 397

Further Readings 399

CHAPTER 21:
MARRIAGE 401

A. Constitutional Framework 401

B. Formal Validity 402
1) General 402
2) Proxy Marriages 404
3) Parental Consent 404
4) Exceptions to the Law of the Place of Celebration 406

C. Essential Validity: Capacity to Marry 406
1) General 406
2) Prohibited Degrees of Consanguinity and Affinity 408
3) Lack of Age 409
4) Previous Marriage 410
    a) Remarriage after Invalid Divorce or Annulment 411
    b) Remarriage after Valid Divorce or Annulment 412
5) Lack of Consent 414
6) Same-Sex Marriages 414
7) Relevance of the Law of the Place of Celebration 414
8) Public Policy 416

D. Subsequent Validation of a Marriage 416

E. Physical Incapacity 418

F. Polygamous Marriages 419

G. Civil Unions 422

Further Readings 423

CHAPTER 22:
DIVORCE 425

A. Jurisdiction to Grant a Divorce 425
1) Existence of Jurisdiction 425
2) Exercise of Jurisdiction: Parallel Proceedings 429

B. Choice of Law 432

C. Recognition of Foreign Divorce Decrees 432
   1) Statutory Grounds for Recognition 433
   2) Common Law Grounds for Recognition 434
      a) Domicile 435
      b) Reciprocity 436
      c) Real and Substantial Connection 436
D. Extra-judical Divorces 438
E. Defences to the Recognition of Foreign Divorce Decrees 442
F. The Effect of an Invalid Foreign Divorce: The Doctrine of Preclusion 446
G. Dissolution of Civil Unions 449

Further Readings 450

CHAPTER 23:
NULLITY 451

A. Void and Voidable Marriages 451
B. Jurisdiction to Grant a Nullity Decree 453
   1) Domicile 454
   2) Residence 455
   3) Place of Celebration of the Marriage 456
C. Choice of Law 457
D. Recognition of Foreign Nullity Decrees 457
   1) Domicile 458
      a) Decree Granted by the Courts of the Parties' Common Domicile 458
      b) Decree Granted by the Courts of the Domicile of One Party 458
      c) Decree Recognized by the Courts of the Parties' Domicile 459
   2) Reciprocity 459
      a) Residence 459
      b) Place of Celebration of the Marriage 460
   3) Real and Substantial Connection 461
E. Defences to the Recognition of Foreign Nullity Decrees 462

Further Readings 463

CHAPTER 24:
CHILDREN 464

A. Introduction 464

B. Custody 465

   1) Jurisdiction 465
   2) Choice of Law 467
   3) Recognition and Enforcement 468
   4) Defences 469
   5) Varying and Superseding Foreign Custody Orders 470

C. International Child Abduction 471

   1) Scope 472
   2) Protection Provided 473
   3) Process 474
   4) Grounds for Refusing to Order a Child's Return 475
   5) Rights of Access 478
   6) Interplay between the *Hague Convention* and Legislation 479

D. Adoption 480

   1) Jurisdiction 480
   2) Choice of Law 481
   3) Intercountry Adoptions 481
   4) Recognition of Foreign Adoptions 483

Further Readings 485

CHAPTER 25:
SUPPORT OBLIGATIONS 487

A. Introduction 487

B. Jurisdiction under the *Divorce Act* 487

   1) Ordinary Residence 488
   2) Support Orders and Foreign Divorces 489

C. Provincial Jurisdiction 490

   1) Interjurisdictional Support Orders Statutes 493
      a) Claimant in the Province 493
      b) Respondent in the Province 494
      c) Variation Orders 495

D. Choice of Law 496

E. Recognition and Enforcement 497

   1) Statutory Provisions 497
   2) At Common Law 499

Further Readings 500

CHAPTER 26:
MATRIMONIAL PROPERTY 501

A. Introduction 501

B. Jurisdiction 502

C. Choice of Law 504
  1) At Common Law 504
  2) Statutory Rules 506
  3) Marriage Contracts 507

D. Recognition and Enforcement 509

Further Readings 510

TABLE OF CASES 511

INDEX 549

ABOUT THE AUTHORS 559

PREFACE

This book is the second edition of a text originally published in 2010. My co-author on the first edition, Professor Nicholas Rafferty, has since retired. I am solely responsible for the revisions made in the second edition. But more than enough of Professor Rafferty's original work remains intact in this edition to justify his continued co-authorship. I will always be grateful for his invitation to collaborate with him on this text.

Our aim in this text is to explain, clearly and concisely, the rules of the conflict of laws in force in common law Canada. We want this book to be both readable and thoughtful and for it to appeal to both legal practitioners and law students. The conflict of laws takes on greater importance with each passing year. Globalization is eroding borders in commercial transactions and family relationships, yet much law remains highly territorial. Understanding the conflict of laws allows lawyers, judges, scholars, and students to better address any legal situation that crosses borders, whether international or interprovincial.

In the first edition, Professor Rafferty and I each took responsibility for specific chapters. Professor Rafferty wrote chapters 5, 7, 16, 17, 19, 21, 22, and 23 and I wrote the others. As indicated, I have updated all of the chapters for this edition. Some required relatively minor revisions, but others, such as the one on jurisdiction (Chapter 5), have evolved considerably. In particular, this edition addresses the Supreme Court of Canada's significant decision in *Club Resorts Ltd v Van Breda*, 2012 SCC 17. Of note, as well, is a new chapter on matrimonial property (Chapter 26). I have set out the law as it stood on 15 March 2016, although in some areas I have been able to make the text more current during the editorial process.

I am fortunate to have the support of Irwin Law for this project, especially in its willingness to publish new texts on traditional subjects. It has been a pleasure to work with Irwin Law throughout the process.

For the first edition, thanks are due to the Faculties of Law at Western University in London, Ontario and the University of Calgary. The former institution funded three excellent research students: Dara Lambie, Jean-Michel Corbeil, and Jesse Harper. In addition, my colleague Professor Berend Hovius provided helpful comments on some of the chapters dealing with family law. The University of Calgary provided teaching relief to accommodate Professor Rafferty's physical disability. Professor Rafferty also received a Borden Ladner Gervais Fellowship, which provided him with the proficient research services of Alex Ramsvig. In addition, his assistant, Shirl Roch, worked tirelessly to transform his illegible script into a finished product. Professor Joost Blom of the University of British Columbia read the entire manuscript and provided helpful comments.

For the second edition, thanks are again due to the Faculty of Law, Western University. Generous funding was provided by the Foundation for Legal Research. My research students both did an excellent job. Liam Ledgerwood identified developments in the law and potential improvements to the entire text and Lyndsey Kiser did background research for Chapter 26, the new matrimonial property chapter. Professor Vaughan Black of Dalhousie University and Professor Joost Blom of the University of British Columbia provided helpful comments on the heavily revised chapter on jurisdiction (Chapter 5).

Both Professor Rafferty and I remain grateful for the efforts of our own mentors in the conflict of laws, our academic colleagues who are contributing to the ongoing development of the field, and our former students for all they have done to stimulate us. Above all, we appreciate the ongoing support of our families.

Stephen GA Pitel

CHAPTER 1

INTRODUCTION

A. INTRODUCTION

The conflict of laws deals with three central questions. The first is whether a court has jurisdiction to hear a particular dispute. The second is what law a court will apply in resolving a dispute. The third is whether a court will recognize and enforce a decision of a court in another jurisdiction.

It is important to appreciate the highly procedural nature of these questions. Conflict of laws rules, in general, do not resolve substantive disputes in the same way that, for example, tort and contract rules do. At the risk of oversimplification, they regulate the process of dispute resolution rather than determine the outcome. They are more closely related to the rules of civil procedure and can in a sense be seen as civil procedure rules for cases with connections to more than one jurisdiction. The subject is therefore of central importance in civil litigation, particularly in light of increasing globalization and cross-border transactions and events. The conflict of laws is important, for example, when Canadians buy and sell goods and services in others countries, marry people from other countries, and own real and personal property outside Canada.

It is essential for civil litigators to have a solid understanding of the conflict of laws: to know the rules and be able to apply them to concrete problems as they arise. But this area of the law is also important for non-litigators. Lawyers who negotiate contracts for clients and who advise clients on how best to organize their affairs to avoid exposure also need to understand this area, at a minimum to recognize when a conflict of laws issue arises for consideration.

The subject can involve complex fact patterns and covers many different areas of substantive law, and so has a reputation as being difficult. William Prosser colourfully claimed that "the realm of the conflict of laws is a dismal swamp filled with quaking quagmires and inhabited by learned but eccentric professors who theorize about mysterious matters in a strange and incomprehensible jargon."[1] The aim of this book is to clearly explain the conflict of laws for academics, lawyers, judges, and students.

This book focuses on the conflict of laws in the common law provinces and territories of Canada.[2] It does not purport to cover the subject under the civil law of Quebec.

B. TERMINOLOGY

This area of law was called the "conflict of laws" by the English legal scholar AV Dicey in his foundational textbook in 1896.[3] It is not the most accurate name for the area, but it has very much taken hold. When different legal systems formulate their answers to legal problems, there is a distinct likelihood that their answers will differ. These differing answers give rise to the name "conflict of laws." Suppose that under California law, manufacturers are strictly liable for any physical injuries caused by their products. Suppose that under British Columbia law, an injured person must show that the manufacturer was somehow careless before liability will be imposed. The two jurisdictions have different substantive legal rules. On the identical facts, a plaintiff might win under California law and lose under British Columbia law. We could say that there is a conflict between the laws of the two jurisdictions.

---

1   William L Prosser, "Interstate Publication" (1953) 51 *Michigan Law Review* 959 at 971. It has been suggested that this metaphor is unfair to swamps, which are an important part of the ecosystem, and that "landfill" or "sinkhole" should instead be the chosen analogue: William M Richman & David Riley, "The First Restatement of Conflict of Laws on the Twenty-Fifth Anniversary of Its Successor: Contemporary Practice in Traditional Courts" (1997) 56 *Maryland Law Review* 1196 at 1218–19.
2   Unless otherwise indicated, references to provinces include the territories.
3   AV Dicey, *A Digest of the Law of England with Reference to the Conflict of Laws* (London: Stevens & Sons, 1896).

If this is, in some sense, a conflict, what impact does it have? Cases that are wholly local to either California or British Columbia would be decided under the relevant local law and the fact that a different result would be reached under another legal system is unlikely to be considered very important. However, the conflict takes on greater importance in cases that are not wholly local but instead have factual connections to both California and British Columbia. In these cases, debate about which system's legal rules will be applied raises the conflict very directly. Much of the law on the conflict of laws relates to resolving this sort of conflict.

This explanation shows how focused this name, "conflict of laws," is on the question of the applicable law. It is harder to explain what the question of jurisdiction and the question of recognition and enforcement have to do with the notion of conflicting laws. This is one of the reasons this name is not considered ideal for the area.[4]

This area of the law is also known as "private international law," and this term can freely be interchanged with the conflict of laws. This term distinguishes the area from public international law, which is quite different and centres on relationships between nations and international organizations. It is also international in quite a different sense than is public international law. In the latter, the law is supra-national: it operates above national law. In private international law, the law is very much national, in the sense that it is formulated by each individual jurisdiction. The notion of international is meant to indicate that this area of law applies to situations with some foreign element or international dimension.[5]

The conflict of laws also sometimes uses words such as "country" and "nation" in a special sense. The subject is concerned with the division of the world into separate geographic entities that each have a separate legal system. The country of New Zealand would be one such entity, but so would the various states of the United States of America or Australia and the various provinces of Canada. This was implicit in the example above about California and British Columbia law. Factual situations that span interstate or interprovincial borders give rise to conflict of laws issues in the same way that those spanning international borders do. In any situation the focus needs to be on the specific entity

---

4   When Morris took over the authorship of Dicey's text, he commented on the area's unsatisfactory name: see JHC Morris, *Dicey's Conflict of Laws* (London: Stevens & Sons, 1949) at 7.
5   Briggs has suggested it would be more accurate to call the area "international private law": Adrian Briggs, *The Conflict of Laws*, 2d ed (Oxford: Oxford University Press, 2008) at 2.

and its legal system. Often these entities are called "jurisdictions" but sometimes they are called countries or nations. So for the purposes of the conflict of laws, Ontario and Michigan can be considered countries.

C. THE THREE CENTRAL QUESTIONS

The first question is whether a court has jurisdiction to hear and resolve a particular dispute. At issue here is the court's power to render a decision that will be treated as binding on the parties. The analysis involves examining the relationship between the country in which the dispute is to be heard and both the parties to the dispute and the facts on which the dispute is based.

Some aspects of jurisdiction are not generally treated as part of the conflict of laws. These relate to aspects of the court's jurisdiction over the subject matter of the dispute. For example, a plaintiff cannot sue for breach of contract in the Ontario Court of Justice because that court, under the statute giving it jurisdiction, hears only criminal and family law matters.[6] As another example, a plaintiff cannot sue for $500,000 for breach of contract in the Ontario Small Claims Court, also because that court's jurisdiction is statutorily limited to claims for not more than $25,000.[7] These types of jurisdictional issues are more properly studied as part of the civil procedure for a particular country.

One central issue in the analysis of jurisdiction is the connection between the country where the dispute is to be heard and the defendant. The plaintiff, in choosing where to commence proceedings, has indicated his or her satisfaction with having the dispute resolved by that country's courts. But the defendant has made no such choice: he or she becomes a defendant unwillingly. So we need to examine whether the court's jurisdiction over the defendant flows simply from the plaintiff's choice or, if that is considered insufficient, from something more. The topic of jurisdiction is examined in detail in Chapter 5.

There is a further element to the question of jurisdiction, which can be expressed as a subsidiary question: if a court does have jurisdiction over a dispute, will it nonetheless exercise discretion not to hear it? While it is possible to have a legal system without such discretion, so that the court must hear every case within its jurisdiction, modern common law legal systems provide that the court has the discretion to

---

6 *Courts of Justice Act*, RSO 1990, c C.43, s 38.
7 *Ibid*, s 23(1), and O Reg 626/00, s 1(1).

decline to hear a dispute. The principles on which this discretion is exercised are explained in Chapter 6.

The subject's second central question is what law a court will apply in resolving a dispute. For many people this seems to be an unusual question since the answer appears obvious: a court applies its own law—the law of the country it is in. An Alberta court therefore applies Alberta law. But the real answer is more complex. The court does not always apply its own law. If it did, there would be no need for this second question, and the applicable law would simply be a consequence of taking jurisdiction. But jurisdiction and the applicable law are separate questions. In certain circumstances, an Alberta court will resolve a dispute using a foreign legal system. If two Albertans make a contract and they expressly agree that it is governed by the law of New York, it at a minimum seems inconvenient that an Alberta court could not resolve the dispute and that only a New York court could do so.

The issue of the applicable law is referred to as choice of law. Some important overarching issues in choice of law are considered in Chapters 10, 11, and 12. Beyond these issues, choice of law rules are generally subdivided by area of law into choice of law for contract, choice of law for tort, and so on. From Chapter 13 onwards each chapter examines the specific choice of law rules for a particular area.

The third central question is whether a court will recognize and enforce a decision of a court in another jurisdiction. This issue can arise in different ways. In one, a plaintiff might obtain judgment against a defendant in another country but the defendant does not satisfy the judgment and does not have sufficient assets in that country to do so. If the defendant has assets elsewhere, the plaintiff will want to enforce the foreign judgment against those assets. In another, a court might render judgment for the defendant but the plaintiff then brings the same claim against the defendant in another country. The defendant will want the courts of that country to recognize the foreign judgment as precluding the further proceedings. As we will see, the analysis of whether to recognize and enforce a foreign judgment is closely linked to the basis on which the foreign court took jurisdiction. This topic is considered in detail in Chapter 8.

In the historical development of the conflict of laws, the second of these questions—the issue of choice of law—was by far the most important, generating the most interest and scholarly analysis. Today, from a practical standpoint the most important question is the first: the issue of jurisdiction. The main reason for the current emphasis is that approximately 95 percent of civil cases are resolved before trial. The choice of law issue is largely, though certainly not exclusively, one that comes up at trial, when the substantive issues are being resolved by the court. While the parties must pay attention to choice of law issues from the outset of the litigation, in practice these issues are formally addressed in relatively few cases. In contrast, jurisdiction issues arise at the outset of the litigation, and so are formally addressed in far more cases.

D. TYPES OF DISPUTES

As we have seen, the conflict of laws is primarily concerned with the resolution, through litigation, of civil disputes involving factual connections to more than one country. It is important to appreciate what this does not include.

Many international civil disputes are resolved not through litigation but rather through arbitration. For example, parties to a cross-border contract may have expressly included a clause requiring the arbitration of any disputes. There is a separate body of law on international arbitrations, addressing issues such as the procedure to be used, the scope of the arbitration, and the jurisdiction of the arbitrator. Within this book, Chapter 9 is the only one that specifically addresses arbitration, examining the recognition and enforcement of foreign arbitral awards.

The conflict of laws is also not concerned with certain international civil disputes covered by specific methods of resolution. One major source of such disputes is the area of international trade. For example, challenges to various trade practices under the *North American Free Trade Agreement*[8] or the rules of the World Trade Organization follow the particular rules and processes of those international arrangements rather than using the litigation process.

Within civil litigation, some issues cross borders but are not strictly considered part of the conflict of laws. One such issue is the extent to which foreign procedures can be used to gather evidence for use in litigation in the forum. Litigation might be occurring in Ontario but key documents or witnesses might be in California. The reverse scenario is also possible: the forum court might be asked to provide assistance in gathering evidence for foreign litigation.[9] Another such issue is the possible geographic scope of a local order. A British Columbia court

---

8   *North American Free Trade Agreement between the Government of Canada, the Government of Mexico, and the Government of the United States*, 17 December 1992, Can TS 1994 No 2, 32 ILM 289 (entered into force 1 January 1994).

9   See, for example, *Re Friction Division Products, Inc v EI Du Pont de Nemours & Co Inc (No 2)* (1986), 56 OR (2d) 722 (HCJ).

might be asked to make an order freezing a defendant's assets in another jurisdiction.[10] These topics are considered in more detail in texts on civil procedure, evidence, and remedies.

E. SOURCES OF RULES AND KEY RESOURCES

In common law Canada the majority of the rules dealing with the conflict of laws are found in the decided cases, and as a result it is very important to understand the leading decisions. Statutes and regulations are another important source of the rules, particularly on the issues of jurisdiction and recognition and enforcement of foreign judgments. The Constitution of Canada[11] does not directly address the conflict of laws, but in their decisions the courts have drawn on aspects of the Constitution for guidance in developing the rules. The conflict of laws also involves several international treaties, particularly those created by the Hague Conference on Private International Law. Finally, this is an area in which the opinions of leading academics have historically been given weight by the courts. A particular example of this is the role of what is now the *Dicey, Morris and Collins* text in English law.

At the end of each chapter in this book is a list of further readings, going beyond the sources identified within the chapter itself. For this first chapter the list is of general references from Canada and other common law jurisdictions. For more than twenty years the leading reference work in Canada has been Jean-Gabriel Castel's text, now written by Janet Walker, and the only published casebook is the one now under the general editorship of Stephen Pitel. These two works contain additional information on the subjects of almost every chapter in this book, but to avoid repetition they are not listed again as further readings.

FURTHER READINGS

BRIGGS, ADRIAN. *Private International Law in English Courts* (Oxford: Oxford University Press, 2014).

BRIGGS, ADRIAN. *The Conflict of Laws*, 3d ed (Oxford: Oxford University Press, 2013).

---

10 See, for example, *Mooney v Orr* (1994), 98 BCLR (2d) 318 (SC).
11 *The Constitution Act, 1982*, being Schedule B to the *Canada Act 1982* (UK), 1982, c 11.

CLARKSON, CMV, & JONATHAN HILL. *The Conflict of Laws*, 4th ed (Oxford: Oxford University Press, 2011).

COLLINS, LAWRENCE, ED. *Dicey, Morris and Collins on the Conflict of Laws*, 15th ed (London: Sweet & Maxwell, 2012).

DAVIES, MARTIN, ANDREW BELL, & PAUL LE GAY BRERETON. *Nygh's Conflict of Laws in Australia*, 9th ed (Chatswood, NSW: LexisNexis Butterworths, 2013).

FAWCETT, JAMES J, & JANEEN CARRUTHERS. *Cheshire, North & Fawcett Private International Law*, 14th ed (Oxford: Oxford University Press, 2008).

FENTIMAN, RICHARD. *International Commercial Litigation*, 2d ed (Oxford: Oxford University Press, 2015).

FORSYTH, CHRISTOPHER F. *Private International Law*, 5th ed (Kenwyn, South Africa: Juta & Co, 2012).

HAY, PETER, PATRICK BORCHERS, & SYMEON C SYMEONIDES. *Conflict of Laws*, 5th ed (St Paul, MN: West Group, 2010).

HILL, JONATHAN, & ADELINE CHONG. *International Commercial Disputes: Commercial Conflict of Laws in English Courts*, 4th ed (Oxford: Hart, 2010).

MACDONALD, KENNETH C. *Cross-Border Litigation: Interjurisdictional Practice and Procedure* (Aurora, ON: Canada Law Book, 2009).

MCCLEAN, DAVID, & VERONICA RUIZ ABOU-NIGM. *Morris: The Conflict of Laws*, 8th ed (London: Sweet & Maxwell, 2012).

MORTENSEN, REID, RICHARD GARNETT, & MARY KEYES. *Private International Law in Australia*, 2d ed (Chatswood, NSW: LexisNexis Butterworths, 2011).

PITEL, STEPHEN GA ET AL. *Private International Law in Common Law Canada: Cases, Text and Materials*, 4th ed (Toronto: Emond Montgomery, 2016).

ROGERSON, PIPPA. *Collier's Conflict of Laws*, 4th ed (Cambridge: Cambridge University Press, 2013).

WALKER, JANET. *Castel & Walker: Canadian Conflict of Laws*, 6th ed (Markham, ON: LexisNexis Butterworths, 2005) (loose-leaf).

WALKER, JANET. *Halsbury's Laws of Canada: Conflict of Laws* (Markham, ON: LexisNexis, 2011).

CHAPTER 2

DOMICILE AND RESIDENCE

A. INTRODUCTION

Chapter 1 identified the three fundamental questions in the conflict of laws, and the first question is addressed starting in Chapter 5. This chapter and the two that follow deal with subjects that cannot easily be encompassed by one of the three fundamental questions. These chapters deal with subjects that are relevant, in differing ways, to each question, and so it is useful to consider them separately. Despite where they appear in this book, it is not essential that they be considered at the outset. Analysis of these subjects could be postponed until they become relevant to a specific conflicts problem. This chapter is a good example. Domicile and residence are quite important in certain areas—the former in the law of succession and the latter in family law, among others—but often play only a small role in corporate and commercial cases.

The conflict of laws has long been interested in identifying an individual's "personal law," thought to be the law of the place to which the individual has the closest ongoing connection. The notion was that individuals carried their personal law with them, as a part of them, wherever they went in the world and that it governed issues relating to their personal status. This approach was important, for example, under Roman law as people travelled across the empire. There are several different ways that an individual's personal law can be ascertained. Civil law systems frequently use the concept of nationality or citizenship, which can be formally acquired in different ways. However, these have not tended to be used in common law systems, which instead have used the concepts of domicile and residence.

B. DOMICILE

There are three main types of domicile, each of which may be obtained by an individual according to a complex set of rules.[1] First, a "domicile of origin" is ascribed to every individual at birth. This domicile stays with the individual for life and is the most tenacious. Second, once an individual reaches the age of majority, he or she is free to adopt a "domicile of choice" by taking up residence in a particular country and intending to remain there indefinitely. Third, individuals who are legally dependent on another will be ascribed the domicile of that other person as their "domicile of dependency." Each of these is discussed in detail below. The rigid requirements of the types of domicile often make it difficult to ascertain an individual's domicile at a particular time in his or her life. In addition, several rules regulate any change between the types of domicile.

Because domicile is used as a means of identifying an individual's personal law and thereby linking an individual to a particular legal system, the central rule is that an individual may have only one domicile at any given time.[2] More technically, an individual may have only one domicile for a particular purpose at any given time. This is especially true in a federal country such as Canada.[3] Depending on which level of government—federal or provincial—has jurisdiction to regulate an issue, an individual can be domiciled in both Canada and in Ontario. Nevertheless, when a court is required to identify an individual's domicile for a particular purpose, it must identify a single domicile.

1) Domicile of Origin

The development of the concept of domicile of origin is largely shaped by the rule that no individual may be without a domicile at any particular time.[4] It must always be possible to identify a person's domicile

---

1 In the context of the analysis of domicile, the individual concerned is sometimes called the "propositus."
2 *Udny v Udny* (1869), LR 1 Sc & Div 441 (HL) [*Udny*]; *Re Foote Estate*, 2009 ABQB 654 at para 23, aff'd 2011 ABCA 1 at para 19. This gives domicile a conceptual advantage over citizenship, since many people are citizens of more than one country.
3 This illustrates another advantage that domicile has over citizenship, as this concept is less meaningful in the context of federal countries.
4 *Udny*, above note 2.

and so identify his or her personal law. Accordingly, every individual is ascribed a domicile of origin at birth. Traditionally, children were ascribed the domicile of their father if they were legitimate and the domicile of their mother if illegitimate.[5] However, most provinces have abolished legal distinctions based on whether a child was born within or outside a marriage.[6] So what is an individual's domicile of origin if the parents each have a different domicile at the time of the birth? The answer is unclear.[7] One approach would be to hold that whatever domicile of dependence, discussed below, the individual first acquires is also his or her domicile of origin. Another is to use the law of the place with which the individual has the closest connection at the time of birth.

As will be discussed further below, an individual can go from having a domicile of origin to having a domicile of choice. In the past, a change of domicile and thus of personal law had potentially important implications. As a result, a person's domicile of origin was treated as difficult to change.[8] The courts held that a claim that a domicile of choice had been adopted to displace a domicile of origin "is a serious matter not to be lightly inferred from slight indications or casual words."[9] There must be clear and unequivocal evidence that the domicile of origin is to be replaced by the domicile of choice. The domicile of origin persists until strong evidence suggests otherwise.[10] Under this approach, individuals sometimes spent decades living in other countries without losing their domicile of origin. More recently, some cases have held that while clear evidence is important, there is no justification for making it particularly or especially difficult to move from having a domicile of origin to a domicile of choice.[11] As in all cases, the burden of proof lies on the person claiming a change in domicile.[12]

---

5 Ibid.
6 See, for example, *Children's Law Reform Act*, RSO 1990, c C.12, s 1.
7 In part, this is because modern statutory reforms like s 67 of the Ontario *Family Law Act*, RSO 1990, c F.3, appear to address a minor's domicile of dependency, discussed below, but not the minor's domicile of origin.
8 *Haut v Haut* (1978), 20 OR (2d) 126 (HCJ). See also *R v R (Divorce: Jurisdiction: Domicile)*, [2006] 1 FLR 389 at 398.
9 *In the Estate of Fuld (No 3)*, [1968] P 675 at 686; *Smallman v Smallman Estate* (1991), 35 CCEL 146 (Ont Ct Gen Div).
10 *Henderson v Henderson*, [1967] P 77 at 80.
11 *Mark v Mark* (2005), [2006] 1 AC 98 (HL). In *Re Foote Estate*, above note 2 at paras 71–74 (QB), the court, relying on *FH v McDougall*, [2008] 3 SCR 41, rejected the use of a higher burden of proof relating to the domicile of origin and held that the ordinary civil standard of proof on the balance of probabilities was to be used.
12 *Zehring v Zehring* (1965), 55 DLR (2d) 283 (Man QB); *Armstrong v Armstrong*, [1971] 3 OR 544 at 547 (HCJ).

An individual's domicile of origin is not lost when he or she leaves that country with no intention of ever returning. Rather, the domicile of origin persists until a domicile of choice is adopted.[13] This ensures that an individual who leaves his or her domicile of origin without adopting a domicile of choice is not, for a time, without a domicile. Even when an individual leaves a domicile of origin with no intention of ever returning and remains away for many years, the domicile of origin persists so long as he or she does not adopt a domicile of choice.

Similarly, an individual can acquire a domicile of choice and then subsequently abandon it without adopting a new domicile of choice. Because everyone must have a domicile, the law holds that the domicile of origin revives and becomes the person's domicile. This revival of the domicile of origin in such situations is one of the key aspects of its tenacity. The logic for the revival of the domicile of origin was explained by the House of Lords in *Udny*:

> That original domicil [sic] depended not on choice but attached itself to its subject on his birth, and it seems to me consonant both to convenience and to the currency of the whole law of domicil to hold that . . . the domicil of origin cast on him by no choice of his own, and changed for a time, be the state to which he naturally falls back when his first choice has been abandoned *animo et facto*, and whilst he is deliberating before he makes a second choice.[14]

Rather than having the abandoned domicile of choice continue as the individual's personal law, the domicile of origin revives until a new domicile of choice is adopted. The strong persistence of domicile of origin made sense in the traditional English society where the concept was developed, since individuals were generally more connected to their place of birth and moved between countries less frequently. While there was early judicial questioning of whether to apply this traditional English rule in Canada,[15] it has been overwhelmingly adopted. It has also been repeatedly criticized.[16]

Interesting issues can arise when a country's borders move or disappear. Consider, for example, a person born in 1935 whose parents were lifelong residents of Breslau and as such were domiciled in Germany. In 1945 Breslau became part of Poland and is today known as Wroclaw. Consider also a person who acquired a domicile of origin of

---

13 *Trottier v Rajotte* (1939), [1940] SCR 203.
14 Above note 2 at 450.
15 *Nelson v Nelson*, [1925] 3 DLR 22 (Alta SC).
16 See below note 38. See also *Vanston v Scott*, 2014 SKQB 64 at paras 43–44.

East Germany in 1985. East Germany became part of modern Germany in 1990.

2) Domicile of Choice

Once an individual has reached the age of majority, it is possible for him or her to adopt a domicile of choice. To adopt a new country as one's domicile of choice, an individual must have a fixed intention to remain in the country forever and must be resident there.[17] These two elements have to overlap at a particular moment in time.[18] The elements can begin at different times—one or the other can start first—but at the first moment of overlap a domicile of choice is acquired.

a) Intention

In order to adopt a domicile of choice, an individual must have the intention to remain in the particular country indefinitely (referred to as *animus manendi*).[19] The intention must be fixed and permanent. This does not mean that the intent to remain is forever irrevocable, but at the time of acquiring a domicile of choice the intent must be to reside in the particular country for the rest of one's life.

The necessary intent is not to be lightly inferred. There must be a positive intention to reside permanently. Other explanations for residence in a country (such as imprisonment and military posting) can often be fatal to the acquisition of a domicile of choice.[20] This is not to say that one cannot acquire a domicile of choice in a situation where the residence is forced, but in such a situation there must be a positive intention to remain indefinitely even after the compulsive element is removed.[21] For example, an individual performing military service that is stationed in a particular country is not *prima facie* precluded from obtaining a domicile of choice in that country should there be an intention to remain once the order to be stationed there is rescinded.[22]

An issue arises as to whether an individual can have the *animus manendi* in situations where he or she has in mind a future contingency

---

17 *Bell v Kennedy* (1868), LR 1 Sc & Div 307 at 319 (HL); *Gillespie v Grant* (1992), 132 AR 288 at para 50 (Surr Ct) [*Gillespie*]; *Re Urquhart Estate* (1990), 74 OR (2d) 42 at 45 (HCJ), aff'd (1991), 3 OR (3d) 699 (Div Ct); *Re Foote Estate*, above note 2 at paras 25–29 (QB) and para 22 (CA).
18 *Waggoner v Waggoner* (1956), 20 WWR 74 (Alta SC).
19 *Osvath-Latkoczy v Osvath-Latkoczy*, [1959] SCR 751 at 752–53; *Re Foote Estate*, above note 2 at paras 40–50 (QB).
20 *In the Estate of Fuld (No 3)*, above note 9 at 684.
21 *Stephen v Stephen* (1961), 51 MPR 65 (NBCA).
22 *Wilton v Wilton*, [1946] OR 117 (HCJ).

that would affect the intention to remain indefinitely. For example, if a refugee plans to stay in Canada for the rest of his or her life unless the oppressive regime in his or her home country is overthrown, does he or she have the requisite intent to acquire a domicile of choice in Canada? This specific issue was addressed in *Osvath-Latkoczy v Osvath-Latkoczy*,[23] where the Supreme Court of Canada applied the principle in *Lord v Colvin* that the intent required was

> not for a mere special and temporary purpose, but with a present intention of making it his permanent home, unless and until something (which is unexpected or the happening of which is uncertain) shall occur to induce him to adopt other permanent home.[24]

The court held that the future event was uncertain enough so as to allow the individual to acquire a domicile in Canada. This suggests that the relevant consideration is the probability of the contingency. As such, an Englishman living in Canada who intended to return to England if his wife died before him did not acquire a Canadian domicile, since there was a real possibility of the contingency occurring.[25] No definitive statement has been made about the exact probability required to negate the acquisition of a domicile of choice. This is a difficult area of the law for consistency and predictability because of the need to determine subjective probabilities of future events.

Further, the federal nature of Canada produces another potential anomaly. Suppose an individual moves to Canada with the intention of staying in the country indefinitely but makes no decision about which province to live in permanently. Has this person acquired a Canadian domicile? This question has not been dealt with directly, but in a similar case an Alberta court stated that

> Because a person leaves a country temporarily intending to return but not necessarily to the same spot he does not thereby abandon his domicile, it still will remain at the place where it was when he left until he resumes it again in the country and if he takes up his residence on his return at a different location he will be then domiciled at a different place but will nevertheless have continued to be domiciled all the while in the country.[26]

This seems to allow for the possibility that an individual may be domiciled in a country even when undecided on where to live within that

---

23 Above note 19 at 753.
24 (1859), 62 ER 141 at 145.
25 *IRC v Bullock*, [1976] 1 WLR 1178.
26 *Nelson v Nelson*, above note 15 at 28–29.

country. However, this case dealt with an individual who had already established a domicile in the state of Colorado and had then left the United States, uncertain about the state to which he would return. This situation is not directly analogous to an individual who has yet to obtain a domicile in a country, being undecided about which state or province to settle in permanently. Some Commonwealth jurisdictions have a legislative answer to this question.[27] It is unclear how Canadian courts would deal with such a case. The fact that courts have allowed a change of domicile between provinces using a lower burden of proof than for a change of domicile between countries[28] suggests that in such a case the clear intent of the individual to be domiciled in Canada may be sufficient.

The question has arisen as to whether an individual can form the intent to reside in a country indefinitely if that residence would be illegal, such as in the case of a person without the legal right to be in a particular country. The Canadian position seems to be that the intention to remain indefinitely may be formed prior to having a right to remain in a country.[29] As the intent to remain is a state of mind, it can be formed whether or not remaining is legally possible.[30]

Intention is entirely within the mind of the individual. Direct testimony as to intention will be taken into consideration, but will increasingly be questioned the more self-serving it becomes.[31] Objective evidence, used to infer an individual's intention, includes a wide range of relevant factors such as the time spent in the proposed domicile, the purchase of real property, becoming naturalized or obtaining citizenship, and the types of activities carried out while in the proposed domicile.

b) Residence

The second element required to establish a domicile of choice is residence. A subjective intention to move to Canada and remain there forever is insufficient unless it overlaps with residence in Canada. As the court held in *Mainguy v Mainguy*, "It is impossible on the law as I perceive it, to conclude that anyone can create domicile solely by expressed

---

27 See, for example, Australia's *Domicile Act 1982*, (Cth), s 11.
28 *Young v Young* (1959), 67 Man R 108 at 117 (CA).
29 *Canada (Deputy Minister of National Revenue, Customs and Excise—MNR) v White* (1995), 92 FTR 285 at 287 (TD); *Jablonowski v Jablonowski*, [1972] 3 OR 410 (HCJ).
30 See *Mark v Mark*, above note 11 for a discussion of the interplay between this issue and that of future contingencies.
31 *Trottier v Rajotte*, above note 13 at 215.

intent, and obviously actual geographic occupation is an essential ingredient with that intent."[32] However, no specific length of residence in the country is required. As such, a domicile of choice can be obtained by an individual who has the intent to remain in a country as soon as he or she arrives in that country.[33] What is important for residence is not length or quality but rather contiguity of the residence with the intent. While lengthy residence is a factor that can allow the necessary intent to be inferred since people generally remain in places they have lived in for a long time, a lengthy residence is not necessary. Further, even the longest periods of residence will not suffice to establish a domicile of choice in the absence of intention. For example, an Englishman who lives in Canada for most of his life will not obtain a domicile there if he has in his mind an intention to spend his final years back in England.[34]

While the orthodox definition of domicile of choice continues to require residence, this might be misleading. Since no length of time in the country is required, some commentators have suggested that this element should be described as presence rather than as residence.[35] However described, the threshold is reasonably low. As long as the individual is living in the country, as opposed to merely passing through, the physical element will be satisfied and the main focus will be on the issue of intention.

c) Loss of Domicile of Choice

In order to lose a domicile of choice, it is necessary for an individual to leave the country with *animus non revertendi* (intention of not returning). As with the adoption of a domicile of choice, neither the loss of intention to remain nor the loss of residence is alone sufficient to lose a domicile of choice. The two elements must coincide or overlap.[36]

If a domicile of choice is abandoned without the individual acquiring a new domicile of choice, the domicile of origin revives. There is no need for residence in, or an intention to return to, the domicile of origin.[37] Consider a person born domiciled in France who adopts a domicile of choice in Ontario for many decades. If he or she then abandons that domicile to travel the world without deciding where to live

---

32 (1984), 42 CPC 84 at 89 (Ont HCJ).
33 *Schwebel v Ungar* (1964), [1965] SCR 148.
34 See, for example, *Ramsay v Liverpool Royal Infirmary*, [1930] AC 588 (HL).
35 See Law Commission, *Private International Law: The Law of Domicile*, Law Com No 168 (London: Her Majesty's Stationery Office, 1987), published jointly with the Scottish Law Commission as No 107, at para 5.7.
36 *Gunn v Gunn* (1956), 2 DLR (2d) 351 (Sask CA); *Breen v Breen* (1929), 38 Man R 409 (CA); *Re Foote Estate*, above note 2 at paras 24–27 (CA).
37 *Bonbright v Bonbright* (1901), 1 OLR 629 at 632 (HCJ).

permanently, he or she becomes domiciled in France, even if actively committed to never setting foot there again. This common law rule has been heavily criticized, chiefly because it can lead to an individual being domiciled in a country with which he or she has no connections except in the distant past.[38] Manitoba has abolished the revival of domicile of origin by statute.[39]

3) Domicile of Dependency

At common law, certain individuals were not able to acquire a domicile of choice of their own because they were considered to be legally dependent on another individual. As such, they were ascribed the domicile of the person on whom they were dependent as a domicile of dependency. If that other person's domicile changed, for example through acquiring a new domicile of choice, the dependant person's domicile changed also. The three groups to which this concept traditionally applied were minors, married women, and individuals without the cognitive ability to form the intention necessary to obtain a domicile of choice.

a) Minors

Until a minor reaches the age of majority he or she has a domicile of dependency. Traditionally, the identity of this domicile depended on whether the child was legitimate. If legitimate, a minor's domicile was that of the father.[40] If not, his or her domicile was that of the mother. It was possible for an illegitimate child to later be legitimated by the subsequent marriage of the parents, but the effect this had on the child's domicile was largely dependent on where the father was domiciled at the time.[41]

As noted above in the discussion of domicile of origin, Canadian provinces have enacted legislation that virtually eliminates legitimacy as a relevant legal consideration.[42] The domicile of minors is now addressed

---

38 Law Commission, above note 35 at paras 5.23–5.25. See the discussion in *Re Foote Estate*, above note 2 at para 97 (QB), where the court suggests that if revival of the domicile of origin would produce an "absurd" result, the court has "residual authority to instead conclude that a person has retained [his or her] last domicile of choice."
39 See the *Domicile and Habitual Residence Act*, RSM 1987, c D96, s 6. Under this statute, a person's domicile of choice persists until a new domicile is obtained.
40 *Kilpatrick v Kilpatrick* (1929), 42 BCR 88 (SC).
41 See *Udny*, above note 2 at 447–48 for the difference between English and Scottish law on this point.
42 Above note 6.

by specific provisions. For example, in Ontario the *Family Law Act* states that:

> The domicile of a person who is a minor is,
> (a) if the minor habitually resides with both parents and the parents have a common domicile, that domicile;
> (b) if the minor habitually resides with one parent only, that parent's domicile;
> (c) if the minor resides with another person who has lawful custody of him or her, that person's domicile; or
> (d) if the minor's domicile cannot be determined under clause (a), (b), or (c), the jurisdiction with which the minor has the closest connection.[43]

These provisions focus heavily on residence, but note that the minor is not simply domiciled where he or she resides. Rather, the general structure is that the minor has the domicile of a person with whom he or she resides. As explained above, that person could have a domicile of a different country.

b) Married Women

A married woman was considered to be legally dependent on her husband and so was unable to obtain an independent domicile.[44] Her domicile of dependency was the domicile of her husband. This reflected the archaic concept of married women not having distinct legal personalities. This rule led to some very unjust decisions, especially in cases where spouses had separated for many years but had not obtained a divorce.[45]

Reform in this area did not come as rapidly as might have been expected, but by the time of broader family law reforms of the 1970s the notion of a married woman as dependent on her husband was very much at odds with the times, and the law was changed by legislation. For example, the Ontario *Family Law Act* now states that "for all purposes of the law of Ontario, a married person has a legal personality that is independent, separate and distinct from that of his or her spouse."[46] Even without such legislation, the common law rules on domicile would have had to evolve in a manner consistent with the

---

43 Above note 7, s 67.
44 *Re Murray Estate* (1921), 31 Man R 362 (KB).
45 See, for example, *Lord Advocate v Jaffrey*, [1921] 1 AC 146 (HL).
46 Above note 7, s 64.

Canadian Charter of Rights and Freedoms.[47] The modern law is that a married woman is now free to obtain, lose, or otherwise change her domicile in the same way as any other competent individual.

c) The Mentally Incapable

In light of the test for domicile of choice and, in particular, the intention requirement, an individual unable to form the necessary intention will be unable to acquire a domicile of choice. The domicile of such individuals has only infrequently been considered by the courts, leaving uncertainty in this area.

It is generally assumed that the domicile of an individual who is mentally incapable is fixed as his or her domicile at the time the mental incapacity arose. This domicile cannot be changed either by the individual or by steps taken by a person on whom the individual is dependent.[48] However, there may be an exception that applies when the individual has become mentally incapable before reaching the age of majority. Here it is possible that the individual's domicile continues to be determined by the laws applying to minors, so that it continues to change with that of his or her parents.[49] It is arguable that the same approach should apply to individuals who lose capacity as adults, although some concern has been expressed about extending the law in this way.[50]

The uncertainty of the common law and a concern for the well-being of individuals who lack the required mental capacity call out for legislative intervention. Under Manitoba's *Domicile and Habitual Residence Act*, the domicile of an individual who becomes mentally incapable after birth is fixed at the time of the mental incapability.[51] However, the individual's substitute decision maker can apply to the court for a change in domicile.[52] Judicial scrutiny aims to alleviate concerns that the interests of the mentally incapable individual might be disregarded if another person could unilaterally affect such a change.

---

47 Part I of the *Constitution Act, 1982*, being Schedule B to the *Canada Act 1982*, (UK), 1982, c 11 [*Charter*]. On the interplay of the *Charter* and the common law, see *Hill v Church of Scientology*, [1995] 2 SCR 1130.
48 *Manella v Manella*, [1942] OR 630 (CA). See also *Cariello v Perrella*, 2013 ONSC 7605 at para 62.
49 *Sharpe v Crispin* (1869), 1 LR P & D 611. This approach is adopted, but only for minors who are born mentally incompetent, in Manitoba's *Domicile and Habitual Residence Act*, above note 39, s 10(1).
50 *Ibid* at 618.
51 Above note 39, s 10(2).
52 *Ibid*, ss 10(3) & 10(4).

4) Choice of Law

In determining a person's domicile, courts apply the forum's understanding of what domicile means.[53] They do not determine domicile using the law of any other country. As discussed in more detail in Chapter 10, the forum interprets and construes its private international law rules, including the meaning of concepts like domicile, using its own law. This means that different countries can reach different conclusions about where the same individual is domiciled. In particular, it should be noted that the law of domicile in the United States is in several respects quite different from that in England and other Commonwealth countries.

C. RESIDENCE

The concept of domicile was originally developed in an English society that was quite different from modern English society, and even more so from modern Canadian society. As such, we have to question the utility of domicile in modern private international law. In light of increased mobility, the easing of border controls, and large-scale immigration, domicile might no longer be the most effective way of identifying an individual's personal law. Domicile has long been a controversial topic. Its relevance was questioned by Canadian judges almost one hundred years ago[54] and modern commentators have advocated a broad move away from the concept of domicile.[55] While the law of domicile can be reformed—witness Manitoba's abolishing of the common law of domicile and replacing it with a codified version[56]—we are still left to wonder whether to reform the concept or abandon it altogether.[57]

The leading alternative to domicile is to use an individual's place of residence to identify his or her personal law. More and more legislatures are following the lead of international organizations such as the Hague Conference on Private International Law and are drafting statutes using residence rather than domicile. For example, the connecting factor for a court to have jurisdiction under the federal *Divorce*

---

53 *Re Annesley*, [1926] Ch 692; *Gillespie*, above note 17 at paras 51–52; *Re Foote Estate*, above note 2 at paras 14–16, 86, and 99 (QB).
54 *Nelson v Nelson*, above note 15.
55 See, for example, Law Commission, above note 35 at para 4.24.
56 *Domicile and Habitual Residence Act*, above note 39.
57 One way that domicile could be abandoned would be to use a rule that an individual's personal law was that of the legal system to which he or she was most closely connected. Such a rule would dramatically change the law in this area.

Act is one year of ordinary residence, not domicile.[58] As this statute illustrates, over time the notion of residence has become subdivided, yielding such concepts as ordinary residence and habitual residence.

In general, domicile is a unitary concept. This means that an individual's domicile is the same for all purposes, and the analysis does not change with the context.[59] In contrast, residence is context sensitive.[60] In part this is because residence tends to be used in statutory rules of private international law and the courts have been willing to approach each statute differently rather than insisting on the same meaning across different statutes. As a result, it is entirely possible that an individual can have a different residence depending on the legislative scheme that is applied. For example, in determining residence for purposes of immigration, it is not necessary that the court follow the definition of residence used in cases dealing with taxation.[61] There is value in this flexibility, but of course it does fragment the jurisprudence. It also makes it difficult to develop a general definition of residence and related terms. One point that is clear is that residence as used in these statutes does not have the meaning that it has as one of the two elements used to determine a domicile of choice.

1) Citizenship Cases

A leading source of judicial decisions on the meaning of residence has been the *Citizenship Act*, which until recently required an applicant to accumulate three years of residence in Canada within a four-year period.[62] The jurisprudence developed two opposing lines of authority considering the definition of residence in this context. One adopted the view that residence was

> not as strictly limited to actual presence in Canada throughout the period . . . but can include, as well, situations in which the person concerned has a place in Canada which is used by him during the period as a place of abode to a sufficient extent to demonstrate the

---

58 RSC 1985 (2nd Supp), c 3, s 3(1).
59 See *Mark v Mark*, above note 11 at 113. Despite this general position, trends can be identified in tax and succession cases that suggest there may be some sensitivity to context in determining domicile.
60 See the discussion in *Lor v Lor* (1978), 25 NSR (2d) 243 at para 12 (SCAD). See also the analysis in *Haig v Canada (Chief Electoral Officer)*, [1993] 2 SCR 995 of ordinary residence in the context of the right to vote. See also *Hipperson v Newbury District Electoral Registration Officer*, [1985] QB 1060 (CA).
61 *Blaha v Canada (Minister of Citizenship & Immigration)*, [1971] FC 521 (CA).
62 RSC 1985, c C-29.

reality of his residing there . . . even though he is away from it part of the time.⁶³

Under this interpretation, actual presence in Canada was not required on any particular day as long as the individual resided in Canada in a more general sense. This approach led to debate about when being outside Canada was temporary and transient enough to constitute being "away from it part of the time" and when it indicated that the applicant was not, in fact, resident in Canada. In *Re Papadogiorgakis* the applicant was found to meet the three-year residence requirement even though he had only been physically present in Canada for seventy-nine days during the four-year period.⁶⁴

This approach was further developed in *Re Koo*.⁶⁵ The Federal Court of Canada indicated that the focus should be on whether Canada is "the country in which [the applicant] has centralized his or her mode of existence" and it outlined six factor-based questions to ask in assessing the residence requirement.⁶⁶ These included identifying where the applicant's immediate family and dependants were resident and the reasons behind any physical absences from Canada.

Some judges expressed concern with this line of cases. One concern was that applicants were being allowed to circumvent the residence requirement by keeping

> Canadian bank accounts, magazine subscriptions, medicare cards, lodgings, furniture, other property and good intentions to meet the statutory criterion, in a word, everything except really residing among Canadians in Canada.⁶⁷

If the purpose of the legislation is to ensure that potential Canadians are present in Canada long enough to become accustomed to the values, virtues, and dangers of Canadian society,⁶⁸ it is difficult to see how this can occur for an individual who is physically present in Canada only for a few months. As a result, a second line of cases held that residence

---

63 *Re Papadogiorgakis*, [1978] 2 FC 208 at 213–14 (TD).
64 *Ibid* at 215. See also *Re Chien* (1992), 51 FTR 317 at 318 (TD).
65 (1992), [1993] 1 FC 286 (TD).
66 *Ibid* at 293–94. See also *Thomson v Minister of Natural Revenue*, [1946] SCR 209 at 225 [*Thomson*], where the court stated that residence "is chiefly a matter of the degree to which a person in mind and fact settles into or maintains or centralizes his ordinary mode of living with its accessories in social relations, interests and conveniences at or in the place in question."
67 *Re Pourghasemi* (1993), 62 FTR 122 at para 4. See also *Canada (Minister of Citizenship and Immigration) v Naveen*, 2013 FC 972.
68 *Re Pourghasemi*, above note 67 at paras 3–8.

is to be interpreted as actual presence in Canada, such that days spent outside the country cannot be counted at all.[69]

Regrettably, this issue could not be resolved by an appellate court, since the statute precluded further appeal beyond the Federal Court.[70] In *Huang v Canada (Minister of Citizenship and Immigration)*, the Chief Justice of the Federal Court called for legislative intervention: "something needs to be done to address the unacceptable state of affairs concerning the test for citizenship in this country."[71]

The issue has now been resolved: the *Citizenship Act* was amended in 2015.[72] The requirement based on residence, the meaning of which was open to interpretation by the courts, was replaced with detailed requirements for specific numbers of days of physical presence in Canada during the period prior to the application. This approach clearly comes down on the side of the second of the two approaches outlined above. It also means that, going forward, the citizenship context will generate much less jurisprudence on the meaning of residence.[73]

2) Ordinary Residence

Ordinary residence has often been either confused or amalgamated with "mere" residence. A majority of the Supreme Court of Canada held that the adjective "ordinary" does not necessarily add anything to the meaning of residence.[74] However, this was in the context of a statutory provision that called for either residence or ordinary residence, so the importance of the distinction may not have been evident. On basic principles of statutory interpretation, the use of an additional word, "ordinary," to modify residence should alter the meaning.

Lord Scarman provided considerable insight into the difference between the two concepts when he stated that the natural and ordinary meaning of "ordinary resident" added two elements to residence:

> The residence must be voluntarily adopted. Enforced residence by reason of kidnapping or imprisonment . . . may be so overwhelming a factor as to negative the will to be where one is. And there must be a

---

69 *Ibid*; *Re Harry* (1998), 144 FTR 141 (TD); *Chen v Canada (Minister of Citizenship and Immigration)* (2001), 213 FTR 137 at para 15 (TD); *Martinez-Caro v Canada (Minister of Citizenship and Immigration)*, 2011 FC 640.
70 *Citizenship Act*, above note 62, s 14(6).
71 2013 FC 576 at para 1.
72 Above note 62, s 5 in general and s 5(1)(c) in particular.
73 In February 2016 the government proposed changes to the residence requirements, but they maintain the approach to assessing residence adopted in 2015.
74 *Thomson*, above note 66.

degree of settled purpose.... This is not to say that the "propositus" intends to stay where he is indefinitely; indeed his purpose, while settled, may be for a limited period.... All that is necessary is that the purpose of living where one does has a sufficient degree of continuity to be properly described as settled.[75]

This is similar to the definition used by Rand J in *Thomson v Minister of National Revenue*: "It is held to mean residence in the course of the customary mode of life of the person concerned, and it is contrasted with special or occasional or casual residence."[76] This appears to adopt a middle position between the fairly loose requirements for residence and the strict requirements for domicile. It is not necessary that an individual intend to make his or her home indefinitely in the country, as it is for domicile, and it follows that an individual is not prohibited from having more than one ordinary residence, assuming a sufficient degree of settled purpose is evident in both countries.[77] This would potentially allow an individual away from a country to remain ordinarily resident in that country, though while away he or she would not be resident there.

The question then arises as to what constitutes a settled purpose or a customary mode of life. The purpose need not involve staying forever: much shorter periods, even with a definitive end in sight as close as six months away, can qualify as a settled purpose.[78] A comprehensive analysis considers the residence of family members, location of furniture, ownership of property, and other relevant aspects of an individual's life. What seems to be most important is that for some period of time the individual used the country for his or her customary routine of life and then retained sufficient connections to the country.

An ordinary residence is not necessarily lost on the adoption of a new ordinary residence because, subject to statutes stipulating to the contrary, it is possible for an individual to have more than one ordinary residence at a given time.[79] Ordinary residence is also not lost merely because an individual is physically absent from the country for some

---

75 *R v Barnet London Borough Council, Ex Parte Shah*, [1983] 2 AC 309 (HL) at 344 [*Barnet London Borough Council*].
76 Above note 66 at 224. See also *Quigley v Willmore*, 2008 NSCA 33; *Armoyan v Armoyan*, 2013 NSCA 99 at para 214; *Nafie v Badawy*, 2015 ABCA 36.
77 *Thomson*, above note 66 at 224. See also *Knowles v Lindstrom*, 2014 ONCA 116 at para 32.
78 *Al Habtoor v Fotheringham*, [2001] 1 FLR 951 at 966 (CA); *Re R (Abduction: Habitual Residence)*, [2004] 1 FLR 216.
79 *Mester v Kummu* (1957), 11 DLR (2d) 217 (Ont HCJ).

period of time, as long as sufficient ties to the residence persist.[80] However, if the absence is in order to live in another country where the individual intends to make his or her home for an indefinite period, the ordinary residence in the former country may be lost.[81]

3) Habitual Residence

There is debate about the difference between habitual residence and ordinary residence. In the leading decision from the House of Lords, "habitual" was used simply as one of the words defining ordinary residence.[82] This lack of distinction has been adopted by the leading English textbooks.[83] Although some Canadian jurisprudence suggests that the two terms are in fact different, there is little real discussion about the difference between the two.[84] Rather, it seems as though the desire to distinguish habitual residence from ordinary residence arises because some courts equate the latter with mere residence. If these two concepts are properly distinguished, there may be no reason to further distinguish habitual residence from ordinary residence.

Manitoba's *Domicile and Habitual Residence Act* refers extensively to habitual residence.[85] However, it probably does not offer much guidance for cases outside Manitoba because it adopts a somewhat unusual approach. The statute merges the concepts of domicile and habitual residence in that it stipulates a joint definition for both: where a person's principal home is located and where that person intends to reside.[86] Further, unless a contrary intention is shown, an individual is presumed to intend to reside indefinitely in the country where that individual's principal home is located.[87] It has been suggested that what

---

80 *Marsellus v Marsellus* (1970), 13 DLR (3d) 383 (BCSC).
81 *Ibid*. See also *Macrae v Macrae*, [1949] 2 All ER 34 at 36–37 (CA); *Molson v Molson* (1998), 222 AR 130 (QB).
82 *Barnet London Borough Council*, above note 75 at 342. See also *Ikimi v Ikimi*, [2001] 3 WLR 672 at para 31 (CA).
83 See James Fawcett & Janeen M Carruthers, *Cheshire, North & Fawcett Private International Law*, 14th ed (Oxford: Oxford University Press, 2008) at 185.
84 *Adderson v Adderson* (1987), 77 AR 256 (CA). In this case the court discussed habitual residence in much the same terms as those used by Lord Scarman about ordinary residence in *Barnet London Borough Council*, above note 75. The court suggested that "habitual" refers to the quality of residence rather than the length and that habitual residence falls somewhere between domicile and residence. See *Cruse v Chittum*, [1974] 2 All ER 940 at 942–43 (Fam D).
85 Above note 39.
86 *Ibid*, s 8(1).
87 *Ibid*, s 8(2).

these provisions do is define habitual residence very much in the terms of the common law of domicile, with the only real difference being the added presumption as to intention.[88] In contrast, in other provinces habitual residence is seen as something quite distinct from domicile.

4) Future Directions

Given the confusion in the jurisprudence, it would be beneficial if future legislative drafting using residence, ordinary residence, or habitual residence included a more detailed explanation as to how the chosen term is to be interpreted.[89] This would ensure that legislative intent is not frustrated by inconsistent judicial interpretation, which is the central problem in the current cases. In the absence of statutory precision, it would also be useful if the courts could agree on a common or core definition of each type of residence to be employed where no guidance is given. However, as noted earlier, a context-specific interpretive approach to residence mitigates against such a development.

As a link to an individual's personal law, residence tends to work best in contexts that do not require an exclusive answer. This is in part because an individual can have more than one residence. If the link is being used to determine which country's courts have jurisdiction, it is acceptable to conclude that the courts in each country in which the individual is resident have jurisdiction. But if the link is being used to identify the law to resolve a dispute, a unitary answer is required—something domicile, but not residence, provides. If domicile is to be replaced by residence in all contexts, this problem would have to be overcome, perhaps through some concept of residence that does provide a single answer.

D. CORPORATIONS

Domicile and residence are concepts that are mainly relevant to individuals. However, there are times when it is necessary to apply them to corporations. In *National Trust Company Ltd v Ebro Irrigation and Power Company Ltd* the court confirmed the well-established principle that a

---

88 Peter North, "Domicile" in *Private International Law Problems in Common Law Jurisdictions* (Dordrecht: Martinus Nijhoff, 1993) at 21.
89 See, for example, Canada Revenue Agency, "Determining an Individual's Residence Status," Income Tax Folio S5-F1-C1, 26 November 2015.

corporation's domicile is the country in which it was incorporated.[90] It is harder to generalize for residence, since different definitions can be used in different contexts. Several contexts adopt the approach that a corporation is resident where its central management and control are located.[91]

FURTHER READINGS

ACORN, ANNALISE. "Gender Discrimination in the Common Law of Domicile and the Application of the *Canadian Charter of Rights and Freedoms*" (1991) 29 *Osgoode Hall Law Journal* 419.

CARTER, PB. "Domicil: The Case for Radical Reform in the United Kingdom" (1987) 36 *International and Comparative Law Quarterly* 713.

FAWCETT, JAMES. "Result Selection in Domicile Cases" (1985) 5 *Oxford Journal of Legal Studies* 378.

FENTIMAN, RICHARD. "Activity in the Law of Status: Domicile, Marriage and the Law Commission" (1986) 6 *Oxford Journal of Legal Studies* 353.

FENTIMAN, RICHARD. "Domicile Revisited" [1991] *Cambridge Law Journal* 445.

FORSYTH, CHRISTOPHER. "The Domicile of the Illegal Resident" (2005) 1 *Journal of Private International Law* 335.

HALPERN, JOHN. "Residence or Domicile: A State of Mind?" (1993) 41 *Canadian Tax Journal* 129.

MANITOBA LAW REFORM COMMISSION. *Report on the Law of Domicile* (Winnipeg: Manitoba Law Reform Commission, 1982).

MCELEAVY, PETER. "Regression and Reform in the Law of Domicile" (2007) 56 *International and Comparative Law Quarterly* 453.

PILKINGTON, MP. "Illegal Residence and the Acquisition of a Domicile of Choice" (1984) 33 *International and Comparative Law Quarterly* 885.

---

90 [1954] OR 463 at 476 (HCJ). See also *Gasque v Commissioners of Inland Revenue*, [1940] 2 KB 80 at 84; *Axis Management Inc v Alsager* (2000), 197 Sask R 234 at 237 (QB).
91 For a broad definition, see *Court Jurisdiction and Proceedings Transfer Act*, SBC 2003, c 28, s 7.

RAFFERTY, NICHOLAS. "Domicile: The Need for Reform" (1977) 7 *Manitoba Law Journal* 203.

ROGERSON, PIPPA. "Habitual Residence: The New Domicile?" (2000) 49 *International and Comparative Law Quarterly* 86.

SMART, P ST J. "Domicile of Choice and Multiple Residence" (1990) 10 *Oxford Journal of Legal Studies* 572.

TRAKMAN, LEON. "Domicile of Choice in English Law: An Achilles Heel?" (2015) 11 *Journal of Private International Law* 317.

WADE, JA. "Domicile: A Re-Examination of Certain Rules" (1983) 32 *International and Comparative Law Quarterly* 1.

CHAPTER 3

EXCLUSION OF FOREIGN LAW

A. INTRODUCTION

Canadian private international law gives considerable effect to foreign law. It does this, for example, when it respects a foreign court's taking of jurisdiction over a dispute, when it applies foreign law to resolve a dispute in the forum, and when it recognizes and enforces a foreign judgment or arbitral award. However, there are situations in which Canadian courts will refuse to give effect to foreign law and they will exclude that law from their analysis. Some of these situations will be discussed throughout this book, such as in Chapter 8 when looking at reasons why a court might not recognize a foreign judgment and in Chapter 14 when looking at mandatory rules in choice of law for contract. However, some of the fundamental principles relating to exclusion of foreign law cut across the whole subject, so it is useful to identify them at the outset.

A court can exclude foreign law in several ways. As noted, it can refuse to recognize or enforce the judgment of a foreign court. In deciding a case it can refuse to apply foreign legal rules that are, under the relevant choice of law rules, otherwise applicable. It can even refuse to give effect to a jurisdiction agreement requiring litigation in another country. These are all different areas of the conflict of laws, but the principles in this chapter can justify the exclusion of foreign law in each of them.

This chapter highlights the tension between comity—being a good neighbour in the international community—and the protection of domestic interests. These exclusions allow the court to disregard foreign law and instead apply the law of the forum. The broader their scope, the more insular and chauvinistic the courts can become. However, as comity has taken on increased importance, the scope of these exclusions has diminished. They are particularly narrow in the interprovincial context. But the debate about whether the balance has been struck in the right place is far from resolved.

The effect of excluding foreign law is clearer in some cases than in others. In the recognition and enforcement context, the effect is straightforward: the forum refuses to give any effect to the foreign judgment. Similarly, if a plaintiff advances a claim under a foreign law that the forum excludes, the claim fails. In a more complex case, the claim might be governed by a foreign applicable law, but only one aspect of that law causes the forum court concern. Here the approach to exclusion is less clear. The forum could exclude the entirety of the foreign law and apply the law of the forum instead. This response is too extreme. Alternatively, the forum could exclude only the specific foreign legal rule in question and resolve the dispute by applying the balance of the foreign law. This is viable when the foreign law provides a coherent response without the specific provision. For example, if the forum excludes a foreign law that prevents a gratuitous passenger involved in a car accident from suing the driver in tort, it can still apply the rest of the foreign tort law to resolve the dispute. In the further alternative, the forum could apply a combination of foreign and forum law, using the latter in place of the specific foreign rule being excluded.[1]

B. PUBLIC POLICY

A central basis for excluding foreign law is that the foreign law conflicts with the forum's public policy. This basis is not established simply because a foreign law or decision has a different policy basis than that of the forum. Canadian courts are quite willing to apply foreign laws that are very different from those in effect where those courts sit.[2] For this exclusion to apply, the foreign law must violate the "essential morality" or "fundamental values" of the forum.[3] The court would, for example,

---

1 For additional discussion, see the analysis of mandatory rules in choice of law for contract in Chapter 14.
2 *Boardwalk Regency Corp v Maalouf* (1992), 6 OR (3d) 737 at 748 (CA).
3 *Ibid* at 743; *Society of Lloyd's v Meinzer* (2001), 55 OR (3d) 688 at para 48 (CA) [*Society of Lloyd's*]; *Dash 224, LLC v Vector Aerospace Engine Services-Atlantic Inc*, 2015 PESC 27 at paras 32–33 [*Dash 224*]. See also *Loucks v Standard Oil Co of New York*, 120 NE 198 at 202 (NY 1918).

refuse to apply a law that confiscated property on religious or racial grounds.[4]

In *Boardwalk Regency Corp v Maalouf* the plaintiff attempted to enforce a New Jersey judgment in respect of gaming debts.[5] The original transaction was illegal under Ontario law. The defendant raised public policy, but a majority of the Court of Appeal for Ontario held that the judgment was enforceable. It considered the evolution of Ontario's laws on gambling, the current legislation, and the prevailing values in the community. The majority found that the New Jersey law was not immoral and did not violate the fundamental values of Ontario, drawing support from the Ontario government's own significant involvement in gambling.[6] In dissent, Arbour JA distinguished between state involvement in gambling and gambling between private entities, the latter still being illegal in Ontario. Her approach appears to treat the criminal law prohibition as more directly expressing a moral standard and thus the forum's fundamental values than does that of the majority.

More controversially, in *Society of Lloyd's v Meinzer* the Court of Appeal for Ontario held that a failure to comply with disclosure requirements for certain investment transactions under the *Securities Act*[7] was a breach of "what in today's society are viewed as fundamental and essential values."[8] Disclosure requirements are certainly important, but it is difficult to see them as in the same vein as laws involving slavery or religion-based property confiscation. The breadth of this view of public policy could expand the courts' ability to exclude foreign law in many different modern situations.[9] This decision is doubly interesting, for having concluded that enforcing the decision of the English court would violate Ontario's public policy, the court nonetheless enforced it. The court held that other public policy considerations, including the disruption that a refusal to enforce would cause to the international insurance markets, outweighed the disclosure requirement violations.[10]

---

4 See *Oppenheimer v Cattermole*, [1976] AC 249 at 277–78 (HL). As another example, double recovery by a plaintiff has been held to be contrary to our "general moral outlook": *Re Lambert* (2001), 26 CBR (4th) 235 at para 76 (Ont SCJ).

5 Above note 2.

6 *Ibid* at 749–50. See also *Re iTV Games Inc* (2001), 18 BLR (3d) 312 (BCSC), leave to appeal denied (2002), 21 BLR (3d) 258 (BCCA).

7 RSO 1990, c S.5, s 53(1).

8 Above note 3 at para 70.

9 It seems that the Court of Appeal did not consider its analysis to be broadening the scope of public policy. It expressly noted that "the case law confirms that the public policy exemption is narrow": *ibid* at para 60.

10 *Ibid* at para 87. Another interesting example is *Branco v American Home Assurance Co*, 2015 SKCA 71 at paras 170–79, which held that a foreign rule prohibiting punitive damages in a claim by an insured against an insurer "is so deeply

The threshold for invoking the public policy exclusion may be challenging to apply in family law cases. Some foreign decisions have been denied recognition and enforcement because the foreign law applied did not accord with Canadian policy objectives in areas such as spousal and child support and division of matrimonial property on marital breakdown.[11] Cases in which the foreign law, for example, provides no or a trivial award are easy enough, but the analysis is more complicated when an award of some value is made but at a level lower than what would be awarded under Canadian law.[12]

In an important development, the House of Lords has confirmed that a law that violates rules of public international law can be excluded on the basis of the forum's public policy.[13] This decision is significant in using public international law rules in this way. In 1990 Iraq invaded Kuwait and seized ten airplanes owned by Kuwait Airways Corporation (KAC). The planes were flown to Iraq and given to Iraq Airways Company (IAC) and Iraq passed a law transferring all of KAC's property to IAC. KAC sued IAC in England for return of the planes or their value. To succeed in its claim, KAC had to show that it owned the planes. But, as is explained in Chapter 18, the law of the place where movable property is located governs the legality of any transfer, so the Iraqi law, passed while the planes were in Iraq, meant IAC, not KAC, owned the planes. KAC therefore argued that the English court should, as a matter of public policy, not give effect to the Iraqi law. Under English law, public policy had not generally been defined in terms of compliance with public international law. Yet the House of Lords held that the seizure and transfer of the planes was a serious violation of public international law—Iraq had failed to comply with resolutions of the United Nations Security Council—and on this basis the law could be excluded.[14]

As indicated, public policy is most frequently invoked to exclude a foreign applicable law or as a defence to recognizing and enforcing a foreign judgment.[15] But in more unusual cases it could be used to exclude a jurisdiction clause in a contract.[16] In *Agro Co of Canada Ltd v The "Regal Scout"* a Canadian company shipped goods to Japan using a

---

inconsistent with Saskatchewan legal policy interests that it can and should be disregarded on public policy grounds."

11 See, for example, *Zhang v Lin*, 2010 ABQB 420 at paras 68–71; *Marzara v Marzara*, 2011 BCSC 408 at paras 77–79.
12 See, for example, *Dashtarai v Shahrestani*, [2006] OJ No 5367 (SCJ).
13 *Kuwait Airways Corporation v Iraqi Airways Company*, [2002] 2 AC 883 (HL).
14 *Ibid* at para 29, Lord Nicholls.
15 On the latter, see the analysis of the public policy defence in *Beals v Saldanha*, [2003] 3 SCR 416, discussed in Chapter 8, Section C(4).
16 Jurisdiction clauses are discussed in detail in Chapters 5 & 6.

Japanese carrier.[17] The contract of carriage was expressly governed by Japanese law and contained an exclusive jurisdiction clause in favour of Japan. When a dispute arose, the Canadian company sued in Federal Court in British Columbia. The defendants argued that because of the exclusive jurisdiction clause, the proceedings should be stayed in favour of Japan. However, the court rejected this argument and refused to give any effect to the clause. It did so not because litigation in Japan in itself violated Canadian public policy. The court's concern was that the litigation in Japan would apply Japanese law and thereby give effect to a clause in the contract excluding all liability for the carrier. Under Canadian law, this clause was null and void and of no effect.[18]

The approach in this decision is aggressive.[19] We have already seen that a court hearing a dispute might exclude an otherwise applicable foreign law based on public policy. That would justify the Federal Court, were it hearing the dispute, not applying the chosen Japanese law. But it is a significant step from there to exclude not only the choice of law clause but also the exclusive jurisdiction clause. The court's position is that the relevant Canadian law is of such fundamental importance that not only can it not be derogated from by contract through the choice of a foreign applicable law, it cannot be avoided through litigation in another jurisdiction.

C. PENAL LAW

This section and the two that follow examine more specific bases for excluding foreign law. In one sense, they can be seen as subsets of the broader notion of public policy discussed above.[20] However, it is useful to consider them separately, both for ease of analysis and because they are each more specifically concerned with protecting the forum's territorial sovereignty than is public policy.[21]

---

17 (1983), 148 DLR (3d) 412 (FCTD).
18 Under what was then the *Carriage of Goods by Water Act*, RSC 1970, c C-15. The court held that the jurisdiction clause was to be excluded based on its interpretation of the language in the statute. But the court applied this Canadian statute as a rule of the forum without any analysis of the issue of choice of law, which suggests that the statute was applied as a matter of public policy.
19 It is consistent with an earlier English decision on similar facts: see *The Hollandia*, [1983] 1 AC 565 (HL).
20 See *Moore v Mitchell*, 30 F2d 600 at 604 (2d Cir 1929).
21 See *Re State of Norway's Application (Nos 1 & 2)*, [1990] 1 AC 723 at 807–8 (HL).

Criminal law is highly territorial. There are no choice of law rules for crimes: each jurisdiction applies its own criminal law. Countries do not enforce the criminal law of other countries.[22] A person alleged to have committed crimes in England would not be tried for those crimes in Canada. Instead, the system of extradition can be used so that the person is taken to England to be tried there. Even in more modern cases where the strict territorial principle is eroded, an accused is still tried under the law of the forum, not under the law of the place of acting. For example, a Canadian citizen who sexually exploits children in Cambodia can be tried for that conduct in Canada, but this occurs not under Cambodian law but rather under Canadian law that is extraterritorially applied to conduct outside Canada.[23]

This view of criminal law has influenced our treatment of foreign penal laws in a civil context. Under the penal law exclusion, courts do not apply the penal law of foreign countries and do not recognize or enforce the penal law judgments of foreign countries.[24] As noted by Lord Denning, "No one has ever doubted that our courts will not entertain a suit brought by a foreign sovereign, directly or indirectly, to enforce the penal or revenue laws of that foreign state. We do not sit to collect taxes for another country or to inflict punishments for it."[25] This makes it important to define penal law. A key early case, *Huntington v Attrill*, held that penal law included any claim advanced by the state aiming to recover monetary penalties for a violation of statute.[26] In that case a creditor had successfully sued the defendant in New York and then sought to enforce the judgment in Ontario. The defendant argued the original claim was based on New York's penal law. The Privy Council disagreed. The claim was by a private party, not the state, and the money would be paid to that private party.

In *United States of America v Ivey* the plaintiff had obtained two judgments against the defendants in Michigan and then sought to enforce them in Ontario.[27] The judgments were based on American

---

22 Courts do, however, recognize the criminal law of other countries and can factor it into their analysis. A leading example of this is discussed in Chapter 14, looking at situations when the performance of a contract is illegal under the law of the place where it is to be performed.
23 See *Criminal Code of Canada*, RSC 1985, c C-46, s 7(4.1). The validity of this extraterritorial legislation was upheld in *R v Klassen*, [2008] BCJ No 2485 (SC). See, more generally, *Libman v The Queen*, [1985] 2 SCR 178.
24 See *Pro Swing Inc v Elta Golf Inc*, [2006] 2 SCR 612 at paras 34 and 100. This decision is discussed in more detail in Chapter 8.
25 *Attorney-General of New Zealand v Ortiz*, [1984] 1 AC 1 at 20 [*Ortiz*].
26 [1893] AC 150 (PC).
27 (1995), 26 OR (3d) 533 (Gen Div), aff'd (1996), 30 OR (3d) 370 (CA) [*Ivey*].

legislation that imposed liability on specific people for environmental cleanup costs, here in respect of a waste disposal operation in Michigan. In resisting the enforcement proceedings in Ontario, the defendants raised the penal law exclusion. They argued that the American statute was penal law, so that a judgment under it should not be enforced. The claim was clearly brought by the state and payment would flow to the state. However, the Ontario courts held that this was not penal law. In their view, making the defendants repay costs that had been incurred was not a penalty. The amount awarded was not arbitrary but rather was directly linked to what the plaintiff had spent.[28]

Ivey illustrates another important point, namely that it is the law of the forum that determines whether a foreign law is penal law.[29] The foreign law's view, or characterization,[30] is not determinative although it can and should be considered. In *Ivey* the court specifically referred to how American courts had noted that the statute "does not exact punishment. Rather it creates a reimbursement obligation .... The restitution of cleanup costs was not intended to operate, nor does it operate in fact, as a criminal penalty or a punitive deterrent."[31]

The way in which the foreign law is formulated can make a significant difference. If the American statute had made it an offence to own a company that polluted and had imposed a fine on conviction, it is much more likely that the foreign judgments would have been excluded as penal law. This is probably the case even if the fine had been based on the amount of the cleanup costs incurred.

The boundary of penal law can be pushed beyond the traditional cases involving fines payable to the state. In *Attorney-General of New Zealand v Ortiz* the plaintiff sued in England, attempting to enforce a New Zealand statute that provided for the forfeiture of cultural property improperly exported from the country.[32] The law did not impose any monetary penalty. Nonetheless, two judges of the Court of Appeal held that this was penal law and so subject to exclusion. The trial judge had disagreed, holding that the purpose of the law was to protect the cultural property rather than to punish its owners.[33] The majority view

---

28   See also *United States of America v Yemec* (2009), 97 OR (3d) 409 at paras 167–68 (SCJ), rev'd on other grounds 2010 ONCA 414.
29   See also *Iran v The Barakat Galleries Limited*, [2007] EWCA Civ 1374 at para 106 [*Barakat*]; *United States of America v Inkley*, [1989] QB 255 at 265.
30   For more on the process of characterization, see Chapter 10.
31   *United States v Monsanto Co*, 858 F2d 160 (4th Cir 1988), quoted in *Ivey*, above note 27 at 544 (Gen Div).
32   Above note 25.
33   The decision was appealed to the House of Lords, which resolved the case without having to address the penal law exclusion. It found that on its wording the statute

of the Court of Appeal is consistent with other cases that have held that expropriation at less than fair market value is penal law.[34]

However, the judicial mood in this area may be changing, in part based on greater sensitivity to the need to protect cultural and historical property. In *Iran v The Barakat Galleries Limited* the government of Iran sued in England, claiming ownership of certain antiquities.[35] Under the law of Iran the government had an immediate right to possession of illegally excavated antiquities, a right that would vest ownership on its taking possession.[36] However, the defendant argued that the Iranian law should be excluded in the English litigation as penal law. The trial judge agreed, on the basis that the Iranian law gave the state title by compulsory process of law and also imposed penalties for illegal excavation, including imprisonment. The Court of Appeal reversed this decision. The Iranian law did impose penalties but those were not at issue in the litigation. The court had to focus on the specific rule in question, namely the rule dealing with title. The ownership provisions were not retroactive, did not deprive anyone of title, and thus were not penal.[37]

Another English case concerned proceedings in Massachusetts brought by the Securities and Exchange Commission (SEC) against alleged fraudsters.[38] The SEC sought an order in England freezing the fraudsters' assets pending the results of the claim. The fraudsters argued that the claim was based on American penal law and so the resulting judgment would not be enforceable in England, so that their assets there should not be frozen in the meantime. In its Massachusetts action, the SEC was seeking both disgorgement of gains and civil penalties, with the former to be paid out to defrauded investors. The Court of Appeal held that the substance of the claim was to require disgorgement of the proceeds of fraud, and so the claim was not one based on penal law. Like *Barakat*, this decision may signal a narrowing of the penal law exclusion.

A judgment for the plaintiff on the underlying claim is not penal simply because it results from the foreign court's sanctioning of the

---

did not apply to the property once it was in England. For the statute to have applied, the property would have had to be seized prior to its being exported.

34 See *Laane v Estonian State Cargo & Passenger Steamship Line*, [1949] SCR 530.

35 Above note 29. On the need to protect this sort of property, see paras 152–63.

36 *Ibid* at paras 82 and 84.

37 *Ibid* at paras 110–11. For a more detailed analysis of cases involving the expropriation of foreign property, see James Fawcett & Janeen M Carruthers, *Cheshire, North & Fawcett Private International Law*, 14th ed (Oxford: Oxford University Press, 2008) at 132–39. Consider also the facts of *Dash 224*, above note 3.

38 *United States Securities and Exchange Commission v Manterfield*, [2009] EWCA Civ 27.

defendant's conduct of the litigation. A default judgment, for example, which can be said to sanction the defendant's failure to appear, is not on that basis penal. The same is true for substantive judgments resulting from a defendant's violations of various pretrial rules such as those dealing with disclosure.[39] The judgment sought to be enforced is in respect of the underlying claim, not the defendant's conduct in the litigation.

Historically the penal law exclusion has been applied as between Canadian provinces. An Ontario court would therefore refuse to enforce a British Columbia judgment ordering the defendant to pay fines to the British Columbia government and it would not allow a claim by that government to recover the fines owing to be brought against the defendant in Ontario. However, the operation of this exclusion within Canada is ripe for reconsideration in light of the principles in *Morguard Investments Ltd v De Savoye*.[40] The requirement that full faith and credit be given to the laws and judgments of other provinces may mean the penal law exclusion is unconstitutional within Canada. Indeed, the foundations of the entire penal law exclusion may be increasingly shaky. In the modern world, there should be much less concern that a country's territorial sovereignty is at risk if foreign penal laws are allowed to have effect. Increasing commercial globalization and economic interdependence militate against maintaining this exclusion in its current form.

D. REVENUE LAW

Under this long-standing exclusion, a foreign tax judgment will not be recognized or enforced and a claim based on a foreign tax law will not be allowed.[41] In *United States of America v Harden* the plaintiff obtained a tax judgment against the defendant in California.[42] When the defendant did not pay, the plaintiff brought an enforcement action in British Columbia. The Supreme Court of Canada refused to recognize or enforce the judgment. It held that whether a foreign government sued

---

39 *Dingwall v Foster*, 2014 ABCA 89 at paras 47–49.
40 [1990] 3 SCR 1077 [*Morguard*]. For more discussion of this important decision, see Chapters 5 and 8.
41 *Holman v Johnson* (1775), 98 ER 1120 at 1121; *Government of India, Ministry of Finance (Revenue Division) v Taylor*, [1955] AC 491; *Prince v ACE Aviation Holdings Inc*, 2014 ONCA 285 at paras 50–52. See also the quotation from Lord Denning in *Ortiz*, above note 25.
42 [1963] SCR 366.

directly in Canada to recover taxes or sued on a judgment previously obtained elsewhere, the underlying liability of the defendant was to pay tax: the exclusion applied.

Courts have held that the revenue law exclusion applies both to claims advanced by a foreign government and to indirect claims in which the plaintiff is not the government but the result of the claim will be the indirect application or enforcement of foreign tax laws. In *Stringam v Dubois* a woman died in Arizona and left a farm in Alberta to her niece.[43] In Alberta the executor sought a sale of the farm to satisfy American estate taxes. The Court of Appeal held that this would amount to giving indirect effect to the foreign government's claim for taxes. It ordered the farm transferred to the niece.

Perhaps to a greater degree than with the penal law exclusion, there is considerable reason to question the continued operation of the revenue law exclusion.[44] In *Stringam*, the Alberta Court of Appeal noted that "the Supreme Court may wish to re-examine the problem in the light of more modern international notions of comity."[45] The historical hostility between nations and focus on territorial sovereignty has evolved into a much more international approach, leaving it difficult to justify why the courts of one country should exclude the tax laws or judgments of another country. It has been suggested that removing the exclusion would force courts into having to draw invidious distinctions between foreign laws and judgments, applying and enforcing some but not others.[46] Central to this suggestion is concern that foreign tax laws are frequently discriminatory or otherwise not in accordance with the public policy of the forum. This considerably overstates the problem. In a large number of cases, the foreign revenue law would not be contrary to Canadian public policy. This is particularly so as concerns the law of other provinces and American states. Furthermore, those cases that do raise genuine public policy concerns can be addressed by Canadian courts under the public policy exclusion in the same way they handle non-revenue laws and judgments.

---

43   (1992), 135 AR 64 (CA) [*Stringam*].
44   In contrast, for a recent defence of the rule see David Bishop Debenham, "From the Revenue Rule to the Rule of the 'Revenuer': A Tale of Two Davids and Two Goliaths" (2008) 56 *Canadian Tax Journal* 1.
45   Above note 43 at para 33.
46   Hans W Baade, "Operation of Foreign Public Law" in Kurt Lipstein, ed, *International Encyclopedia of Comparative Law*, vol 3 (Tübingen, Germany: JCB Mohr, 1970–) ch 12 at 52. In addition, a statement that a foreign tax rule violates the forum's public policy could embarrass the foreign country. For a recent American case upholding the revenue exclusion, see *Attorney General of Canada v RJ Reynolds Tobacco Holdings, Inc*, 268 F3d 103 (2d Cir 2001).

Today, it is doubtful that the revenue law exclusion applies between provinces, at least in the context of proceedings to enforce a foreign judgment.[47] It is more of an open question whether the government of one province can sue for taxes in the courts of another province, though the *Morguard* principle of full faith and credit strongly suggests this should be possible.[48] In addition, at least one Canadian decision has shown a willingness to modify the exclusion in the international context. In the context of bankruptcy proceedings, the court in *Re Sefel Geophysical Ltd* noted that "given the present trends of international comity in the recognition of foreign bankruptcy proceedings, I am not certain that [the revenue rule] is compatible with the current judicial climate."[49]

Beyond these changes in the common law, the revenue law exclusion has become less important because of certain provincial statutes and bilateral conventions. Canada has agreed to enforce the tax judgments of several other countries, including the United States.[50] Within Canada, provincial legislation provides for the recognition and enforcement of tax judgments of other provinces.[51]

E. OTHER PUBLIC LAW

The exclusions discussed in the two previous sections both concern foreign public law. Going beyond these two specific areas of public law, courts have concluded that a similar exclusion exists for other foreign public law. However, this exclusion has proven to be very difficult to define. As noted in *Attorney-General (United Kingdom) v Heinemann Publishers Australia Pty Ltd*, nearly all statutory law is in a sense public law, having a political and public element.[52] A wide definition of public law would give this exclusion a wide scope, which would be quite contrary to comity and the narrow

---

47 See *Weir v Lohr* (1967), 65 DLR (2d) 717 (Man QB); Vaughan Black, "Old and in the Way? The Revenue Rule and Big Tobacco" (2003) 38 *Canadian Business Law Journal* 1 at 16.
48 Above note 40.
49 [1989] 1 WWR 251 at 260 (Alta QB). See also *Re Matol Botanical International Ltd*, [2001] QJ No 4195 (CS).
50 *Canada–United States Convention with Respect to Taxes on Income and on Capital*, 26 September 1980, art 26A, as enacted by the *Canada–United States Tax Convention Act, 1984*, SC 1984, c 20.
51 See, for example, the *Income Tax Act*, RSO 1990, c I.2, s 54. Note also that the Uniform Law Conference of Canada's *Enforcement of Canadian Judgments and Decrees Act* specifically excludes penal judgments from its scope but not tax judgments.
52 (1988), 165 CLR 30 (HCA) [*Heinemann*].

scope of the other grounds for exclusion. Accordingly, the presence of a public interest underlying a foreign law should not automatically be a ground for exclusion. Other public law is best defined as law under which a foreign government is asserting its particular interests over people or property outside its own territory.[53]

In *Ivey*, discussed above under the penal law exclusion, the courts also considered whether the claim by the American government was other public law, and in doing so looked to whether the claim could "be characterized as an attempt by a foreign state to assert its sovereignty within the territory of Ontario."[54] The courts noted the importance of having states create regulatory schemes in areas like environmental law and expressed concern that a wide meaning of other public law would make such schemes, and judgments under them, unenforceable abroad. The Ontario courts found the exclusion did not apply and enforced the judgment.[55] To the extent that the line between what is private law and what is public law is increasingly blurred, this exclusion could become more difficult to apply.

This ground of exclusion has been considered in a variety of cases, often in conjunction with the penal law exclusion. In *Ortiz*, Lord Denning considered that the statute providing for forfeiture of cultural property was other public law and could thus be excluded, but the other two judges of the Court of Appeal did not agree.[56] This exclusion also arose in the *Spycatcher* litigation. The United Kingdom government sued Heinemann in Australia and New Zealand to prevent publication of a book, titled *Spycatcher*, by a former member of the British Security Service. The High Court of Australia held that this was a claim advancing the interests of the United Kingdom government and thus was excluded as other public law.[57] In contrast, the identical claim was allowed in New Zealand.[58] There is room to question the analysis in the Australian decision. Much of the government's claim was not based on its statutory law dealing with official secrets but rather was based on common law and equitable causes of action such as breach of contract and breach of confidence. It was clear that the government's motive was to act in what

---

53 See *Mbasogo v Logo Ltd*, [2007] 2 WLR 1062 at para 51 (CA); *Robb Evans v European Bank Limited*, [2004] NSWCA 82 at para 37. See also *Bienstock v Adenyo Inc*, 2014 ONSC 4997 at para 12.
54 Above note 27 at 548 (Gen Div).
55 See also *United States of America v Levy* (1999), 45 OR (3d) 129 (Gen Div).
56 Above note 25 at 20–21. However, see now the analysis in *Barakat*, above note 29, at paras 131–50.
57 *Heinemann*, above note 52.
58 *Attorney General for the United Kingdom v Wellington Newspapers Ltd*, [1988] 1 NZLR 129 at 174.

it perceived was the public interest, but the focus should not be on the motivation for the claim. It should instead be on the law relied upon for that claim, and in this case much of that was pure private law.

In *Robb Evans v European Bank Limited* the New South Wales Court of Appeal rejected the argument that the proceedings had been brought to secure a "governmental interest" and thus fell into this category of exclusion.[59] That only a public body could advance the claim and that a public interest was being furthered by the claim were relevant considerations but were not determinative. While it was possible that any surplus recovered in the proceedings would be paid to the United States Treasury, this was not considered likely on the facts and so did not alter the substance of the claim, which was to recover funds to compensate victims of fraud.

F. BLOCKING STATUTES

A blocking statute aims to provide a legal justification for not complying with an otherwise applicable foreign law. For example, the Ontario *Business Records Protection Act* prohibits the removal of business records from Ontario in response to any "requirement, order, direction or summons of any legislative, administrative or judicial authority in any jurisdiction outside Ontario," except in certain situations.[60] Based on a belief that such a request for documents has been made or is likely to be made, the attorney general or any person with an interest in the business concerned can apply for an order requiring any person to undertake not to remove the records from Ontario. If, while such an application is pending, that person does remove business records, he or she is deemed to be in contempt of court and is liable to imprisonment for one year.[61] Similar legislation is in force in at least one other province.[62]

These provisions were enacted because of concerns about litigation in the United States. American antitrust and other litigation can have a wide scope, drawing in businesses from around the world. American litigation also has significant pretrial disclosure requirements, under which parties can be ordered to produce a wide range of documents. Some Canadian provinces wanted to protect Canadian businesses from being ordered to reveal potentially incriminating documents in American proceedings, and so they adopted these blocking statutes.

---

59 Above note 53 at paras 57–89.
60 RSO 1990, c B19, s 1.
61 *Ibid*, s 2.
62 See *Business Concerns Records Act*, CQLR c D-12.

In *Hunt v T&N plc* the plaintiffs, residents of British Columbia, sued several defendants for injuries suffered as a result of exposure to asbestos fibres.[63] Defendants based in Quebec refused to produce business records to the plaintiffs, relying on Quebec's blocking statute.[64] While this and similar statutes had been drafted to prevent business records from being removed to another country, and had not generally been raised as an issue in interprovincial litigation, on the clear wording of the statute it applied to removal to another province. The Supreme Court of Canada applied the principles from *Morguard*, considering the extent to which comity is implicit in the federal nature of the country.[65] While *Morguard* did not squarely raise constitutional issues, *Hunt* did: at issue was whether it was beyond the power of Quebec to enact a statute with such an extraterritorial effect on proceedings in another province. The court framed the central principles from *Morguard* as constitutional requirements that provincial legislatures were obliged to respect. In its view, the blocking statute discouraged interprovincial commerce by hampering the legal system's ability to efficiently resolve commercial disputes. Routine application of these provisions would have a serious impact on corporations operating across provincial borders. The court therefore held that as a matter of constitutional law the Quebec provision could not have the intended effect on litigation in another province. It was held inapplicable to litigation in other provinces, although it remained effective for litigation in foreign countries.

Canadian courts also have to consider this issue from the opposite vantage point, namely how to handle a party's refusal to produce documents in litigation in the forum as a result of a foreign blocking statute. For example, a French corporate defendant could rely on a similar French rule and refuse to disclose documents to the plaintiff in Ontario proceedings. While it may seem hypocritical in light of Canadian blocking statutes, Canadian courts will generally not allow a foreign rule to excuse a party from its pretrial disclosure obligations under the law of the forum. The court usually starts by attempting to determine the scope of the foreign provision, making an effort to see if compliance is possible. In the face of a true conflict, however, the party must produce the documents.[66]

---

63 [1993] 4 SCR 289 [*Hunt*].
64 Above note 62.
65 Above note 40.
66 See *Ed Miller Sales & Rentals Ltd v Caterpillar Tractor Co* (1988), 90 AR 323 (CA); *Spencer v The Queen*, [1985] 2 SCR 278. A different approach is taken for non-parties, like witnesses, who are generally not required to violate the law of the place where they reside: see *Frischke v Royal Bank of Canada* (1977), 17 OR (2d) 388 (CA).

FURTHER READINGS

BAADE, HANS W. "The Operation of Foreign Public Law" (1995) 30 *Texas International Law Journal* 429.

BLOM, JOOST. "Public Policy in Private International Law and Its Evolution in Time" (2003) 50 *Netherlands International Law Review* 373.

BRIGGS, ADRIAN. "The Revenue Rule in the Conflict of Laws: Time for a Makeover" [2001] *Singapore Journal of Legal Studies* 280.

CARTER, PB. "The Role of Public Policy in English Private International Law" (1993) 42 *International and Comparative Law Quarterly* 1.

CHONG, ADELINE. "Transnational Public Policy in Civil and Commercial Matters" (2012) 128 *Law Quarterly Review* 88.

DODGE, WILLIAM S. "Breaking the Public Law Taboo" (2002) 43 *Harvard International Law Journal* 161.

ENONCHONG, NELSON. "Public Policy in the Conflict of Laws: A Chinese Wall around Little England" (1996) 45 *International and Comparative Law Quarterly* 633.

KOVATCH, WILLIAM J, JR. "Recognizing Foreign Tax Judgments: An Argument for the Revocation of the Revenue Rule" (2000) 22 *Houston Journal of International Law* 265.

LAGARDE, PAUL. "Public Policy," in Kurt Lipstein, ed, *International Encyclopedia of Comparative Law*, vol 3 (Tübingen, Germany: JCB Mohr, 1970–) ch 11.

MANN, FA. "The International Enforcement of Public Rights" (1987) 19 *New York University Journal of International Law and Politics* 603.

MCCONNAUGHAY, PHILIP J. "Reviving the 'Public Law Taboo' in International Conflict of Laws" (1999) 35 *Stanford Journal of International Law* 255.

MILLS, ALEX. "The Dimensions of Public Policy in Private International Law" (2008) 4 *Journal of Private International Law* 201.

SAUMIER, GENEVIEVE. "What's in a Name?: Lloyd's, International Comity and Public Policy" (2002) 37 *Canadian Business Law Journal* 388.

SMART, P ST J. "Public Policy and the Conflict of Laws" (1983) 99 *Law Quarterly Review* 24.

SULLIVAN, JOHN P, & JONATHAN M WOOLLEY. "*Oakwell Engineering Limited v Enernorth Industries Inc*: Questions of Burden and Bias in the Enforcement of Foreign Judgments" (2007) 85 *Canadian Bar Review* 605.

WALKER, JANET. "Foreign Public Law and the Colour of Comity: What's the Difference between Friends?" (2003) 38 *Canadian Business Law Journal* 36.

CHAPTER 4

FOREIGN CURRENCY OBLIGATIONS

A. INTRODUCTION

Dividing up the world into different countries not only gives rise to conflict of laws issues relating to foreign legal rules and judicial decisions but also issues relating to foreign currencies. Consider the following simple and typical example. An Ontario company sells goods to a company in Ghana. The contract is governed by Ontario law and the buyer is to pay 500,000 cedi, the currency of Ghana, into the seller's bank account in Ghana. The goods are supplied but the buyer does not pay and the seller sues for breach of contract in Ontario. There are several ways we could describe the seller's claim. It could be for 500,000 cedi, such that the court would make its order in that currency. It could instead be for an amount in Canadian dollars, obtained by converting the cedi into dollars. If so, that conversion could be done at various times: the date of the breach, the date of the claim, the date of the judgment, or the date of the payment.

Sometimes these are only academic questions. If the rate of exchange between the dollar and the cedi does not change from the time of the breach to the time the buyer eventually satisfies the judgment, it does not matter which currency is used or when any conversion takes place. As we know, however, exchange rates usually do change over time. Even small changes could have a significant impact on what the seller recovers, depending on the size of the claim. A more dramatic change in the exchange rate raises these issues more starkly. If during the trial the value of the cedi falls 90 percent against the dollar, the seller will want an award in dollars, converted as of a date before the trial, and the buyer will want either to pay an award in cedi or to have any conversion to dollars done as of a date after the trial.[1] Put another way, the issue is which party bears the risk of the change in the exchange rate.

B. CURRENCY OF JUDGMENT

The traditional common law rule is that the court cannot order payment in a foreign currency: the court's order must be expressed in the local currency.[2] In several cases, central among them *Re United Railways of the Havana and Regla Warehouses Ltd*, the English courts held that under this rule the amount in issue between the parties had to be converted to the local currency as of the date the cause of action arose.[3] Particularly from its application to contract claims, this was known as the "breach-date rule."

The central benefit of this rule lay in establishing the extent to which the parties bore the risk of currency fluctuations after the date of the loss. The rule was not based on a sense of which party was in the better position to plan for changes in the exchange rate or which party should bear more responsibility for doing so. With knowledge of the rule, each party could take some steps to guard against changes in the exchange rate. This was easier for the defendant, who, at least once proceedings had commenced, could choose to purchase the relevant amount of the local currency so as to have it on hand to meet an eventual judgment. In a more sophisticated currency market, the defendant could purchase currency futures on margin, and so avoid tying up the full amount in issue pending the litigation. Similarly, if the plaintiff wanted not the local currency but rather a foreign currency, it could use a currency futures contract to agree to exchange the amount of local currency it expected to recover for a specified amount of the foreign currency.

The breach-date rule came under pressure in *Miliangos v George Frank (Textiles) Ltd*.[4] The contract between the parties required the English buyer to pay the Swiss seller in Swiss francs. Since the date of

---

1 For a case involving a dramatic change in the exchange rate, see *The Texaco Melbourne*, [1994] 1 Lloyd's LR 473 (HL).
2 This rule had been well established for hundreds of years: see *Rastell v Draper* (1605), 80 ER 55 (KB).
3 [1961] AC 1007 (HL) [*Havana Railways*]. See also *Di Ferdinando v Simon, Smits & Co Ltd*, [1920] 3 KB 409 (CA).
4 [1976] AC 443 (HL) [*Miliangos*].

the breach, the franc had risen sharply against the pound. Applying the breach-date rule, the pounds the seller would receive would only, as at the time of payment, convert to 50 percent of the francs it was expecting to receive. As explained above, with knowledge of the breach-date rule, the seller could have taken steps to guard against a rise in the franc's value. But the House of Lords was concerned about whether these were steps that the seller, acting reasonably, should have had to take. The seller had contracted to receive a certain amount, in francs, and was simply seeking to enforce that contract. The House of Lords therefore held that the English court could award damages in a foreign currency.[5] It considered the *Havana Railways* rule as too rigid and not reflecting commercial reality. Given the contract, the risk of a change in the exchange rate was on the buyer, not the seller.

This change in the law also responds to another concern with the breach-date rule, which is that it promotes forum shopping. Under that rule, a plaintiff could choose to sue in a country where conversion into the local currency at the time of breach produced a greater recovery.[6]

In Canada, the rule in *Havana Railways* had been adopted by the Supreme Court of Canada.[7] It had also been incorporated into section 12 of the *Currency Act*, which provides that "any reference to money or monetary value in . . . legal proceedings shall be stated in the currency of Canada."[8] In *Batavia Times Publishing Co v Davis* the court held that this provision precluded the making of awards in foreign currency.[9] However, the court did agree with the reasoning behind the change in approach in *Miliangos*, and so accepted that, while the amount awarded had to be stated in dollars, it was not required to follow the breach-date rule for conversion. As a result, the conversion could be ordered as of the date of the judgment. On facts like those in *Miliangos*, this would allow the court to protect the seller's position up to the date of judgment. However, if the exchange rate fluctuated significantly after that date and before the buyer had paid, the seller would still have had to take its own steps to protect itself.

As a matter of precedent, the decision in *Batavia Times* is of a court of first instance. It cannot, strictly speaking, overturn earlier appellate

---

5   Ibid at 463, 466–67, and 497. For this development in the United States, see *The Amoco Cadiz*, 954 F2d 1279 (7th Cir 1992).
6   See Vaughan Black, "Foreign Currency Obligations in Private International Law" (2003) 302 *Recueil des Cours* 9 at 180–81.
7   *Custodian v Blucher*, [1927] SCR 420; *Gatineau Power Co v Crown Life Insurance Co*, [1945] SCR 655.
8   RSC 1985, c C-52. The original version of this provision was enacted in 1871.
9   (1978), 20 OR (2d) 437 (HCJ) [*Batavia Times*].

decisions supporting the *Havana Railways* rule. But the Supreme Court of Canada has not addressed the issue in more than sixty years.[10] It is therefore an open question, at common law, whether *Miliangos* is the prevailing approach in Canada. Most recent decisions consider that it is.[11]

In addition, three provinces have devised a way around section 12 of the *Currency Act*. For example, section 121(1) of the Ontario *Courts of Justice Act* provides that "where a person obtains an order to enforce an obligation in a foreign currency," the order is to be phrased so as to require payment, in dollars, of the amount required to purchase the foreign currency on the day before the payment.[12] The order is expressed in dollars, to satisfy the *Currency Act*, but no particular amount of dollars is specified: the specified amount is of the foreign currency. This has the effect of postponing the date of conversion to the date of payment. While this is stated as a general rule, section 121(3) gives the court the power to order conversion as of any other day if using the date of payment would be "inequitable" and section 121(4) gives priority to the manner of conversion, if any, provided for in the obligation between the parties (such as under a foreign judgment or a contract). It is clear that section 121(1) would cover a claim to enforce a foreign judgment in a foreign currency, but it appears that it would also cover any claim to an amount owing in a foreign currency.[13] It has been held that the change in exchange rates, in itself, cannot constitute the inequity required to deviate from the general rule, though it can be difficult to insist on this position when the change is dramatic.[14]

In addition to this type of general statutory provision, some more specific statutes address the conversion-date issue. For example, some provincial statutes providing for the registration of foreign judgments (an enforcement mechanism discussed in Chapter 8) stipulate that if the judgment is in a currency other than Canadian dollars, conversion into the local currency is to be done as of the date of the original judgment.[15]

---

10 See the extended discussion in *Kellogg Brown & Root Inc v Aerotech Herman Nelson Inc*, 2004 MBCA 63 at paras 89–103 and 129–39.
11 Black, above note 6 at 85. See, for example, *Stevenson Estate v Siewert*, 2001 ABCA 180; *Albionex (Overseas) Ltd v Conagra Ltd*, 2011 MBCA 95 at para 141. In contrast, the Federal Court has insisted on the rigid breach-date rule: see, for example, *Kuehne + Nagel Ltd v Agrimax Ltd*, 2010 FC 1303.
12 RSO 1990, c C.43. See also the *Foreign Money Claims Act*, RSBC 1996, c 155, ss 1–3; *Judicature Act*, RSPEI 1988, c J-2.1, s 54.
13 See, for example, *General Refractories Co of Canada v Venturedyne*, [2002] OJ No 54 at paras 285–98 (SCJ). This case is discussed in more detail later in this chapter.
14 See the discussion in *Hollowcore Inc v Visocchi*, 2014 ONSC 6802 at paras 252–56.
15 See, for example, *Reciprocal Enforcement of Judgments Act*, RSA 2000, c R-6, s 3. In contrast, the *Reciprocal Enforcement of Judgments Act*, RSO 1990, c R-5, does

As another example, conversion as of the date of judgment is required in cases involving damages awarded under the *Warsaw Convention* on carriage by air.[16]

In provinces that have not enacted this type of general provision, there are some examples of judges simply ignoring the impact of the *Currency Act* and making awards in foreign currency.[17] While such an award cannot be correct, it is at least arguable that even without relying on a provision like Ontario's section 121, a court could, if it so chose, phrase its order so as to comply with the *Currency Act* while still providing for conversion as of the date of payment. The formulation in section 121, in other words, could be adopted as a matter of the common law, consistent with the principles in *Miliangos*.

The approach underlying *Miliangos*, *Batavia Times*, and these provincial statutory provisions moves away from a stable, clear, but arguably unfair rule to a situation of considerable flexibility. In the face of section 121, the Ontario court is required to determine, in each case, the appropriate date of conversion from the foreign currency into dollars. Some cases will be clear. If the plaintiff sues on a foreign judgment, or for non-payment of a contracted price, and an amount in foreign currency has been stipulated in either the judgment or the contract, the courts generally follow the reasoning in *Miliangos*, preserving the creditor's reasonable expectations of receipt, and order the conversion as of the date of payment.[18] But other cases will be less clear and courts will use some other conversion date.[19]

This area of the law starkly raises the debate between certainty and flexibility. A fixed conversion date is predictable. It can promote settlements and allow the parties to plan their affairs. In contrast, the law's current flexibility can accommodate a wide range of factual circumstances but it increases the complexity and expense of litigation.[20] As

---

not contain such a provision. There are also specific provisions dealing with support or maintenance orders expressed in foreign currencies: see, for example, *Interjurisdictional Support Orders Act*, SA 2002, c I-35, s 41; *Interjurisdictional Support Orders Act, 2002*, SO 2002, c 13, s 44.

16 *Carriage by Air Act*, RSC 1985, c C-26, s 2(6). On this, see the discussion in Black, above note 6 at 146–50.
17 See *Sandy Frank Film Syndication Inc v CFQC Broadcasting Ltd* (1983), 23 Sask R 241 (CA).
18 See, for example, *Litecubes, LLC v Northern Light Products Inc (cob Glowproducts. com)*, 2009 BCSC 427 at para 17.
19 See *Old North State Brewing Co v Newlands Services Inc* (1997), 47 BCLR (3d) 254 (SC), aff'd (1998), 58 BCLR (3d) 144 (CA); *Stott v Merit Investment Corp* (1988), 63 OR (2d) 545 (CA).
20 See Black, above note 6 at 21–22.

mentioned above, this area of the law also gives rise to possible forum shopping. If different jurisdictions, including different provinces, adopt a different approach to the date of conversion, then where the plaintiff sues can make a significant difference to the eventual award.[21] Between provinces this is particularly true where there could be a change in the exchange rate for a foreign currency between the date of judgment and the date of payment.

C. CURRENCY OF LOSS

Thus far, the focus has been on cases where it is clear that the currency of loss, or, to put it another way, the currency of the obligation between the plaintiff and the defendant, is easy to identify. If the currency of loss is the local currency, no issues of conversion arise. If the currency of loss is a foreign currency, the foregoing analysis is used to determine the appropriate conversion date.

However, in some cases the currency of loss will itself be unclear and it must, as a preliminary matter, be identified. For example, an Ohio seller might sell a machine to an Ontario buyer for $150,000 without any indication as to whether the price is in American or Canadian dollars. If the buyer does not pay and the seller sues in Ontario, the court must determine the currency under the contract.[22] If it is in Canadian dollars, no issues of foreign currency are raised. If it is in American dollars, the court must then consider issues about conversion. Consistent with the approach outlined in Chapter 14, the court would use the contract's governing law to determine the currency. However, this does not mean that if the contract is governed by Ohio law that it is in American dollars; rather, it means that Ohio law would be used to determine the currency.[23] In doing this analysis, most common law legal systems look to factors such as the place of payment and any past course of dealings.

In a more complex case, *The Folias*,[24] a French company chartered a ship from an English company under a contract governed by English law. The French company used the ship to carry cargo to Brazil and the cargo arrived damaged due to defects in the ship's refrigeration

---

21 *Ibid* at 22–23.
22 It is possible that the court could conclude that there was no meeting of the minds on the issue of currency and thus that there is no contract. For another example, see *Jones v Kansa General Insurance Co* (1992), 10 OR (3d) 56 (CA).
23 See *Weiss Estate v State Life Insurance Co*, [1935] SCR 461.
24 [1979] AC 685 (HL). See also *The Despina R*, [1977] 3 WLR 617 (CA).

system. As a result, the French company had to pay the buyer of the cargo an amount in Brazilian cruzeiros. It then brought proceedings in England against the English company to recover what it had to pay out. Crucially, between the time of the payment to the buyer and the time of trial, the cruzeiro fell dramatically against other world currencies. The claim looks like one for a specific amount of a foreign currency. Yet if the court ordered the English company to pay the French company the specific amount of cruzeiros,[25] the latter would in reality recover little.

To avoid this result, the French company argued that the true currency of its loss was not cruzeiros, but rather French francs, because it did not hold substantial funds in cruzeiros as part of its business. When called upon to compensate the buyer of the damaged cargo, it used its primary currency, francs, to buy the cruzeiros. So it sought an award of the amount of francs it had used to buy the cruzeiros. The House of Lords accepted this argument and made that award. Under English law, which applied to the claim in light of the contract, the currency of account between the parties was the currency in which the plaintiff had suffered its loss.[26] This approach to identifying the currency of loss has also been applied in tort cases.

More complex cases can thus raise two different but closely related issues. The court must first identify the currency of loss. If it is a foreign currency, it must then consider issues as to the appropriate conversion date. As has been shown, the analysis for each of these issues is open-ended and fact-specific, leaving considerable room for argument by the parties and scope for the court's decision.

Both issues arose in *General Refractories Co of Canada v Venturedyne*, where the plaintiff, an Ontario corporation, purchased an industrial press from the defendant's corporate predecessor, an American corporation, in 1982.[27] The plaintiff sued for return of the purchase price, paid in American dollars from an account in that currency maintained by the plaintiff. The plaintiff argued that the currency of loss was American dollars and that conversion should be as of the date of payment.

In contrast, the defendant argued that the plaintiff, as an Ontario corporation, had used Canadian dollars to purchase the American dollars it then used to buy the press, so that its currency of loss was Canadian dollars. In the alternative, the defendant argued that the Canadian dollar had fallen significantly against the American dollar, such that

---

25   Transposing the situation to a Canadian province, the same problem would arise if the court made an order requiring conversion into dollars as of the date of judgment or the date of payment.
26   *The Folias*, above note 24 at 701–2 and 705.
27   Above note 13.

conversion as of the date of payment would give the plaintiff a windfall. The defendant asked for conversion as of the date of breach. The court did not accept these arguments, though its analysis on each was quite minimal. It did not explain why it held that the currency of loss was American dollars, although this is a reasonable conclusion given the plaintiff's maintaining of an ongoing bank account in that currency. As to the conversion date, the court held that section 121(1) was the presumptive rule and the fall in the Canadian dollar was not a reason to depart from that rule.[28]

FURTHER READINGS

BAXTER, IAN. "Foreign Currency Obligations" (1957) 35 *Canadian Bar Review* 697.

BLACK, VAUGHAN. *Foreign Currency Claims in the Conflict of Laws* (Oxford: Hart, 2010).

BLACK, VAUGHAN. "Foreign Money Obligations in Ontario" (2016) 45 *Advocates' Quarterly* 268.

BLACK, VAUGHAN. "Loose Change: Problems with Foreign Currency Conversions" (2001) 35 *Canadian Business Law Journal* 123.

BOWLES, RA, & CJ WHELAN. "The Currency of Suit in Actions for Damages" (1979) 25 *McGill Law Journal* 236.

KAHN-FREUND, OTTO. "Foreign Currency Obligations and the Devaluation of Sterling" (1952) 68 *Law Quarterly Review* 163.

KNOTT, JOHN. "A Quarter of a Century of Foreign Currency Judgments" [2004] *Lloyd's Maritime and Commercial Law Quarterly* 325.

LAW REFORM COMMISSION OF BRITISH COLUMBIA. *Report on Foreign Money Liabilities* (Vancouver: Law Reform Commission of British Columbia, 1983).

MANN, FA. *The Legal Aspect of Money*, 4th ed (Oxford: Clarendon Press, 1982).

NUSSBAUM, ARTHUR. *Money in the Law: National and International* (Brooklyn: Foundation Press, 1950).

---

28 *Ibid* at paras 297–98. See also *Corporate Bank and Trust Co v Toronto Dominion Bank*, [1987] OJ No 418 (HCJ).

CHAPTER 5

JURISDICTION *IN PERSONAM*

A. INTRODUCTION

The first major issue in the conflict of laws is that of jurisdiction. Jurisdiction refers to the power of the court to hear a dispute. A court must have jurisdiction over the parties to the dispute and over the subject matter of the dispute. Subject matter jurisdiction, however, rarely raises issues in the conflict of laws.[1] One major exception relates to the traditional rule that Canadian courts have no jurisdiction to determine title to foreign immovable property. The intricacies of that topic are considered in Chapter 17.

While the court needs to have jurisdiction over both parties, jurisdiction over the plaintiff is a simple matter. Having chosen to sue in the forum, the plaintiff voluntarily submits to the court's jurisdiction. Accordingly, this chapter concentrates on jurisdiction over the defendant. In addition, its focus is jurisdiction in actions *in personam*. The purpose of such an action is to impose a personal obligation on the defendant owed to the plaintiff. For example, the obligation might be to pay damages for a breach of contract or tort committed or to comply with an order of specific performance. This chapter considers jurisdiction *in personam* generally. The special jurisdictional rules that apply

---

1   For a discussion of subject matter jurisdiction in the context of British Columbia's *Court Jurisdiction and Proceedings Transfer Act*, SBC 2003, c 28, see *Scott v Hale*, [2009] BCJ No 327 (SC).

in the context of, for example, the administration of estates and matrimonial causes are covered in later chapters. Jurisdiction in actions *in rem*, which are most frequently admiralty actions relating to vessels, where the resultant judgment is enforced against the thing itself and is binding on anyone who has an interest in the thing, is not considered in this book.[2]

At common law, there were two bases for jurisdiction *in personam*: presence and submission. First, since jurisdiction was grounded traditionally in territorial power, the local courts were regarded as having jurisdiction over defendants who could be served with an originating process within the territory of the forum. The court had jurisdiction based on the defendant's presence in the forum at the time the litigation was commenced. Second, defendants could vest jurisdiction in a court in an action *in personam* by their consent or voluntary submission to the proceedings against them. Such submission could be shown by defending in the proceeding on its merits or, in advance of proceeding, by agreeing to submit the dispute to the jurisdiction of the courts of a particular territory.

Beginning in England in the nineteenth century with the passage of the *Common Law Procedure Act, 1852*,[3] courts were authorized to assume jurisdiction over defendants who resided outside the forum by provisions allowing for service of the originating process *ex juris*. In turn, each Canadian province adopted rules governing service *ex juris*. The various Canadian regimes for service *ex juris* are not uniform. Under the typical approach, the provisions set out enumerated situations in which the plaintiff is allowed to serve an originating process *ex juris* without the leave of the court. However, the plaintiff can apply to the court for leave to serve *ex juris* in any other case.[4] This basis for taking jurisdiction is called "assumed jurisdiction."[5]

This approach meant, for many years, that the rules about service *ex juris* were more than just procedural rules dealing with how litigation was commenced. They were rules about the court's jurisdiction, since the court assumed jurisdiction in any dispute in which the defendant

---

2   For a detailed treatment of this topic, see Janet Walker, *Castel & Walker: Canadian Conflict of Laws*, 6th ed (Markham, ON: Butterworths, 2005) (loose-leaf) ch 12. For a discussion of the distinction between actions *in personam* and actions *in rem*, see *Pattni v Ali*, 2006 UKPC 51 at paras 19–23.
3   (UK), 15 & 16 Vict, c 76.
4   See, for example, *Rules of Civil Procedure*, RRO 1990, Reg 194, r 17 [Ontario Rules].
5   See, for example, *Chevron Corp v Yaiguaje*, 2015 SCC 42 at para 82 [*Chevron*]. It has also been called "exorbitant jurisdiction," though it is important not to see in this phrasing something negative about the basis for jurisdiction: see *Abela v Baadarani*, [2013] UKSC 44 at paras 45 and 53.

could be validly served under the rules. As is explained below, this is no longer true. Canada has now developed rules about assumed jurisdiction. These rules are independent of the procedural rules about service of the originating process. The latter are still important, since the defendant must be served, but service itself is no longer the basis for jurisdiction.[6]

1) Constitutional Considerations

The language of the *Constitution Act, 1867* makes it clear that provincial legislative power is restrained territorially.[7] Thus, section 92(13), for example, assigns exclusive legislative authority to the provincial legislatures in respect of "Property and Civil Rights in the Province." Similar wording is evident in the other provisions allocating power to the provincial legislatures. Over the years, the courts have developed a substantial body of law for determining the meaning and scope of the constitutional prohibition against extraterritorial provincial legislation.[8]

Conflict of laws principles are designed to resolve disputes containing some "foreign" or extraterritorial element. Traditionally, the courts have elaborated those principles with little or no regard for any constraints imposed by the Canadian Constitution. It has been argued, however, that constitutional doctrine restricts the extraterritorial reach of provincial law generally and that the entire body of conflict of laws principles—such as those dealing with the jurisdiction of the courts, the recognition of extraprovincial judgments, and choice of law—must be evaluated according to a constitutional standard.[9] That suggestion bore fruit in the important decision of the Supreme Court of Canada in *Morguard Investments Ltd v De Savoye*,[10] with its confirmation as a principle of Canadian constitutional law in *Hunt v T & N plc*.[11] As a result of *Morguard*, it has become clear that, in the context of taking jurisdiction, the courts are constitutionally restrained so that they can assume jurisdiction only where a real and substantial connection exists between the province in question and the dispute. The application of the *Morguard* principle

---

6 This has, in turn, led to some provinces modifying their rules on service *ex juris* so that they mirror the rules on jurisdiction. See, for example, *Supreme Court Civil Rules*, BC Reg 168/2009, r 4-5 [British Columbia Rules].
7 (UK), 30 & 31 Vict, c 3.
8 See Peter W Hogg, *Constitutional Law of Canada*, 5th ed (Toronto: Thomson Carswell, 2007) (loose-leaf) ch 13.3.
9 See, for example, John Swan, "The Canadian Constitution, Federalism and the Conflict of Laws" (1985) 63 *Canadian Bar Review* 271.
10 [1990] 3 SCR 1077 [*Morguard*].
11 [1993] 4 SCR 289 [*Hunt*]. Both *Morguard* and *Hunt* are considered in depth in Chapter 8. See Hogg, above note 8, ch 13.5.

arises typically in cases of service *ex juris*. There are still questions, however, as to whether it could be applicable to cases falling within one of the two traditional common law bases for jurisdiction *in personam*, such as cases in which the defendant is served with process while on a temporary visit to the forum.

Morguard was the catalyst for the development, mentioned above, of rules of assumed jurisdiction independent from procedural rules about service *ex juris*. Those rules will be discussed in detail later in this chapter.

2) Existence and Exercise of Jurisdiction

It is important to draw a distinction between the existence of jurisdiction and its exercise. This chapter focuses on the existence of jurisdiction or jurisdiction *simpliciter*, as it has come to be known.[12] It thus discusses the circumstances in which a court has the authority to hear a case involving foreign elements. A court, however, also possesses discretion to decline to exercise its jurisdiction. Typically, such a decision would be reached on grounds of *forum non conveniens*, namely that there is another forum clearly more appropriate for the pursuit of the action and in the interests of the parties. Thus, a court may stay an action on the basis of principles of *forum non conveniens* or, on similar principles, it may refuse to grant a plaintiff leave to serve an originating process *ex juris* in those circumstances where leave is required. The circumstances in which a court may decline jurisdiction are explained in Chapter 6.

Issues of jurisdiction *simpliciter* and *forum non conveniens* are logically distinct. In *Jordan v Schatz*, Cumming JA wrote:

> [W]hether a court has jurisdiction *simpliciter* over a case is a distinct issue from whether it is the *forum conveniens*. The existence of jurisdiction and the declining of jurisdiction, if there is any, are to be considered sequentially.[13]

Nevertheless, the courts do not always differentiate clearly between the two questions that must be addressed,[14] and the factors to be considered under each can overlap. For example, some courts have clearly indicated that fairness is not to be ignored at the jurisdiction *simpliciter*

---

12 See, for example, *Canadian International Marketing Distributing Ltd v Nitsuko Ltd* (1990), 56 BCLR (2d) 130 at 132 (CA).
13 (2000), 77 BCLR (3d) 134 at para 21 (CA).
14 See Cheryl Dusten & Stephen Pitel, "The Right Answers to Ontario's Jurisdictional Questions: Dismiss, Stay or Set Service Aside" (2005) 30 *Advocates' Quarterly* 297 at 301–6.

stage. In *Oakley v Barry*, Pugsley JA for the Nova Scotia Court of Appeal stated that fairness to both parties was a "theme . . . emphasized by Justice La Forest in [both] *Morguard* and *Hunt*."[15] In that regard, he relied upon the words of La Forest J in *Hunt* that "the assumption of, and the discretion not to exercise jurisdiction must ultimately be guided by the requirements of order and fairness, not a mechanical counting of contacts or connections."[16] Justice Pugsley therefore concluded:

> The concept of fairness in determining jurisdiction should be considered from the point of view of both the [plaintiff], as well as the [defendants]. While this issue, as well as the issue of juridical advantage, are matters that are usually considered on a *forum non conveniens* issue, it is appropriate and relevant to consider them in this case involving jurisdiction *simpliciter*.[17]

More importantly, in *Muscutt v Courcelles*, which for a time was a leading authority on the application of the *Morguard* test to issues of jurisdiction, the Court of Appeal for Ontario, despite taking care to distinguish the existence of jurisdiction based on the "real and substantial connection test from the discretionary *forum non conveniens* doctrine," included as relevant to the first question factors normally associated with the second.[18] Thus in determining whether they could assume jurisdiction, courts had to consider, *inter alia*, unfairness to the defendant in assuming jurisdiction, unfairness to the plaintiff in not assuming jurisdiction, and the involvement of other parties to the litigation so as to avoid an unnecessary multiplicity of proceedings and the consequent risk of inconsistent decisions.

In *Club Resorts Ltd v Van Breda*, the Supreme Court of Canada reiterated the importance of maintaining a clear distinction between the tests for jurisdiction *simpliciter* and *forum non conveniens*.[19] However, the court was highly critical of the approach in *Muscutt*. It held that "[j]urisdiction must . . . be established primarily on the basis of objective factors that connect the legal situation or the subject matter of the litigation with the forum . . . . Abstract concerns for order, efficiency or fairness in the system are no substitute for connecting factors that give rise to a 'real and substantial' connection."[20] As will be discussed below, this approach both aims at a greater analytical separation between the issue

---

15 (1998), 158 DLR (4th) 679 at 692 (NSCA) [*Oakley*].
16 Above note 11 at 326, cited *ibid* at 690.
17 Above note 15 at 699.
18 (2002), 60 OR (3d) 20 at para 42 (CA) [*Muscutt*].
19 2012 SCC 17 at para 101 [*Club Resorts*].
20 *Ibid* at para 82.

of jurisdiction *simpliciter* and *forum non conveniens* and seeks to make the analysis of the former more straightforward and less case-specific.

3) Statutory Reform

In 1994 the Uniform Law Conference of Canada proposed for adoption in common law Canada the *Court Jurisdiction and Proceedings Transfer Act*.[21] Its purposes, in part, were to establish a uniform set of standards for determining jurisdiction and to ensure that Canadian jurisdictional rules were consistent with the principles underlying *Morguard*. The provisions of the statute are discussed throughout this chapter.[22] To date, the statute is in force in British Columbia,[23] Saskatchewan,[24] and Nova Scotia[25] and under consideration in several other provinces and territories.[26] The statute will frequently yield the same result as the approach under the common law, especially in the wake of *Club Resorts*.

The *CJPTA*, as it is known, is drafted using the language of "territorial competence" rather than jurisdiction. Territorial competence is defined in section 1 as "the aspects of a court's jurisdiction that depend on a connection between (a) the territory or legal system of the state in which the court is established, and (b) a party to a proceeding in the court or the facts on which the proceeding is based." It is roughly equivalent to the concept of jurisdiction *in personam*. The *CJPTA* also refers to "subject matter competence," which is defined in section 1 as "the aspects of a court's jurisdiction that depend on factors other than those pertaining to the court's territorial competence." In *Scott v Hale* the court made it clear that subject matter competence refers to the ability of the court to hear the type of dispute in question, considering issues such as whether its jurisdiction was limited by statute. It

---

21 Uniform Law Conference of Canada, *Proceedings of the 1994 Annual Meeting* at 48 [*CJPTA*].
22 For a detailed analysis of the *CJPTA* and the decisions interpreting and applying it, see Vaughan Black, Stephen GA Pitel, & Michael Sobkin, *Statutory Jurisdiction: An Analysis of the Court Jurisdiction and Proceedings Transfer Act* (Toronto: Thomson Reuters Canada, 2012).
23 Above note 1. For commentary, see Elizabeth Edinger, "New British Columbia Legislation: The *Court Jurisdiction and Proceedings Transfer Act*; The *Enforcement of Canadian Judgments and Decrees Act*" (2006) 39 *University of British Columbia Law Review* 407.
24 *The Court Jurisdiction and Proceedings Transfer Act*, SS 1997, c C-41.1.
25 *Court Jurisdiction and Proceedings Transfer Act*, SNS 2003 (2nd Sess), c 2.
26 In Prince Edward Island, for example, the statute has been passed (SPEI 1997, c 61) but not yet proclaimed in force. The Alberta Law Reform Institute has recommended its adoption in that province: *Enforcement of Judgments* (Edmonton: Alberta Law Reform Institute, 2008) at 22.

deals with criteria that are not connected to the territorial reach of the court's authority and rarely raise issues of private international law.[27]

4) Organization of the Topic

This chapter first examines the traditional common law bases for jurisdiction *in personam* of presence and consent. It then explores assumed jurisdiction over defendants outside the forum. In doing so, it considers the *Morguard* principle requiring a real and substantial connection between the forum and the action, particularly as now explained and applied by the Supreme Court of Canada in *Club Resorts*. The chapter also discusses some of the jurisdictional problems posed by class actions in which the facts cut across provincial or national boundaries. Finally, it addresses the emerging notion of forum of necessity.

B. PRESENCE-BASED JURISDICTION

The central basis for jurisdiction *in personam* has always been territorial power. Therefore, if the plaintiff serves the defendant with process while the defendant is present in the forum then the local courts have jurisdiction to hear an action *in personam* against that particular defendant. It is unnecessary to establish that the defendant is resident or domiciled in the forum. Purely transitory presence is sufficient to meet the requirements for jurisdiction. In this situation, the local courts are said to have jurisdiction "as of right."[28] The only exception is where the defendant's presence in the forum is involuntary through duress or fraud.

The traditional position at common law is exemplified by the decision of the English Court of Appeal in *Maharanee of Baroda v Wildenstein*.[29] The plaintiff, who lived in France, bought a painting from the defendant, a renowned art dealer who also lived in France. Doubts later arose as to the painting's authenticity. The plaintiff then sued the defendant, claiming rescission of the contract and repayment of the purchase price. She served the defendant while he was on a temporary visit to England to watch horse racing at Ascot. The court had no doubt that it possessed jurisdiction to adjudicate the action. Lord Justice Edmund Davies said:

---

27 Above note 1. See the analysis in Black, Pitel, & Sobkin, above note 22 at 43–50.
28 See, for example, *Spiliada Maritime Corp v Cansulex Ltd*, [1987] AC 460 at 474 (HL), Lord Goff.
29 [1972] 2 All ER 689 (CA).

> [The plaintiff] did no wrong in taking out a High Court writ in the first place (foreigner though she is) and serving it here at the first available opportunity upon the defendant (foreigner though *he* also is). Both in taking it out and serving it (albeit when the defendant was only fleetingly on British soil) she was doing no more than our law permits, even though it may have ruined his day at the races.[30]

Of course, the effect of this traditional basis for jurisdiction is that the courts of the forum may well possess jurisdiction in a totally inappropriate case because of minimal connections between the forum and the parties or the cause of action. It is, therefore, quite likely that the local court will decline to exercise its jurisdiction where the defendant is served while on a temporary visit to the forum.[31]

The merits of grounding jurisdiction on presence have been questioned, especially because of the possibility that the presence might be fleeting. But this is a long-standing basis for taking jurisdiction and it has recently been confirmed by the Supreme Court of Canada in *Chevron Corp v Yaiguaje*.[32]

There has been some debate, in the aftermath of *Morguard*, as to whether the real and substantial connection requirement can be used to limit the scope of jurisdiction based on presence.[33] Part of the problem flowed from what the Supreme Court of Canada said in *Beals v Saldanha*.[34] In his dissenting judgment, LeBel J was clear. In his view, the *Morguard* test "should supersede, rather than complement, the traditional common law bases of jurisdiction."[35] Thus, the sole question to be addressed was whether the real and substantial connection test had been met. Justice LeBel also indicated that his preferred approach had not been adopted by the majority. In fact, the majority's reasoning is a little ambiguous. Thus, on the one hand Major J stated:

> A real and substantial connection is the overriding factor in the determination of jurisdiction. The presence of more of the traditional indicia of jurisdiction (attornment, agreement to submit, residence and presence in the . . . jurisdiction) will serve to bolster the real and substantial connection to the action or parties.[36]

---

30 *Ibid* at 694 [emphasis in original].
31 See Chapter 6.
32 Above note 5.
33 See Stephen Pitel & Cheryl Dusten, "Lost in Transition: Answering the Questions Raised by the Supreme Court of Canada's New Approach to Jurisdiction" (2006) 85 *Canadian Bar Review* 61 at 63–70.
34 [2003] 3 SCR 416 [*Beals*].
35 *Ibid* at para 207.
36 *Ibid* at para 37.

On the other, he said that the parties were still free to select the jurisdiction in which their dispute was to be resolved by attorning or agreeing to the jurisdiction of the court; he did not, however, state that the defendant's presence or residence in the jurisdiction was sufficient.

On this issue, in *Incorporated Broadcasters Ltd v Canwest Global Communications Corp* the Court of Appeal for Ontario indicated that the real and substantial connection test was inapplicable where the defendant was present in the jurisdiction. Thus, Rosenberg JA stated:

> The real and substantial connection test applies where a court seeks to assume jurisdiction over defendants that have no presence in the jurisdiction. The real and substantial connection test serves to extend jurisdiction of the domestic courts over out-of-province defendants. It is not a prerequisite for the assertion of jurisdiction over defendants, even out-of-province defendants, that are present in the jurisdiction.[37]

As a result, the court concluded that it had jurisdiction over the corporate defendants based purely upon their presence in Ontario through their conduct of business in that province. A difficulty arose, however, with respect to the individual defendant. The court said that it would assume that, although a resident of Manitoba, he had been served properly in Ontario. Despite that assumption, Rosenberg JA determined that "since he [was] an extra-provincial defendant, Ontario courts only [had] jurisdiction over him if the real and substantial connection test [was] met."[38] Although it is not entirely clear, the court seems to have drawn a distinction between residence and transitory presence and, if so, to have changed the common law concept of presence-based jurisdiction.

In *Ward v Canada (Attorney General)* Freedman JA applied *Incorporated Broadcasters* to support the proposition that the traditional jurisdictional rules had not been subsumed under the real and substantial connection test.[39] Yet he stated that where the parties were within the jurisdiction, "jurisdiction *simpliciter* would *ordinarily* be satisfied without consideration of whether there [was] a 'real and substantive connection' between the claim and the province."[40] Justice Freedman also stated that there was no need to consider the real and substantial connection test where the parties had a presence in the province and

---

37 (2003), 63 OR (3d) 431 at para 29 (CA) [*Incorporated Broadcasters*].
38 *Ibid* at para 37.
39 (2007), 220 Man R (2d) 224 (CA) [*Ward*].
40 *Ibid* at para 38 [emphasis added].

there was "a connection such as the sustaining of damages within the province."[41]

The recent decisions of the Supreme Court of Canada in *Club Resorts* and *Chevron* make it clear that presence is an independent basis for jurisdiction which has not been subsumed into the real and substantial connection requirement. In *Chevron* the court stated, "where jurisdiction stems from the defendant's presence in the jurisdiction, there is no need to consider whether a real and substantial connection exists."[42] Nonetheless, it did not reject the suggestion from counsel that, as a constitutional principle, the real and substantial connection requirement could somehow limit presence-based jurisdiction.[43] So to a degree the question remains open. If at all, this argument is most likely to succeed in a situation of purely transitory presence.

It should be noted that the CJPTA does not include presence as a ground for jurisdiction. Instead, it provides for jurisdiction when the defendant is "ordinarily resident" in the forum at the time of the commencement of the proceedings.[44] This is a significant change to the common law.

1) Corporations

The various provincial rules of court typically provide that service on a corporation can be effected by service on an officer, director, or agent of the corporation.[45] Nonetheless, such a rule does not mean that a corporation is present any time one of its representatives can be served in the province. A corporation can be served pursuant to these provincial rules only when the corporation is carrying on business in the province.[46] Only in that way can it be said that the corporation is present in the province. Carrying on business by a corporation equates to physical

---

41 *Ibid* at para 41.
42 Above note 5 at para 87. See also *Prince v ACE Aviation Holdings Inc*, 2014 ONCA 285 at para 48.
43 Above note 5 at para 88. The court was content to indicate that it did not do so on the facts before it: para 89.
44 Above note 21, s 3(d). Under this provision the defendant could be served inside or outside the forum. See Chapter 2 for the meaning of "ordinary residence."
45 See, for example, Ontario Rules, above note 4, r 16.02(1)(c).
46 See *Chevron*, above note 5 at para 85: "[t]o establish traditional, presence-based jurisdiction over an out-of-province corporate defendant, it must be shown that the defendant was carrying on business in the forum at the time of the action." See, for example, *Santa Marina Shipping Co SA v Lunham & Moore Ltd* (1978), 18 OR (2d) 315 (HCJ); *Kroetsch v Domnik Industries Ltd* (1985), 60 AR 69 (QB); *Na v Renfrew Security Bank & Trust (Offshore) Ltd* (2003), 16 BCLR (4th) 345 (SC).

presence on the part of an individual.[47] Thus, once the requisite nexus has been established by way of carrying on business, there is no restriction on the subject matter of the dispute for which service has been effected. In other words, the litigation need not relate to that aspect of the corporation's business that is being conducted in the province.

Many of the cases determining when a corporation is to be regarded as carrying on business in a particular jurisdiction have arisen in the context of the enforcement of foreign judgments. In *Littauer Glove Corp v FW Millington (1920) Ltd*, for example, Salter J held that a corporation was present in a particular jurisdiction when it engaged in "some carrying on of business at a definite, and, to some reasonable extent, permanent place" in that locality.[48] The English cases on the point are summarized as follows in an earlier edition of the leading English textbook:

> The question whether a corporation is carrying on business here is one of fact not always easy to determine. In order that the jurisdiction may exist, [certain] conditions must be fulfilled.
> (1) The activity carried on by the foreign corporation must be a business . . . .
> (2) The business must have been carried on for a substantial period of time. But nine days have been held sufficient in appropriate circumstances, as where a foreign manufacturer of motor-cars occupied a stand at an exhibition in London.
> (3) The business must have been carried on at some fixed and definite place in England.
> (4) The business must be that of the corporation, not that of the agent who acts for it in England. This condition is fulfilled if the agent has authority to make contracts on behalf of the corporation, even if he is paid only by commission, pays the rent of his office, and also acts as agent for another foreign corporation. But it is not fulfilled if the agent has no general authority to make contracts on behalf of the corporation but merely to obtain orders and submit them to the foreign corporation for approval.[49]

---

47 In *Research in Motion Ltd v Visto Corp* (2008), 93 OR (3d) 593 (SCJ), the court intimated (at paras 50–57) that presence-based jurisdiction could be established by a corporation's carrying on business in the province even where the corporation was served *ex juris*. That is contrary to the traditional position at common law where service in the province is essential.
48 (1928), 44 TLR 746 at 747 (KB).
49 Albert Venn Dicey & JHC Morris, *Dicey and Morris on the Conflict of Laws*, 9th ed (London: Stevens & Sons, 1973) at 164–65.

This passage has influenced Canadian courts.[50] In *Adams v Cape Industries Plc*, the English Court of Appeal elaborated on the circumstances in which a corporation could be regarded as carrying on business in a particular jurisdiction through some agent or representative.[51] Lord Justice Slade said that the question of whether the representative had been carrying on the business of the corporation depended to some degree upon a detailed examination of the precise relationship between the representative and the corporation. In particular, Slade LJ indicated that answers to the following questions were likely to be relevant:

> (a) whether or not the fixed place of business from which the representative operates was originally acquired for the purpose of enabling him to act on behalf of the overseas corporation; (b) whether the overseas corporation has directly reimbursed him for (i) the cost of his accommodation at the fixed place of business; (ii) the cost of his staff; (c) what other contributions, if any, the overseas corporation makes to the financing of the business carried on by the representative; (d) whether the representative is remunerated by reference to transactions, e.g. by commission, or by fixed regular payments or in some other way; (e) what degree of control the overseas corporation exercises over the running of the business conducted by the representative; (f) whether the representative reserves (i) part of his accommodation, (ii) part of his staff for conducting business related to the overseas corporation; (g) whether the representative displays the overseas corporation's name at his premises or on his stationery, and if so, whether he does so in such a way as to indicate that he is a representative of the overseas corporation; (h) what business, if any, the representative transacts as principal exclusively on his own behalf; (i) whether the representative makes contracts with customers or other third parties in the name of the overseas corporation, or otherwise in such manner as to bind it; (j) if so, whether the representative requires specific authority in advance before binding the overseas corporation to contractual obligations.[52]

Recently in *Club Resorts* the Supreme Court of Canada held that carrying on business "requires some form of actual, not only virtual, presence in the jurisdiction, such as maintaining an office there or regularly visiting the territory of the particular jurisdiction."[53] But the court ex-

---

50 See, for example, *Moore v Mercator Enterprises Ltd* (1978), 90 DLR (3d) 590 at 601 (NSSC).
51 [1990] Ch 433 (CA).
52 *Ibid* at 530–31.
53 Above note 19 at para 87.

pressly left open the issue of "whether and, if so, when e-trade in the jurisdiction would amount to a presence in the jurisdiction."[54]

In some situations, service on a foreign corporation is straightforward because, typically, such a corporation is required to register or be licensed as an extraprovincial corporation in a particular province when it carries on business there.[55] The precise requirements do differ, however, from province to province. Thus, as an example, both Alberta[56] and Ontario[57] define an extraprovincial corporation as one incorporated otherwise than under an act of the provincial legislature. In Ontario,[58] however, such corporations are divided into three classes: those incorporated in other provinces, those incorporated federally, and those incorporated outside Canada. Only corporations in the third class are required to obtain a licence to carry on business in Ontario.[59] The various statutes also define, for the purposes of the statute, what constitutes carrying on business in the province.[60]

In order to register or obtain a licence, the foreign corporation ordinarily must appoint some agent upon whom process can be served.[61] Where, however, a foreign corporation fails to register and appoint an agent for service, despite carrying on business in the province, a plaintiff can serve the corporation in accordance with the local rules of practice.[62]

Under the CJPTA, jurisdiction is based not on presence but rather on the defendant's ordinary residence in the province.[63] Section 7 provides that a corporation is ordinarily resident in the province only if

(a) the corporation has or is required by law to have a registered office in [the province],
(b) pursuant to law, it (i) has registered an address in [the province] at which process may be served generally, or (ii) has nominated

---

54 Ibid. See the analysis in *Equustek Solutions Inc v Google Inc*, 2015 BCCA 265, aff'g 2014 BCSC 1063, leave to appeal to SCC granted, [2015] SCCA No 355.
55 See, for example, *Business Corporations Act*, RSA 2000, c B-9, s 279; *Extra-Provincial Corporations Act*, RSO 1990, c E.27, s 4(3).
56 *Business Corporations Act*, above note 55, s 1(r).
57 *Extra-Provincial Corporations Act*, above note 55, s 1.
58 Ibid, s 2(1).
59 Ibid, s 4.
60 See, for example, Ontario's *Extra-Provincial Corporations Act*, ibid, s 1(2); and Alberta's *Business Corporations Act*, above note 55, s 277(1).
61 See, for example, Alberta's *Business Corporations Act*, above note 55, s 280(2)(c); and Ontario's *Extra-Provincial Corporations Act*, above note 55, s 19.
62 *Kroetsch v Domnik Industries Ltd*, above note 46. Interestingly, the court determined that the defendant corporation was carrying on business in the province by examining the definition in the legislation rather than by directly applying common law principles.
63 Above note 21, s 3(d).

an agent in [the province] upon whom process may be served generally,
(c) it has a place of business in [the province], or
(d) its central management is exercised in [the province].

2) Partnerships

The local courts have jurisdiction over a partner if that partner, as with any other individual, is served with process while physically present in the forum. Where, however, two or more persons are alleged to be liable as partners, they may be sued in the name of their firm if there is one.[64] Typically, local practice rules provide that personal service on a partnership is effected by serving an individual partner or any person at the partnership's principal place of business in the jurisdiction who appears to have management or control of that place of business.[65]

There are also special statutory provisions that deal with the conditions under which limited partnerships and limited liability partnerships are allowed to operate in a province despite their having been formed in a jurisdiction outside the province. In general, the legislation provides for a system of registration and for a place or manner of service of documents.[66]

As noted earlier, under the CJPTA the focus is on ordinary residence in the province, not presence. Section 8 states that a partnership is ordinarily resident in the province only if

  (a) the partnership has, or is required by law to have, a registered office or business address in [the province],
  (b) it has a place of business in [the province], or
  (c) its central management is exercised in [the province].

C. CONSENT-BASED JURISDICTION

The second basis for jurisdiction *in personam* at common law is the defendant's consent to having the dispute resolved in the local courts.

---

64 See, for example, Ontario Rules, above note 4, r 8.01.
65 See, for example, Ontario Rules, *ibid*, r 16.02(1)(m). It could be questioned whether, like the rules discussed above for serving a corporation, these rules should be interpreted as requiring that the partnership be carrying on business in the province. If not, a partnership could be present in a province if one of its partners was served while there temporarily.
66 See, for example, *Partnership Act*, RSA 2000, c P-3, ss 52 and 93–104.1; *Limited Partnerships Act*, RSO 1990, c L.16, s 25; *Partnerships Act*, RSO 1990, c P.5, s 44.4.

Consent is also known as submission or attornment and it can take a variety of forms. Plaintiffs who launch actions in the local courts are taken to have consented to the jurisdiction of those courts, including in respect of any counterclaims that may be brought against them by the defendants.[67] Equally, defendants submit when they contest the case on the merits, such as by filing statements of defence or even notices of an intent to defend.[68] However, the filing of a notice to defend by an insurer purportedly on behalf of the defendant did not constitute submission where the defendant had indicated through its own solicitor that it did not intend to attorn to the jurisdiction and that instead it was going to challenge the court's jurisdiction.[69]

MJ Jones Inc v Kingsway General Insurance Co raised the interesting question of whether the filing of a statement of defence in compliance with a court order would constitute a submission to the jurisdiction.[70] A defendant in an Ontario action, without attorning to the jurisdiction of the Ontario courts, had brought a motion seeking dismissal of the action on the grounds that Ontario lacked jurisdiction *simpliciter* and that Ontario was an inconvenient forum for the trial of the action. The Ontario courts had rejected the motion.[71] The defendant immediately sought leave to appeal the decision to the Supreme Court of Canada on the issue of jurisdiction *simpliciter*. He also moved for a stay of proceedings pending the outcome of the leave application and, if successful, any subsequent appeal. The defendant argued that, if a stay was not granted and he was ordered to file a statement of defence, compliance with that order would amount to submission to Ontario's jurisdiction and the application before the Supreme Court of Canada would be moot. Justice Lang recognized that a defendant who argued the merits of a dispute would ordinarily be held to have submitted to the court's jurisdiction and would be precluded from contesting jurisdiction *simpliciter*. She observed, however, that it was unclear whether a defendant would be regarded as having attorned by participating on the merits only because ordered to do so. Since the law was uncertain on this point, there was the possibility that the defendant would suffer irreparable harm if a stay were denied. Consequently, Lang JA granted the defendant's motion.

---

67   See, for example, *CJPTA*, above note 21, s 3(a).
68   See, for example, *Kinch v Pyle* (2004), 8 CPC (6th) 66 (Ont SCJ).
69   *Coldmatic Refrigeration of Canada Ltd v Leveltek Processing LLC* (2004), 70 OR (3d) 758 (SCJ), aff'd on different grounds (2005), 75 OR (3d) 638 (CA).
70   (2004), 72 OR (3d) 68 (CA). See also *Stuart Budd & Sons Ltd v IFS Vehicle Distributors ULC*, 2014 ONCA 546.
71   [2003] OJ No 4409 (SCJ), aff'd [2004] OJ No 1087 (CA).

The key issue is whether the defendant has taken steps that go beyond challenging the court's jurisdiction.[72] Even conduct short of this threshold can be problematic, since some questions remain as to the extent to which a defendant can challenge the existence or the exercise of jurisdiction without being taken to have submitted to the jurisdiction of the court.[73] Some answers are supplied by the provincial rules of court, though rarely are those answers complete. The British Columbia *Supreme Court Civil Rules*, for example, provide that a party who has been served with an originating pleading, whether in or outside British Columbia, may, after filing a "jurisdictional response," apply to stay or dismiss the proceeding on the ground of lack of jurisdiction.[74] The rules further provide that a party who, within thirty days of filing the jurisdictional response, does in fact challenge the jurisdiction of the court does not submit to the court's jurisdiction by doing so.[75] Indeed, pending the resolution of the challenge, the party is even allowed to defend on the merits.[76] Interestingly, however, the rules do not provide explicitly that the defendant is free to ask that the court decline to exercise its jurisdiction without being held to have submitted. Under an earlier version of the rules the British Columbia Court of Appeal had concluded that "it has now been settled that . . . challenges to jurisdiction, both *simpliciter* and *forum conveniens*, can now be brought in this jurisdiction without the applicant being deemed to have thereby submitted to the jurisdiction of the court."[77] Despite the change in the wording of the rules, it is unlikely that any substantive change was intended and so, in all probability, an application to the court to decline jurisdiction would not constitute a submission to the jurisdiction.[78]

---

72 See *Fraser v 4358376 Canada Inc (cob Itravel 2000 and Travelzest PLC)*, 2014 ONCA 553.

73 The *CJPTA*, above note 21, does not resolve these questions. It merely incorporates the existing common law by providing in s 3(b) that a court has jurisdiction where the defendant submits to the court's jurisdiction during the course of the proceedings.

74 Above note 6, r 21-8(1).

75 *Ibid*, r 21-8(5).

76 *Ibid*, r 21-8(5)(b)(ii).

77 *Mid-Ohio Imported Car Co v Tri-K Investments Ltd* (1995), 13 BCLR (3d) 41 at para 14 (CA) [*Mid-Ohio*].

78 This seems to be a reasonable inference from cases like *Ezer v Yorkton Securities Inc*, [2005] BCJ No 30 (CA), but see *O'Brien v Simard* (2006), 230 BCAC 120 (CA). In *Borgstrom v Korean Air Lines Co* (2007), 70 BCLR (4th) 206 (CA), the British Columbia Court of Appeal appeared to interpret the rules strictly so that only a protest to jurisdiction *simpliciter* would protect a defendant from being found to have attorned to the jurisdiction. The court made it clear, however, that such a challenge to the existence of jurisdiction could be made simply as a matter of

Rule 17.06 of Ontario's *Rules of Civil Procedure* deals specifically with cases of service *ex juris*. It provides that a party who has been served with an originating process outside Ontario may move, before delivering a defence or notice of intent to defend, for an order setting aside the service (or the order for service) or for an order staying the proceedings.[79] The court may make either order where it is satisfied that service *ex juris* was not authorized by the rules or that Ontario is an inconvenient forum.[80] The Ontario Rules also provide specifically that the making of such a motion "is not in itself a submission to the jurisdiction of the court" over the defendant.[81] Rule 17.06, however, does not explicitly address the situation in which a defendant wishes to contest jurisdiction *simpliciter*.[82] Nor is there any similar rule dealing with service of an originating process within Ontario.[83]

Many of the authorities dealing with the questions of whether a protest to the existence or the exercise of jurisdiction constitutes a submission to the jurisdiction have arisen in the context of the enforcement of foreign judgments.[84] In the difficult case of *Henry v Geoprosco International Ltd*, the English Court of Appeal appeared to leave open the question of whether a protest solely to the existence of jurisdiction constituted a voluntary submission.[85] It did, however, indicate that an invitation to a court to decline to exercise its jurisdiction would constitute a voluntary submission.[86] It is still unclear to what extent *Henry* represents the Canadian position. It has certainly been doubted by the Court of Appeal for Ontario.[87]

Finally, it is well recognized that a defendant can submit to the jurisdiction of a court by an agreement to submit.[88] Thus, parties to a contract may agree that all disputes arising thereunder are to be referred to the courts of, for example, Ontario. Such a choice of forum clause will

---

form, on arguably specious grounds, so as to allow the defendant to also apply to the court to decline jurisdiction without being taken as having submitted.

79 Above note 4, r 17.06(1).
80 *Ibid*, r 17.06(2).
81 *Ibid*, r 17.06(4).
82 This focus on service illustrates the point, made earlier, that historically it has been equated with jurisdiction.
83 For a discussion of some of the gaps in Ontario's procedural framework, see Dusten & Pitel, above note 14.
84 See Chapter 8. That was true, for example, in *Mid-Ohio*, above note 77.
85 [1975] 3 WLR 620 at 637–39 (CA).
86 *Ibid* at 637.
87 *McCain Foods Ltd v Agricultural Publishing Co* (1979), 26 OR (2d) 758 (CA). See also *Mid-Ohio*, above note 77.
88 See *CJPTA*, above note 21, s 3(c).

bestow jurisdiction on the Ontario courts. If the defendant happens to be outside the chosen jurisdiction, there is a standard provision in the provincial rules permitting service *ex juris* based on the agreement.[89] On occasion, courts have held that an exclusive jurisdiction clause in a contract ousts the jurisdiction of the courts of any other country to hear a dispute arising under that contract. Thus, in *EK Motors v Volkswagen Canada Ltd*, the Saskatchewan Court of Appeal held that a clause that provided that a contract was "subject . . . to the exclusive jurisdiction of [Ontario's] Courts" was sufficient to "oust the jurisdiction of the Saskatchewan courts in respect of litigation arising out of that contract."[90] The clearly accepted view, however, is that the parties cannot by their private stipulation oust the jurisdiction of the courts.[91] Nevertheless, courts will enforce exclusive choice of forum clauses by staying actions launched in defiance of such provisions unless there are substantial reasons to ignore their existence.[92]

It should be noted that no amount of consent can confer jurisdiction on a court which lacks subject matter jurisdiction.[93] Thus, before a court can assume jurisdiction in a divorce case, for example, the jurisdictional requirements of the *Divorce Act* must be satisfied; the consent of the respondent to the proceedings is irrelevant.[94] Equally, given the rule that Canadian courts have no jurisdiction over foreign land, including, it appears, actions for tortious damage to foreign land,[95] jurisdiction in such proceedings cannot be conferred by the defendant's submission.[96]

Consent and assumed jurisdiction under the real and substantial connection principle are separate bases of jurisdiction. The latter has

---

89 See, for example, Ontario Rules, above note 4, r 17.02(f)(iii).
90 [1973] 1 WWR 466 at 467 and 470 (Sask CA). For this conclusion, the court relied upon the words of Furlong CJ in *Wescott v Alsco Products of Canada Ltd* (1960), 26 DLR (2d) 281 at 284 (Nfld CA). See also *Momentous.ca Corp v Canadian American Association of Professional Baseball Ltd*, 2012 SCC 9, discussed in Chapter 6.
91 *Volkswagen Canada Inc v Auto Haus Frohlich Ltd* (1985), 65 AR 271 at para 4 (CA). In *2249659 Ontario Ltd v Sparkasse Siegen*, 2013 ONCA 354 at para 25 the court observed "[a] forum selection clause applicable to the relevant litigation identifying a forum other than Ontario as the forum of choice cannot deprive Ontario of jurisdiction *simpliciter*."
92 *ZI Pompey Industrie v Ecu-Line NV*, [2003] 1 SCR 450. See the discussion in Chapter 6.
93 See, for example, *Rothgiesser v Rothgiesser* (2000), 46 OR (3d) 577 (CA); and *Ashad v Deutsche Lufthansa Aktiengesellschaft (cob Lufthansa German Airlines)*, [2009] OJ No 4979 (SCJ).
94 RSC 1985 (2nd Supp), c 3, s 3(1).
95 For an examination of this proposition, see Chapter 17.
96 *Albert v Fraser Companies Ltd*, [1937] 1 DLR 39 at 42 (NBSCAD).

not subsumed the former. In *Shekhdar v K & M Engineering & Consulting Corp*, for example, the Court of Appeal for Ontario rejected the position of Matlow J in the court below that consent could not constitute a basis of jurisdiction separate from assumed jurisdiction.[97]

D. ASSUMED JURISDICTION

1) The *Morguard* Principle

Originally, the grounds for service *ex juris* set the boundaries of a court's jurisdiction over foreign defendants. The scope of a court's assumed jurisdiction was as broad or as narrow as its rules permitting service abroad. Now, through the *Morguard* principle, it has been recognized that the rules for service *ex juris* do not by themselves confer jurisdiction on the courts. They are rules of procedure and service in accordance with them is simply designed to ensure that "the parties to an action receive timely notice of the proceeding so that they have an opportunity to participate."[98]

In *Morguard*, the Supreme Court of Canada reinvented the law relating to jurisdiction *in personam*. The case actually concerned the enforceability of a foreign judgment and focused upon the circumstances in which a foreign court would be regarded as having jurisdiction for that purpose. Justice La Forest, however, indicated that the decision was just as important on the issue of local jurisdiction. He pointed out:

> The conditions governing the taking of jurisdiction by the courts of one province and those under which [their judgments] are enforced by the courts of another province should be viewed as correlative. If it is fair and reasonable for the courts of one province to exercise jurisdiction over a subject matter, it should as a general principle be reasonable for the courts of another province to enforce the resultant judgment.[99]

According to La Forest J, what had to "underlie a modern system of private international law [were] principles of order and fairness, principles that ensure[d] security of transactions with justice."[100] He continued:

---

97 [2006] OJ No 2120 (CA), rev'g (2004), 71 OR (3d) 475 (SCJ).
98 *Muscutt*, above note 18 at para 50.
99 *Morguard*, above note 10 at 1094.
100 *Ibid* at 1097.

It may meet the demands of order and fairness to recognize a judgment given in a jurisdiction that had the greatest or at least significant contacts with the subject matter of the action. But it hardly accords with principles of order and fairness to permit a person to sue another in any jurisdiction, without regard to the contacts that jurisdiction may have to the defendant or the subject matter of the suit.[101]

Justice La Forest said that jurisdictional difficulties arose where the defendant had been served *ex juris*. There had to be "some limits to the exercise of jurisdiction against persons outside the province."[102] Those limits could not be found in the various provincial rules for service *ex juris*, some of which were overly broad. He considered that the correct approach was to allow a proceeding where there was "a real and substantial connection with the action" because that approach provided "a reasonable balance between the rights of the parties."[103]

Morguard itself was an interprovincial case and much of the court's reasoning was restricted to that context. In *Hunt v T & N plc*, the Supreme Court of Canada transformed the *Morguard* principle from a common law proposition into a constitutional one, again in the interprovincial context.[104] Nevertheless, from the outset the courts assumed that the principle was applicable, at least as a matter of common law, where the defendant was to be served outside Canada. The Supreme Court of Canada, however, undermined this assumption in *Spar Aerospace Ltd v American Mobile Satellite Corp*.[105] The plaintiff launched an action in Quebec against four corporations situated in the United States for damages it incurred in connection with the testing of the communications payload of a satellite. The plaintiff asserted that the court had jurisdiction on the basis of article 3148(3) of the *Civil Code of Quebec*,[106] which provided *inter alia* that the Quebec courts had jurisdiction over actions in respect of damage suffered in Quebec. The defendants, however, contested the jurisdiction of the Quebec courts, in part on the ground that there was no real and substantial connection between the action and Quebec. In his judgment for the court, LeBel J held that there was no need for the plaintiff to satisfy the real and substantial connection requirement in an international case. The only question was whether the provisions of the *Civil Code* had been met. He empha-

---

101 *Ibid* at 1103.
102 *Ibid* at 1104.
103 *Ibid* at 1108.
104 Above note 11.
105 [2002] 4 SCR 205 [*Spar*].
106 CQLR c C-1991 [*Civil Code*].

sized that "*Morguard* and *Hunt* were decided in the context of interprovincial jurisdictional disputes."¹⁰⁷

Despite *Spar*, however, Canadian courts, including the Supreme Court of Canada, have continued to insist that the *Morguard* principle applies even in international cases.¹⁰⁸ For example, the subsequent decision of the Supreme Court of Canada in *Beals* is inconsistent with *Spar*.¹⁰⁹ That case concerned the related question of the enforcement in Canada of a foreign judgment. The judgment was from Florida. Justice Major, for the majority, was in no doubt that the *Morguard* principle, which had arisen in the context of the enforcement of a judgment from another Canadian province, applied equally to the enforcement of a judgment from a foreign country. *Spar* has simply been ignored on this point and the courts routinely apply the *Morguard* principle in international cases.

2) Application of the *Morguard* Principle

In *Morguard* the Supreme Court of Canada did not offer much detail as to how, in operation, the real and substantial connection principle would be applied. Over the years, different approaches have been used. Until recently the most frequent approach at common law was that from the Court of Appeal for Ontario in *Muscutt*. A different approach was adopted under the *CJPTA*. Recently, the Supreme Court of Canada articulated the current common law approach in *Club Resorts*. Each of these approaches is discussed below.

a) *Muscutt*: Eight Factors

In 2002 in *Muscutt* the Court of Appeal for Ontario engaged in a thorough analysis of the *Morguard* principle.¹¹⁰ The plaintiff in the dispute was a passenger in a motor vehicle that was involved in a traffic accident in Alberta. He wanted to sue the owner and driver of the vehicle in which he was travelling and the owner and driver of the other vehicle involved in the collision. At the time of the accident, all the defendants were Alberta residents, though one of them later moved to Ontario. The

---

107 Above note 105 at para 51.
108 See the discussion by Pitel & Dusten, above note 33 at 77–81.
109 Above note 34.
110 On the same day as it released *Muscutt*, above note 18, the court released judgments in four companion cases decided using the principles set out in *Muscutt*: see *Leufkens v Alba Tours International Inc* (2002), 60 OR (3d) 84 (CA) [*Leufkens*]; *Lemmex v Bernard* (2002), 60 OR (3d) 54 (CA); *Sinclair v Cracker Barrel Old Country Store Inc* (2002), 60 OR (3d) 76 (CA); *Gajraj v DeBernardo* (2002), 60 OR (3d) 68 (CA).

plaintiff was an Ontario resident who, just before the crash, had moved
to Alberta to work on a contract for his Ontario-based employer. While
in Alberta, the plaintiff had accepted an offer from his employer to
work at a new Alberta office and he would have moved permanently to
Alberta to take that job had it not been for the accident. Instead, upon
his release from a Calgary hospital, the plaintiff had returned to Ontario to live with his mother. He required extensive and ongoing medical care in Ontario. He launched an action in Ontario and served the
defendants *ex juris* on the basis of rule 17.02(h) of the Ontario Rules,
which allowed such service where a claim is in respect of damage sustained in Ontario arising from a tort wherever committed.

Justice Sharpe pointed out that the task in applying *Morguard* was
to identify whether there was a real and substantial connection between the action and the forum. There was no requirement that the
forum have the most real and substantial connection.[111] In other words,
the forum might not be the only one with jurisdiction over the case.
That was why there was a residual discretion to decline jurisdiction on
forum non conveniens grounds even though the *Morguard* test had been
satisfied. He also emphasized that the analysis was flexible and that the
Supreme Court of Canada had not attempted any precise definition of
the required connection. Indeed, Sharpe JA pointed out that the court
in *Morguard* had been somewhat ambiguous in its formulation of the
required connection:

> While certain passages in *Morguard* suggest that the connection must
> be with the defendant, others suggest that the connection must be
> with the subject matter of the action or with the damages suffered by
> the plaintiff.[112]

Justice Sharpe noted that two different approaches to the application of
Morguard were evident from the authorities: the "personal subjection"
approach and the "administration of justice" approach.[113] The personal
subjection approach focused on the connection between the defendant and the forum. The question was whether the defendant's conduct
and connection with the forum made it reasonable for the defendant to
anticipate that he or she might be sued there. In contrast, the administration of justice approach was broader in scope. It concentrated more
generally on whether the forum was a fair and reasonable place for the

---

111 Above note 18 at para 44.
112 *Ibid* at para 56.
113 Justice Sharpe drew this language from Joost Blom, "Case Comment: *Morguard Investments Ltd. v. De Savoye*" (1991) 70 *Canadian Bar Review* 733 at 741.

action to proceed in the interests of both parties. Under this approach the search was for a connection between the forum and the subject matter of the action. In this respect, the defendant's connection with the forum was important but not determinative.

Justice Sharpe held that the weight of authority supported this broader approach, and he himself favoured it. In the interests of clarity, Sharpe JA then isolated eight factors that the courts should consider in determining whether the *Morguard* principle had been satisfied. He said that no single factor was determinative but that they all had to be considered and weighed together. He indicated that he was dealing with the specific question of whether a court could assume jurisdiction against an out-of-province defendant on the basis of damage sustained in the province as a result of a tort committed elsewhere. Not surprisingly, however, later courts considered these factors to be more generally relevant.

The eight *Muscutt* factors, as they became known, are as follows: (1) the connection between the forum and the plaintiff's claim; (2) the connection between the forum and the defendant; (3) the unfairness to the defendant in assuming jurisdiction; (4) the unfairness to the plaintiff in not assuming jurisdiction; (5) the involvement of other parties; (6) the court's willingness to recognize and enforce extraprovincial judgments rendered on the same jurisdictional basis; (7) the nature of the dispute (interprovincial or international), with a more lenient approach taken to the assumption of jurisdiction in an interprovincial case; and (8) comity and standards of jurisdiction, recognition, and enforcement prevailing elsewhere.

Ultimately, the court concluded that a fair weighing of the identified factors favoured the assumption of jurisdiction in *Muscutt*. Despite Sharpe JA's assertion that no single factor was determinative and that all eight had to be considered and weighed together to answer the jurisdictional question, it can be argued that in practice the most important are the connection between the forum and the action and between the forum and the defendant.[114] It also seems clear, as Sharpe JA indicated, that the real and substantial connection requirement would be more difficult to satisfy in international cases. It is worth observing that the four companion decisions to *Muscutt* were international cases and the Court of Appeal held in each of those cases that a real and substantial connection had not been established.[115]

---

114 See Jeff Berryman, "Real and Substantial: The Ontario Court of Appeal's View on Service *Ex Juris: Muscutt v. Courcelles*" (2003) 26 *Advocates' Quarterly* 492.
115 Above note 110.

Under the *Muscutt* approach, it became common to refer to the "real and substantial connection test." For over a decade this approach was used in Ontario as the test for assumed jurisdiction. The approach was also used outside Ontario.[116] The British Columbia courts, however, tended not to apply the eight *Muscutt* factors specifically but to rely simply on the general proposition that there must be a real and substantial connection between the court and the defendant or between the court and the subject matter of the litigation.[117] In addition, the New Brunswick Court of Appeal in *Coutu v Gauthier (Estate)* cast doubt on the need for courts to adopt the eight-point *Muscutt* test.[118] Chief Justice Drapeau stressed the importance of distinguishing issues of jurisdiction *simpliciter* from issues of *forum non conveniens* and of not conflating the applicable tests. It was essential for counsel to be able to determine with reasonable certainty, prior to launching an action, whether the court had jurisdiction. To his mind, most of the *Muscutt* factors were directed towards the ascertainment of the convenient forum.[119] The question was whether there was a real and substantial connection with the forum, not whether the forum had the most real and substantial connection. According to Drapeau CJ, the *Muscutt* test might "be straying from the former into the latter."[120] He thought that the essence of the real and substantial connection test was captured by the first *Muscutt* factor: the connection between the forum and the plaintiff's claim. He determined that, in *Coutu* itself, a sufficiently substantial connection could be established either on the ground that the defendant could reasonably have foreseen that the plaintiff would suffer harm in New Brunswick through his negligent act or simply on the basis that the plaintiff had indeed sustained significant damage in the province.

As will be explained below, the *Muscutt* approach was rejected by the Supreme Court of Canada in 2012 in *Club Resorts*. Yet courts con-

---

116 See, for example, Alberta cases *Deuruneft Deutsche-Russische Mineralol Handelsgesellschaft mbH v Bullen* (2003), 21 Alta LR (4th) 349 (QB); *Royal and Sun Alliance Insurance Co of Canada v Wainoco Oil & Gas Co* (2004), 364 AR 151 (QB), aff'd (2005), 367 AR 177 (CA); *Wheeler v 1000128 Alberta Ltd* (2008), 431 AR 209 (QB), aff'd (sub nom *Wheeler v China Natural Petroleum Corp*) (2008), 433 AR 234 (CA); and the Nova Scotia case of *Bouch v Penny (Litigation Guardian of)* (2009), 281 NSR (2d) 238 (CA) [*Penny*].
117 See, for example, *British Columbia v Imperial Tobacco Canada Ltd* (2006), 56 BCLR (4th) 263 (CA); *UniNet Technologies Ltd v Communication Services Inc* (2005), 38 BCLR (4th) 366 (CA) [*UniNet*].
118 (2006), 296 NBR (2d) 34 (CA) [*Coutu*].
119 *Ibid* at paras 56 and 67.
120 *Ibid* at para 68. See also *Fewer v Sayisi Dene Education Authority*, 2011 NLCA 17 [*Fewer*].

tinue to grapple with the appropriate weight, if any, of several of the *Muscutt* factors in the jurisdictional analysis.

b) The *CJPTA*: Some Presumptions

The *CJPTA* draws directly on the *Morguard* principle in its provisions on territorial competence. It provides in section 3(e) for territorial competence in situations in which "there is a real and substantial connection between [enacting province or territory] and the facts on which the proceeding against that person is based." Had the drafters stopped at this point, the analysis under this provision would be expected to develop along lines similar to those in provinces relying on the common law. However, section 10 goes on to develop the concept of real and substantial connection by providing a list of connections that are presumed, subject to being rebutted, to satisfy the test. The list is explicitly open-ended: the plaintiff remains free to establish other circumstances that constitute a real and substantial connection between the forum and the facts on which a proceeding is based.[121]

The specific presumptions are discussed in more detail below. A real and substantial connection is presumed, for example, in a proceeding concerning contractual obligations that were, to a substantial extent, to be performed in the forum. It is also presumed in a proceeding concerning a tort committed in the forum.

Because it is open-ended, the *CJPTA* approach requires that the court have a means to analyze whether there is a real and substantial connection to the forum in cases falling outside the presumptions. In *Bouch v Penny (Litigation Guardian of)*,[122] the Nova Scotia Court of Appeal had to determine whether there was jurisdiction based on a real and substantial connection under Nova Scotia's *CJPTA*. The case concerned an action brought by a mother on behalf of herself and her infant son for medical malpractice against four Alberta physicians who had treated her during her pregnancy and an Alberta hospital. At the time that the medical services were provided, the plaintiff resided in Alberta though she had been born and raised in Nova Scotia. She moved back to Nova Scotia shortly after the birth so as to have the benefit of the support of her family since she was a single mother. She later left Nova Scotia for brief periods in Saskatchewan and Ontario but returned again to settle permanently. Her son had a serious disability.

The case did not fit any of the presumptive circumstances for the existence of a real and substantial connection. The question, therefore,

---

121 For a detailed analysis of the approach to assumed jurisdiction under the *CJPTA*, see Black, Pitel, & Sobkin, above note 22, ch 6.
122 Above note 116.

was whether the plaintiff had established other circumstances that constituted such a connection with the province. In answering that question, the Court of Appeal agreed with the motions judge[123] in the application of the eight factors from *Muscutt*. Justice Saunders stressed that fairness to both parties was important at the jurisdiction *simpliciter* stage as well as at the *forum non conveniens* stage.[124] It had therefore been appropriate for the motions judge to take into account what he saw as extreme unfairness to the plaintiff if Nova Scotia did not assume jurisdiction. The mother was financially incapable of suing anywhere else, and her son required her constant care and attention. Justice Wright had concluded:

> Given the marginal financial resources at her disposal, and the personal care requirements and immobility of her son Caiden, this becomes an access to justice issue for the plaintiffs. The submission of their counsel was that if this case were to be moved to Alberta, the personal hardships of the plaintiffs may well be such that they are not able to proceed with the litigation at all.[125]

The Nova Scotia Court of Appeal stressed the conventional wisdom that the *Morguard* test required only a real and substantial connection with the province and not that the province had the most real and substantial connection with the action and the parties. Despite that assertion, the connection to Nova Scotia in *Penny* seems minimal at best.

In stark contrast to the approach in Nova Scotia, the British Columbia Court of Appeal indicated that "any reliance on the *Muscutt* factors as a guide to determining the question of jurisdiction came to an end in British Columbia with the coming into force of the *CJPTA*."[126] The statute itself does not mandate this conclusion, since it leaves open the means of analysis to be used in cases not fitting one of the presumptions. But this conclusion is consistent with the general hostility, mentioned above, of the British Columbia courts to the *Muscutt* approach.

c) *Club Resorts*: **Presumptive Connecting Factors**

In *Club Resorts* the plaintiff travelled from Ontario to Cuba for a holiday, staying at a resort managed by Club Resorts Ltd, a Cayman Islands

---

123 (2008), 305 DLR (4th) 412 (NSSC).
124 In that regard, the court also relied on the earlier Nova Scotia appellate authority of *Oakley*, above note 15, and *O'Brien v Canada (Attorney General)* (2002), 210 DLR (4th) 668 (NSCA).
125 Above note 123 at para 50.
126 *Stanway v Wyeth Pharmaceuticals Inc*, 2009 BCCA 592 at para 73.

corporation.[127] While at the resort she was very seriously injured. She returned to Canada and became a resident of British Columbia. She sued Club Resorts Ltd in Ontario. The Ontario courts, using the *Muscutt* approach, found that they had jurisdiction.[128] The Supreme Court of Canada agreed, but in doing so it significantly changed the test for assumed jurisdiction.

The most important development of the law by the court was its conclusion that the real and substantial connection test should no longer be used directly to assess the taking of jurisdiction.[129] It held that it is a constitutional principle which operates at a higher level of generality. Instead, the real and substantial connection required for assumed jurisdiction has to be found in each case through a "presumptive connecting factor," a factor that triggers a presumption of such a connection.[130] Where a presumptive connecting factor is established, the defendant can rebut the presumption.[131]

The court stated that it would not set out a definitive list of presumptive connecting factors. The claims before the court were in tort, and so the court identified four presumptive connecting factors for tort claims: that the defendant is domiciled or resident in the forum, that the defendant carries on business in the forum, that the tort was committed in the forum, and that a contract connected with the dispute was made in the forum.[132] The court acknowledged that additional presumptive connecting factors would need to be identified by lower courts. It held that "[i]n identifying new presumptive factors, a court should look to connections that give rise to a relationship with the forum that is similar in nature to the ones which result from the listed factors."[133] Such a court is to consider the similarity of the new factor to the recognized presumptive connecting factors and the treatment of the new factor in the jurisprudence, in statutes, and in the private international law of other legal systems.

---

127 Above note 19. The analysis of this decision in this chapter is based on Stephen GA Pitel, "Checking In to *Club Resorts*: How Courts Are Applying the New Test for Jurisdiction" (2013) 42 *Advocates' Quarterly* 190.
128 The Court of Appeal reformulated the *Muscutt* approach in reaching its decision. As that reformulation was rejected by the Supreme Court of Canada, it is not discussed here.
129 *Club Resorts*, above note 19 at paras 30 and 70.
130 *Ibid* at paras 75, 78, and 100.
131 *Ibid* at paras 81, 95, and 100.
132 *Ibid* at paras 68, 80, and 90.
133 *Ibid* at para 91.

The court held that where no presumptive connecting factor is established, a court cannot take jurisdiction.¹³⁴ It is not open to the plaintiff to establish jurisdiction by identifying factual connections that, while not amounting to a presumptive connecting factor, collectively warrant the court hearing the dispute. This is the most significant change from the *Muscutt* approach and its weighing of the eight factors.

In *Club Resorts* the court was concerned by the criticism that the test for assumed jurisdiction under the *Muscutt* approach was too open-ended and fact-specific, leading to uncertainty and protracted disputes about jurisdiction *simpliciter*.¹³⁵ Its objective was to create a more certain approach. The court was also influenced by the *CJPTA*. The move to assumed jurisdiction based on presumptive connecting factors is very similar to the approach in section 10 of the statute. However, as noted above, the structure of the *CJPTA* does allow a court to take jurisdiction based on a real and substantial connection even in the absence of a section 10 presumption. That flexibility is not replicated in the *Club Resorts* approach.

Indeed, while *Club Resorts* was not a case under the *CJPTA*, the decision raises issues about whether it has an effect on the approach under the statute. Both sections 3(e) and 10 use the real and substantial connection requirement not as a constitutional principle but as the direct test for assumed jurisdiction. In all likelihood this has not been invalidated by the Supreme Court of Canada.¹³⁶ More subtly, the *Club Resorts* approach could change the way courts apply the *CJPTA* in cases that do not involve a section 10 presumption. It could lead courts in those provinces to develop additional presumptions beyond those listed in section 10 and to refuse to take jurisdiction where such a presumption is not established, directly mirroring the *Club Resorts* approach.¹³⁷

3) Presumptive Connecting Factors

Prior to *Club Resorts*, there was some debate in the jurisprudence as to whether falling within an enumerated ground for which service *ex juris* was authorized in and of itself satisfied the real and substantial

---

134 *Ibid* at paras 81 and 93.
135 *Ibid* at paras 30, 67, and 73.
136 Justice LeBel observed that "all my comments about the development of the common law principles of the law of conflicts are subject to provisions of specific statutes and rules of procedure": *ibid* at para 68.
137 This approach was adopted in *Aleong v Aleong*, 2013 BCSC 1428, and in *Li v MacNutt & Dumont*, 2015 NSSC 53. But other decisions have treated *Club Resorts* as not requiring this change: see, for example, *Kilderry Holdings Ltd v Canpower International BV*, 2013 BCCA 82; *Original Cakerie Ltd v Renaud*, 2013 BCSC 755.

connection requirement. In *Spar*, LeBel J held that the provisions of the *Civil Code* dealing with the circumstances in which a Quebec court had jurisdiction were "designed to ensure that there [was] a 'real and substantial connection' between the action and the Province of Quebec and to guard against the improper assertion of jurisdiction."[138] He examined the language of article 3148 which provided that Quebec had jurisdiction where "(3) a fault was committed in Quebec, damage was suffered in Quebec, an injurious act occurred in Quebec or one of the obligations arising from a contract was to be performed in Quebec." He indicated that each of the listed grounds was an example of a real and substantial connection between the province and the action and that a plaintiff who established one of the four grounds must "be considered to have satisfied the 'real and substantial connection' criterion, at least for the purposes of jurisdiction *simpliciter*."[139]

This reasoning was difficult to accept. If the *Morguard* principle restrains courts from taking jurisdiction, then the courts cannot simply defer to various grounds for service *ex juris* established in any given province. As a result, courts outside Quebec tended not to follow this aspect of *Spar*. In *Muscutt*, which was released just before *Spar*, the Court of Appeal for Ontario made it clear that the rules for service *ex juris* did not in themselves confer jurisdiction and that the rules had to be read in light of the principles of order and fairness.[140] The grounds for service *ex juris* were not determinative of the issue of jurisdiction.[141] It is clear from subsequent cases that the authority of *Muscutt* was not impaired by *Spar*.[142]

The context of this debate has been shifted by *Club Resorts*. As noted above, that decision identified only four presumptive connecting factors. Additional ones have been, and will continue to be, identified by lower courts. This raises questions about the sources for the additional presumptive connecting factors. It is reasonably well established that the presumptions in section 10 of the *CJPTA* are also presumptive connecting factors under *Club Resorts*, though small differences might emerge. Less clear is whether the grounds for service *ex juris* of the various provinces will become presumptive connecting factors. Taken on its face, *Spar* suggests that they would. But the better view is that we cannot generalize: some of those grounds will, but others will not.[143]

---

138 Above note 105 at para 55.
139 *Ibid* at para 56.
140 Above note 18 at paras 48–49.
141 *Ibid* at para 51.
142 See the discussion in Pitel & Dusten, above note 33.
143 *Club Resorts*, above note 19 at paras 64 and 89. See also *Misyura v Walton*, 2012 ONSC 5397.

Some potential presumptive connecting factors can be rejected at the outset because of their breadth. Traditionally provinces have accepted, as grounds for service *ex juris*, that the claim was in respect of damage sustained in the province, even if primarily caused elsewhere, or that the claim is against a "necessary or proper party" to a proceeding against another defendant served in the province.[144] Both these grounds have been identified as illustrations of the undue breadth of the grounds for service *ex juris* and the need for the *Morguard* principle. Neither of these bases was adopted as a presumption in section 10 of the *CJPTA*. In *Club Resorts*, the Supreme Court of Canada expressly rejected damage sustained in the province as a presumptive connecting factor.[145] It seems quite unlikely that "necessary or proper party" will be accepted as a presumptive connecting factor.[146] In addition, the Court of Appeal for Ontario has rejected the contention that a third-party claim, brought in the context of proceedings over which the court otherwise has jurisdiction, constitutes a presumptive connecting factor.[147]

a) Property

i) Property in the Jurisdiction

Section 10(a) of the *CJPTA* creates a presumption for a proceeding "to enforce, assert, declare or determine proprietary or possessory rights or a security interest in immovable or movable property" in the province. This has some overlap with section 10(c) which creates a presumption for a proceeding "to interpret, rectify, set aside or enforce any deed, will, contract or other instrument" relating to either immovable or movable property in the province or movable property of a deceased person, wherever located, if at the time of death, he or she was ordinarily resident in the province. These provisions parallel the traditional grounds for service *ex juris*. In Ontario, for example, service *ex juris* without leave is available for a claim in respect of property, real or personal, situated in the jurisdiction; a claim that concerns the interpret-

---

144 See, for example, former Ontario Rules, above note 4, rr 17.02(h) "in respect of damage sustained in Ontario arising from a tort, breach of contract, breach of fiduciary duty or breach of confidence, wherever committed" and (o) "against a person outside Ontario who is a necessary or proper party to a proceeding properly brought against another person served in Ontario." Both are now repealed.
145 Above note 19 at para 89. The position in Quebec may be, or at least appears to be, different: see *Infineon Technologies AG v Option Consommateurs*, 2013 SCC 59.
146 Although it has been in at least one decision: *Turner v Bell Mobility Inc*, 2014 ABQB 36.
147 *Export Packers Co v SPI International Transportation*, 2012 ONCA 481 [*Export Packers*].

ation, rectification, enforcement, or setting aside of some instrument, like a will or contract, in respect of real or personal property in the jurisdiction or in respect of the personal property of a deceased person who died resident in the jurisdiction; and a claim for foreclosure, sale, payment, possession, or redemption in respect of some mortgage or other charge on real or personal property in the jurisdiction.[148]

In *Knowles v Lindstrom* the plaintiff asserted an interest in real property located in Ontario. The Court of Appeal for Ontario held that the location of the property was a presumptive connecting factor.[149]

The most interesting interpretive issues about this presumption concern identifying the location of intangible property in order to establish that it is located in the province.[150] This issue is discussed in greater detail in Chapter 18.

ii) Trusts and Administration of Estates

Section 10(b) of the *CJPTA* creates a presumption for a proceeding which concerns the administration of an estate in relation to immovable property in the province or in respect of movable property anywhere when the deceased, at the time of death, ordinarily resided in the province. Section 10(d) creates a presumption for a proceeding against a trustee in relation to the carrying out of a trust when relief is claimed against trust property situated in the province, the trustee is ordinarily resident in the province, the administration of the trust is principally carried on in the province, or the trust is governed expressly by the law of the province. This presumption is generally consistent with the service *ex juris* provisions of several provinces.[151]

It is open to question whether the presumption for trust claims extends to those involving constructive trusts. It has been suggested that the wording of section 10(d), while not limited to express trusts, is not so broad as to cover constructive trusts.[152]

b) Contracts

A contract can be connected to a province in different ways. It could be made in the province, performed in whole or in part in the province, breached in the province, or governed expressly or objectively by the law of the province. The current debate is about which of these connections

---

148 Ontario Rules, above note 4, rr 17.02(a), (c), and (e).
149 2014 ONCA 116 at paras 21–22.
150 See, for example, *Columbia Pictures Industries Inc v Wang*, 2007 SKCA 133; *Tucows.com Co v Lojas Renner SA*, 2011 ONCA 548.
151 See, for example, Ontario Rules, above note 4, rr 17.02(b) and (d).
152 Black, Pitel, & Sobkin, above note 22 at 101–2.

will be accepted as a presumptive connecting factor under the *Club Resorts* approach.

Section 10(e)(i) of the *CJPTA* creates a presumption for a proceeding concerning contractual obligations when those obligations were, to a substantial extent, to be performed in the province. More narrowly, section 10(e)(iii) of the *CJPTA* creates a presumption for a proceeding concerning contractual obligations when the contract resulted from a solicitation of business in the province by the seller of property or services for use other than in the purchaser's business. This provides special protection for consumers, allowing them to sue in their home forum. It could have a significant impact, especially as concerns contracts made over the Internet. Both these presumptions are different from the traditional grounds for service *ex juris* in contract claims.[153]

Section 10(e)(ii) of the *CJPTA* creates a presumption for a proceeding concerning contractual obligations when the contract in dispute is expressly governed by the law of the province. This mirrors one of the traditional service *ex juris* grounds,[154] and it has been accepted as a presumptive connecting factor.[155] There must be an express provision: the presumption is not triggered by ascertaining, in accordance with the analysis in Chapter 14 for contracts without an express provision, that the province's law is the applicable law.

contract of / Place of formation

In some provinces the fact that the action is in respect of a contract made in the province is a ground for service *ex juris*.[156] However, the view that this particular connection is not sufficiently strong led to it being omitted from the *CJPTA*.[157] At common law, several cases have treated it as a presumptive connecting factor despite this lack of strength.[158] In *Club Resorts* the Supreme Court of Canada suggested in passing that this is a presumptive connecting factor.[159] If a dispute arises as to where any contract was made for jurisdictional purposes, the law of

---

153 For an analysis of these presumptions, see Black, Pitel, & Sobkin, *ibid* at 106–11.
154 See, for example, Ontario Rules, above note 4, r 17.02(f)(ii).
155 See, for example, *Pavilion Financial Corp v Highview Financial Holdings Inc*, 2013 MBQB 95 at para 19. But it has also been rejected: *Christmas v Fort McKay First Nation*, 2014 ONSC 373. For a cautionary view, see Maria Hook, "The Choice of Law Agreement as a Reason for Exercising Jurisdiction" (2014) 63 *International and Comparative Law Quarterly* 963.
156 See, for example, Ontario Rules, above note 4, r 17.02(f)(i).
157 Except in Saskatchewan: see Black, Pitel, & Sobkin, above note 22 at 35–36 and 104.
158 See, for example, *Edward Jones v Raymond James Ltd*, 2013 ONSC 4640 at paras 5–6; *Tyoga Investments Ltd v Service Alimentaire Desco Inc*, 2015 ONSC 3810, aff'd 2016 ONCA 15.
159 Above note 19 at para 88.

the forum settles that question. Thus, in *Entores Ltd v Miles Far East Corp* a contract was concluded by a telexed acceptance sent from Holland to England.[160] The English Court of Appeal applied English law to determine that the contract was made in the jurisdiction in which the telex was received and not in the jurisdiction from which it was sent. Thus, the contract was made in England. Recently, the Court of Appeal for Ontario has suggested that "the arbitrary common law rules for determining the place of a contract may not always be apposite in jurisdictional cases .... A broader, more contextual analysis is required, which would inevitably engage the same considerations as the real and substantial connection test itself."[161] Further, at the risk of significantly undercutting any utility the place of contract formation might have as a presumptive connecting factor, some courts have held that in this context a contract can be made at more than one place.[162]

Another connection not included in the *CJPTA* but typically used as a ground for service *ex juris* is a breach of the contract in the province.[163] As discussed below, in tort cases the location of the tort is considered highly important. It might be thought, then, that in contract cases the location of the breach of contract would be similarly important. Yet in *Central Sun Mining Inc v Vector Engineering Inc* the Ontario Superior Court of Justice refused to accept this as a presumptive connecting factor.[164] If this does become a presumption, it will not always be straightforward for the court to identify where the breach occurred. In *Rhodes v Shorter*,[165] for example, the British Columbia Court of Appeal relied on English authority[166] for the proposition that an express repudiation of contractual obligations by letter occurs in the jurisdiction in which the letter originates, not in the jurisdiction in which it is received. The court then determined that the same principle applied to telephone calls. The plaintiff alleged that he had entered into a contract with the defendant to render personal services to the defendant in Calgary from 1 April 1979. He then argued that the defendant had committed an anticipatory breach of contract in British Columbia when,

---

160 [1955] 2 All ER 493 (CA).
161 *Trillium Motor World Ltd v General Motors of Canada Ltd*, 2014 ONCA 497 at para 70, aff'g 2013 ONSC 2289, aff'd (*sub nom Lapointe Rosenstein Marchand Melançon LLP v Cassels Brock & Blackwell LLP*) 2016 SCC 30, but see paras 31–40 endorsing the traditional rules.
162 See, for example, *Inukshuk Wireless Partnership v 4253311 Canada Inc*, 2013 ONSC 5631 at paras 30–32; *Brown v Mar Taino SA*, 2015 NSSC 348 at para 65.
163 See, for example, Ontario Rules, above note 4, r 17.02(f)(iv).
164 2012 ONSC 7331 at para 87, rev'd 2013 ONCA 601 [*Central Sun Mining*].
165 (1981), 27 BCLR 60 (CA).
166 *Cherry v Thompson* (1872), LR 7 QB 573.

in a telephone conversation between the defendant in California and the plaintiff's wife in British Columbia, the defendant informed the wife that operations in Calgary would not commence until later. The court held that any breach of contract had occurred in California.

In the case of a failure to perform a particular obligation under a contract, it appears that in order for there to be a breach of contract committed in the jurisdiction, it is necessary that some part of the contract was to be performed in the jurisdiction and that there was a breach in respect of that part. For example, in the case of a failure to pay money owing under a contract, in order for the breach to have been committed in the jurisdiction, there must either have been an express provision in the contract that payment was to be made in the jurisdiction or it must have been the intention of the parties as inferred from all the circumstances that payment was to be made in the jurisdiction.[167]

c) Restitutionary Obligations Arising in the Jurisdiction

Section 10(f) of the *CJPTA* creates a presumption for a proceeding which concerns restitutionary obligations that, to a substantial extent, arose in the province. This presumption raises some significant issues of definition: What is a restitutionary obligation? Where does it arise? It can be expected to include unjust enrichment claims since in them the plaintiff seeks restitution. But is it broad enough to cover any claim in which disgorgement is sought, such as breach of confidence, breach of fiduciary duty, or torts and breaches of contract that support such a remedy?[168] If it is not broad enough, then courts will need to consider creating new presumptive connecting factors, especially for equitable claims.

d) Torts Committed in the Jurisdiction

As noted earlier, in *Club Resorts* the Supreme Court of Canada held that a tort committed in the province was a presumptive connecting factor. This is not controversial: it has been a standard ground for service *ex juris* and is a presumption in section 10(g) of the *CJPTA*.[169] The core issue is determining the place where a given tort occurs. This issue is discussed at some length in the choice of law context in Chapter 13. But there are also many cases in the jurisdiction *simpliciter* context. Crucially, the test for determining the place of a tort for choice of law purposes may well differ from the test employed for jurisdictional purposes. In *Moran v Pyle National (Canada) Ltd*, Dickson J wrote:

---

167 *International Power and Engineering Consultants Ltd v Clark* (1963), 41 DLR (2d) 260 (BCSC), aff'd (1964), 43 DLR (2d) 394 (BCCA).
168 See Black, Pitel, & Sobkin, above note 22 at 111–16.
169 See, for example, Ontario Rules, above note 4, r 17.02(g).

The rules for determining *situs* for jurisdictional purposes need not be those which are used to identify the legal system under which the rights and liabilities of the parties fall to be determined.[170]

It is essential for choice of law purposes that a single place of the tort be identified, whereas in the jurisdictional context there is no need to locate one place of a tort since several countries might appropriately assume jurisdiction.

The difficulty of isolating the place of a tort arises typically where each constituent element of the tort takes place in a different country. A classic instance is where a defendant negligently manufactures a product in one jurisdiction that harms the plaintiff in another. The leading case is the decision of the Supreme Court of Canada in *Moran*. Moran was an electrician working in Saskatchewan. He was killed when removing a light bulb manufactured by the defendant. The plaintiffs claimed that the defendant had negligently manufactured the bulb. The issue was whether Saskatchewan was the place of the alleged tort for jurisdictional purposes. The defendant did not carry on business in Saskatchewan. It had neither assets nor agents there. All of its manufacturing and assembling operations took place in Ontario. It sold its products to distributors, not directly to consumers.

Earlier authority had tended to favour the view that the tort of negligence was committed where the negligent act or omission took place.[171] In *Moran*, Dickson J characterized that approach as an application of the "place of acting theory."[172] He rejected that theory as too arbitrary. Plaintiffs sued because they had been hurt and, therefore, Dickson J said that "a paramount factor in determining *situs* must be the place of the invasion of one's right to bodily security."[173] Moreover, the theory lacked logic. Justice Dickson stated:

> [I]t would seem that if a tort is to be divided and one part occurs in state A and another in state B, the tort could reasonably for jurisdictional purposes be said to have occurred in both states or, on a more restrictive approach, in neither state. It is difficult to understand how it can properly be said to have occurred only in state A.[174]

---

170 [1975] 1 SCR 393 at 397 [*Moran*].
171 See, for example, *Anderson v Nobel's Explosives Co* (1906), 12 OLR 644 (Div Ct); and *George Monro Ltd v American Cyanamid & Chemical Corp*, [1944] 1 KB 432 (CA).
172 Above note 170 at 398.
173 *Ibid* at 405.
174 *Ibid* at 398.

Justice Dickson also rejected other existing theories for determining the place of the tort such as the one embodied in the first *Restatement*[175] — the "last event theory." Section 377 provided that "[t]he place of wrong is in the State where the last event necessary to make an actor liable for an alleged tort takes place." The last event necessary to complete the tort of negligence is, of course, damage. According to Dickson J, however, such a theory was "too arbitrary and inflexible to be recognized in contemporary jurisprudence."[176] Not surprisingly, he also rejected the restrictive view, suggested by some courts, that in order for a tort to have been committed in the jurisdiction every element of the tort must have occurred in the jurisdiction.[177] Instead, Dickson J favoured a flexible test. He approved of the following formulation from a leading English textbook on private international law:

> It would not . . . be inappropriate to regard a tort as having occurred in any country which is substantially affected by the defendant's activity or its consequences and the law of which is likely to have been in the reasonable contemplation of the parties.[178]

He then formulated a specific test for the tort of negligent manufacture:

> [W]here a foreign defendant carelessly manufactures a product in a foreign jurisdiction which enters into the normal channels of trade and he knows or ought to know both that as a result of his carelessness a consumer may well be injured and it is reasonably foreseeable that the product would be used or consumed where the plaintiff used or consumed it, then the forum in which the plaintiff suffered damage is entitled to exercise judicial jurisdiction over that foreign defendant.[179]

According to Dickson J, such an approach gave full rein to the interest of a state in injuries suffered by people within its territory. A manufacturer should be prepared and obliged to assume the burden of defending its products in jurisdictions in which it has enjoyed the benefit of the foreseeable distribution of its goods. Justice Dickson therefore concluded that the tort had been committed in Saskatchewan and that,

---

175 American Law Institute, *Restatement of the Law of Conflict of Laws* (St Paul, MN: American Law Institute, 1934).
176 *Moran*, above note 170 at 408.
177 See, for example, *Abbott-Smith v Governors of University of Toronto* (1964), 45 DLR (2d) 672 (NSSC).
178 Geoffrey C Cheshire & Peter M North, *Cheshire's Private International Law*, 8th ed (London: Butterworths, 1970) at 281, cited in *Moran*, above note 170 at 408.
179 *Moran, ibid* at 409.

consequently, Saskatchewan could exercise jurisdiction over the plaintiff's claim.

Canadian courts have applied the *Moran* test to torts other than that of negligent manufacture. For example, in *Ichi Canada Ltd v Yamauchi Rubber Industry Co* the British Columbia Court of Appeal determined that the tort of inducing breach of contract had been committed in the province for the purposes of service *ex juris*.[180] The court reached this conclusion despite the fact that the acts of inducement had taken place outside the province, that those acts had been designed to persuade a non-British Columbia party to break its contract with the plaintiff, and that the performance of the contract by the party in breach was to have taken place outside British Columbia. The court determined that British Columbia was substantially affected by the defendant's activities and that British Columbia law was likely to have been in the reasonable contemplation of the parties. The plaintiff, whose head office was in the province, had lost profits from numerous customers in British Columbia and had incurred a considerable loss of prestige in the province.

In *Gulevich v Miller*, a medical negligence case, the Alberta Court of Appeal held that Alberta was the place of the tort even though the wrongful conduct had occurred in Ontario.[181] The court insisted on a "contextual" analysis of the place of the tort, and since the injury had subsequently manifested in Alberta, the tort had "crystallized" in Alberta. The court claimed that its approach was consistent with *Moran*, but arguably it would have been more consistent had the court expressly stated that for jurisdiction purposes the tort could be committed in more than one place rather than insisting that it had been committed in Alberta. Courts have recently taken a similarly broad view of the issue of where the tort of negligent misrepresentation, or a related statutory tort, has occurred.[182]

The tort of defamation has always raised particular problems, especially in cases where the same defamatory statements are published in a variety of jurisdictions. The traditional common law position is illustrated by cases like *Jenner v Sun Oil Co Ltd*, which involved a radio broadcast that had originated in the United States but that had also been received in Ontario.[183] One issue was whether Ontario was

---

180 (1983), 43 BCLR 215 (CA).
181 2015 ABCA 411.
182 See, for example, *Central Sun Mining*, above note 164 (CA); *Ontario (Attorney General) v Rothmans Inc*, 2013 ONCA 353 [*Rothmans*]; *Kaynes v BP, Plc*, 2014 ONCA 580.
183 [1952] 2 DLR 526 (Ont HCJ) [*Sun Oil*].

the place of the tort for the purposes of service *ex juris*. Chief Justice McRuer determined that the tort had been committed in Ontario because Ontario was a place of publication of the defamation. He emphasized that the "tort consist[ed] in making a third person understand actionable defamatory matter."[184] He indicated that when the plaintiff might have little connection to, and hence no real reputation in, that place, it would be best for the court to exercise its discretion not to hear the case.[185] In other common law countries, jurisdiction has been exercised based on publication in the forum when the plaintiff has strong connections to the forum and a reputation there.[186] In *Éditions Écosociété Inc v Banro Corp* the Supreme Court of Canada found that the tort of defamation had been committed in Ontario based on fifteen copies of a book circulating in libraries there and on the plaintiff showing evidence that its reputation in Ontario was vital to its business.[187] More problematic are cases where, although there is publication in the forum, it is relatively minimal and neither the plaintiff nor the defendant has significant connections to the forum.[188]

i) *Contract Connected with the Tort Made in the Jurisdiction*

In *Club Resorts* the Supreme Court of Canada held, with only minimal analysis, that in a tort claim a contract connected to the dispute and made in the province constituted a presumptive connecting factor.[189] This is surprising because such a presumption is not included in the CJPTA or in any province's list of enumerated grounds for service *ex juris*. The presumption raises several issues. First, as explained earlier in the context of contract claims, the place of making a contract is arguably not a strong connection to a particular forum, and it seems even weaker in the context of tort claims. Even if a connected contract matters in analyzing the tort claim, the focus on its place of formation, as opposed to its place of performance, may be misplaced. Second, courts

---

184 *Ibid* at 537. See also *Szalatnay-Stacho v Fink*, [1947] 1 KB 1. In the Internet context, see *Breeden v Black*, 2012 SCC 19 at para 20; *Court v Debaie*, 2012 ABQB 640 at para 40.
185 *Sun Oil*, above note 183 at 538.
186 *Dow Jones & Company Inc v Gutnick* (2002), 210 CLR 575 (HCA); *Harrods v Dow Jones & Co Inc*, [2003] EWHC 1162 (QB). See Megan Richardson & Richard Garnett, "Perils of Publishing on the Internet: Broader Implications of *Dow Jones v. Gutnick*" (2004) 13 *Griffith Law Review* 74.
187 2012 SCC 18 at para 38. See also *Paulsson v Cooper*, 2011 ONCA 150.
188 See, for example, *Lewis v King*, [2004] EWCA Civ 1329.
189 Above note 19 at paras 88 and 90.

now are faced with the difficult issue of determining when a contract is sufficiently "connected" to a tort claim.[190]

In *Trillium Motor World Ltd v General Motors of Canada Ltd* the Ontario Superior Court of Justice expressed concern about the operation of this factor. It was critical of the lack of clarity provided by the Supreme Court of Canada, noting that the court "did not really explain how it came up with this fourth presumptive connecting factor."[191] It suggested a narrow interpretation: that the factor should be understood to mean that "an Ontario court has jurisdiction over a tort claim brought by a non-party to an Ontario contract that is connected with the dispute, if the non-party can be brought within the scope of the contractual relationship by the terms of the contract, and if the events that gave rise to the claim flowed from the relationship created by that contract."[192] The Court of Appeal for Ontario and the Supreme Court of Canada (in a split decision) agreed with the motions judge that the presumptive connecting factor was established on the facts.

e) Injunctions

Section 10(i) of the *CJPTA* creates a presumption for a proceeding that is "a claim for an injunction ordering a party to do or refrain from doing anything" in the province or "in relation to immovable or movable property" in the province. This is also a standard ground for service *ex juris*.[193] The Court of Appeal for Ontario analyzed this ground in *Barrick Gold Corp v Lopehandia*.[194] The plaintiff, an Ontario company with its head office in Toronto, brought an action in Ontario for defamation against the defendant, a businessman who resided in British Columbia. The defendant had embarked upon an Internet smear campaign by posting messages on bulletin or message boards on various websites. In part, the plaintiff sought a permanent injunction restraining the defendant from posting further defamatory statements on the Internet. One issue was whether the case fell within rule 17.02(i) of the Ontario Rules. The trial judge held that it did not because the defendant was not doing anything in Ontario. The Court of Appeal reversed the trial judgment for two reasons. First, it pointed out that the Ontario provision

---

190 See, for example, *Export Packers*, above note 147. This issue could arise frequently in respect of insurance contracts: see, for example, *Forsythe v Westfall*, 2015 ONCA 810; *Tamminga v Tamminga*, 2014 ONCA 478. In these decisions the court held the insurance policies were not connected contracts.
191 Above note 161 at para 5 (SCJ). See also para 88 (SCC).
192 *Ibid* at para 12 (SCJ). See also para 47 (SCC).
193 See, for example, Ontario Rules, above note 4, r 17.02(i).
194 (2004), 71 OR (3d) 416 (CA).

covered an injunction affecting property, real or personal, in Ontario. It then concluded that the plaintiff's goodwill, which was being damaged by the defendant's statements, constituted personal property in Ontario.[195] Second, the court held that, in any event, the defendant was acting in Ontario because at least one of the bulletin boards on which messages were posted was located in Ontario through its operation by an Ontario company.

An issue in respect of this presumption is whether it covers what is called a "stand-alone" injunction: an injunction granted in one jurisdiction in support of proceedings in another jurisdiction.[196] A leading example is an order freezing a defendant's assets in one jurisdiction to await the result of litigation elsewhere. The language of the presumption is broad and would on its face appear to catch such an injunction. However, some older cases have held that the court does not have jurisdiction in such a situation: the injunction sought must involve substantive rights which are being resolved in the forum.[197] More recent cases have questioned this view and shown a willingness to take jurisdiction.[198]

f) Enforcement of Foreign Judgments

Section 10(k) of the *CJPTA* creates a presumption for a proceeding to enforce a domestic or foreign judgment of a court or arbitral award. This is a typical basis for service *ex juris*.[199] The wording is broad: it does not require any connection with the province other than that enforcement is sought there. Until recently, debate about this presumption had thus been about whether it would be narrowed by judicial interpretation, for example to require assets of the defendant in the province. However, the Supreme Court of Canada has adopted a very different approach. In *Chevron Corp v Yaiguaje* the court concluded that in a proceeding to enforce a foreign judgment, there is no need for a presumptive connecting factor because there is no need for a real and substantial connection at all. The court stated:

---

195 *Ibid* at para 71.
196 See generally Black, Pitel, & Sobkin, above note 22 at 127–31.
197 See *The Siskina*, [1977] 3 All ER 803 (HL); *Mercedes Benz AG v Lieduck*, [1996] 1 AC 284 (PC).
198 See *Transat Tours Canada Inc v Tescor, SA de CV*, 2007 SCC 20; *Obégi Chemicals LLC v Kilani*, 2011 ONSC 1636; *United States v Friedland* (1996), 13 CPC (4th) 296 (BCSC); Stephen GA Pitel & Andrew Valentine, "The Evolution of the Extra-Territorial Mareva Injunction in Canada: Three Issues" (2006) 2 *Journal of Private International Law* 339; Vaughan Black & Edward Babin, "*Mareva* Injunctions in Canada: Territorial Aspects" (1997) 28 *Canadian Business Law Journal* 430.
199 See, for example, Ontario Rules, above note 4, r 17.02(m).

In an action to recognize and enforce a foreign judgment where the foreign court validly assumed jurisdiction, there is no need to prove that a real and substantial connection exists between the enforcing forum and either the judgment debtor or the dispute. It makes little sense to compel such a connection when, owing to the nature of the action itself, it will frequently be lacking. Nor is it necessary, in order for the action to proceed, that the foreign debtor contemporaneously possess assets in the enforcing forum. Jurisdiction to recognize and enforce a foreign judgment within Ontario exists by virtue of the debtor being served on the basis of the outstanding debt resulting from the judgment.[200]

While the court did not go so far as to say that no jurisdictional basis is required for the enforcement action, it did state that the basis is found simply and wholly in the defendant being served with process.[201] This view runs contrary to *Morguard*, which, as has been explained, separated the issue of service of process from the issue of jurisdiction. For the court to now say the service itself founds jurisdiction is arguably to have no jurisdictional requirement at all for assumed jurisdiction in these cases. This decision is discussed in more detail in Chapter 8.

g) Defendant's Domicile, Ordinary Residence, or Carrying on Business in the Jurisdiction

In *Club Resorts* the Supreme Court of Canada held that the defendant's domicile, residence, or carrying on business in the province is a presumptive connecting factor in a tort claim.[202] In subsequent decisions these connections have been used beyond the tort context, such that they are becoming general presumptive connecting factors for all types of claims.[203] Section 10(h) of the *CJPTA* creates a presumption in a proceeding which "concerns a business carried on" in the province,[204] and more directly, section 3(d) provides that the court has territorial

---

200 Above note 5 at para 3.
201 *Ibid* at para 27. The court acknowledged that the approach under the *CJPTA* is different, using the s 10(k) presumption, and so confined its approach to the common law of assumed jurisdiction: para 73.
202 Above note 19 at paras 86–87.
203 See, for example, *Sears Canada Inc v C & S Interior Designs Ltd*, 2012 ABQB 573; *Avanti Management & Consulting Ltd v Argex Mining Inc*, 2012 ONSC 4395; *Royal Bank of Canada v DCM Erectors Inc*, 2013 ONSC 2864; *Sullivan v Four Seasons Hotels Ltd (cob Four Seasons Hotels & Resorts)*, 2013 ONSC 4622.
204 While not specified in the statutory language, the better view is that this must be the defendant's business and that the plaintiff's carrying on business in the province cannot be sufficient: see Black, Pitel, & Sobkin, above note 22 at 122–24. This view is consistent with *Club Resorts*.

competence in a proceeding brought against a person who is ordinarily resident in the province at the time the proceeding is commenced. In addition, section 10(j) creates a presumption in a proceeding for a determination of "the personal status or capacity of a person" who is ordinarily resident in the province. This goes beyond section 3(d) in that the person need not be a defendant.

Some comments can be offered about these presumptive connecting factors. First, they are at least partially reflective of the traditional grounds for service *ex juris*.[205] Second, using domicile is problematic because of the difficulties, discussed in Chapter 2, associated with that concept. At least as traditionally understood at common law, domicile may be too tenuous a connection on which to base jurisdiction. Third, there is the potential for significant overlap between these factors and jurisdiction based on presence, discussed above. A defendant domiciled, resident, or carrying on business in a province is, in many cases, able to be served in the province, making recourse to assumed jurisdiction unnecessary. So these presumptive connecting factors will be needed only when the defendant is domiciled, resident, or carrying on business in the province but, for some reason, cannot be served there. As discussed in Chapter 2, a domiciliary might indeed be a full-time resident of another country, and a resident might be away from the province for an extended period of time, so these situations can certainly arise. But care must be taken to keep presence-based jurisdiction and assumed jurisdiction analytically separate.[206]

What domicile and residence mean is discussed at length in Chapter 2. The meaning of carrying on business is discussed earlier in this chapter in the analysis of whether a defendant is present in the forum.

While not free from doubt, it appears that the plaintiff's claim against the defendant does not have to specifically relate to the business being carried on in the province.[207] That makes this a relatively broad presumptive connecting factor, though, as discussed below, one basis on which the presumption can be rebutted is the lack of connection between the claim and the business carried out in the province.

h) Family Law
The common law on assumed jurisdiction in family law cases has historically operated alongside detailed statutory rules for taking juris-

---

205 See, for example, Ontario Rules, above note 4, r 17.02(p).
206 For unnecessary analysis of assumed jurisdiction in cases of presence see, for example, *Wilson v Riu*, 2012 ONSC 6840 [*Riu*]; *Lixo Investments Ltd v Gowling, Lafleur, Henderson*, 2013 ONSC 4862, aff'd 2014 ONCA 114.
207 See *Club Resorts*, above note 19 at para 96.

diction. It has also developed differently than in commercial cases in order to meet the specific needs of family law cases. *Club Resorts* does not change this. Indeed, LeBel J noted that "all my comments about the development of the common law principles of the law of conflicts are subject to provisions of specific statutes and rules of procedure."[208]

In *Ghaeinizadeh v Ku De Ta Capital Inc* the Court of Appeal for Ontario noted that the *Club Resorts* list of presumptive connecting factors had to be modified in the family context.[209] However, the court did not identify a presumptive connecting factor on which jurisdiction was based. It simply noted an amalgamation of several factual connections that, in its view, gave it jurisdiction.[210] Similarly in *Wang v Lin* the same court, after first considering whether it had jurisdiction under statute, turned to the common law and held that "in the context of marriage breakdown, the presumptive connecting factors are necessarily different from those identified" in *Club Resorts*.[211] The court accepted that if the "real home" or "ordinary residence" of the applicant was in Ontario, this would constitute a presumptive connecting factor. On the facts this was not established and so the court did not have jurisdiction under the common law.[212]

In contrast, in *Aleong v Aleong* the British Columbia Supreme Court appears to have rejected the notion that family law cases are to be analyzed differently.[213] It observed that "[t]here is no suggestion that a family law case should be accorded any special status or that special, more relaxed, rules should apply. I do not find support in the *CJPTA*, or in the discussion in [*Club Resorts*], for the proposition that, in family law cases generally, there should be special or more relaxed rules in relation to establishing jurisdiction."[214] However, the fact that neither the *CJPTA* nor *Club Resorts* addresses the issue is not determinative.

---

208 *Ibid* at para 68.
209 2013 ONCA 2 at para 15. See Vaughan Black, "Choice of Law and Territorial Jurisdiction of Courts in Family Matters" (2013) 32 *Canadian Family Law Quarterly* 53 at 61: "The articulation of presumptive connecting factors for family-related disputes is in its infancy and presumably will be the matter of considerable litigation over the coming years."
210 *Ibid*. These included the parties residing together in Ontario for a substantial period of time, the parties residing in Ontario with the child at the time of separation, the child's enrolment in a preschool program in Toronto, and the parties' Canadian citizenship.
211 2013 ONCA 33 at para 46.
212 *Ibid* at paras 46–47.
213 Above note 137.
214 *Ibid* at para 122. This view is somewhat undermined by the court's subsequent comment (at para 126) that "the spouses' last common habitual residence has the qualities of an acceptable presumptive connecting factor," indicating at least

i) Other Factors

Section 10(1) of the *CJPTA* creates a presumption in a proceeding brought by the Crown or a local authority, such as a municipality, "for the recovery of taxes or other indebtedness." This has parallels in the grounds for service *ex juris*.[215] At common law, for reasons discussed in Chapter 3, the traditional view is that a claim to recover taxes owing can be brought only in the plaintiff's home jurisdiction: the Crown or a local authority cannot sue for them abroad. The meaning of "other indebtedness" remains a somewhat open question.

4) Rebutting a Presumption

The issue of whether a presumptive connecting factor has been rebutted must be kept analytically separate from the issue, discussed above, of whether such a factor has been established. If such a factor is not established by the plaintiff, there is no jurisdiction and no need to consider rebuttal.

The test for rebutting a presumptive connecting factor is that the defendant must establish facts that "demonstrate that the presumptive connecting factor does not point to any real relationship between the subject matter of the litigation and the forum or points only to a weak relationship between them."[216] Two key issues arise. The first is the relative strength of the presumptions: how easy or difficult will it be to rebut them. The second is the framework for the analysis: what the courts will consider.

The cases since *Club Resorts* demonstrate different ways of addressing the rebuttal issue. In some, the court does not refer to this stage of the analysis at all. This creates the appearance that an analytical step has been missed. When the defendant does not attempt to rebut the presumption, the court should note that fact explicitly. Since the defendant bears the onus, its failure to seek to rebut the presumption is a sufficient basis for the court to say nothing further. In *2249659 Ontario Ltd v Sparkasse Siegen* the Court of Appeal for Ontario properly stated that the rebuttal was not addressed because the defendants did not advance such an argument.[217]

In other cases, the court states that the presumption has not been rebutted without providing any reasons. By doing this, the court is

---

some willingness to create a new and distinctive presumptive connecting factor for family law cases.
215 See, for example, Ontario Rules, above note 4, r 17.02(r).
216 *Club Resorts*, above note 19 at para 95.
217 Above note 91 at para 37.

acknowledging this stage of the analysis but providing no insight into how it has reached its conclusion. This is insufficient. If the defendant does seek to rebut the presumption, the court must explain how it has reached its conclusion.

In cases that devote more analysis to the rebuttal of the presumption, the courts are focusing on the specific facts of the cases to assess the strength of the connection. While it would be possible to create a framework with which to analyze this connection, the courts do not appear to be moving in that direction. The analysis is general and unstructured.[218] One interesting question is whether the factors considered in the *Muscutt* analysis, while no longer to be used as the jurisdictional test, can be considered on the issue of whether the presumption is rebutted.[219]

Several of the presumptions raise interpretation questions that will bear on the rebuttal analysis. If a presumption is interpreted broadly, applying in relatively more cases, then greater resort will be had to the rebuttal analysis. In contrast, if the courts build limitations into the presumptions themselves, many cases will not trigger them and the rebuttal stage is not reached. One could easily see the same set of facts being alternatively analyzed as (1) not triggering the presumption or (2) triggering it but having it rebutted.

It is possible to identify specific considerations in the rebuttal analysis that relate to specific presumptive connecting factors. Indeed, this process was started in *Club Resorts*. Justice LeBel noted that "where the presumptive connecting factor is the commission of a tort in the province, rebutting the presumption of jurisdiction would appear to be difficult, although it may be possible to do so in a case involving a multi-jurisdictional tort where only a relatively minor element of the tort has occurred in the province."[220] The first part of this statement was relied on in *Ontario (Attorney General) v Rothmans Inc* to support the conclusion that the presumption had not been rebutted.[221] In that case the tort had clearly happened in the forum. The second part was relied on in *Central Sun Mining* at first instance to support the opposite conclusion. In that case the plaintiff sued various foreign defendants in Ontario in respect of the operation of a mine in Costa Rica. In respect

---

218 See, for example, *Mining Technologies International, Inc v Krako Inc*, 2012 ONCA 847 at para 7; *Nagra v Malhotra*, 2012 ONSC 4497 at paras 11–12.
219 This notion has been rejected in the context of rebuttal under British Columbia's statute: see *Laxton v Jurem Anstalt*, 2011 BCCA 212 at para 42. It is also arguably contrary to the spirit of *Club Resorts*.
220 Above note 19 at para 96.
221 Above note 182 at paras 48–52.

of the claims for negligence and negligent misrepresentation, the court accepted that "[t]his is plainly a case involving multi-jurisdictional torts."²²² In the context of the facts as a whole, the connection to Ontario was relatively minor, and as a result the presumption was rebutted. But the Court of Appeal disagreed, finding that "the misrepresentation was received and acted upon in Ontario. It cannot be said that only a relatively minor element of the tort occurred in this province."²²³

Similarly, the court in *Club Resorts* stated that the presumption based on carrying on business could be rebutted by showing that the subject matter of the litigation is unrelated to the business activities in the province.²²⁴ This suggests that the presumption itself could have a wide scope and that the more nuanced analysis will be done as part of the rebuttal. In *Wilson v Riu* the plaintiffs booked a holiday to Jamaica with Thomas Cook.²²⁵ In Jamaica they arranged to go horse riding and on that excursion one of the plaintiffs was injured. The Ontario Superior Court of Justice found that Thomas Cook did conduct business in Ontario but that it had no involvement in the horse-riding excursion. It therefore held that the presumption had been rebutted.²²⁶ In contrast, the presumption was not rebutted in *Edward Jones v Raymond James Ltd*.²²⁷ The individual defendant had left the plaintiff's employment and gone to work for a competitor. This happened in Manitoba, but the plaintiff sued in Ontario. The Superior Court of Justice found that the competitor did business in Ontario but noted that "the presumption might be rebutted if the subject matter of the litigation were unrelated to its business activity in Ontario."²²⁸ The presumption was not rebutted because there were some factual connections to Ontario relating to the change of employment.

The court in *Club Resorts* also stated that the presumption based on a related contract could be "rebutted by showing that the contract has little or nothing to do with the subject matter of the litigation."²²⁹ In *Paraie v Cangemi* the plaintiff, an Ontario resident, sued a New York resident for injuries resulting from a car accident in New York.²³⁰ The plaintiff argued that because the damages might exceed the value of

---

222 Above note 164 at para 43 (SCJ).
223 *Ibid* at para 38 (CA). See also *Goldhar v Haaretz.com*, 2016 ONCA 515.
224 Above note 19 at para 96.
225 Above note 206.
226 *Ibid* at para 13. The plaintiffs did not attend to contest the defendants' jurisdiction motion.
227 Above note 158.
228 *Ibid* at para 10.
229 Above note 19 at para 96.
230 2012 ONSC 6341.

the coverage held by the defendant under a New York insurance policy, his own Ontario policy providing underinsured motorist coverage was a contract made in the province and connected with the dispute. The Superior Court of Justice held that the possible connection to Ontario was speculative and contingent, and accordingly the presumptive connecting factor was not present. The judge went on to hold in the alternative that, for the same reasons, any presumption that was established would be rebutted.[231]

The issue of rebuttal arises in a very similar way under the *CJPTA*.[232] It is open to the defendant to argue that a section 10 presumed real and substantial connection is rebutted on the facts of the particular case. The presumptions in section 10 are narrower than the four set out by the Supreme Court of Canada in *Club Resorts*, with the result that it has proven difficult to rebut those presumptions.[233] To the extent that the section 10 presumptions are taken to be presumptive connecting factors under the *Club Resorts* analysis, they should similarly be difficult to rebut.

5) Concurrent Claims

In cases in which plaintiffs advance more than one cause of action, courts have historically held that they require jurisdiction over each of them, analyzed separately. In some cases, the court has held that it has jurisdiction over some, but not all, of a plaintiff's claims. It is therefore of considerable interest that in *Club Resorts* the Supreme Court of Canada held that

> it is possible for a case to sound both in contract and in tort or to invoke more than one tort. Would a court be limited to hearing the specific part of the case that can be directly connected with the jurisdiction? Such a rule would breach the principles of fairness and efficiency on which the assumption of jurisdiction is based. The purpose of the conflicts rules is to establish whether a real and substantial connection exists between the forum, the subject matter of the litigation and the defendant. If such a connection exists in respect of a factual and legal situation, the court must assume jurisdiction over all aspects of the case.[234]

---

231 *Ibid* at paras 19–22.
232 For analysis of rebuttal of the presumptions under the *CJPTA*, see Black, Pitel, & Sobkin, above note 22 at 146–52.
233 See *Lailey v International Student Volunteers, Inc*, 2008 BCSC 1344 at para 33.
234 Above note 19 at para 99.

This suggests that if a plaintiff can base jurisdiction for at least one cause of action on a presumptive connecting factor, the court could take jurisdiction over all claims made without additional analysis. The difficulty here is in understanding how far the court meant to take this point. There is a considerable difference between concurrent claims in tort and contract arising from the same facts and completely different claims each arising from different facts advanced against a defendant in the same action. It is hard to accept that the court meant that all claims that the rules of joinder allow to be advanced are within the court's jurisdiction so long as one presumptive connecting factor applies to any one of them.

One would expect that, for truly concurrent claims, if there is a presumptive connecting factor that applies to one of the claims, then there should equally be a presumptive connecting factor that separately applies to the other claim. It should not, in basic cases of concurrency, be necessary to "piggyback" one claim on the other in order to establish jurisdiction in the manner suggested by the court. No hardship is caused by insisting on a presumptive connecting factor for each cause of action. The benefit of this approach, which is more in keeping with the traditional one, is that courts will not be faced with the problem the *Club Resorts* approach creates, namely how different any additional claims can be and yet still be within the court's jurisdiction from the initial presumptive connecting factor. It is possible that the court has replaced one analytic approach with another, moving from having to analyze jurisdiction for each claim to now having to analyze whether additional claims are sufficiently related to the initial presumptive connecting factor.

In *Re Ghana Gold Corp* the Ontario Superior Court of Justice relied specifically on *Club Resorts* to conclude that if it had jurisdiction over the tort claim, it had jurisdiction over the entire claim, including a claim for breach of contract.[235] Nevertheless the court conducted an independent analysis of whether it had jurisdiction over the contract claim, suggesting a cautious approach. In contrast, in *Cesario v Gondek* the plaintiff was involved in two separate car accidents, the first in New York and the second in Ontario. She sued in Ontario in respect of both accidents. The New York defendants challenged jurisdiction. The Ontario Superior Court of Justice found a presumptive connecting factor, in that one of the other defendants was resident in Ontario. It then relied on *Club Resorts* to hold that the court had jurisdiction over the

---

235 2013 ONSC 3284 at paras 59–60.

entire claim, including the claim against the New York defendants.[236] It is open to question whether this is the type of situation contemplated by the Supreme Court of Canada in *Club Resorts*.

6) Process and Manner of Service *Ex Juris*

The focus in this part of the chapter has been on the jurisdictional rules for situations in which the defendant is not present in the forum and does not submit. As explained, these rules are independent from the procedural rules about service of the originating process. However, some points about the service itself should be noted.

In most provinces, if the plaintiff is satisfied that the claims fall within the enumerated grounds for service *ex juris*, the plaintiff serves the defendant without leave of the court.[237] In other situations, the plaintiff will need leave of the court to serve the defendant *ex juris*.[238] The court's permission is sought *ex parte* and it is possible that the court will refuse to grant leave if it concludes that the forum does not have jurisdiction.[239] Typically, however, the plaintiff is initially successful. The validity of the service, and any dispute about the court's jurisdiction, arises as a contested issue between the parties only if the defendant, having been served, objects rather than defends. This illustrates an overlap between jurisdiction based on consent and assumed jurisdiction: in both situations, the defendant must be properly served *ex juris*. If the defendant defends rather than objects, he or she submits by consent. If the defendant objects, jurisdiction might still be found based on consent, under a jurisdiction clause. Otherwise it will be a situation of assumed jurisdiction.

Challenges to service *ex juris*, and to jurisdiction, can raise evidentiary issues. The orthodox approach is that plaintiffs are required to establish only that they have a "good arguable case" that the claim falls within one of the enumerated grounds for service *ex juris*.[240] They are not required to prove their case as they would at trial because the "need

---

236 2012 ONSC 4563.
237 See, for example, Ontario Rules, above note 4, r 17.02.
238 See, for example, Ontario Rules, *ibid*, r 17.03.
239 The court does not have to be satisfied, to grant leave, that the province is the most appropriate forum. This contrasts with the approach to granting leave in England: see *VTB Capital Plc v Nutritek International Corp*, [2013] UKSC 5 at paras 18, 80, and 190.
240 See, for example, *AG Armeno Mines and Minerals Inc v PT Pukuafu Indah* (2000), 77 BCLR (3d) 1 (CA) [*AG Armeno*]; *Nova, an Alberta Corporation v Grove* (1982), 39 AR 409 (CA) [*Nova*]; *Dreco Energy Services Ltd v Wenzel Downhole Tools Ltd* (2008), 443 AR 116 (QB), aff'd 440 AR 351 (CA).

for service *ex juris* arises, of necessity, before pleading is complete and before there has been production of documents or oral examinations."[241] Even where the defendant challenges service *ex juris* successfully on the basis that the case does not fit within one of the enumerated grounds, the plaintiff may be able to persuade the court to validate the service *ex post facto* where he or she can meet the test for assumed jurisdiction.[242]

Normally, issues of jurisdiction *simpliciter* are decided on the sufficiency of the plaintiff's pleadings alone. Where, however, the defendant introduces evidence that contradicts material facts pleaded by the plaintiff, the plaintiff must establish a good arguable case on the evidence with respect to facts put in issue by the defendant's evidence.[243]

Typically, service of an originating process outside the province depends on whether it is served in a contracting state under the Hague Convention on the Service Abroad of Judicial and Extrajudicial Documents in Civil or Commercial Matters.[244] If it is, it must be served through the central authority in the contracting state or in a manner permitted by both the convention and by the province's rules for service in the prov-

---

241 *Nova*, above note 240 at para 10, Laycraft JA dissenting but not on this point.
242 *UniNet*, above note 117.
243 *AG Armeno*, above note 240 at para 19. See also *Purple Echo Productions Inc v KCTS Television* (2008), 76 BCLR (4th) 21 (CA); *Rothmans*, above note 182 at para 110; *Shah v LG Chem Ltd*, 2015 ONSC 2628. Sometimes the courts indicate that a plaintiff need merely establish that there is "a good arguable case that the [real and substantial] connection exists": *Schreiber v Mulroney* (2007), 88 OR (3d) 605 at para 18 (SCJ). This formulation has been criticized by Stephen Pitel, "Nuances in the Analysis of Jurisdiction: *Schreiber v. Mulroney*" (2008) 34 *Advocates' Quarterly* 126 at 129:

> The plaintiff does not only have to show a good argument that there is a real and substantial connection — the plaintiff must show such a connection does exist. If facts relevant to the analysis of jurisdiction are in dispute, then it is generally correct to say that only a good arguable case need be shown that those facts can be established before the court can then make use of them in its analysis of the connection. But that analysis looks for a real and substantial connection, not a good arguable case for such a connection.

It is not clear how this analysis will be affected by the new focus on presumptive connecting factors. The question of the appropriate standard of proof for factual issues on motions challenging jurisdiction, with particular emphasis on choice of forum clauses, is considered in depth by Stephen Pitel & Jonathan de Vries, "The Standard of Proof for Jurisdiction Clauses" (2008) 46 *Canadian Business Law Journal* 66. Consider also the approach in *Newfoundland and Labrador (Attorney General) v Rothmans Inc*, 2013 NLTD(G) 180 at paras 329 and 335–38, which imposes a higher standard.
244 16 ILM 1339 (1977); Can TS 1989 No 2 [*Hague Convention*]. For a discussion of this convention, see Walker, above note 2 at para 11.15.

ince.²⁴⁵ If it is not, it may be served in a manner provided for service in the province or in a manner provided by the law of the place where service is made if, by that manner of service, the document could reasonably be expected to come to the notice of the person to be served.²⁴⁶ Equally, proof of service abroad may be in a manner provided for proof of service in the province, in a manner provided for proof of service by the law of the place where service was effected, or, if service was made pursuant to the *Hague Convention*, in accordance with that convention.²⁴⁷

E. CLASS ACTIONS

Most provinces now have legislation providing for the institution of class actions to deal with common issues of fact or law.²⁴⁸ This section explores the way in which the courts have adapted the jurisdictional principles of private international law to deal with the special problems such actions pose.

1) Jurisdiction over Defendants

Ward concerned a proposed class action brought by the plaintiff, a Manitoba resident, in the Manitoba courts against the federal Crown.²⁴⁹ The action arose from chemical spraying at CFB Gagetown in New Brunswick between 1956 and 2005. The plaintiff had been a member of the Canadian military stationed at the base in the mid-1970s. He claimed that he and others had encountered various serious medical problems as a result of the spraying. The Crown moved to have the action dismissed on the ground that the court lacked jurisdiction *simpliciter*. It acknowledged that, if this had been an individual action, there would have been no doubt that the Manitoba courts would have possessed jurisdiction because the federal Crown was resident in every province in Canada, including Manitoba. In the case of a proposed national class action, however, the Crown argued that the Manitoba

---

245 See, for example, Ontario Rules, above note 4, r 17.05(3). The service regime under the convention has been held to be a complete code which cannot be varied: see *Metcalfe v Yamaha Motor Powered Products Co*, 2012 ABCA 240; *Khan Resources Inc v Atomredmetzoloto JSC*, 2013 ONCA 189.
246 See, for example, Ontario Rules, above note 4, r 17.05(2).
247 See, for example, Ontario Rules, *ibid*, r 17.05(4).
248 See, for example, *Class Proceedings Act*, SO 1992, c 6; *Class Proceedings Act*, RSBC 1996, c 50; *Class Proceedings Act*, SA 2003, c C-16.5.
249 Above note 39.

courts could have jurisdiction only if there were a real and substantial connection between the claim and Manitoba. According to the defendant, New Brunswick was the only province with the required connection for jurisdiction since that was where the alleged wrongful conduct took place. The Manitoba Court of Appeal rejected the Crown's argument. Justice Freedman held that the prospective certification of the proceeding as a class action did not deprive the court of its jurisdiction, which had been established on the traditional basis of the defendant's presence in the province.

In other cases, jurisdiction over the defendants will depend upon satisfaction of the *Morguard* principle. *Vitapharm Canada Ltd v F Hoffmann-La Roche Ltd* involved five class actions based on alleged losses and damages in Canada, including Ontario, due to a worldwide conspiracy to fix prices, lessen competition, and allocate markets with respect to various vitamins and vitamin components.[250] The foreign defendants were twenty-six corporations and officers and directors of some of the corporate defendants. They were served *ex juris* on various grounds, including the commission of a tort in Ontario, the sustaining of damage in Ontario, and as necessary or proper parties to an action brought in Ontario. The defendants challenged the jurisdiction of the Ontario courts. They argued that it was essential that a foreign defendant have a substantial connection with the forum. Justice Cumming characterized that approach as harkening back to the pre-*Morguard* test for jurisdiction based on territorial power. Although the fact that a defendant was not present in the forum was a relevant factor to consider, the ultimate test for jurisdiction *simpliciter* was whether the subject matter of the action had a real and substantial connection with Ontario and whether the foreign defendant was connected to that subject matter. Justice Cumming determined that the alleged conspiracy in each of the class actions established the requisite real and substantial connection with Ontario. He concluded:

> The participants in a conspiracy entered into geographically beyond Canada with the purpose of fixing prices and allocating markets within Canada (amongst other countries) would know, and indeed would intend, that damages (through artificially high prices) would be sustained in Canada, including Ontario, as a result of their agreement. As I have already said, in my view such an agreement would be a tort committed within Ontario. The most significant aspect of the alleged conspiracy, being the artificial raising of prices in Can-

---

250 (2002), 20 CPC (5th) 351(Ont SCJ), appeal quashed (2002), 23 CPC (5th) 230 (Ont CA).

ada, is implemented within Canada and the agreement is directed at Canadian consumers.... The centre of gravity for each of the class actions, initially on behalf of putative plaintiff "national classes," is Ontario. The participants in any such conspiracies have voluntarily exposed themselves to the risk of litigation in Ontario.[251]

2) Jurisdiction over Non-resident Plaintiffs

The central difference between class actions and traditional proceedings is not the identity of the defendants. Rather, it is the concept of a class of plaintiffs rather than one or more individual plaintiffs. In traditional litigation, jurisdiction over the plaintiffs is readily established based on consent, since they choose to sue in the forum. That same analysis cannot be used in a class action: the representative plaintiff chooses the forum, but each member of the proposed class does not.[252] Additional analysis is required to establish jurisdiction over the class as a whole. If all members of the class are in the forum, jurisdiction might be based on their presence. Difficulties arise, however, when the proposed class covers members outside the forum. A national class could cover anyone in Canada, and a global class could cover anyone anywhere.

In part because the stakes are significant, there has been considerable debate about whether, and in what circumstances, national or global classes should be certified.[253] The courts have been willing to certify such classes, in part because they consider that doing so furthers the access to justice and administrative efficiency rationales of class actions. In *Excalibur Special Opportunities LP v Schwartz Levitsky Feldman LLP*, for example, Perell J stated "the question to be decided is not whether there can be a global class action, the question is when is it appropriate to certify a global class."[254]

In *Harrington v Dow Corning Corp*, for example, the plaintiffs alleged that they had suffered injury from silicone gel breast implants.[255] They brought an action in negligence against the defendant manufacturers and distributors. The motions judge issued an order certifying the action as a

---

251 *Ibid* at para 101 (SCJ).
252 This flows from the opt-out nature of class actions, under which the class, as defined, binds all members except those who expressly opt out. Under an opt-in model, each member would expressly join the class and thus consent to the court's jurisdiction.
253 See, for example, Janet Walker, "Are National Class Actions Constitutional? A Reply to Hogg and McKee" (2010) 48 *Osgoode Hall Law Journal* 95.
254 2014 ONSC 4118 at para 109, aff'd 2015 ONSC 1634 (Div Ct).
255 (2000), 82 BCLR (3d) 1 (CA), aff'g (1996), 22 BCLR (3d) 97 (SC) [*Harrington*].

class proceeding and he described a resident and non-resident subclass.[256] He determined the common issue to be whether silicone breast implants were reasonably fit for their intended purpose. On appeal to the British Columbia Court of Appeal, the defendants contested the court's jurisdiction, in particular to adjudicate the claims of non-resident plaintiffs who had received their implants outside British Columbia. They argued that British Columbia lacked a real and substantial connection with those plaintiffs and those claims. The motions judge had agreed that the court would not have jurisdiction over those claims in the absence of the class proceeding. He determined that it was the "common issue which establish[ed] the real and substantial connection necessary for jurisdiction."[257] The Court of Appeal supported that approach. Justice Huddart stressed the fact that the manufacturers marketed their product throughout Canada and there could be no injustice in requiring them to submit to judgment in any Canadian province. In those circumstances, the existence of a certified class action with a common issue provided a sufficient connection to British Columbia to justify the assertion of jurisdiction. She concluded:

> The appellants are manufacturers of an allegedly defective product for personal use which they market throughout Canada. Such a person must anticipate the possibility of being haled into any Canadian court. The issue of that product's fitness is common to all purchasers wherever they reside. The Supreme Court has properly accepted jurisdiction over all claims by purchasers resident in British Columbia. The appellants are defending those claims. The Supreme Court has certified an issue common to all purchasers for resolution in a class proceeding. These are compelling reasons for British Columbia courts to accept jurisdiction. British Columbia has more than a little interest in accommodating a national resolution of this dispute.[258]

In *Wilson v Servier Canada Inc*, the plaintiff, an Ontario resident, launched an action against a Quebec drug company and its French parent.[259] She alleged that she had suffered a life-threatening disease from taking a weight-loss drug that had been marketed by the defendants in Canada. There was no doubt that the Ontario courts had jurisdiction over the plaintiff's claim and the claim of other Ontario residents because the alleged facts established a real and substantial connection with Ontario based on torts committed within the province. The plain-

---

256 *Ibid* (SC).
257 (1997), 29 BCLR (3d) 88 at para 18 (SC).
258 *Harrington*, above note 255 at para 98 (CA).
259 (2000), 50 OR (3d) 219 (SCJ) [*Wilson*].

tiff, however, sought to have the action brought on behalf of a national class. The defendant objected to the certification of a national class on the ground that proposed class members who resided outside Ontario had no connection to Ontario: they had obtained their prescriptions from doctors practising outside Ontario, they had purchased the drugs from pharmacists carrying on business outside Ontario, and they had allegedly sustained injuries outside Ontario. The defendants argued that the Ontario courts lacked jurisdiction with respect to non-resident members of the class under principles of constitutional law and private international law.

Justice Cumming rejected those arguments. He held that the *Morguard* principle was satisfied when, as in the case before him, there was a real and substantial connection between the province assuming jurisdiction and the defendants or the subject matter of the litigation. Ontario's *Class Proceedings Act* was procedural in nature. It allowed the court to establish a national class in a class proceeding. It was not unconstitutional as a piece of extraterritorial legislation. It allowed the court "to include non-residents as parties in an action in which Ontario ha[d] unquestioned jurisdiction with respect to Ontario residents."[260] Justice Cumming summarized what he saw as the legal position:

> *Morguard* and *Hunt* stand for the proposition that if there is a real and substantial connection between the subject matter of the action and Ontario, then the Ontario court has jurisdiction with respect to the litigation and can apply Ontario's procedural law. Ontario may not necessarily apply its substantive law since there must be a determination of the choice of law that applies. In cases where Ontario has properly assumed jurisdiction, other jurisdictions on the basis of the principle of comity should recognize the Ontario judgment. (In my view, this analysis does not involve any extra-territorial application of Ontario law, and *Morguard* and *Hunt* do not stand for the proposition that Ontario law should be applied extra-territorially.)[261]

The issue of jurisdiction over non-resident plaintiffs in a class action also arose in *McCutcheon v The Cash Store Inc.*[262] Justice Cullity pointed out that there had been no definitive decision on the question from either the Court of Appeal for Ontario or the Supreme Court of Canada. The basic question related to how the *Morguard* principle was to be adapted to the special features of class actions. He saw the problems as being particularly acute in jurisdictions such as Ontario and Alberta

---

260 *Ibid* at para 66.
261 *Ibid* at para 83.
262 (2006), 80 OR (3d) 644 (SCJ) [*McCutcheon*].

where the legislation enabled the court to bind class members who failed to opt out of the proceedings. While there was an analogy to be drawn between the position of non-resident class members and that of defendants in individual actions in the sense that the issue involved the power of the court to bind them, there were differences. Thus, Cullity J said:

> One is that the class members are also in the position of plaintiffs—albeit passive plaintiffs. The purpose of the litigation is, or should be, to confer benefits upon them and even where—as is most commonly the case—the proceedings end with a settlement, this purpose is reflected in the requirement that the court must approve it as being in the class members' interests.
>
> The potential detriment to class members is the reverse of that confronting defendants contesting jurisdiction in individual proceedings. The members face the risk of being bound by a decision in favour of the defendants, or one that will provide them with less compensation than they believe is their entitlement. Depending on the significance to be attributed to the right to opt out, these consequences effect a loss of autonomy and, even independently of them, such a loss will result from the members' compelled involvement with proceedings in which they may not desire to participate.[263]

The court indicated that the difficult cases were those in which the claims of the non-resident class members were based entirely on material facts that occurred outside the province:

> In such a case, the only connecting factor between Ontario, on the one hand, and such members and their claims, on the other, may be that they have claims against the same defendants and that these raise the same common issues as the claims of class members resident in Ontario over whom—and whose claims against the defendants—the court has jurisdiction.[264]

In such a case, a court could demand some connection with Ontario in respect of each class member's cause of action or, as in *Harrington* and *Wilson*, it could base jurisdiction on "a commonality of interest between non-resident class members and those who are resident in the forum and whose causes of action have sufficiently real and substantial connections to it to ground jurisdiction over their claims against the defendants."[265] In the final analysis, Cullity J preferred the latter approach.

---

263 *Ibid* at paras 33–34.
264 *Ibid* at para 37.
265 *Ibid* at para 49.

More recently, courts have had to consider the refinement of the *Morguard* principle by *Club Resorts*. Some courts have thus identified presumptive connecting factors unique to class actions. In *Meeking v Cash Store Inc*, a decision about the recognition of a foreign decision rather than the analysis of jurisdiction *simplicter*, the Manitoba Court of Appeal sought to identify a presumptive connecting factor which would have given the Ontario court jurisdiction over non-resident class members. It held that "in circumstances where the court has territorial jurisdiction over both the defendant and the representative plaintiff in a class action proceeding, common issues between the claim of the representative plaintiff and that of non-resident plaintiffs is a presumptive connecting factor, sufficient to give the court jurisdiction over non-resident plaintiffs."[266] Since the common issues are required for the class action to have been certified, this new factor appears quite easy to satisfy. This factor has been applied in the context of taking jurisdiction,[267] but its appropriateness in the context of a global class has also been questioned.[268] Courts have expressed the concern that taking jurisdiction over a global class on this basis exposes defendants to added liability because courts of other countries will refuse to recognize the Canadian decision, allowing class members in those countries to advance additional claims.[269]

The related question of the jurisdiction of foreign courts to bind non-resident class members by their judgments is considered in Chapter 8, which looks at the recognition and enforcement of foreign judgments.

F. FORUM OF NECESSITY

Section 6 of the *CJPTA* provides that a court that lacks territorial competence may still hear a dispute if it considers that

(a) there is no court outside [the forum] in which the plaintiff can commence the proceeding; or
(b) the commencement of the proceeding in a court outside [the forum] cannot reasonably be required.[270]

---

266 2013 MBCA 81 at paras 97 and 106.
267 See, for example, *Abdula v Canadian Solar Inc*, 2015 ONSC 53 at paras 58–59.
268 See, for example, *Airia Brands v Air Canada*, 2015 ONSC 5332 at para 173.
269 See, for example, *Airia Brands v Air Canada*, ibid at paras 115 and 189–90.
270 For a detailed analysis of this provision, see Black, Pitel, & Sobkin, above note 22, ch 7.

This provision is modelled on similar provisions in Quebec and Switzerland.[271] It has been enacted in British Columbia and Nova Scotia but not in Saskatchewan.[272]

In *Club Resorts* the Court of Appeal for Ontario held that concern for access to justice required the adoption of forum of necessity at common law, for cases in which there was "no other forum in which the plaintiff [could] reasonably seek relief." Justice Sharpe observed that "the overriding concern for access to justice that motivates the assumption of jurisdiction despite inadequate connection with the forum should be accommodated by explicit recognition of the forum of necessity exception."[273] These comments were *obiter dicta* and on appeal the Supreme Court of Canada expressly declined to comment on the existence of forum of necessity jurisdiction.[274] Nevertheless, lower courts have taken jurisdiction on this basis. In *Bouzari v Bahremani*, for example, the plaintiffs sued regarding torture that occurred in Iran.[275] The court concluded there was no reasonable basis on which they could be required to sue in Iran.

Under both the *CJPTA* and the common law, the test for forum of necessity is high, and in most cases in which it has been raised it has been rejected by the court. The courts have cited *Lamborghini (Canada) Inc v Automobili Lamborghini SPA*, a decision applying the Quebec provision, to the effect that it applies only "when the foreign forum that would normally have jurisdiction is unavailable for exceptional reasons such as a nearly absolute legal or practical impossibility. This includes, for example, the breakdown of diplomatic or commercial relations with a foreign State, the need to protect a political refugee, or the existence of a serious physical threat if the debate were to be undertaken before the foreign court."[276] Claims that the limitation period had expired in a

---

271 See *Josephson (Litigation guardian of) v Balfour Recreation Commission*, 2010 BCSC 603 at para 86 [*Josephson*]. See Janet Walker, "*Muscutt* Misplaced: The Future of Forum of Necessity Jurisdiction in Canada" (2009) 48 *Canadian Business Law Journal* 135.
272 On the situation in Saskatchewan, see Black, Pitel, & Sobkin, above note 22 at 174–77 and also 35–36.
273 *Van Breda v Village Resorts Ltd*, 2010 ONCA 84 at para 100.
274 *Club Resorts*, above note 19 at para 52.
275 [2011] OJ No 5009 (SCJ). For subsequent developments, see *Bouzari v Bahremani*, 2015 ONCA 275.
276 [1996] JQ No 4175 at para 44 (CA) [translation from *Anvil Mining Ltd v Association canadienne contre l'impunité*, 2012 QCCA 117 at para 98].

foreign forum or that it would be difficult to obtain counsel in a foreign forum are quite unlikely to trigger this threshold.[277]

However, even at this early stage some cases have relied on somewhat broader views of this jurisdiction. These cases tend to have somewhat unusual fact situations.[278] Even so, they can be criticized for expanding a jurisdiction which, to be coherent, needs to be exercised sparingly.

An important issue is whether forum of necessity jurisdiction is constitutional.[279] If *Morguard* requires that there must be a real and substantial connection between the dispute and the forum for a court to take jurisdiction over a defendant who is not present and does not submit, and if this is a constitutional requirement, then forum of necessity arguably cannot be constitutional. Yet given the rationale that underlies forum of necessity, it seems unlikely that a court would want to reach that conclusion. This issue remains to be analyzed by the courts.[280]

FURTHER READINGS

BEAUMONT, PAUL. "Hague Choice of Court Agreements Convention 2005: Background, Negotiations, Analysis and Current Status" (2009) 5 *Journal of Private International Law* 125.

BIGOS, OREN. "Jurisdiction over Cross-Border Wrongs on the Internet" (2005) 54 *International and Comparative Law Quarterly* 585.

BLACK, VAUGHAN. "Simplifying Court Jurisdiction in Canada" (2012) 8 *Journal of Private International Law* 411.

BLACK, VAUGHAN. "The Other Side of *Morguard*: New Limits on Judicial Jurisdiction" (1993) 22 *Canadian Business Law Journal* 4.

BLACK, VAUGHAN, & STEPHEN GA PITEL. "Reform of Ontario's Law on Jurisdiction" (2009) 47 *Canadian Business Law Journal* 469.

BLACK, VAUGHAN, & JANET WALKER. "The Deconstitutionalization of Canadian Private International Law?" (2003) 21 *Supreme Court Law Review* (2d) 181.

BLOM, JOOST. "New Ground Rules for Jurisdictional Disputes: The *Van Breda* Quartet" (2012) 53 *Canadian Business Law Journal* 1.

---

277 See *Mitchell v Jeckovich*, 2013 ONSC 7494; *West Van Inc v Daisley*, 2014 ONCA 232; *Cook v 1293037 Alberta Ltd (cob Traveller's Cloud 9)*, 2015 ONSC 7989.
278 See, for example, *Ibrahim v Robinson*, 2015 ONCA 21; *Josephson*, above note 271.
279 For a detailed analysis of this issue, see Black, Pitel, & Sobkin, above note 22 at 177–85. See also Edinger, above note 23 at 417.
280 See the comments in *Fewer*, above note 120 at para 48.

BLOM, JOOST. "The Challenge of Jurisdiction: *Van Breda v. Village Resorts* and *Black v. Breeden*" (2010) 49 *Canadian Business Law Journal* 400.

BLOM, JOOST, & ELIZABETH EDINGER. "The Chimera of the Real and Substantial Connection Test" (2005) 38 *University of British Columbia Law Review* 373.

BRIGGS, ADRIAN. "The Hidden Depths of the Law of Jurisdiction" [2016] *Lloyd's Maritime and Commercial Law Quarterly* 236.

CASTEL, JEAN-GABRIEL. "The Uncertainty Factor in Canadian Private International Law" (2007) 52 *McGill Law Journal* 555.

CASTEL, MATTHEW. "Jurisdiction and Choice of Law Issues in Multistate Defamation on the Internet" (2013) 51 *Alberta Law Review* 153.

DRURY, ROBERT. "Jurisdiction over Foreign Corporations: A Survey" [2007] *Lloyd's Maritime and Commercial Law Quarterly* 494.

EDINGER, ELIZABETH. "*Club Resorts Ltd. v. Van Breda*: Extraterritoriality Revisited" (2014) 55 *Canadian Business Law Journal* 263.

EDINGER, ELIZABETH. "*Spar Aerospace*: A Reconciliation of *Morguard* with the Traditional Framework for Determining Jurisdiction" (2003) 61 *Advocate* 511.

GREGORY, JOHN D. "The Hague Service Abroad Convention" (1990) 11 *Advocates' Quarterly* 327.

KAIN, BRANDON, ELDER MARQUES, & BYRON SHAW. "Developments in Private International Law: The 2011–12 Term—The Unfinished Project of the *Van Breda* Trilogy" (2012) 59 *Supreme Court Law Review* (2d) 277.

MCEVOY, JOHN P. "'After the Storm: The Impact of the Financial Crisis on Private International Law': Jurisdiction" (2010) 60 *University of New Brunswick Law Journal* 55.

MONESTIER, TANYA J. "Is Canada the New Shangri-La of Global Securities Class Actions?" (2012) 32 *Northwestern Journal of International Law & Business* 305.

MONESTIER, TANYA J. "Personal Jurisdiction over Non-resident Class Members: Have We Gone Down the Wrong Road?" (2010) 45 *Texas International Law Journal* 537.

MONESTIER, TANYA J. "A 'Real and Substantial' Mess: The Law of Jurisdiction in Canada" (2007) 33 *Queen's Law Journal* 179.

MONESTIER, TANYA J. "(Still) A 'Real and Substantial' Mess: The Law of Jurisdiction in Canada" (2013) 36 *Fordham International Law Journal* 396.

NWAPI, CHILENYE. "A Necessary Look at Necessity Jurisdiction" (2014) 47 *University of British Columbia Law Review* 211.

PITEL, STEPHEN GA. "Reformulating a Real and Substantial Connection" (2010) 60 *University of New Brunswick Law Journal* 177.

ROGERSON, PIPPA. "Problems of the Applicable Law of the Contract in the English Common Law Jurisdiction Rules: The Good Arguable Case" (2013) 9 *Journal of Private International Law* 387.

TU, GUANGJIAN. "Finding a Proper Nexus for Constructing Specific (Special) Jurisdiction Regarding Commercial Contract and Tort Cases: A Comparative Study of the US and European Approaches" (2009) 5 *Journal of Private International Law* 243.

VON MEHREN, ARTHUR TAYLOR. *Theory and Practice of Adjudicatory Authority in Private International Law* (The Hague: Martinus Nijhoff, 2003).

WALKER, JANET. "Coordinating Multijurisdictional Class Actions through Existing Certification Processes" (2005) 42 *Canadian Business Law Journal* 112.

WATSON, GARRY, & FRANK AU. "Constitutional Limits on Service *Ex Juris*: Unanswered Questions from *Morguard*" (2000) 23 *Advocates' Quarterly* 167.

CHAPTER 6

FORUM NON CONVENIENS

A. INTRODUCTION

As earlier chapters have explained, the first central question in the conflict of laws considers whether a court has jurisdiction to resolve a dispute. This chapter addresses a subsidiary question. It is quite possible to have a legal system in which a court is required to resolve all disputes that fall within its jurisdiction. But it is equally possible to allow a court with jurisdiction to decline, in certain situations, to resolve a dispute. On this approach, which has been adopted in Canada, the subsidiary question is whether the court will exercise its jurisdiction.

As a matter of procedure, the obligation rests with the defendant to request, by motion, that the court decline to exercise jurisdiction and that it accordingly stay the proceedings.[1] Such a motion can be brought regardless of the basis on which the court has taken jurisdiction: presence, submission, or service *ex juris* based on a presumptive connecting factor with the forum. It is not only available to defendants who have been served abroad. In addition, a motion for a stay of proceedings can be brought even after the defendant has taken steps which in law constitute acceptance of the court's jurisdiction, such as defending on the merits. This is because the motion is not a challenge to the court's

---

1   *Club Resorts Ltd v Van Breda*, 2012 SCC 17 at para 102 [*Club Resorts*].

jurisdiction. Quite the opposite: It accepts the court's jurisdiction but requests that the court not exercise it.²

B. EVOLUTION OF THE DOCTRINE

Historically, the ability of the court to refuse to hear a dispute falling within its jurisdiction flowed from its inherent power to prevent an abuse of process. In English law, the courts established a high hurdle for defendants seeking a stay of proceedings. They had to show that the action was vexatious or oppressive.³ In part, this test, which made it hard to stop proceedings in England, reflected the judges' belief in the superiority of English procedural and substantive law. In contrast, courts in nineteenth-century Scotland were considerably more willing to decline to exercise jurisdiction. Gradually, the Scottish principles began to influence English law. In *MacShannon v Rockware Glass Ltd*, the court accepted that English proceedings could be stayed if the defendant could (1) identify another forum in which justice could be done between the parties with "substantially less inconvenience and expense" and (2) establish that the stay would not deprive the plaintiff of a "legitimate personal or juridical advantage."⁴

In Scottish law this doctrine was called *forum non conveniens*, meaning "not a convenient forum." This name is something of an oversimplification since the court's concern is not solely with convenience. Rather, under this approach the court is engaged in a comparison of the relative merits of having the dispute resolved either in the local forum or in another forum. If the court concludes that it should decline jurisdiction in favour of another forum, then it pronounces itself to be a *forum non conveniens* and the other forum is the *forum conveniens*.

The formulation in *MacShannon* still favoured plaintiffs, since defendants had to show that the alternative forum would involve "substantially less" inconvenience and expense and plaintiffs were not to be deprived of legitimate advantages flowing from litigating in England. But within a decade the English courts abandoned these aspects of the doctrine and accepted the more neutral Scottish approach. The leading case is *Spiliada Maritime Corp v Cansulex Ltd*, in which the House of

---

2   Notwithstanding this logic, the position in British Columbia has been that a defendant who attorns cannot seek a stay of proceedings: *O'Brien v Simard*, 2006 BCSC 814. This may be changing: see *Blazek v Blazek*, 2010 BCCA 188.
3   *Egbert v Short*, [1907] 2 Ch 205; *St Pierre v South American Stores Ltd*, [1936] 1 KB 382 at 398 (CA).
4   [1978] AC 795 at 812 (HL), Lord Diplock [*MacShannon*].

Lords held that the doctrine of *forum non conveniens* had two elements or limbs.⁵ Under the first limb, the court has to be satisfied that there is another available forum in which the case could be resolved more suitably for the interests of all of the parties and the ends of justice. This inquiry involves more of a pure balancing of the merits of the competing forums than under *MacShannon*, although the court did say that the other forum had to be "clearly or distinctly" more appropriate.⁶ The aim, said the court, was to ensure that the action was tried in the jurisdiction that had the closest connection to the dispute and the parties. If, under the first limb, there was no such alternative forum, the inquiry ends and the motion for a stay fails. If there is such a forum, the analysis moves to the second limb, which considers whether justice nonetheless requires, in the circumstances of the case, trial in the forum. The analysis involves considering whether the plaintiff would be deprived of personal or juridical advantages by being prevented from proceeding in the chosen forum. The court held that under the second limb, the existence of such an advantage was not decisive and that a plaintiff could be deprived of such an advantage in appropriate cases.

The Supreme Court of Canada confirmed that *forum non conveniens* is part of Canadian law in *Amchem Products Inc v British Columbia (Workers' Compensation Board)*.⁷ However, the court rejected the division of the analysis into two distinct limbs as adopted in *MacShannon* and *Spiliada*. The court held that there was no principled reason why the loss of advantage should be treated separately rather than weighed with the other factors. The test can therefore be stated quite simply: a stay is to be granted when there is a clearly more appropriate forum for resolution of the dispute. More recently, some provinces have chosen to codify the doctrine. For example, in British Columbia the *Court Jurisdiction and Proceedings Transfer Act* provides in section 11 that "[a]fter considering the interests of the parties to a proceeding and the ends of justice, a court may decline to exercise its territorial competence in the proceeding on the ground that a court of another state is a more appropriate forum in which to hear the proceeding."⁸

---

5   [1987] AC 460 (HL) [*Spiliada*]. For a recent discussion, see *VTB Capital Plc v Nutritek International Corp*, [2013] UKSC 5 [*VTB Capital*].
6   *Spiliada*, above note 5 at 477.
7   [1993] 1 SCR 897 [*Amchem*]. See also *Club Resorts*, above note 1 at paras 101–4.
8   SBC 2003, c 28, s 11 [*CJPTA* (BC)]. Similar statutes are in force in Saskatchewan (*The Court Jurisdiction and Proceedings Transfer Act*, SS 1997, c C.41.1) and Nova Scotia (*Court Jurisdiction and Proceedings Transfer Act*, SNS 2003 (2nd Sess), c 2).

C. RATIONALE FOR THE DOCTRINE

Several lines of reasoning support the evolution and continued operation of *forum non conveniens*. First, it serves as a check on the combined effect of allowing the plaintiff to choose where to commence proceedings and the broad jurisdictional rules in many countries. If countries are, through broad rules on service *ex juris*, quite willing to hear disputes involving foreign defendants, then plaintiffs have significant tactical ability to choose a forum that best advantages them. In contrast, defendants have little say in where the dispute is to be heard. In Canada this was certainly the case prior to *Morguard Investments Ltd v De Savoye*, when jurisdiction over a foreign defendant was almost wholly dependent on fitting within broad rules for service out.[9] The development of the real and substantial connection requirement for service outside the province, now formulated as the need for a presumptive connecting factor, has mitigated this concern, but only in part. The analysis in *Spar Aerospace Ltd v American Mobile Satellite Corp*, if taken literally, would have restricted that requirement to interprovincial situations, leaving broad service *ex juris* rules free to catch defendants outside Canada.[10] Further, even if the real and substantial connection requirement is applied equally to international cases, the cases (reviewed in Chapter 5) have demonstrated that this standard is not overly difficult to satisfy, so that the plaintiff still has a fair degree of choice of forum. The doctrine of *forum non conveniens* gives defendants a counterweight against the broad choice afforded to plaintiffs. It serves to restrain plaintiffs from choosing a forum with little genuine connection to the dispute based solely on tactical considerations.

Second, the doctrine allows disputes to be resolved in the forum with which they have the strongest and best connection. This is a laudable goal for private international law and one that cannot be achieved without a willingness to stay proceedings in favour of another forum. There may be several available forums with at least a real and substantial connection to a dispute, and yet the connection to one of those forums may be much stronger than that to any of the others. The doctrine allows the dispute to be channelled into that forum.

Third, *forum non conveniens* is critical to holding parties to contractual jurisdiction agreements. In the absence of the doctrine, a party could sue in a forum other than that exclusively chosen by contract, as long as the other forum would take jurisdiction under its rules. This

---

9 [1990] 3 SCR 1077.
10 [2002] 4 SCR 205. It was not taken literally by subsequent decisions, including those of the Supreme Court of Canada.

would be in breach of the agreement. One way the defendant could enforce the jurisdiction agreement would be to sue for damages for the breach, but this remedy is at best imperfect. Damages could be quite difficult to ascertain and could well not provide true compensation for the breach. What the defendant wants is specific performance of the jurisdiction agreement. This cannot be achieved in a forum that cannot stay its proceedings. In contrast, *forum non conveniens* allows the court to hold parties to their bargain on jurisdiction.

Fourth, the doctrine enables courts to avoid the "unseemly rush to judgment" that can result from parallel proceedings in different jurisdictions. When multiple forums are available for a dispute, it is possible for one party to sue in one country and the other party to sue in another. Each is both a plaintiff and a defendant, depending on the jurisdiction. If both actions proceed, time and money can be wasted doing twice what arguably should be done only once. Each party has an incentive to simultaneously try to speed along the proceedings in which it is a plaintiff and to delay the proceedings in which it is a defendant, so as to have the dispute resolved first in the preferred forum. These incentives rarely assist in the efficient resolution of disputes or in co-operation between opposing counsel. *Forum non conveniens* allows the court in one of the two jurisdictions to stay its proceedings in favour of those in the other country, removing these problems.

These reasons have collectively led to courts across the common law world adopting the doctrine of *forum non conveniens*.[11] Yet the analysis is not one-sided. Several criticisms can be advanced against the doctrine. It is arguable that the overall goal of having a dispute resolved in the most appropriate forum, while laudable in theory, is unworkable in practice. Stay motions are typically brought at the very outset of the litigation, when many factual connections are unclear or in dispute. This timing increases the difficulty for the court in identifying the *forum conveniens*.[12] Further, the test is vague and open-ended. The extent to which decisions on motions to stay are reversed on appeal indicates how different judges can reach different results on the same facts. This reduces predictability and confidence in the litigation process. Ultimately, the doctrine has led to parties spending more time on prelimin-

---

11 For example, see *Inter Metal Group Ltd v Worslade Trading Ltd*, [1998] 2 IR 1, for the adoption of the doctrine in Ireland. Australia has adopted it but under a different, narrower formulation. In order to obtain a stay, the defendant must establish that the forum chosen by the plaintiff is inappropriate for the dispute. If it is not, a stay will not be granted, notwithstanding that some other forum is more appropriate. See *Voth v Manildra Flour Mills Pty Ltd* (1990), 171 CLR 538 (HCA).

12 For judicial disagreement as to how to assess facts in dispute on a stay motion, see *Young v Tyco International of Canada Ltd* (2008), 92 OR (3d) 161 (CA).

ary jurisdictional issues, which delays moving the dispute forward and addressing the merits.

In light of these criticisms, it is possible to support a very different approach. Rather than striving to have a dispute heard in the best possible forum, it may be more efficient to instead have it heard in an acceptable forum. Beyond that, stays of proceedings should be based not on relative appropriateness but rather on the timing of when proceedings are started. This is, in oversimplified terms, the approach adopted as between the member states of the European Union.[13] That approach has its own problems, especially those stemming from basing priority on timing, but it does avoid many of the problems with *forum non conveniens*.

It would also be possible to narrow, rather than abandon, the doctrine so that it would apply only in cases involving jurisdiction agreements or parallel proceedings elsewhere. Arguably these are the situations that generate the greatest pressures for a stay of proceedings, so the doctrine is essential to address them. However, it would be relatively easy for a defendant to commence parallel proceedings in a foreign forum so as to access even this more limited version of the doctrine, so this might not amount to much of an improvement in practice.

The current trend in Canada remains highly supportive of *forum non conveniens*. Statutory reforms on the issue of jurisdiction in several provinces chose to codify rather than alter the doctrine, so that it continues to operate as it did under the common law.[14] The best response to the argument that the doctrine is too vague and flexible and so encourages wasteful preliminary motions is to analyze the decided cases. As this chapter will explain, the principles in the cases applying the doctrine provide significant guidance as to which factors will have the most weight in particular disputes, allowing for reasonable predictability of outcome and guarding against arbitrary decisions.

D. PROCESS ISSUES

1) Relationship to Taking Jurisdiction

It is not uncommon for lawyers and judges to confuse the issue of jurisdiction and the doctrine of *forum non conveniens*. This confusion can lead to

---

13   See EC, *Commission Regulation (EU) No 1215/2012 of 12 December 2012 on jurisdiction and the recognition and enforcement of judgments in civil and commercial matters (recast)*, [2012] OJ, L 351/1 (known as the "Recast Brussels I Regulation").

14   See, for example, the analysis of s 11 of the *CJPTA* (BC), above note 8, in *Teck Cominco Metals Ltd v Lloyd's Underwriters*, 2009 SCC 11 at para 22, aff'g (2007), 67 BCLR (4th) 101 (CA) [*Teck Cominco*].

unclear decisions staying proceedings for lack of jurisdiction or dismissing proceedings because another forum is more appropriate.[15] One cause of this confusion is the structure and the wording of the various provincial statutes and rules of court dealing with these issues. Another is that defendants frequently raise both issues together, challenging a proceeding both for lack of jurisdiction and on the basis of *forum non conveniens*.

It must first be determined that the court has jurisdiction in the proceeding, and then, if it does, the court must consider whether it should use its discretion to stay its jurisdiction. The Supreme Court of Canada made reference to the distinction between jurisdiction and *forum non conveniens* in *Tolofson v Jensen* when it stated:

> [the real and substantial connection] test has the effect of preventing a court from unduly entering into matters in which the jurisdiction in which it is located has little interest. In addition, through the doctrine of *forum non conveniens* a court may refuse to exercise jurisdiction where, under the rule elaborated in *Amchem* . . . there is a more convenient or appropriate forum elsewhere.[16]

In *Muscutt v Courcelles*, the Court of Appeal for Ontario made it clear that a two-stage approach is necessary.[17] In that case, Sharpe JA quoted from the Ontario Divisional Court's decision granting leave to appeal in *Lemmex v Bernard*:[18]

> [T]he question of whether Ontario has jurisdiction to hear these actions is a different question from whether this court should decline to exercise its jurisdiction because another forum is the more convenient forum. Using other terminology, the concept of jurisdiction *simpliciter* is different from that of *forum non conveniens*. The second question of whether Ontario should decline to exercise jurisdiction because another forum is the more convenient forum only needs to be considered once an Ontario court has determined that it has jurisdiction to hear the action.[19]

---

15 See Cheryl Dusten & Stephen GA Pitel, "The Right Answers to Ontario's Jurisdictional Questions: Dismiss, Stay or Set Service Aside" (2005) 30 *Advocates' Quarterly* 297.
16 [1994] 3 SCR 1022 at 1049. See also *GreCon Dimter Inc v JR Normand Inc*, [2005] 2 SCR 401 at para 58.
17 (2002), 60 OR (3d) 20 (CA) [*Muscutt*]. See also *Coutu v Gauthier (Estate)* (2006), 296 NBR (2d) 34 at paras 52–55 (CA) [*Coutu*]; *Bouch v Penny (Litigation Guardian of)*, 2009 NSCA 80 at paras 29–30 [*Penny*].
18 (2000), 51 OR (3d) 164 (Div Ct).
19 *Ibid* at para 19, cited in *Muscutt*, above note 17 at para 43. See also *Club Resorts*, above note 1 at para 101: "a clear distinction must be drawn between the existence and the exercise of jurisdiction."

This separation of analysis also needs to be maintained on the question of the appropriate remedy. If the court lacks jurisdiction, the proceeding should be dismissed. In contrast, if the court has jurisdiction but there is a more convenient forum elsewhere, the proceeding should be stayed. This distinction between a stay and a dismissal needs to be observed. One aspect of this is that courts should not be encouraged to avoid reaching a conclusion on the issue of jurisdiction by holding that, in any case, the forum is not the convenient forum and so stay proceedings. This might seem convenient where the jurisdiction issue is complex but the circumstances point quite clearly to another forum as the *forum conveniens*. This nonetheless amounts to having accepted jurisdiction without truly resolving that issue, since the court must have jurisdiction in order to impose a stay.

2) Onus of Proof

Another important procedural question is who bears the onus on a motion for a stay of proceedings. Canadian provinces have differed in their answer to this question. One approach would be to put the onus of showing that another forum is more appropriate on the defendant as the moving party. This has been the approach in some provinces, such as New Brunswick and Manitoba.[20] But in other provinces the situation has been more complicated. In *Frymer v Brettschneider* a majority of the Court of Appeal for Ontario held that who bears the onus depends on whether the defendant has been served inside or outside the province.[21] If the defendant is served in the province, the defendant bears the onus. If the defendant is served *ex juris*, then the plaintiff bears the onus of showing that the forum is the *forum conveniens*.[22] In contrast, the dissenting judge held that the onus should depend not on the location of service but instead on whether the defendant had been served as of right or with leave of the court. If the defendant had been served as of right, which would include both service in the province and any situations under the rules of court that allowed for service *ex juris* without leave, then the defendant would bear the onus.[23] If the plaintiff had first had to obtain leave of the court before serving the defendant, then the plaintiff would bear the onus. Arguably, the dissenting view is more consistent with Sopinka J's

---

20   *Coutu*, above note 17 at para 80; *Craig Broadcast Systems Inc v Magid (Frank N) Associates Inc* (1998), 123 Man R (2d) 252 at para 31 (CA).
21   (1994), 19 OR (3d) 60 (CA) [*Frymer*].
22   See also *Bushell v T & N Plc* (1992), 67 BCLR (2d) 330 (CA).
23   See *Landmark Sport Group Atlantic Ltd v Karpov* (1995), 142 NSR (2d) 280 at paras 13–16 (SC).

statement in *Amchem* that "[w]hether the burden of proof should be on the plaintiff in *ex juris* cases will depend on the rule that permits service out of the jurisdiction."[24]

This difference in approach may have recently been resolved. In *Club Resorts Ltd v Van Breda* the Supreme Court of Canada, in summarizing the doctrine of *forum non conveniens*, indicated that the burden of proof is always on the defendant.[25] In doing so, however, it did not refer to *Frymer* or the Ontario approach. However, it is likely that the court's decision will be treated as having settled this issue.[26] The court's approach has the benefit of uniformity across all provinces.

In any event, it is important to question whether the burden of proof is of much importance to the doctrine of *forum non conveniens*. In *Amchem*, Sopinka J stated that "[t]he burden of proof should not play a significant role in these matters as it only applies in cases in which the judge cannot come to a determinate decision on the basis of the material presented by the parties."[27] But this does not sit entirely well with the court's emphasis that the alternative forum must be "clearly" more appropriate.[28] A judge hearing a stay motion thus has two approaches to difficult or close cases. On one, despite the difficulty, he or she simply identifies the forum that is the most appropriate as the *forum conveniens*. On another, he or she can hold that the appropriateness of a particular forum has not been clearly established, such that the party bearing the onus will lose. The many cases applying the doctrine illustrate both of these approaches.[29]

3) Statutory and Regulatory Provisions

While *forum non conveniens* is a common law doctrine, provincial statutes and rules of court frequently contain specific provisions addressing the staying of proceedings. Defendants seeking a stay should be familiar with these provisions, in part because they can vary in their

---

24   Above note 7 at 921.
25   Above note 1 at para 103.
26   See, for example, *Avanti Management & Consulting Ltd v Argex Mining Inc*, 2012 ONSC 4395 at para 23; *Eco-Tec Inc v Lu*, 2015 ONCA 818 at para 23; *Kaynes v BP, Plc*, 2014 ONCA 580 at para 35.
27   Above note 7 at 921.
28   *Club Resorts*, above note 1 at paras 108–9.
29   The statutory codification of *forum non conveniens* does not use the word "clearly" and is phrased more in terms of a pure balancing: see *CJTPA* (BC), above note 8, s 11. Despite this, the Nova Scotia Court of Appeal has refused to grant a stay on the basis that the defendants had not met the burden of proof: *Penny*, above note 17 at paras 61–62.

scope. For example, in Ontario section 106 of the *Courts of Justice Act* is broadly worded: "A court, on its own initiative or on motion by any person, whether or not a party, may stay any proceeding in the court on such terms as are considered just."[30] Ontario's *Rules of Civil Procedure* also deal with the doctrine, but the scope is more restrictive: it applies only in cases of service outside Ontario and in which the defendant has not delivered a defence, notice of intent to defend, or notice of appearance.[31] In cases falling outside this rule, defendants can still rely on the more general language in section 106.[32]

E. THE ANALYSIS

Despite the decision in *Amchem* to reject the two distinct analytical limbs from *Spiliada*, the factors considered by the courts in evaluating the appropriateness of competing forums can still be divided into two groups. The first group of factors deals with how well connected a forum is with aspects of the dispute. The second group looks less at that sort of proximity and more at the consequences, in terms of injustice, of litigating in one forum rather than the other.

The factors have been set out in key cases like *Eastern Power Ltd v Azienda Communale Energia*.[33] That case involved a breach of contract, and the court listed the following factors:

> the location where the contract in dispute was signed, the applicable law of the contract, the location in which the majority of witnesses reside, the location of key witnesses, the location where the bulk of the evidence will come from, the jurisdiction in which the factual matters arose, and the residence or place of business of the parties.[34]

---

30 RSO 1990, c C.43.
31 RRO 1990, Reg 194, r 17.06 [Ontario Rules].
32 *Occidental Chemical Corp v Sovereign General Insurance Co* (1997), 32 OR (3d) 277 (Gen Div). This is arguably the better procedural solution for *Momentous.ca Corp v Canadian American Association of Professional Baseball Ltd*, 2012 SCC 9 [*Momentous.ca*] rather than the court's resort to r 21.01(3) of the Ontario Rules. The issue should not have been whether Ontario lacked jurisdiction but rather whether Ontario's proceedings should have been stayed. On that issue, the fact that the defendant had delivered a statement of defence is irrelevant, since, as explained above, submitting to the court's jurisdiction in no way precludes seeking a stay.
33 (1999), 178 DLR (4th) 409 (Ont CA). See also *472900 BC Ltd v Thrifty Canada, Ltd* (1998), 57 BCLR (3d) 332 (CA); *Muscutt*, above note 17 at para 41.
34 *Ibid* at para 19, quoting from *SDI Simulation Group Inc v Chameleon Technologies Inc* (1994), 34 CPC (3d) 346 at 350–51 (Ont Ct Gen Div).

In provinces that have enacted a specific provision on *forum non conveniens*, similar factors are listed. The British Columbia statute, for example, lists:

> (a) the comparative convenience and expense for the parties to the proceeding and for their witnesses, in litigating in the court or in any alternative forum, (b) the law to be applied to issues in the proceeding, (c) the desirability of avoiding multiplicity of legal proceedings, (d) the desirability of avoiding conflicting decisions in different courts, (e) the enforcement of an eventual judgment, and (f) the fair and efficient working of the Canadian legal system as a whole.[35]

Under both the common law approach and these statutory provisions, the lists of factors are open-ended, so that factors not listed can still be considered.

As long as all relevant factors are considered, the specific organizational framework is not critical, but two potentially interesting observations can be offered. First, in the provinces with a statutory provision, decisions have varied as to whether they centre their analysis on the listed factors or the factors from earlier leading cases.[36] This is possible because, as noted earlier, the Supreme Court of Canada has held that the statutory provision is simply a codification of the common law doctrine.[37] Second, and more important, the analysis in provinces without a statutory provision has been influenced by the language of the statute. In *Breeden v Black*, a case from Ontario, the Supreme Court of Canada used the statutory provision quoted above as the framework even though it did not apply as a matter of law.[38] Subsequently several decisions have used the same approach,[39] to the extent that we may find it becomes the standard framework in all provinces. If so, we must still remember that it is an open-ended list and that it omits some of the key considerations, discussed below, such as jurisdiction clauses and juridical advantages to the plaintiff from suing in the chosen forum.

---

35 *CJPTA* (BC), above note 8, s 11(2). See, generally, Stephen GA Pitel, "The Canadian Codification of *Forum Non Conveniens*" (2011) 7 *Journal of Private International Law* 251.

36 For more detailed analysis, see Vaughan Black, Stephen GA Pitel, & Michael Sobkin, *Statutory Jurisdiction: An Analysis of the Court Jurisdiction and Proceedings Transfer Act* (Toronto: Carswell, 2012) at 195–98.

37 *Teck Cominco*, above note 14.

38 2012 SCC 19 at paras 29–36 [*Breeden*].

39 See, for example, *Nagra v Malhotra*, 2012 ONSC 4497; *Court v Debaie*, 2012 ABQB 640. For detailed analysis of each of the factors listed in the statutory framework, see Black, Pitel, & Sobkin, above note 36 at 198–213.

Where relevant, these additional factors must be considered alongside those listed in the statutory formulation.

It should be noted that, while straightforward in most cases, to be a clearly more appropriate forum for resolution of the dispute the foreign forum must be able to take jurisdiction under its own rules. A forum that lacks jurisdiction cannot be claimed to be an alternative forum, much less a clearly more appropriate one.[40]

In light of the rationale for the doctrine, a motion for a stay of proceedings based on *forum non conveniens* should be brought in a timely manner. Procedural delay can be considered by the court as a factor against granting a stay.[41]

1) Physical Connections

In a simple case there may be three central physical connections: the residence of the plaintiff, the residence of the defendant, and the location where the acts giving rise to the dispute took place. But there are many possible variations on these basic connections. Individuals may be resident in more than one country. Corporations and other legal persons may not truly have a residence: they instead can have a head office, a registered office, a place of business, or all of the above. The acts giving rise to the dispute may have occurred in multiple countries and the injuries that result could be suffered in a different country. The analysis of these factors is very fact-specific. In this area one principle sometimes invoked by the courts is that it should be relatively difficult for a defendant to allege that his or her home jurisdiction is an inconvenient forum.

Another group of physical connections includes the location of documents, physical evidence, and witnesses. The relative importance of these factors will be different depending on whether the key evidence in the case is documentary or based on testimony. The analysis should focus not only on where the evidence is located but also on what procedures are available in each forum for getting the evidence before the court. There may be many witnesses in Panama, but if they cannot be compelled to testify there then that factor loses importance. Other relevant considerations are the language used in the documents and by the witnesses. In litigation in Canada, German documents would have

---

40 See *Douez v Facebook, Inc*, 2015 BCCA 279, leave to appeal to SCC granted, [2015] SCCA No 367 [*Douez*], in which the court rejected the submission that a provincial statute deprived California courts of jurisdiction over the dispute. California was not shown to be an unavailable forum.

41 See, for example, *Loat v Howarth*, 2011 ONCA 509 [*Loat*].

to be translated for the court, whereas that would not be needed if the litigation were in Germany.

2) Applicable Law

In terms of expense, convenience, and accuracy there is a strong sense that it is better to have a dispute resolved by courts fully familiar with the applicable law. So, if the applicable law is Dutch, it is easy to conclude that the courts of the Netherlands will be in a better position to apply that law than the courts of any Canadian province. More detailed reasoning for this conclusion is outlined in Chapter 12. It is important, however, to consider the role the applicable law will play in the overall litigation. If the points of law involved are complex or contentious, the general rule above holds true. But in some cases, the legal rule in issue may be quite simple, possibly not even disputed by the parties. The real dispute may be factual, not as to the law.[42] Consider a breach of contract case. The parties may dispute the applicable law as being either that of Ontario or of Greece. If, however, Greek law applies, they may agree on the relevant rule of Greek contract law. In such a case, the role of this factor in the *forum non conveniens* analysis is much reduced.

A further point can be made here. In general, jurisdiction issues receive much more attention from lawyers and courts than choice of law issues. This is largely because most disputes settle at some point between when they are started and the time of trial. Jurisdiction issues usually arise at the very beginning, so they arise much more often than choice of law issues, which mainly arise at trial. However, the role of the applicable law in the *forum non conveniens* analysis is an exception. Its role in the doctrine requires consideration, at an earlier stage in the proceedings, of the applicable law and therefore of the choice of law rules to identify that law.

3) Specialized Expertise

One of the most important factors in *Spiliada* that led the court to refuse to stay the English proceedings was the fact that a very similar action had already proceeded to trial in England. In both actions, the plaintiff corporation was the owner of a bulk carrier ship and the defendant—the same in both actions—had used the ship to transport

---

42 See *Molson Coors Brewing Co v Miller Brewing Co* (2006), 83 OR (3d) 331 at para 21 (SCJ) [*Molson*]. See also *VTB Capital*, above note 5 at paras 45–49.

sulphur. The plaintiffs claimed that the sulphur had caused severe corrosion and pitting to the holds of their ships. The House of Lords stated:

> ... anyone who has been involved, as counsel, in very heavy litigation of this kind, with a number of experts on both sides and difficult scientific questions involved, knows only too well what the learning curve is like: how much information and knowledge has to be, and is, absorbed ... .[43]

The court went on to say that this factor also encompasses specialized expertise a court has developed in resolving a particular type of dispute. In *Spiliada*, the parties would benefit from having the second, highly similar dispute resolved in the same country as the first. The earlier dispute involved the ship *The Cambridgeshire* and so this has become known in some circles as the Cambridgeshire factor.

Some caution needs to be exercised in considering this factor. First, the similar proceedings need to be at quite an advanced stage in order for any expertise to have been developed. Second, the court should be mindful that even where there is expertise in the forum, similar expertise may also exist in other jurisdictions. Third, and perhaps most important, this factor should not be used to mask judicial chauvinism. It would go beyond the permissible limits of this factor for a court to weigh its overall expertise in handling commercial litigation with that of the courts of another country. The expertise in question must be specific, not general; cases truly raising the Cambridgeshire factor are infrequent.

4) Jurisdiction Clauses

Parties to international contracts often aim to achieve further certainty in their arrangements through the use of jurisdiction clauses.[44] A jurisdiction clause is a provision in a contract under which the parties agree to submit some or all disputes arising under or in connection with the contract to the courts of a particular country. Under Canadian private international law, jurisdiction clauses will generally be enforced unless a party can demonstrate that there are strong reasons for not doing so.[45]

---

43 *Spiliada*, above note 5 at 485.
44 These clauses are also called forum selection clauses, choice of court clauses, and jurisdiction agreements.
45 In *ZI Pompey Industrie v ECU-Line NV*, [2003] 1 SCR 450 at para 20 [*ZI Pompey*], Bastarache J noted for the court that "these clauses are generally to be encouraged by the courts as they create certainty and security in transaction, derivatives of order and fairness, which are critical components of private international law."

Jurisdiction clauses play a major role in the issue of whether a court will exercise its discretion to stay proceedings. A jurisdiction clause pointing to the country where the litigation has been started makes it difficult for the defendant to stay the proceedings, and a jurisdiction clause pointing away from that country has the opposite effect. Courts have consistently held that there is a heavy onus on a party seeking to avoid a jurisdiction clause.[46] There is some difference in approach depending on whether the clause is exclusive or non-exclusive. The heavy onus is typically imposed in cases involving exclusive clauses. Non-exclusive clauses are still given reasonably strong weight in the balancing process, but less weight than exclusive clauses.[47]

A key case is *ZI Pompey Industrie v ECU-Line NV*.[48] The plaintiffs had contracted with the defendant to ship goods to Seattle. The goods arrived damaged and the plaintiffs commenced litigation against the defendant in the Federal Court of Canada. The defendant brought a motion for a stay of proceedings, arguing that the bill of lading contained an exclusive jurisdiction clause in favour of Antwerp. The court held that the party opposing the enforcement of a jurisdiction clause, in this case the plaintiff, must show "strong cause" as to why the clause should not be given effect. The plaintiff could not do so and the stay was granted.

There is some question in the law as to whether an exclusive jurisdiction clause is of such importance that it warrants an even greater change from the normal approach. In *ZI Pompey* Bastarache J stated: "I am not convinced that a unified approach to *forum non conveniens*, where a choice of jurisdiction clause constitutes but one factor to be considered, is preferable." He suggested that, at least in cases involving bills of lading, "a separate approach" should be followed which would honour the clause in all but "exceptional circumstances."[49] This language goes beyond the heavy onus traditionally imposed in jurisdiction-clause cases and moves to an approach that makes all other factual connections and juridical advantages irrelevant, focusing the entire analysis on the clause. This view of *ZI Pompey* has since been adopted in

---

46   See *ZI Pompey*, ibid; *Oulton Agencies Inc v Knolloffice Inc* (1988), 69 Nfld & PEIR 65 (PEISCAD); *Ash v Lloyd's Corporation* (1992), 9 OR (3d) 755 (CA); *Fairfield v Low* (1990), 71 OR (2d) 599 (HCJ). The classic English case on this point is *The Eleftheria*, [1969] 2 All ER 641.
47   See, for example, *Loat*, above note 41 at paras 29–31.
48   Above note 45.
49   *Ibid* at para 21. See Genevieve Saumier & Jeffrey Bagg, "Forum Selection Clauses before Canadian Courts: A Tale of Two (or Three?) Solitudes" (2013) 46 *University of British Columbia Law Review* 439 at 454–62.

several recent decisions. In *Expedition Helicopters Inc v Honeywell Inc* the Court of Appeal for Ontario elaborated, stating:

> The few factors that might be considered include the plaintiff was induced to agree to the clause by fraud or improper inducement or the contract is otherwise unenforceable, the court in the selected forum does not accept jurisdiction or otherwise is unable to deal with the claim, the claim or the circumstances that have arisen are outside of what was reasonably contemplated by the parties when they agreed to the clause, the plaintiff can no longer expect a fair trial in the selected forum due to subsequent events that could not have been reasonably anticipated, or enforcing the clause in the particular case would frustrate some clear public policy. Apart from circumstances such as these, a forum selection clause in a commercial contract should be enforced.[50]

However, other cases have preferred a more holistic approach, analyzing a wider range of factors. In *Microcell Communications Inc v Frey*, for example, the Saskatchewan Court of Appeal expressed concern about limiting the scope of the analysis.[51] There are cases where notwithstanding an exclusive jurisdiction clause other considerations pointed to a different forum. For example, in *Skyway Canada Ltd v Clara Industrial Services Ltd* the court did not give effect to an exclusive jurisdiction clause in favour of New York.[52] The clause was between only two of several parties involved in a complex dispute. The court held that it made more sense to have all of the parties involved in one proceeding in Ontario rather than separating out one aspect of the larger dispute and having it resolved in New York because of the clause. Decisions such as this one suggest that some courts may continue to consider jurisdiction clauses alongside other *forum non conveniens* factors.[53]

In the provinces that have adopted a statute on jurisdiction, this issue—whether consideration of jurisdiction clauses is part of *forum non conveniens* or a separate doctrine—gives rise to a related debate about where that consideration fits within the scheme of the statute.[54]

---

50 2010 ONCA 351 at para 24. See also *Viroforce Systems Inc v R&D Capital Inc*, 2011 BCCA 260 at para 14.
51 2011 SKCA 136 at para 115 [*Microcell*]. See also *Hudye Farms Inc v Canadian Wheat Board*, 2011 SKCA 137.
52 (2005), 47 CLR (3d) 311 (Ont SCJ).
53 See also *Château des Charmes Wines Ltd v Sabate, USA, Inc*, [2005] OJ No 4604 (SCJ); *Sarabia v The "Oceanic Mindoro"* (1996), 26 BCLR (3d) 143 at para 36 (CA); *Winvan Paving Ltd v Gencor Industries Inc*, 2015 BCSC 233.
54 See Black, Pitel, & Sobkin, above note 36 at 207–11; Saumier & Bagg, above note 49 at 462–69.

As noted earlier, the statutory provision on staying proceedings has been held by the Supreme Court of Canada to be a codification of the common law approach.[55] But the court also held that the statutory provision is a complete code on the issue of staying jurisdiction based on *forum non conveniens*,[56] and it does not mention jurisdiction clauses, much less accord them special status. In *Microcell* the court held the analysis fits within the statutory provision, which is consistent with considering a broader range of factors. In contrast, in *Preymann v Ayus Technology Corp* the British Columbia Court of Appeal held that "applications for a stay of proceedings based on forum selection clauses constitute a different inquiry than *forum non conveniens* applications" and so are outside the statutory provision.[57]

Exclusive jurisdiction clauses can be used in a wide range of contractual contexts and the "strong cause" test might not apply to all of them. In *Stubbs v ATS International BV* the Court of Appeal for Ontario suggested that it might not apply to employment contracts.[58]

In *Momentous.ca Corp v Canadian American Association of Professional Baseball Ltd* the Supreme Court of Canada confirmed, in brief reasons, the important role of jurisdiction clauses in staying proceedings.[59] Depending on how the decision is understood, the court may have gone even further and held that an exclusive jurisdiction clause in favour of a foreign forum does not relate to staying the proceedings but rather deprives the court of subject matter jurisdiction.[60] This would be counter to the orthodox view that such a clause does not, and cannot as a matter of law, have an impact on the domestic court's ability to take jurisdiction on any available basis such as presence or submission.[61]

---

55 *Teck Cominco*, above note 14.
56 *Ibid* at para 22.
57 2012 BCCA 30 at paras 39 and 48. See to similar effect *Douez*, above note 40 at para 31.
58 2010 ONCA 879 at para 58.
59 Above note 32.
60 Support for this understanding is based on the court's reliance on Ontario Rules, above note 31, r 21.01(3), which on its clear wording deals with situations in which the court has "no jurisdiction over the subject matter of the action" and on the fact that the remedy granted in the case was a dismissal, not a stay, of the proceedings: *Momentous.ca*, above note 32 at paras 7–8 and 10. Yet the court also referred to *ZI Pompey* and the "strong cause" test for exercising jurisdiction, a point in the analysis which would not be reached if the court lacked jurisdiction *simpliciter*: *ibid* at paras 9–10.
61 The position in Quebec is different: see Saumier & Bagg, above note 49 at 451–54.

Subsequent decisions have not relied on *Momentous.ca* as depriving the court of jurisdiction, and that is welcome.[62]

On 30 June 2005, the Hague Conference on Private International Law concluded the *Convention on Choice of Court Agreements*.[63] Canada has not yet ratified this convention but it is likely to do so, which would be followed by implementing statutes in each province. The convention has important implications for the issue of taking jurisdiction, but it also has an impact on the operation of *forum non conveniens*. Under the convention, courts given exclusive jurisdiction under a jurisdiction clause would be required to hear the dispute, and all other courts would equally be required not to do so.[64] The chosen court could therefore not stay its proceedings, and a province that was not the chosen court would be required to order a stay. The aim of such a rigid rule is to promote certainty, particularly in light of the reasonable expectations of the contracting parties. But there may be reason for concern. As mentioned above, there have been cases where other factors have appropriately been found to outweigh even an exclusive jurisdiction agreement in the *forum non conveniens* analysis. Under the convention such a conclusion would no longer be possible.

An important issue in cases involving jurisdiction clauses is whether the particular dispute falls within the scope of the clause. If it does not, the clause should not be relevant to the *forum non conveniens* analysis.[65] The courts generally interpret such clauses broadly, refusing to draw fine distinctions based on the language used.[66] In some recent

---

62 See, for example, *2249659 Ontario Ltd v Sparkasse Siegen*, 2013 ONCA 354 at para 25 [*Sparkasse*].

63 30 June 2005, reprinted in 44 ILM 1294 (2005) [*Hague Convention*]. See Vaughan Black, "The Hague Choice of Court Convention" (2006) 6 *Canadian International Lawyer* 181 at 184; Louise Ellen Teitz, "The Hague Choice of Court Convention: Validating Party Autonomy and Providing an Alternative to Litigation" (2005) 53 *American Journal of Comparative Law* 543 at 550–51; Richard Garnett, "The Hague Choice of Court Convention: Magnum Opus or Much Ado about Nothing?" (2009) 5 *Journal of Private International Law* 161.

64 *Hague Convention*, above note 63, arts 5(2) and 6. There are some limited exceptions to this general approach, such as where a stay in favour of the chosen forum would lead to a "manifest injustice."

65 See, for example, *Sparkasse*, above note 62; *Nalcor Energy—Oil and Gas Inc v Husky Oil Operations Ltd*, 2016 NLTD(G) 5.

66 See *Mantini v Smith Lyons LLP* (2003), 64 OR (3d) 505 at para 19 (CA); *Woolcock v Bushert* (2004), 246 DLR (4th) 139 at para 22 (Ont CA); *Dalimpex Ltd v Janicki*, (2003), 64 OR (3d) 737 at paras 41–43 (CA) [*Dalimpex*]; *Kaverit Steel and Crane Ltd v Kone Corp* (1992), 85 Alta LR (2d) 287 (CA). See also the analysis of Lord Hoffmann, in a different context, in *Premium Nafta Products Limited v Fili Shipping Company Limited*, [2007] UKHL 40 at para 12.

cases the courts have distinguished between claims that rely on elements of the contract containing the clause, which will usually fall inside the scope, and claims of conspiracy or breach of fiduciary duty that are not dependent on the contract, which usually fall outside the scope.[67] A different but related issue is to identify which parties in a dispute are bound by the clause. While there are few Canadian cases on the issue,[68] it is possible that a court might hold a non-contracting party bound by a jurisdiction clause based either on that party's close relation to the clause or on the circumstances of an overall transaction.[69]

5) Lis Alibi Pendens

As explained earlier in this chapter, one aim of *forum non conveniens* is to avoid a multiplicity of proceedings and the possibility of inconsistent decisions. Accordingly, one of the key factors is whether the same or similar litigation is already under way in another forum. This issue is often referred to as *lis alibi pendens*, which means "a proceeding pending elsewhere."

It is important to examine how far along the other litigation is: if it has started only recently or if it has not advanced beyond the initial pleadings then this factor is of reduced weight.[70] The court should also consider whether the other litigation has been commenced purely for tactical reasons in an attempt to forum shop. One indication of this is if the proceedings are for a negative declaration, such that the plaintiff is asking the court to declare that he or she is not liable to the defendant. Such a request is the reverse of the normal pattern of litigation and can indicate that one party, concerned about being sued in one country, pre-emptively commenced proceedings first in another country.

The conventional view is that *lis alibi pendens* is an important factor in the *forum non conveniens* analysis but it is not determinative. However, there have been some suggestions that in the interests of comity and out of respect to foreign courts it should be elevated above the other factors. Elements of this can be found in *Westec Aerospace Inc v Raytheon Aircraft Co*, in which the plaintiff, a British Columbia company, sued the defendant, a Kansas company, in British Columbia for breach of

---

67 See *Precious Metal Capital Corp v Smith* (2008), 92 OR (3d) 701 (CA); *Matrix Integrated Solutions Ltd v Naccarato* (2009), 97 OR (3d) 693 (CA).
68 See *Aldo Group Inc v Moneris Solutions Corp*, 2013 ONCA 725.
69 See Vaughan Black & Stephen GA Pitel, "Forum-Selection Clauses: Beyond the Contracting Parties" (2016) 12 *Journal of Private International Law* 26.
70 *Cleveland Museum of Art v Capricorn Art International SA*, [1990] 2 Lloyd's Rep 166.

contract.⁷¹ Two months before that litigation was started, the defendant had sued the plaintiff in Kansas, seeking a negative declaration that it had not breached the contract. The defendant sought a stay of the British Columbia action on the basis that Kansas was the *forum conveniens*. The stay was granted by the Court of Appeal. It held that despite the reversal of roles in the Kansas action, those proceedings involved the same parties and the same subject matter as the British Columbia action. The court appears to have given significant weight to the Kansas proceedings, since it did not otherwise hold that Kansas was clearly the more appropriate forum. Rather, it held that Kansas was an appropriate forum, as was British Columbia, and beyond that "[b]y fashioning rules that attempt to avoid or minimize the inefficiencies and injustices that can result from parallel proceedings, the court, to some degree, will necessarily favour *on the jurisdiction question* the party who initiates proceedings first."⁷² The action in Kansas was expected to be tried before a jury later that same year, suggesting that those proceedings were further advanced than the ones in the forum. It is difficult to disagree with the decision, but the court may have gone beyond what was needed to reach that conclusion in its suggestion that the analysis must necessarily favour the proceedings that were started first.

This suggestion of elevated priority for *lis alibi pendens* was raised in *Teck Cominco Metals Ltd v Lloyd's Underwriters*.⁷³ Teck had mining and smelting operations in British Columbia. In 2004 it was sued in Washington State for environmental property damage caused by the discharge of waste material into the Columbia River, which flows from Teck's Canadian operations into the United States. Teck notified its insurers, looking to them to defend the claim, but they refused. Teck therefore sued the insurers in Washington State to establish its entitlement under the insurance policies. Shortly afterwards, the insurers sued Teck in British Columbia to establish their lack of responsibility under the same policies. So the issue became where the coverage issue would be resolved. Stay applications were brought in both coverage actions. The application failed in the United States. In Canada, Teck wanted the courts to take a different approach to applications for a stay in cases where a foreign court had already asserted jurisdiction. It argued that, despite all the factual connections the coverage dispute had to British Columbia, the existence of *lis alibi pendens* should take precedence over all other factors and be virtually conclusive of the analysis. The Court of Appeal and Supreme Court of Canada rejected this

---

71   (1999), 67 BCLR (3d) 278 (CA) [*Westec*].
72   *Ibid* at para 38 [emphasis in original].
73   Above note 14.

argument. They were not prepared to sanction a "race to the courthouse" and create a principle whereby the litigation that was first to be started had to be allowed to proceed.[74] This decision is welcome. Parallel proceedings are an important factor in the analysis, but there is no basis for treating them as conclusive against all other factors.[75] Even if the court was satisfied that the alternative forum had a sufficient connection to the dispute to found jurisdiction, it would be quite mechanical and artificial to base a rigid rule on the time when proceedings were commenced. Doing so would severely impair the flexibility of *forum non conveniens*.

The leading decisions on *lis alibi pendens* involve competing actions across international borders. The orthodox view is that the same general approach should apply across provincial borders, so that an Alberta court would not have to treat parallel proceedings in Ontario as anything other than one factor in the stay analysis. But it is possible that a different approach could emerge. One reason could be the fact that either or both applications for a stay in competing interprovincial actions could be appealed to the same ultimate appellate court, the Supreme Court of Canada, which would resolve the issue as to which was the more appropriate forum. Another, more speculative reason could be a growing willingness for provincial courts to recognize even the interlocutory decisions of sister provinces.[76]

Parallel proceedings are also an important issue in multi-jurisdictional class actions. A useful example is *Mignacca v Merck Frosst Canada Ltd*, in which both the courts of Ontario and Saskatchewan certified class proceedings against the same defendants in respect of the same conduct.[77] Both actions certified multi-jurisdictional classes, so that residents of some provinces were covered by both classes. The defendants moved to stay the Ontario action, arguing that the courts in Ontario were required to allow the Saskatchewan action, which had been certified first, to proceed. The court rejected this argument and denied the stay, holding that "[s]uch a rigid technical approach encourages unfair tactics and undermines the integrity of the justice system."[78] The parallel proceedings were only one factor to be taken into account. That factor was seen as more de-

---

74 *Ibid* at paras 25–30 (SCC) and para 74 (CA).
75 See *Molson*, above note 42 at paras 39–42; *Invar Manufacturing, a Division of Linamar Holdings Inc v Giuliani, a Division of IGM USA Inc* (2008), 235 OAC 202 at paras 19–20 (CA); *Ingenium Technologies Corp v McGraw-Hill Companies, Inc* (2005), 49 BCLR (4th) 120 at para 9 (CA).
76 For more on this, see Chapter 8.
77 (2009), 95 OR (3d) 269 (Div Ct).
78 *Ibid* at para 49.

terminative in *Kaynes v BP, Plc*, in which the Court of Appeal for Ontario stayed a class action in favour of litigation in the United States and the United Kingdom in order to avoid a multiplicity of proceedings.[79]

While not strictly a question of *lis alibi pendens*, a related factor considers the ability of the competing forums to consolidate parties and claims into one action within the forum. If a dispute involves five parties, and Ontario will take jurisdiction over only claims by or against two of them but Michigan will do so in respect of all five, then proceedings in Michigan are more efficient. All issues arising from the same factual matrix can be resolved in one action as opposed to having a smaller proceeding in Ontario and then further proceedings elsewhere.

6) Juridical Advantages

The factors considered above evaluate appropriateness in terms of physical connections with one or more countries. In English law they would be analyzed under the first limb of the *Spiliada* test. The second limb of that test evaluates appropriateness in different terms, looking at whether the strength of those physical connections warrant depriving the plaintiff of certain advantages in the chosen forum. The Canadian approach in *Amchem* does not have the two separate limbs, but the issue of judicial advantage to the plaintiff is still very relevant.

The courts have identified different possible advantages. One of these concerns limitation periods. If the plaintiff has commenced proceedings in the forum within the applicable limitation period but is outside the time for suing in the alternative forum, a decision to stay the forum's proceedings will effectively put an end to the litigation in both forums. The plaintiff's claim will be time-barred in the *forum conveniens*. In such cases plaintiffs have claimed a juridical advantage in being able to maintain the action in the chosen forum. The courts have not adopted an all-or-nothing approach to this issue. Rather, they have asked whether it was reasonable for the plaintiff not to have commenced proceedings within the limitation period in the alternative forum. Because multiple forums may have jurisdiction, it is open for the plaintiff to commence proceedings in respect of the same claim in different countries and to then choose to move ahead either in his or her preferred forum or in whichever forum remains after jurisdictional challenges. A plaintiff who does not recognize an obvious *forum conveniens* and start proceedings there, even if only to guard against the running of the time bar, runs the risk of the court in the chosen forum

---

79 Above note 26.

concluding that he or she did not act reasonably and therefore staying the proceedings.[80] On the other hand, if the court is satisfied that the plaintiff has acted reasonably, it would be unusual for it to force the plaintiff into a jurisdiction where the claim is barred.

The courts have also considered differences in issues relating to the expense of litigation. In some countries the successful party can recover part of his or her legal expenses from the losing party through an award of costs. In some other countries no awards are made for costs: each side bears its own expenses, win or lose. A plaintiff could argue that his or her ability to be awarded costs in the chosen forum is a juridical advantage over litigation in a forum where these expenses will go uncompensated.[81] English cases have divided over whether this is a true advantage or only a neutral factor, since of course the advantage or disadvantage depends on the outcome of the case. A related but more serious issue is whether the plaintiff will be able to fund the litigation. In *Connelly v RTZ Corporation plc* the House of Lords held that the availability of legal aid in the chosen forum was a legitimate juridical advantage that favoured denying the stay.[82]

Plaintiffs have raised other differences and alleged that they indicate a juridical advantage in the chosen forum, but the courts have been more skeptical.[83] Differences in the extent and scope of pretrial discovery procedures have usually been seen as neutral, affecting each party relatively equally. Differences in the quantum of damages or prejudgment interest have not generally been seen as an advantage, though a derisory award or complete denial of interest could amount to the plaintiff being denied an effective remedy in the alternative forum. In such cases this factor could play a role. Differences in litigation procedure relating to speed or availability of a jury trial are generally entitled to respect under principles of comity and so are treated as neutral.[84] However, a truly inordinate delay can amount to injustice to the plaintiff.[85]

In *Club Resorts* the Supreme Court of Canada commented on the role of juridical advantage. It suggested that this factor should, in the interests of comity between jurisdictions, be downplayed or given a reduced role, especially in interprovincial cases.[86] In *Breeden* the same

---

80 See, for example, *Hurst v Société Nationale de L'Amiante* (2008), 93 OR (3d) 338 at para 51 (CA).
81 See *Gemstar Canada Inc v George A Fuller Co*, [2009] OJ No 4878 at para 47 (SCJ).
82 [1998] AC 854 (HL).
83 See *Herceg Novi v Ming Galaxy*, [1998] 4 All ER 238 (CA).
84 See *Westec*, above note 71 at paras 50–55.
85 *The Vishva Ajay*, [1989] 2 Lloyd's Rep 558.
86 Above note 1 at para 112.

court stated that "[j]uridical advantage therefore should not weigh too heavily in the *forum non conveniens* analysis."[87] While these comments indicate a need for caution, they do not preclude continued reliance on juridical advantage considerations in appropriate cases. A court that recognizes a legitimate juridical advantage is not, simply by doing so, improperly favouring the domestic forum and showing a homeward bias. Overall, decisions since *Club Resorts* and *Breeden* have continued to consider juridical advantage in the analysis in much the same way as in earlier cases, though references to the need to respect comity have increased.[88]

7) Other Factors

Courts in the United States have explicitly considered the impact that cases involving non-residents have on the legal system. Non-residents are not paying the taxes that support the local court system, and the cases they bring to a country can strain the pool of available local jurors. These considerations are interesting, but they have not been adopted in English or Canadian law.[89]

In a very small number of cases the plaintiff alleges that regardless of the strength of the factual connections to an alternative forum, it is a foregone conclusion that he or she will be unsuccessful there on the merits.[90] These cases are difficult for courts to handle. Regrettably, there are parts of the world where a person of a particular race, ethnicity, or religion will not receive a fair trial. Political bias is also possible. While a Canadian court would need highly compelling evidence to support such an allegation, in such a case a stay would be inappro-

---

87 Above note 38 at paras 26–27. See also *Prince v ACE Aviation Holdings Inc*, 2014 ONCA 285 at paras 62–66. For a proposal narrowing the scope of juridical advantage, see Ardavan Arzandeh, "Should the *Spiliada* Test Be Revised?" (2014) 10 *Journal of Private International Law* 89.
88 Some decisions have even analyzed comity as a separate factor, but "[c]omity is not a stand-alone factor. It is part and parcel of the *forum non conveniens* assessment in a given case": *James Bay Resources Ltd v Mak Mera Nigeria Ltd*, 2015 ONCA 781 at para 12. See also Black, Pitel, & Sobkin, above note 36 at 212–13.
89 In *Cunningham v Hamilton* (1997), 209 AR 123 at para 28 (CA), the court noted "[w]e can think of no reason for the Alberta Courts to permit their already overtaxed resources to be used for an action that has so little connection to this jurisdiction," but this was more by way of conclusion, based on the traditional factors, than reasoning. See also *Right Business Ltd v Affluent Public Ltd*, 2011 BCSC 783 at para 89, aff'd 2012 BCCA 375.
90 See, for example, *AK Investment CJSC v Kyrgyz Mobile Tel Ltd*, [2011] UKPC 7. See also the cases mentioned in Arzandeh, above note 87 at 94.

priate.⁹¹ Equally challenging are cases where the plaintiff can establish that the alternative forum will apply an applicable law under which he or she will certainly lose. If the Canadian court considers this to be a refusal by the foreign court to apply what it perceives to be the objectively correct applicable law, should it refuse a stay?⁹² In this area the risk of invidious comparisons and judicial chauvinism is high.

F. CONDITIONS AND UNDERTAKINGS

The doctrine of *forum non conveniens* requires courts to choose between possible forums for the resolution of a dispute. On the surface, the choice is a stark one: the court either stays its proceedings or allows them to continue. There is no room for a compromise. But in practice, conditions and undertakings allow the court to reach a compromise on some aspects of a dispute over the best forum for the litigation. These conditions and undertakings increase the flexibility of the result on a stay motion and allow for more creativity.⁹³

On a motion for a stay, either party can give an undertaking to the court. For example, a defendant moving for a stay in favour of litigation in California might undertake, in the proceedings there, not to raise an available limitation defence. In part this is a sacrifice, since one reason for seeking the stay would be to obtain the benefit of the limitation defence in California. But it is a tactical sacrifice, made in an attempt to convince the court to grant the motion. If the defendant thinks this limitation issue will lead the court to deny the stay motion and would prefer California proceedings to those in the forum even without that benefit, then the undertaking makes sense. There are many possible undertakings. Examples for a defendant include not requesting a civil jury trial, agreeing on a particular level of pretrial discovery of documents and information, and agreeing to pay costs if the other party is successful on the merits.

Undertakings can pose a trap for the unwary. The party being offered the undertaking should make sure that it will have the intended effect. For example, a defendant might undertake not to raise a limitation defence. That would be sufficient in a jurisdiction where this is an

---

91 See *Pei v Bank Bumiputra Malaysia Berhad* (1998), 41 OR (3d) 39 (Gen Div); *Somji v Somji* (2001), 292 AR 337 (QB); *Oppenheimer v Louis Rosenthal & Co AG*, [1937] 1 All ER 23.
92 See *Banco Atlantico SA v British Bank of the Middle East*, [1990] 2 Lloyd's Rep 504.
93 See, for a detailed analysis, Vaughan Black, "Conditional *Forum Non Conveniens* in Canadian Courts" (2013) 39 *Queen's Law Journal* 41.

affirmative defence that must be invoked by a defendant but not in a jurisdiction where the court can raise, on its own, such a defence.

Conditions are similar to undertakings, except that rather than being offered by a party they are required by the court as part of the order on the stay motion. In *Spiliada*, Lord Goff indicated that if he had been minded to order a stay of the English action, he would have made the order conditional on the defendants waiving the limitation defence in proceedings in British Columbia.[94] A condition could equally be imposed on the plaintiff, such as one requiring him or her to bear the costs of the more extensive pretrial discovery available in the chosen forum. In either case the party subject to the condition must choose whether to agree or not, and the outcome of the stay motion hinges on that choice.

G. THE DOCTRINE IN PRACTICE: AN EXAMPLE

Several aspects of *forum non conveniens* can be further fleshed out through a study of the efforts of some South African employees to sue the parent company of their local employers in England. In *Lubbe v Cape plc* the defendant was an English corporation involved in the mining and processing of asbestos.[95] It created many subsidiary companies which in turn employed local workers in asbestos mines in South Africa. Many of those employees became ill through exposure to the asbestos and wanted to bring a claim for damages. However, the subsidiary companies had virtually no assets and were effectively judgment-proof. The employees thus focused on suing the English parent company.

In February 1997 five former employees sued Cape in England. Cape moved for a stay on the basis that South Africa was the *forum conveniens*. The Queen's Bench Division granted the motion in January 1998. It held that the key factual connections were with South Africa, where the plaintiffs resided and had worked and where the medical evidence as to their illness and records of their employers' operations were located. It found the only connection to England was the location of the defendant.

The employees appealed and in July 1998 the Court of Appeal held that the stay should not have been granted. It held that the motions judge had failed to appreciate the true nature of the claim against Cape. The plaintiffs were alleging that Cape had failed in its obligations to

---

94 Above note 5 at 484.
95 [2000] 1 WLR 1545 (HL).

ensure that its subsidiaries followed safe working practices. In such a claim, the key decisions were taken in England by Cape and not in South Africa by the subsidiary employers. An important underlying consideration in the court's reasoning is the need to hold multinational enterprises accountable for their global operations in the courts of countries where they are based. It was not unfair for Cape to be sued in the jurisdiction where it chose to maintain its head office.

The Court of Appeal's decision and the House of Lords' refusal of leave to appeal in December 1998 appeared to clear the way for the employees' claims to proceed in England. In their wake more than three thousand more former employees sued Cape there. Cape alleged this was an abuse of process: that the lawyers for the initial five plaintiffs had known of these possible additional claims but had not raised them with the court in the earlier arguments. Cape moved to stay these further claims and in July 1999 the Queen's Bench Division concluded that South Africa was clearly the more appropriate forum for the litigation. With this number of plaintiffs, the factual connections pointed much more strongly there and not to England. The employees appealed on several grounds. First, they presented evidence that they would be unable to afford to litigate these claims in South Africa. They could not obtain legal aid or find lawyers to take the case on a contingency fee basis. Second, they argued that the South African courts lacked the ability to handle the dispute given its size and the scientific evidence involved. The Court of Appeal rejected these arguments in November 1999 and confirmed the stay. Its view of the evidence was that the plaintiffs would in fact be able to fund the litigation in South Africa through legal aid or contingency fees.

The House of Lords granted leave to appeal. It also changed its position and agreed to hear the appeal in the initial action involving the five employees. Both appeals were heard together. In July 2000, the House of Lords refused to stay any of the actions. It acknowledged that the factual connections involved in the case clearly pointed to South Africa as the appropriate forum. The number of plaintiffs involved meant that the personal injury elements of the action—issues involving causation, diagnosis, and prognosis—outweighed the corporate responsibility elements. However, contrary to the views of the Court of Appeal, the House of Lords accepted that the plaintiffs would not obtain legal aid in South Africa and that no lawyers there would handle the case on contingency. The plaintiffs' lack of financial resources meant that a stay would amount to a denial of justice: they would be unable to sue in South Africa. The House of Lords held that it would be unjust to deprive the plaintiffs of the ability to sue in England.

These proceedings show the courts engaged in considering and balancing several of the important factors in the *forum non conveniens* analysis. They also illustrate one of the main concerns about the doctrine, in that it took some three years for the disputing parties to resolve the preliminary question of where the dispute was to be litigated.

H. STATUTORY TRANSFER SCHEME

The statutes on jurisdiction that have been enacted in some provinces go beyond codifying the doctrine of *forum non conveniens*: they also provide a transfer mechanism.[96] At common law, if the courts of one province stay proceedings in favour of another province, the plaintiff is expected to commence proceedings in that other province if none have as yet been commenced. The transfer scheme is designed to avoid repetition of steps already taken before the proceeding was stayed. The scheme applies only between provinces. It requires the court of one province to request that the court in another province accept the transfer and then also requires the requested court to accept the transfer. This process can have important procedural advantages for the plaintiff on the issue of limitation periods.[97]

I. STAY OF PROCEEDINGS IN FAVOUR OF ARBITRATION

Arbitration has been increasing in popularity as an alternative dispute resolution mechanism. It has several advantages over litigation. Arbitration can take place in private rather than in open court. Parties can select an arbitrator with specialized expertise in the relevant area. Arbitrations allow for innovative procedural steps that can increase efficiency. As a result, parties to transnational contracts are frequently choosing to include an arbitration clause in their contract.

If, in the face of an arbitration clause, one party commences litigation, the other party will often seek to enforce the clause by seeking a stay of proceedings in favour of arbitration. This is not done under the doctrine of *forum non conveniens*. The court does not balance the relative merits of arbitration and litigation. The modern approach, spelled

---

96 See, for example, *CJPTA* (BC), above note 8 at ss 13–23. For a detailed analysis of the transfer scheme, see Black, Pitel, & Sobkin, above note 36 at 214–49.
97 *CJPTA* (BC), above note 8, s 23(2).

out in various statutes dealing with arbitration, is that the courts should stay proceedings and give effect to the arbitration clause. This approach has the dual benefit of holding contracting parties to their agreement and promoting arbitration as a way to resolve disputes. It operates in both the wholly domestic context, when litigation is stayed in favour of arbitration in the same forum, and in the cross-border context, when litigation is stayed in favour of arbitration abroad.

For example, the Ontario *International Commercial Arbitration Act* adopts, as part of the law of Ontario, the Model Law on International Commercial Arbitration adopted by the United Nations Commission on International Trade Law on 21 June 1985.[98] The Model Law contains a broad definition of an international commercial arbitration in article 1.[99] Under article 8(1), "A court before which an action is brought in a matter which is the subject of an arbitration agreement shall, if a party so requests not later than when submitting his first statement on the substance of the dispute, refer the parties to arbitration unless it finds that the agreement is null and void, inoperative or incapable of being performed." Canadian courts have indicated that the use of the word "shall" in this provision means that the court does not have discretion: if the provision is triggered the proceedings must be stayed.[100] The courts have also held that the threshold for whether a particular dispute falls within the terms of an arbitration clause is not high—it only needs to be "arguable" that it does for a stay to be required.[101]

An important issue in this context is whether an arbitration clause requires the court to stay a class action. Class actions aim to promote access to justice, especially for consumers, and so concluding that each consumer is required to proceed to arbitration could significantly frustrate that objective. Some provinces have enacted legislation favouring class actions over arbitration clauses in such cases.[102] Even absent specific legislation, courts have favoured consumer access to

---

98 RSO 1990, c I.9. There is similar legislation adopting the Model Law in other provinces.
99 See, however, the interpretation of "commercial" in *Patel v Kanbay International Inc*, [2008] OJ No 5256 at paras 11–13 (CA).
100 See, for example, *BWV Investments Ltd v Saskferco Products Inc* (1994), 119 DLR (4th) 577 (Sask CA).
101 See *Dalimpex*, above note 66 at para 21; *Gulf Canada Resources Ltd v Arochem International Ltd* (1992), 66 BCLR (2d) 113 at paras 39–40 (CA). See also *Dell Computer Corp v Union des consommateurs*, [2007] 2 SCR 801 at para 84; *Donaldson International Livestock Ltd v Znamensky Selekcionno-Gibridny Center LLC* (2008), 305 DLR (4th) 432 (Ont CA).
102 See, for example, *Consumer Protection Act, 2002*, SO 2002, c 30, Sch A, ss 7–8, applied in *Griffin v Dell Canada Inc*, 2010 ONCA 29.

class actions over arbitration clauses.[103] The leading cases involve arbitration clauses mandating a local arbitration, but a similar analysis can be applied to clauses mandating arbitration elsewhere.

FURTHER READINGS

BELL, ANDREW. *Forum Shopping and Venue in Transnational Litigation* (Oxford: Oxford University Press, 2003).

BLACK, VAUGHAN, & JOHN SWAN. "Concurrent Judicial Jurisdiction: A Race to the Court House or to Judgment? *Lloyd's Underwriters v. Cominco Ltd.*" (2008) 46 *Canadian Business Law Journal* 292.

BLOM, JOOST. "Concurrent Judicial Jurisdiction and *Forum Non Conveniens*—What Is to Be Done?" (2009) 47 *Canadian Business Law Journal* 166.

BRIGGS, ADRIAN. "The Subtle Variety of Jurisdiction Agreements" [2012] *Lloyd's Maritime and Law Quarterly* 364.

BRIGGS, ADRIAN. *Agreements on Jurisdiction and Choice of Law* (Oxford: Oxford University Press, 2008).

EDINGER, ELIZABETH. "The Problem of Parallel Actions: The Softer Alternative" (2010) 60 *University of New Brunswick Law Journal* 116.

FAWCETT, JJ. *Declining Jurisdiction in Private International Law* (Oxford: Oxford University Press, 1995).

HAYES, ELLEN L. "*Forum Non Conveniens* in England, Australia and Japan: The Allocation of Jurisdiction in Transnational Litigation" (1992) 26 *University of British Columbia Law Review* 41.

HILL, JONATHAN. "Jurisdiction in Civil and Commercial Matters: Is There a Third Way?" (2001) 54 *Current Legal Problems* 439.

MERRETT, LOUISE. "Uncertainties in the First Limb of the *Spiliada* Test" (2005) 54 *International and Comparative Law Quarterly* 211.

MICHELL, PAUL. "Forum Selection after *Z.I. Pompey Industrie v. ECU-Line N.V., The Canmar Fortune*" (2003) 39 *Canadian Business Law Journal* 262.

NWAPI, CHILENYE. "Re-evaluating the Doctrine of *Forum Non Conveniens* in Canada" (2013) 34 *Windsor Review of Legal and Social Issues* 59.

---

103 See *Seidel v TELUS Communications Inc*, 2011 SCC 15.

Parrish, Austen L. "Comity and Parallel Foreign Proceedings: A Reply to Black and Swan, *Lloyd's Underwriters v. Cominco Ltd.*" (2009) 47 *Canadian Business Law Journal* 209.

Robertson, DW. "*Forum Non Conveniens* in America and England: 'A Rather Fantastic Fiction'" (1987) 103 *Law Quarterly Review* 398.

Saumier, Genevieve. "Judicial Jurisdiction in International Cases: The Supreme Court's Unfinished Business" (1995) 18 *Dalhousie Law Journal* 447.

Walker, Janet. "Parallel Proceedings—Converging Views: The *Westec* Appeal" (2000) 38 *Canadian Yearbook of International Law* 155.

Walker, Janet. "*Teck Cominco* and the Wisdom of Deferring to the Court First Seised, All Things Being Equal" (2009) 47 *Canadian Business Law Journal* 192.

CHAPTER 7

ANTI-SUIT INJUNCTIONS

A. INTRODUCTION

In *Amchem Products Inc v British Columbia (Workers' Compensation Board)*,[1] Sopinka J noted that the courts had developed two remedies to control the choice of forum by the parties. The first remedy is a stay of the local proceedings on the ground of *forum non conveniens*.[2] The second remedy is an anti-suit injunction from the local courts which purports to restrain proceedings launched or threatened abroad. Justice Sopinka described such an injunction as a "more aggressive remedy, which [might] be granted by the domestic court at the request of a defendant or defendants . . . in a foreign suit."[3] He continued:

> In the usual situation the plaintiff in the domestic court moves to restrain the defendant or defendants from launching or continuing a proceeding in the courts of another jurisdiction. Occasionally . . . the defendants in a foreign jurisdiction who allege that the plaintiff in that jurisdiction has selected an inappropriate forum seek an injunction from the courts of the alleged appropriate forum, in which no proceeding is pending, to restrain continuation of the foreign proceedings.[4]

---

1 [1993] 1 SCR 897 [*Amchem*].
2 See Chapter 6.
3 *Amchem*, above note 1 at 912.
4 *Ibid* at 912–13.

Justice Sopinka emphasized that the injunction did not operate directly on the foreign court but rather *in personam* on the foreign plaintiff. It was, therefore, essential that the foreign plaintiff be subject to the jurisdiction of the issuing court.[5] Despite the fact that the injunction was not directed at the foreign court, it did constitute an indirect attack on the foreign proceedings and, therefore, its issuance "raise[d] serious issues of comity."[6] Justice Sopinka said that a case could be made for the view that anti-suit injunctions should be restricted to those situations in which it was necessary to protect the jurisdiction of the issuing court or to prevent the evasion of some important public policy.[7] In his view, a court should entertain an application for an anti-suit injunction only where "a serious injustice [would] be occasioned as the result of the failure of a foreign court to decline jurisdiction."[8]

The question of whether to issue an anti-suit injunction typically arises in what are described as "alternative forum" cases. In these cases, a choice has to be made between the domestic forum, which is alleged to be the natural forum for the action, and the proposed foreign forum. Occasionally, however, the question of whether to grant an injunction may arise in a "single forum" case in which an attempt is made "to restrain a party from proceeding in a foreign court which alone has jurisdiction over the relevant dispute."[9] In such cases, the English courts have indicated that the relevant question to be addressed is whether, in all the circumstances, the foreign proceedings are unconscionable and unjust.[10]

In *Airbus Industrie GIE v Patel*,[11] Lord Goff suggested that, as a general rule, before an anti-suit injunction could properly be granted, comity required that the domestic forum have a sufficient interest in the matter so as to justify the indirect interference with the foreign court. In an alternative forum case, that interest was provided by the fact that

---

5   In *Hudon v Geos Language Corp* (1997), 34 OR (3d) 14 (Div Ct) [*Hudon*], which is discussed in detail below in Section C(1), the jurisdiction of the Ontario court to issue an injunction seems to have been based solely on the foreign plaintiff's participation in the domestic litigation because it was a Japanese corporation with no obvious presence in Ontario.
6   *Amchem*, above note 1 at 913.
7   *Ibid* at 914.
8   *Ibid*.
9   *Airbus Industrie GIE v Patel*, [1998] 2 All ER 257 at 265 (HL), Lord Goff [*Airbus*]. See Lawrence Collins, ed, *Dicey, Morris and Collins on the Conflict of Laws*, 14th ed (London: Sweet & Maxwell, 2006) at para 12-077.
10 See, generally, *British Airways Board v Laker Airways Ltd*, [1985] AC 58 (HL); *Midland Bank Plc v Laker Airways Ltd*, [1986] QB 689 (CA).
11 Above note 9.

the domestic forum was the natural forum for the action. In a single forum case, the court would have to consider the extent to which the relevant transactions were connected to the domestic forum or the extent to which the injunction was required to protect the policies of the domestic forum.[12]

B. THE ENGLISH APPROACH

Originally, the test for granting an anti-suit injunction mirrored the test for determining whether to stay local proceedings on the ground of *forum non conveniens*. Thus in *Castanho v Brown and Root (UK) Ltd*, Lord Scarman stated explicitly that the criteria governing the exercise of the court's discretion were the same "whether the remedy sought [was] a stay of English proceedings or a restraint on foreign proceedings."[13] However, because an anti-suit injunction is a more intrusive remedy than a stay of proceedings, this was too aggressive an approach. Accordingly, the link between the two situations was broken by the Privy Council's judgment in *Société Nationale Industrielle Aérospatiale v Lee Kui Jak*.[14] In that case, Lord Goff indicated that a party should be restrained from pursuing proceedings in a foreign court only where the ends of justice required such restraint because the pursuit would be "vexatious or oppressive."[15] He continued:

> This presupposes that, as a general rule, the English ... court must conclude that it provides the natural forum for the trial of the action, and further, since the court is concerned with the ends of justice, that account must be taken not only of injustice to the defendant if the plaintiff is allowed to pursue the foreign proceedings, but also of injustice to the plaintiff if he is not allowed to do so. So, as a general rule, the court will not grant an injunction if, by doing so, it will deprive the plaintiff of advantages in the foreign forum of which it would be unjust to deprive him.[16]

Lord Goff also made it clear that, as with the granting of a stay of domestic proceedings, it was within the court's discretion to grant

---

12   Ibid at 269.
13   [1981] AC 557 at 574 (HL).
14   [1987] AC 871 (PC) [*SNIA*].
15   Ibid at 896.
16   Ibid. See also *Star Reefers Pool Inc v JFC Group Co Ltd*, [2012] EWCA Civ 14 at paras 25–27 [*Star Reefers*]; *Tadros v Barratt*, [2014] EWHC 2860 at paras 43–45 (Ch).

an injunction on terms. Indeed, potential problems could be avoided by undertakings given by the foreign defendant to undermine the supposed advantages to the plaintiff of the foreign forum. In *SNIA* itself, for example, the defendant in the foreign (Texas) proceedings gave various assurances to the court to the effect that such evidence as had been obtained under the broad discovery process in Texas would be available in the local proceedings, that every effort would be made to ensure that the plaintiff's Texas lawyers would be allowed to argue the case in the local forum, and that the defendant would co-operate in obtaining an early trial date. These undertakings effectively neutralized many of the alleged advantages to the plaintiff of suing in Texas. The Privy Council granted the anti-suit injunction on the terms of the defendant's undertakings.

While the vexatious or oppressive basis is the leading one for an anti-suit injunction, two other bases can be identified. One is the violation of a legal right to be sued in a particular forum, such as under an exclusive jurisdiction agreement. That basis is discussed later in this chapter. A second, more specialized basis operates in insolvency proceedings. An anti-suit injunction can issue to prevent a party, through litigation elsewhere, from undermining the forum's statutory scheme of priorities and distribution. This does not require showing that the foreign proceedings are vexatious or oppressive. As recently noted by the Privy Council, "the court has an equitable jurisdiction to restrain the acts of persons amenable to the court's jurisdiction . . . calculated to violate the statutory scheme of distribution."[17]

C. THE CANADIAN APPROACH

The leading Canadian decision on the anti-suit injunction is *Amchem*.[18] A group of asbestos manufacture and supply companies sought an anti-suit injunction from the British Columbia courts to prevent the plaintiffs from suing them in Texas in tort. Most of the plaintiffs were British Columbia residents and had been at the time that they sustained their injuries. The alleged tortious conduct took place in the United States. None of the companies had any connection with British Columbia. Most of the companies were incorporated and had their principal place of business and manufacture in the United States, though there was no

---

17 *Stichting Shell Pensioenfonds v Krys*, [2014] UKPC 41 at para 18, relying on *Carron Iron Co Proprietors v Maclaren* (1855), 5 HLC 415. See also paras 24–25.
18 Above note 1.

concentration in a single state. None of the companies was incorporated in Texas although most did carry on business there. A majority of the companies had sought a stay of the Texas action on the ground of *forum non conveniens*. The Texas court had dismissed that motion without reasons, though seemingly on the basis that Texas had abolished the doctrine.

Surprisingly, the British Columbia courts[19] exercised their discretion by granting the injunction on the terms, *inter alia*, that the companies would attorn to the jurisdiction of the British Columbia courts should the plaintiffs launch a fresh action in that province. In a unanimous judgment by Sopinka J, the Supreme Court of Canada allowed the plaintiffs' appeal and dismissed the application for an injunction.

Before delving into the specific principles relating to anti-suit injunctions, Sopinka J made several general points with respect to choice of forum in modern litigation. He pointed out that the business of litigation was increasingly becoming international. As a result, often it could not be said that any single forum was clearly more appropriate than any other. Rather, there were various appropriate forums and the best that could be achieved by the courts was the selection of an appropriate forum. In that endeavour, there were two potential remedies available to control a party's choice of forum: the stay of a domestic action or the restraint of foreign proceedings by injunction.

Justice Sopinka stressed that the injunction operated *in personam* on the foreign plaintiff and not directly on the foreign court. Nevertheless, it raised serious issues of comity because the court granting the injunction was effectively determining for the foreign court the appropriateness of the foreign forum. Justice Sopinka indicated that in a perfect world where comity was universally respected, courts would not have to resort to extraordinary remedies like the anti-suit injunction. They would be able to rely on a foreign court's staying the proceedings where it was an inappropriate forum. He also pointed out that there would be occasions where both jurisdictions might justifiably refuse to decline jurisdiction because no one forum was clearly more appropriate than another. The result might be the institution of parallel proceedings which, in itself, would not be disastrous. At present, however, comity was not universally respected. The granting of an anti-suit injunction could therefore be justified where a foreign court had breached the basic requirements of *forum non conveniens* and a serious injustice would ensue from that breach.

---

19   *Amchem Products Inc v British Columbia (Workers' Compensation Board)* (1989), 42 BCLR (2d) 77 (SC), aff'd (1990), 50 BCLR (2d) 218 (CA).

On the issue of timing, Sopinka J held that there was no requirement that alternative proceedings had to have been started in the domestic forum. However, the exceptional nature of the remedy and respect for comity demanded that, ordinarily, such relief should not be granted until the foreign proceedings had been started and the applicant had sought a stay of those proceedings and had been unsuccessful.

On the test for the injunction, Sopinka J drew on, but also varied, the analysis used by Lord Goff in *SNIA*.[20] It was important to consider the first part of the *SNIA* test, namely whether the domestic forum was the natural forum for the trial of the action. Moreover, to justify an injunction, a key question to be addressed was whether the foreign court could reasonably have concluded, in accordance with principles of *forum non conveniens*, that there was no alternative forum that was clearly more appropriate. If it could, then its assumption of jurisdiction should not be pre-empted by the issuance of an injunction. It did not matter, however, whether the foreign court had applied the doctrine of *forum non conveniens*. The question was whether the result was consistent with that doctrine. This aspect of the test, having regard for the foreign court's assessment, was not an aspect of the *SNIA* analysis.

If the court concluded that the foreign court's assumption of jurisdiction was inconsistent with principles of *forum non conveniens*, then it had to address the second part of the test from *SNIA*. The injunction would be granted only if the continuation of the foreign proceedings would lead to serious injustice. Thus, the court had to determine whether the restraint of the foreign action would deprive the foreign plaintiff of some personal or juridical advantage available in that forum that it would be unjust to deny that plaintiff having regard to the extent that the plaintiff and the facts were connected to the foreign forum. Of course, "[a]ny loss of advantage to the foreign plaintiff must be weighed against the loss of advantage, if any, to the defendant in the foreign jurisdiction if the action [were] tried there rather than in the domestic forum."[21] Justice Sopinka did, however, reject Lord Goff's view in *SNIA* that the foreign proceedings must be vexatious or oppressive. He thought that those words could not be satisfactorily defined and that the concept of injustice to the foreign defendant was sufficient to introduce some flexibility into the process.[22] Justice Sopinka summarized his version of the applicable principles in the following manner:

---

20   Above note 14.
21   *Amchem*, above note 1 at 933.
22   *Ibid* at 932.

The result of the application of these principles is that when a foreign court assumes jurisdiction on a basis that generally conforms to our rule of private international law relating to the *forum non conveniens*, that decision will be respected and a Canadian court will not purport to make the decision for the foreign court. The policy of our courts with respect to comity demands no less. If, however, a foreign court assumes jurisdiction on a basis that is inconsistent with our rules of private international law and an injustice results to a litigant or "would-be" litigant in our courts, then the assumption of jurisdiction is inequitable and the party invoking the foreign jurisdiction can be restrained. The foreign court, not having, itself, observed the rules of comity, cannot expect its decision to be respected on the basis of comity.[23]

In applying these principles, the Supreme Court of Canada held that no injunction should be granted. First, Texas could reasonably have concluded that there was no alternative forum that was clearly more appropriate than Texas. All of the asbestos companies had some connection with Texas and they had no connection with British Columbia. Further, the claim was based on acts that had taken place outside British Columbia and in the United States. The fact that Texas did not apply *forum non conveniens* principles, even if true, was irrelevant because its assumption of jurisdiction was consistent with those principles.

Second, in any event, the companies had failed to establish that the continuation of the Texas proceedings would cause them injustice by depriving them of legitimate personal or juridical advantages. In the British Columbia Supreme Court,[24] Esson CJ had suggested injustice by characterizing the action of the Texas court as oppressive because of its failure to apply the doctrine of *forum non conveniens*. Justice Sopinka, however, stressed that the test, no longer one of oppression and comity, required only that the foreign court's decision be consistent with the *forum non conveniens* doctrine.

Despite Sopinka J's modifications of the *SNIA* test, his judgment has been approved in some later English decisions. In *OT Africa Line Ltd v Magic Sportswear Corp*,[25] for example, Lord Justice Longmore said:

[I]f the issue is one of *forum non conveniens* and a foreign court applies rules of private international law generally conforming to English

---

23 *Ibid* at 934.
24 Above note 19.
25 [2005] 2 Lloyd's Rep 170 (CA) [*OT Africa*].

rules of *forum non conveniens* and decides that its own court should retain jurisdiction, that decision will usually be respected.[26]

Indeed, it can be argued that the Canadian approach is more sensitive to comity concerns than the orthodox English test, since it emphasizes a willingness to defer to the foreign court's assessment of the propriety of the proceedings before it.

In the jurisprudence applying *Amchem*, courts have differed somewhat in their organization of the analysis. The approach has been said to have as few as two and as many as five steps. The most common structure is to consider the foreign court's assumption and exercise of jurisdiction first, then to consider whether the domestic forum is the natural forum for the litigation, and finally to consider the injustice involved in allowing the foreign proceedings to continue. The following sections consider specific elements of the analysis in more detail.

1) Assessing the Foreign Court's Analysis

As explained above, the first part of the test for an anti-suit injunction considers the foreign court's assessment of the proceedings before it. If the continuation of the foreign proceedings accords with our sense of taking and exercising jurisdiction then our courts will not issue an injunction.[27] On some occasions, Canadian courts appear to have misunderstood this point. For example, in *Hudon v Geos Language Corp* the plaintiff had been employed by the defendant to teach English in Japan.[28] During a break in her teaching duties, she took a short vacation to China where she was seriously injured in a motor vehicle accident. By virtue of her employment contract, the plaintiff had the benefit of not overly generous insurance coverage. She launched an action in Ontario for both breach of contract and in tort against her employer. Ontario was her place of residence, the place where she received the bulk of her medical treatment, and the place where the employment contract was made. She claimed that it was an implied term of her employment contract that the defendant would provide complete health, disability, and accident coverage. Alternatively, she claimed that the defendant had misrepresented the scope of the coverage that would be provided for her. The contract contained a provision that it was to be governed by the law of Japan.

Initially, the defendant had sought a stay of the Ontario proceedings on the ground of *forum non conveniens*. Ultimately, the court re-

---

26 *Ibid* at para 25. See also *Airbus*, above note 9 at 269, Lord Goff.
27 See, for example, *Armoyan v Armoyan*, 2013 NSCA 99 at para 197.
28 Above note 5.

jected that motion. In the interim, the defendant instituted an action in Japan against the plaintiff in which it sought a declaration that it was under no liability to her. The plaintiff obtained an order from the Ontario courts granting her an injunction restraining the defendant from proceeding with its action in Japan. The defendant appealed that order to the Ontario Divisional Court and so the question was whether the injunction was justified on the basis of the test from *Amchem*.

In *Amchem*, Sopinka J had made it clear that, as a matter of comity, the domestic court had to take cognizance of the fact that the foreign court had assumed jurisdiction. Therefore, the first branch of the test required the domestic court to determine whether the foreign court could reasonably have concluded that there was no clearly more appropriate alternative forum. If it could have so concluded, then there was no basis for interfering with the foreign court's assumption of jurisdiction because "the courts of this country should not arrogate to themselves the decision for both jurisdictions."[29]

The court in *Hudon* seemed to overlook that point. Instead, Southey J indicated that it was sufficient to clear the first leg of the *Amchem* test that Ontario was an appropriate forum. He said:

> Although Japan might be an appropriate forum, as recognized by Corbett J. [who granted the anti-suit injunction], it has been settled between the parties by the decision of German J. [who refused to stay the Ontario proceedings] that Ontario is an appropriate forum.[30]

Indeed, Corbett J had stated that she was prepared to assume that Japan might "well be an appropriate forum having regard to, *inter alia*, the law of Japan applying to the contract and the employment being in Japan."[31] On that basis, it is difficult to see how the first leg of the *Amchem* test was satisfied. Undoubtedly, a significant factor in Southey J's decision was the fact that the Ontario courts had already denied a stay of the Ontario action on *forum non conveniens* grounds.

Hudon was applied by Nordheimer J in *Bell'O International LCC v Flooring and Lumber Co.*[32] He granted an anti-suit injunction to restrain the plaintiff from proceeding with an action in New Jersey. Again, the court made no mention of the requirement that the domestic court must be satisfied that the foreign court could not reasonably have concluded that there was no other clearly more appropriate forum. Instead, Nordheimer J intimated that it was sufficient that there was no other

---

29 Above note 1 at 932.
30 Above note 5 at 23.
31 Her reasons are quoted by Southey J, *ibid* at 20.
32 [2001] OJ No 1871 (SCJ) [*Bell'O*].

forum clearly more appropriate than the domestic forum, Ontario. Undoubtedly in granting the injunction the court was heavily influenced by the fact that the plaintiff had originally chosen to commence its action in Ontario. It had brought an action in New Jersey against the same defendant for the same claim only after the Ontario courts had rejected the plaintiff's request for interlocutory injunctive relief.

Given that this part of the test looks at the foreign court's handling of the proceedings before it, obtaining an anti-suit injunction in respect of foreign proceedings that have not yet been started should be quite rare.[33] In such a case, presumably the court would have to form some conclusion as to how the foreign court would analyze the issue of its own jurisdiction.

2) Need to Seek Stay of Foreign Proceedings

In *Amchem*, Sopinka J had stressed the importance of ensuring that the foreign court be given the opportunity to decide for itself whether or not to assume jurisdiction over the dispute. Thus, ordinarily an application for an anti-suit injunction should not be entertained until "a proceeding ha[d] been launched in [the foreign] court and the applicant for an injunction in the domestic court ha[d] sought from the foreign court a stay or other termination of the foreign proceedings and failed."[34]

Interestingly, in both *Hudon*[35] and *Bell'O*[36] the court granted an injunction despite the fact that no stay had been sought of the foreign proceedings. In *Hudon*, Southey J emphasized that Sopinka J in *Amchem* had stated only that it was preferable that the applicant first seek a stay of the foreign proceedings: "He did not say that such proceedings in the foreign jurisdiction were a condition precedent."[37] In *Bell'O*, Nordheimer J accepted the defendant's contention that it would have been prohibitively expensive for it to have retained and briefed lawyers in the United States in order to bring an application to stay the New Jersey proceedings. The defendant was already incurring considerable expenses in defending the plaintiff's original action that had been instituted in Ontario.

In *Elga Laboratories Ltd v Soroko Inc*,[38] however, Hoy J underlined the point that only in rare circumstances should a court grant an anti-suit

---

33 See, for example, the comments in *Veritas Investment Research Corp v Indiabulls Real Estate Ltd*, 2015 ONSC 6040 at paras 47–48 [*Veritas Investment*].
34 Above note 1 at 931. See also *Veritas Investment*, above note 33 at para 49.
35 Above note 5.
36 Above note 32.
37 Above note 5 at 21.
38 (2002), 61 OR (3d) 324 (SCJ).

injunction before the applicant had sought a stay from the foreign court. Elga Laboratories was an Ontario corporation that manufactured a cosmetic product in Ontario. Soroko, a New Jersey company, took delivery of the product in Ontario. The product, which was sold in New Jersey, was recalled because of bacterial contamination. Soroko brought an action in New Jersey against Elga Laboratories and others in negligence and for breach of contract. Elga Laboratories and others applied in Ontario for an anti-suit injunction to restrain Soroko from proceeding with its action in New Jersey. Justice Hoy dismissed the application for an injunction, saying that there was no justification for granting "a restraining order over residents of New Jersey without first giving the courts of New Jersey the opportunity to pass on the issue of whether they should assume jurisdiction."[39]

Justice Hoy did support the decisions reached in both *Hudon* and *Bell'O*. She regarded the facts in *Hudon* as unique because "a stay motion had previously been brought unsuccessfully in Ontario by the foreign party against which the anti-suit injunction was sought."[40] Equally, Hoy J determined that *Bell'O* was something of a special case because the plaintiff had first sued the defendant in Ontario. It then brought a similar action against the defendant in New Jersey in which it sought the same relief after the Ontario court had refused to grant an interlocutory injunction. Justice Hoy seemed to agree with Nordheimer J's view that the plaintiff's original decision to sue in Ontario warranted the "pre-emptive jurisdictional intrusion in order to restrain the plaintiffs from continuing another proceeding, the commencement of which ha[d] all the appearances of 'forum shopping.'"[41]

The most recent decisions continue to reflect tension on this issue. Some have held that a stay must first be sought in the foreign court.[42] Others have held that while preferable, it is not required.[43]

3) Inappropriate Domestic Jurisdiction

In *Amchem*, Sopinka J made it clear that if no action had been commenced in the domestic forum, then that forum had no juridical basis for entertaining an application for an anti-suit injunction unless the applicant argued that the action should have been commenced in the do-

---

39 Ibid at para 8.
40 Ibid at para 7.
41 Bell'O, above note 32 at para 20.
42 McMillan v McMillan, 2012 BCSC 32 at para 17.
43 Canadian Imperial Bank of Commerce v Glasford, 2015 ONSC 197 at para 39, aff'd 2015 ONCA 523.

mestic forum as the most appropriate place for the trial. At a minimum, it had to be an appropriate forum.[44] In *Airbus*,[45] the House of Lords had to face the problem of what was to be done when the domestic forum was not an appropriate forum. The case arose from an airplane crash in India. Some of the passengers aboard were British citizens with homes in London. They or their personal representatives launched an action against various parties in India. Subsequently they commenced another action in Texas in which the primary defendant was Airbus, the designer and manufacturer of the aircraft. At Airbus's behest, the Indian courts issued an injunction to restrain the passengers from proceeding with the action in Texas. The passengers ignored the Indian order, which they could do safely because they were resident in England. Airbus instituted an action in England seeking enforcement of the Indian injunction or, instead, an English anti-suit injunction. The trial judge refused to enforce the Indian order, and Airbus did not appeal on that question. Lord Goff clearly stated the issue before the House of Lords:

> [T]he first and crucial question which arises in the present case is whether the English court will grant an anti-suit injunction in circumstances where there is no relevant connection between the English jurisdiction and the proceedings in question other than that the defendants, who are resident in this country, are subject to the jurisdiction and so can effectively be restrained by an injunction granted by an English court.[46]

Lord Goff determined that comity required that the domestic forum have a sufficient interest in the case to justify the interference with the foreign court through the issuance of an anti-suit injunction. In an alternative forum case, comity demanded that, as a general rule, the domestic forum be the natural forum for the trial of the action. On this basis, the House of Lords rejected Airbus' application for an injunction. Lord Goff said:

> In a world which consists of independent jurisdictions, interference, even indirect interference, by the courts of one jurisdiction with the exercise of the jurisdiction of a foreign court cannot in my opinion be justified by the fact that a third jurisdiction is affected but is powerless to intervene. The basic principle is that only the courts of an interested jurisdiction can act in the matter; and if they are powerless to

---

44 Above note 1 at 931.
45 Above note 9.
46 *Ibid* at 264–65.

do so, that will not of itself be enough to justify the courts of another jurisdiction to act in their place. Such are the limits of a system which is dependent on the remedy of an anti-suit injunction to curtail the excesses of a jurisdiction which does not adopt the principle, widely accepted throughout the common law world, of *forum non conveniens*.[47]

Lord Goff indicated[48] that the normal way for the English court to come to the assistance of the Indian court would be through enforcement of the Indian judgment. Traditionally, such a course of action would have been impossible because only foreign monetary judgments could be enforced. The decision of the Supreme Court of Canada in *Pro Swing Inc v Elta Golf Inc*[49] has opened up the possibility of enforcing foreign non-monetary judgments. The question therefore is whether the reasoning in *Pro Swing* can incorporate the enforcement of a foreign anti-suit injunction.[50]

4) Interprovincial Anti-Suit Injunctions

The majority of the cases dealing with anti-suit injunctions involved an application to restrain a party from bringing proceedings in a foreign country. There are few cases in which the applicant is seeking an injunction to prevent a party from suing elsewhere in Canada. In one such case, *Gentra Canada Investments Inc v Lehndorff United Properties (Canada)*,[51] Lefsrud J determined that the same *Amchem* test was applicable where the "foreign" jurisdiction involved was another Canadian province. He did intimate, however, that in light of the basic similarity between the courts of different provinces, the issuance of an injunction was likely to be rarer. He said:

> [H]aving regard to the foundation on which Canadian laws, certainly those in Provinces such as Ontario and Alberta, are based, and having regard to the fact that the Supreme Court of Canada is the Court of final resort for appeals emanating from Provincial Courts, coupled with the fact that judges of the Superior Courts in each Canadian Province are appointed by the Government of Canada, I find it

---

47 *Ibid* at 270–71.
48 *Ibid* at 270.
49 [2006] 2 SCR 612 [*Pro Swing*]. See Chapter 8.
50 Doubts are expressed in Janet Walker, *Castel & Walker: Canadian Conflict of Laws*, 6th ed (Markham, ON: Butterworths, 2005) (loose-leaf) at para 13.4: "lending assistance of this sort would be far from straightforward as it would amount to the recognition and enforcement of an interim measure from the court of the natural forum."
51 (1995), 31 Alta LR (3d) 322 (QB), aff'd (1995), 34 Alta LR (3d) 360 (CA).

difficult in the true sense to categorize the Ontario Courts as foreign Courts.[52]

Nevertheless, Lefsrud J issued an injunction to restrain the defendants in an Alberta action from suing in Ontario. The Alberta Court of Appeal upheld his decision despite the fact that the Ontario courts had rejected the applicant's motion for a stay of the Ontario proceedings pending the resolution of the Alberta action. The Ontario judge's decision was characterized as "unreasonable."[53]

D. ANTI-SUIT INJUNCTIONS IN FURTHERANCE OF EXCLUSIVE JURISDICTION AND ARBITRATION CLAUSES

The English courts have shown a readiness to grant an anti-suit injunction to prevent a party from suing abroad in breach of an agreement that all disputes are to be referred to the jurisdiction of the English courts. Thus, in *Donohue v Armco Inc*,[54] Lord Bingham, in accordance with the principles governing the stay of an English action brought in defiance of an exclusive jurisdiction clause, determined that an injunction should be granted in the absence of strong reasons as to why the foreign action should proceed. He said:

> If contracting parties agree to give a particular court exclusive jurisdiction to rule on claims between those parties, and a claim falling within the scope of the agreement is made in proceedings in a forum other than that which the parties have agreed, the English court will ordinarily exercise its discretion (whether by granting a stay of proceedings in England, or by restraining the prosecution of proceedings in the non-contractual forum abroad, or by such other procedural order as is appropriate in the circumstances) to secure compliance with the contractual bargain, unless the party suing in the non-contractual forum (the burden being on him) can show strong reasons for suing in that forum.[55]

---

52 *Ibid* at para 42 (QB). See also *Speers Estate v Reader's Digest Association (Canada) ULC*, 2009 CanLII 28404 at paras 45–46 (Ont SCJ).
53 *Ibid* at para 5 (CA).
54 [2002] 1 All ER 749 (HL).
55 *Ibid* at para 24. See also *Star Reefers*, above note 16 at para 25; *Impala Warehousing and Logistics (Shanghai) Co Ltd v Wanxiang Resources (Singapore) PTE Ltd*, [2015] EWHC 811 at paras 108–11 (Comm).

In *OT Africa*,⁵⁶ the English Court of Appeal indicated that comity had a smaller role to play when the court was dealing with the issuance of an injunction in support of an exclusive jurisdiction clause. Lord Justice Longmore stated:

> Whatever country it is to the courts of which the parties have agreed to submit their disputes is the country to which comity is due. It is not a matter of an English court seeking to uphold and enforce references to its own courts; an English court will uphold and enforce references to the courts of whichever country the parties agree for the resolution of their disputes. This is to uphold party autonomy not to uphold the courts of any particular country.⁵⁷

In *OT Africa* the Court of Appeal upheld an anti-suit injunction to restrain proceedings being brought in Canada in respect of a contract of carriage governed by English law which provided that England had exclusive jurisdiction over the dispute. The case was complicated by the fact that in 2001 Canada had enacted section 46(1) of the *Marine Liability Act*.⁵⁸ The purpose of that provision was to deal with the prevalence of choice of exclusive forum clauses in contracts for the carriage of goods by sea. It was designed to alleviate the position of Canadian shippers who were otherwise forced to incur the high cost and inconvenience of litigating claims for loss of cargo in a foreign forum. The section allowed a plaintiff to institute proceedings in Canada, despite the presence of a choice of foreign forum clause, where the port of loading or discharge was in Canada, the defendant resided or had a place of business in Canada, or the contract was made in Canada. In *OT Africa*, the defendant had a place of business in Canada and the contract was made there. The Court of Appeal made it clear, however, that, in the absence of an exceptional provision like section 46(1), Canadian courts would typically stay actions brought in defiance of an exclusive jurisdiction clause in the absence of strong cause to the contrary.⁵⁹

Interestingly, the Federal Court of Appeal,⁶⁰ despite section 46(1) of the *Marine Liability Act*, eventually stayed the Canadian proceedings on general *forum non conveniens* grounds. In the course of giving judgment for the court, Evans JA said that, were it not for section 46(1), a Canadian court would typically have reached the same conclusion as

---

56 Above note 25.
57 *Ibid* at para 32.
58 SC 2001, c 6.
59 The leading decision is *ZI Pompey Industrie v ECU-Line NV*, [2003] 1 SCR 450, which is discussed in Chapter 6.
60 *Magic Sportswear Corp v OT Africa Line Ltd*, [2007] 2 FCR 733 (CA).

the English court when it decided to grant the anti-suit injunction. He continued:

> That is, if the applicable law of the contract had been Canadian, a court in Canada would, in the absence of strong reasons, have given effect to a clause in the contract specifying a court in Canada as the exclusive forum, in the interests of commercial certainty and on the basis of party autonomy in determining the terms of the contract . . . .[61]

For this proposition, he cited the Supreme Court of Canada's decisions in *Amchem* and *ZI Pompey Industrie v ECU-Line NV*.[62]

It is important to appreciate that these cases involve exclusive jurisdiction clauses, which can be said to give a party a legal right to be sued in a particular forum. If in contrast the clause is non-exclusive, a party cannot be said to have a right to be sued in that forum, merely a right to sue in that forum. So an anti-suit injunction in respect of a non-exclusive jurisdiction clause would have to be based on the *SNIA* test.[63]

The English courts have also been willing to grant an anti-suit injunction to ensure that the parties abide by their agreement to submit disputes to an English arbitration. In *Aggeliki Charis Compania Martima SA v Pagnan SpA, The Angelic Grace*,[64] for example, Millett LJ said that he saw "no difference in principle between an injunction to restrain proceedings in breach of an arbitration clause and one to restrain proceedings in breach of an exclusive jurisdiction clause."[65] Moreover, in both cases there was "no good reason for diffidence in granting an injunction to restrain foreign proceedings on the clear and simple ground that the defendant ha[d] promised not to bring them."[66]

One of the few Canadian authorities on point is *Lincoln-General Insurance Co v Insurance Corp of British Columbia*.[67] The Ontario courts granted an anti-suit injunction to prevent a party from suing in British Columbia in breach of an agreement to arbitrate. The applicant had argued that the *Amchem* test was inapplicable because the issue

---

61 *Ibid* at para 75.
62 Above notes 1 and 59 respectively.
63 See *Highland Crusader Offshore Partners LP v Deutsche Bank AG*, [2009] EWCA Civ 725.
64 [1995] 1 Lloyd's Rep 87 (CA) [*The Angelic Grace*].
65 *Ibid* at 96. See also *Ust-Kamenogorsk Hydropower Plant JSC v AES Ust-Kamenogorsk Hydropower Plant LLP*, [2013] UKSC 35.
66 *The Angelic Grace*, above note 64. A further variant is an anti-arbitration injunction, brought to stop arbitral proceedings abroad in violation of an agreement to litigate or arbitrate in the forum: *Claxton Engineering Services Ltd v TXM Olaj-Es Gazkutato KTF*, [2011] EWHC 345 (Comm).
67 [2001] OJ No 1903 (SCJ), aff'd [2002] OJ No 2059 (CA).

was simply "one of enforcement of the provisions of an agreement to arbitrate, and as such, the *forum non conveniens* principles of *Amchem* [were] not relevant."[68] Justice Croll seemed to accept this argument and to issue the injunction on the basis that the question was one "of the enforcement of arbitration provisions."[69] Nevertheless, she also applied the *Amchem* test and found that "an injunction [was] the appropriate remedy on the basis of the *forum non conveniens* test and a consideration of juridical advantage."[70] In the Court of Appeal, Abella JA simply observed that Croll J's conclusion that an injunction was warranted was, "in the circumstances of this case, fully justified."[71]

FURTHER READINGS

BLACK, VAUGHAN. "The Standard for Issuing Antisuit Injunctions" (1991) 44 *Carswell's Practice Cases (Second Series)* 30.

CASTEL, MATTHEW. "Anti-Foreign Suit Injunctions in Common Law Canada and Quebec Revisited" (2012) 40 *Advocates' Quarterly* 195.

EDINGER, ELIZABETH R. "Conflict of Laws—Jurisdiction—British Columbia Residents Bringing Action for Damages in Texas against Non British Columbia Resident Defendants—Defendants Seeking Anti-Suit Injunction in British Columbia: *Amchem Products v. Workers' Compensation Board*" (1992) 71 *Canadian Bar Review* 117.

HO, LOOK CHAN. "Anti-Suit Injunctions in Cross-Border Insolvency: A Restatement" (2003) 52 *International and Comparative Law Quarterly* 697.

MCEVOY, JOHN P. "International Litigation: Canada, *Forum Non Conveniens* and the Anti-Suit Injunction" (1995) 17 *Advocates' Quarterly* 1.

RAPHAEL, THOMAS. *The Anti-Suit Injunction* (Oxford: Oxford University Press, 2008).

SIM, CAMERON. "Choice of Law and Anti-Suit Injunctions: Relocating Comity" (2013) 63 *International and Comparative Law Quarterly* 703.

---

68 *Ibid* at para 72 (SCJ).
69 *Ibid* at para 74.
70 *Ibid* at para 81.
71 *Ibid* at para 1 (CA).

CHAPTER 8

RECOGNITION AND ENFORCEMENT OF FOREIGN JUDGMENTS

A. INTRODUCTION

The third central question in the conflict of laws is whether a court will recognize and enforce a decision of a court in another jurisdiction. The previous three chapters have focused on the first central question, that of jurisdiction. So it may seem odd to now take up the third question rather than the second. However, as will be developed, there are strong connections between the question of jurisdiction and the question of recognition and enforcement. They have more in common with each other than either does with the second central question, choice of law. As a result, it makes sense to examine these topics in this order.

Under the principle of territorial sovereignty, the judgment of a court has effect only inside the territory within which the court is located. Consider an Ontario court order requiring a defendant to pay money. The plaintiff is entitled to enforce that order against the defendant in Ontario. For example, the defendant's assets in Ontario can be seized by the sheriff and sold, and the proceeds paid to the plaintiff. This makes eminent sense; the order would be of little value otherwise. But that same order cannot simply be applied in the same way to the defendant's assets outside Ontario. If the defendant has assets in Alberta or New York, the plaintiff cannot present the Ontario order to the local sheriff in the foreign jurisdiction and expect him or her to act on it. The Ontario order is not operative beyond Ontario's borders.

Modern commerce makes it imperative that these territorial limitations are overcome. While a defendant may have sufficient assets to satisfy a plaintiff's claim, those assets may be spread across several different jurisdictions. It would be very inefficient to require the plaintiff to bring separate substantive proceedings against the defendant in each such jurisdiction. In addition, it is increasingly easy for certain types of assets to be moved across borders. Even if the defendant has sufficient assets in the forum where the dispute is to be resolved, there is often no guarantee those assets will remain there at the conclusion of the litigation. It is therefore important that the eventual judgment be useful outside the forum.

Similar considerations arise for injunctive relief. If the plaintiff seeks an injunction against a defendant who is not present in the forum and who has no assets there, then the injunction could end up being of little value. The plaintiff will not be able, in the forum, to enforce the injunction against either the person or the assets of the defendant. As with money judgments, it is important to consider whether the judgment could become enforceable beyond the forum.

The main way the limitations of territorial sovereignty have been overcome is through jurisdictions accepting that when certain conditions are satisfied they will recognize and enforce the judgment of a foreign court. This is a sovereignty compromise: a foreign court's order ends up having an extraterritorial effect, but each jurisdiction gets to establish its own conditions for when this will occur.

At the outset we should distinguish between recognition and enforcement, even though the two terms are often loosely used interchangeably. Recognition is the first step: it is the process by which the court accepts the validity of the decision on its merits and that it has resolved the issue between the parties. Enforcement is the second step: it involves lending assistance to a party to follow through on the judgment. The seizure and sale process, for example, is an enforcement mechanism. A decision must be recognized before it can be enforced. However, not all decisions need to be enforced: recognition is often enough. Sometimes the defendant might pay the plaintiff once the decision is recognized in a jurisdiction where he or she has assets, so the plaintiff does not need to move on to enforcement. In quite a different type of case, the defendant might be seeking to have the court recognize a foreign judgment in which the plaintiff's claim was dismissed. The defendant seeks to use this earlier judgment as the basis for a defence of *res judicata* or issue estoppel. If the court recognizes the foreign judgment, the defendant does not need to have it enforced: he or she simply relies on it in support of these defences.[1]

---

1 See, for example, *Armoyan v Armoyan*, 2013 NSCA 99 at para 355. See also the use made of a foreign judgment by the plaintiff in *Monteiro v Toronto Dominion Bank* (2008), 89 OR (3d) 565 (CA).

B. THE TEST FOR RECOGNITION AND ENFORCEMENT

The common law gives the plaintiff who has obtained a foreign judgment two options. First, the plaintiff can bring an action on the foreign judgment. While this is a separate action, requiring all the procedural steps of an action, it is based not on the original claim the plaintiff had pursued against the defendant but rather on the obligation created by the foreign judgment, typically a debt obligation.[2] This remains the standard common law method for having a foreign judgment recognized and enforced.[3] The enforcement proceedings typically follow an accelerated procedure available for cases where facts are not in dispute, such as an application or a motion for summary judgment.[4]

The second option is for the plaintiff to bring an action on the original cause of action. This has nothing to do with recognition and enforcement of the foreign judgment. Rather, the plaintiff simply sues the defendant again on the same cause of action. The doctrine of merger provides that once a plaintiff has been successful in an action against the defendant, the original cause of action merges into the resulting judgment. It prevents the plaintiff from suing the defendant again. But the doctrine of merger does not apply to foreign judgments, so that it is always open for the successful plaintiff to re-litigate the original case in a different forum. Although available, this option is very unpopular. It raises limitation-period problems, is time-consuming and expensive, and raises the possibility of inconsistent results on the same underlying facts.

In an action on a foreign judgment, the test for whether a court will recognize and enforce the foreign judgment has three requirements. First, the judgment must be final. Second, the court granting the judgment must have had jurisdiction on a particular basis. This sometimes called jurisdiction in the international sense or jurisdictional competence. Third, for enforcement, the judgment must be for a fixed sum of money and not a tax or penalty or must be a non-monetary judgment the court is willing to enforce. Each of these requirements will be further explained, after a brief discussion of the issue of jurisdiction.

---

2   See *Schibsby v Westenholz* (1870), LR 6 QB 155.
3   *Nouvion v Freeman* (1889), 15 App Cas 1 (HL) [*Nouvion*], relying on *Williams v Jones* (1845), 13 M & W 628 at 633.
4   In Ontario, see *Rules of Civil Procedure*, RRO 1990, Reg 194, rr 14.05 and 20 [Ontario Rules]. While some cases may be sufficiently complex that a summary process is not appropriate, the suggestion, seen in decisions such as *Noël et Associés, SENCRL v Sincennes*, 2012 ONSC 3770, that as a matter of law recognition and enforcement must be by way of action and not application cannot be correct.

1) Jurisdiction

Because an action on the foreign judgment is a new legal proceeding, issues of jurisdiction, as discussed in Chapter 5, must be considered at the outset. If the defendant is resident in the country in which recognition and enforcement is sought, it will be easy to establish jurisdiction.[5] But in many cases the defendant will not be resident there: he or she will only have assets there, which the plaintiff is going after to enforce the judgment. Typically, the presence of assets in a province is an insufficient basis for taking jurisdiction over a foreign defendant. But most provinces have made specific provision to allow for service *ex juris* in such cases. For example, in Ontario, service outside the province can be made as of right where the claim is "on a judgment of a court outside Ontario."[6]

However, as explained in Chapter 5, the rules on service *ex juris* are not in themselves rules of jurisdiction. The plaintiff would still need to show a presumptive connecting factor with the province in which enforcement was sought. Under this approach, the presence of assets may be insufficient to ground substantive proceedings, but they should virtually always be sufficient to ground proceedings for recognition and enforcement. Put another way, assets in the jurisdiction should be considered a presumptive connecting factor in an action on a foreign judgment.

Recently, however, the Supreme Court of Canada adopted a very different approach. In *Chevron Corp v Yaiguaje* the court concluded that because, as discussed below, the analysis of the claim on the foreign judgment considers the sufficiency of the rendering court's jurisdiction, that is the only required analysis of jurisdiction and there is no need for separate consideration of the enforcing court's jurisdiction. The court stated:

> In an action to recognize and enforce a foreign judgment where the foreign court validly assumed jurisdiction, there is no need to prove that a real and substantial connection exists between the enforcing forum and either the judgment debtor or the dispute. It makes little sense to compel such a connection when, owing to the nature of the action itself, it will frequently be lacking. Nor is it necessary, in order for the action to proceed, that the foreign debtor contemporaneously possess assets in the enforcing forum. Jurisdiction to recognize and enforce a foreign judgment within Ontario exists by virtue of the

---

5   See, for example, *Chevron Corp v Yaiguaje*, 2015 SCC 42 at paras 81–87 [*Chevron*].
6   Ontario Rules, above note 4, r 17.02(m).

debtor being served on the basis of the outstanding debt resulting from the judgment.[7]

While the court did not go so far as to say that no jurisdictional basis is required for the enforcement action, it stated that the basis is found simply and wholly in the defendant being served with process.[8] This statement runs contrary to the court's foundational decision in *Morguard Investments Ltd v De Savoye*,[9] discussed in Chapter 5, which separated the issue of service of process—a purely procedural requirement—from the issue of jurisdiction. For the court to now say that the service itself founds jurisdiction is arguably to have no jurisdictional requirement at all.

While the court was correct to note that the considerations in defending the underlying substantive claims are different from those involved in defending enforcement proceedings,[10] the latter nonetheless allow reasonable scope for defences, such as fraud, denial of natural justice or contravention of public policy, to be raised. These are all discussed in detail below. With no threshold jurisdiction requirement for an enforcement action, judgment debtor defendants can now be required to advance and establish those defences in a forum that may have no connection with them or the judgment. It would have been preferable, and more consistent with the constitutional dimension of *Morguard*, for the court to have maintained the requirement of a jurisdictional nexus or connection between the dispute and the forum for actions on foreign judgments and to have adjusted the analysis of a presumptive connecting factor accordingly.

Time will tell as to whether the difference in analysis matters. It might raise problems only in cases in which enforcement is sought in a jurisdiction where the defendant is not present and does not have assets. It is unlikely many cases will fit that profile: *Chevron* was unusual in that it did.

As explained in Chapter 5, because of the *Court Jurisdiction and Proceedings Transfer Act* the analysis of jurisdiction is different in British Columbia, Nova Scotia, and Saskatchewan.[11] Most significantly, the statute provides that in a proceeding to enforce a foreign judgment, a real and substantial connection to the forum is presumed to exist, though it can be rebutted.[12]

---

7   Above note 5 at para 3.
8   *Ibid* at para 27.
9   [1990] 3 SCR 1077 [*Morguard*].
10 *Chevron*, above note 5 at para 48.
11 See, for example, *Court Jurisdiction and Proceedings Transfer Act*, SBC 2003, c 28.
12 *Ibid*, s 10(k). See Chapter 5, Section D(3)(f).

2) Final Judgment

Most legal systems recognize a distinction between final and interlocutory orders. The orthodoxy is that only final decisions of foreign courts can be recognized. In *Nouvion v Freeman* the English court was asked to recognize a Spanish judgment that had been obtained using an executive or fast-track procedure.[13] The relevant Spanish procedural rules allowed a defendant to bring a proceeding to overturn such a judgment. The court saw the initial judgment as analogous to an interlocutory order: it was final in itself, but was not a final determination of the issue between the parties. The court refused to recognize the judgment.

A judgment is considered to be final even though there is time remaining within which to launch an appeal or an appeal has in fact been launched.[14] However, in such a situation it is relatively straightforward for the defendant in the enforcement proceedings to obtain a stay of the action on the basis that the court should await the results of the appeal.[15] Even if the enforcement proceedings are stayed, starting them pending an appeal can still have advantages to the plaintiff. With proceedings now pending in a forum where the defendant has assets, the plaintiff could attempt to obtain a *Mareva* injunction to freeze the assets so they will be available to satisfy the judgment.[16]

Until quite recently, there has been little Canadian jurisprudence to suggest that courts are becoming willing to give effect to foreign interlocutory decisions. However, the Court of Appeal for Ontario has enforced an English interlocutory order. It stated that "in an age where the rules of private international law are evolving to accommodate the increasingly transnational nature of commerce, [we] see no reason why [enforcement] should be precluded by those rules just because the foreign order to be recognized is not final."[17] This decision is somewhat in tension with the considerable stress the Supreme Court of Canada has put on the finality requirement in *Pro Swing Inc v Elta Golf Inc*.[18] Nonetheless, this Ontario decision is in line with some provincial statutes, discussed later in this chapter, which allow for interprovincial registration

---

13 Above note 3. See also *Four Embarcadero Venture Center v Mr Greenjeans Corp* (1988), 64 OR (2d) 746 (HCJ).
14 *Nouvion*, above note 3 at 10–11 and 13. See also *Continental Casualty Co v Symons Estate*, 2015 ONSC 6394 [*Continental Casualty*].
15 See, for example, *Van Damme v Gelber*, 2012 ONSC 6277 at paras 71–72, aff'd 2013 ONCA 388 [*Van Damme*]; *Continental Casualty*, ibid.
16 See *Aetna Financial Services Ltd v Feigelman*, [1985] 1 SCR 2.
17 *Re Cavell Insurance Co* (2006), 80 OR (3d) 500 at para 54 (CA), aff'g (2004), 6 CBR (5th) 11 (Ont SCJ).
18 [2006] 2 SCR 612 at paras 29 and 91 [*Pro Swing*].

of non-monetary judgments, and so could signal a major change to this requirement.[19]

3) Jurisdictional Competence of the Foreign Court

The enforcing court does not examine whether the foreign court properly followed the foreign country's rules of taking jurisdiction.[20] It also does not examine whether the taking of jurisdiction by the foreign court was done in a way that would comply with its own rules for taking jurisdiction. Rather than use either of these approaches, the common law has developed a separate and special test to evaluate the foreign court's taking of jurisdiction. Prior to *Morguard*, to satisfy this test the foreign court had to have taken jurisdiction in one of two ways: based on the defendant's presence in the foreign country at the start of the litigation or based on the defendant's submission to the foreign country's jurisdiction.[21] In *Morguard*, a groundbreaking decision by the Supreme Court of Canada, the court created an additional permissible basis. If there was a real and substantial connection between the dispute and the foreign forum, then this test of jurisdictional competence would be satisfied. There are therefore three ways to meet this part of the test: presence, submission, or a real and substantial connection. If the foreign court has taken jurisdiction on some other basis, its decision will not be enforced.

There were some suggestions that these three ways of taking jurisdiction have been replaced by a single test: one that subsumes presence and submission into the real and substantial connection analysis. One basis for these suggestions is the somewhat loose language in *Beals v Saldanha*, a leading case about recognition and enforcement.[22] Justice Major for the majority stated:

> A real and substantial connection is the overriding factor in the determination of jurisdiction. The presence of more of the traditional indicia of jurisdiction (attornment, agreement to submit, residence

---

19 Another recent decision on the issue is *Fédération des producteurs acéricoles du Québec v SK Export Inc*, 2015 NBCA 30.
20 See *Buchanan v Rucker* (1808), 9 East 192.
21 Above note 9. This approach originated in English law: see *Emanuel v Symon*, [1908] 1 KB 302 (CA), rev'g [1907] 1 KB 235; *Re Trepca Mines Ltd*, [1960] 3 All ER 304 (CA). For a recent confirmation, see *Rubin v Eurofinance SA; New Cap Reinsurance Corporation (In Liquidation) v AE Grant*, [2012] UKSC 46 [*Rubin*].
22 [2003] 3 SCR 416 [*Beals*].

and presence in the foreign jurisdiction) will serve to bolster the real and substantial connection to the action or parties.[23]

It is very difficult to see how this is consistent with *Morguard*. It is worded so as to suggest that the real and substantial connection test has replaced the traditional three bases for international jurisdiction. Yet for all that, it is decidedly unclear. There is no indication in any of Major J's surrounding statements that he intended to make a significant change to the law on international jurisdiction. In fact, in the next sentence he confirmed that submission to the court remains an independent basis for jurisdiction.

The vague nature of these statements by the majority in *Beals* contrasts with the clarity in LeBel J's dissent. In his view:

> the logic on which the *Morguard* test is founded suggests that it should supersede, rather than complement, the traditional common law bases of jurisdiction. In my view, it is not necessary to ask whether any of the traditional grounds are present and then go on to ask whether there is a real and substantial connection (as the majority reasons suggest, at para. 37). There should be just one question: is the "real and substantial connection" test made out?[24]

Justice LeBel is firmly of the view that in all cases a real and substantial connection must be established for the court to have international jurisdiction. That this position is expressed in dissent, expressly criticizing the majority's position, lends support to the argument that the majority did not intend to change the traditional approach. Otherwise, there would have been common ground on this issue between Major J and LeBel J. The Supreme Court of Canada has not amalgamated the three bases.[25] They remain independent and require separate analysis. Most importantly, the plaintiff only needs to satisfy any one of them. If the plaintiff shows that the foreign court had jurisdiction based on presence, or on submission, there is no need to analyze whether there was a real and substantial connection between the dispute and the foreign country.

---

23 Ibid at para 37.
24 Ibid at para 207.
25 This is very clear in the context of taking jurisdiction, as opposed to recognition and enforcement: see *Chevron*, above note 5 at paras 82–84. See also Stephen GA Pitel & Cheryl Dusten, "Lost in Transition: Answering the Questions Raised by the Supreme Court of Canada's New Approach to Jurisdiction" (2006) 85 *Canadian Bar Review* 61.

a) Presence

As discussed in Chapter 5, it is quite common for legal systems to assume jurisdiction over defendants who are present within their territory. This has long been accepted as a valid basis for exercising jurisdiction, so that a court that has jurisdiction on this basis is accepted as having had jurisdictional competence. For individuals, this should be distinguished from jurisdiction based on a person's citizenship, which does not satisfy this requirement. Presence needs to be considered as of a particular time, namely when proceedings were commenced. Presence in the country at some earlier time, such as when a contract was made, is not sufficient.[26]

For individuals, this test raises few concerns in cases where the presence has some degree of permanence, such as those in which the defendant is ordinarily resident in the country. The controversial cases are those of temporary or fleeting presence. As explained in Chapter 5, the common law considers temporary presence, however brief, to be sufficient for taking jurisdiction. Consistent with that position, at the recognition and enforcement stage it similarly considers a foreign court's reliance on temporary presence as sufficient to ground international jurisdiction.[27] Some Canadian cases have expressed concern about this,[28] but the orthodoxy is that it remains sufficient to meet this test.

The presence of a corporation is a more complex issue. In the easier cases, the corporation has a head office, a registered office, or a permanent place of business in the country. In the more difficult cases, the analysis is similar to that in Chapter 5, looking at whether the corporation is carrying on business in the country. However, the court being asked to recognize the foreign judgment applies its own test for carrying on business, not the test that is used in the foreign country.[29] A leading authority on corporate presence is the English case of *Adams v Cape Industries Plc*.[30] American factory workers who had been exposed to asbestos sued the defendant in Texas. The defendant was an English company involved in mining and selling asbestos in South Africa. It had no assets in America and did no business there, so it did not defend the Texas proceedings. The plaintiffs sought to enforce the default judgment in England, and to meet the test for recognition and enforcement had to show that the defendant was present in Texas. They advanced two interesting arguments. First, they argued that as the de-

---

26 *Sirdar Gurdyal Singh v Rajah of Faridkote*, [1894] AC 670 (PC).
27 *Forbes v Simmons* (1914), 20 DLR 100 (Alta SC).
28 *Re Carrick Estates Ltd and Young* (1987), 43 DLR (4th) 161 at 163 (Sask CA).
29 See the analysis in *Moore v Mercator Enterprises Ltd* (1978), 90 DLR (3d) 590 (NSSC).
30 [1990] Ch 433 (CA).

fendant owned subsidiary corporations that clearly carried on business in the United States, it was part of a "single economic unit" that met the test for presence. Second, they argued that it was present because its subsidiaries were acting as its agents. The Court of Appeal rejected both arguments. The defendant was entitled to divide its operations up using subsidiary corporations. The "single economic unit" theory, if accepted, would defeat this entitlement. Further, on the evidence the subsidiary corporations were clearly present but they were conducting their own business, not acting as agents conducting the defendant's business. As a result, the judgment was not enforceable in England.[31]

b) Submission

The common law considers that it would be inconsistent for a defendant to accept the jurisdiction of a foreign court by submitting to it, and then object to having that court's decision recognized and enforced elsewhere on jurisdictional grounds. Submission is therefore a well-accepted basis for international jurisdiction.[32] Submission can occur in one of two ways: by appearance or by contract.

A defendant who defends against the merits of the plaintiff's claim has submitted by appearance. Engaging with the substantive issues of a dispute in a court indicates acceptance that the court has jurisdiction to deal with those issues.[33] Easy cases involve filing a statement of defence: this is clear submission. But a defendant can submit by appearance in other, lesser ways. Some jurisdictions require defendants to "enter an appearance" to acknowledge the proceeding. Entering an unqualified appearance, as opposed to one indicating a challenge to the court's jurisdiction, can constitute submission.[34]

Submission by appearance can be a trap for unwary defendants. They have to closely consider the procedural steps available in the foreign forum and yet remain focused on the fact that it will be the law of the place of eventual enforcement proceedings, not the law of that forum, that will be used to determine whether they submitted through their conduct. Intention is not a determining factor: defendants can

---

31 The defendant advanced a further argument in case it lost either of these points, namely that the subsidiaries were not present in Texas but only in other states. In *obiter dicta* the court indicated this argument would have failed because, since the Texas litigation was in federal rather than state court, presence anywhere in the United States would have been sufficient.
32 *Emanuel v Symon*, [1908] 1 KB 302 (CA).
33 See, for example, *Van Damme*, above note 15 at paras 21–27 (CA); *Nackawic Mechanical Ltd (cob SDI Aviation) v Ward*, 2015 NBCA 1 at paras 18–24 [*Nackawic Mechanical*].
34 *First National Bank of Houston v Houston E & C, Inc* (1990), 47 BCLR (2d) 347 (CA).

submit inadvertently, without being aware of doing so.[35] It is also easy, in the course of interlocutory motions, to be drawn into arguments about the merits of the case, and yet this must be avoided so as not to submit.[36]

There are older cases that indicate that even appearing to challenge jurisdiction constituted submission by appearance.[37] Their logic was that defendants who had raised the issue of jurisdiction and had it resolved against them should not be able to then withdraw from the proceedings and claim lack of jurisdiction at the enforcement stage. These cases have been heavily challenged. They put defendants in a very difficult position. It is preferable that jurisdictional concerns are first raised with the court purporting to exercise jurisdiction, and yet the position in these cases undercuts that approach and leads defendants to wait until the enforcement proceedings to raise the issue. The better view is that appearing solely to challenge jurisdiction is not a submission.[38]

A conceptually more difficult question is whether seeking a stay of proceedings, for example based on *forum non conveniens*, constitutes submission. As discussed in Chapter 6, implicit in seeking a stay is acceptance of the court's jurisdiction. On that logic, seeking a stay is submission. But this raises the same concerns as the earlier cases on challenging jurisdiction, especially since a motion for a stay is frequently brought at the same time, in the alternative, as a motion challenging jurisdiction. Again, the better view is that seeking a stay is not submission. To a limited extent this issue has been resolved in some of the provincial rules of civil procedure. Ontario's rule 17.06(4) provides that "the making of a motion under subrule (1) [for an order setting service aside or for a stay] is not in itself a submission to the jurisdiction of the court over the moving party."[39] On its face this provision indicates only what conduct will not constitute a submission to Ontario. Another country may have a quite different rule. But in an enforcement action in Ontario, the court would not be concerned with the foreign country's rule. Whether the defendant submitted is a matter for the law of the place where enforcement is sought. But even as a matter of Ontario law, this provision is silent on whether a motion for a stay brought abroad constitutes submission. It could have a different rule for foreign

---

35 *Ibid* at 352.
36 See *Mid-Ohio Imported Car Co v Tri-K Investments Ltd* (1995), 129 DLR (4th) 181 (BCCA) [*Mid-Ohio*].
37 *Harris v Taylor*, [1915] 2 KB 580 (CA); *Henry v Geoprosco International Ltd*, [1975] 2 All ER 702 (CA).
38 *Clinton v Ford* (1982), 137 DLR (3d) 281 at 285 (Ont CA) [*Clinton*].
39 Ontario Rules, above note 4.

stay motions than for local stay motions. But this is unlikely, and one should expect the philosophy in the rule to equally apply to the question of whether a foreign motion for a stay amounts to submission.[40]

It is also possible to appear in an effort to preserve local assets without this being a submission. If specific property is seized on an interlocutory basis, the defendant can challenge the validity and scope of the seizure.[41] However, this point cannot be extended to cover concerns about local assets that might become subject to an eventual judgment in the forum. This broader concern arises in many cases and does not warrant special treatment.

Thus far we have focused on submission by appearance. The other way that submission can occur is by contract. In a contract the parties can agree that the courts of a country are to have either exclusive or non-exclusive jurisdiction over the dispute. If the plaintiff sues in that country, and the defendant is not present and does not submit by appearing, the defendant can nonetheless be held to have submitted by contract. Even if the defendant takes no part in the proceedings, the foreign court would have had international competence based on the contractual submission.

A somewhat unusual case draws on both types of submission. In *Batavia Times Publishing Co v Davis* the defendant borrowed money from the plaintiff.[42] The contract contained a somewhat unusual clause. Under it the defendant "authorize[d] and empower[ed] any attorney of any court of record of Pennsylvania, New York, Canada or elsewhere to appear for and to enter judgment against [him] in favour of the [plaintiff]." The plaintiff used the clause to obtain judgment in Pennsylvania. The defendant resisted enforcement proceedings in Ontario. The court held that through the clause the defendant had contracted to submit to the forum in which the proceedings were brought. Further, the defendant had appeared through the authorized attorney used under the clause, also amounting to submission.

c) Real and Substantial Connection

Prior to *Morguard*, the test for international jurisdiction was quite restrictive, to the detriment of plaintiffs seeking to enforce foreign judgments. A defendant who was sued in a country where he or she was not present and had no assets could decide to take no part in the proceedings, confident that without presence or submission the default

---

40 See *Mid-Ohio*, above note 36.
41 *Clinton*, above note 38. In this case, however, the defendant did not limit the appearance in this way and defended on the merits, thereby submitting.
42 (1977), 18 OR (2d) 252 (HCJ).

judgment would not be enforced in Canada. This restrictive test was based on a refusal to recognize as acceptable a foreign country's taking of jurisdiction through service *ex juris*. Yet provinces were routinely taking jurisdiction over foreign defendants on precisely such a basis. This contradiction put pressure on the traditional test.

In *Morguard* the issue was the enforceability of an Alberta judgment in British Columbia. Under the traditional common law test for jurisdiction, the decision could not be recognized in British Columbia. However, the Supreme Court of Canada expanded the test. It is now sufficient for recognition if the plaintiff can show a "real and substantial connection" with the jurisdiction that rendered the judgment.[43] This development was based on two important facts. The first was the federal nature of Canada. Justice La Forest found that the aim of the Canadian Constitution was to create a single, economically integrated country.[44] To achieve this aim, judgments of one province had to be recognized more willingly in other provinces than was the case under the traditional test. He held that "a regime of mutual recognition of judgments across the country is inherent in a federation."[45] The second fact was increasing economic globalization. Justice La Forest stated:

> The business community operates in a world economy, and we correctly speak of a world community even in the face of decentralized political and legal power. Accommodating the flow of wealth, skills and people across state lines has now become imperative. Under these circumstances, our approach to the recognition and enforcement of foreign judgments would appear ripe for reappraisal. Certainly, other countries, notably the United States and members of the European Economic Community, have adopted more generous rules for the recognition and enforcement of foreign judgments, to the general advantage of litigants.[46]

Subsequent cases have clarified several important aspects of the real and substantial connection requirement. First, while *Morguard* was interprovincial, it is clear from the subsequent cases that the same approach applies to judgments from outside Canada.[47] In *Beals*, Major J

---

43   Above note 9 at 1108–109.
44   *Ibid* at 1099. For an extended economic analysis of this point, see Stevan Pepa, "Extraterritoriality and the Supreme Court's Assertion of the Economic Constitution" (2001) 34 *Canadian Business Law Journal* 231.
45   *Morguard*, above note 9 at 1100.
46   *Ibid* at 1098.
47   This development is explained in Joost Blom, "The Enforcement of Foreign Judgments: Morguard Goes Forth into the World" (1997) 28 *Canadian Business Law Journal* 373 at 379–84.

stated for the majority that "while there are compelling reasons to expand the test's application, there does not appear to be any principled reason not to do so."[48] He relied on the above quotation from *Morguard* about accommodating the flow of wealth, skills, and people in a world economy, and noted that this was "as much an imperative internationally as it is interprovincially."[49]

Second, there has been some clarification as to what has to have a real and substantial connection to the jurisdiction. In *Old North State Brewing v Newlands Services Inc*, the British Columbia Court of Appeal adopted a broad approach, stating that the connection had to be between the jurisdiction and "the action."[50] In *United States of America v Ivey*, the Court of Appeal for Ontario affirmed the analysis of Sharpe J, who had referred to the connection as being with the "subject matter of the action" and then, in applying the test, went on to consider a broad range of factual connections.[51] More recently, in *Beals* the majority stated that jurisdiction would have been properly exercised if there was a real and substantial connection "with either the subject matter of the action or the defendant."[52] It also referred to the connection being with "the action or the parties."[53] The breadth inherent in these various formulations is welcome, but it would be simpler and clearer to state that the real and substantial connection is between the foreign country and either "the action," "the proceedings," or "the dispute," each of which is functionally equivalent.

Third, a framework has been developed for determining whether a real and substantial connection exists. In *Morguard* La Forest J left "real and substantial connection" largely undefined. In *Hunt v T&N plc*, he acknowledged that this test was not meant to be rigid: the exact limits of what would constitute a reasonable assumption of jurisdiction could not be precisely defined.[54] Since these decisions, most of the efforts to flesh out the meaning of a real and substantial connection came from courts assessing their own ability to take jurisdiction over a dispute: they have not been in the enforcement context. These cases, the most important of which was *Muscutt v Courcelles*,[55] were mentioned in

---

48 Above note 22 at para 19.
49 *Ibid* at para 26.
50 (1998), 58 BCLR (3d) 144 at paras 24 and 31 (CA) [*Old North*]. See also *Moses v Shore Boat Builders Ltd* (1993), 83 BCLR (2d) 177 at paras 30 and 32 (CA).
51 (1995), 26 OR (3d) 533 at 541–43 (Gen Div), aff'd (1996), 30 OR (3d) 370 (CA) [*Ivey*].
52 Above note 22 at para 23.
53 *Ibid* at paras 37 and 68.
54 [1993] 4 SCR 289 at 325 [*Hunt*].
55 (2002), 60 OR (3d) 20 (CA) [*Muscutt*].

Chapter 5. In *Beals*, the judges did not devote much time to this issue, likely because the connection to Florida was clearly quite strong.

In *Muscutt*, Sharpe J set out eight factors to consider in assessing the connection. Applied in the context of recognition and enforcement, the factors are as follows: (1) the connection between the rendering forum and the plaintiff's claim; (2) the connection between the rendering forum and the defendant; (3) unfairness to the defendant in assuming jurisdiction; (4) unfairness to the plaintiff in not assuming jurisdiction; (5) the involvement of other parties to the proceedings; (6) the rendering forum's willingness to recognize and enforce a foreign judgment rendered on the same jurisdictional basis; (7) the nature of the case (interprovincial or international); and (8) comity and the standards of jurisdiction, recognition, and enforcement prevailing elsewhere.[56] This approach, weighing a wide range of factors to assess the connection, is consistent with what judges have been doing in enforcement cases since *Morguard*. Several provinces have expressly referenced the *Muscutt* factors. However, in British Columbia there is debate about whether these factors are to be used.

In the enforcement context, this broad approach to the real and substantial connection test has been relatively easy to satisfy. Indeed, there are few cases where enforcement has been refused because the test was not met.[57] One of these was *Braintech, Inc v Kostiuk*, in which the court refused to enforce a Texas judgment.[58] The connections between the dispute and Texas were tenuous. The defendant, who resided in British Columbia, was alleged to have posted defamatory statements on the Internet, which could be read by people in, among other places, Texas. Tellingly, though, the plaintiff did not allege in its claim that anyone in Texas had even seen the posted statements. The plaintiff corporation had its head office in Vancouver, although it did conduct research operations in Texas at the time the litigation was commenced. The court found that the dispute did not have a real and substantial connection with Texas.

As discussed in Chapter 5, the Supreme Court of Canada held in *Club Resorts Ltd v Van Breda* that the real and substantial connection test could no longer be used directly in the context of taking jurisdiction. Rather, a presumptive connecting factor had to be identified.[59] Given

---

56 *Ibid* at paras 76–111.
57 These cases have tended to involve somewhat specialized contexts. See *Re Singer Sewing Machine Co of Canada Ltd* (2000), 259 AR 364 (QB); *Ontario v Mar-Dive Corp* (1996), 141 DLR (4th) 577 (Ont Ct Gen Div).
58 (1999), 63 BCLR (3d) 156 (CA).
59 2012 SCC 17 at paras 30, 70, 75, 78, and 100 [*Club Resorts*].

the strong linkage, forged in *Morguard* and noted frequently since, between the taking of jurisdiction and the assessment of a foreign court's taking of jurisdiction in recognition and enforcement proceedings, this change raises the issue of whether the test has also changed in the latter context. Many decisions continue to examine whether there was a real and substantial connection between the dispute and the foreign forum, but some decisions have reframed the analysis and sought to identify a presumptive connecting factor.[60]

d) Criticisms of the Real and Substantial Connection Test

This additional basis for determining that a foreign court had jurisdiction in the international sense means that Canadian common law is, among the world's legal systems, one of the most willing to recognize and enforce a foreign judgment. This willingness could pose several problems. The real and substantial connection test promotes the liberal flow of judgments across borders. Globally, this is a phenomenon that requires the support of many countries. If Canada is one of only a few countries to liberalize in this area, it risks having to enforce foreign judgments it might rather not while not having its own similar judgments enforced elsewhere. Those with assets in Canada could find themselves more exposed to foreign plaintiffs than those who locate their assets elsewhere. Whether Canada will benefit economically from having liberalized judgment enforcement rules while other countries do not is an important question for debate.[61]

In addition, the real and substantial connection test imposes practical difficulties on Canadians who are sued abroad. Even with the *Muscutt* factors the test is relatively open-ended, which can impair predictability. It is one thing to assess whether a court has a real and substantial connection with a dispute at the outset of litigation. The parties will find out the court's answer and proceed accordingly. It is quite another thing to predict in advance what a Canadian court, when later asked to enforce a foreign judgment, will decide. An Ontario defendant in Texas proceedings has to assess whether the courts of Ontario, in subsequent enforcement proceedings, will hold that there was a real and substantial connection to Texas. Neither the Texas nor the Ontario court will answer this question at an early stage of the litigation.

---

60 See, for example, *Sincies Chiementin SpA (Trustee of) v King*, 2012 ONCA 653.
61 Ireland recently considered and rejected the Canadian approach: David Kenny, "*Re Flightlease*: The 'Real and Substantial Connection' Test for Recognition and Enforcement of Foreign Judgments Fails to Take Flight in Ireland" (2014) 63 *International and Comparative Law Quarterly* 197. For the United Kingdom, see *Rubin*, above note 21.

Of course, this is not a problem as between provinces, since the same test will be used for jurisdiction and enforcement. If the Alberta court holds that there is a real and substantial connection to Alberta at the jurisdiction stage, it is then clear that the Ontario court would enforce the resulting Alberta judgment on that same basis. But the predictability problem remains for foreign countries. As a result, many Canadian defendants have decided that when they are sued abroad their most sensible option is to defend on the merits in the foreign jurisdiction.

e) A Note about New Brunswick and Saskatchewan

Most provinces have not enacted legislation to address actions to enforce foreign judgments, leaving it to the common law. New Brunswick and Saskatchewan, however, have long had statutes that specified the test for enforcement.[62] That test generally requires the defendant to have been resident in the foreign jurisdiction at the time the litigation started or to have submitted to that jurisdiction.[63] The appellate courts of these provinces initially held that *Morguard* had changed only the common law and could not alter these specific statutory provisions.[64] But in the wake of *Hunt*, making the *Morguard* test a constitutional requirement as far as interprovincial enforcement was concerned, this position could not stand. Both provinces have since enacted new statutes dealing with the registration of judgments, discussed below, from other parts of Canada.[65] In so doing, they preserved the older statutes but limited their application to judgments from outside Canada. Saskatchewan subsequently repealed its statute and replaced it with a more modern version.[66]

In these provinces, an action to enforce a judgment from outside Canada is governed by statute. Because the New Brunswick statute does not establish a real and substantial connection as a sufficient basis for jurisdictional competence, the scope of enforceable foreign judgments is narrower in that province than in the rest of the country. So a judgment of a Florida court, in a dispute with a real and substantial connection to

---

62 *Foreign Judgments Act*, RSNB 1973, c F-19 (now RSNB 2011, c 162); *The Foreign Judgments Act*, RSS 1978, c F-18.
63 For Saskatchewan, see *The Foreign Judgments Act*, ibid, s 3. For New Brunswick, see *Foreign Judgments Act*, above note 62, s 2. Both also accepted the jurisdiction of other Canadian provinces or territories if the defendant, at the time the judgment was obtained, carried on business in that province or territory.
64 *Sims v Bower* (1993), 138 NBR (2d) 302 (CA); *Noyes v Cardinal Couriers Ltd* (1993), 109 Sask R 108 (CA).
65 *Canadian Judgments Act*, SNB 2000, c C-0.1 (now RSNB 2011, c 123); *The Enforcement of Canadian Judgments Act, 2002*, SS 2002, c E-9.1001.
66 *The Enforcement of Foreign Judgments Act*, SS 2005, c E-9.121.

Florida, would be enforceable in Ontario and now also in Saskatchewan, but not in New Brunswick.[67] This situation is not welcome. It would be better if all provinces followed a national standard.

4) Monetary Judgments

Money judgments are enforceable as long as they are for a fixed sum of money and not a penalty or a tax.[68] The amount owing has to be either expressly stated or ascertainable by a simple mathematical process.[69] An order that the defendant pay the plaintiff 50 percent of the value of a business is not for a fixed sum until that value has been determined. An order including an award of costs is not for a fixed sum until the amount of the costs is established. An order against two or more defendants should be clear whether it is against them jointly, severally, or jointly and severally.[70]

Concerns about foreign penal and revenue judgments were explained in Chapter 3. The refusal to enforce such decisions is a matter of public policy. Historically this restriction has applied even to judgments from other provinces. For penal judgments this might still be the case today, such that an Ontario court would refuse to enforce a decision of an Alberta court ordering the defendant to pay a fine to the Alberta government. For revenue judgments this restriction may no longer operate interprovincially and in any event has largely been overtaken by provincial tax legislation allowing for enforcement.[71]

Several commentators have argued that the penal and revenue restrictions on enforcement are inconsistent with the federal nature of Canada and the principles in the *Morguard* line of cases and therefore they should be eliminated at least for interprovincial judgments.[72] Even for judgments from other countries, it is difficult to accept in the current age of internationalism that courts should continue to refuse

---

67 See *Nackawic Mechanical*, above note 33 at para 16.
68 *Huntington v Attrill*, [1893] AC 150 (PC) [*Huntington*]; *Holman v Johnson* (1775), 98 ER 1120; *Ivey*, above note 51.
69 *Beatty v Beatty*, [1924] 1 KB 807.
70 *South Pacific Import, Inc v Ho*, 2009 BCCA 163 at paras 53 and 56 [*South Pacific Import*].
71 See *Weir v Lohr* (1967), 65 DLR (2d) 717 (Man QB); Vaughan Black, "Old and in the Way? The Revenue Rule and Big Tobacco" (2003) 38 *Canadian Business Law Journal* 1 at 16.
72 Blom, above note 47 at 395–96; Elizabeth Edinger, "New British Columbia Legislation: The *Court Jurisdiction and Proceedings Transfer Act*; The *Enforcement of Canadian Judgments and Decrees Act*" (2006) 39 *University of British Columbia Law Review* 407 at 410–11.

enforcement of foreign revenue judgments. Concerns about foreign discriminatory or invidious tax laws can be appropriately addressed in the defences to enforcement and thus do not justify blanket exclusion. At least one Canadian case has illustrated a willingness to relax the revenue judgment restriction.[73] It is therefore likely that Canadian courts will be under continued pressure to reconsider the enforcement requirement that a money judgment not be for a penalty or tax.

While it has been suggested that a foreign award of punitive damages should not be enforced on the basis that it is a penal judgment, Canadian courts have not adopted this view. An essential hallmark of a penalty is that the sum imposed is paid to the state, not to a private litigant.[74] There is a tenable distinction between state penalties and punitive damages, a distinction which goes beyond the basic observation that both serve to punish. For the former, the state establishes the triggering conditions and amount for the penalty and takes active steps to impose it. For the latter, the state's role is much more limited, providing the administrative mechanism under which a private litigant seeks an award. Moreover, the meaning of a penalty has generally been interpreted narrowly, which is consistent with the view that punitive damages are not a penalty. In *Ivey*, the court analyzed an award of damages payable to the United States under an environmental protection statute and concluded that the damages were restitutionary, not punitive, and so did not amount to a penalty.[75]

As noted in Chapter 3, a judgment is not penal simply because it results from the foreign court's sanctioning of the defendant's conduct of the litigation. A default judgment, for example, which can be said to sanction the defendant's failure to appear, is not on that basis penal. The same is true for substantive judgments resulting from a defendant's violations of various pretrial rules such as those dealing with disclosure.[76] The judgment being enforced is in respect of the underlying claim, not the defendant's conduct in the litigation.

---

73 *Re Sefel Geophysical Ltd* (1989), 62 Alta LR (2d) 193 (QB). See also *Re Matol Botanical International Ltd*, [2001] QJ No 4195 (CS). In his analysis of the revenue exclusion, Vaughan Black has concluded that the arguments in support of maintaining it, for the most part, "seem risibly weak": above note 71 at 30. In contrast, for a recent defence of the rule, see David Bishop Debenham, "From the Revenue Rule to the Rule of the 'Revenuer': A Tale of Two Davids and Two Goliaths" (2008) 56 *Canadian Tax Journal* 1.
74 *Huntington*, above note 68 at 156–57.
75 Above note 51 at 544. See also *Uniforêt Pâte Port-Cartier Inc v Zerotech Technologies Inc* (1998), 50 BCLR (3d) 359 (SC).
76 *Dingwall v Foster*, 2014 ABCA 89 at paras 47–49.

5) Non-monetary Judgments

The Supreme Court of Canada broke new ground in *Pro Swing Inc v Elta Golf Inc*, holding that "the time has come to permit the enforcement of foreign non-money orders where the general principles of *Morguard* are met and other considerations do not render recognition and enforcement of the foreign judgment inadvisable or unjust."[77] The plaintiff had obtained a consent decree in an Ohio court against the Ontario-based defendant. The defendant subsequently violated the terms of that judgment and the plaintiff obtained a further order finding the defendant in contempt. The decree and order were not enforceable against the defendant in Ohio because it had no presence or assets there, so the plaintiff brought enforcement proceedings in Ontario, asking the court to recognize and enforce the two Ohio judgments. The defendant opposed enforcement on two grounds: first, that the decree and order were both non-monetary, and second, that the order, being concerned with contempt, was penal. The Supreme Court of Canada unanimously held that the time had come to allow enforcement of foreign non-monetary judgments. But it was quite divided on important subsidiary issues. The majority held that the scope of the judgments was uncertain and also held that the contempt order was penal.[78] In stark contrast, the dissent held that civil contempt orders, as distinguished from criminal contempt orders, were not penal and that on a "plain reading" of the judgments they were unambiguous in their scope.[79]

The change in the law brought about by *Pro Swing* is welcome. Over the past two decades historic suspicion of foreign judgments has been eroded by a more international spirit. *Morguard*, discussed above, is a leading expression of that change in tone. Its reliance on comity, not as a doctrine or theory but as an informing principle for private international law, applies equally to non-monetary judgments. In *Pro Swing* Deschamps J observed that "frontiers remain relevant to national identity and jurisdiction, but ... the globalization of commerce and mobility of both people and assets make them less so."[80]

There are important differences between monetary and non-monetary judgments. Traditionally the sense has been that in enforcing a money judgment the forum court does not have to understand the factual situation giving rise to the judgment and uses its own familiar local mechanisms of enforcement. In contrast, concern has been expressed that

---

77 Above note 18 at para 87, McLachlin CJC. See also paras 15–16, Deschamps J.
78 *Ibid* at para 62.
79 *Ibid* at paras 106–8 and 116–17.
80 *Ibid* at para 1.

enforcing non-monetary judgments will require courts to invest time and energy to understand the foreign order and will require enforcement using concepts from foreign law.[81]

There are several reasons why these differences should not stand in the way of enforcing foreign non-monetary judgments. First, not all such judgments will require the plaintiff to invoke the local enforcement mechanisms. Just as with money judgments, once the court recognizes the foreign judgment the defendant will, in many cases, comply with the terms of the judgment. Second, it is reasonable to expect that in many cases the non-monetary judgment will be clear and precise, so that the court can indeed enforce it without having to delve into the underlying facts of the original litigation. In other, less clear-cut cases, the court's involvement will have to be more substantial. But this is not a good reason to refuse enforcement. The presence of the defendant or of his or her assets in the jurisdiction should be considered a sufficient basis to warrant judicial resources being used in this way. Third, the enforcement will still occur under the local procedures, with which the court is highly familiar. Many foreign non-monetary judgments will involve remedies well known to our courts, such as an injunction or mandatory order. In those cases where the remedy is truly foreign, the court would work from the closest domestic analogy. The foreign elements of the judgment are not sufficient reason to deny enforcement.

a) The Test for Enforcement

In the majority decision in *Pro Swing* Deschamps J pointed to the differences between money and non-monetary judgments as reason for "a cautious approach,"[82] and this caution drives much of the majority's reasoning for not enforcing the two Ohio judgments. In reality, the differences are not so great as to warrant this much caution, so it is unfortunate that the court's step forward in this area is in such guarded language. In contrast, the dissent is far stronger. Chief Justice McLachlin did not place stress on the need for caution, referred to this development as "an incremental step" in the common law, and noted that concerns about judicial economy "should not be overemphasized."[83] In future cases, it will be important for lower courts to look at both the majority and minority decisions to extract the leading principles, since the latter may well contain a better formulation of the test.

---

81 See Vaughan Black, "Enforcement of Foreign Non-monetary Judgments: *Pro Swing v. Elta*" (2006) 42 *Canadian Business Law Journal* 81 at 89.
82 Above note 18 at paras 1, 17, 19, and 64.
83 *Ibid* at paras 86 and 99.

Now that the court has removed the fixed sum of money requirement, we must consider whether the test for enforcement of foreign non-monetary judgments is identical to that for money judgments. On this the court in *Pro Swing* could have provided more guidance. As a starting point, both the majority and the minority stressed that the foreign judgment must be clear and specific.[84] This is important for the enforcing court to properly supervise its enforcement. Of course, money judgments must also be clear and specific, so this requirement is not new. But the court is correct to observe that non-monetary judgments raise more difficulties in this regard, especially as to their territorial scope. What the foreign court may consider clear and specific may not seem so to the enforcing court. The court also stressed the need for finality.[85]

In the majority decision, Deschamps J did suggest some additional elements forming part of the test for enforcement:

> the domestic court should ... scrutinize the impact of the order. Relevant considerations may thus include the criteria that guide Canadian courts in crafting domestic orders, such as: ... Is the enforcement the least burdensome remedy for the Canadian justice system? Is the Canadian litigant exposed to unforeseen obligations? Are any third parties affected by the order? Will the use of judicial resources be consistent with what would be allowed for domestic litigants?[86]

While some of these may be relevant considerations for a domestic court considering whether to make its own non-monetary order, it is difficult to see why these are factors at the stage of enforcing a foreign non-monetary judgment. Little real justification, beyond the need for flexibility, is provided. Further, to the extent that some aspects of these considerations are already part of the traditional defences to enforcement, discussed below, this approach has the potential for duplicative analysis. These additional elements were not endorsed in the dissenting judgment.

These additional considerations have the potential to significantly limit enforcement. To take just one as an example, one reason the majority refused to enforce the consent decree and contempt order is because the plaintiff could have instead used letters of request, from Ohio into Ontario, to obtain some of the information it sought from the defendant.[87] Should this kind of judicial second-guessing be encouraged? The plaintiff had obtained two judgments from the court in Ohio,

---

84   *Ibid* at paras 24 and 91.
85   *Ibid* at paras 29 and 91.
86   *Ibid* at para 30. See also *United States of America v Yemec*, 2010 ONCA 414.
87   *Pro Swing*, above note 18 at paras 40–48.

and it seems contrary to comity that Ontario would refuse to enforce them simply because other procedures might produce a similar result.

Overall, while the principle of foreign non-monetary judgment enforcement has been accepted, the court has not provided much guidance on how the test for enforcement will be different, if at all, from when money judgments are involved. The language used by the majority in *Pro Swing* suggests a preference for a significant degree of discretion in whether to enforce these orders, while the minority's view treats them more like money judgments: if the test is met, they are to be enforced subject to any defences. The differences between these positions will have to be worked out in future litigation.

In the wake of *Pro Swing*, Canadian courts have enforced foreign non-monetary orders in several cases, including injunctions, constructive trusts, and other equitable orders.[88] Overall these decisions appear more consistent with the minority's approach, showing a general willingness to enforce the foreign orders.

b) Contempt Orders

The enforcement of foreign contempt orders raises some difficult issues. Canadian law has historically distinguished between criminal and civil contempt. In *Poje v Attorney General for British Columbia*, the Supreme Court of Canada held:

> The Court of Chancery has for centuries enforced its orders by contempt proceedings, but it is well settled that such orders, when made merely in aid of execution of process for the benefit of a party, are to be regarded as purely civil in nature. It is equally well settled that conduct which renders appropriate contempt proceedings in aid of execution may have a criminal aspect as well.[89]

In subsequent cases the courts have maintained the distinction and developed the notion that elements of public defiance, the tarnishing of the administration of justice, and damaging the authority of the court are all factors that can convert an otherwise civil contempt into a criminal contempt. Civil contempt orders are mainly restitutionary since their objective is to enforce private rights. In contrast, a criminal

---

88 See, for example, *Bienstock v Adenyo Inc*, 2015 ONCA 310; *PT ATPK Resources TBK (Indonesia) v Diversified Energy and Resource Corporation (appeal by Hopaco Properties Ltd)*, 2014 ONCA 466; *Van Damme*, above note 15; *Blizzard Entertainment, Inc v Simpson*, 2012 ONSC 4312.

89 [1953] 1 SCR 516 at 517. See also *United Nurses of Alberta v Alberta (Attorney General)*, [1992] 1 SCR 901 [*United Nurses*].

contempt order is intended to be punitive and a deterrent.⁹⁰ Criminal contempt involves "punishment for conduct calculated to bring the administration of justice by the courts into disrepute" while civil contempt involves securing "compliance with the process of a tribunal including, but not limited to, the process of a court."⁹¹

In *Pro Swing*, the defendant argued that the Ohio contempt order was not enforceable in Ontario because it was penal in nature. In accordance with the traditional distinction between civil and criminal contempt, the dissent was prepared to enforce the Ohio order. Chief Justice McLachlin stated that "[w]hen a foreign court issues a contempt order to secure compliance with a private remedy flowing from a private dispute, the order does not necessarily contain a 'penal' aspect that should preclude enforcement by Canadian courts."⁹² In contrast, the majority held that all contempt orders have a "quasi-criminal" nature and thus are penal law.⁹³ In so doing, it adopted a "unified approach" to contempt orders, rejecting the traditional distinction.

In the context of enforcement of foreign judgments, this move to the unified approach raises concerns. The effect of the majority's unification of civil and criminal contempt was that the contempt order, which was not penal in and of itself, was characterized as penal. This has the potential to restrict the enforcement of foreign non-monetary judgments. Even if Canadian common law comes to recognize all contempt orders as involving elements of public law, some distinction should still be made for enforcement purposes between contempt orders that are issued to protect private rights and those that truly have penal components.

One of the central ways non-monetary judgments are enforced is through contempt orders. For example, the Ontario Rules provide that "an order requiring a person to do an act, other than the payment of money, or to abstain from doing an act, may be enforced against the person refusing or neglecting to obey the order by a contempt order."⁹⁴ So if the courts are unwilling to enforce foreign contempt orders, they will nonetheless find themselves asked to make their own contempt orders in support of foreign non-monetary judgments.

---

90 Christopher Miller, *Contempt of Court* (Oxford: Oxford University Press, 2000) at 1.05 and 1.07.
91 *United Nurses*, above note 89 at 943, Sopinka J dissenting but not on this point.
92 Above note 18 at para 108.
93 *Ibid* at paras 35–36.
94 Above note 4, r 60.05.

c) Making Extraterritorial Non-monetary Orders

Pro Swing is not based on notions of reciprocity. However, it is likely that one consequence of its evolution of the common law will be a greater willingness on the part of Canadian courts to render non-monetary judgments that depend on enforcement by a foreign court. In *Barrick Gold Corp v Lopehandia* the plaintiff alleged that the defendant had posted defamatory statements about it on the Internet.[95] It sought a permanent injunction against the defendant restraining such conduct. The proceedings were brought in Ontario but the defendant lived and acted in British Columbia. The Court of Appeal for Ontario observed:

> The more troubling point respecting the claim for injunctive relief is the *in personam* nature of the remedy, the marginal presence of the defendant in the jurisdiction, and the concerns about enforceability of such an order. The motions judge was correct to be worried about this. Courts have traditionally been reluctant to grant injunctive relief against defendants who are outside the jurisdiction.[96]

Yet the court granted the injunction. In part, the decision was based on the court's sense that the courts of British Columbia might, in accordance with the principles of *Morguard*, enforce the order in that province.[97] Only a few years later, *Pro Swing* confirmed these earlier suspicions.

C. DEFENCES TO RECOGNITION AND ENFORCEMENT

The common law has developed several defences to recognition and enforcement. If the test, outlined above, for recognition and enforcement is satisfied it is then open to the defendant to raise one or more of these defences. If the court accepts the defence then the judgment will not be recognized or enforced.

At the outset, it is important to appreciate what is not a defence. First, the defendant cannot argue that the foreign court lacked jurisdiction under its own rules. Arguments on that issue must be raised in the foreign court, not the court being asked to recognize the judgment. Second, the defendant cannot seek to reopen the merits of the case, either on issues of fact or of law.[98] On these issues the foreign court's

---

95 (2004), 71 OR (3d) 416 (CA).
96 *Ibid* at para 73.
97 *Ibid* at para 77.
98 *Old North*, above note 50 at paras 40–41.

decision is taken as final. An extreme example can illustrate the point. In *Godard v Gray* the French court ruled on a point of English law.[99] In English enforcement proceedings the defendant argued that the French court had erred. Despite the English court's superior knowledge of the content of English law, it refused to question the merits of the foreign decision. Errors of fact or law should be raised on appeal in the foreign forum, not as defences to enforcement.

1) The Scope of the Defences

Traditionally, each of the defences has been narrowly interpreted and the courts have resisted the creation of new defences. However, the extension of the *Morguard* test to international judgments has led to the suggestion that a new defence should be recognized or that the traditional defences should be expanded. In *Beals*, the trial judge thought that in the wake of *Morguard* the court would be required to develop "some sort of judicial sniff test in considering foreign judgments" to handle cases that did not meet the narrow definitions of fraud and public policy.[100] But the Supreme Court of Canada was more circumspect. The majority of the court resisted expansion of the defences. Justice Major acknowledged that "unusual" situations might arise that would justify the creation of a new defence to the enforcement of an international judgment. However, such a defence would have to be narrow, like the existing defences.[101] In contrast, LeBel J concluded that the scope of the existing natural justice defence needed to be expanded and that "serious consideration" should be given to refusing to enforce judgments whose enforcement "would shock the conscience of Canadians."[102] Thus far, the defences have retained their traditional scope.

In the wake of *Pro Swing*, a further issue is whether enforcing non-monetary judgments should lead to an expansion of the current defences or to the creation of new defences. As the majority decision noted, this issue closely parallels the post-*Morguard* debate about the scope of the defences for money judgments. In *Pro Swing*, the court did not have to analyze either expansion or creation of defences. Both the majority and the minority did mention Major J's acknowledgement in *Beals* that a new defence could someday be created and seemed to accept this as sufficient, for the time being, in the non-monetary judgment context.

---

99 (1870), LR 6 QB 139.
100 (1998), 42 OR (3d) 127 at 144 (SCJ).
101 *Beals*, above note 22 at paras 41–42.
102 *Ibid* at paras 216–18, 238–39, and 252–53.

In *United States of America v Yemec*, a proceeding to enforce both a money judgment and an injunction from Illinois, the Ontario Superior Court of Justice created a new defence, "loss of meaningful opportunity to be heard." However, this was reversed by the Court of Appeal which held this was indistinguishable from the denial of natural justice defence.[103]

2) Fraud

It is well established that a judgment obtained by fraud will not be recognized. However, there are many different ways that fraud can affect the outcome of proceedings, and not all will satisfy this defence. In English law the courts have adopted a broad meaning of fraud.[104] Fraud going either to whether the court had jurisdiction or to the merits of the dispute is a defence to enforcement. This allows the defendant, in enforcement proceedings, to challenge the evidence that was before the foreign court. The evidence could be challenged, for example, on the basis that a witness had lied or that documents had been forged. The defendant can raise this defence even if he or she did not challenge the evidence in the foreign court or, in contrast, did challenge it and the court rejected the challenge.

The Canadian approach to this defence is narrower. Historically the courts have drawn a distinction between intrinsic fraud and extrinsic fraud.[105] The former relates to the merits of the dispute and the latter relates to the process used by the court. Intrinsic fraud cannot be raised as a defence.[106] These issues should have been challenged in the foreign forum. Extrinsic fraud, in contrast, can be challenged. So if the plaintiff's fraud has misled the court such that it took jurisdiction where otherwise it would not, this is extrinsic or procedural fraud and is properly a defence.

Over time, the Canadian courts have relaxed this position somewhat. They have allowed a defendant to resist a foreign judgment based on intrinsic fraud as long as the challenge is based on fresh evidence, discovered since the trial, and which could not have, with reasonable diligence, been discovered any earlier.[107] More recently, the Supreme Court of Canada has indicated that the language of extrinsic and intrinsic fraud is unhelpful. It is clearer to say that fraud going to the

---

103 Above note 86 at paras 26–28.
104 The leading cases are *Abouloff v Oppenheimer* (1882), 10 QBD 295; *Owens Bank Ltd v Bracco*, [1992] 2 AC 443 (HL).
105 *Beals*, above note 22 at para 45.
106 *Stanton v Gudbranson* (1999), 45 RFL (4th) 85 (BCSC).
107 *Beals*, above note 22 at paras 47 and 50. See also *Sutcliffe v Sotvedt*, 2015 NSSC 194.

foreign court's jurisdiction can always be challenged, while fraud going to the merits of the dispute requires fresh evidence for a challenge.[108]

3) Denial of Natural Justice

The common law will not recognize a foreign judgment obtained in proceedings in which one of the parties was denied procedural rights considered by the forum to be fundamental or essential. Central among these rights are the right to be notified of the proceedings, the right to present evidence, and the right to make submissions. If a defendant is unaware of foreign litigation and only learns of the judgment in enforcement proceedings, he or she will be able to resist enforcement based on the lack of notice.

In *Ivey*, the defendant raised several concerns about the process that had been followed in the United States District Court in Michigan.[109] The court found no basis for his argument that he had not had the opportunity to be heard. The court also rejected his allegation that the imposition of strict liability by statute was a denial of natural justice, in part because Canadian law frequently imposes the same type of liability.

The natural justice defence was a point of some debate in *Beals*.[110] At issue was the adequacy of the notice the defendants received about the Florida litigation. In his dissent, Binnie J outlined several key aspects of the Florida litigation about which the defendants had no notice. He held that, taken together, this constituted a failure of notice and thus a denial of natural justice.[111] In contrast, in a relatively brief analysis, Major J addressed only the defendants' concern that they were not told the amount being claimed by the plaintiffs but rather just that the claim was for more than US$5,000. Justice Major held that, in the circumstances of this case, the failure of the defendants to be told the amount claimed did not amount to a lack of notice. After all, the defendants knew that the plaintiffs were claiming repayment of the purchase price, losses

---

108 *Beals*, above note 22 at para 51. See *Cabaniss v Cabaniss*, 2010 BCCA 348. For the suggestion that in certain circumstances even fraud as to jurisdiction must be raised in the foreign forum and cannot be raised as a defence, see *Monte Cristo Investments LLC v Hydroslotter Corp*, 2011 ONSC 6011 at paras 31–32, aff'd without comment on this point 2012 ONCA 213.
109 Above note 51. Another case in which several procedural concerns were raised but rejected is *SHN Grundstuecksverwaltungsgesellschaft MBH & Co Seniorenresidenz Hoppegarten—Neuenhagen KG v Hanne*, 2014 ABCA 168.
110 Above note 22.
111 *Ibid* at paras 83 and 125.

resulting from the failed model home construction, lost revenue for their construction business, punitive damages, and treble damages.[112]

This disagreement at the Supreme Court of Canada raises the question of the extent to which a defendant is expected to seek out information about foreign litigation of which he or she has at least some notice. Under our domestic law, we expect defendants to take reasonable and proper steps to respond to proceedings that have been validly commenced. As a general rule, we should expect the same reasonable conduct in the face of foreign proceedings. The defendants in *Beals* could have obtained additional information but instead chose not to become involved. Justice Binnie, in contrast, would impose a higher obligation on plaintiffs suing defendants abroad, especially those who are self-represented, to inform them about the litigation. In his dissent in *Beals*, LeBel J went even further. He held that (1) the defendant had to be informed of the approximate amount claimed by the plaintiff and (2) the defendant had to be alerted to the consequences of "any procedural steps taken or not taken" if those consequences would not otherwise be reasonably apparent.[113] This would be a significant widening of the natural justice defence. It also raises vagueness concerns because while the standard procedural rules the plaintiff must follow are easy to ascertain, it is not clear what the plaintiff would be required to do to comply with this higher standard.

Some Canadian courts have had to consider the fairness of the justice system in Singapore. In *Oakwell Engineering Ltd v Enernorth Industries Inc* the plaintiff obtained a judgment against the defendant in Singapore and then sought to enforce it in Ontario.[114] The defendant argued that the Singapore justice system was biased and corrupt. It alleged that the judiciary was not independent of the government and that the plaintiff's close ties to the government meant that the courts were bound to decide in its favour. The court rejected these arguments on the basis that insufficient evidence had been presented to establish these very serious allegations. However, in another case, the Ontario Superior Court of Justice refused to grant summary judgment in a proceeding to enforce another Singapore judgment.[115] The court thought more facts were needed to resolve the issues, including whether the defendant had a reasonable opportunity to be heard in Singapore and whether the courts consciously favour the interests of banks as litigants.

---

112 *Ibid* at paras 65–66.
113 *Ibid* at paras 238–39 and 252–53.
114 (2006), 81 OR (3d) 288 (CA).
115 *State Bank of India v Navaratna*, [2006] OJ No 1125 (SCJ).

Interplay between civil and criminal proceedings can raise possible concerns about natural justice. In part this stems from the different law in Canada and the United States on self-incrimination. This can require defendants to make important choices about what to say in each type of proceeding. In two cases the defendants sought to avoid recognition in Ontario of an American judgment because the impact of parallel criminal charges against them was to restrict their opportunity to defend the foreign civil litigation.[116] In both cases the court rejected the defence. The Court of Appeal for Ontario did not consider it appropriate that defendants could avoid civil liability simply because their conduct had also triggered criminal proceedings. The fact that the protection against self-incrimination operated differently in the two countries did not amount to a denial of natural justice.

4) Public Policy

This defence has to some extent already been addressed in Chapter 3. The forum reserves to itself the right to refuse to recognize and enforce foreign judgments that are contrary to the forum's public policy. This defence needs to be interpreted narrowly, since otherwise it would allow courts to significantly undermine international comity through insular, chauvinistic decisions. It is not established simply because a foreign decision is based on law that has a different policy basis than that of the forum. Canadian courts are quite willing to recognize foreign judgments based on laws that are very different from those in effect where those courts sit.[117] For this defence to apply, the foreign judgment must be based on laws that violate the "essential morality" or "fundamental values" of the forum.[118] The court would, for example, refuse to recognize a decision based on a law that confiscated property on religious or racial grounds.[119]

In *Boardwalk Regency Corp v Maalouf* the plaintiff attempted to enforce in Ontario a New Jersey judgment in respect of gaming debts.[120] The original transaction was illegal under Ontario law. The defendant

---

116 *United States of America v Levy* (2002), 1 CPC (6th) 386 (Ont SCJ), aff'd [2003] OJ No 56 (CA); *King v Drabinsky* (2008), 91 OR (3d) 616 (CA).
117 *Boardwalk Regency Corp v Maalouf* (1992), 6 OR (3d) 737 at 748 (CA).
118 *Ibid* at 743; *Society of Lloyd's v Meinzer* (2001), 55 OR (3d) 688 at 713 (CA); *Dash 224, LLC v Vector Aerospace Engine Services-Atlantic Inc*, 2015 PESC 27 at paras 32–33.
119 See *Oppenheimer v Cattermole*, [1976] AC 249 (HL). As another example, double recovery by a plaintiff has been held to be contrary to our "general moral outlook": *Re Lambert* (2001), 26 CBR (4th) 235 at para 76 (Ont SCJ).
120 Above note 117.

raised the public policy defence, but a majority of the Court of Appeal for Ontario held that the judgment was enforceable. The court examined Ontario's statutory provisions on gaming, the evolution of the law, and related community beliefs and values. The majority concluded that the conduct was not immoral and did not violate Ontario's fundamental values. In part, this conclusion was based on the province's own role in state-run gaming. The dissent was more willing to separate legal state-run gaming from illegal private gaming and also quicker to equate the criminal prohibition on the conduct with the prevailing standard of morality.

a) Punitive Damages

One of the key issues arising under the public policy defence is the enforcement of foreign punitive damages awards. American courts, in particular, often create headlines with the size of these awards, often made by local juries against foreign defendants. Some scholars have argued that foreign punitive damages awards should not be enforceable in Canada.[121] However, this argument goes too far, beyond the protection that defendants with assets in Canada require or merit.

In some situations, there is little merit to invoking public policy to stop such enforcement. For example, if a New York court orders that a New York defendant pay punitive damages to the plaintiff, and that defendant has assets in Ontario, those assets should not be, by Ontario's public policy, sheltered from satisfying the punitive damages portion of the judgment. As another example, if an Ontario defendant submits to proceedings in Texas, then a resulting punitive damages award should arguably be enforceable in Ontario.

In addition, Canadian courts award punitive damages in a variety of cases, so it is difficult to accept that all such awards made by a foreign court are against our own public policy.[122] The Supreme Court of Canada has upheld a jury's punitive damages award in the Ontario Court (General Division) of one million dollars.[123] Other jurisdictions are equally capable of imposing proportional awards of punitive damages, such that Canadian notions of public policy are not violated by their enforcement. While certainly true that Canadian courts would consider some punitive damages awards made in the United States to

---

121 Jacob Ziegel, "Enforcement of Foreign Judgments in Canada, Unlevel Playing Fields, and *Beals v. Saldanha*: A Consumer Perspective" (2003) 38 *Canadian Business Law Journal* 294 at 295.
122 *Old North*, above note 50 at para 53. See also *Clancy v Beach* (1994), 92 BCLR (2d) 82 at para 44 (SC).
123 *Whiten v Pilot Insurance Co*, [2002] 1 SCR 595.

be grossly excessive, this cannot justify a blanket rule against all such enforcement.

A better solution is to provide for review, by the enforcing court, of foreign punitive damage awards. At common law, this could be incorporated as part of the public policy defence.[124] The review should be based on the following principles. First, the ability to deny enforcement should be discretionary, not mandatory. It should be up to the enforcing court, on a case-by-case basis. Second, the focus for what is reasonable should be on an amount comparable to what the enforcing court could have awarded, but not necessarily what it would have awarded.[125] Third, in assessing whether punitive damages could have been awarded, the court should consider the applicable law as applied by the foreign court rather than the law of the forum. This is essential to avoid screening out reasonable foreign punitive damages awards in cases where, on the facts, Canadian law does not allow punitive damages. The court should also be sensitive to the role that punitive damages occupy in the system of law under which they were awarded. They might be awarded in a case where there is a strong sense that the compensatory damages, as assessed, do not truly make the plaintiff whole or in a case where a successful plaintiff is unable to recover legal costs. Fourth, the enforcing court should be able to consider, as part of the review, the basis on which the foreign court took jurisdiction over the defendant. If the defendant is a resident of the foreign jurisdiction or submitted to the litigation there, it should be more difficult for the enforcing court to refuse to enforce the resulting punitive damages award. In sum, the enforcing court should enforce the punitive damages award unless it considers it to be truly unreasonable.

Support for limited review of punitive damages awards can be found in *Beals*. In that case, US$50,000 of the award was punitive damages. In the context of stressing that the public policy defence was to continue to have a narrow scope, Major J stated:

> The award of damages by the Florida jury does not violate our principles of morality. The sums involved, although they have grown large, are not by themselves a basis to refuse enforcement of the foreign judgment in Canada. Even if it could be argued in another case that the arbitrariness of the award can properly fit into a public policy

---

124 For a statutory analogy, see *The Enforcement of Foreign Judgments Act*, above note 66, s 6.
125 Janet Walker, "*Beals v. Saldanha*: Striking the Comity Balance Anew" (2002) 5 *Canadian International Lawyer* 28 at 32.

argument, the record here does not provide any basis allowing the Canadian court to re-evaluate the amount of the award.¹²⁶

While Major J did not distinguish, in this statement, between the punitive damages and the compensatory damages, the result was that the punitive damages were enforceable. Canadian courts have enforced punitive damages awards in several other cases.¹²⁷ In dissent, LeBel J held that the natural justice defence, not public policy, should apply to "unimaginably large" punitive damages awards where "the applicable law does not, in theory at least, support the size of the damage award."¹²⁸ In his view the punitive damages had likely been awarded without proof that the defendants deserved to be punished, since they had done nothing deserving of punishment.¹²⁹

b) Multiple Damages

Much of the analysis of punitive damages applies equally to multiple damages awards, such as an award of treble damages. However, unlike punitive damages, multiple damages are generally not available under Canadian law. This gives greater force to the argument that they should not be enforced under the defence of public policy. Indeed, some jurisdictions such as the United Kingdom have enacted statutes to specifically block the enforcement of foreign multiple damages awards.¹³⁰ Canada, however, has adopted a different statutory approach. Under the *Foreign Extraterritorial Measures Act*,¹³¹ the Attorney General of Canada has the discretion to hold multiple damages awards made in foreign antitrust actions unenforceable in Canada. As was noted by the British Columbia Court of Appeal in *Old North*, that statute could have instead declared all multiple damages awards made by foreign courts unenforceable in Canada. It also could have covered awards based upon statutes other than antitrust laws. Yet it did neither.¹³² The specific provision drafted by Parliament therefore suggests that in general the enforcement of foreign multiple damages awards does not violate Canadian public policy.

Consistent with this reasoning, in *Old North* the court enforced a North Carolina award in which the damages had been trebled under an

---

126 *Beals*, above note 22 at para 76.
127 In an extreme example, *Tracy v The Iranian Ministry of Information and Security*, 2016 ONSC 3759 at paras 106–9 [*Tracy*], the court enforced foreign judgments awarding hundreds of millions of dollars in punitive damages.
128 *Beals*, above note 22 at paras 226 and 229.
129 *Ibid* at paras 257 and 265.
130 *Protection of Trading Interests Act 1980* (UK), 1980, c 11, s 5(2).
131 RSC 1985, c F-29, ss 8–9.
132 Above note 50 at para 51.

unfair trade practice statute. In addition, Binnie J's judgment in *Beals* suggested that the approximately US$210,000 awarded by the Florida jury as compensatory damages represented an actual loss of about US$70,000, which was then trebled.[133] If Binnie J was correct, *Beals* is a leading example of straightforward enforcement of a multiple damages award. As a general rule, foreign multiple damages awards should be enforced in Canada. However, it would not be inappropriate for the courts to adopt a review process similar to that proposed for punitive damages awards to screen out awards that are truly unreasonable.

5) Other Defences

Two other defences arise less frequently. Under the first, a foreign judgment will not be recognized if there is already a prior judgment of the forum that is inconsistent with that foreign judgment.[134] This defence is quite important in cases of parallel litigation in different jurisdictions. It can also be posited that recognition would be refused if an inconsistent foreign judgment had previously been recognized in the forum.[135] Under the second, a foreign judgment that purports to resolve a question of title to immovable property in the forum will not be recognized.[136] This is a corollary of the special jurisdictional rules for cases involving immovable property, discussed in Chapter 17. While better explained as a defence, this could also be seen as a particular instance of the foreign court not having jurisdictional competence to deal with the subject matter of the dispute, namely immovable property outside its territory.

6) Foreign Negative Declarations

One possible remedy available in litigation is a declaration. In a proceeding for a "negative declaration" the plaintiff seeks a declaration that it does not owe any money to the defendant. Such proceedings are almost always brought for tactical reasons: the plaintiff either is being sued in another forum or anticipates being sued there and so sues as plaintiff in its preferred forum for a negative declaration.

While Canadian courts have shown hostility to this sort of proceeding, no specific defence precludes the recognition of foreign nega-

---

133 Above note 22 at para 97. A clearer example is *Bank of Mongolia v Taskin*, 2011 ONSC 6083, aff'd 2012 ONCA 220.
134 *Vervaeke v Smith*, [1983] 1 AC 145 (HL). See also *South Pacific Import*, above note 70 at paras 55–56.
135 See *Showlag v Mansour*, [1995] 1 AC 431 (PC).
136 *Duke v Andler*, [1932] SCR 734. On this basis it is difficult to accept the majority decision in *Chapman Estate v O'Hara*, [1988] 2 WWR 275 (Sask CA).

tive declarations. If they meet the test for recognition and are not defeated by any of the established defences, negative declarations can be invoked as a defence to proceedings in the forum on the basis of *res judicata* or issue estoppel. However, the Supreme Court of Canada has held that these bases are equitable and so, in limited circumstances, the court can refuse to apply them.[137] In one recent decision, the Court of Appeal for Ontario concluded that even if the foreign negative declaration it was considering otherwise met the test for recognition, in its discretion it would not give it preclusive effect.[138] There had not been a hearing on the merits in the foreign forum and the underlying claim for compensation was integrally tied to Ontario.

7) Limitation Periods

Because the common law process for enforcement involves commencing a new action, the issue of limitation periods should be considered. The enforcement action must be started within the relevant period. However, it may be difficult to identify that period. The analysis proceeds under the law of the enforcing forum, since it is its substantive law that governs the enforcement action. The characterization of the enforcement action in part depends on the wording of the limitation statute. Older statutes prescribe periods for particular types of claim. In *Lax v Lax* the issue was whether an action to enforce a California judgment in Ontario was an action on a contract debt or an action on a judgment.[139] Historically a foreign judgment was treated as having created a simple contract debt between the parties and was therefore subject to the limitation period applicable to actions in contract.[140] But in *Girsberger v Kresz* the court had rejected that characterization as based on an outdated legal fiction and instead held that a claim on a foreign judgment should be characterized as a claim on a judgment.[141] This made a significant difference: the contract period was six years and the judgment period was twenty years. However, in *Lax v Lax* the court insisted on the orthodox view and applied the period for contract debts.[142]

---

137 *Danyluk v Ainsworth Technologies Inc*, [2001] 2 SCR 460 at 492.
138 *Amtim Capital Inc v Appliance Recycling Centers of America*, 2014 ONCA 62.
139 (2004), 70 OR (3d) 520 (CA).
140 *Rutledge v The United States Savings and Loan Co* (1906), 37 SCR 546; *Livesley v E Clemens Horst Co*, [1924] SCR 605 at 609–10.
141 (2000), 47 OR (3d) 145 (SCJ), aff'd (2002), 50 OR (3d) 157 (CA).
142 For a critical evaluation of this decision, see Stephen GA Pitel & Jonathan de Vries, "The Ontario Limitation Period for Actions to Enforce Foreign Judgments" (2004) 29 *Advocates' Quarterly* 312.

More modern limitation statutes contain a general limitation period to be applied to a broad range of claims. For example, section 4 of the Ontario *Limitations Act, 2002* states that unless the statute provides otherwise, all proceedings must be commenced within a two-year limitation period.[143] The statute also provides for certain proceedings to be exempt from any limitation period. One such proceeding, in section 16(1)(b), is "a proceeding to enforce an order of a court, or any other order that may be enforced in the same way as a court order." So there is still an issue about whether an action to enforce a foreign judgment fits under the general period or the specific period in section 16, and the choice is even starker: either the period is two years or there is no limitation at all.[144]

Under either type of statute, a short limitation period is arguably not appropriate for enforcement proceedings. As a practical matter, it is more difficult to enforce a foreign judgment than a domestic one. It is therefore difficult to understand why a plaintiff should have only a short time for the former but a longer or indefinite time for the latter. During the limitation period, even if the foreign judgment is under appeal and thus years away from the eventual and uncertain outcome, the plaintiff has to find the defendant's assets, retain local lawyers, and start proceedings. For this, two years in particular seems impracticably short. In addition, at least for judgments from other provinces, a two-year limitation is much shorter than the time available under alternative statutory registration schemes, discussed below, and erects, rather than reduces, barriers to interprovincial enforcement. In the wake of *Morguard*, this is an odd approach.

Ideally, provincial limitation statutes should contain an express provision dealing with actions on a foreign judgment. There are valid policy reasons for treating foreign judgments differently from judgments of the forum, particularly in light of the need to assess possible defences. But these policy reasons do not require such a short limitation period. Rather, a period of ten or fifteen years would be more appropriate.[145]

---

143 SO 2002, c 24, Sch B.
144 In *Commission de la Construction du Québec v Access Rigging Services Inc*, 2010 ONSC 5897, the court held a claim on a foreign judgment did not fall within s 16(1)(b). The opposite view was endorsed in *PT ATPK Resources TBK (Indonesia) v Diversified Energy and Resource Corporation*, 2013 ONSC 5913 at paras 41–43. In Alberta, see *Laasch v Turenne*, 2012 ABCA 32, applying the general limitation period.
145 See, for example, *Limitation Act*, SBC 2012, c 13, s 7(b).

D. CLASS ACTIONS

In recent years, Canadian courts have been coming to terms with the recognition of foreign class action judgments. These cases raise several considerations that differ from those in litigation between individual parties. One of the key features of class actions in many jurisdictions is an open-ended definition of the class covered by the claim. Any individuals meeting the class description are intended to be covered, and so bound by the decision, unless they specifically opt out and retain their individual rights. For example, a class action might be brought on behalf of all people who bought a particular product in a particular year.

For conflict of laws purposes, the most important development has been the willingness of courts in various jurisdictions—both provinces and other countries—to certify class actions which, in the description of the class, cover individuals outside the particular jurisdiction. So a class action could be brought in Ontario on behalf of a class that includes people from across Canada. This has become known as a "national class."[146] It is also possible to have a class that either covers individuals in two or more specific countries or covers individuals wherever they are located.[147] Increasing the size of the class in this way is consistent with some of the most important underlying aims of class actions: efficiency and access to justice.[148]

Most class actions are settled and the settlement is approved by a judgment. In settling the claim, the defendant wants to put an end to the claims that could be brought by those covered by the class description. The effectiveness of this, however, depends in national and international class cases on the extent to which other jurisdictions will recognize the judgment and hold that it is binding on class members in the forum.

Two examples can illustrate the problem. First, suppose class actions are started in both Ontario and Saskatchewan. Each purports to cover the same national class. If the defendant quickly settles the Saskatchewan action and obtains court approval, what is the effect on the Ontario action? The defendant's position will be that the Ontario

---

146 See, for example, *Harrington v Dow Corning Corp* (2000), 193 DLR (4th) 67 (BCCA); *Carom v Bre-X Minerals Ltd* (1999), 44 OR (3d) 173 (SCJ); *Wilson v Servier Canada Inc* (2000), 50 OR (3d) 219 (SCJ).

147 See, for example, *Robertson v Thomson Corp* (1999), 43 OR (3d) 161 (Gen Div); *Silver v IMAX Corp* (2009), 86 CPC (6th) 273 (Ont SCJ).

148 Craig Jones, "The Case for a National Class" (2004) 1 *Canadian Class Action Review* 29. There is a considerable body of recent scholarship on the legality of national and worldwide class actions. See the discussion in Chapter 5.

court should recognize the judgment and, under the doctrine of *res judicata*, it has a complete defence to the action.[149] Second, suppose a class action is started in Texas that purports to cover individuals in the United States and Canada. If that action is settled with judicial approval, what is the impact on any attempt to launch a class action on behalf of individual Canadians in a Canadian court? As in the first example, the defendant will want to rely on the Texas judgment as precluding any further claim. To do so it will have to show that the judgment is recognized in the Canadian court.

In *Currie v McDonald's Restaurants of Canada Ltd* the Court of Appeal for Ontario addressed the recognition of a foreign class action judgment.[150] A class action had been brought in Illinois on behalf of customers, both national and international, of McDonald's, alleging fraud in connection with one of its promotional contests. A settlement of that action was approved by the court. Currie started a class action against McDonald's in Ontario on behalf of Canadian residents, raising allegations similar to those in the Illinois action. The defendant sought to have the Illinois judgment recognized by the Ontario court. The court held that foreign class action judgments could be recognized under the traditional common law principles. However, Sharpe JA stated that "[b]efore enforcing a foreign class action judgment against Ontario residents, we should ensure that the foreign court had a proper basis for the assertion of jurisdiction and that the interests of Ontario residents were adequately protected."[151]

The court held that there was a real and substantial connection between the dispute and Illinois. This is consistent with the analysis in Canadian class action cases taking jurisdiction over non-resident plaintiffs. Nonetheless, the court refused to recognize the Illinois judgment. It had serious concerns about the adequacy of the notice given to Canadian residents. In the Illinois class action, notice had been given to Canadian residents by means of two advertisements in *Maclean's* magazine and one advertisement in each of three French language newspapers in Quebec. Canadian residents were required to opt out of the settlement by a specified date or else they would be bound by its terms. The court held that this was procedurally insufficient to protect the rights of Canadian residents.

---

149 See John CL Dixon, "The *Res Judicata* Effect in England of a U.S. Class Action Settlement" (1997) 46 *International and Comparative Law Quarterly* 134.
150 (2005), 74 OR (3d) 321 (CA) [*Currie*]. See also *Silver v IMAX Corp*, 2013 ONSC 1667 at paras 91–131.
151 *Currie, ibid* at para 17.

One interesting thing about the court's analysis in *Currie* is the apparent blurring of the distinction between international competence—the question of the foreign court's jurisdiction—and the defences. Arguably the issue of adequate notice is best considered as part of the natural justice defence. But the court instead treated the question of procedural fairness in the foreign forum as part of its analysis of whether the foreign court had jurisdiction.[152] It is not clear whether this blurring will improve the analysis in these cases, have no effect, or impair the analysis. At a minimum, little seems to have been gained by moving away from the orthodox separation of jurisdiction and the defences.

Concerns with notice were also prominent in *Lepine v Canada Post Corp*, in which both the Quebec courts and the Supreme Court of Canada refused to recognize an Ontario judgment approving a class action settlement in a national class case.[153] The courts held that the notice did not adequately inform Quebec residents of their rights. This meant that the Ontario judgment was in violation of fundamental procedural rights, which is a bar to recognition under article 3155(4) of the *Civil Code of Quebec*.[154]

In *Meeking v Cash Store Inc* the Manitoba Court of Appeal was asked to recognize an Ontario class action judgment which purported to cover class members in Manitoba.[155] It followed the approach in *Currie*, looking first at the basis on which the Ontario court took jurisdiction and second at issues of notice. On the first point, mindful of *Club Resorts*, it sought to identify a presumptive connecting factor which would have given the Ontario court jurisdiction over non-resident class members. It held that "in circumstances where the court has territorial jurisdiction over both the defendant and the representative plaintiff in a class action proceeding, common issues between the claim of the representative plaintiff and that of non-resident plaintiffs is a presumptive connecting factor, sufficient to give the court jurisdiction over non-resident plaintiffs."[156] Since the common issues are required for the class action to have been certified, this new factor appears quite easy to satisfy. On the second point, it agreed with the lower court's decision that notice to class members in Manitoba was adequate in respect of some claims

---

152 *Ibid* at paras 30–31. See *McCutcheon v The Cash Store Inc* (2006), 80 OR (3d) 644 at para 56 (SCJ): "By incorporating fairness considerations into the rules for jurisdiction, the reasoning in *Currie* abandons some of the traditional distinctions between jurisdiction and recognition."
153 2009 SCC 16, aff'g [2007] RJQ 1920 (CA), aff'g [2005] JQ no 9806 (CS). See also *HSBC Bank of Canada v Hocking*, [2006] RJQ 804 (CS), aff'd [2008] RJQ 1189 (CA).
154 CQLR c C-1991.
155 2013 MBCA 81.
156 *Ibid* at paras 97 and 106.

but inadequate in respect of others. As a result, the Ontario decision was recognized only in part.[157]

E. STATUTORY REGISTRATION

In an effort to improve the process of recognition and enforcement of foreign judgments, each Canadian common law province has enacted legislation that provides for the registration of judgments from specified jurisdictions. Once the registration process has been followed, the foreign judgment becomes enforceable as though it had been granted in the forum. The aim of these statutes, which draw heavily on model legislation drafted by the Uniform Law Conference of Canada, is to make the process easier and quicker. There is some debate about whether this aim has been achieved. These statutes operate alongside the common law—they do not replace it—and so the plaintiff has a choice of process. However, there are limitations in the scope of the legislation so that in some cases only the common law route is available. There are differences in the legislation as between provinces so close attention must be paid to the specific language in any particular province.[158]

1) Scope

Some statutory schemes are limited to the judgments of other provinces. For example, the Ontario *Reciprocal Enforcement of Judgments Act* covers judgments only from other common law provinces.[159] In contrast, the scheme in some provinces extends to judgments from outside Canada.[160]

Some schemes are limited to judgments for the payment of money. In some other provinces, either the same statute or a separate statute covers non-monetary judgments or decrees. For example, the definition of "Canadian judgment" in British Columbia's *Enforcement of Canadian Judgments and Decrees Act* includes non-monetary judgments,

---

157 *Ibid* at paras 111–15.
158 References to statutes in this section are chiefly to provide examples. Space does not permit comprehensive reference to all relevant statutes.
159 RSO 1990, c R.5, s 7 [REJA (Ont)].
160 Under Man Reg 319/87 R, made under *The Reciprocal Enforcement of Judgments Act*, CCSM c J20, s 12(1) [REJA (Man)], the Manitoba scheme applies to all common law provinces and territories of Canada, seven of the Australian states and territories, and two American states (Washington and Idaho).

including interlocutory orders.¹⁶¹ Saskatchewan has gone one step further. In *The Enforcement of Foreign Judgments Act*, which applies to judgments from outside Canada, the definition of "foreign judgment" includes non-monetary judgments.¹⁶²

Some of the provincial statutes exclude the registration of foreign maintenance and support orders. This is because the registration of these orders is governed by a separate provincial statute. These orders are more complex than most money judgments, largely because they provide for ongoing payments and can be varied as circumstances change. This issue is covered in more detail in Chapter 25.

In *Solehdin v Stern Estate* the British Columbia Court of Appeal held that an Ontario judgment rendered in an action to enforce a Louisiana judgment in Ontario could be registered, as a "Canadian judgment," under the British Columbia legislation.¹⁶³ In contesting the registration, the judgment debtors argued it amounted to indirect registration of the Louisiana judgment. The court disagreed, noting that it was the Ontario judgment which was being registered.

2) Process

Taking the scheme in Ontario as an example, the process starts with the plaintiff applying to have the foreign judgment registered. In most cases, this can be done without notice to the defendant.¹⁶⁴ If notice is not given, the plaintiff is under the standard obligation in *ex parte* matters to make full and frank disclosure to the court.¹⁶⁵ The application must be made within the time limit set out in the statutory scheme, for example within six years of the foreign judgment.¹⁶⁶ In response to the application, the court orders the judgment registered. The plaintiff then must notify the defendant of the registration and the defendant has the opportunity, within a specified time, to move to set the registration aside.¹⁶⁷

---

161 SBC 2003, c 29, ss 1(1) and 2(1) [*ECJDA* (BC)]. For a detailed analysis of the statute, see Edinger, above note 72. Similar legislation is in force in Manitoba: *The Enforcement of Canadian Judgments Act*, CCSM c E116 [*ECJA* (Man)]; Nova Scotia: *Enforcement of Canadian Judgments and Decrees Act*, SNS 2001, c 30; and Saskatchewan: *The Enforcement of Canadian Judgments Act, 2002*, SS 2002, c E-9.1001.
162 Above note 66, s 2.
163 2014 BCCA 482. See also *Tracy*, above note 127 at para 177.
164 *REJA* (Ont), above note 159, s 2.
165 See, for example, *Central Guaranty Trust Co v Deluca*, [1995] NWTR 200 (SC) [*Central Guaranty Trust Co*].
166 *REJA* (Ont), above note 159, s 2. Some statutes set a deadline of the earlier of ten years from the judgment and the date when the time for enforcement ends in the rendering jurisdiction: see *ECJA* (Man), above note 161, s 5(1).
167 *REJA* (Ont), above note 159, ss 5–6.

There is conflicting authority on the strictness of the time limits under the statutes. In some cases, the courts have insisted on strict compliance.[168] In others, the courts have allowed registration to be challenged beyond the time period when "basic requirements to obtain the order on an *ex parte* basis were falsely or fraudulently put before the court."[169]

3) Defences

It is difficult to generalize about the defences because of the differences between the statutes. Typically the defences of fraud, denial of natural justice, and public policy are all available and operate very much as they do at common law. Some statutes provide that an appeal period being open or an appeal being pending in the foreign jurisdiction is a defence to registration. Some statutes preserve any other common law defence to an enforcement action not otherwise listed in the legislation.

Because of the process these schemes follow, lack of jurisdiction is generally framed as a defence, to be raised by the defendant in objecting to registration, rather than as part of a test for registration. Most statutes preserve the common law approach for international competence: presence, submission, or a real and substantial connection. Sometimes this is done in quite broad language: for example, making it a defence that "the original court acted without jurisdiction."[170] In other schemes each of these elements is expressly indicated and may be varied from the common law. For example, some statutes require that the defendant was ordinarily resident in the foreign forum rather than merely present, and others take some steps towards defining what constitutes a real and substantial connection.

Under the Ontario statute, it is a defence to registration that the defendant was neither ordinarily resident nor carrying on business in the foreign jurisdiction and did not submit to the proceedings.[171] This means that in such a case, even if there was a real and substantial connection between the dispute and the foreign jurisdiction, the defendant could successfully oppose registration. There has been some debate about whether it is permissible for a province to have defences to registration that encompass judgments that, under *Morguard* and the common law, are enforceable. The courts have decided that this is possible because the registration scheme operates alongside and not instead of the common

---

168 See *Central Guaranty Trust Co*, above note 165.
169 See *James C Bennett Holdings Ltd v EMD Management Ltd* (1991), 74 Man R (2d) 92 at para 23 (QB).
170 REJA (Ont), above note 159, s 3(a). See also REJA (Man), above note 160, s 3(6)(a).
171 REJA (Ont), above note 159, s 3(b). See also REJA (Man), above note 160, s 3(6)(b).

law.[172] It is therefore important for a plaintiff, in deciding whether to commence enforcement proceedings or apply for registration, to consider which defences are open to the defendant under each of the two routes.

In the wake of *Morguard*, some provinces have significantly limited the defences to registration for judgments from other provinces. For example, under the *Canadian Judgments (Enforcement) Act* in Prince Edward Island it is no defence to registration that the court in the rendering province did not have jurisdictional competence.[173] The registering province's approach is to assume that the rendering province's court must have taken jurisdiction under the proper principles and it puts the onus on the defendant to raise any concerns about jurisdiction in the original proceedings rather than at the registration stage. These schemes have also removed fraud as a defence on the basis that any concerns about fraud should be raised in the rendering provinces and not at the registration stage. There are concerns about this approach. It can be argued that a defendant, under *Morguard*, must have the ability to resist registration on jurisdictional grounds. Under this argument, if improper proceedings are commenced elsewhere, the defendant should not bear the burden of having to object to the jurisdiction of the plaintiff's chosen forum but rather should be entitled to await the attempt at local registration.

4) Bilateral Agreements

All common law provinces have implemented a 1984 convention between Canada and the United Kingdom that creates a scheme for the recognition and enforcement of judgments between the two countries.[174] This provides a further alternative to the common law. The process is very similar to that under the more general provincial statutory schemes and the defences are similar too.

A similar convention was finalized in 1996 between Canada and France but has not yet been implemented. Rather than have a separate provincial statute for each reciprocating country, some provinces have enacted a model statute prepared by the Uniform Law Conference of Canada that would allow the province to give effect to each new convention as it comes into effect.[175]

---

172 *Acme Video Inc v Hedges* (1993), 12 OR (3d) 160 (CA); *TDI Hospitality Management Consultants Inc v Browne*, [1994] 9 WWR 153 (Man CA).
173 RSPEI 1988, c C-1.1, s 7(2). See also *ECJA* (Man), above note 161, s 6(3)(a); *ECJDA* (BC), above note 161, s 6(3)(a).
174 See, for example, *Reciprocal Enforcement of Judgments (U.K.) Act*, RSO 1990, c R.6.
175 See, for example, *Enforcement of Judgments Conventions Act, 1999*, SO 1999, c 12, Sch C.

FURTHER READINGS

BARNETT, PETER. *Res Judicata, Estoppel, and Foreign Judgments: The Preclusive Effects of Foreign Judgments in Private International Law* (Oxford: Oxford University Press, 2001).

BLACK, VAUGHAN. "A Canada-United States Full Faith and Credit Clause?" (2012) 18 *Southwestern Journal of International Law* 595.

BLACK, VAUGHAN. "Commodifying Justice for Global Free Trade: The Proposed Hague Judgments Convention" (2000) 38 *Osgoode Hall Law Journal* 237.

BRIGGS, ADRIAN. "Crossing the River by Feeling the Stones: Rethinking the Law on Foreign Judgments" (2004) 8 *Singapore Year Book of International Law* 1.

BRIGGS, ADRIAN. "Enforcing and Reinforcing an English Judgment" [2008] *Lloyd's Maritime and Commercial Law Quarterly* 421.

BRIGGS, ADRIAN. "Recognition of Foreign Judgments: A Matter of Obligation" (2013) 129 *Law Quarterly Review* 87.

BRIGGS, ADRIAN. "Which Foreign Judgments Should We Recognise Today?" (1987) 36 *International and Comparative Law Quarterly* 240.

CHONG, ADELINE. "Recognition of Foreign Judgments and Cross-Border Insolvencies" [2014] *Lloyd's Maritime and Commercial Law Quarterly* 241.

GLENN, H PATRICK. "A North American Transformative Judgment?" (2002) 81 *Canadian Bar Review* 469.

HARDER, SIRKO. "The Effects of Recognized Foreign Judgments in Civil and Commercial Matters" (2013) 62 *International and Comparative Law Quarterly* 441.

HO, HL. "Policies Underlying the Enforcement of Foreign Commercial Judgments" (1997) 46 *International and Comparative Law Quarterly* 443.

LA FOREST, ANNE WARNER. "New Brunswick's Continuing Policy of Splendid Isolation in the Recognition and Enforcement of Judgments" (2016) 58 *Canadian Business Law Journal* 57.

MANGAN, JAMES. "The Need for Cross-Border Clarity—Recognizing American Class Action Judgments in Canada" (2009) 35 *Advocates' Quarterly* 375.

MONESTIER, TANYA J. "Foreign Judgments at Common Law: Rethinking the Enforcement Rules" (2005) 28 *Dalhousie Law Journal* 163.

MONESTIER, TANYA J. "Jurisdiction and the Enforcement of Foreign Judgments" (2013) 42 *Advocates' Quarterly* 107.

MONESTIER, TANYA J. "*Lepine v. Canada Post*: Ironing Out the Wrinkles in the Interprovincial Enforcement of Class Judgments" (2008) 34 *Advocates' Quarterly* 499.

OPPONG, RICHARD. "Enforcing Foreign Non-money Judgments: An Examination of Some Recent Developments in Canada and Beyond" (2006) 39 *University of British Columbia Law Review* 257.

PENGELLEY, NICHOLAS. "'We All Have Too Much Invested to Stop': Enforcing *Chevron* in Canada" (2012) 40 *Advocates' Quarterly* 213.

PITEL, STEPHEN GA. "Enforcement of Foreign Judgments: Where *Morguard* Stands after *Beals*" (2004) 40 *Canadian Business Law Journal* 189.

PITEL, STEPHEN GA. "Enforcement of Foreign Non-monetary Judgments in Canada (and Beyond)" (2007) 3 *Journal of Private International Law* 241.

SAUMIER, GENEVIEVE. "Competing Class Actions across Canada: Still at the Starting Gate after *Canada Post v. Lepine*?" (2010) 48 *Canadian Business Law Journal* 462.

SAUMIER, GENEVIEVE. "The Recognition of Foreign Judgments in Quebec—The Mirror Crack'd?" (2002) 81 *Canadian Bar Review* 677.

SAUMIER, GENEVIEVE. "What's in a Name?: Lloyd's, International Comity and Public Policy" (2002) 37 *Canadian Business Law Journal* 388.

SNOW, ELLEN. "Protecting Canadian Plaintiffs in International Class Actions: The Need for a Principled Approach in Light of *Currie v. McDonald's Restaurants of Canada Ltd.*" (2005) 2 *Canadian Class Action Review* 217.

SULLIVAN, JOHN, & JONATHAN WOOLLEY. "*Oakwell Engineering Limited v. Enernorth Industries Inc.*: Questions of Burden and Bias in the Enforcement of Foreign Judgments" (2007) 85 *Canadian Bar Review* 605.

WALKER, JANET. "Crossborder Class Actions: A View from across the Border" (2003) *Michigan State Law Review* 755.

WALKER, JANET. "Recognizing Multijurisdictional Class Action Judgments within Canada: Key Questions—Suggested Answers" (2008) 46 *Canadian Business Law Journal* 450.

CHAPTER 9

RECOGNITION AND ENFORCEMENT OF FOREIGN ARBITRAL AWARDS

A. INTRODUCTION

The number of civil disputes resolved by arbitration has increased significantly over the past thirty years. In many cases the disputing parties are required, by contract or statute, to arbitrate rather than litigate. In many other cases the parties voluntarily choose arbitration once the dispute has arisen, perceiving it to have advantages over the judicial process. The potential advantages are well known: the ability to resolve the dispute in private rather than in open court, the availability of a specialist decision maker with expertise in the relevant area, and procedures that allow the dispute to proceed more rapidly and efficiently.

At the conclusion of an arbitration, the arbitrator renders an award. It looks very similar to a judicial decision but there are important differences when it comes to enforcement. Unlike a judgment, the machinery of the state is not automatically available to force the unsuccessful party to comply. As a result, most countries have enacted legislation dealing with the enforcement of domestic arbitral awards.[1] In very general terms, this legislation allows a party to apply to the court to have the award enforced. If the conditions for enforcement are met, the court grants judgment enforcing the award.

---

1   See, for example, the *Arbitration Act, 1991*, SO 1991, c 17 [*AA* (Ont)]; *Arbitration Act*, RSNS 1989, c 19.

The issue in this chapter is the recognition and enforcement of foreign arbitral awards. In Canada, the domestic enforcement statutes generally cover awards from within the province or, going somewhat farther afield, other parts of Canada.[2] This leaves as a separate question the process and test for enforcing awards from other countries. There are three separate regimes for recognizing and enforcing a foreign arbitral award: the *New York Convention on the Recognition and Enforcement of Foreign Arbitral Awards*,[3] the UNCITRAL Model Law, and the common law. Each is available only in certain situations.

B. THE *NEW YORK CONVENTION*

The *New York Convention* was adopted by the United Nations Conference on International Commercial Arbitration in 1958. Every common law province except Ontario has legislation implementing the *New York Convention*.[4] Ontario had previously implemented it but repealed that legislation.[5] The Government of Canada has also implemented the convention.[6]

Under article 1(3), two reservations are possible under the *New York Convention*. The first is that a contracting state may insist on reciprocity and thereby elect to give effect only to arbitral awards made in another contracting state. The second is that a contracting state may choose to apply the convention only to disputes arising from legal relationships, contractual or otherwise, which are considered "commercial" by the laws of the contracting state. The federal government and all common law provinces have made the second reservation but not the first. This means that in common law Canada, other than Ontario, the *New York Convention* applies to commercial arbitrations from any other country. If the arbitration is, according to the law of the province, not a commercial arbitration, the convention does not apply and cannot be used.

---

2   See, for example, the *Arbitration Act*, RSA 2000, c A-43, s 49 [*AA* (Alta)]; *AA* (Ont), above note 1, s 50.
3   330 UNTS 38 (1959) [*New York Convention*].
4   See, for example, the *International Commercial Arbitration Act*, RSA 2000, c I-5, s 2 [*ICAA* (Alta)]. The legislation typically includes the convention as a schedule.
5   SO 1988, c 30, s 14, repealing the *Foreign Arbitral Awards Act, 1986*, SO 1986, c 25.
6   *United Nations Foreign Arbitral Awards Convention Act*, RSC 1985 (2nd Supp), c 16. In *Compania Maritima Villa Nova SA v Northern Sales Co* (1991), [1992] 1 FC 550 at 561 (CA), aff'g (1989), 29 FTR 136 (TD) [*Compania Maritima*], the court held that this federal statute is constitutionally valid when applied to the recognition and enforcement of foreign arbitral awards "having a federal character in a constitutional sense."

The central obligation imposed on states by the *New York Convention* is in article 3, which provides that "each Contracting State shall recognize arbitral awards as binding and enforce them in accordance with the rules of procedure of the territory where the award is relied upon." Pursuant to the convention, therefore, recognition and enforcement of a commercial arbitral award from another country is mandatory.[7] A party can have such an award enforced by applying to a court of competent jurisdiction, according to the applicable rules of procedure. Generally speaking, this entails commencing an action or an application for the relief set out in the foreign award.[8] Article 4(1) of the convention requires the party seeking enforcement of the award to supply the court with the duly authenticated original award and with the original arbitration agreement between the parties or with duly certified copies of these documents.

A party can resist the application for recognition and enforcement by invoking one of the specific grounds enumerated in article 5(1) of the *New York Convention*. There are five such grounds. The first covers cases where the parties to the agreement to arbitrate were under some incapacity or where the agreement is not valid under its express governing law or, if none, under the law of the country where the award was made. The issue of capacity is to be evaluated using "the law applicable to" the parties. While not specified, this law arguably could be that of their respective domicile or place of ordinary residence. The second ground applies where a party was not given proper notice of the appointment of the arbitrator or of the arbitration proceedings or was otherwise unable to present his or her case. The third ground refuses recognition of that part of an award that goes beyond the terms of the arbitration.[9] The fourth covers cases where the composition of the arbitral authority or the arbitral procedure was not in accordance with the agreement of the parties or, if none, with the law of the country where the arbitration took place. Finally, the fifth ground applies when the award has not yet become binding on the parties or has been set aside or suspended by a competent authority of the country in which, or under the law of which, the award was made.

In addition, article 5(2) sets out two more grounds for refusing to recognize and enforce the arbitral award. These are (1) that the subject

---

7   See, for example, the analysis in *Sociedade-de-fomento Industrial Private Ltd v Pakistan Steel Mills Corp (Private) Ltd*, 2014 BCCA 205.
8   The taking of jurisdiction in respect of such an action or application raises comparable issues to proceedings brought to recognize and enforce a foreign judgment. See Chapter 8.
9   See the discussion in *Compania Maritima*, above note 6 (TD).

matter of the dispute is not capable of being resolved by arbitration under the law of the country in which recognition and enforcement is sought and (2) that recognition or enforcement of the award would be contrary to the public policy of that country.[10]

C. THE MODEL LAW

In 1985 the United Nations Commission on International Trade Law (UNCITRAL) adopted the Model Law on International Commercial Arbitration. Its aim was to assist countries in the reform and modernization of their legislation on arbitration. The Model Law is more comprehensive than the 1958 *New York Convention*, since the Model Law covers all stages of the arbitral process. Chapter 8 of the Model Law covers recognition and enforcement of arbitral awards.

Each common law province has enacted legislation adopting the Model Law.[11] As part of its adoption of the Model Law, Ontario repealed its earlier adoption of the *New York Convention*. In contrast, most provinces adopted the Model Law while leaving the *New York Convention* in force, so both are available. The Government of Canada has adopted the Model Law,[12] but in a slightly amended form called the Commercial Arbitration Code.[13] The federal legislation applies the Code (1) when at least one of the parties to the arbitration in question is Her Majesty in right of Canada, a department corporation, or a Crown corporation and (2) to maritime or admiralty matters.[14]

---

10 Some of the key English cases dealing with the public policy ground are *Deutsche Schachtbau-und Tiefbohrgesellschaft mbH v Shell International Petroleum Co Ltd*, [1990] 1 AC 295 (HL); *Westacre Investments Ltd v Jugoimport-SPDR Holding Co Ltd*, [2000] QB 288 (CA); *Soleimany v Soleimany*, [1999] QB 785 (CA). See Nelson Enonchong, "The Enforcement of Foreign Arbitral Awards Based on Illegal Contracts" [2000] *Lloyd's Maritime and Commercial Law Quarterly* 495; and Jonathan Harris & Frank Meisel, "Public Policy and the Enforcement of International Arbitration Awards: Controlling the Unruly Horse" [1998] *Lloyd's Maritime and Commercial Law Quarterly* 568.
11 See *ICAA* (Alta), above note 4, s 4(1); *International Commercial Arbitration Act*, RSO 1990, c I.9, s 2(1) [*ICAA* (Ont)]. In British Columbia, the *International Commercial Arbitration Act*, RSBC 1996, c 233, does not expressly adopt the Model Law but its preamble refers to it as "a consensus of views" on judicial intervention in international commercial arbitration. The provisions of the statute closely follow those of the Model Law.
12 *Commercial Arbitration Act*, RSC 1985 (2nd Supp), c 17, s 5(1).
13 The amendment removes the requirement in the Model Law that the arbitration be "international" as defined in arts 1(3) and 1(4).
14 *Commercial Arbitration Act*, above note 12, s 5(2).

Canadian courts, in interpreting the Model Law, are expressly authorized to consider two international documents: the Report of the United Nations Commission on International Trade Law on the work of its eighteenth session, dated 3–21 June 1985,[15] and the Analytical Commentary contained in the Report of the Secretary General to the eighteenth session of the United Nations Commission on International Trade Law.[16]

The scope of the Model Law is limited by article 1(1) to "international commercial arbitration." Under article 1(3), an arbitration is "international" in the following situations. First, it is international if the parties to the arbitration agreement have, at the time the agreement is made, their places of business in different states. If a party does not have a place of business, his or her habitual residence is considered instead. If a party has more than one place of business, the one with the closest relationship to the agreement is used. Second, an arbitration is international if the place of arbitration determined pursuant to the arbitration agreement is outside the state in which the parties have their places of business. Third, it is international if a place where a substantial part of the obligations of the commercial relationship is to be performed, or the place to which the subject matter of the dispute is most closely connected, is outside the state in which the parties have their places of business. Fourth, it is international if the parties have expressly agreed that the subject matter of the arbitration agreement relates to more than one country.[17] If a foreign arbitration does not fall into one of these situations, then the Model Law does not apply.[18]

Under article 1(1), the arbitration must also be "commercial" for the Model Law to apply. As is the case with the *New York Convention*, whether an arbitration is commercial will depend on the law of the jurisdiction in which enforcement of the award is sought. The Model Law is not based on reciprocity and so each province is bound to recognize and enforce an international commercial arbitral award regardless of whether it was issued in another signatory state.[19]

Under the Model Law, an international commercial arbitral award is enforced by an application to a court of competent jurisdiction.[20] The

---

15   A/40/17.
16   A/CN.9/264. *ICAA* (Alta), above note 4, s 12(2); *ICAA* (Ont), above note 11, s 13.
17   In Ontario, the statute implementing the Model Law removes this as a basis for an arbitration being international: *ICAA* (Ont), *ibid*, s 2(3).
18   The statute implementing the Model Law in Ontario provides that the articles on recognition and enforcement apply even if the arbitration is not "international," covering "a commercial arbitral award made outside Canada": *ibid*, s 10.
19   Model Law, art 35(1).
20   The taking of jurisdiction in respect of such an application raises comparable issues to proceedings brought to recognize and enforce a foreign judgment. See Chapter 8.

party seeking to enforce the award is required to supply the court with the original award and arbitration agreement or duly authenticated copies.[21] In *Schreter v Gasmac Inc* the court addressed a procedural issue relating to the Model Law.[22] The plaintiff had been successful in an arbitration in Georgia. The plaintiff then took steps there to have the award confirmed by a judgment of the court. Subsequently the plaintiff applied in Ontario to enforce the foreign award under the provisions of the Model Law. The defendant argued that the Model Law applied only to arbitral awards, not judgments, and that by obtaining the judgment in Georgia the plaintiff could no longer enforce the award: he had to instead enforce the foreign judgment. The court refused to treat the award as having merged into the Georgia judgment. The award remained and could be enforced under the Model Law. The contrary result would have severely limited the usefulness of the Model Law.[23]

Like the *New York Convention*, the Model Law allows the court to refuse to enforce an arbitral award based only on an enumerated list of grounds. The grounds, found in article 36, are identical to those discussed above under the *New York Convention*.[24] Under article 36(2) of the Model Law, the court where enforcement is sought can, if the award is being challenged in the courts of the place where it was made, adjourn its decision to await the results of the challenge. In the meantime, it can order the defendant to provide security.[25]

One of the grounds more frequently raised by defendants is that of public policy. However, as in the area of the enforcement of foreign judgments, this ground for refusal must be interpreted narrowly. In *Schreter* the court noted that

> [t]he concept of imposing our public policy on foreign awards is to guard against enforcement of an award which offends our local principles of justice and fairness in a fundamental way, and in a way

---

21 Model Law, art 35(2). For discussion of the meaning of "duly certified" see *Kan-to Yakin Kogyo Kabushiki-Kaisha v Can-Eng Manufacturing Ltd* (1992), 7 OR (3d) 779 (Gen Div), aff'd (1995), 22 OR (3d) 576 (CA). There is some debate as to whether this requirement is truly mandatory: see *ACTIV Financial Systems, Inc v Orbixa Management Services, Inc*, 2011 ONSC 7286 at paras 54–62.
22 (1992), 7 OR (3d) 608 (Gen Div) [*Schreter*].
23 The court rejected the approach adopted earlier in *Stolp & Co v WB Browne & Co*, [1930] 4 DLR 703 (Ont HCJ) as contrary to the Model Law. See also *Dalimpex Ltd v Janicki* (2003), 64 OR (3d) 737 at paras 51–53 (CA).
24 See, for example, *Aamco Transmissions Inc v Kunz* (1991), 97 Sask R 5 (CA).
25 See *Europcar Italia SpA v Alba Tours International Inc*, [1997] OJ No 133 (Gen Div); *Empresa Minera Los Quenuales SA v Vena Resources Inc*, 2015 ONSC 4408. See also, in the English context, *Soleh Boneh International Ltd v Government of the Republic of Uganda*, [1993] 2 Lloyd's LR 208 at 212 (CA).

which the parties could attribute to the fact that the award was made in another jurisdiction where the procedural or substantive rules diverge markedly from our own, or where there was ignorance or corruption on the part of the tribunal which could not be seen to be tolerated or condoned by our courts.[26]

There is an issue about whether parties to an arbitration agreement can waive, in advance, any defences to recognition and enforcement otherwise available under article 36. In *Food Services of America Inc (cob Amerifresh) v Pan Pacific Specialties Ltd*,[27] the parties expressly waived the grounds for refusal listed in section 36 of the British Columbia *International Commercial Arbitration Act*,[28] which mirror those in article 36 of the Model Law. The court held that the waiver was effective. However, in light of the importance of the protection provided through these grounds, there is room to question whether this approach is correct as a matter of public policy.

D. THE COMMON LAW

The overwhelming majority of foreign arbitral awards fall within the federal and provincial legislation giving effect to the New York Convention and the UNCITRAL Model Law. As a result, scant consideration is usually given to other options for recognition and enforcement. However, it is not beyond the realm of possibility for a foreign award to fall outside the ambit of both schemes. As discussed above, awards that do not satisfy the definition of "international" are not covered by the Model Law, and awards that are not commercial according to the jurisdiction where enforcement is sought are not covered by either the New York Convention or the Model Law.

In such cases, a further option is available. A foreign arbitral award may be enforced by an action at common law.[29] The conditions under which a common law court will recognize and enforce a foreign arbitral

---

26 Above note 22 at 623. See also *Depo Traffic Facilities (Kunshan) Co v Vikeda International Logistics and Automotive Supply Ltd*, 2015 ONSC 999. For a case in which the defence succeeded, see *Subway Franchise Systems of Canada Ltd v Laich*, 2011 SKQB 249.
27 (1997), 32 BCLR (3d) 225 (SC).
28 Above note 11.
29 See the discussion in *Trade Fortune Inc v Amalgamated Mill Supplies Ltd* (1994), 89 BCLR (2d) 132 (SC). As this case indicates, it is also open to the plaintiff to commence an entirely new substantive action, rather than rely on the award at all, since the substantive claims do not merge into the arbitral award.

214 CONFLICT OF LAWS

award were explained in *Norske Atlas Ins Co v London General Ins Co*.³⁰ The parties to the arbitration must have agreed to submit to the arbitral process that took place, the arbitration producing the award must have been conducted in accordance with the agreement, and the agreement to arbitrate must have been valid according to the law of the jurisdiction where the arbitration was conducted.³¹ The award must also be final and conclusive.³² The party resisting enforcement can seek to impeach the foreign award using the various grounds available for resisting the enforcement of foreign judgments.

If a foreign arbitral award can be enforced under either the *New York Convention* or the Model Law, resort to the common law may be precluded. In *ACTIV Financial Systems, Inc v Orbixa Management Services, Inc* the court held, as a matter of statutory interpretation, that Ontario's adoption of the Model Law was as a "complete code" for enforcement such that enforcement at common law was not available.³³

E. LIMITATION PERIOD ISSUES

As with the enforcement of foreign judgments, limitation period issues can arise in the enforcement of foreign arbitral awards. In part this is because the statutory schemes implementing the *New York Convention* and the Model Law do not contain specific limitation period provisions. As a result, the general provincial provisions come into play. In *Yugraneft Corp v Rexx Management Corp* the plaintiff obtained an arbitral award against the defendant following arbitration proceedings in Russia.³⁴ Some three years later the plaintiff applied to enforce the award against the defendant in Alberta. The defendant argued that the application was outside the general two-year provincial limitation period. The Supreme Court of Canada agreed. As a threshold point, it confirmed that it was open to each province to impose a limitation period for such applications. It then rejected, as a matter of statutory interpretation, the argument that an application to enforce a foreign arbitral award is akin to a claim based on a "judgment or order for the

---

30 (1927), 28 Ll LR 104 (KB).
31 *Ibid* at 107.
32 See *Dalmia Dairy Industries Ltd v National Bank of Pakistan*, [1978] 2 Lloyd's LR 223 at 246 (CA).
33 Above note 21 at paras 63–69.
34 2010 SCC 19.

payment of money."³⁵ It also noted, as a point of consistency, that the statutory limitation period to enforce a domestic arbitral award was two years.³⁶ The court therefore held that the application to enforce the foreign award was caught by the general two-year limitation period.

This approach is open to some of the same criticisms made in Chapter 8 in the context of enforcing foreign judgments. In particular, it seems unduly narrow and restrictive to deprive a successful plaintiff of the results of his or her award by using such a relatively short limitation period. Comity and the internationalization of commerce suggest that plaintiffs should be allowed more time to enforce both foreign judgments and foreign arbitral awards.

FURTHER READINGS

GRAHAM, WILLIAM. "International Commercial Arbitration: The Developing Canadian Profile" in Robert Paterson & Bonita Thompson, eds, *UNCITRAL Arbitration Model in Canada* (Toronto: Carswell, 1987).

GRAHAM, WILLIAM. "The *New York Convention* of 1958: A Canadian Perspective" in Nabil Antaki & Alain Prujiner, eds, *International Commercial Arbitration* (Montreal: Wilson & Lafleur, 1986).

GRAY, WAYNE D, & ROBERT WISNER. "The Russians Are Coming, But Can They Enforce Their Foreign Arbitral Award?" (2009) 47 *Canadian Business Law Journal* 244.

HILL, JONATHAN. "The Significance of Foreign Judgments Relating to an Arbitral Award in the Context of an Application to Enforce the Award in England" (2012) 8 *Journal of Private International Law* 159.

HILL, JONATHAN, & ADELINE CHONG. *International Commercial Disputes: Commercial Conflict of Laws in English Courts*, 4th ed (Oxford: Hart, 2010) ch 24.

PENGELLEY, NICHOLAS. "Alberta Says *Nyet*! Limitation Act Declares Russian Arbitral Award DOA: Supreme Court to Give Kiss of Life?" (2009) 5 *Journal of Private International Law* 105.

PENGELLEY, NICHOLAS. "This Pig Won't Fly: Death Threats as Grounds for Refusing Enforcement of an Arbitral Award" (2010) 37 *Advocates' Quarterly* 386.

---

35 *Ibid* at paras 42–47. Such claims benefit from a longer limitation period: *Limitations Act*, RSA 2000, c L-12, s 11.
36 See the *AA* (Alta), above note 2, s 51.

ST JOHN SUTTON, DAVID, JUDITH GILL, & MATTHEW GEARING. *Russell on Arbitration*, 24th ed (London: Sweet & Maxwell, 2015) at 8-020.

TWEEDDALE, ANDREW, & KEREN TWEEDDALE. *Arbitration of Commercial Disputes: International and English Law and Practice* (Oxford: Oxford University Press, 2007) ch 13.

CHAPTER 10

THE CHOICE OF LAW PROCESS

A. INTRODUCTION

As explained in Chapter 1, the second central question private international law seeks to answer is what law the court will use to resolve a dispute. Implicit in this question is that the court does not always simply use its own law, the law of the forum. This may at first seem surprising, since we are so familiar with courts resolving cases according to the law of the forum, and indeed this is what happens in the vast majority of cases. But sometimes the court resolves a dispute using the law of some other legal system. The choice of law process explains how the court determines what legal system applies to a particular dispute.

B. THE RATIONALE FOR CHOICE OF LAW

A preliminary question is why a court would be willing to resolve a dispute using a foreign law. Laws are in essence highly territorial and so it might seem problematic for a court in Ontario to resolve a dispute using German law rather than Ontario law. Some might even consider the application of German law to violate Ontario's sovereignty. Throughout the history of the conflict of laws, the leading preoccupation of its scholars has been the issue of choice of law, and over time three leading theories emerged to attempt to explain why the court would resolve a dispute using foreign law.

The first theory is the theory of comity. It posits that the courts of one country apply the laws of another country as a courtesy to that country and in the hope that its courts will reciprocate. In a sense, resolving all disputes using the law of the forum would be discourteous or rude.[1] There are significant flaws in this theory. The common law cases rarely analyze the extent to which the foreign legal system does or might reciprocate, casting doubt on the reciprocity aspect. In addition, courts have resolved disputes by applying the foreign law of an unfriendly or enemy country, for example in times of war,[2] casting doubt on the courtesy aspect.

In recent years Canadian appellate courts have placed considerable emphasis on notions of comity.[3] But it is important to be clear that in doing so they are not using comity in the sense described above and are not affirming the concept as a theory which would explain the use of foreign law to resolve disputes.[4] Rather, the courts are using comity in the way it was subsequently defined in *Hilton v Guyot*, in which the United States Supreme Court stated "[c]omity, in the legal sense, is neither a matter of absolute obligation, on the one hand, nor of mere courtesy and good will, upon the other."[5]

The second theory is the theory of vested rights. It asserts that a person, by acting in a particular country, acquires rights under the law of that country. These rights must then be treated as having vested in the person so that all other countries must give effect to them. Universal application of the law of the forum would deny these vested rights.[6] The vested rights theory was widely adopted by common law courts in

---

1   Leading advocates of this theory are Ulrich Huber, "Of the Conflict of Diverse Laws in Diverse Governments (*de Conflictu Legum*) (1689)" in Ernest G Lorenzen, *Selected Articles on the Conflict of Laws* (New Haven, CT: Yale University Press, 1947) at 164; and Melville M Bigelow, *Story's Commentaries on the Conflict of Laws*, 8th ed (Boston: Little, Brown, 1883) at 33–34.
2   Otto Kahn-Freund, "General Problems of Private International Law" (1974) 143 *Recueil des Cours* 139 at 464. See also Perry Dane, "Vested Rights, 'Vestedness,' and Choice of Law" (1987) 96 *Yale Law Journal* 1191 at 1213–214.
3   As a leading example, see *Morguard Investments Ltd v De Savoye*, [1990] 3 SCR 1077 at 1095–96.
4   In *Davies v Collins*, 2011 NSCA 79 at para 33, the court noted that "The Supreme Court's resurrection of comity has not escaped criticism which argues the difficulty, if not irrelevance of applying 'comity' to choice of law questions in a private setting." See Peter Kincaid, "*Jensen v. Tolofsen* and the Revolution in Tort Choice of Law" (1995) 74 *Canadian Bar Review* 537 at 541–45.
5   159 US 113 at 163–64 (1875).
6   Albert Venn Dicey, *A Digest of the Law of England with Reference to the Conflict of Laws* (London: Stevens & Sons, 1896) at 22; Joseph Beale, *A Selection of Cases on the Conflict of Laws*, vol 3 (Cambridge: Harvard University Press, 1902) at

the early part of the twentieth century.[7] However, this theory also has its flaws. An appeal to vested rights is possible where the country in which these rights allegedly vested is easily identified but if the person's conduct has connections to multiple countries, how is the court to know under which legal system any rights have vested?[8] In addition, this theory does not fit the decided cases particularly well, as courts in some cases have expressly not applied the law of the place of acting and have instead resolved disputes using either the law of the forum or of some other country.[9]

The third theory is the local law theory. It claims that courts do not, in fact, resolve disputes using foreign law. They always apply the law of the forum, but in doing so they modify that law by developing special rules modelled on the foreign law.[10] This theory is particularly controversial. It tries to define away the problem: clearly there is no need to explain why the court would apply foreign law if, in fact, it does not do so. But this just begs a further question: namely, why the court would apply this modified forum law.[11] A rationale remains lacking. In addition, there is little sense in the cases that the courts are behaving as the theory suggests. According to the courts' own explanation, they are applying foreign law, not modified rules of domestic law.

Much has been written about each of these theories and yet ultimately none offer a particularly satisfying explanation. In part this is because the theories have been attempting to address an overstated concern, that of territorial sovereignty. Once we accept that any decision to resolve a dispute using foreign law is a decision for our own courts, not something being imposed on us or demanded of us, there is no true concern about sovereignty. We control the application of foreign law in

---

517. See also Geoffrey Chevalier Cheshire, *Private International Law* (Oxford: Clarendon Press, 1935) at 4–6.

7   In Canada, see *Livesley v E Clements Horst Co*, [1924] SCR 605.

8   Friedrich Carl von Savigny, *Private International Law: A Treatise on the Conflict of Laws*, trans by William Guthrie (Edinburgh: T & T Clark, 1869) at 102–3.

9   Walter Wheeler Cook, *The Logical and Legal Bases of the Conflict of Laws* (Cambridge: Harvard University Press, 1942) at 19–20. Only three years after espousing vested rights, Cheshire recanted and called the theory of vested rights "fallacious": Geoffrey Chevalier Cheshire, *Private International Law*, 2d ed (Oxford: Clarendon Press, 1938) at 86.

10 Cook, above note 9 at 20–21.

11 Hessel E Yntema, "The Objectives of Private International Law" (1957) 35 *Canadian Bar Review* 721 at 722; David F Cavers, "The Two 'Local Law' Theories" (1950) 63 *Harvard Law Review* 822 at 826; George W Stumberg, *Principles of Conflict of Laws*, 3d ed (Brooklyn: The Foundation Press, 1963) at 15.

our courts.¹² Nonetheless, we still need some explanation for why we do not just always apply the law of the forum.

The most convincing explanation is based on notions of justice and convenience.¹³ This explanation was put best by the English scholar Cheshire who wrote "when the circumstances indicate that the internal law of a foreign country will provide a solution more just, more convenient, and more in accord with the expectations of the parties than the internal law of England, the English judge does not hesitate to apply the foreign rules."¹⁴ It is important to explain what is meant by "justice" in this context. This refers not to the fairness of the eventual outcome but rather to whether a just decision is being made about which legal system to apply. Central to this idea of justice is the principle of proximity, which provides that a dispute should be resolved by the most proximate law: the legal system with the closest and most real connection to the dispute.¹⁵

---

12 For an early case on this point, see *Holman v Johnson* (1775), 98 ER 1120 at 1121, Lord Mansfield. In Canada see, for example, *Stephens v Falchi*, [1938] SCR 354 at 363: "The courts of Quebec administer the law of Quebec and no other law. If they apply the rules of the law of another country, it is because the law of Quebec commands them to do so in the circumstances. Whether or not the conditions are such as to require the application of the rules of law of another country is a question they must decide under their own law."

13 See Ronald Harry Graveson, "Philosophical Aspects of the English Conflict of Laws" (1962) 78 *Law Quarterly Review* 337 at 348–54 and 370; Ronald Harry Graveson, "The Special Character of English Private International Law" in *Comparative Conflict of Laws: Selected Essays*, vol 1 (Oxford: North-Holland, 1977) at 7; Ronald Harry Graveson, *Conflict of Laws: Private International Law*, 7th ed (London: Sweet & Maxwell, 1974) at 7; AJE Jaffey, *Introduction to the Conflict of Laws* (London: Butterworths, 1988) at 275; David F Cavers, "Contemporary Conflicts Law in American Perspective" (1971) 131 *Recueil des Cours* 75 at 101–2; John O'Brien, *Conflict of Laws*, 2d ed (London: Cavendish, 1999) at 7–8; Kahn-Freund, above note 2 at 464.

14 Cheshire, above note 9 at 90. Virtually the same statement appears in James Fawcett & Janeen Carruthers, *Cheshire, North and Fawcett Private International Law*, 14th ed (Oxford: Oxford University Press, 2008) at 37.

15 Frank Vischer, "Connecting Factors" in Kurt Lipstein, ed, *International Encyclopedia of Comparative Law*, vol 3 (Tübingen, Germany: Mohr Siebeck, 1970) at 3. In *Macmillan Inc v Bishopsgate Investment Trust Plc (No 3)*, [1995] 3 All ER 747 (Ch D), aff'd [1996] 1 All ER 585 (CA) [*Macmillan*], Millett J stated (at 760), "[i]t is impossible to quarrel with the contention that the governing law should be the law which has 'the closest and most real connection with the transaction.'"

C. THE CHOICE OF LAW PROCESS

The traditional choice of law process uses a series of rules, each of which links a legal category or issue with a particular system of law by means of a connecting factor.[16] For example, one such rule could be that claims in tort are governed by the law of the place where the tort was committed. In this example, tort is the legal category or issue and the connecting factor is the place of the tort. To apply the rule, we identify the place of the tort and that place, as the connecting factor, leads us to the applicable law. This rule covers only tort, and so we would need a separate rule for other legal categories or issues such as contract, unjust enrichment, the transfer of property, trusts, and so on.

One hallmark of the traditional process is that it chooses the applicable law without focusing on the content of that law or on the result it will reach when applied. An Ontario court could use the rule in the example above to identify Texas law as the law applicable to a tort claim without first knowing anything about that law. In this sense the choice of law process operates at one step removed from the resolution of the underlying dispute.

As we will see, the selection of the connecting factor is critical in formulating a choice of law rule. There are many possible connecting factors. Some are relatively certain and predictable. These include a person's domicile or habitual residence and the place where a specific act occurs, such as the commission of a tort or the making of a contract. These sorts of connecting factors have a relatively narrow focus. They are quite specific and can therefore be described as rigid connecting factors. Other connecting factors have a broader focus and are thought to be more flexible. These include the "proper law" of a contract, ascertained by weighing several factual connections to various legal systems. One of the core debates in choice of law is how rigid or how flexible the connecting factor should be for a particular rule.

Most choice of law rules use a single connecting factor, whether rigid or flexible. However, it is possible to have a choice of law rule that uses multiple connecting factors. For example, a rule could provide that the formal validity of a contract is governed by either the law of the place of contracting or the proper law of the contract. If each connecting factor pointed to a different legal system, the contract would need to be formally valid only under one of the two. For another example, a rule could provide that claims in tort are governed by both the law of the place where the tort occurred and by the law of the forum.

---

16 See von Savigny, above note 8 at 27, 89, and 148–51.

Here, the plaintiff would have to show entitlement under both systems of law in order to recover.

Traditional choice of law rules are multilateral. This means that they are framed from a neutral perspective, indicating which of several potential legal systems applies. In contrast, a unilateral choice of law rule is framed from the perspective of only one legal system and specifies when that legal system's rules are to apply.

D. CHARACTERIZATION

Characterization is central to the choice of law process. It is the means by which we identify which choice of law rule to use to determine the applicable law. Often little thought is given to characterization—the parties know their dispute is about breach of contract and so they turn automatically to the choice of law rule for contract. But in other cases it is less clear what legal category or issue is involved, making it unclear which choice of law rule should be used.

Take the example of a construction crew on its way to a day of work. It spots a warehouse in danger of imminent collapse and so instead spends the day shoring up temporary supports for the warehouse to prevent a collapse. The crew then contacts the warehouse owner and demands payment for its services. If the owner refuses to pay and the crew sues, we have a variety of ways to explain the crew's claim. It could be in contract: the law might imply a promise by the owner to pay for the work. It could be in tort: the owner might have negligently created a dangerous situation which required immediate attention. It could be in unjust enrichment: the owner has been enriched by the value of the services, the enrichment is at the expense of the crew, and there is no juristic reason for the enrichment. It could be a *sui generis* claim, in its own special category: some legal systems recognize a claim based on *negotiorum gestio*, rooted in Roman law and dealing with the uninvited intervention by one party in the affairs of another.[17]

In a purely domestic case not much may turn on how we characterize the crew's claim.[18] But if the crew and the owner were both from Detroit and the warehouse was in Windsor, characterization becomes very important. To determine whether Michigan or Ontario law ap-

---

17 For a description, see Peter Birks, *Unjust Enrichment*, 2d ed (Oxford: Oxford University Press, 2005) at 22–23.
18 In some jurisdictions the relevant statute of limitations has different periods for different causes of action.

plies, we have to characterize the claim and then use the relevant rule, whether for contract, tort, unjust enrichment, or something else.

This is a good place to make a suggestion about pleadings. In much Canadian civil litigation the parties are not required to plead domestic law.[19] It is sufficient to plead the material facts on which the claim is based and then to indicate what is being claimed, such as damages, as a result of those facts. However, in the example above, if the crew does not plead any law, it is open for the owner to ask the court, for purposes of determining the applicable law, to characterize the claim in a way that leads to using the law that is more favourable to its position. The crew would likely disagree and the parties would be into a dispute about the proper characterization, and much might then depend on the court's answer. It would be better for the crew to have indicated how it characterizes its claim. In fact, it would be better still for the crew to plead a series of concurrent or alternative causes of action. If, for example, the crew pleaded claims in both contract and tort, the choice of law process would be applied separately to each of those claims. One rule would determine what law governs the contract claim and another would determine what law governs the tort claim. These laws could be different: Michigan law might govern the former and Ontario law the latter.

Characterization raises two central issues. First, there is debate about what is characterized. Second, there is debate about whether characterization is done with reference to the *lex fori*, the *lex causae*, or some other legal framework.

1) What Is Characterized

Common law courts have not attempted a coherent answer to the question of what is characterized. In *Macmillan Inc v Bishopsgate Investment Trust Plc (No 3)*[20] the three members of the Court of Appeal variously referred to characterizing the issue, the judicial concept or category, the question in the action, and the relevant rule of law.[21] This is not sloppiness because in certain situations all of these different answers can be correct. Causes of action, issues, and legal rules are all characterized in different situations. However, it is not correct to consider that facts are characterized. Until legal rules are applied to them, facts lack independent meaning. There are no choice of law rules for facts.[22] It is

---

19 As discussed in Chapter 12, they are required to plead foreign law.
20 Above note 15.
21 *Ibid* at 589 and 591 (CA), Staughton LJ; at 604, Auld LJ; and at 614, Aldous LJ.
22 See John D Falconbridge, *Essays on the Conflict of Laws*, 2d ed (Toronto: Canada Law Book, 1954) at 58 and 69; AH Robertson, *Characterization in the Conflict of*

also unhelpful to say that connecting factors are characterized.[23] It is analytically clearer to consider the interpretation of connecting factors, such as determining the meaning of domicile or identifying the place of a tort, as an entirely separate question.

The difference between characterizing a cause of action and an issue is well illustrated in *Macmillan*. The plaintiff, a Delaware company, owned shares in Berlitz Inc, a New York company. The plaintiff transferred these shares to the defendant to hold as its nominee. In violation of that arrangement, the defendant treated the shares as its own, using them as security for other debts such that the defendant's creditors acquired an interest in the shares. The defendant became insolvent, leaving the plaintiff and the creditors in a dispute over the shares.

The plaintiff considered that English law would be more favourable to its claim and so sought to characterize the dispute in a way that would lead to the application of that law. The plaintiff asserted that it was advancing a "receipt-based restitutionary claim" so that the court should apply the choice of law rule for unjust enrichment and look to the law of the place of enrichment, which it said was England. The Court of Appeal did not disagree with the plaintiff's characterization of its claim but it nonetheless did not apply that choice of law rule. Instead, it determined that the central issue in the dispute was whether the creditors were, in respect of the shares the plaintiff sought to recover, bona fide purchasers. The court therefore applied the choice of law rule that issues of ownership of shares were governed by the *lex situs* of the shares, namely the place of incorporation of the company, which was New York. Lord Justice Staughton held "the rules of conflict of laws must be directed at the particular issue which is in dispute, rather than at the cause of action on which the plaintiff relies."[24] This approach properly recognizes that different aspects of a dispute can be governed by different applicable laws.

Nevertheless, it is likely that courts will continue to characterize causes of action as well as legal issues, as it is appropriate to do so in cases where no issues of subdivision arise. We do not have separate choice of law rules for each element of a cause of action in negligence: for the existence of a duty of care, for whether the standard of care was

---

Laws (Cambridge, MA: Harvard University Press, 1940) at 61–63; Christopher Forsyth, "Characterisation Revisited: An Essay in the Theory and Practice of the English Conflict of Laws" (1998) 114 *Law Quarterly Review* 141 at 147; Pippa Rogerson, *Collier's Conflict of Laws*, 4th ed (Cambridge: Cambridge University Press, 2013) at 269.

23   Janet Walker, *Castel & Walker: Canadian Conflict of Laws*, 6th ed (Markham: LexisNexis Canada, 2005) (loose-leaf) at para 3.3, suggests that connecting factors are characterized.

24   *Macmillan*, above note 15 at 596 (CA).

breached, and for remoteness of loss. We do not even have separate choice of law rules for separate torts: for negligence, for nuisance, and for battery. Instead we have a choice of law rule formulated at the more general level of a cause of action: a choice of law rule for tort. In that context it is sensible, notwithstanding *Macmillan*, to explain things in terms of characterization of a cause of action.[25]

We need to characterize causes of action and legal issues because we divide up our legal system into a series of categories such as tort, contract, and property. Characterization allows us to access the proper category within the legal system. But we also divide up our legal system in a very different way: into substance, on the one hand, and procedure, on the other hand. This division cuts across the whole of our system of law. As we will see in Chapter 11, there are times when, as part of the choice of law process, we will have to determine what is substance and what is procedure. Indeed, sometimes we need to do this as part of our domestic law. If, for example, legislative changes to substantive law are presumptively only forward-looking and such changes to procedural law are presumptively retroactive, it might be very important to know if a particular statutory rule is one of substance or procedure. Making this determination is equally a form of characterization, but not of causes of action — there are no causes of action within the law of procedure — or even legal issues. Here, legal rules are characterized, identified as either rules of substance or of procedure.[26]

These characterization problems can be divided into two stages, further complicating the issue. In the first stage, the cause of action or issue is characterized in order to determine which choice of law rule to apply. The choice of law rule then indicates the applicable law. The second stage involves determining which rules from the whole of the relevant legal system comprise the law applicable to the dispute.[27] For example, a cause of action may be characterized as being in unjust enrichment and the choice of law rule may indicate that the law of France is the applicable law. This does not mean, however, that the entirety of French law is applicable to the dispute. Only the French law of unjust enrichment is applicable and so the characterization process

---

25 A recent example is *Bieberstein v Kirchberger*, 2012 ONSC 6524, in which the court had to determine whether the plaintiff's cause of action was one to enforce a foreign judgment or one based on a foreign obligation or agreement. Another is *Quadrangle Holdings Ltd v Coady*, 2015 NSCA 13, in which the court had to determine whether the plaintiff's claim was in tort or in equity.
26 For an example of this kind of characterization in the succession context, see *Re Cohn*, [1945] Ch 5.
27 On this process, see Falconbridge, above note 22 at 51–53; O'Brien, above note 13 at 95–99.

must determine which French legal rules are part of that law.²⁸ Causes of action, issues, and legal rules are all characterized in different situations.

A related issue at the second stage flows from statutes with explicit territorial limitations. If Ontario law has been identified as the applicable law in a contract case, this includes its legislation relating to contract. But if a particular aspect of that legislation provides that it applies only to cases with a specific territorial connection to Ontario, can it be applied even where that connection is absent, by virtue of having been determined to be the applicable law? For example, *The Arthur Wishart Act (Franchise Disclosure), 2000*, applies only if the "the business operated by the franchisee under the franchise agreement or its renewal or extension is to be operated partly or wholly in Ontario."²⁹ Ontario courts have held that if, on a choice of law analysis, the applicable law is that of Ontario then the statute applies notwithstanding this provision.³⁰

2) The Approach to Characterization

Characterization cannot be done in a vacuum: it must be done within the context of a specific system of law. A cause of action is only in tort, for example, if within a particular legal system it is characterized as such. There is no such thing as a tort claim in the abstract. This raises the second debate, which concerns whether characterization is done with reference to the law of the forum or some other system of law.

The mainstream approach is to characterize using forum law. Just as the choice of law rules are those of the forum, the process of interpreting those rules to determine what causes of action or issues they cover would also use forum law. If a plaintiff brings a claim in Ontario, we ask how Ontario law characterizes the claim and then use the relevant choice of law rule. This approach almost seems so obvious that it is hard to see any other viable approach.

But the situation becomes less clear in certain cases. Suppose the plaintiff is alleging a claim that is available only under German law and does not exist in Ontario law. How can the Ontario court characterize that claim under Ontario law? Doing so seems to demand that a square peg be fitted into a round hole. To address such cases, some

---

28 As *Re Cohn*, above note 26, and *Re Maldonado's Estate*, [1954] P 223 (CA), illustrate, at this second stage the characterization can concern either the distinction between substance and procedure (as in the former) or the difference between two legal categories (as in the latter).
29 SO 2000, c 3, s 2(1).
30 *405431 Ontario Ltd v Midas Canada Inc*, 2010 ONCA 478; *Trillium Motor World Ltd v General Motors of Canada Ltd*, 2015 ONSC 3824 at paras 119–42.

commentators have proposed that the characterization should be done not with reference to the law of the forum but instead with reference to the law that would end up governing the claim, often called the *lex causae*. Under this approach, the Ontario court would characterize the claim as German law would. In this example, the likely result is that Ontario would then not have a choice of law rule for that legal category and would need to formulate one.

The idea that characterization should be done according to the *lex causae*, the law which the choice of law rule is itself trying to identify, has been widely criticized as entirely circular. The plaintiff cannot simply assert a claim under German law and then insist the choice of law process follow German characterization; the point of the choice of law process is to see whether there is any basis for looking to German law rather than the law of the forum to resolve the dispute. In addition, *lex causae* characterization breaks down if there are two possibly applicable foreign legal systems, for example German law and Austrian law, and they each characterize the cause of action or issue differently, leaving no answer to the question of which is to be preferred.[31]

As a result, the common law characterizes using the law of the forum. However, some modifications are made to attempt to better address these more difficult cases. First, if the claim is unknown to the law of the forum, it is characterized as its closest functional equivalent under that law. For example, German law recognizes contracts of inheritance. There is no directly comparable legal institution in Ontario law, but using a functional analysis it seems likely that the closest analogy would be to a will and the law of succession rather than to contract law.[32]

Second, there is some limited willingness to adjust the forum legal system's domestic divisions to better align with international norms. Kahn-Freund and others call this approach one using the "enlightened" law of the forum.[33] The leading example of this is in the choice of law rules on property. As will be explained in Chapter 16, while the common law generally distinguishes between real and personal property, most other legal systems instead distinguish between immovable

---

31 Rogerson, above note 22 at 270; Kahn-Freund, above note 2 at 372. Forsyth addresses additional problems with *lex causae* characterization such as those of cumulation and gap: above note 22 at 152.
32 See Kahn-Freund, above note 2 at 376.
33 *Ibid* at 373–77; Forsyth, above note 22 at 153–54. Kurt Lipstein is a leading advocate of this approach: see his "Characterization" in Kurt Lipstein, ed, *International Encyclopedia of Comparative Law*, vol 3, above note 15 at 5–7; and also Kurt Lipstein, *Principles of the Conflict of Laws, National and International* (The Hague: Martinus Nijhoff, 1981) at 96–97.

and movable property. So under Ontario's domestic law, a mortgagee's interest is personal property, not real property, because the debt and not the security interest is considered the transaction's central feature. But for characterization purposes, the Ontario court would consider the mortgagee's interest as immovable property, not movable property.[34]

While some variation from a purely domestic characterization is welcome, this approach is still very much dominated by the *lex fori*. In the difficult cases where competing applicable laws use different legal institutions to accomplish the same end result—for example, one using contract and the other using tort to handle the same kind of claim—no amount of enlightenment will resolve the conflict.[35] Each system can be expected to maintain its own characterization according to its own law.

The debate over which law governs the characterization process continues into the second stage of characterization. In *Re Maldonado's Estate*[36] the English Court of Appeal, having determined the law applicable to an issue of intestate succession to movable property was Spanish law, looked to what Spanish law considered to be within that legal category. While the first stage of characterization used the law of the forum, the second stage used the *lex causae*. This approach to the second stage can create considerable problems. Suppose an issue is characterized by Manitoba law as part of the law of tort and by Spanish law as part of the law of contract. A Manitoba court will apply the choice of law rule for tort. If the applicable law is Spanish and the *lex causae*, Spanish law, is used for the second stage of characterization, the focus will be on ascertaining what Spanish law considers to be its tort law. This will not properly address the issue, because, as noted, Spanish law characterizes that issue as contractual.

To avoid the problem in cases like *Re Maldonado's Estate*, and in keeping with the overall analysis of the approach to characterization, the law of the forum should be used for both the first and second stages of characterization. This approach will at times be sensitive to differences between legal systems, as in its treatment of the types of property, but it is firmly grounded in the forum legal system's own internal divisions of law.

---

34 See *Hogg v Provincial Tax Commission*, [1941] 3 WWR 605 (Sask CA). See the further discussion in Chapter 16.
35 Kahn-Freund, above note 2 at 378.
36 Above note 28.

E. AMBIGUITIES IN APPLYING THE CHOICE OF LAW RULE

1) Renvoi

The choice of law rule indicates which system of law will be applied to resolve a dispute. So if the rule for tort is to apply the law of the place of the tort, and the tort clearly happened in France, the court applies French law. By "French law" we mean here the internal or domestic tort law of France. We do not, as a rule, mean all of French law, including in particular its choice of law rules.

However, in some circumstances the court could instead consider the choice of law rules of the applicable legal system. If French law were applicable, the court would then examine the French rule for choice of law in tort. If it also pointed to French law, its internal law would be applied. But if it pointed to another legal system, the rules of that system would be applied. This approach uses the doctrine of *renvoi*.

Renvoi means "reference back" but there are two related types of *renvoi*: remission, where the reference is back to the law of the forum, and transmission, where the reference is to another system of law. Under remission, the Ontario rule points to France and the French rule points to Ontario. Under transmission, the Ontario rules points to France and the French rule points to Germany.

There are various arguments in favour of *renvoi*.[37] First, it prevents forum shopping by ensuring that whatever court hears the dispute, the same substantive law will be applied to the claim. Without *renvoi*, in the remission example above a French court would apply Ontario law and an Ontario court would apply French law. Second, it avoids the arguably absurd result of a court applying foreign law to a claim that the courts of that foreign country would in fact consider governed by a different legal system.[38]

Yet there are strong arguments against *renvoi*. In those areas of choice of law where it is used, it has been applied inconsistently, leading to the charge that it operates mainly as an "escape device" to allow courts to avoid the otherwise applicable law. Further, *renvoi* is arguably either infinitely circular or unprincipled. If the court is prepared to

---

37 See Adrian Briggs, "In Praise and Defence of *Renvoi*" (1998) 47 *International and Comparative Law Quarterly* 877.
38 An important Australian case discussing *renvoi* at length and applying it in the context of choice of law in tort is *Neilson v Overseas Projects Corporation of Victoria Ltd*, [2005] HCA 54. See Reid Mortensen, "'Troublesome and Obscure': The Renewal of *Renvoi* in Australia" (2006) 2 *Journal of Private International Law* 1.

consider a foreign choice of law rule and thus refer back to the law of the forum, why is not that reference also seen as looking to all of forum law, including its choice of law rules? If it is, to be consistent in what we mean by the law of a foreign jurisdiction, we are caught in an infinite loop, being referred back and forth. However, if it is not, why not? What principled reason allows *renvoi* to operate for some references to a jurisdiction's law but not for others?

The doctrine of *renvoi* has the potential to significantly complicate the choice of law analysis. As indicated above, *renvoi* is not generally used as part of common law choice of law rules. It has virtually no role in choice of law for obligations. Those cases where it has been used or discussed, which tend to involve succession or matrimonial property issues, are not overly persuasive.[39]

2) The Incidental Question

In unusual cases the result can differ depending on the order in which the court proceeds through interrelated conflict of laws issues. An example of such a case is *Schwebel v Ungar*, in which the issue was whether the parties had validly married in Ontario.[40] The husband was domiciled in Ontario and the wife was domiciled in Israel. The wife had been married before and divorced before a rabbi in Italy. The divorce was recognized under Israeli but not Ontario law. The husband alleged that the wife had lacked the capacity to marry.

There are two ways the court could proceed. In one sense the case concerns the wife's capacity to marry, an issue which would normally be resolved using the law of her domicile (Israel), but in another sense the case is about whether the divorce is recognizable in Ontario, since if it is not the wife was still married at the time of her Ontario marriage. Here the validity of the divorce is the incidental question: it arises within the context of a larger choice of law issue, the capacity to marry, but it has its own separate conflict of laws rule. If the court resolves the incidental question using Ontario law, the marriage will be invalid. If the court allows the incidental question to be resolved by the law governing the larger issue, capacity to marry, the marriage will be valid since the law of her domicile, Israel, recognizes the earlier divorce. In *Schwebel* the court adopted the latter approach, but in reasoning highly tied to the specific facts of the case. There is no better or worse general

---

39 See *Ross v Ross* (1894), 25 SCR 307; *Vladi v Vladi* (1987), 39 DLR (4th) 563 (NSSC). In English law the leading case is *Re Annesley*, [1926] Ch 692.
40 [1965] SCR 148 [*Schwebel*].

solution to incidental question problems. Courts will have to continue to resolve them on a case-by-case basis.⁴¹

3) Time

In conflict of laws cases, as in domestic ones, there is typically a temporal difference, measured in months or more often years, between when the facts giving rise to the dispute occurred and when the court resolves the dispute. If the law changes during that time, issues can arise. Does the court use the law as of the time of the incident or as of the current date?

In most choice of law situations, a reference to a foreign legal system is understood to be to its current law, not its law of the past. Changes since the incident are applied in resolving the dispute. Exceptions are made, however, where the changes to the foreign law are intended to operate only prospectively. Exceptions are also sometimes made in cases that involve retroactive changes to a person's status, such as whether he or she was validly married, or entitlement to property, such as whether he or she validly inherited property under a will. In these cases, it can at times seem unfair to the court for it to disadvantage the person by applying the current law.⁴²

F. CHALLENGES TO THE CHOICE OF LAW PROCESS

The traditional choice of law process has been criticized on three main grounds. First, important considerations are omitted if the content of the possibly applicable legal systems does not play a central role in the analysis. Second, the various connecting factors are often not adequate for the task, being either too rigid so as to produce unacceptable results or too flexible so as to defeat predictability. Third, the process of characterization allows courts to manipulate the result. If the court does not like the answer produced by one choice of law rule, it is possible for the issue to be re-characterized so that a different rule, with a different connecting factor, is applied.

---

41   See AE Gotlieb, "The Incidental Question Revisited—Theory and Practice in the Conflict of Laws" (1977) 26 *International and Comparative Law Quarterly* 734.
42   See, for example, *Lynch v Provisional Government of Paraguay* (1871), LR 2 P & D 268; *Starkowski v Attorney General*, [1954] AC 155 (HL).

These shortcomings have led some commentators, mainly based in the United States, to propose alternative choice of law methods. One of these is rule selection. Under this method, courts identify the substantive difference between possibly applicable legal systems and then choose directly which of the competing legal rules to apply.[43] Under this approach, choice of law rules in the traditional sense cannot be formulated. Instead, courts are urged to develop "principles of preference." These general principles would guide courts in deciding which rule to apply. For example, one such principle could be to choose whichever law favours contractual validity, so as to preserve the consensual arrangement between the parties.

Another choice of law method is interest analysis. It builds on the rule-selection approach, in that it also aims to choose between competing legal rules rather than identify an applicable system of law. It requires the court to identify the governmental policy or interest expressed in each of the competing legal rules. Under this approach, the court should apply the law of the forum unless the forum has no interest in having its rule applied to the particular case. If it does not, and if the foreign country has an interest in having its rule applied, then the court should apply the foreign rule.[44]

A case on which advocates of interest analysis have focused is *Milliken v Pratt*.[45] A woman from Massachusetts guaranteed her husband's debts to a supplier in Maine. The guarantee was executed in Massachusetts and mailed to the supplier. The husband defaulted and the supplier sued the woman in Massachusetts. The law of Massachusetts prohibited married women from guaranteeing their husbands' debts. The court used a choice of law rule that focused on the place of contracting, which it held was Maine, finding the woman had made an offer to the supplier which it accepted in Maine. The supplier therefore was successful.

Using interest analysis, a court would determine the policy expressed in the Massachusetts prohibition. The policy might be, for example, to protect married women domiciled in Massachusetts from commercial exposure. A court would also determine the policy expressed by the lack of such a prohibition in the law of Maine. The policy

---

43 See David F Cavers, "A Critique of the Choice-of-Law Problem" (1933) 47 *Harvard Law Review* 173.
44 See Brainerd Currie, *Selected Essays on the Conflict of Laws* (Durham, NC: Duke University Press, 1963) at 183–84 and 188–89 [Currie, *Selected Essays*]; Brainerd Currie, "Comment on *Babcock v. Jackson*" (1963) 63 *Columbia Law Review* 1233 at 1242–243. For a more recent defence of interest analysis, see Robert A Sedler, "A Real World Perspective on Choice of Law" (1997) 48 *Mercer Law Review* 781.
45 125 Mass 374, 28 Am Rep 241 (1878) [*Milliken*].

might be, for example, to preserve the reasonable expectations of the parties and the security of commercial transactions. With both states having an interest in having their rule applied, this method would fall back on the law of the forum. Of greater interest, consider the analysis if the facts of the case remained the same but the legal systems were reversed, so that it was the law of Maine that contained the prohibition. Now the court could well conclude that Maine had no interest in having its rule applied to a woman in Massachusetts.[46]

Babcock v Jackson is a famous American conflict of laws case that illustrates both rule selection and interest analysis.[47] The plaintiff was a passenger in the defendant's car. Both parties were from New York. They drove to Ontario for a weekend visit, where they were involved in a single-vehicle accident. The plaintiff sued the defendant in New York and the court had to consider whether the claim was governed by the law of New York or the law of Ontario. Ontario law at that time included a statutory prohibition on guest passengers—people who had not paid the driver for the transport—suing the driver of the vehicle.

The court noted that the traditional choice of law rule for tort was to apply the law of the place of the tort, which was Ontario. However, instead of using that rule to determine the legal system that would govern the dispute, the court directly examined the two competing rules. It held that New York had a strong interest in having its law applied so that the injured plaintiff could receive compensation. It also held that Ontario had no interest in having its law applied. The court stated that the policy underlying the Ontario statute, which it took as being to protect insurance companies from fraudulent claims concocted by drivers and passengers, was not concerned with protecting New York insurers. Accordingly, the court did not apply the Ontario statute.

Several American states have adopted rule selection or interest analysis as their choice of law process.[48] But Canadian courts have generally not followed suit, and with good reason. Both of these approaches have a pronounced bias in favour of applying the law of the forum, which runs counter to comity and the principle of proximity. Rule selection leaves it open for courts to choose what they perceive to be the "better" law, which, given their high degree of familiarity with the law of the forum, is likely to be that law.[49] In *Clark v Clark* the court openly observed that

---

46 Currie, *Selected Essays*, above note 44 at 108–9.
47 191 NE2d 279 (NY 1963) [*Babcock*].
48 See Symeon C Symeonides, "Choice of Law in the American Courts in 2014: Twenty-Eighth Annual Survey" (2015) 63 *American Journal of Comparative Law* 299.
49 JHC Morris, "Law and Reason Triumphant or How Not to Review a Restatement" (1973) 21 *American Journal of Comparative Law* 322 at 324.

"[w]e prefer to apply the better rule in conflicts cases . . . . If the law of some other state is outmoded, an unrepealed remnant of a bygone age, 'a drag on the coat-tails of civilization,' we will try to see our way clear to apply our own law instead."[50] Interest analysis gives too much deference to the forum's interest, so that even a minimal interest it has in its law being applied outweighs the foreign country's interest, however considerable.[51] Returning to *Milliken*, interest analysis would apply either the law of Massachusetts or of Maine, dependent on which was the forum, so that the outcome of the dispute would depend on where the litigation occurred. In addition, it may be extremely hard for a court to identify the policy that underlies a foreign legal rule.[52] In *Babcock* the New York court relied on the view of Ontario's legislative policy expressed by a law student in a brief published note.[53]

Overall, rule selection and interest analysis, if viable at all, may operate as intended only within the confines of a federal country where the degrees of difference between competing laws are relatively small.[54] It is, for example, much easier to accept a Michigan court purporting to identify the policy behind an Ohio rule than doing the same thing for a French, Russian, or Chinese rule.

---

50 222 A2d 205 at 209 (NH 1966). See Sagi Peari, "Better Law as a Better Outcome" (2015) 63 *American Journal of Comparative Law* 155.

51 Patrick J Borchers, "Back to the Past: Anti-pragmatism in American Conflicts Law" (1997) 48 *Mercer Law Review* 721 at 724.

52 See Lea Brilmayer, "Interest Analysis and the Myth of Legislative Intent" (1980) 78 *Michigan Law Review* 392; JJ Fawcett, "Is American Governmental Interest Analysis the Solution to English Tort Choice of Law Problems?" (1982) 31 *International and Comparative Law Quarterly* 150.

53 See Kurt Lipstein, "Private International Law with a Social Content—A Super Law?" in Herbert Bernstein, Ulrich Drobnig, & Hein Kotz, eds, *Festschrift fur Konrad Zweigert* (Tubingen: JCB Mohr, 1981) at 189, n 61.

54 This point is acknowledged by Cavers, above note 43 at 203. See also Friedrich K Juenger, "Choice of Law: How It Ought Not to Be" (1997) 48 *Mercer Law Review* 757 at 758–60. In *Prudential Insurance Company of America v O'Grady*, 396 P2d 246 (1964), the Supreme Court of Arizona stated at 248 that "the conditions are totally different [from an international case] in the sister states of this country. The law of another state is in our language; its principles are substantially the same and its tenor is readily ascertained."

FURTHER READINGS

AMERICAN LAW INSTITUTE. *Restatement of the Law Second: Conflict of Laws*, 2d (St Paul, MN: American Law Institute, 1971).

BRILMAYER, LEA. *Conflict of Laws*, 2d ed (Boston: Little, Brown, 1995).

CAVERS, DAVID. *The Choice-of-Law Process* (Ann Arbor, MI: University of Michigan Press, 1965).

EDINGER, ELIZABETH. "*Renvoi* in Canada—Form and Availability" (1984) 14 *Manitoba Law Journal* 35.

GOTLIEB, ALLAN EZRA. "The Incidental Question in Anglo-American Conflict of Laws" (1955) 33 *Canadian Bar Review* 523.

HUGHES, DAVID ALEXANDER. "The Insolubility of *Renvoi* and Its Consequences" (2010) 6 *Journal of Private International Law* 195.

MARTIN, JAMES, ED. *Perspectives on Conflict of Laws: Choice of Law* (Boston: Little, Brown, 1980).

PITEL, STEPHEN GA. "Characterisation of Unjust Enrichment in the Conflict of Laws" in Jason Neyers, Mitchell McInnes, & Stephen GA Pitel, eds, *Understanding Unjust Enrichment* (Oxford: Hart, 2004).

SWAN, JOHN. "Federalism and the Conflict of Laws: The Curious Position of the Supreme Court of Canada" (1995) 46 *South Carolina Law Review* 923.

SYMEONIDES, SYMEON C. "The American Choice-of-Law Revolution in the Courts: Today and Tomorrow" (2002) 298 *Recueil des Cours* 9.

SYMEONIDES, SYMEON C. "The Choice-of-Law Revolution Fifty Years after Currie: An End and a Beginning" [2015] *University of Illinois Law Review* 1847.

CHAPTER 11

SUBSTANCE AND PROCEDURE

A. INTRODUCTION

The previous chapter introduced the process of characterizing particular legal rules as either substantive or procedural. This characterization is chiefly important because the forum nearly always applies its own procedural law, even in cases where a choice of law rule leads to foreign law being applied to resolve the dispute. For example, a claim in contract may be governed by New York law but the Ontario court will still use Ontario rules of evidence in the dispute. It does not sit as though it was a New York court and does not apply any procedural law of New York. The court will therefore have to determine which rules from each legal system are substantive and which are procedural.

Exceptionally, a court might apply a procedural rule of another country. A possible example is in assessing the validity of the service of documents on a party outside the forum. Rather than insisting that such a service be made in accordance with the forum's procedural rules, the forum might accept the service as valid if it was made in accordance with the law of the place where the party was served.[1]

In developing definitions of procedure and of substance, it is important to fully appreciate what is at stake. The choice of law process is

---

1   See, for example, r 17.05(2) of *Rules of Civil Procedure*, RRO 1990, Reg 194 [Ontario Rules]. On this and other exceptions to the general rule, see Richard Garnett, *Substance and Procedure in Private International Law* (Oxford: Oxford University Press, 2012) at 3 and 37.

based on a willingness to have certain disputes resolved using foreign law rather than forum law. However, the more broadly the courts define procedure, the more foreign law is thereby excluded and forum law is applied. A broad definition of procedure produces a marked trend in favour of the law of the forum. This trend can undermine much of the central objective of choice of law rules and can lead to forum shopping.[2]

Traditionally, one view was that substance involved legal rights and procedure involved remedies and enforcement.[3] This view was both too simplistic and too broad in its definition of procedure. In *243930 Alberta Ltd v Wickham* the court indicated that the best approach was to use a relatively narrow definition of procedure. In its view, courts should consider how "inconvenient" it would be for them to apply a foreign rule, and if the foreign rule can be conveniently applied then that should be done.[4] It would clearly be confusing and inconvenient, for example, to exchange pleadings using foreign rules about the required format for court documents or to conduct a trial using foreign rules of evidence. It also may not be practical, or possible, to apply foreign rules regarding the local enforcement of a foreign order. But in many cases the court may well be able to give effect to a remedy available under foreign law without inconvenience. This approach to the substance–procedure distinction characterizes as procedure those rules needed to ensure the orderly functioning of the local justice system.

A narrow definition of procedure makes it more difficult for a court to use characterization as a mechanism for applying a particular forum rule. A court might still apply the forum rule, for example as a matter of public policy (as discussed in Chapter 3). But doing so on that basis rather than as a matter of characterization is arguably more transparent and principled.[5]

B. REMEDIES

As noted, the traditional view was that remedies were governed by the law of the forum. This meant that a successful plaintiff could be awarded

---

2   See Garnett, *ibid* at 8.
3   See, for example, the discussion in *Vogler v Szendroi*, [2008] NSJ No 71 at paras 16–21 (CA) [*Vogler*].
4   (1990), 75 OR (2d) 289 (CA) [*Wickham*]. See also *Block Bros Realty Ltd v Mollard* (1981), 122 DLR (3d) 323 at 327–28 (BCCA). For a similarly broad definition of substance in Australia, see *Tipperary Developments Pty Ltd v The State of Western Australia*, [2009] WASCA 126 at paras 79–81.
5   Garnett, above note 1 at 339.

only those remedies available under the forum's domestic law.[6] English law, for example, does not include a remedial constructive trust. This remedy would therefore not be available in English proceedings, even to a plaintiff who had succeeded in a claim that was governed by a legal system that did include a remedial constructive trust.

However, the modern view, in line with cases like *Wickham*, is that courts should fashion local remedies that are consistent with the applicable law. It would not be inappropriate for the plaintiff in a conflicts case to be awarded different remedies than the plaintiff in a wholly domestic case. The central aim should be giving a broad scope to the applicable law, including its remedies. The court's limiting concern should be whether a foreign remedy can be made effective and enforceable within the forum's legal system. This is especially warranted where there is a close connection between a particular right and a specific remedy, as is often the case for claims under a statutory scheme.[7]

Most legal systems provide for a monetary award of damages, but they can vary as to what types of loss will lead to recovery. In a personal injury case, for example, types of loss include costs of care, loss of earnings, pain and suffering, and loss of enjoyment of life. Whether a particular type or "head" of loss is recoverable is generally considered to be substantive and so governed by the applicable law. In contrast, the actual quantification or calculation of the amount to be awarded for any of these heads is procedural and uses the law of the forum.[8] This can produce difficulties. Consider a court in a country that does not award damages for pain and suffering. If in a conflicts case the plaintiff is, under the applicable law, entitled to an award for pain and suffering, the court will have few or no domestic principles to assist it in calculating those damages under the law of the forum. Consider also the issue of punitive damages. These damages can be significantly larger under the law of some American states than in Canada. In Ontario proceedings, a plaintiff's claim and entitlement to punitive damages, as a head of loss, might be governed by Texas law but the calculation of the amount of those damages would use Ontario law.

This can give rise to concerns about forum shopping, with plaintiffs seeking to sue in the jurisdiction where the calculation, under the law of the forum, would be most favourable. This can produce, for ex-

---

6   See, for example, *Khalij Commercial Bank Ltd v Woods* (1985), 50 OR (2d) 446 (HCJ); *Barrick Gold Corp v Goldcorp Inc*, 2011 ONSC 3725 at para 990.
7   See *Wickham*, above note 4.
8   *Wong v Wei* (1999), 65 BCLR (3d) 222 at para 40 (SC). See *Boys v Chaplin*, [1971] AC 356 (HL); *Harding v Wealands*, [2006] UKHL 32 at para 24 [*Harding*]; *Cox v Ergo Versicherung AG (formerly known as Victoria)*, [2014] UKSC 22.

ample, more product liability cases being brought in the United States and more defamation cases being brought in the United Kingdom. In response to this concern, one solution would be to allow the applicable law to have some role, along with the law of the forum, in the quantification of damages. One way to do this would be to require courts to consider, as a factor in making the award, what would be awarded under the applicable law. Another would be to treat that amount as an upper limit on the award under forum law.

An important issue in personal injury cases is the characterization of the Canadian upper limit on recovery of damages for non-pecuniary loss. In 1978 the Supreme Court of Canada held that as a general rule $100,000 was the upper limit for these losses.[9] Adjusted for inflation, as of 2013 the limit was around $330,000.[10] In imposing a limit, the court was concerned about the social burden of rising awards. How should this limit be characterized? A strong argument can be made that there is little difference between a rule that no damages are available for non-pecuniary loss in personal injury cases and a rule that limits such damages to a nominal amount. Both rules would, in effect, be about whether such damages were practically available. Yet the $330,000 limit is not a nominal amount: it is a sizable sum, though far below what some American courts might award.

In *Somers v Fournier* the Court of Appeal for Ontario characterized the limit as procedural.[11] It accepted the view that the availability of any recovery for a particular head of damage was substantive but that other provisions addressing the scope of such recovery were about calculation and therefore procedural.[12] If this seems overly semantic, in support of this conclusion it held that the policy considerations behind the limit, which aimed at avoiding excessive and unpredictable damages awards, justified this result. Two questions can be posed in response. First, is it appropriate to take these considerations into account in the characterization process? Recall that in *Wickham* the approach to separating procedure from substance focused on convenience and efficiency. The reasoning in *Somers* is somewhat result-oriented: the court has policy reasons for wanting the limit to be applied and achieves that result through characterizing it as procedural. Second, do the policy considerations behind the limit, developed in Canadian domestic law,

---

9   Andrews v Grand & Toy Alberta Ltd, [1978] 2 SCR 229.
10 See *Kim v Toronto (City)*, 2013 ONSC 6831; *Afonina v Jansson*, 2015 BCSC 10.
11 (2002), 60 OR (3d) 225 at 244 (CA) [*Somers*]. For the contrary view, see *John Pfeiffer Pty Ltd v Rogerson* (2000), 203 CLR 503 (HCA).
12 On this the court followed *Stevens v Head* (1993), 176 CLR 433 at 458 (HCA). See also *Harding*, above note 8 at paras 39 and 77.

apply equally to conflicts cases? If New York law is the applicable law, and it does not have any such limit, then how does it violate the Canadian policy for a court to make a larger award, especially if the defendant is from outside the province?

This issue can be considered from different perspectives. If litigation were under way in England concerning a personal injury claim governed by Canadian tort law, would we expect the plaintiff's claim for non-pecuniary loss to be limited to $330,000? If not, does this encourage the plaintiff to sue in England rather than in Ontario? Consider instead similar litigation in Ontario, with the substantive claim governed by the law of a foreign country that has a limit of only $100,000. The Canadian characterization of the limit as procedural means that the Ontario court would ignore the foreign limit, even if it were based on the same policy considerations underpinning the Canadian limit. In short, despite the converging appellate authority on this issue, there is room for further analysis here and continuing debate should be expected.

The court in *Somers* also had to characterize two other sets of rules relating to damages: those on costs and those on prejudgment interest. Under the law applicable to the tort claim in the case, which was New York law, lawyers' fees could not be recovered by the successful party. Under Ontario law, the law of the forum, the general rule is that the successful party does receive some indemnity for these fees from the unsuccessful party in the form of an award of costs. The court noted that costs awards were not solely concerned with compensation and were routinely used to facilitate and control the litigation process and to promote settlement. In this sense, the rules on costs were best understood as part of the mechanism of the local court, allowing it to run more smoothly, and so were characterized as procedural.[13]

In contrast, the court held that the core function of prejudgment interest was compensatory, to account for the time value of the money from when the entitlement accrued to the time of judgment. In this sense it was closely analogous to a head of damages. Under the old distinction between right and remedy, the plaintiff had a right to receive prejudgment interest on an award of damages. The court therefore characterized rules on prejudgment interest as substantive.[14] These two characterization decisions accord with the general principles in *Wickham*. Although tempting to conclude that it would be quite convenient for the Ontario court to adopt New York's no-costs rule, it is difficult to see as a more general matter how a local court could apply the intricacies of various

---

13 *Somers*, above note 11 at 233–34.
14 *Ibid* at 236–37.

costs regimes from different legal systems.[15] In contrast, there is much less practical difficulty in using the prejudgment interest rules of the applicable law rather than those of the forum.

C. LIMITATION PERIODS

The common law traditionally characterized limitation periods as procedural.[16] They were considered to deprive the plaintiff of access to the process of suing and obtaining a remedy rather than to abolish the underlying legal entitlement. This characterization also meant that all litigants in the court would be subject to the same limitation periods, achieving a kind of procedural equality. This characterization was subject to significant criticism, such that the United Kingdom eventually passed legislation to reverse it and characterize limitation periods as substantive.[17]

In Canada, a similar change occurred by judicial decision. In *Tolofson v Jensen* the Supreme Court of Canada reviewed the historic treatment of this issue.[18] For the court, La Forest J rejected both reasons underlying the traditional view. First, limitation periods could equally be understood as giving a defendant a right, after the passage of time, not to be sued, and extinguishing a plaintiff's substantive right.[19] Arguably this view is, in modern times, the more correct of the two views of what limitation periods do.[20] But even more fundamentally, the decision as to whether limitation periods are substantive or procedural should not flow from this sort of semantics, which has strong links back to the more general divide between right and remedy. As indicated above, that divide is much less important today. Looking back to the approach in *Wickham*, the courts can conveniently apply foreign limitation periods in cases governed by foreign law, and so they should.

Second, aiming to treat all litigants as procedurally equal clashes with the aims of the choice of law process. If the court is willing to resolve a plaintiff's claim using a foreign law, it is more consistent with

---

15 Especially considering costs awards are often made on an ongoing basis at various interlocutory stages of litigation, such as after a motion.
16 See *Allard v Charbonneau*, [1953] 2 DLR 442 (Ont CA).
17 *Foreign Limitation Periods Act, 1984* (UK), 1984, c 16. For a detailed criticism of the characterization of limitation periods as procedural, see Garnett, above note 1 at 262–63.
18 [1994] 3 SCR 1022 [*Tolofson*].
19 See *Yew Bon Tew v Kanderaan Bas Mara*, [1983] 1 AC 553 at 563 (PC); *Martin v Perrie*, [1986] 1 SCR 41.
20 The decision in *Tolofson* has itself subsequently fostered this view: see *Aucoin v Murray*, 2013 NSSC 37.

doing so to apply that legal system's limitation period rather than the forum's. Insisting on having all cases use the same limitation periods looks like equality for its own sake, not for any principled reason.

1) Transitional Issues

The modern law's tendency to characterize more as substantive and less as procedural raises a related issue: how will the courts handle transitional issues that arise when traditional characterizations are altered? Consider, as a hypothetical situation, a lawyer in Nova Scotia acting for a local resident who was injured in a car accident in Saskatchewan. The lawyer is planning to commence proceedings in Nova Scotia, where the limitation period for the client's claim is two years from the accident. The client consulted the lawyer soon after the accident, but eighteen months later the lawyer has still not started proceedings. The lawyer's thinking, relying on the forum's limitation period, is that all will be fine as long as the litigation is started in the next few months. The Supreme Court of Canada then releases its decision in *Tolofson*. Limitation periods are held to be substantive, and the Saskatchewan limitation period for the client's claim is one year. If the lawyer now starts the proceedings, how should the limitation issue be resolved?

One approach would be to work by analogy from legislative changes. Sometimes a limitation period is shortened by statute. In the absence of explicit transitional provisions, the general rule is that changes to procedural law operate retroactively and changes to substantive law do not. If limitation periods are substantive, then the change would not operate retroactively and the client would get the benefit of the original, longer period.

However, this analogy may be flawed in two ways. First, *Tolofson* did not shorten any legal system's limitation period, so it is not like a statutory change to that effect. What *Tolofson* did was change the characterization of limitation periods. Second, unlike a legislative change, the presumption in the common law is that judicial decisions operate retroactively, in accordance with the fiction that judges do not change the law but rather state what it has always been. In the scenario above, it is difficult to escape the conclusion that the Saskatchewan limitation period would be applied in Nova Scotia and the client would lose. However, some courts have been troubled by that result.[21]

---

21 See *Hendsbee v Khuber* (1995), 148 NSR (2d) 270 (SC); *Dipalma v Smart* (1995), 35 Alta LR (3d) 119 (QB), rev'd (1996), 43 Alta LR (3d) 161 (QB); *Stewart v Stewart* (1997), 30 BCLR (3d) 233 (CA).

2) Statutory Developments

Following the decision in *Tolofson*, which held that limitation periods are substantive, Alberta amended its *Limitations Act* in 1996 to provide in section 12 that "[t]he limitations law of the Province shall be applied whenever a remedial order is sought in this Province, notwithstanding that, in accordance with conflict of law rules, the claim will be adjudicated under the substantive law of another jurisdiction."[22] As a statutory provision, it takes precedence over the common law. On one reading of this provision, it prevents *Tolofson* from having an effect in Alberta: instead of using the limitation period from the applicable law, the court is directed to apply the forum's limitation period.

In *Castillo v Castillo* the plaintiff sued the defendant in Alberta for a tort committed in California.[23] The claim was commenced just inside Alberta's two-year limitation period and so outside California's one-year period. Based on the characterization in *Tolofson*, the defendant argued that as California law applied to the tort claim, its limitation period also applied. The plaintiff sought to rely on section 12.

The Supreme Court of Canada adopted an interesting interpretation of section 12. It did not conclude that it ousted or took priority over the California limitation period. Rather, it held that consideration had to be given to both limitation periods, and as the California period had expired the claim was statute-barred.[24] This conclusion is unsettling in two ways. First, it seems more plausible that the legislature's intention in enacting section 12 was to require courts to use the forum's limitation period exclusively than to make it an additional requirement alongside the limitation period from the applicable law. Second, despite the opportunity, the court provides no indication as to how it would treat an amended version of a provision like section 12 that made it more explicit that the foreign law's limitation period is not to be considered.[25]

Justice Bastarache's separate concurring reasons in *Castillo* highlight important issues that the other judges, on their interpretation, did

---

22 RSA 2000, c L-12. See the similar language in *The Limitations Act*, SS 2004, c L-16.1, s 27, and see also the *Limitations Act*, SNL 1995, c L-16.1, s 23. In contrast, some provinces have enacted provisions that are consistent with *Tolofson*: see the *Limitations Act, 2002*, SO 2002, c 24, Sch B, s 23, which provides that the limitations law of Ontario or of any other jurisdiction is substantive law.
23 [2005] 3 SCR 870 [*Castillo*].
24 *Ibid* at paras 3–4 and 8.
25 Alberta did not press the issue. Instead, it revised s 12 to expressly codify the court's interpretation in *Castillo* (*Limitation Statutes Amendment Act*, SA 2007, c 22, s 1). Similar provisions in other provinces (above note 22) have not been revised, so the issue could arise again.

not have to address. He held that section 12 was an unconstitutional attempt by Alberta to legislate extraterritorially.[26] He stated that "the question of whether limitation periods are procedural or substantive is not something the province can decide."[27] In part this flowed from the limits on a province's power to enact laws. A province must not be able, merely by characterizing particular rules as procedural, to apply those rules to any cases in its courts. It was therefore not open to the province to in effect reverse the characterization in *Tolofson*. This analysis is provocative and will likely have significant influence in subsequent cases dealing with the distinction between substance and procedure.

3) Related Issues

In *Vogler v Szendroi* the plaintiff, a resident of Nova Scotia, was injured in a car accident in Wyoming.[28] Three years after the accident the plaintiff commenced proceedings in Nova Scotia but did not serve one of the defendants until another three years had passed. Wyoming's law of limitations required that the action be commenced within four years. In accordance with *Tolofson*, the court applied the Wyoming limitation period. However, there was a further complication. Under Nova Scotia law, the action was commenced by the filing of the originating notice. But under Wyoming law, because of the delay in serving the defendant, the proceeding was deemed to have been commenced on the date of service. The court therefore had to determine which rule to apply as to when the litigation was commenced.

The motions judge held that the Wyoming rule on timing was "integral" to its law on the limitation of actions and so had to be characterized as substantive law.[29] The judge therefore applied the Wyoming rule and held that the claim was started outside the limitation period. The Court of Appeal reversed, holding that the rule was not concerned with the timing within which proceedings had to be commenced but rather with the way in which they were commenced.[30] The Wyoming rule addressed the manner of starting the action, which required both filing and service. Put another way, the law of the forum, as procedural law, determines what event will stop the limitation period from running.[31]

---

26 *Castillo*, above note 23 at paras 16–18.
27 *Ibid* at para 37.
28 Above note 3.
29 *Vogler v Szendroi* (2007), 255 NSR (2d) 190 at para 27 (SC).
30 *Vogler*, above note 3 at paras 26–28 and 31–34.
31 *Ibid* at para 37, relying on Janet Walker, "Twenty Questions (about Section 23 of the *Limitations Act, 2002*)" in Wayne Gray, Lisa Kerbel-Caplan, & Jacob Ziegel,

D. PARTIES

A common preliminary issue in litigation is the status, standing, or capacity of either the plaintiff to commence proceedings or the defendant to be sued. This is in no way primarily a conflicts issue: it arises often in domestic litigation and is considered in detail in the civil procedure literature. Each jurisdiction has to determine rules for claims by or against individuals under a certain age, individuals with a mental illness, partnerships, trusts, unincorporated associations, and the like.[32]

In conflicts cases, the general rule is that issues concerning a party's status are governed by the law of the forum, on the basis that these are issues of procedure, not of substance.[33] Even if the dispute will be resolved using a foreign law, that law cannot, by virtue of being the applicable law, give to the plaintiff a status he, she, or it otherwise lacks under the law of the forum. For example, for an individual to sue in Ontario independently in his or her own name, he or she must be eighteen years old.[34] It is not relevant that he or she is sixteen years old and is resident or domiciled in a country where that is a sufficient age to so sue. The forum's requirement governs.

However, this rule would cause significant problems if strictly applied to non-natural persons. For example, for a corporation to sue in Ontario, must it meet Ontario's requirements for a valid corporation in terms of share structure, number of directors, and so on? In practice this would mean a large number of foreign corporations would lack status to sue in Ontario. Each jurisdiction can allow non-natural persons such as corporations, partnerships, and trusts to be created in slightly different ways. Strict insistence on the law of the forum for status questions would be a major barrier to cross-border litigation.

Accordingly, the status of non-natural persons is governed by the law of the person's "home" jurisdiction, such as the place of incorporation for a corporation. If the person has the status to sue or be sued under that law, that will be accepted by the forum. In *International Association of*

---

eds, *The New Ontario Limitations Regime: Exposition and Analysis* (Toronto: Ontario Bar Association, 2005) at 110.
32   See, for example, Ontario Rules, above note 1, rr 7–10.
33   *Regas Ltd v Plotkins*, [1961] SCR 566 at 571–72; *International Association of Science and Technology for Development v Hamza* (1995), 28 Alta LR (3d) 125 at para 9 (CA) [*IASTD*].
34   See Ontario Rules, above note 1, r 1.03(1), which defines "disability" to include being a minor; and r 7.01(1), which requires those under a disability to use a litigation guardian; see also the *Age of Majority and Accountability Act*, RSO 1990, c A.7, s 1, which sets the age of majority at eighteen.

Science and Technology for Development v Hamza the plaintiffs, which were Swiss societies, were recognized as legal entities under Swiss law but had no such status under Alberta law. They sued in Alberta and the defendants challenged their status to sue. The Court of Appeal noted the general rule that foreign corporations, validly created under the law of a foreign country, could sue as corporations in a common law province of Canada.[35] It extended that rule to unincorporated foreign entities, holding that "the law tends to support a granting of status in cases where the entity in question is recognized as a legal or juridical person by the laws of its home jurisdiction, in the sense of having status to sue."[36] In the court's view this approach was consistent with the comity principle.

This can lead to some interesting results. In *Bumper Development Corp Ltd v Commissioner of Police of the Metropolis* the English Court of Appeal had to consider whether a ruined Hindu temple had the status to sue, as a plaintiff, in the English courts.[37] The court noted the "formidable conceptual difficulty in recognizing as a party entitled to sue in our courts something which on one view is little more than a pile of stones."[38] This object lacked status under the law of the forum but under Indian law it had the status of a legal person. The court concluded that it was consistent with comity that its status under its home legal system be respected and it was therefore able to sue in England.[39]

In *Cirque du Soleil Inc v Volvo Group Canada Inc* the issue was whether a California corporation which had been dissolved could be sued in Ontario.[40] Under California law a dissolved corporation could be sued whereas under Ontario law it could not. The court held that the issue was governed by California law, in part relying on *IASTD*. But the court also stated that "the narrow issue of the capacity to be sued in Ontario is a substantive one."[41] Labelling the issue as substantive is unusual. Having resort to the procedural rules of a foreign legal system does not make the issue substantive. It remains procedural.

---

35 *IASTD*, above note 33 at para 27.
36 *Ibid* at para 37. See also, on the issue of limited partnerships, *Devon Canada Corp v PE-Pittsfield, LLC (cob as Pittsfield Generating Co, LP)*, [2008] AJ No 1263 (CA).
37 [1991] 4 All ER 638 (CA).
38 *Ibid* at 647.
39 The resulting English judgment was subsequently enforced in Alberta, with the Alberta court similarly concluding that the ruined temple had the necessary status to bring the enforcement proceedings: *India v Bumper Development Corp* (1995), 29 Alta LR (3d) 194 at para 71 (QB), aff'd 4 December 1995 (Alta CA).
40 2015 ONSC 2698.
41 *Ibid* at paras 26–27.

A related issue is whether an entity is immune from being sued on the basis of sovereign immunity. The orthodox view is that this issue is resolved by the law of the forum. Under the *State Immunity Act* a foreign state is, subject to some exceptions, immune from the jurisdiction of Canadian courts.[42] This immunity encompasses "any government of the foreign state or of any political subdivision of the foreign state, including any of its departments, and any agency of the foreign state." An agency of a foreign state is defined as "any legal entity that is an organ of the foreign state but that is separate from the foreign state."[43] Whether an entity is caught by this definition is thus determined by forum law.[44]

FURTHER READINGS

AILES, EDGAR. "Substance and Procedure in the Conflict of Laws" (1941) 39 *Michigan Law Review* 392.

CARRUTHERS, JANEEN. "Substance and Procedure in the Conflict of Laws: A Continuing Debate in Relation to Damages" (2004) 53 *International and Comparative Law Quarterly* 691.

CASTEL, JEAN-GABRIEL. "Procedure and the Conflict of Laws" (1970) 16 *McGill Law Journal* 603.

ELIAS, OLUSOJI. *Judicial Remedies in the Conflict of Laws* (Oxford: Hart, 2001).

GRAY, ANTHONY. "Loss Distribution Issues in Multinational Tort Claims: Giving Substance to Substance" (2008) 4 *Journal of Private International Law* 279.

KEYES, MARY. "Substance and Procedure in Multistate Tort Litigation" (2010) 18 *Torts Law Journal* 201.

MALCAI, OFER, & RONIT LEVINE-SCHNUR. "Which Came First, the Procedure or the Substance? Justificational Priority and the Substance-Procedure Distinction" (2014) 34 *Oxford Journal of Legal Studies* 1.

---

42 RSC 1985, c S-18, s 3(1).
43 *Ibid*, s 2.
44 *University of Calgary v Colorado School of Mines* (1995), 179 AR 81 (QB). One case, *Collavino Inc v Yemen (Tihama Development Authority)*, 2007 ABQB 212 at para 107, suggests that both forum law and foreign law are relevant to resolving this issue. See Garnett, above note 1 at 139–41.

PALMER, DUSTIN. "Should Prejudgment Interest Be a Matter of Procedural or Substantive Law in Choice-of-Law Disputes?" (2002) 69 *University of Chicago Law Review* 705.

PORRETTA, CHRISTINA. "Assessing Tort Damages in the Conflict of Laws: *Loci, Fori*, Illogical" (2012) 91 *Canadian Bar Review* 97.

SCOTT, ANDREW. "Substance and Procedure and Choice of Law in Torts" [2007] *Lloyd's Maritime and Commercial Law Quarterly* 44.

WALKER, JANET. "*Castillo v. Castillo*: Closing the Barn Door" (2006) 43 *Canadian Business Law Journal* 487.

WEINTRAUB, RUSSELL. "Choice of Law for Quantification of Damages: A Judgment of the House of Lords Makes a Bad Rule Worse" (2007) 42 *Texas International Law Journal* 311.

CHAPTER 12

PLEADING AND PROOF OF FOREIGN LAW

A. INTRODUCTION

An important issue in cases involving choice of law is how the court becomes aware of the content of foreign law. If, for example, a contract dispute before the Ontario court is governed by the law of California, how does the court come to know California's law? The domestic court is taken to know its own law but there is no basis for assuming the same degree of familiarity with foreign law.

B. THE VOLUNTARY NATURE OF CHOICE OF LAW

Choice of law is voluntary in the sense that it is an issue raised by the parties rather than by the court. It is up to one or both parties to a dispute to allege that it should be resolved by foreign rather than domestic law. If neither party makes such an allegation, the court resolves the dispute using the law of the forum, no matter how strong the factual connections to another legal system.[1] To take a striking example, a contract may expressly provide that it is to be interpreted using the law of Germany but if neither party alleges that the dispute is to be resolved using German law then the clause will be ignored and forum law will

---

1   See *Pettkus v Becker*, [1980] 2 SCR 834 at 853–54, Dickson J [*Pettkus*].

249

be used. There will be no need to identify the content of German law. Interestingly, this approach has led to some decisions becoming leading cases on the law of a particular jurisdiction when arguably they could have been resolved under a different law. In Canada, *Pettkus v Becker* became a leading common law case on the law of constructive trusts, yet on its facts it could have been resolved under the civil law of Quebec instead.[2]

There are different reasons why a choice of law issue would not be raised by the parties.[3] One is that they might not notice it. They may be unfamiliar with the relevant choice of law rule and simply think that forum law is the only law available. Another is that they might notice the issue but choose not to raise it. It might not make any difference: the parties might consider the result likely to be the same, or equally acceptable, under the law of the forum as under the foreign law. In addition, as we will see, proceeding under foreign law can add to the expense and complexity of the litigation. The parties might therefore prefer to proceed under the cheaper, more familiar forum law.[4]

Should choice of law be entirely voluntary? Within a federal country like Canada, the argument can be made that the courts of one province should be required to consider whether an issue is governed by the law of another province. This requirement would show respect for that province's law and prevent the parties from avoiding its application. An argument of this sort could be rooted in elements of the reasoning in *Morguard Investments Ltd v De Savoye* dealing with the inherent constitutional principles of a federal country.[5] However, there is little authority to support this argument.[6] Even in relatively recent cases, such as *Boulanger v Johnson & Johnson Corp*,[7] the courts have retained the traditional approach to the pleading and proof of foreign law even in the interprovincial context.

---

2   Ibid.
3   See Richard Fentiman, *Foreign Law in English Courts* (Oxford: Oxford University Press, 1998) at 164–72.
4   See *Tolofson v Jensen*, [1994] 3 SCR 1022 at 1053, La Forest J: "the parties may either tacitly or by agreement choose to be governed by the *lex fori* if they find it advisable to do so."
5   [1990] 3 SCR 1077.
6   Some Australian commentators have argued that judges in the states of that country can, on their own, raise the issue of the applicability of the law of another state: see Edward I Sykes & Michael C Pryles, *Australian Private International Law*, 3d ed (Sydney: Law Book Company, 1991) at 275–76.
7   (2003), 64 OR (3d) 208 (Div Ct) [*Boulanger*].

C. FOREIGN LAW AS FACT

In domestic proceedings we are accustomed to a general distinction between facts, which must be proven to the court, and laws, which do not require proof and which are simply understood to be known to the court.[8] In Ontario litigation, the lawyers do not call evidence of Ontario law: they submit copies of cases and statutes and make submissions on them. However, foreign laws are considered to be facts.[9]

The central consequence of this classification is that foreign laws, like other facts, cannot be assumed to be within the knowledge of the court: they must be proven. If an issue in Ontario litigation is governed by New York law, the lawyers cannot simply provide the court with copies of New York cases and statutes and make submissions on them. Each point of New York law will need to be proven in evidence. As discussed below, this is typically done by calling, as a witness, an expert in the foreign law.

In domestic cases judges are not allowed to conduct their own research into the facts,[10] and the same principle applies to foreign laws. In *Bumper Development Corp Ltd v Commissioner of Police of the Metropolis* the Court of Appeal held that the motions judge had overstepped his role in doing his own research into Indian law.[11]

There is one well-established gloss on the classification of foreign laws as facts. This lies in their treatment on appeal. Typically, on an appeal the rule is that the facts must be taken as found by the court below and cannot be challenged absent exceptional circumstances. However, appellate courts have held that findings of fact as to the content of foreign law are not subject to this usual deference, so that the appellate court can substitute its view of foreign law, based on the evidence presented, for that of the court below.[12]

---

8 There are exceptions both ways: the court can take judicial notice of some notorious facts even without proof and certain delegated laws such as municipal bylaws sometimes require formal proof.

9 *Hunt v T&N plc*, [1993] 4 SCR 289 at 308 [*Hunt*]. For a statutory enactment of this rule, see *The Evidence Act*, SS 2006, c E-11.2, s 4(2). In contrast, it is important to appreciate that many legal systems in Europe and Latin America treat foreign law as law.

10 See, for example, *Phillips v Ford Motor Co of Canada*, [1971] 2 OR 637 (CA).

11 [1991] 4 All ER 638 (CA) [*Bumper Development*].

12 *Bumper Development*, ibid. See also *General Motors Acceptance Corp of Canada v Town and Country Chrysler Ltd* (2007), 88 OR (3d) 666 at paras 28–35 (CA).

D. PLEADING OF FOREIGN LAW

Parties are required, in their pleadings, to plead the material facts on which they rely for their claim or defence. One consequence of foreign law being classified as fact is that it must therefore be pleaded. A party seeking to have an issue resolved by foreign law is required to plead, concisely and with precision, the content of that law.[13] For legislation, regulations, or similar sources of law, the full citation, including specific section numbers, should be pleaded.[14] For decided cases, the pleading should summarize the key legal propositions that flow from the decisions but should generally not cite specific cases.[15]

There is some debate about whether to include, in the pleading, extracts from legislation or quotations from cases. A party might choose to do so for added impact and persuasion, even if not necessary. But a countervailing danger is that the pleading could become unduly lengthy. Some cases have suggested that the text of foreign statutes must be pleaded but the better view is that this is not always necessary and its utility should be assessed in each case.[16] One factor to consider is whether the opposing party will, from the pleading, be able to plead in response and whether, on a motion to strike, the court will, without further evidence, be able to properly assess the claim or defence. This can be important in situations where it might not be easy to access authoritative sources of the foreign law due to distance and language issues. In *Yordanes v Bank of Nova Scotia* the judge struck out the plaintiffs' lengthy statement of claim because it did not plead foreign law sufficiently for the defendants to plead in response.[17]

It is also important for a party to plead the facts that would lead the court to apply a choice of law rule resulting in the application of the pleaded foreign law. The connecting factors favouring the application of that law need to be identified.[18]

---

13   See *Yordanes v Bank of Nova Scotia* (2006), 78 OR (3d) 590 (SCJ) [*Yordanes*]; *Anand v Rumpal*, 2014 ONSC 7560 at para 47.
14   *Bryant Press Ltd v Acme Fast Freight Inc*, [1951] OWN 665 (HCJ).
15   *Ontario Stone Corp v RE Law Crushed Stone Ltd*, [1964] 1 OR 303 (HCJ). In a sense, pleading the specific cases would cross the line from pleading material facts to pleading evidence.
16   See the discussion in *Yordanes*, above note 13 at paras 38–45.
17   *Ibid*. See also *Slegers v Sullivan* (2009), 84 CPC (6th) 156 at para 14 (Ont SCJ).
18   *Yordanes*, above note 13 at paras 15–16.

E. PROOF OF FOREIGN LAW

1) Methods

The most common way of proving foreign law is by calling an expert in that law as a witness.[19] As with other types of expert witness, issues can arise as to whether the court will accept the witness's qualifications and treat him or her as an expert. Possible witnesses include lawyers, judges, law professors, police officers, and government officials. This list is not closed: anyone with the required level of expertise in the foreign law could be an expert. The witness does not need to be qualified to practise in the foreign jurisdiction. A party should look for a witness with expertise in the specific area of law in issue and with more rather than less experience overall.

Parties need to be alert to the general rules in the province governing experts. These can stipulate whether a written report is required and how far in advance and how many expert witnesses can testify for a party.[20] An expert must be careful to provide evidence of the foreign law as it would be applied by the foreign court, rather than his or her own views as to what the law should be, because the court "must apply the foreign law as it exists and not as reformers think it ought to be."[21]

Beyond using expert witnesses, there are several other methods of proof, each with its own limitations. First, some provincial legislation provides that copies of statutes, regulations, and similar sources of law are to be admitted to prove the contents of the foreign law.[22] However, this legislation often applies only to the law of particular countries, such as members of the Commonwealth, so in many cases it will not assist. In addition, it often does not extend to include judicial decisions, including such decisions as may be needed to interpret and understand the printed text.[23]

Second, parties can avoid the need to prove foreign law by agreement. Just as the parties can agree on other facts, such as in an admission in

---

19 See *Gold v Reinblatt*, [1929] 1 DLR 959 (SCC).
20 See, for example, Ontario's *Rules of Civil Procedure*, RRO 1990, Reg 194, r 53.03 [Ontario Rules] and its *Evidence Act*, RSO 1990, c E.23, s 12.
21 *Foresight Shipping Co v Union of India*, 2004 FC 1501 at para 31.
22 See, for example, Ontario's *Evidence Act*, above note 20, s 25.
23 The Ontario provision has both of these limitations. In contrast, r 54.04(1) of the *Civil Procedure Rules of Nova Scotia*, online: http://courts.ns.ca/Civil_Procedure_Rules/cpr_home.htm [Nova Scotia Rules], allows the law of any foreign country to be proven by "reference to official publications of legislation, judicial decisions, and authoritative sources." To similar effect, see r 54.03 on proving the law of another province.

a pleading or in a joint statement of agreed facts, and thus dispense with the need for proof, they can do the same for the content of foreign law.[24] Other types of agreement are possible. For example, where the parties remain divided in their view of the content of foreign law, they could agree that each of their experts will present his or her evidence in writing rather than orally, to save time at the hearing. Even without any agreement, a party could make use of a procedure like a request to admit facts to simplify the proof process.[25]

Third, it may be possible to proceed by way of a stated case. Under this mechanism, the forum court stops its proceedings and seeks judicial assistance from a court in the foreign jurisdiction. Typically, the forum court would set out the facts as found and the issues, thus stating a case for the foreign court to resolve under its law. This procedure is rarely used. It can be quite time-consuming, producing a lengthy delay in the forum proceedings. There is no guarantee the foreign court will decide to answer the question. In some senses this procedure undermines the choice, made by the plaintiff in commencing the litigation, that the case should be decided by the forum court. A further challenge for a party seeking to use a stated case is to identify an appropriate authority or basis for the request. It is possible the request could simply be made under the common law and the court's inherent powers, as was done between provinces in *Re Komer*.[26] Historically, some British legislation has provided for such requests within the Commonwealth,[27] and they may also be possible under some international conventions.[28]

Fourth, in limited circumstances the court may take judicial notice of foreign law. The Supreme Court of Canada has held that in a case originating from one province, it can take judicial notice of the statutory and other laws of the other provinces.[29] This ability is rarely of much importance, since it is an appellate court and the material facts, including foreign law, typically need to be proven in the court of first instance. If a party attempted to first raise the application of the law of another province on an appeal to the Supreme Court of Canada, the court could indeed take judicial notice of that law but likely would decline to do so,

---

24 See *Holt Cargo Systems Inc v ABC Containerline NV (Trustees of)*, [2001] 3 SCR 907 at 933.
25 See, for example, Ontario Rules, above note 20, r 51.
26 [1925] 2 DLR 86 (Ont SC).
27 British Law Ascertainment Act, 1859 (UK), 22 & 23 Vict, c 63.
28 See, for example, *Inter-American Conference on Private International Law, Convention on Proof of and Information on Foreign Law*, 18 ILM 1231 (1979).
29 *Pettkus*, above note 1 at 853–54; *Hunt*, above note 9 at 306.

the issue not having earlier been raised.[30] More helpful are the statutory provisions in most provinces that either require or permit the court to take judicial notice of either the statute law or all of the laws of another province.[31] It is important to consider the precise wording of each such provision to ascertain its scope. When the statutory provision is permissive rather than mandatory, it is open to the court to refuse to take judicial notice and to require proper proof.[32]

The idea, discussed earlier, that the federal nature of Canada might require courts to raise at least interprovincial choice of law issues on their own initiative has strong connections to courts being required to take judicial notice of the law of other provinces. If a court is going to raise the issue on its own, it needs a mechanism that allows it to examine the foreign law that does not rely on the evidence the parties choose to submit. As noted above, this view is far from the orthodox position and is not supported by recent cases.[33]

2) Validity of Foreign Law

A potentially controversial issue is whether the analysis of foreign law can include an assessment of its validity. For example, if in Ontario litigation the parties call evidence of Michigan law, can that evidence include expert opinion that a particular rule of Michigan law violates the Constitution of the United States and so is of no force and effect? On the one hand, it would seem very odd for an Ontario court to consider and decide this issue, rather than a Michigan court. If the rule has not been challenged in Michigan, how can this properly be raised in Ontario? It could be considered a serious violation of comity for an Ontario court to make such a pronouncement about Michigan law. On the other hand, the Ontario court is attempting to ascertain and apply Michigan law and it would be wrong to apply a rule that was not legally valid.

This issue does not arise often, usually because issues of validity have been addressed and resolved in the foreign jurisdiction. The experts rely

---

30 *Upper Ottawa Improvement Co v Hydro-Electric Power Commission of Ontario*, [1961] SCR 486.
31 For example, see *Judicature Act*, RSA 2000, c J-2, s 12; *Evidence Act*, RSBC 1996, c 124, ss 24–25; *Manitoba Evidence Act*, CCSM c E150, s 30; *Evidence Act*, RSNB 1973, c E-11, s 70(1); *Evidence Act*, RSNL 1990, c.E-16, s 26; *Evidence Act*, RSNS 1989, c 154, s 3(3); *Evidence Act*, RSPEI 1988, c E-11, s 21; Saskatchewan's *The Evidence Act*, above note 9, s 40. See also the *Canada Evidence Act*, RSC 1985, c C-5, s 17.
32 See, for example, *Nystrom v Tarnava* (1996), 44 Alta LR (3d) 355 (QB).
33 In *Boulanger*, above note 7, the Ontario Divisional Court held that the statutes of other provinces were material facts and had to be formally proven at trial.

on, rather than reopen, those conclusions. However, when it does arise, the better view is that the forum court can and should determine any issues of the foreign law's validity.[34] In *Hunt v T&N plc*, the Supreme Court of Canada stated that "in determining what constitutes foreign law, there seems little reason why a court cannot hear submissions and receive evidence as to the constitutional status of foreign legislation."[35] It is crucial to remember that the inquiry into foreign law is factual. If a foreign rule is invalid, it is hard to see how it can be accepted as a fact. In addition, the court's decision, being factual, does not create a legal precedent on the point of law. If the decision was recognized in the foreign jurisdiction, it would not support, as a matter of law, the rule's invalidity. This lessens concerns about comity.

3) Failure of Proof

It is possible for a party to plead that an issue is governed by a foreign law but then not tender any evidence of that foreign law. The court, in light of the pleading, can apply the relevant choice of law rule and could, indeed, determine that the issue is governed by the foreign law. But how can it then proceed in the absence of evidence? To overcome this difficulty, the common law developed the presumption of similarity. Under this concept, the law of the foreign country is, in the absence of proof of its content, presumed to be the same as the law of the forum.[36] This approach has been codified in Saskatchewan, where section 4(4) of *The Evidence Act* provides "In an action or matter, if a foreign law is not proved, it shall be presumed to be identical to the law of Saskatchewan."[37]

The presumption of similarity leads to some unsettling results. For example, it can lead an Alberta court to presume that Chinese tort law is the same as Alberta tort law and thus resolve the dispute under the latter law. This is highly artificial. The presumption will, in fact, be wrong in a good many cases. Is it really logical to presume that China and Alberta have the same tort law? The presumption is even more troubling in areas dominated by statutes, where we would expect a high degree of variation between different jurisdictions. Yet the presumption would lead an Alberta court to presume, in the absence

---

34 *Hunt*, above note 9 at 310.
35 *Ibid* at 308.
36 *Canadian National Steamships Co v Watson*, [1939] SCR 11 at 13–14; *Morgardshammar AB v HR Radomski & Co Ltd* (1983), 145 DLR (3d) 111 (Ont HCJ), aff'd (1984), 5 DLR (4th) 576 (Ont CA); *United States of America v Mgbolu*, 2015 ONSC 1273 at para 18.
37 Above note 9. See also Nova Scotia Rules, above note 23, r 54.04(2).

of evidence, that China's securities disclosure laws were the same as those of Alberta.

To address these concerns, Canadian courts have modified the presumption, but without much real success. Aware that specific statutes are likely to differ from country to country, the courts use the presumption to apply, in the absence of proof, the "general" law of the forum but not particular, jurisdiction-specific laws. In *Gray v Kerslake*, Cartwright J held that

> [i]t is contended that the Court of Appeal were right in presuming that the law of the State of New York was the same as that of Ontario, but the presumption relates to the general law and does not extend to the special statutory provisions of particular statutes altering the common law.[38]

The aim in this approach is to avoid the worst absurdities of the presumption and apply law that could plausibly be the same in each jurisdiction. But it creates a new problem, namely how to identify which aspects of the forum law are sufficiently general so as to fall within the presumption. In *Amosin v "The Mercury Bell"*[39] the Federal Court of Appeal had to decide whether the provisions in the *Canada Labour Code*[40] relating to recognizing the role of unions, giving effect to collective agreements, and allowing employees to sue for wages were sufficiently general as to be applied under the presumption in the absence of proof of Liberian law. In more of a conclusion than a process of analysis, a majority of the court held that these provisions "are fundamental and have that potential degree of universality" while holding that other provisions in the same statute were specific to Canadian law.[41] In so doing the court avoided some difficulties that would have arisen if the entire *Canada Labour Code* had been applied to the facts. Be that as it may, there is room to debate whether the provisions the court applied truly had the requisite degree of universality. There is even more scope to question an approach that requires this sort of distinction to be drawn.

Accordingly, it would be a welcome development for courts to abandon the presumption of similarity. In the absence of proof of the foreign law, the better approach is for the court to simply apply the law of the forum as the only law the court can apply. Under this approach the whole law of the forum, and not only its "general" law, would be applied. In *The Mercury Bell*, the majority acknowledged the arguments in favour

---

38   [1958] SCR 3 at 10. See also *Hellens v Densmore*, [1957] SCR 768 at 780.
39   [1986] 3 FC 454 (CA) [*The Mercury Bell*].
40   At that time, RSC 1970, c L-1.
41   *The Mercury Bell*, above note 39 at 467.

of this alternative approach and Hugessen J in a separate concurring decision indicated that the presumption was outdated and made "little or no sense."[42] Some more recent decisions have not applied the presumption and instead have applied the forum law as the only option open in the absence of proof.[43] These are welcome developments and should point the way forward.

The presumption of similarity was examined by the High Court of Australia in *Neilson v Overseas Projects Corporation of Victoria Ltd*.[44] The court was considering China's choice of law rule for tort claims and, in particular, whether that rule's exception to using the law of the place where the tort occurred was triggered. The court was concerned about the lack of evidence as to how, under Chinese law, the exception was to be triggered. The judgments adopted different approaches to this problem. A bare majority of the court relied on the presumption of similarity and therefore considered the circumstances that might trigger the exception if it had been a rule of Australian law.[45]

In contrast, three judges refused to adopt the presumption of similarity. The presumption was "devoid of content" in this case,[46] since the court could not ignore the fact that while the Chinese rule had an exception, the Australian rule did not. There were thus no similar Australian principles that could be applied in place of Chinese law. It was "straining even credulity to impose on an Australian court the fiction of presuming that the law of China . . . is the same as the law in Australia."[47] These three judges held that the onus was on the plaintiff and if her evidence of Chinese law was insufficient then she could not succeed. The minority's approach, refusing to fill the evidentiary gap with the law of the forum and instead ruling against the party bearing the onus on the particular point of law, not only eliminated the presumption but also adopted a fairly radical solution to the lack of evidence of foreign law.

The first development is welcome but the second is not. A better approach would have been, in the absence of Chinese law on what triggers the exception, to use the law of the forum as the only available law. While

---

42 *Ibid* at 468.
43 See *Triathlon Leasing Inc v Juniberry Corp* (1995), 157 NBR (2d) 217 (CA); *Guarantee Co of North America v Mercedes-Benz Canada Inc* (2005), 83 OR (3d) 316 (SCJ), aff'd (2006), 86 OR (3d) 479 (CA); *Brown v Pulley*, 2015 ONCJ 186 at para 143.
44 [2005] HCA 54 [*Neilson*].
45 *Ibid* at paras 125, Gummow and Hayne JJ; at 249, Callinan J; and at 275, Heydon J. The presumption of similarity was also recently confirmed in England in *OPO v MLA*, [2014] EWCA Civ 1277 at para 108, rev'd on other grounds (*sub nom Rhodes v OPO*) [2015] UKSC 32.
46 *Neilson*, above note 44 at para 16, Gleeson CJ.
47 *Ibid* at paras 202–4, 208, and 219, Kirby J. See also para 36, McHugh J.

Australian law has no such exception, it does have general principles of statutory interpretation that it could apply to interpret the exception as set out in Chinese law.

In some cases the issue is not a complete absence of evidence of foreign law but rather evidence the court considers insufficient. The court is not bound to accept the evidence presented by a party, even if it is unchallenged, but it should refuse to do so only in rare cases. Instances could include situations where the evidence lacks a ring of truth, is unsupported by authority, or has obvious gaps.[48] In *Bumper Development*, the English Court of Appeal held that the trial judge was not, on the facts of that case, entitled to reject the agreed evidence of opposing experts and instead reach his own conclusion as to the foreign law.[49] In *Kollaras v Olympic Airways SA* the plaintiff in a tort action attempted to prove Greek law through an expert.[50] The trial judge found that the expert was insufficiently familiar with the relevant Greek law and had failed to research judicial decisions interpreting the applicable civil code provisions. The judge thus held that the foreign law had not been sufficiently proven and so applied Ontario law under the presumption of similarity.[51]

FURTHER READINGS

CASTEL, JEAN-GABRIEL. "Proof of Foreign Law" (1972) 22 *University of Toronto Law Journal* 33.

DOLINGER, JACOB. "Application, Proof, and Interpretation of Foreign Law: A Comparative Study in Private International Law" (1995) 12 *Arizona Journal of International and Comparative Law* 225.

FENTIMAN, RICHARD. "Foreign Law in English Courts" (1992) 108 *Law Quarterly Review* 142.

GEEROMS, SOFIE. *Foreign Law in Civil Litigation: A Comparative and Functional Analysis* (Oxford: Oxford University Press, 2004).

HARTLEY, TREVOR. "Pleading and Proof of Foreign Law: The Major European Systems Compared" (1996) 45 *International and Comparative Law Quarterly* 271.

---

48 See, for example, *Lear v Lear*, [1973] 3 OR 935 at 941 (HCJ), rev'd on other grounds (1974), 5 OR (2d) 572 (CA); *Allen v Hay* (1922), 64 SCR 76 at 80–81.
49 Above note 11 at 644–46.
50 [1999] OJ No 1447 (SCJ), aff'd (2000), 132 OAC 67 (CA).
51 *Ibid* at paras 19 and 23–25.

JANTERA-JAREBORG, MAARIT. "Foreign Law in National Courts: A Comparative Perspective" (2003) 304 *Recueil des Cours* 181.

KLOTZ, ROBERT. "Proving Foreign Law in Canadian Courts" (1994) 1 *Canadian International Lawyer* 8.

RODGER, BARRY, & JULIETTE VAN DOORN. "Proof of Foreign Law: The Impact of the *London Convention*" (1997) 46 *International and Comparative Law Quarterly* 151.

SASS, STEPHEN. "Foreign Law in Federal Courts" (1981) 29 *American Journal of Comparative Law* 97.

SPIGELMAN, JJ. "Proof of Foreign Law by Reference to the Foreign Court" (2011) 127 *Law Quarterly Review* 208.

WOOD, GAVIN. "Proof of Foreign Law in the Manitoba Courts" (1985) 15 *Manitoba Law Journal* 53.

CHAPTER 13

TORT

A. INTRODUCTION

The amount of tort litigation has increased significantly over the past fifty years and an increasing number of these cases involve factual connections to more than one country. Choice of law rules for tort claims are therefore quite important so that the applicable law can be ascertained. Much has been written by academics and judges about choice of law in tort and yet it remains a controversial topic. To this day different common law countries have quite different views about what the rule should be and some of these countries, including Canada, have witnessed dramatic changes to the rule. It is therefore important in this area, more so than in others, to have an understanding of how and why the rule has evolved over time.

B. HISTORICAL DEVELOPMENT

The earliest English choice of law rule for tort was to use the *lex loci delicti*: the law of the place of the tort. Tort evolved from the criminal law, which is highly territorial. People are expected to comply with the criminal law of the place where they act. So tort law also focused on the law of the place of acting. This approach was considerably strengthened by the vested rights theory, discussed in Chapter 10.

However, the law was changed in *The Halley*.¹ In that case a British ship was involved in a collision in Belgian waters. Under Belgian law the British ship was liable for the collision. Yet in proceedings in England the court held that a defendant could not be liable in tort in an English court unless the defendant was liable under the law of the forum. This new approach to choice of law, which imposed the *lex fori* as the applicable law, was highly chauvinistic and nearly impossible to justify. Yet it was confirmed two years later in *Phillips v Eyre*, a famous case that became the leading word on choice of law in tort for many decades.² To sue in tort in England, the conduct in question had to be actionable under English law and "not justifiable" under the law of the place of acting. This formulation of the rule had two parts or branches: the first followed *The Halley* and the second, additional requirement was rooted in the notion of vested rights. Over time this became known as a rule of "double actionability" under which the plaintiff had to satisfy both branches.

There was some debate as to the meaning of the second branch of the rule. Some thought "not justifiable" meant that the conduct had to be civilly actionable under the law of the place of acting. Others thought it had to be actionable in tort as opposed to under any other part of the law. In *Machado v Fontes* the court adopted a very wide meaning of "not justifiable," holding that any conduct that was contrary to law could not be said to be justified.³ This made it significantly easier for a plaintiff to satisfy the second branch, since most injurious conduct was at least a violation of some legal rule. This was taken close to its extreme limit in *McLean v Pettigrew*, in which the Supreme Court of Canada held, in respect of a negligence action brought in Quebec, that conduct in Ontario which was not civilly actionable under Ontario law satisfied the second branch of the rule because it was conduct that could be caught by a provincial statute that imposed a minor fine.⁴

These decisions illustrate the ebb and flow in the law in this area. While the rule as stated in *Phillips* raises the hurdle for the plaintiff, the interpretation of the second branch in these subsequent cases lowers that same hurdle. It also increases the overall importance of the first hurdle: liability under the law of the forum.

---

1   (1868), LR 2 PC 193.
2   (1870), LR 6 QB 1 (Ex Ct) [*Phillips*]. For a historical analysis of the litigation in this case, see Rande W Kostal, *A Jurisprudence of Power: Victorian Empire and the Rule of Law* (Oxford: Oxford University Press, 2005).
3   [1897] 2 QB 231 (CA) [*Machado*].
4   [1945] SCR 62 [*McLean*]. This conclusion is difficult to reconcile with the fact that the defendant was acquitted in Ontario proceedings under the provincial statute.

The rule evolved again in the House of Lords' decision in *Boys v Chaplin*.⁵ The case involved two British soldiers, one of whom injured the other while they were stationed in Malta. The plaintiff sued in tort in England. The central issue that arose was whether the plaintiff could recover damages for non-pecuniary loss (for pain and suffering). Such damages were available under the law of England but not under the law of Malta. The case was complex because, in addition to the issue of choice of law in tort, it also involved the issue of whether recovery for a particular head of damages was a matter of substance or procedure (see Chapter 11). The five Law Lords hearing the appeal each wrote a decision, making it difficult to identify the core principle of the decision.

Subsequently academics and judges have focused on Lord Wilberforce's reasoning. Lord Wilberforce held that the rule of double actionability should be maintained, but he varied it in two important respects. First, he overruled *Machado*, reformulating the second branch to require that the conduct was civilly actionable under the law of the place of acting. By doing this he introduced a rule of true double actionability.

Second, Lord Wilberforce expressed concern about the second branch and its rigid application of the *lex loci delicti*. He noted that applying the law of the place of the tort could lead to unfair results, particularly in cases where the factual connections between the dispute as a whole and that place were relatively weak. In *Boys* two English people, working for an English employer, were temporarily in Malta when one injured the other. Should the law of Malta thereby determine the plaintiff's degree of recovery or is the place of the tort merely fortuitous? The principle of proximity, central to choice of law justice, is difficult to reconcile with always applying the *lex loci delicti*. As a result, Lord Wilberforce created a flexible exception to the second branch of the rule, under which the *lex loci delicti* can be ignored and the only applicable law is the law of the forum. On this approach, the plaintiff was entitled to recover non-pecuniary damages.

The scope of this flexible exception was not entirely clear from Lord Wilberforce's reasons, but it came to be understood as expressed in *Dicey and Morris*: rather than applying the *lex loci delicti*, "a particular issue between the parties ... may be governed by the law of the country which, with respect to that issue, has the most significant relationship with the occurrence and the parties."⁶

Three important questions remained after *Boys*. First, could the exception be applied to the whole dispute or only to a specific issue

---

5   [1971] AC 356 (HL) [*Boys*].
6   Lawrence Collins, ed, *Dicey and Morris on the Conflict of Laws*, 12th ed (London: Sweet & Maxwell, 1993) at 1487–88.

within the dispute? Second, was there a parallel flexible exception to the first branch of the rule? Third, in using the phrase "most significant relationship" was the intention to adopt elements of American interest analysis (as discussed in Chapter 10)? After all, Lord Wilberforce had expressly referred to Malta's lack of interest in having its law applied to the dispute before the English courts.[7] Two of these questions were definitively answered by the Privy Council in *Red Sea Insurance Co Ltd v Bouygues SA*.[8] There the court held that there was indeed a parallel flexible exception that could displace the first branch of the rule (the law of the forum) and that the exception to either branch could be applied to the whole tort dispute. On the third question, the court did not expressly adopt interest analysis or conduct any analysis of the policies behind the law of the forum, which was Hong Kong. Instead, the court engaged in a weighing of factual connections, much as would occur under a proper law of the tort rule, and found that the connections to Saudi Arabia, the place of the tort, were much stronger than to Hong Kong. The court accordingly invoked the exception to the first branch and applied only the *lex loci delicti*. The English rule had thus evolved into a double actionability rule with flexible exceptions to both branches.

C. THE MODERN CANADIAN RULE

As indicated above in the discussion of *McLean*, Canadian courts adopted double actionability as the rule and accepted the wide formulation of the second branch. This approach came under attack in cross-border automobile accident cases. In a case in which an Ontario driver was driving in Ontario and was involved in a two-vehicle accident, significant differences arose hinging on whether the other driver was from Ontario or from another province. If he or she was from Ontario, all issues would end up resolved under Ontario law. But if he or she was from another province, the litigation could end up taking place in that province and the issues would be resolved mainly by its law. The law of the place of accident would be almost entirely irrelevant, examined only to determine whether the defendant's conduct was not justifiable there. One consequence of this was that plaintiff drivers were in effect able to carry the law of their home province with them when driving in other provinces. If injured, they could sue upon returning home and expect the court, under double actionability, to base recovery on the

---

7 *Boys*, above note 5 at 392.
8 [1995] 1 AC 190 (PC).

law of the forum. This was seen as imposing inappropriate burdens on defendants driving within their own home province.

One solution, of course, was that adopted in *Boys* which was to overrule *Machado* and require true double actionability. This would at least give equal weight to the law of the forum and the law of the place of the tort. But this was not the approach taken in Canada. In *Grimes v Cloutier* the plaintiff, from Ontario, was injured in an automobile accident in Quebec caused by a Quebec driver.[9] In Quebec at the time, a system of no-fault automobile insurance removed the right to sue in tort. But the plaintiff sued in Ontario, arguing that under *McLean* the defendant's conduct was an actionable tort under Ontario law and was not justifiable under Quebec law, since it amounted to a provincial offence for which he had been convicted. This argument was successful at trial but on appeal the Court of Appeal for Ontario, while bound by *McLean*, held that the double actionability rule required exceptions when its strict application would lead to an unjust result. The court held that while the wide meaning of the second branch was to be applied in cases where the plaintiff and defendant were from the same province and the accident occurred in another, it did not have to be applied in cases where the plaintiff and defendant were from different provinces. In those cases, it was open to the court to require civil actionability under the law of the place of the accident. While this decision attempted to reach a just result, particularly for the Quebec defendant, it added considerable uncertainty to the tort choice of law rule.

After decades of struggling with the limitations of the double actionability rule, in 1994 the Supreme Court of Canada broke with the past and adopted a new rule in *Tolofson v Jensen*.[10] The fact pattern of the case is a familiar one. Two cars collided in Saskatchewan. The driver of one was resident in Saskatchewan while the driver and passenger in the other were residents of British Columbia. The passenger was seriously injured and he sued both drivers in British Columbia. There were two central differences in the law of the two provinces. Under Saskatchewan law, the limitation period for the claim had expired and any gratuitous passenger such as the plaintiff had to show "willful or wanton misconduct" to recover against the driver of the vehicle in which he or she was riding. Under British Columbia law the limitation period had not expired and there was no reduced standard of care for the duty owed to gratuitous passengers.[11]

---

9   (1989), 69 OR (2d) 641 (CA) [*Grimes*]. See also *Prefontaine Estate v Frizzle* (1990), 71 OR (2d) 385 (CA).
10 [1994] 3 SCR 1022 [*Tolofson*].
11 *Ibid* at 1033.

Central to the court's analysis is a vigorous critique of applying the law of the forum. For the court, La Forest J explained how applying the first branch of *Phillips* to conduct in other countries could amount to improper extraterritorial application of forum law. Accordingly, the court rejected applying the law of the forum as part of the new rule and thus overruled double actionability. This was a very welcome development.

In place of double actionability, the court held that the new rule for choice of law in tort would be to apply the law of the place of the tort: the *lex loci delicti*. Justice La Forest based this decision on the theory that a state has exclusive jurisdiction within its own territory and on the practical need for a certain and predictable rule. He reasoned that people would ordinarily expect that their conduct would be governed by the law of the territory where it occurred.[12]

The court considered at some length whether the new rule should have an exception. In the end La Forest J indicated that a rigid rule could lead to injustice in international cases and so accepted that, in certain circumstances, the court could instead apply the law of the forum. However, he stressed that he could "imagine few cases where this would be necessary."[13] For interprovincial cases, he held that there could be no exception to the law of the place of the tort. He acknowledged that the twin underlying principles of private international law were order and fairness but stated that "order comes first."[14]

So after decades of cases and volumes of scholarly analysis, the court returned the law to where it started, coming back to the original common law rule. One commentator compared the adopting of such an ancient rule for modern tort disputes to going to the mall and finding a practising alchemist![15] There can be no doubt that the *lex loci delicti* is of central importance to choice of law in tort but adopting it as a rigid rule is controversial. It has overtones of the rejected theory of vested rights. The rule is open to the criticism that under the principle of proximity fairness, not order, should come first. Fairness is rarely well served by a rigid rule.[16]

---

12 *Ibid* at 1050.
13 *Ibid* at 1058.
14 *Ibid*. Justices Major and Sopinka dissented on this specific issue: they would have allowed an exception for both international and interprovincial cases.
15 John Swan, "Federalism and the Conflict of Laws: The Curious Position of the Supreme Court of Canada" (1995) 46 *South Carolina Law Review* 923 at 948.
16 See Adrian Briggs, *The Conflict of Laws*, 3d ed (Oxford: Oxford University Press, 2013) at 269: "experience shows that the need to make an exception in the interests of flexibility becomes irresistible when the facts are sufficiently unusual . . . the courts in Canada . . . may yet have to eat some of their words."

The decision in *Tolofson* clashes with the American experience of the past fifty years, which has shown a tendency by many courts to reject an absolute rule in favour of greater flexibility. In the landmark case of *Babcock v Jackson*, a group of New York residents driving in Ontario had a single-vehicle accident.[17] One of the passengers sued the driver in New York. Under Ontario law gratuitous passengers could not sue the driver of the vehicle in which they were travelling but such a claim was open under New York law. The court rejected rigid application of the law of the place of the tort. Instead, it adopted a "center of gravity" or "grouping of contacts" approach. Under that approach, it held that the vast majority of the factual connections in the dispute were to New York while Ontario's only connection was "the purely adventitious circumstance that the accident occurred there."[18] The court applied New York law to the tort claim.

When adopted in 1994, the *lex loci delicti* rule was controversial. It remains so more than twenty years later. Even without radical change to the rule, such as a move to a proper law of the tort approach, arguably it could be significantly improved by two relatively minor changes. First, the flexible exception should be less exceptional than as interpreted thus far by the courts, particularly in cases where the plaintiff and the defendant have the same habitual residence. Second, the flexible exception should apply interprovincially as well as internationally.[19]

1) Interpreting the Rule and the Exception

Some courts have struggled with the rigidity of the *lex loci delicti* rule. For example, in *Lau v Li* a single vehicle accident occurred in Quebec.[20] The passenger and the driver were both from Ontario and the passenger brought a tort claim in Ontario. No such claim was available under Quebec law. The court held that *Tolofson* did not require the application of Quebec law. In cases where applying the law of the place of the tort would cause an injustice, the law did not have to be applied. On an application for leave to appeal this decision, the court held that *Tolofson* was only intended to cover cases where the plaintiff and defendant were from different provinces.[21] This analysis, as subsequent decisions have

---

17　191 NE2d 279 (NY 1963).
18　*Ibid* at 284.
19　This argument is expanded in Stephen GA Pitel & Jesse R Harper, "Choice of Law for Tort in Canada: Reasons for Change" (2013) 9 *Journal of Private International Law* 289.
20　(2001), 53 OR (3d) 727 (SCJ).
21　[2001] OJ No 5437 (SCJ).

held, must be incorrect.²² The language in *Tolofson* expressly rejects any flexibility in interprovincial cases. Drawing a distinction based on the residence of the parties is hard to reconcile with the language or the spirit of *Tolofson*. It would seem to move the law back towards the confusion of cases like *Grimes*. This is an example of a case where the court clearly felt uncomfortable with a rigid rule for interprovincial cases.

There are also issues involving the scope of the rule: does *Tolofson* apply to all torts, or a particular subgroup of torts, or only to automobile accidents? In his decision, La Forest J described the *lex loci delicti* as a general rule and in no way confined it to car crashes. However, he stated:

> There are situations, of course, notably where an act occurs in one place but the consequences are directly felt elsewhere, when the issue of where the tort takes place itself raises thorny issues. In such a case, it may well be that the consequences would be held to constitute the wrong. Difficulties may also arise where the wrong directly arises out of some transnational or interprovincial activity. There territorial connections may become muted; they may conflict and other considerations may play a determining role.²³

A crucial question is whether this analysis contemplates that, in the cases described above, the rule is not to apply the law of the place of the tort but rather some other choice of law rule. After all, the law of torts covers a wide range of possible claims. It may be that one choice of law rule is not appropriate for all of them. Some tort claims arise out of facts that occur in one place, such as an automobile accident. But the conduct and harms involved in many other torts such as conspiracy, intentional interference with economic relations, defamation, and negligent misrepresentation can easily span borders. Does the *lex loci delicti* rule apply to these torts? The notion that in *Tolofson* the court was laying down a general rule indicates that it does, but the passage quoted above might suggest otherwise. Since *Tolofson* courts have generally treated the *lex loci delicti* rule as applicable to all torts, but there has been a recent suggestion that this might change. In *Éditions Écosociété Inc v Banro Corp* the Supreme Court of Canada referred to La Forest J's language quoted above and indicated that the *lex loci delicti* might not be the choice of law rule for defamation.²⁴ The court did not express a firm view on the issue but its comments leave the issue open. This is discussed in more detail later in this chapter in the context of Internet defamation.

---

22 See, for example, *Bezan v Vander Hooft*, 2004 ABCA 44 at paras 10–11.
23 *Tolofson*, above note 10 at 1050.
24 2012 SCC 18 at paras 56–62 [*Éditions Écosociété*].

This issue of the scope of the rule in *Tolofson* gives rise to two subsidiary questions. If, for a particular tort, the *lex loci delicti* rule does apply, the court will be required to identify the place of the tort. So in a case where a product is manufactured in one province and injures someone in another, to apply *Tolofson* the court must identify the place of the tort. Recall that this same issue arose in Chapter 5 in the context of taking jurisdiction based on the place of a tort. However, in that context the court could hold that the tort took place in both provinces, so that both could assert jurisdiction.[25] The same answer is not available for choice of law: the claim cannot be governed by both systems of law. Here a definitive answer is required.

There are different ways of identifying the place of the tort. One would be to develop definitive rules for particular torts. For example, the court could hold that the tort of negligent product manufacture always occurs in the place where the plaintiff suffered injury. A rule of this nature would be required for each tort. Another approach would be to develop principled criteria to identify the place in a specific case. Using the same example, in some cases the court would use the place of manufacture and in others it would use the place of injury, depending on the criteria. An even broader approach is to aim to identify the place of the tort by weighing the various connecting factors in each case.[26] Such an approach would make using the law of the place of the tort very similar to using the law of the place with the closest and most real connection to the claim. Although not likely what the court had in mind in *Tolofson*, it may nonetheless be an appropriate solution for tort claims where the facts are not neatly grouped within one jurisdiction.

In *Barrick Gold Corp v Goldcorp Inc* the court noted that "In the absence of a physical event causing injury, the determination of the *lex loci delicti* in respect of the torts of inducing breach of contract, interference with contractual relations and conspiracy is not straightforward."[27] The court determined the place of the torts by looking to the place where the "defining activities of the parties" giving rise to the tort claims occurred. It also looked to the place where the consequences of the wrong were felt. On the facts, these both pointed to the same place and thus the same applicable law.[28]

In *Huang v Silvercorp Metals Inc* the plaintiff was detained, investigated, and imprisoned by Chinese authorities.[29] He sued the defendant,

---

25 See *Moran v Pyle National (Canada) Ltd*, [1975] 1 SCR 393.
26 See *Ostroski v Global Upholstery*, [1995] OJ No 4211 (Gen Div).
27 2011 ONSC 3725 at para 646.
28 *Ibid* at paras 648–55.
29 2015 BCSC 549.

a Vancouver-based corporation, alleging that it had initiated and directed these events. In the context of a motion for a stay of proceedings the court had to consider whether the tort of false imprisonment had been committed in China or in British Columbia. It found the issue sufficiently in doubt that it refused to resolve the issue.

The second subsidiary question is that if the *Tolofson* rule does not apply to a particular tort, an alternative choice of law rule must be identified. One could argue that as a matter of precedent, torts not coming within *Tolofson* are still covered by cases such as *McLean*, so that double actionability is the rule. But it is highly unlikely that a court, in the wake of *Tolofson*, would apply that rule to any claim in tort. The criticisms in *Tolofson* and elsewhere of applying the law of the forum are simply too telling. So what choice of law rule would apply? In circumstances where using the law of the place of the tort is inappropriate, the best option available might be to work by analogy from choice of law in contract and to aim to identify the system of law with the closest and most real connection to the tort claim. However, it is also possible that a more specific rule could be developed for certain torts such as defamation (discussed below).

The exception in *Tolofson* to the *lex loci delicti* rule for international cases also raises interpretation issues. Some early decisions interpreted the exception quite broadly. In *Hanlan v Sernesky* the plaintiff and defendant, both from Ontario, were involved in a single-vehicle accident in Minnesota.[30] The plaintiff sued in Ontario and invoked the exception, arguing that the law of Ontario, not the law of Minnesota, should be applied. The Court of Appeal for Ontario agreed with the motions judge that it would "work an injustice" to apply the law of the place of the tort and so held that Ontario law was applicable. But it is difficult to identify precisely what, on the facts, gave rise to the injustice that triggered the exception, beyond the fact that the plaintiff and defendant were both from Ontario. Recall that in *Tolofson* La Forest J had stressed how narrow and rare the exception would be, in order for the rule to be certain and predictable. In *Hanlan* neither the motions judge nor the appellate court addressed this underlying consideration.

Subsequent cases have rejected the approach in *Hanlan*. In *Wong v Lee* the fact pattern was identical to that in *Hanlan* except it involved an accident in New York rather than Minnesota.[31] A majority of the Court of Appeal for Ontario held that the exception was intended to be narrow, available only in unusual cases and not intended to apply each

---

30 (1998), 38 OR (3d) 479 (CA) [*Hanlan*].
31 (2002), 58 OR (3d) 398 (CA).

time the plaintiff and defendant were from the same jurisdiction. This approach was confirmed in *Somers v Fournier*.[32] The Court of Appeal for Ontario held that the law of the place of the tort applies notwithstanding a high degree of connection between the parties and the forum. It also held that differences in the law between jurisdictions that had an impact on the amount a plaintiff could recover and differences in limitation periods that could lead to the claim being barred did not amount to an injustice so as to trigger the exception.[33] Indeed, in *Tolofson* the application of the law of the place of the tort led to the claim being outside the limitation period under that law. It is fair to say that these more recent cases have clarified the situations that will not trigger the exception. What unfortunately remains unclear is what situations, if any, will trigger it. The relatively small degree of flexibility in the *lex loci delicti* rule left open in *Tolofson* appears to be further diminished.

In *Tolofson*, La Forest J explained the exception in language that, read literally, can lead only to the application of the law of the forum instead of the law of the place of the tort. His explanation is silent as to whether the law of a third country could be applied under the exception. The reasoning that gives rise to having an exception is more consistent with the view that under the exception the court has the ability to apply the law of any country, and not only the forum, when that country has the closest and most real connection with the tort claim. As an example, consider a driver and passenger both resident in England who have a single-vehicle accident while on holiday in Florida, and then both subsequently move to Ontario. In proceedings in Ontario, under the exception it should be possible for the passenger's claim against the driver to be governed by the law of England.

2) Maritime and Airborne Torts

One difficulty with using the law of the place of the tort as the applicable law is that torts can occur outside the territorial jurisdiction of any country. Consider a battery committed on a ship in international waters, a misstatement made on an airplane flying across Europe, or even a product failure on the international space station. In these situations a *lex loci delicti* rule produces no answer, and so special rules are needed. The orthodox answer is to use the law of the place where the ship or

---

32 (2002), 60 OR (3d) 225 (CA).
33 See also *Roy v North American Leisure Group Inc* (2004), 73 OR (3d) 561 (CA); *Anand v Rumpal*, 2014 ONSC 7560 at paras 31–43.

aircraft is registered.[34] But this could give rise to injustice. If two Ontario residents take a cruise in the Caribbean on a ship that happens to be registered in Liberia, and one commits a tort against the other, it is difficult to accept the conclusion that Liberian tort law should govern a subsequent claim in Ontario. In the modern world it is important to at least consider a possible flexible exception to any such rule and perhaps to go further to consider whether, in these situations, it would be more appropriate to identify the country with the closest and most real connection to the dispute.

3) Interplay with Statutory Accident Legislation

Most provinces have adopted some form of statutory scheme to govern automobile accidents. These schemes typically provide for benefits to be paid to those who are injured and remove the injured person's right to sue in tort. Cross-border issues can complicate the operation of these schemes. In *Britton v O'Callaghan*, for example, the Ontario plaintiff was injured in a car accident in Ohio.[35] He applied for and received statutory no-fault benefits under Ontario's statutory accident benefits scheme. But he also sued in tort. If that claim was governed by Ontario law, it was precluded by the statutory scheme. However, consistent with *Tolofson*, the court held that it was governed by Ohio law and therefore could proceed. The statutory scheme applied to preclude a tort claim only when such a claim was governed by Ontario law. The fact that the plaintiff had received statutory benefits was irrelevant to the choice of law analysis.

In this area, much depends on the wording of the legislation and regulations and of the standard-form insurance policies. It would be possible to create a scheme that prevented a plaintiff who had taken benefits under it from claiming in tort at all, regardless of the applicable law. A scheme could also provide for an offset of recovery, so that payments under the scheme had to be deducted from any amounts recovered in a tort claim, or vice versa.[36] A central concern here is avoiding double recovery in the face of different statutory approaches between jurisdictions.

---

34 See *R v Anderson* (1868), LR 1 CCR 161 at 168; *Canadian National Steamships Co v Watson*, [1939] SCR 11. Some specific guidance on this issue was formerly provided by the *Canada Shipping Act*, RSC 1985, c S-9, s 275, in respect of masters and seamen but that statute has been repealed and its replacement contains no similar provision: *Canada Shipping Act, 2001*, SC 2001, c 26. There is little authority concerning torts on aircraft.
35 (2002), 62 OR (3d) 95 (CA).
36 See the discussion in *Gurniak v Nordquist*, [2003] 2 SCR 652 at paras 36–46.

D. RECENT DEVELOPMENTS IN OTHER COUNTRIES

1) The United Kingdom

As in Canada, the rule of double actionability was the subject of considerable criticism in the United Kingdom. As early as 1984 the Law Commissions of England and Wales and Scotland published a working paper as a basis for further consultation about possible reform of the choice of law rule for tort.[37] The working paper recommended that double actionability be abolished and offered two possible models for replacement rules. The first of these models adopted, as a general rule, the law of the place where the tort occurred, subject to a flexible exception. It provided that

> [t]he applicable law is that of the country where the tort or delict occurred.
> ...
> The law of the country where the tort or delict occurred may be disapplied, and the law of the country with which the occurrence and the parties had, at the time of the occurrence, the closest and most real connection applied instead, but only if the occurrence and the parties had an insignificant connection with the country where the tort or delict occurred and a substantial connection with the other country.[38]

The second model used a modified proper law approach. The general rule was that the applicable law was "that of the country with which the occurrence and the parties had, at the time of the occurrence, the closest and most real connection."[39] However, specific presumptions as to that country were proposed for claims involving personal injury, damage to property, death, and defamation. Finally, the exception to the presumptions provided that

> [a] presumption may be departed from only if the occurrence and the parties had an insignificant connection with the country indicated by the presumption and a substantial connection with another country.[40]

The Law Commissions rejected, in formulating the second model, an approach solely based on the proper law. They did so because the proper law was "too uncertain." In their view, the proper law approach could

---

37 Law Commission, *Private International Law: Choice of Law in Tort and Delict*, Working Paper No 87 (London: HMSO, 1984).
38 *Ibid* at 263–64.
39 *Ibid* at 264–65.
40 *Ibid*.

not be made sufficiently certain even with the listing of a series of factors or guidelines to be considered by the courts. Sufficient certainty could be achieved only through the presumptions.[41]

In 1990 the Law Commissions went one step further and issued a report on choice of law in tort that included a draft statute designed to implement the proposed reforms.[42] They stated that they had identified a strong consensus in favour of proceeding using the first model proposed in the 1984 working paper rather than the second model. Accordingly, the Report proposed the adoption of the place of the tort as a general rule subject to a flexible exception. Significantly, the wording of that exception changed markedly from what had been suggested in the working paper. The Report rejected the earlier threshold, which had required that the connection to the place of the tort be insignificant before the exception could apply, in favour of a threshold which compared the strength of the connection to the place of the tort with the connection to another country. If, from this comparison, it appeared that it would be "substantially more appropriate" to use the law of that other country then it became the applicable law.[43]

The bill that became the *Private International Law (Miscellaneous Provisions) Act 1995* was introduced in the House of Lords in 1994.[44] As enacted, section 11(1) provided that the general rule was that the applicable law is the law of the country in which the events constituting the tort occur. This was a general rule based on the place of the tort. However, three further rules in section 11(2) purported to directly identify the applicable law, and not the place of the tort, in cases in which elements of those events occur in different countries. For claims concerning personal injury or death, the applicable law was that of the country where the person was when the injury was sustained. For claims concerning property damage, the applicable law was that of the country where the property was located when damaged. And in any other case, the applicable law was the law of the country "in which the most significant element or elements" of the events occurred. As a result of section 11(2), the place of the tort rule in section 11(1) applied only in cases where all the events constituting the tort occurred in one country, a situation which could be handled by almost any viable choice of law rule.[45]

---

41 Ibid at 157–58 and 268.
42 Law Commission, *Private International Law: Choice of Law in Tort and Delict*, Law Com No 193 (London: HMSO, 1990) [the Report].
43 Ibid at 30.
44 *Private International Law (Miscellaneous Provisions) Act 1995* (UK), 1995, c 42 [the 1995 Act].
45 See Adrian Briggs, *The Conflict of Laws*, 2d ed (Oxford: Oxford University Press, 2008) at 195.

Section 12(1) then provided:

> If it appears, in all the circumstances, from a comparison of (a) the significance of the factors which connect a tort or delict with the country whose law would be the applicable law under the general rule; and (b) the significance of any factors connecting the tort or delict with any other country, that it is substantially more appropriate for the applicable law for determining the issues arising in the case, or any of those issues, to be the law of the other country, the general rule is displaced and the applicable law for determining those issues or that issue (as the case may be) is the law of that other country.

The most important issue in the relationship between the general rule and the exception was the threshold for triggering the exception. Section 12 was somewhat long-winded but the process it set out is what occurs in the search for the proper law. The significance of the various factors pointing to different countries must be assessed, aggregated, and compared. Had section 12 omitted the word "substantially" it would, on its face, have made the general rule into a neutral presumption. Wherever the tort occurred, the applicable law would have been the law of the country found to be most appropriate to resolve the dispute using the proper law approach. The effect achieved by using the word "substantially" to modify "more appropriate" was central to the exception.[46]

It was noteworthy that the new statutory rule did not cover all claims in tort, as one specific area was expressly excluded. Under section 13, defamation remained governed by the former double actionability rule. This exception was the result of considerable concern, expressed by the English press, about possible liability under the defamation law of other countries. It is, however, debatable whether these concerns justified this exception.

After less than fifteen years under the choice of law rule in the 1995 Act, the landscape in the United Kingdom changed again. The European Community adopted a regulation, known colloquially as "Rome II," on the law applicable to non-contractual obligations, which encompasses torts.[47] In January 2009, the domestic choice of law rule for tort in member states across Europe, including common law countries such as the United Kingdom and Ireland, was replaced by the provisions of Rome II.

The new general rule is in article 4(1), which provides that tort claims are governed by the law of the place where the damage occurs. This is not

---

46 See *Roerig v Valiant Trawlers Ltd*, [2002] 1 WLR 2304 at para 12, Waller LJ.
47 EC, *Commission Regulation (EC) No. 864/2007 of 11 July 2007 on the law applicable to non-contractual obligations*, [2007] OJ, L 199 [Rome II].

strictly speaking a *lex loci delicti* rule because the focus on the place of the damage is narrower than a focus on the place of the tort. The general rule requires using the law of the place of damage "irrespective" of the place where the events giving rise to the damage occur and of the place where any "indirect" consequences occur. This removes the flexibility that used to exist in the identification of the place of the tort.

The general rule has two exceptions. First, under article 4(2), if the plaintiff and defendant have the same habitual residence at the time the damage occurs, the law of that country of residence applies instead. This exception would catch cases like *Boys*. Second, under article 4(3), if it is clear from "all the circumstances of the case" that the tort is "manifestly more closely connected" with another country than that identified by article 4(1) or (2), the law of that other country shall apply. Article 4(3) indicates that a pre-existing relationship, such as a contract, closely connected to the tort and governed by a different system of law, could trigger this exception. Recent cases have interpreted the exception narrowly and as difficult to trigger.[48]

Rome II contains specific provisions for some particular tort issues, such as product liability, environmental damage, and infringement of intellectual property rights. It also provides that the applicable law for a tort claim governs, among other things, "the existence, the nature and the assessment of damage or the remedy claimed."[49] For English law, this is a significant modification of the traditional distinction between substance and procedure, which would have considered the assessment of a plaintiff's damages to be a matter for the law of the forum.[50] Rome II explicitly excludes tort claims relating to privacy and rights of personality, including those in defamation.[51] Such claims therefore remain subject to the common law's choice of law rules.

A provision of some interest in Rome II is article 14, which in part provides that "where all the parties are pursuing a commercial activity" they can choose the law to govern future tort claims that might arise between them "by an agreement freely negotiated before the event giving rise to the damage occurred." Party autonomy is not typically given much of a role in choice of law for tort and so it will be interesting to see how the jurisprudence under article 14 develops.

---

48   See, for example, *Stylianou v Toyoshima*, [2013] EWHC 2188 (QB); and *Winrow v Hemphill*, [2014] EWHC 3164 (QB).
49   Art 15(c).
50   See the discussion in Chapter 11.
51   Art 1(2)(g).

2) Australia

The current Australian choice of law rule for tort claims was established in two decisions of the High Court.[52] Under the rule, claims in tort are governed, without exception, by the law of the place where the tort occurred. This rule has led the court, in *Neilson v Overseas Projects Corporation of Victoria Ltd*, to adopt a surprising approach to choice of law in tort.[53] The defendant, a corporation owned by the state of Victoria, employed the plaintiff's husband under a contract that required him to live and work in China. The defendant provided a residential unit there, but there was no railing around the stairway opening on the second floor. In 1991 the plaintiff suffered severe injuries when she fell into the opening. She sued the defendant in negligence in Western Australia, where she was ordinarily resident.

The place of the tort was clearly China and under the law of China not only was the defendant not likely liable to her but her claim was outside the limitation period. The plaintiff therefore advanced an unusual argument. China's choice of law rule for tort claims was also that they were governed by the law of the place of the tort, but the rule had an exception such that if both the plaintiff and the defendant were from the same country, the law of that country could instead be applied.[54] The plaintiff therefore argued that in identifying the law of China as the applicable law, the court should not only consider China's rules of substantive tort law but should also consider China's choice of law rule for tort. If the court did so, it could rely on the exception since both she and the defendant were from Australia and it could therefore apply the law of Australia to the claim.[55] The court accepted this argument, holding that the claim was, as a result of the Chinese choice of law rule, governed by the law of Australia.

The plaintiff's argument amounted to asking the court to apply the doctrine of *renvoi* to choice of law in tort. The orthodox view is that *renvoi* does not apply in tort cases. In the United Kingdom, where choice of law in tort had been almost exclusively governed by the 1995 Act, *renvoi* was expressly excluded.[56] In one of the few Canadian cases to even mention the issue, Reed J noted "the general rejection of *renvoi* as applicable

---

52 *John Pfeiffer Pty Ltd v Rogerson* (2000), 203 CLR 503; *Regie Nationale des Usines Renault SA v Zhang* (2002), 210 CLR 491.
53 (2005), 223 CLR 331 [*Neilson*].
54 *Ibid* at para 75, Gummow and Hayne JJ.
55 The plaintiff and defendant were from different Australian states but the court considered her claim to be based on the common law of Australia, which was the same in both Victoria and Western Australia: *ibid* at para 135, Gummow and Hayne JJ.
56 Above note 44, s 9(5). Rome II also excludes *renvoi*: above note 47, art 24.

to conflict of law issues, especially tort claims."⁵⁷ In neither of its two previous decisions about choice of law in tort did the High Court even mention *renvoi*. Yet the court has now held that *renvoi* is part of Australia's choice of law rule for tort. In light of the criticisms generally directed at the doctrine, outlined in Chapter 10, this is a dramatic development.

The decision in *Neilson* may offer lessons for Canadian law. Admittedly a Canadian court faced with similar facts might rely on *Tolofson*'s flexible exception to apply the law of the forum. Yet, as explained above, Canadian courts recently have adopted a very narrow interpretation of the exception. For example, expiry of the limitation period under Chinese law would not constitute an injustice. So a plaintiff might well fail to trigger the Canadian exception to using the law of the place of the tort. He or she might then, in light of *Neilson*, argue that reference to that law should include its choice of law rules: in other words, argue for *renvoi*. So if the Canadian exception is interpreted too narrowly, the issue could indeed arise in a Canadian court.

The similarities between the Australian and Canadian rules also mean that some guidance can be obtained from Australian cases on identifying the place of a tort. In *Amaca Pty Ltd v Bernard George Frost* the plaintiff had inhaled asbestos fibres manufactured in New South Wales while working in New Zealand.⁵⁸ The trial judge held that the place of manufacture was the place of the tort but the Court of Appeal held that the place of the exposure was the place of the tort. Other cases are consistent with this approach but in at least one case the court has held that the place where the defendant acted, not the place where the plaintiff was injured, was the place of the tort.⁵⁹

E. INTERPLAY BETWEEN TORT AND CONTRACT

In many cases the plaintiff will be able to claim in both tort and contract. This can be handled in a straightforward manner by the choice of law process. The pleaded claims would be analyzed separately, with the contract choice of law rule applied to the contract claim and the tort choice of law rule applied to the tort claim. It is possible that this will result in the two claims each having a different applicable law, but there is nothing alarming about this: it is a natural consequence of concurrent claims and choice of law rules organized by cause of action.

---

57 *Ferguson v Arctic Transportation Ltd* (1998), 147 FTR 96 at para 48 (TD).
58 [2006] NSWCA 173.
59 See *Nicholls v Brisbane Slipways and Engineering P/L*, [2003] QSC 193.

A more complicated interplay between tort and contract arises when a defendant seeks to rely on a contractual provision as a defence to a claim in tort. For example, the defendant may have committed a tort in Ontario but a contract between the plaintiff and the defendant, governed by New York law, excludes liability for negligence. The cases illustrate two different ways of handling this situation. The orthodox approach considers whether the exclusion clause is valid under the law that governs the contract. If it is, it is given effect.[60] This approach has been criticized for failing to consider the position of the law governing the tort claim. In the example above, Ontario law might prohibit the particular exclusion of liability, yet this might not be a mandatory rule of Ontario law. An alternative approach would add, to the orthodox approach, the requirement that the exclusion clause also be analyzed under the law of the tort.[61] In order for the clause to provide a valid defence, it would therefore have to be valid under both the law applicable to the contract and the law applicable to the tort.

F. INTERNET DEFAMATION

The tort of libel consists of the communication of a written defamatory statement to someone other than the plaintiff. The rise of the Internet has made it much easier for people to commit this tort. It has also multiplied the number of cases in which there are factual connections to more than one country. Consider a defendant in Oregon who posts a defamatory statement about a plaintiff in Manitoba on a website hosted in New South Wales. In proceedings in Manitoba, what law would govern the tort claim? At the outset this raises the issue, discussed earlier, about the scope of the rule in *Tolofson*: is the choice of law rule here the law of the place of the tort? If it is, then that place has to be identified. If it is not, then an alternative choice of law rule must be identified.

One possible place of this tort is where the statement has been posted on the Internet, namely New South Wales. But on a strict understanding of the tort, the mere posting of the statement is not libel. The statement must be communicated to third parties, so the tort is not completed by the posting but rather by its downloading by readers of the website. However, those readers could be in many different countries, increasing the complexity of the choice of law question. As a result, some commentators have argued for a "single publication rule." Rather than treating this as a case of multiple publications of the statement,

---

60 See *Sayers v International Drilling Co NV*, [1971] 1 WLR 1176 (CA).
61 See *Brodin v A/R Seljan*, [1973] SC 213.

occurring each time it is downloaded, the law would treat it as a single publication in the place of posting. Such a rule has been advocated by those who post statements on websites in the United States, since it would require use of American law, which tends to provide significant protection to the defendant in libel cases.[62] In the common law this approach has not been adopted outside the United States.

Another possible place of this tort is where the statement was read by the third party. The law of defamation treats each communication to a third party as a separate tort, so each download of the posting would be a separate libel, committed in the place where the reader was located.[63] This would mean a separate claim for libel committed in each different country, each with a different applicable law. Such an approach would make the plaintiff's claim very complex. It could be factually difficult to establish where readers were when they downloaded the statement. The plaintiff may have suffered no loss in one or more of these different countries. This approach also creates problems for defendants in planning their conduct. In general, print media publishers can control the distribution of their products into different countries. But many websites are open access. Once a statement is published it can be accessed immediately from any country. This raises significant compliance concerns, especially for smaller publishers. For these reasons, courts have not been attracted to this approach. However, it is possible that courts might yet adopt a narrower version of this approach, applying the law of each place where the defendant has reasonably targeted readers, for example through its marketing.

A third possible place of this tort is the country in which the plaintiff resides and works. Defamation protects a person's reputation and so the ultimate injury or loss suffered by the plaintiff has most likely occurred in his or her home country, regardless of where the statements were posted or read. This approach has been adopted in some of the recent leading cases. In *Dow Jones & Company Inc v Gutnick* the plaintiff lived in the Australian state of Victoria.[64] He alleged that he had been defamed in articles posted on the defendant's website, maintained on computers located in New Jersey. The High Court of Australia held that the place of the tort should be identified based on where the damage to the plaintiff's reputation had occurred.[65]

---

62   See, for example, the defendant's arguments in *Dow Jones & Company Inc v Gutnick* (2002), 210 CLR 575.
63   Building on the approach in *Szalatnay-Stacho v Fink*, [1947] 1 KB 1.
64   Above note 62.
65   See also *Australian Broadcasting Corp v Waterhouse* (1991), 25 NSWLR 519 (CA).

Finally, the court could maintain its focus on damage to reputation but recognize some flexibility as to where that damage occurs. While the courts have indicated that this will, in most cases, be where the plaintiff is habitually resident, it is possible for a plaintiff to have a reputation in another country. In *Berezovsky v Michaels* a Russian businessman sued an American corporation in England for defamation.[66] As part of the arguments about whether the court should decline jurisdiction, he provided evidence that he had a reputation in England that was worthy of protection and that accordingly the place of the tort was England, not Russia. While the House of Lords did not resolve that issue, it held that the court should not decline jurisdiction, in part based on the strength of the plaintiff's connections to England.

Recently in *Éditions Écosociété* the Supreme Court of Canada noted, without reaching a conclusion on the point, that the choice of law rule for defamation might not be the *lex loci delicti*. Instead, "one possible alternative . . . which has gained some significant support, may be the place of most substantial harm to reputation."[67] A primary purpose of the tort is to protect the plaintiff's reputation, so a focus on the place of that reputation is sensible. It is not clear, however, whether this should be understood as a true alternative to the *lex loci delicti* rule or as an application of that rule using the place of substantial harm as the place of the tort. Language in the decision, and in *Tolofson* itself, can support either approach. Further, there may be difficulties in identifying the place of the plaintiff's reputation. A plaintiff, however, can make this easier for the court. For example, in *Breeden v Black* the plaintiff explicitly limited his claim to damages to his reputation in Ontario and undertook not to bring a defamation action in any other jurisdiction.[68]

A further issue for choice of law for defamation is whether a separate rule should be developed for purely interprovincial cases. In the United States, the *Restatement (Second)* contains a specific choice of law rule for multistate defamation.[69] The rule aims to identify a single law to govern defamation arising from an "aggregate communication" such as a single issue of a newspaper that reaches readers in multiple

---

66 [2000] 1 WLR 1004 (HL).
67 Above note 24 at para 56. See Jean-Gabriel Castel, "Multistate Defamation: Should the Place of Publication Rule Be Abandoned for Jurisdiction and Choice of Law Purposes?" (1990) 28 *Osgoode Hall Law Journal* 153 at 177; Craig Martin, "*Tolofson* and Flames in Cyberspace: The Changing Landscape of Multistate Defamation" (1997) 31 *University of British Columbia Law Review* 127 at 149 and 158.
68 2012 SCC 19 at para 33. See also *Goldhar v Haaretz.com*, 2015 ONSC 1128 at para 50, aff'd 2016 ONCA 515 at paras 83–88.
69 American Law Institute, *Restatement of the Law Second: Conflict of Laws 2d* (St Paul, MN: American Law Institute, 1971) at § 150.

countries. In response to a proposal from the Australian Law Reform Commission,[70] Australian states adopted a rule which applies "the substantive law applicable in the Australian jurisdictional area with which the harm occasioned by the publication as a whole has its closest connection."[71] It would be open to Canadian courts to formulate a specific rule to cover interprovincial defamation cases. However, the pressure to do so is relatively slight since the law of defamation is very similar in each of the common law provinces.

One reason cross-border defamation raises difficult issues is because of the different policy considerations underlying each country's defamation law. The law in this area must balance rights to reputation against public concerns like freedom of expression. A leading example is the difference between American and English defamation law: while the latter historically has emphasized vindicating a person's right to reputation, the former accords greater weight to free speech considerations.

G. CONSTITUTIONAL ISSUES

Common law jurisdictions continue to debate the best formulation of a tort choice of law rule. In Canada, criticisms of the rigid *lex loci delicti* rule from *Tolofson* have led to calls for legislative reform, similar to the kind of reform adopted in the United Kingdom in the 1995 Act. For example, the Manitoba Law Reform Commission has proposed legislative reform of the law in this area.[72]

If *Tolofson* is simply a common law rule, it can be changed by statute. Two key changes that could be made are the introduction of a flexible exception to the law of the place of the tort for interprovincial cases and the relaxation of the threshold required to trigger the exception in both international and interprovincial cases. One concern that should be noted is that provincial action in this area could lead to significant differences in the tort choice of law rule as between different provinces. One problem with tort litigation in the United States is that across the different states there are many different choice of law rules used for tort. Some states use the place of the tort, others use a more flexible analysis of connecting factors, and still others use rule

---

70 Australian Law Reform Commission, *Unfair Publication, Defamation and Privacy* (Canberra: Australian Government Publications Service, 1979).
71 See, for example, *Defamation Act 2005* No 77 (NSW), s 11(2).
72 See Manitoba Law Reform Commission, *Private International Law*, Report No 119 (Winnipeg: Manitoba Law Reform Commission, 2009).

selection and interest analysis.[73] This can lead to forum shopping and increased complexity. Despite concerns about *Tolofson*, there may be merit to a uniform rule across the common law provinces.

But is *Tolofson* just a common law rule? Since *Morguard Investments Ltd v De Savoye* the Supreme Court of Canada has elevated several private international law rules to constitutional status.[74] Much of this has been based on elements essential to a federal country. One of these elements is the extent to which a province has the power, as a matter of legislative competence, to have its law apply beyond its territory. It is therefore arguable that at a minimum a province could not, by statute, either impose a *lex fori* tort choice of law rule or return to a rule of double actionability. The argument would be that the province cannot, as a constitutional matter, insist on applying its own tort law to all disputes where the tort occurred in another province. Rigid application of the law of the forum may well be constitutionally invalid.[75] However, it is a significant leap from that argument to claim that any rule other than the *lex loci delicti* would be unconstitutional. Provinces surely are free to adopt from a range of possible tort choice of law rules, including a rule that could, through a flexible exception, lead to the application of the law of the forum in appropriate cases.

FURTHER READINGS

AHERN, JOHN, & WILLIAM BINCHY, EDS. *The Rome II Regulation on the Law Applicable to Non-contractual Obligations* (Leiden: Martinus Nijhoff, 2009).

CASTEL, JEAN-GABRIEL. "Back to the Future! Are the 'New' Rigid Choice of Law Rules for Interprovincial Torts Constitutionally Mandated?" (1995) 33 *Osgoode Hall Law Journal* 35.

CASTEL, MATTHEW. "Jurisdiction and Choice of Law Issues in Multistate Defamation on the Internet" (2013) 51 *Alberta Law Review* 153.

DICKENSON, ANDREW. *The Rome II Regulation: The Law Applicable to Non-contractual Obligations* (Oxford: Oxford University Press, 2008).

DOLINGER, JACOB. "Evolution of Principles for Resolving Conflicts in the Field of Contracts and Torts" (2000) 283 *Recueil des Cours* 187.

---

73 These different approaches are discussed in Chapter 10.
74 [1990] 3 SCR 1077.
75 See the separate concurring analysis of Bastarache J in *Castillo v Castillo*, [2005] 3 SCR 870.

FAWCETT, JJ. "Policy Considerations in Tort Choice of Law" (1984) 47 *Modern Law Review* 650.

GEORGE, MARTIN. "Choice of Law in Maritime Torts" (2007) 3 *Journal of Private International Law* 137.

HARRIS, JONATHAN. "Choice of Law in Tort—Blending In with the Landscape of the Conflict of Laws?" (1998) 61 *Modern Law Review* 33.

HARTLEY, TREVOR. "Choice of Law for Non-contractual Liability: Selected Problems under the Rome II Regulation" (2008) 57 *International and Comparative Law Quarterly* 899.

JUNGER, ROBIN. "A Proposed Choice of Law Methodology for Tort in Canada: Comparative Evaluation of British and American Approaches" (1994) 26 *Ottawa Law Review* 75.

KINCAID, PETER. "*Jensen v. Tolofson* and the Revolution in Tort Choice of Law" (1995) 74 *Canadian Bar Review* 537.

LEHMANN, MATTHIAS. "Where Does Economic Loss Occur?" (2011) 7 *Journal of Private International Law* 527.

MORRIS, JHC. "The Proper Law of the Tort" (1951) 64 *Harvard Law Review* 881.

MORTENSEN, REID. "Homing Devices in Choice of Tort Law: Australian, British and Canadian Approaches" (2006) 55 *International and Comparative Law Quarterly* 839.

NYGH, PETER. "Some Thoughts on the Proper Law of a Tort" (1977) 26 *International and Comparative Law Quarterly* 932.

RUSHWORTH, ADAM, & ANDREW SCOTT. "Rome II: Choice of Law for Non-contractual Obligations" [2008] *Lloyd's Maritime and Commercial Law Quarterly* 274.

SYMEONIDES, SYMEON C. "Rome II and Tort Conflicts: A Missed Opportunity" (2008) 56 *American Journal of Comparative Law* 173.

WALKER, JANET. "'Are We There Yet?': Towards a New Rule for Choice of Law in Tort" (2000) 38 *Osgoode Hall Law Journal* 331.

WALSH, CATHERINE. "Territoriality and Choice of Law in the Supreme Court of Canada: Applications in Products Liability Claims" (1997) 76 *Canadian Bar Review* 91.

CHAPTER 14

CONTRACT

A. INTRODUCTION

Policy considerations have played an important role in the development of choice of law rules for contract. Four of the more central considerations are as follows: (1) to respect party autonomy, in terms of giving effect to party choice; (2) to honour the reasonable expectations of the parties; (3) to achieve uniformity of results, so that the outcome does not depend on the place where the dispute is resolved; and, more recently, (4) to give effect to laws designed to protect contracting parties, especially in consumer transactions.

B. THE PROPER LAW RULE

The early English and American choice of law rule for contract was the *lex loci contractus* — the law of the place of contracting.[1] This rule drew considerable strength from the vested rights theory, explained in Chapter 10. However, as we have seen, that theory is open to considerable criticism, and likewise this rule came under attack. One problem was that it required somewhat artificial rules to identify the place where a contract was made in cases involving mail or telegraph. For mail, courts used the postal acceptance rule, under which the contract was

---

1   *Wilmot v Shaw* (1881), 14 NSR 343 (CA).

made at the place where the acceptance was mailed rather than the place where it was received by the offeror.[2] A second problem was that the rule did not cover certain contracts, such as those made on board a ship in international waters. A third and more important problem was that the rule did not give sufficient effect to party autonomy. For parties to choose the applicable law of their contract under this rule, they would have to arrange to make the contract in the country of their choice. This would often be inconvenient or impractical. Further, the place of the contracting rule could lead to fortuitous results that do not reflect the reasonable expectations of the parties, such as a contract made by two English residents while on a brief visit to France.[3]

As a result, the courts evolved exceptions to the place of contracting rule. As far back as *Robinson v Bland*, Lord Mansfield held that if the parties had in mind a different applicable law, such as the law of the place where the contract was to be performed, then that law and not the law of the place of contracting would be applied.[4] Over time, these exceptions came to displace the rigid rule. The modern common law rule is that a contract is governed by its "proper law." This is of course a vague concept, and the courts have accordingly fleshed out what is meant by a contract's proper law. It is the law that the parties intended, either expressly or implicitly, to govern the contract, and in the absence of any such intention it is the law with which the transaction has its closest and most real connection.[5]

Canadian courts followed the English courts in adopting the proper law rule, and English decisions in this area have historically had persuasive value in Canada. However, as part of its membership in the European Union, England has, since 1990, rejected the proper law rule and instead adopted the rules formulated for use across Europe.[6] The new rules apply in all cases before the English courts, not just those involving

---

2   *Household Fire & Carriage Accident Insurance Company v Grant* (1879), 4 Ex D 216 at 221.
3   In *Amin Rasheed Shipping Corp v Kuwait Insurance Co*, [1984] AC 50 (HL) [*Amin Rasheed*], Lord Diplock referred to the place of contracting as often being "a mere matter of chance." See also *Sharn Importing Ltd v Babchuk* (1971), 21 DLR (3d) 349 (BCSC).
4   (1760), 2 Burr 1077.
5   *Bonython v Commonwealth of Australia*, [1951] AC 201 at 219 (PC); *Tomkinson v First Pennsylvania Banking and Trust Co*, [1961] AC 1007 at 1068 and 1081 (HL); *Amin Rasheed*, above note 3 at 61; *Etler v Kertesz*, [1960] OR 672 (CA) [*Etler*].
6   *Contracts (Applicable Law) Act 1990* (UK), c 36, implementing the *Convention on the Law Applicable to Contractual Obligations* (1980), OJ C027 26/01/1998 at 34 [*Rome Convention*]. See now Rome I, below note 56.

other member states of the European Union. As a result, modern English cases are much less useful as a comparative source for Canadian courts.

1) Express Choice

Under the proper law rule, an express choice of law clause in a contract is given effect. In *Vita Food Products Inc v Unus Shipping Co* the Privy Council, on appeal from the Nova Scotia Court of Appeal, upheld a clause in a bill of lading that provided for English law to apply.[7] Lord Wright held that "the express words of the bill of lading must receive effect . . . the proper law of the contract 'is the law which the parties intended to apply.'"[8] In *Amin Rasheed Shipping Corp v Kuwait Insurance Co*, Lord Diplock stated that "[i]f it is apparent from the terms of the contract itself that the parties intended it to be interpreted by reference to a particular system of law, their intention will prevail."[9]

In some standard-form contracts, the choice of law clause can be very minimal: "law=New York," for example. A more detailed clause could read: "This contract is governed by the law of Ontario, including the law of Canada applicable therein, excluding its private international law." The final five words in this example are designed to exclude the doctrine of *renvoi*, discussed in Chapter 10. This could also be achieved by expressly referencing the "internal" or "domestic" law of Ontario. While common, these efforts are not generally necessary since *renvoi* is virtually never applied in contract cases in any event.[10]

In most cases involving an express choice, it is clear that the choice of law clause has become part of the contract. But difficulties can arise in certain situations. Sometimes the parties will each purport to contract based on their own standard-form terms, each of which chooses a different applicable law. In other cases one party may not read the "small print" of a contract which includes such a clause.[11] In cases of this nature, the court must determine whether the choice of law clause has become part of the contract. As will be discussed later, a contract's applicable law governs the issue of what terms have become part of the contract. But if the disputed term is itself a choice of law clause, the analysis becomes somewhat circular. Should the chosen law in the clause be taken as the applicable law and thus used to determine whether

---

7   [1939] AC 277 (PC) [*Vita Food*].
8   *Ibid* at 289–90.
9   Above note 3 at 61.
10 *Amin Rasheed*, *ibid* at 62.
11 See, for example, *Roy v North American Leisure Group Inc* (2004), 73 OR (3d) 561 at paras 14–16 (CA) [*Roy*].

the clause is part of the contract? This seems, at least in part, to assume the answer at the beginning. However, as will be explained further in discussing contract formation generally, this is a well-accepted approach known as using the putative proper law. In general, the court would determine the applicable law as if the clause were part of the contract and then use that law to determine whether the clause had become part of the contract.[12] If it has not, it is more sensible for the court to re-determine the applicable law in the absence of the clause than to continue using that applicable law for any other issues.

When parties choose an applicable law, they generally are understood to intend to have that law apply as it stood at the time a dispute arises. So if a contract, made in 2000, chooses the law of New York and a dispute arises in 2008, the contract's governing law will include any changes to New York's law of contract between 2000 and 2008. New York law is not somehow frozen as of the time the contract is made. If the parties want to effect such a freezing, it is open to them to expressly provide that the contract is governed by the law of a particular country as at a particular time.[13]

There are limitations on the extent to which parties can choose the law to govern their contract. First, any such choice must be made bona fide, or with good faith. If the parties randomly selected a country and inserted it into a choice of law clause, this would likely not be a good faith choice of that country's law. The same could be true where the parties somewhat mischievously choose the law of a country with no connections to the transaction. Of course, it is not in itself improper to pick such a law, since it is common for parties to select New York or English law in contracts with no connection to those jurisdictions. They do so because the contract law of those jurisdictions is stable, developed, and well understood.[14] But where there is no connection, there is a concern that the choice is not bona fide. This limitation is in part motivated by a concern that the parties not be allowed to choose a law with no connection to the transaction solely to avoid the application of the law that would otherwise apply. The lack of connection can be evidence of intent to so evade.[15]

12 In *Roy*, *ibid*, however, the court appears to use the law of the forum to determine that the clause is part of the parties' contract. There is no indication that counsel suggested a different law governed the issue.
13 So, in theory, the parties could expressly provide that the contract is governed by the law of Prussia as of 1 January 1850. See, however, the limitations on party choice discussed below.
14 See *Vita Food*, above note 7 at 291: "parties may reasonably desire that the familiar principles of English commercial law should apply."
15 See *2106701 Ontario Inc v 2288450 Ontario Limited*, 2016 ONSC 2673 at paras 27–33.

Second, the choice of the governing law must be legal. It is possible that, under the law of the forum, certain choices are outlawed. For example, a province could enact a provision that required all sales of vehicles located in the province to be governed by the law of that province. If the parties stipulated that their contract was governed by the law of New York, interesting considerations arise. On one approach, the choice of law rule would look to the chosen law and apply it. The provincial statute would not enter the analysis. On this view, the provincial statute would apply only if a choice of law rule first indicated that the province's law was applicable. But on another approach, the court would start the analysis with the statute. It would apply the law of the province and invalidate the parties' choice. This approach is sometimes described as unilateral.[16]

Third, the choice must not be contrary to public policy. The scope of the public policy exclusion was discussed in Chapter 3 and this is a specific instance of its application. This limitation overlaps with the requirement that the choice be bona fide, in that it is also concerned with attempts to avoid the otherwise applicable law. Private wagering contracts are illegal in Alberta. The parties to such a contract in Alberta could not alter that result by expressly making the contract governed by Nevada law. In *Golden Acres Ltd v Queensland Estates Pty Ltd* the court refused to give effect to a Hong Kong choice of law clause. It stated that

> While appreciating that public policy can be an unclear concept, generally speaking it would be contrary to public policy for the legislative intention to be stultified by parties to a contract, of which the proper law would be Queensland, selecting some other law for the purpose of avoiding the application of Queensland law.[17]

In *Nike Infomatic Systems Ltd v Avac Systems Ltd* the defendant argued that the court should refuse to accept a British Columbia choice of law clause.[18] However, the court held that the choice was not contrary to public policy because the parties were not trying to avoid the application of Alberta law.

---

16   This would likely have been the result had *Vita Food, ibid,* been heard in Newfoundland and Labrador rather than in Nova Scotia. For a discussion of cases that take this analysis one step further, beyond choice of law clauses to related choice of forum clauses, see the discussion in Chapter 3 of *Agro Co of Canada Ltd v The "Regal Scout"* (1983), 148 DLR (3d) 412 (FCTD).

17   [1969] Qd R 378 at 385 (SC), aff'd (*sub nom Freehold Land Investments Ltd v Queensland Estates Pty Ltd*) (1970), 123 CLR 418 (HCA). The High Court of Australia reached the same result but by different reasoning. It started with the Queensland statute as the law of the forum and applied it.

18   (1979), 16 BCLR 139 (SC).

Three further points about express choice should be noted. First, the parties cannot provide that the contract is not governed by any system of law, since every contract must have a governing law. If the parties purport to choose no system, the proper law analysis will determine the applicable law objectively, as discussed below. Second, there is an ongoing debate about whether the parties must select the law of a country or can instead choose to have the contract governed by "soft" law, such as the commercial principles of an international organization. The orthodoxy is that the choice must be that of a legal system—the law of a country. Other commercial principles can be made terms of the contract by reference but not through a choice of law clause. But there are signs that this orthodoxy may change. The Hague Conference on Private International Law recently supported the notion that parties to an international commercial contract can validly choose to have the contract governed by non-state rules.[19] Third, the parties are free to vary the chosen law through subsequent agreement. However, the parties cannot creatively choose a "floating" applicable law, for example through a term providing that the contract is governed by the law of the place where any resulting disputes are litigated.[20] The applicable law must be able to be ascertained at any given time, not only at some point in the future.

2) Implied Choice

If the parties have not made an express choice of the applicable law, the proper law rule next considers whether they have implicitly agreed on the applicable law. In order to give effect to the reasonable expectations of the parties, the rule infers a choice from certain indicators. This amounts to finding that the parties have chosen an applicable law but have failed to make this choice explicit in the contract.

The jurisprudence indicates the weight that courts can give to certain factors in assessing whether there has been an implied choice of law. One factor that has been treated as a reasonably strong indication is the place chosen for arbitration of disputes under the contract. Courts have inferred from this choice that the parties wanted the law of that place to govern.[21] Another strong factor is a jurisdiction clause,

---

19 This development is explained in Genevieve Saumier, "The Hague Principles and the Choice of Non-state 'Rules of Law' to Govern an International Commercial Contract" (2014) 40 *Brooklyn Journal of International Law* 1.

20 *The Iran Vojdan*, [1984] 2 Lloyd's Rep 380 at 385. Consider the analysis in *Re Pope & Talbot Ltd*, [2009] BCJ No 2248 (SC).

21 *Compagnie Tunisienne de Navigation SA v Compagnie D'Armement Maritime SA*, [1971] AC 572 at 584, 590, 596, and 604 (HL); *Star Shipping AS v China National*

which can imply that the parties want the law of the chosen forum to apply.[22] This inference is considerably stronger if the jurisdiction clause is exclusive rather than non-exclusive. Courts will also consider the transaction's connection to other contracts. If the contract in question is one of a series of related contracts, and those other contracts have the same applicable law, the court can infer that the parties intended the contract to use that same law. Similarly, if there have been previous similar contracts between the parties, it can be inferred that the parties meant the law previously applied to apply again. Some cases have considered the language or the currency of the contract as pointing to an implied choice of law, but these factors are weak and no inference should be drawn from them.

Some commentators are critical of allowing for an implied choice of law. They advocate that doing so is artificial, imputing intent to the parties that may not exist. They would prefer to have only two parts to the proper law rule: express choice and, absent that, objective determination of the governing law.

3) Absence of Choice

In the absence of party choice, either express or implied, the contract is governed by law with which the transaction has its closest and most real connection. A leading Canadian authority for this proposition is *Imperial Life Assurance Co of Canada v Colmenares*.[23] The Supreme Court of Canada had to determine whether two life insurance contracts were governed by Ontario law or by the law of Cuba. It rejected the outdated rule that the applicable law was that of the place where the contracts were made. It held that

> the problem of determining the proper law of a contract is to be solved by considering the contract as a whole in light of all the circumstances which surround it and applying the law with which it appears to have the closest and most substantial connection.[24]

Foreign Trade Transportation Corp, [1993] 2 Lloyd's Rep 445 (CA); *Re O'Brien and Canadian Pacific Railway Co* (1972), 25 DLR (3d) 230 (Sask CA); *Richardson International, Ltd v Mys Chikhacheva (The)*, 2002 FCA 97 at para 34. No inference can be drawn if multiple places for arbitration are indicated.

22   *Hamlyn & Co v Talisker Distillery*, [1984] AC 202 (HL). See also *Royal Exchange Assurance Corp v Sjoforsakrings Aktiebologet Vega*, [1902] 2 KB 384 (CA); *NV Kwik Hoo Tong Handel Maatschappij v James Finlay & Co Ltd*, [1927] AC 604 (HL).
23   [1967] SCR 443 [*Imperial Life*].
24   *Ibid* at 448.

The approach is objective, looking for the law that the reasonable person would consider applicable to the contract. This approach weighs a wide range of factors including the place of contracting, the place of performance of the contract, the place where the subject matter of the contract is located, the residence of each of the parties, and the style of the language used in the contract.[25] All of the factors discussed above that could have indicated an implied choice of law are also relevant. In *Imperial Life* the court concluded that Ontario law applied because the applications for coverage and the policies were prepared in Ontario using a standard form that complied with the law of the province. The court also indicated that the reasonable expectation of the applicant was that Ontario law would apply.

In *Lilydale Cooperative Ltd v Meyn Canada Inc* the defendant argued that the contract in issue was best understood as one for the sale and delivery of an oven system from Ontario to it in Alberta, such that objectively Alberta law applied. In contrast, the court held that the contract was for both the design and sale of the oven system, and that the design process had been done by the plaintiff in Ontario.[26] This illustrates the importance of properly characterizing the nature of the contract.

At one time, the common law used to employ certain presumptions as to the applicable law in the absence of choice. One such presumption, for example, would be that the applicable law was the law of the place of performance. This had the effect of making certain factors more important than others, which was difficult to justify across a wide range of factual situations and which raised additional issues about what was required to refute the presumption. The use of presumptions as part of identifying the proper law has since been rejected.[27]

The various factors are to be considered as of the time the contract was made, such that subsequent events are excluded.[28] For example, if the plaintiff changes his or her residence after the contract was made, the relevant factor is where he or she formerly resided. However, there are some limited situations in which future events become relevant. In these situations, the future conduct creates an estoppel concerning the applicable law. To take an extreme example, if the parties initially did not choose an applicable law but then subsequently agree on one, the subsequent agreement is taken into account. But this is not a perfect example because the real effect of the subsequent agreement

---

25 Etler, above note 5 at 682–88. See also *Branco v American Home Assurance Co*, 2015 SKCA 71 at paras 162–63.
26 2015 ONCA 281.
27 *Coast Lines Ltd v Hudig and Veder Chartering NV*, [1972] 2 QB 34 (CA).
28 *Amin Rasheed*, above note 3 at 62.

is to make the case one involving an express choice and not one of no choice. A less extreme situation could involve the parties having subsequently conducted themselves as though the contract were governed by a particular law. This conduct could create an estoppel, precluding the parties from alleging that a different law applied, and so would be considered even though it happened after the contract was formed.[29]

Under the doctrine of *depeçage*, which literally means "picking and choosing," it is possible that different parts of a contract can have different applicable laws.[30] The parties could choose to do this expressly, by providing that the law of one country governs certain issues and that the law of another country governs all others. In practice, this is rarely done: parties prefer to have a uniform governing law. This could also occur in the objective assessment of the proper law. A court could conclude that part of a contract has the closest and most real connection with one law and the rest has the closest and most real connection with another law.[31] This is also quite rare, as courts generally try to interpret a contract as an integrated whole rather than as comprised of separate elements.

We have already seen, in Chapters 5 and 6, that tests framed in broad language such as "real and substantial connection" and "most appropriate forum" raise concerns about whether the law is sufficiently certain and predictable. The same concerns arise about determining a contract's proper law by looking for the law with which the transaction has its closest and most real connection. The weighing of the many factors can produce decisions that are quite fact-specific, making it difficult to know what law will govern. However, as in these other areas of private international law, the accumulated jurisprudence provides a valuable guide as to which factors the courts have prioritized in which types of cases. Common fact patterns thus have a reasonably high degree of predictability. Where the proper law is most uncertain is in novel situations, and yet its ability to handle such situations in a flexible way is one of the approach's strengths.

C. SCOPE OF THE APPLICABLE LAW

Contract disputes raise many different types of issues. Not all of these issues are resolved using the applicable law. For example, the applicable

---

29   See *Whitworth Street Estates (Manchester) Ltd v James Miller & Partners Ltd*, [1970] AC 583 (HL).
30   *Libyan Arab Foreign Bank v Bankers Trust Co*, [1989] QB 728. See *Re Pope & Talbot Ltd*, above note 20.
31   This possibility was considered in *Montreal Trust Co v Stanrock Uranium Mines Ltd*, [1966] 1 OR 258 (HCJ).

law does not govern the manner of performance. If an Ontario corporation contracts to deliver goods to a location in Quebec, and the applicable law of the contract is that of Ontario, this does not mean that in driving the goods to the location the corporation's employee can follow Ontario's rules of the road, not Quebec's. The way in which the corporation performs the contract is still governed by the law of the place of performance.[32]

1) Essential Validity

The essential validity of the contract is governed by the applicable law. Essential validity includes issues such as whether the contract, or any one of its particular terms, is legally binding. The validity of an exclusion or limitation clause, for example, is governed by the applicable law. Essential validity also includes (1) the interpretation of the contract, determining what the specific words used mean; (2) the scope of the obligation to perform and any excuses for non-performance; and (3) the way in which the contract is validly discharged, for example by performance or frustration.

2) Formation

In most contract disputes the parties do at least agree that they have entered into a contract. In some cases, however, one of the parties alleges that there is in fact no contract: that, for example, sufficient certainty of terms was not achieved. This raises issues for the question of choice of law. Must the court somehow first resolve whether there is a contract, and if so using what law, before then looking for its applicable law? After all, how can something that is not a contract have an applicable law? This issue has been the subject of academic commentary and two general approaches have been advocated, one using the putative proper law of the contract and the other using the law of the forum.

The putative proper law of the contract is the law that would be the proper law of the contract if the contract were validly created.[33] In other words, whether the contract has come into existence is determined according to the law that would apply to the contract if it were in existence. Such an analysis considers the same factors as a determination of the proper law. Once a contract is determined to exist under the putative proper law, all remaining questions are resolved by the now

---

32 *Auckland Corp v Alliance Assurance Co Ltd*, [1937] AC 587 at 606 (PC).
33 See *Mackender v Feldia AG*, [1967] 2 QB 590 (CA) [*Mackender*]; Elizabeth Crawford, "The Uses of Putativity and Negativity in the Conflict of Laws" (2005) 54 *International and Comparative Law Quarterly* 829.

discernible proper law of the contract. At present, the putative proper law approach is dominant.[34]

This approach has been criticized. One major criticism is that the putative proper law approach operates from an assumption that there is a contract. Adrian Briggs argues that the determination of a contract's proper law, and by extension its putative proper law, is based on subjective intention of the parties to the (purported) agreement.[35] The problem, according to Briggs, is that if the proper law is a subjective idea based on the intentions of the parties, then it should be possible for the parties to not have chosen a proper law and therefore not have made a contract.[36]

The putative proper law approach does not appear to allow for such a situation. In addition, the putative proper law approach is open to abuse. An oft-cited hypothetical case involving a choice of law clause illustrates this:

> [Suppose a] hypothetical case of a written offer made by a Dane to an Englishman with whom the former has had previous dealings. The offer contains a clause providing that the contract shall be governed by Danish law. The Englishman does not reply. By Danish law silence is regarded as acceptance, but of course there is no such rule in English law.[37]

The putative proper law would, in light of the clause, be Danish law, under which the contract would then be valid.

The general position of critics of the putative proper law approach is that it should not be used when there are preliminary disputes as to the existence of the contract.[38] In such situations, recourse must be had to some other method in order to determine this initial issue, with the *lex fori* being the main choice. There are two ways the *lex fori* could be used. Under the first, it would be used to determine whether the parties had made a contract. If they had, then the proper law could be determined, and it could govern various issues in the usual way. Under the second, which is subtler, the *lex fori* would determine not whether the parties had made a contract but whether they had reached

---

34 See *Mackender*, above note 33; *Compania Naviera Micro SA v Shipley International Inc (The Parouth)*, [1982] 2 Lloyd's Rep 351 (CA).
35 Adrian Briggs, "The Formation of International Contracts" [1990] *Lloyd's Maritime and Commercial Law Quarterly* 192 at 200.
36 *Ibid*.
37 David Pierce, "Post-formation Choice of Law in Contract" (1987) 50 *Modern Law Review* 176 at 181. Pierce's hypothetical is based upon the original articulation of the problem in Martin Wolff, *Private International Law*, 2d ed (Oxford: Clarendon Press, 1950) at 439.
38 See Andrew Bell, "Jurisdiction and Arbitration Agreements in Transnational Contracts, Part II" (1996) 10 *Journal of Contract Law* 97 at 98–100.

agreement on a proper law. If they did, then that proper law would be used to determine the existence of the putative contract. If they did not agree, then, since all contracts require a proper law, there would be no contract between the parties.[39]

However, the use of the *lex fori* undermines the idea of party autonomy, a key principle of the law of contract. Further, some of the objections to the putative proper law are based on the notion that all contracts require subjective agreement on an applicable law and do not allow courts to identify the proper law using a wholly objective analysis. This notion is controversial, since, as outlined above, the orthodox understanding of the choice of law rule for contract allows the proper law to be determined objectively. Furthermore, the use of the *lex fori* to determine the existence of a contract could give rise to forum shopping, since parties could seek out jurisdictions whose laws would be more favourable to their position.

The putative proper law approach is dominant in Canadian law.[40] However, criticisms of using the putative proper law in cases involving disputed contracts alleged to contain a choice of law clause have led some courts to consider a modified approach. Rather than use the law of the forum, this approach identifies the putative proper law without considering a choice of law clause. In the hypothetical situation outlined above, the choice of law clause in favour of Danish law would be ignored and the court would objectively identify the proper law. This approach has been called the "objective putative proper law." It retains the strengths of the putative proper law approach while reducing some of the associated concerns. There is little judicial support for this approach but it might be appropriate in certain situations.[41]

3) Formal Validity

The issue of formal validity addresses whether the contract is in the correct form. Most contracts do not have any requirements of form. But in some legal systems some contracts have to be in writing (such as those transferring an interest in real property) and some contracts have particular form requirements (such as the need for two witnesses). The choice of law rule for formal validity provides that a contract must comply with the form requirements of either the proper law of the

---

39 See Briggs, above note 35.
40 See, for example, *Timberwest Forest Ltd v Gearbulk Pool Ltd*, 2001 BCSC 882 at paras 27–31, aff'd 2003 BCCA 39.
41 It was considered in *Mackender*, above note 33, especially for cases in which one of the parties alleges a complete lack of agreement.

contract or of the place of contracting. In *Greenshields Inc v Johnston* the parties' contract was made in Alberta.[42] Under Alberta's *Guarantees Acknowledgement Act* a person giving a guarantee is required to appear before a notary public and sign a required statement.[43] If this is not done, the guarantee has no effect. The court, applying the choice of law rule for formal validity, held that the contract was not formally valid by the law of the place of contracting. However, it found that the proper law of the contract was that of Ontario and since Ontario had no similar statutory requirement the contract was formally valid under that law.

Note that the approach in *Greenshields Inc* uses the traditional multilateral approach to choice of law. The Alberta statute does not invalidate the contract since it is not governed by Alberta law. The court starts with the choice of law rule, finds Ontario law to be the proper law, and applies it. Vaughan Black has argued that a different, unilateral approach should apply.[44] Under such an approach, the Alberta court would start with the Alberta statute and interpret its provisions. If the contract in question fell within them, and there had been no appearance before a notary public, the statute would invalidate the contract. Ontario law would not enter into the analysis. One concern with this approach, however, is that it starts with the law of the forum without explaining why. This has the potential to undercut the whole notion of choice of law rules.

4) Capacity

The capacity of a party to enter into a contract is typically treated as a separate issue. Under most systems of law certain parties do not have capacity to contract. For example, in Canada contracts made by minors—those under the age of majority—that are not for the provision of necessities can be avoided by the minor. The jurisprudence is inconsistent on the choice of law rule for capacity to contract. Options include the law of the place of contracting (though this can be fortuitous), the law of the party's habitual residence, and the putative proper law of the contract (the law that would govern assuming the parties had capacity). The latter option was endorsed in *Charron v Montreal Trust Co*.[45] That case did not involve an express choice of law and so the putative proper law was determined objectively. If a contract did contain an express choice, there is some debate about whether a court would apply the

---

42 (1981), 28 AR 1 (QB), aff'd (1981), 35 AR 487 (CA) [*Greenshields Inc*].
43 RSA 1970, c 163, s 3. See now RSA 2000, c G-11, s 3.
44 Vaughan Black, "The Strange Case of Alberta's *Guarantees Acknowledgement Act*: A Study in Choice-of-Law Method" (1987) 11 *Dalhousie Law Journal* 208.
45 [1958] OR 597 (CA). See also *Bodley Head Ltd v Flegon*, [1972] 1 WLR 680.

chosen law to the issue of capacity. The concern is that parties could pick an applicable law by which they had capacity and so avoid the restrictions—which usually protect one of the contracting parties—of another country's law. In light of this concern, one approach is to always use only the putative proper law as determined objectively. An alternative, which is probably more adaptable to the various circumstances, is to use the putative proper law including any express choice. After all, as explained above, the choice would still need to be bona fide, legal, and not contrary to public policy. In addition, there could still be scope, in cases raising the most concern, for a court to apply the law on capacity from another country as a mandatory rule, as discussed below.

In an interesting and complex case, *Haugesund Kommune v Depfa ACS Bank*, the English Court of Appeal held that "for the purposes of English conflicts of laws, a lack of substantive power to conclude a contract of a particular type is equivalent to a lack of 'capacity.'"[46] The litigation involved "interest rate swap" contracts, expressly governed by English law, between banks and Norwegian municipalities. The court held that under Norwegian law the municipalities did not have capacity to enter into such contracts. While it was possible, as a matter of Norwegian law, that the contracts might nonetheless be valid despite that lack of capacity, the court held that "the consequence of the lack of 'capacity' is something that is to be determined by the putative applicable law of the contract."[47] That was English law, and under English law a contract involving a party that lacks capacity is invalid.

D. MANDATORY RULES

Mandatory rules are those substantive rules of a legal system that apply regardless of the applicable law. They are not confined to contract cases, but that is the area in which they are most common and most developed. They are a counterbalance to the broad scope given to party autonomy in contract choice of law rules. The parties have considerable freedom to choose the applicable law, but this freedom has to be balanced against the interests a country has in applying another law—typically, but not exclusively, its own—to some contract issues. In other areas of choice of law where autonomy plays a much smaller role, like choice of law for tort, there is much less need for mandatory rules. The forum's interests can be accommodated under the much narrower doctrine of

---

46   [2010] EWCA Civ 579 at para 47.
47   *Ibid* at para 60.

public policy. But in contract, situations arise where the forum does not object to the parties' choice of applicable law or to the content of that law yet considers that there are forum rules that it must apply.

A leading example of a mandatory rule is section 27(2) of the United Kingdom's *Unfair Contract Terms Act 1977*.[48] The statute contains provisions that invalidate certain contractual terms, such as excluding liability for death or personal injury caused by negligence. Section 27(2) provides that in certain circumstances these provisions apply notwithstanding a choice of law clause in the contract that selects the law of a place outside the United Kingdom. The statute's provisions are thus express mandatory rules.

Many statutory provisions are much less clear as to whether they constitute mandatory rules, leaving it to the courts to determine this on a case-by-case basis. In *Avenue Properties Ltd v First City Development Corp*[49] the plaintiff refused to complete a purchase agreed to with the defendants in a contract governed by Ontario law because of the defendants' failure to comply with section 62 of the British Columbia *Real Estate Act*.[50] The section required the defendants to have submitted a prospectus and provided a copy to the plaintiff. The defendants alleged that the plaintiff could not avoid the transaction on this basis because section 62 did not apply. The parties litigated the issue of whether proceedings should be in Ontario or in British Columbia, and in that litigation the British Columbia Court of Appeal considered the question of what law would be applied by a court in that province. While it acknowledged that the contract was governed by Ontario law, it held that there was a reasonable possibility that the court would apply section 62 as a mandatory rule. It reached this conclusion based on interpreting the wording of the section, finding that the legislature may well have intended it to apply regardless of the applicable law of the contract.

In determining whether a rule is mandatory, courts both interpret statutory language and consider notions of "public policy." In this context, public policy has a different meaning than discussed in Chapter 3. It is not nearly as narrow as it is in that context. A law need not address fundamental values and essential morality before it is found to be a mandatory rule. Here the public policy is leading not to the exclusion of foreign law—passing a negative judgment—but to the positive application of the law of the forum. This may explain the broader scope given to the concept.

---

48 (UK), 1977, c 50.
49 (1986), 7 BCLR (2d) 45 (CA).
50 RSBC 1979, c 356. This statute has since been repealed.

Mandatory rules are typically found in statutes but it is possible that a common law rule could qualify. As noted above, mandatory rules are usually those of the forum, but it is open to the court to apply the laws of a third legal system as mandatory rules. The most likely such system of law is that of the place of performance.

E. ILLEGALITY

A contract could be illegal under one of four different, potentially relevant legal systems: (1) the law applicable to the contract, (2) the law of the forum, (3) the law of the place of performance, and (4) the law of the place of contracting. In this context, "illegal" generally means not that there is a problem with the contract itself but rather that what the contract requires one or more parties to do under it is prohibited. Put another way, the contract requires performance of an act contrary to one of these four systems of law.

If the contract is illegal under the applicable law, the issue is resolved by looking to how the applicable law treats illegal contracts. Not every legal system treats illegal contracts the same way. One of the most common treatments, used in Canadian provinces, is that the contract is void. In *Etler v Kertesz* the plaintiff sued in Ontario on a contract made in Austria.[51] The court found that there was no express or implied choice of law and so had to identify the law with which the transaction had the closest and most real connection. It held that this was the law of Austria, and under that law the contract was illegal as contrary to specific provisions relating to foreign currency. The court held that Austrian law, like English law, treated an illegal contract as void.[52]

There is a difference of opinion on the effect of illegality under the law of the forum. Under one perspective, this is irrelevant. The contract is not governed by the law of the forum and is not being performed in the forum, so why should the forum law matter? Under the other perspective, this illegality matters a great deal. As a point of public policy, the forum's courts should not allow the parties to do something contrary to the forum's law. Which perspective is correct depends on the view taken of public policy. On a broad view, the illegality under forum law would be sufficient to invalidate the contract. On a narrower view, there would have to be something more before the court could invoke the forum law, for example a sense that the forum law was a

---

51   Above note 5.
52   *Ibid* at 688.

mandatory rule (as discussed in the previous section). As discussed in Chapter 3, public policy should generally be given a narrow scope. Accordingly, the better approach is that illegality under forum law should matter only if there is some basis for the forum law being applied, one of which would be as a mandatory rule.

The most interesting issues deal with illegality under the law of the place of performance. It is generally accepted as a rule of English and Canadian common law that a contract that is illegal where it is to be performed will not be enforced.[53] However, the cases on this issue can be divided into two categories. In the first, the applicable law is also the law of the forum. In the second, these are two different legal systems.

Gillespie Management Corp v Terrace Properties is a case in the first category.[54] The plaintiff sought, in proceedings in British Columbia, to recover commissions due under a contract with the defendant. The contract was governed by British Columbia law. However, under the law of Washington State, where the contract was performed, the plaintiff was required to have a licence to act as a real estate broker to engage in the work it was doing. The plaintiff did not have such a licence, so the contractual performance was illegal in Washington. As a result, the claim failed. This can be seen as an application of the rule in the previous paragraph. But why is the rule applied? It could be applied because it is part of the applicable law, but it could also be applied as the law of the forum. Where these laws are the same, it does not matter.

Suppose, however, that in *Gillespie Management* the applicable law was that of New York. The case would then be in the second category. One option would be for the British Columbia court to hold that the forum's rule that contracts illegal in their place of performance will not be enforced applies regardless of the applicable law. This would have the effect of making that rule a mandatory rule, in that it would apply in all cases. This would be a rare example of a common law mandatory rule: as noted above, most such rules are found in statutes. Support for this approach can be found in *Zivnostenska Banka National Corp v Frankman*, where Lord Reid stated "whatever be the proper law of the contract, an English court will not require a party to do an act in performance of a contract which would be an offence under the law in force at the place where the act has to be done."[55] The other option would be to hold that

---

53 *Ralli Bros v Compania Naviera Sota y Aznar*, [1920] 2 KB 287 (CA). See also *Regazzoni v KC Sethia (1944) Ltd*, [1958] AC 301 (HL) [*Regazzoni*].
54 (1989), 39 BCLR (2d) 337 (CA) [*Gillespie Management*].
55 [1950] AC 57 at 79 (HL). This approach is consistent with a broader public policy against enforcing contracts that require the violation of the law of a foreign "friendly" country: see *Foster v Driscoll*, [1929] 1 KB 470; *Regazzoni*, above note 53.

the forum's rule is only a domestic rule, and so applies only when the domestic law is applied as the proper law of the contract. If British Columbia law does not govern the contract, then that rule of British Columbia law does not apply. Instead, the court would look to the applicable law, the law of New York for this example, and determine how that law handles the situation. If New York law has a similar rule about contracts illegal where performed, then under that rule the court could find that the contract was not enforceable. However, if New York law is willing to give effect to such contracts, then it would not be correct for the British Columbia court to hold otherwise.

Finally, the easiest analysis is of illegality under the law of the place of contracting: this should be entirely irrelevant.[56] The connection between the place of contracting and the transaction is not sufficiently significant for the illegality to affect a contract that is legal under its applicable law, the law of the forum, and the law of the place of performance. To hold otherwise would give undue prominence to the place of contracting.

F. THE ROME I REGULATION

The European Union has a uniform contract choice of law rule, found in the *Regulation on the Law Applicable to Contractual Obligations* (known colloquially as "Rome I").[57] In some respects it is quite similar to the approach in common law Canada but it is quite different in others. The primary rule, preserving party autonomy, is that a contract is governed by the law chosen, expressly or clearly demonstrated by the terms or circumstances, by the parties.[58] In the absence of choice, there are detailed provisions for different types of contract: contracts of carriage, consumer contracts, insurance contracts, and individual contracts of employment.[59] There is also a general provision, article 4, and its approach is quite different from that of the common law. Article 4.1 sets out eight sub-rules as to the applicable law. For example, a contract for the sale of goods is

---

56   *Vita Food*, above note 7.
57   EC, *Commission Regulation (EC) No 593/2008 of 17 June 2008 on the law applicable to contractual obligations*, [2008] OJ, L 177 [Rome I]. For a detailed analysis, see James Fawcett & Janeen Carruthers, *Cheshire, North & Fawcett Private International Law*, 14th ed (Oxford: Oxford University Press, 2008) ch 18.
58   Rome I, above note 57, art 3.1. *Depeçage* is expressly allowed and there is some scope (see arts 3.3 and 9) for mandatory rules to operate. The alternative to express choice, namely a clearly demonstrated choice, is more limited than the common law notion of implied choice. See Pippa Rogerson, *Collier's Conflict of Laws*, 4th ed (Cambridge: Cambridge University Press, 2013) at 304–5.
59   Rome I, above note 57, arts 5–8.

governed by the law of the seller's habitual residence and a franchise contract is governed by the law of the franchisee's habitual residence. If these sub-rules overlap or do not apply, the contract is governed by "the law of the country where the party required to effect the characteristic performance of the contract has his habitual residence."[60] This notion of characteristic performance appears quite strange from a common law perspective but it has been used in European choice of law for some time. Article 4.3 provides that if the contract is "manifestly more closely connected" with a country other than the one identified, the law of that country applies, and article 4.4 provides that if the applicable law cannot otherwise be determined by the earlier rules then the law of the country with which the contract is most closely connected applies. Rome I also contains specific choice of law rules for the issues of formal validity and capacity,[61] and it adopts a putative applicable law approach to issues of consent and material validity: "The existence and validity of a contract, or of any term of a contract, shall be determined by the law which would govern it under this Regulation if the contract or term were valid."[62]

FURTHER READINGS

ARZANDEH, ARDAVAN. "The Law Governing International Contractual Disputes in the Absence of Express Choice by the Parties" [2015] *Lloyd's Maritime and Commercial Law Quarterly* 525.

ATRILL, SIMON. "Choice of Law in Contract: The Missing Pieces of the Article 4 Jigsaw?" (2004) 53 *International and Comparative Law Quarterly* 549.

BLOM, JOOST. "Regulation of Contracts in Canadian Private International Law" (2014) 31 *Arizona Journal of International and Comparative Law* 21.

BRIGGS, ADRIAN. *Agreements on Jurisdiction and Choice of Law* (Oxford: Oxford University Press, 2008).

DOLINGER, JACOB. "Evolution of Principles for Resolving Conflicts in the Field of Contracts and Torts" (2000) 283 *Recueil des Cours* 187.

---

60 *Ibid*, art 4.2.
61 *Ibid*, arts 11 and 13.
62 *Ibid*, art 10(1). A limited exception in art 10(2) allows individuals to establish they did not consent in certain circumstances.

GIULIANO, MARIO, & PAUL LAGARDE. "Report on the Convention on the Law Applicable to Contractual Obligations" (1980) 23 *Official Journal of the European Communities—Information and Notices* C282.

HAGUE CONFERENCE ON PRIVATE INTERNATIONAL LAW. *Principles on Choice of Law in International Commercial Contracts* (The Hague: Hague Conference on Private International Law, 2015).

HARTLEY, TREVOR. "Mandatory Rules in International Contracts: The Common Law Approach" (1997) 266 *Recueil des Cours* 337.

HELLNER, MICHAEL. "Third Country Overriding Mandatory Rules in the Rome I Regulation: Old Wine in New Bottles?" (2009) 5 *Journal of Private International Law* 447.

LIBLING, DF. "Formation of International Contracts" (1979) 42 *Modern Law Review* 169.

LOW, KELVIN. "Choice of Law in Formation of Contracts" (2004) 20 *Journal of Contract Law* 167.

MARSHALL, BROOKE ADELE. "Reconsidering the Proper Law of the Contract" (2012) 13 *Melbourne Journal of International Law* 505.

NYGH, PETER. *Autonomy in International Contracts* (Oxford: Clarendon Press, 1999).

PENADÉS FONS, MANUEL. "Commercial Choice of Law in Context: Looking beyond Rome" (2015) 78 *Modern Law Review* 241.

SWAN, JOHN. "Choice of Law in Contracts" (1991) 19 *Canadian Business Law Journal* 213.

SYMEONIDES, SYMEON C. "The Hague Principles on Choice of Law for International Contracts: Some Preliminary Comments" (2013) 61 *American Journal of Comparative Law* 873.

WALSH, CATHERINE. "The Uses and Abuses of Party Autonomy in International Contracts" (2010) 60 *University of New Brunswick Law Journal* 12.

CHAPTER 15

UNJUST ENRICHMENT

A. INTRODUCTION

The previous two chapters have considered the choice of law rules for two well-known parts of the law of obligations, namely contract and tort. Each of these areas of the law required little introductory explanation. In contrast, unjust enrichment is less well understood, especially by law students. One reason for this is that the law in this area developed much more recently in the common law than did contract and tort. In addition, claims in this area arise less frequently. Accordingly, a brief introduction to the core concepts is required.

In Canada, a claim to reverse an unjust enrichment requires the plaintiff to show (1) that the defendant has been enriched; (2) that the enrichment is at the plaintiff's expense; and (3) that there is no "juristic reason," such as a contract or a gift, for the enrichment.[1] A leading example can be drawn from the area of mistaken payments. Consider Anne, who thinks she owes Brian $100 and pays that amount to him. In reality, Anne owed the $100 to Carrie. When Carrie demands payment, Anne complies and then asks Brian for the first $100 back. If Brian refuses, we must determine the legal basis on which Anne could recover the $100. She has no contract with Brian, and his retention of the $100

---

1   *Pettkus v Becker*, [1980] 2 SCR 834 at 848, Dickson J; *Garland v Consumers' Gas Co*, [2004] 1 SCR 629 at para 30, Iacobucci J; *Kerr v Baranow*, 2011 SCC 10 at para 32, Cromwell J.

paid to him is not a tort, so those areas of the law are of no help. Anne's claim is in unjust enrichment. There is no juristic reason to which Brian can point as basis for his retaining the enrichment. Anne paid him by mistake, which vitiates the intent to transfer the money. This is a very simple example, but it could easily be modified to involve a financial institution mistakenly transferring millions of dollars.

If all of the factual connections in an unjust enrichment case are with the jurisdiction hearing the dispute, there is no choice of law issue. However, it is easy to envisage situations where some of the connections will be with other jurisdictions. Staying with the mistaken payments example, wire transfer payments can easily be made around the world. In such cases, a choice of law rule for unjust enrichment becomes essential.

However, we are immediately confronted with a significant difficulty. Unlike for contract and tort, there is little clear authority for an unjust enrichment choice of law rule. Several factors have combined to produce this situation. First, unjust enrichment was recognized as a distinct area of law in England only in the 1990s and in Canada there are few cases prior to the 1980s. As a result, there was little opportunity to develop a choice of law rule. Second, in light of the first factor, litigants chose not to raise potential choice of law issues when they did arise. They thought doing so would make the proceedings more complex and less predictable. Third, in Canada the substantive law of unjust enrichment is largely common law, and thus quite uniform across the country, reducing the number of possible cases. Fourth, in the few cases that did arise, there was a tendency to accept the choice of law rule proposed by leading academics rather than litigating the issue further.

Unjust enrichment, therefore, is quite different from other areas of choice of law. It is difficult to articulate the current rule with a high degree of confidence, which can be frustrating. Yet as more cases arise, Canadian courts will be required to formulate a choice of law rule for unjust enrichment. This will provide an excellent opportunity to debate, using the core principles of choice of law, what the rule should be.

A final introductory point should be made about characterization.[2] Because unjust enrichment is a developing area of the law of obligations, it is common to see disagreements about whether a claim is one in unjust enrichment or not. Part of this confusion flows from the historic link between unjust enrichment and restitution. Restitution is not a cause of

---

2   See Stephen GA Pitel, "Characterisation of Unjust Enrichment in the Conflict of Laws" in Jason Neyers, Mitchell McInnes, & Stephen GA Pitel, eds, *Understanding Unjust Enrichment* (Oxford: Hart, 2004); Pattarapas Tudsri, "Characterization of Proprietary Restitution in the Conflict of Laws" (2013) 44 *Ottawa Law Review* 261.

action; rather, it is a remedy. It is a remedy measured not by the plaintiff's loss but rather by the defendant's gain. Restitution is the remedy awarded for successful unjust enrichment claims. However, this remedy has also been awarded in other contexts, such as breach of contract, breach of fiduciary duty, and breach of confidence. In some of these other contexts, courts have sometimes seen that the plaintiff was seeking restitution and thought that the case therefore involved unjust enrichment, and so they considered choice of law for unjust enrichment. This is incorrect since those cases were not about unjust enrichment. Nonetheless, because the courts thought they were, they can contain useful commentary on the choice of law rule for unjust enrichment.

B. ENGLISH COMMON LAW

There are only a few relevant Canadian decisions, and they draw heavily on the English common law rules, so those rules are a good starting point for the analysis. In England those rules are now of historical interest only because the current English choice of law rule for unjust enrichment is found not in the common law but rather in European Union law,[3] which is discussed later in this chapter. The best-known formulation of the earlier common law rule was found in the leading text *Dicey, Morris and Collins on the Conflict of Laws*:

> Rule 230:
> (1) The obligation to restore the benefit of an enrichment obtained at another person's expense is governed by the proper law of the obligation.
> (2) The proper law of the obligation is (*semble*) determined as follows:
>   (a) If the obligation arises in connection with a contract, its proper law is the law applicable to the contract;
>   (b) If it arises in connection with a transaction concerning an immovable (land), its proper law is the law of the country where the immovable is situated (*lex situs*);
>   (c) If it arises in any other circumstances, its proper law is the law of the country where the enrichment occurs.[4]

---

3   See Section E(1), below in this chapter.
4   Lawrence Collins, ed, *Dicey, Morris and Collins on the Conflict of Laws*, 14th ed (London: Sweet & Maxwell, 2006) at 1863 [*Dicey, Morris and Collins*]. Because of the change this rule has been removed from the current (15th) edition. All subsequent references in this chapter to r 230 are to the 14th edition.

The authors of the text were modest about the support for the rule, candidly acknowledging that "[n]one of the authorities cited . . . support our Rule as a matter of *ratio decidendi*."[5] More recently, though, they changed their claim somewhat, stating "[t]hose authorities which have approved the Rule are comparatively few; in other cases it has been accepted without discussion. Certainly no English decision has held the Rule to be wrong . . . ."[6] At the outset, therefore, we have to recognize that rule 230 was itself only a scholarly suggestion as to the choice of law rule, if admittedly one the courts seemed reasonably keen to accept as a starting point for their analysis. Elements of rule 230 may be more or less well supported by the actual cases.[7]

There are two quite different ways to understand this rule. Read literally, the flexibility in clause 1, which aims to identify the proper law of the unjust enrichment claim, is entirely removed by clause 2. This is because all claims must fall into one of the sub-rules in clause 2, with clause 2(c) acting as the catch-all for those that do not fit into clause 2(a) or 2(b). On this approach, rule 230 is a hierarchy of three rigid sub-rules with no flexibility and no exceptions.

However, it would be inappropriate to read rule 230 in this way. First, in using the word "*semble*" (meaning "it would seem") in clause 2, the authors indicated a real hesitancy in moving beyond the general rule in clause 1. Moreover, the commentary to the rule indicated that clause 1 "may be regarded as the general principle of which the particular solutions identified in clause (2) of the Rule are examples."[8] So the commentary to rule 230 acknowledged that the sub-rules in clause 2 were not to be rigidly applied. This flexibility, and not the literal rigidity, is borne out in the leading English cases.

In *Arab Monetary Fund v Hashim* the plaintiff retained a building construction firm to build its headquarters in Abu Dhabi.[9] The plaintiff later discovered that the firm had paid a significant sum to the plaintiff's president, Hashim, which it alleged was a bribe or secret commission. The plaintiff sued Hashim and the firm in England in contract, tort,

---

5   Lawrence Collins, ed, *Dicey and Morris on the Conflict of Laws*, 12th ed (London: Sweet & Maxwell, 1993) at 1472, n 9.
6   *Dicey, Morris and Collins*, above note 4 at 1864 [footnotes omitted]. For a contrary view, see Peter North & JJ Fawcett, *Cheshire and North's Private International Law*, 13th ed (London: Butterworths, 1999) at 685–89.
7   See George Panagopoulos, *Restitution in Private International Law* (Oxford: Hart, 2000).
8   *Dicey, Morris and Collins*, above note 4 at 1872. See also (at 1864): "Rule [230](1) states a general principle. Rule [230](2) gives guidance as to the choice of law which will follow from that general principle in certain particular cases."
9   [1996] 1 Lloyd's Rep 589 (CA), rev'g [1993] 1 Lloyd's Rep 543 (QB) [*AMF*].

and unjust enrichment to recover the amount Hashim had received and argued that the law applicable to all of the claims was English law. At trial Evans J referred to the unjust enrichment claim as involving "a claim for money had and received, in other words a restitutionary claim categorized as quasi-contract for the amount of the bribe."[10]

This characterization led him to consider rule 230. Justice Evans held that these restitutionary claims against both Hashim and the firm were claims to enforce obligations that arose in connection with a contract. In other words, he held that they came within the scope of the wording of clause 2(a). In Hashim's case, he was the agent of the plaintiff and received the bribe while acting as such. In the firm's case, it had a building contract with the plaintiff and the claim amounted to an effort to recover part of what had been paid to the firm under that contract. Justice Evans found that both of these contractual relationships were governed by the law of Abu Dhabi. Had Evans J been minded to apply clause 2(a), he could have then done so. Instead, he stated:

> I prefer however to base this conclusion on wider grounds. It seems to me that in such cases the proper law of the restitutionary obligation which the plaintiffs assert is the law of Abu Dhabi. The building transaction was centred there, Dr. Hashim was based there and his duties were owed to the plaintiffs whose headquarters were there. The bribe agreement and the bribe payment were ancillary to the building contract and to Dr. Hashim's employment. If the plaintiffs had contended that the law of Abu Dhabi governed these claims, I doubt whether the contrary suggestion of English law . . . would have appeared seriously arguable.[11]

It is clear from this language that Evans J did not support the mechanical application of clause 2(a) and instead preferred the proper law approach, considering the various connections to Abu Dhabi. His decision cannot be seen as an endorsement of clause 2(a).

The Court of Appeal agreed with Evans J's approach. Having addressed the choice of law issues for the contract and tort claims, Saville LJ stated:

> Much the same considerations apply to the claim in quasi-contract. I accept the proposition stated as r. [230] in Dicey, that . . . the obligation to restore the benefit of an enrichment obtained at another person's expense is governed by the proper law of the obligation.[12]

---

10 Ibid at 563 (QB). Justice Evans's language makes it reasonably clear that he considered this claim to be in unjust enrichment.
11 Ibid at 566 (QB).
12 Ibid at 597 (CA).

Lord Justice Saville did not go on to consider the directive in clause 2(a). Instead, the considerations he referred to are a series of territorial connections examined as part of his choice of law in tort analysis, earlier in the judgment, which formed the basis for the conclusion that the alleged tort was in substance committed in Abu Dhabi. These included the relationships between Hashim, the firm, and the plaintiff, which were governed by the law of Abu Dhabi, and also included the location of the dishonest abuse of these relationships. It was in Abu Dhabi that the firm put forward its tender and Hashim obtained the building contract for the firm. Having completed this analysis, Saville LJ concluded by expressly agreeing with Evans J's reasoning on this issue; reasoning based on his "wider grounds."[13] In *AMF*, therefore, the Court of Appeal considered rule 230 but it did not endorse clause 2(a) and the specific link to the law of the contract. It endorsed the more general principle in clause 1.

Another English case that specifically considered rule 230 is *Macmillan Inc v Bishopsgate Investment Trust Plc (No 3)*.[14] The plaintiff sought to have English law applied to a claim of ownership of certain shares. All three judges of the Court of Appeal held that what was to be characterized, for the purpose of determining the appropriate choice of law rule, was the specific issue involved, which was whether the defendant had a defence to the claim as a result of having given value in good faith. The court held that this issue was essentially proprietary and that the applicable law was the *lex situs*, which was New York law. In passing, however, the court made some important observations about the validity and scope of clause 2(c) of rule 230, which calls for application of the law of the place of enrichment. In particular, Auld LJ was critical of this sub-rule. He labelled it "tentative" and with "insecure" foundations. He stated that "[a]t the highest . . . there is a 'tendency in the cases to endorse Dicey's proposition'" and noted that none of those cases bound the Court of Appeal.[15]

In *AMF*, Evans J had thought that the place of enrichment test made "obvious sense" when a defendant has received a sum of money in a foreign country where either he or she is resident or for some other reason receives the benefit of the enrichment there.[16] In the end, however, Evans J did not apply clause 2(c). In part this appears to have been influenced by his concern that Switzerland, the location of Hashim's bank

---

13 Ibid.
14 [1996] 1 All ER 585 (CA).
15 Ibid at 605. See also *Barros Mattos Junior v Macdaniels Ltd*, [2005] EWHC 1323 at paras 85–86 and 117 (Ch D); *OJSC Oil Company Yugraneft v Abramovich*, [2008] EWHC 2613 at paras 239–47 (Comm).
16 Above note 9 at 565–66 (QB).

account, "was at best a temporary staging post for the money and was never its journey's end."[17] The money then was transferred to several different jurisdictions, although not to Abu Dhabi, whose law Evans J eventually applied. While *obiter dicta*, these observations suggest that, at a minimum, clause 2(c) may be framed too broadly.

The most recent English cases similarly considered the rule to be flexible, perhaps to an even greater degree. In *Fiona Trust & Holding Corp v Privalov* Andrew Smith J noted that "If the Rule is intended to be applied rigidly, it is not supported by authority, and a more flexible approach has been preferred" in other cases.[18] This decision was cited with approval in *OJSC TNK-BP Holding v Beppler & Jacobson Ltd* with the court noting that the three sub-rules were not determinative if "the claim is much more closely connected" to the law of another country.[19]

C. CANADIAN LAW

In *Christopher v Zimmerman* the plaintiff brought a claim for a constructive trust over certain assets owned by the defendant, based on her contribution to those assets during a period of cohabitation.[20] Following *Pettkus v Becker* and other decisions of the Supreme Court of Canada,[21] such claims are part of the law of unjust enrichment in Canada, though they are not under English law. The court expressly characterized the claim as "one concerning unjust enrichment," though less usefully also as "a claim in equity."[22] The court then accepted, without any analysis or consideration of judicial authority, rule 230 of *Dicey, Morris and Collins*, finding that the case fit into clause 2(c) and required the application of the law of the place of enrichment.[23] In the result, the court remitted the issue of the applicable law to trial since the facts needed to apply this rule were not before it.

The narrow approach seen in *Christopher* has not been applied in the more recent cases. *Minera Aquiline Argentina SA v IMA Exploration*

---

17   *Ibid* at 566.
18   [2010] EWHC 3199 at para 161 (Comm).
19   [2012] EWHC 3286 at para 116 (Ch) [*OJSC TNK-BP Holding*].
20   (2000), 80 BCLR (3d) 229 (CA) [*Christopher*].
21   Above note 1. See also *Sorochan v Sorochan*, [1986] 2 SCR 38; *Peter v Beblow*, [1993] 1 SCR 980.
22   *Christopher*, above note 20 at paras 10 and 12.
23   *Ibid* at para 14. See also *Knowles v Lindstrom*, 2014 ONCA 116 at para 47, in which the two disputed properties were both in Ontario and the place of enrichment was Ontario.

Inc was a case about a claim for breach of confidence.[24] As explained earlier, that cause of action is not one in unjust enrichment: it is part of the law of equitable wrongs. However, the parties agreed that "a claim for breach of confidence is a restitutionary claim for unjust enrichment resulting from a breach of duty."[25] Accordingly, the court had to consider the choice of law rule for unjust enrichment. The court accepted the parties' position that "the choice of law rule for unjust enrichment claims is the 'proper law of the obligation.'"[26] It then analyzed rule 230 of *Dicey, Morris and Collins* in some detail. The court refused to resolve the issue simply by deciding whether, on the facts, the case was covered either by clause 2(a) or by clause 2(b). Instead, it indicated that "[t]he essential question to be answered in choosing the appropriate law to govern a claim is, 'what legal system has the closest and most real connection to the obligation?'"[27] This reflects an approach to choice of law that prioritizes clause 1 of rule 230 and downplays clause 2.

In *Minera Aquiline* the court held that a

> more principled approach ... would be to examine all the factors that could be relevant to the strength of the connection between the obligation and the competing legal systems. Such factors should be given weight according to a reasonable view of the evidence and their relative importance to the issues at stake.[28]

The court would weigh not only the connecting factors listed throughout clause 2 of rule 230 but also additional factors, such as the residence and place of business of the parties and the place where the parties had acted. In part the court adopted this approach because the case involved connections to both a pre-existing contractual relationship and to immovable property, giving rise to tension between clauses 2(a) and 2(b) of rule 230. In the result the court held that while the enrichment had occurred in Argentina, the weight of other connecting factors pointed to British Columbia law governing the claim.

In *Barrick Gold Corp v Goldcorp Inc* the court considered a claim to reverse unjust enrichment. It held that the choice of law rule was the proper law of the obligation. It referred to the sub-rules in rule 230 as the "traditional" rules for identifying the proper law. However, the court stated that

---

24 (2006), 58 BCLR (4th) 217 (SC), aff'd (2007), 68 BCLR (4th) 242 (CA) [*Minera Aquiline*].
25 *Ibid* at para 183 (SC).
26 *Ibid* at para 184.
27 *Ibid* at para 195.
28 *Ibid* at para 200.

in recent years, courts have determined which of these rules applies to any particular circumstances by taking a principled approach to the choice of law issue. The issue is decided by asking which legal system has the closest and most real connection to the obligation.[29]

As in *Minera Aquiline*, the court considered an open-ended series of factors. It concluded that Ontario law applied because it had the closest and most real connection to the unjust enrichment claim.

In addition to the few cases, one aspect of choice of law for unjust enrichment is covered at least in part by statute.[30] One way that a contract can fail is by it being frustrated, in that the expected performance becomes impossible. For example, a family rents a banquet hall for a reunion dinner but the hall burns down a week before the dinner. Under the law of contract, the frustrating event puts an end to the contract but does not render it void *ab initio*. This means that if the family has already paid for the rental, it has no claim in contract to recover the money: the loss lies where it fell. To recover the money at common law, the family has to look to the law of unjust enrichment.

However, some provinces have enacted legislation dealing with frustrated contracts. Section 3(1) of Ontario's *Frustrated Contracts Act*, for example, gives the family a right to recover the advance payment.[31] But this section does not apply to all such claims for recovery brought in Ontario. Section 2(1) provides: "This Act applies to any contract that is governed by the law of Ontario and that has become impossible of performance or been otherwise frustrated and the parties to which for that reason have been discharged." In other words, if the contract is governed by Ontario law, a plaintiff can invoke the rights under section 3(1) without further analysis of choice of law for unjust enrichment. If the contract is governed by some other law, the statute is silent as to what happens. The issue would have to be resolved using the common law choice of law rule for unjust enrichment. Moreover, if that rule found the claim was governed by Ontario law, the relevant content would be found in Ontario's common law for unjust enrichment, not in section 3(1).

British Columbia has adopted a different approach. Section 1(1) of its *Frustrated Contract Act* provides: "this Act applies to every contract (a) from which the parties to it are discharged by reason of the application of

---

29 2011 ONSC 3725 at paras 840–41.
30 On the view adopted here, these statutes are characterized as dealing with the law of unjust enrichment. An alternative approach is possible: they could be characterized as dealing with the law of contracts. On that view, it would be the choice of law rules for contract, not for unjust enrichment, that would determine when these statutes apply.
31 RSO 1990, c F.34.

the doctrine of frustration."[32] The statute goes on to set out substantive law for claims based on frustration of contract. These provisions will be applied whether the contract was governed by British Columbia law or another law. However, they can be applied only when the plaintiff's claim is governed by British Columbia law, which must be determined using the common law choice of law rule for unjust enrichment.

As indicated at the outset, it is difficult to definitively state the Canadian choice of law rule for unjust enrichment. The most recent cases appear to be rejecting a mechanical application of rule 230 and instead are using something much closer to a proper law rule, weighing various connecting factors without treating any of them as paramount.

D. OPTIONS FOR FORMULATING A RULE

As we have seen, the decided cases leave considerable scope for courts in the future to formulate a choice of law rule for unjust enrichment. In order to assess possible rules, evaluation criteria must be identified. To a certain extent these criteria are a matter of common sense. For example, a good rule is easy to understand and is not arbitrary or capricious. Beyond this, however, the identification of criteria has to start with the underlying theory of choice of law, developed in Chapter 10. The ultimate aim of choice of law rules is to achieve justice between the parties, to which the principle of proximity is central. A choice of law rule must therefore be assessed in terms of how well it implements the principle of proximity, such that the law with the closest connection to the dispute is applied.[33] In addition, a choice of law rule should (1) further the reasonable expectations of the parties, so that the applicable law is as they anticipated it would be; and (2) achieve uniformity of result across different jurisdictions, so that the same dispute uses the same applicable law regardless of where it is resolved.[34] Other important criteria are certainty, predictability, and ease of application.

Legal academics have proposed several different choice of law rules for unjust enrichment. These include rules using the law of the place of enrichment, the defendant's personal law, the law of the forum, and the law of a related contractual relationship. Some of these rules are

---

32 RSBC 1996, c 166.
33 Frank Vischer, "Connecting Factors" in Kurt Lipstein, ed, *International Encyclopedia of Comparative Law*, vol 3 (Tübingen, Germany: Mohr Siebeck, 1970) at 3.
34 AJE Jaffey, *Topics in Choice of Law* (London: British Institute of International and Comparative Law, 1996) at 17 and 23; Scott Fruehwald, "A Multilateralist Method of Choice of Law" (1996–97) 85 *Kentucky Law Journal* 347 at 370–71.

too rigid and specific and so fail to satisfy the above criteria. More elaborate proposals recognize the great difficulty in formulating a single-factor rule for all unjust enrichment claims. They instead advocate a proper law rule based on weighing connecting factors or a series of more specific sub-rules and flexible exceptions. Some of these rules are considered in more detail below.

1) The Law of a Related Contract

Many unjust enrichment claims arise as a consequence of contractual invalidity. For example, in *Kleinwort Benson Ltd v Glasgow City Council* the interest-rate-swap contracts between the bank and the council were *ultra vires* the council.[35] As a result, the contracts were void *ab initio*. In this situation, the bank, which had been the net payor to the council during the time the parties were complying with the contracts, brought an unjust enrichment claim to recover the money paid to the council. The law of contract held the contracts to be void but it did not address the consequences of the contractual invalidity. These consequences were, instead, addressed by the law of unjust enrichment.

Because unjust enrichment claims often follow contractual invalidity, many choice of law commentators have proposed that those unjust enrichment claims should be governed by the same law that governed the invalid contract. The arguments in support focus on convenience, the links between contract and unjust enrichment within a legal system, and the expectations of the parties.

First, some commentators argue that it is more convenient to have all of the issues that arise from a contractual relationship governed by one law. They argue that in cases involving a contract the court has to determine and apply the law applicable to the contract in any event. A separate choice of law rule for unjust enrichment complicates matters.[36] This argument is true but it does not prove very much. Surely it would be convenient, in the same sense, to have all legal issues in a particular case governed by the same applicable law, determined by one overarching choice of law rule. However, this is at odds with the fundamental approach in choice of law to focus on particular issues.

Second, an argument in favour of using the law of the contract is that the legal rules that resolve issues of whether a contract is valid or not, found in the law of contract, and the legal rules that address the consequences of contractual invalidity, found in the law of unjust

---

35 [1999] 1 AC 153 (HL).
36 Joanna Bird, "Choice of Law" in Francis Rose, ed, *Restitution and the Conflict of Laws* (Oxford: Mansfield Press, 1995) at 122–23.

enrichment, are, within a domestic system of law, interdependent, working and evolving in tandem. To fragment the choice of law issues, such that one system of law governs the contractual issues and another governs the unjust enrichment issues, ignores this interdependence.[37] There is merit to this point, but it should not be taken too far. There is tension between the idea of interdependence, on the one hand, and the perceived hard-won recognition of unjust enrichment as a separate part of the law of obligations on the other hand. For many years, the law of unjust enrichment was treated as an offshoot of the law of contract. Part of the relatively recent emergence of unjust enrichment as a separate branch of the law of obligations has involved considerable criticism of that historic treatment, which perpetuated legal fictions and caused inconsistency in the decided cases.[38] As a result, modern attempts to link aspects of contract and unjust enrichment have been met with suspicion from some academic and judicial quarters.

A further problem with the internal balance argument is its speculative nature. It is not immediately clear how this balance is identified or analyzed and there is a dearth of concrete examples to illustrate the point. In addition, the idea of a united solution has not been adopted in other areas of the law, such as the treatment of tortious and proprietary issues in the context of a contractual dispute. The prevailing approach to choice of law instead accepts that separate issues can be characterized as such and resolved using independent choice of law rules.

Third, one of the strongest arguments in favour of using the law of the contract is based on the reasonable expectations of the parties. The parties may have expressly indicated that a contract is to be governed by a particular law, usually through a choice of law clause. Having done so, the parties have an expectation that most, if not all,[39] issues relating to the contract will be resolved by that law. On the other hand, where the parties do not choose an applicable law, they may be completely unaware of the notion of choice of law in contract and expect a court to apply the law of the forum. Once this misconception is dispelled, however, their expectation may be that the applicable law, however identified, will govern most, if not all, issues. In either case, they are likely

---

37 Ibid at 123; Peter Brereton, "Restitution and Contract" in Rose, ibid at 146.
38 Mitchell McInnes, *The Canadian Law of Unjust Enrichment and Restitution* (Markham, ON: LexisNexis Canada, 2014) at 57–59; Charles Mitchell, Paul Mitchell, & Stephen Watterson, eds, *Goff & Jones: The Law of Unjust Enrichment*, 8th ed (London: Sweet & Maxwell, 2011) at 5–6; Peter Birks, *An Introduction to the Law of Restitution* (Oxford: Clarendon Press, 1989) at 34–39.
39 Not all, because they may appreciate the impact of mandatory rules of another system of law, such as the forum, which will govern some issues regardless of the choice of law.

to be unaware of the distinction drawn by the common law between contract and unjust enrichment and will instead see all issues, including those following contractual invalidity, as matters of contract.[40]

There are some difficulties with this argument. There may be cases in which the parties are sophisticated enough to understand the distinction between contractual issues and issues following contractual invalidity. In such cases, if those parties have not framed their choice of law clause to cover unjust enrichment claims, it may be incorrect to assume that they intend the chosen law to govern such issues. They may be content to leave them to be resolved by recourse to the relevant choice of law rules. There is even less reason to link the two choice of law rules where sophisticated parties have not made an express choice. In such a case, there is less indication that the parties are relying in some way on the law of the contract to govern unjust enrichment issues. Further, in the absence of an express choice, even unsophisticated parties, unaware of the distinction between contract and unjust enrichment, may not rely to any significant extent on a linkage between the two choice of law rules. In other words, they encounter the issue after the fact, in legal proceedings, at a time when there is no expectation interest to be protected. Accordingly, while the reliance aspect is important, such that it may be near-determinative in some cases, there will be other cases in which it is much less important and in which the law of the contract should not necessarily be applied.

There are other situations in which using the law of the contract may be undesirable. Contractual invalidity may flow from the application of a law other than the law applicable to the contract, such as the law of the place of performance or a mandatory rule of the forum. It is hard to accept that the unjust enrichment claim should always be governed by the law of the contract and never by that other law. There are also cases in which the contractual invalidity results from duress or as a result of a fundamental mistake or pre-contractual misrepresentation. Such contracts can be declared void, since there has been no true meeting of the minds. In these cases, it is highly questionable whether the parties can be said to have intended the applicable law of the contract, expressly chosen or not, to govern the consequences of invalidity.[41]

On the foregoing analysis, the arguments in favour of applying the law of a relevant contract are not conclusive. Nonetheless, taken together, these arguments are reasonably persuasive, more so than the arguments for any other connecting factor in unjust enrichment cases

---

40 Brereton, above note 37 at 144–45 and 156–57; Bird, above note 36 at 123–24.
41 See the analysis in *Baring Brothers v Cunninghame District Council*, [1997] CLC 108 (Scotland Court of Session: Outer House).

involving contractual invalidity. They suggest that there is a considerable likelihood that the law of the contract will have the closest and most real connection with the unjust enrichment claim.

2) The Law of the Place of Enrichment

There is considerable academic support for this sub-rule but it is also highly controversial. It is certainly not a new rule.[42] Historically, one of the central arguments in favour of using the place of a specific event was the vested rights theory.[43] The one-time prevalence of this theory is perhaps the main reason for the extent of academic support for a rule based on the *lex loci*. However, the vested rights theory has been discredited, with the consequence that choice of law rules based on the *lex loci* have to look elsewhere for support and justification.

Advocates of the *lex loci* argue that the place of a specific event identifies the legal system that is most closely connected with the obligation to make restitution.[44] However, in some situations the place of a specific event will be entirely fortuitous. This can be the case with the place of enrichment, for example, when funds are deposited electronically into a bank account in a remote country. In this age of wire transfers and electronic banking it is easy to envisage situations in which the place of enrichment is far removed from the other relevant facts surrounding the claim.

Two further arguments can be raised against using the *lex loci*. The first is the considerable artificiality of having to choose, in formulating the rule, between specific events of relatively equal importance. What if the place of the act that leads to the enrichment is different from the place where the enrichment occurs? Some commentators claim that the "decisive criterion" of unjust enrichment is the effect of the act, not the act itself.[45] However, this distinction is difficult to accept. In unjust enrichment, a successful claim requires the identification of both an act and a result. To elevate one aspect over the other is more semantics than logic. Both are relevant, and where each occurs in a different country, a rule based on the *lex loci* is therefore forced to make an invidious choice between relevant elements.

---

42 American Law Institute, *Restatement of the Law of Conflict of Laws* (St Paul, MN: American Law Institute, 1934) at §§ 452–53.
43 See Chapter 10.
44 HC Gutteridge & Kurt Lipstein, "Conflicts of Law in Matters of Unjustifiable Enrichment" [1939] *Cambridge Law Journal* 80 at 90.
45 Konrad Zweigert & Dierk Muller-Gindullis, "Quasi-contracts" in *International Encyclopedia of Comparative Law*, vol 3, above note 33 at 7.

Second, a rule based on the *lex loci* is fraught with the difficulty, already well-known in choice of law for tort, of having to identify the place of the specific event.[46] The enrichment could occur on the high seas or in the air. Advocates of the *lex loci* often praise its simplicity and certainty, but, as in tort cases, the place of an enrichment can be difficult to identify so that the certainty is illusory.[47] Further, the more difficult it is, on the facts, to establish the place where an event happened, the less likely the law of that place will *prima facie* have the best connection to the dispute.

Ultimately, in too many cases the place of enrichment will be a relatively weak connecting factor. It will certainly be weaker in some cases than other competing connecting factors, such as the law of a related contract. Accordingly, the *lex loci* should not be used as a rigid choice of law rule for unjust enrichment. Indeed, its weaknesses are such that it is debatable whether it should even be used as a catch-all within a more detailed hierarchical rule, such as rule 230 of *Dicey, Morris and Collins*.

3) The Proper Law

This approach is modelled on the common law choice of law rule for contract, which provides that in the absence of an express or implied choice of law by the parties, the contract is to be governed by the legal system with which it has its closest and most real connection.[48] The approach is not confined to contract and there have been advocates of a proper law approach to tort and to marriage.[49] The analogy in the context of choice of law for unjust enrichment is that the proper law of the obligation to reverse an unjust enrichment is the system of law with which that obligation has its closest and most real connection.

Under the proper law approach many of the connecting factors discussed in earlier sections of this chapter are considered as relevant indicators of the applicable law and they are weighed against each other. This allows assessment of the personal law of the parties, the *lex loci*, the *lex situs*, and the law of a relevant relationship such as a contract. None is determinative but none is pre-emptively rejected as

---

46 See James Blaikie, "Unjust Enrichment in the Conflict of Laws" [1984] *Juridical Review* 112 at 120; Panagopoulos, above note 7 at 138–40.
47 James Audley McLaughlin, "Conflict of Laws: The Choice of Law *Lex Loci* Doctrine, the Beguiling Appeal of a Dead Tradition, Part One" (1991) 93 *West Virginia Law Review* 957 at 958–60 and 964.
48 See Chapter 14.
49 For tort, the leading article is JHC Morris, "The Proper Law of the Tort" (1951) 64 *Harvard Law Review* 881. For marriage, see Richard Fentiman, "The Validity of Marriage and the Proper Law" [1985] *Cambridge Law Journal* 256.

irrelevant. Further, one benefit of a proper law approach is that the court can consider the law applicable to a relevant contract in different ways. For example, it can consider both the proper law of the contract, objectively determined, and any express choice of law made by the parties.

The most important advantage of a proper law rule is its flexibility. It allows the court to engage in an open-ended inquiry, assessing the strengths and weaknesses of territorial connections that happen to be present in a given case. A proper law approach is able to handle the considerable variety of cases that form part of the law of unjust enrichment. It avoids the need to divide unjust enrichment claims into specific factual contexts, such as those involving an invalid contract or immovable property, thereby avoiding overlap difficulties where a claim could fit more than one category. This is particularly important for a choice of law rule for unjust enrichment since the parameters of this emerging area of the law are still being developed.

There are, of course, traditional concerns about a proper law rule. Such a rule might be too vague to offer meaningful guidance to litigants and judges. The applicable law can be harder to predict, with room for different judges to reach different answers on the same facts, so litigation is riskier. A proper law rule can work well in complex cases like *AMF*, with many factual connections to be weighed. It can present more difficulties in simple cases, such as those with only three significant factual connections—the residence of the plaintiff, the residence of the defendant, and the place of the enrichment.

A proper law rule mitigates against the rigidity in other types of rules. Another way that this can be achieved is by using a rule and exception approach. In such an approach, the rule or sub-rules are only presumptions, subject to be displaced by a flexible exception. There are similarities between this approach and the proper law rule, especially if the presumptions are relatively easy to displace. In recent years rebuttable presumptions and flexible exceptions have become increasingly common within choice of law for contract and tort, especially in English law. This trend could provide a parallel for developments in choice of law for unjust enrichment.

E. COMPARATIVE LAW SOURCES

In light of the lack of an established choice of law rule for unjust enrichment in the common law, there is some value in considering the rules that have been developed in other jurisdictions.

1) European Union

The European Union spent several years formulating a choice of law rule for unjust enrichment. It did so as part of the drafting of the regulation on the law applicable to non-contractual obligations, known as the Rome II Regulation.[50] In January 2009, the domestic choice of law rule for unjust enrichment in member states across Europe, including common law countries such as the United Kingdom and Ireland, was replaced by article 10 of Rome II.

Article 10 is organized into three hierarchical, rigid sub-rules and then allows a flexible exception for each of those rules. If the unjust enrichment claim both (1) arises in the context of a pre-existing relationship between the parties, and (2) is closely connected to that relationship, then the applicable law is that of the relationship. By way of example, paragraph 1 provides that the relationship can be in contract or in tort. If paragraph 1 does not apply, and if both the plaintiff and the defendant have the same country of habitual residence at the time of the event giving rise to the unjust enrichment, then the applicable law is the law of that country. If neither paragraph 1 nor paragraph 2 applies, the applicable law is the law of the place of enrichment. Given the specificity of the first two rules, this is the fall-back or default rule. Finally, paragraph 4 provides that if, from "all the circumstances of the case," it is clear that the unjust enrichment claim is "manifestly more closely connected" with a country other than the one indicated by paragraphs 1 to 3, the applicable law is the law of that other country.[51]

One of the advantages of article 10 is that it imposes a clear rule in place of the vague jurisprudence that previously comprised the rule in the common law countries of Europe. It is now considerably easier to identify and state the rule. Paragraph 1 is highly defensible in light of the fact that many unjust enrichment claims arise in the context of an underlying contractual relationship. Paragraph 2 is unusual, as common law choice of law rules for obligations tend not to accord any particular priority to a common habitual residence. Paragraph 3 is the most disappointing, given the considerable criticisms that have been levelled against elevating the place of the enrichment to any sort of rule. The most important aspect of article 10 is the flexible exception. As noted

---

50 EC, *Commission Regulation (EC) No. 864/2007 of 11 July 2007 on the law applicable to non-contractual obligations*, [2007] OJ, L 199/40 [Rome II].
51 For more detail on art 10, see Stephen GA Pitel, "Rome II and Choice of Law for Unjust Enrichment" in John Ahern & William Binchy, eds, *The Rome II Regulation on the Law Applicable to Non-contractual Obligations* (Leiden: Martinus Nijhoff, 2009).

earlier, the more easily it can be triggered, the more the rule becomes like a proper law rule. The more difficult it is to trigger, the more rigid the sub-rules in the first three paragraphs become. This raises classic considerations of the need to balance certainty and predictability against flexibility and the principle of proximity. It will be important to consider how European courts interpret the exception.[52]

2) American Law Institute

As a document created by a team of scholars, the American Law Institute's *Restatement of the Law (Second), Conflict of Laws* is not legally binding.[53] However, its various choice of law rules have been adopted by many American courts, making it one of the more influential sources for comparative law purposes. Its choice of law rule for unjust enrichment provides:

> *221. Restitution*
>
> (1) In actions for restitution, the rights and liabilities of the parties with respect to the particular issue are determined by the local law of the state which, with respect to that issue, has the most significant relationship to the occurrence and the parties under the principles stated in § 6.
>
> (2) Contacts to be taken into account in applying the principles of § 6 to determine the law applicable to an issue include:
> (a) the place where a relationship between the parties was centered, provided that the receipt of enrichment was substantially related to the relationship,
> (b) the place where the benefit or enrichment was received,
> (c) the place where the act conferring the benefit or enrichment was done,
> (d) the domicile, residence, nationality, place of incorporation and place of business of the parties, and
> (e) the place where a physical thing, such as land or a chattel, which was substantially related to the enrichment, was situated at the time of the enrichment.
>
> These contacts are to be evaluated according to their relative importance with respect to the particular issue.

---

52 In *OJSC TNK-BP Holding*, above note 19 at para 103.3, the court relied on the flexible exception and downplayed the importance of the place of enrichment.
53 American Law Institute, *Restatement of the Law (Second), Conflict of Laws 2d* (St Paul, MN: American Law Institute, 1971).

Several important points can be made about this rule. First, while phrased in part as about restitution, it is a rule dealing with claims in unjust enrichment. Second, it is a true proper law rule, in that the contacts listed in clause 2 are not hierarchical or mandatory or exclusive. It is therefore highly flexible, though this makes it open to complaints that it is insufficiently predictable. Third, while using a traditional choice of law method (as described in Chapter 10), it also involves a uniquely American element, namely, interest analysis, which is included through the reference to the principles in section 6.

FURTHER READINGS

BIRD, JOANNA. "Choice of Law and Restitution of Benefits Conferred under a Void Contract" [1997] *Lloyd's Maritime and Commercial Law Quarterly* 182.

CHONG, ADELINE. "Choice of Law for Unjust Enrichment/Restitution and the Rome II Regulation" (2008) 57 *International and Comparative Law Quarterly* 863.

DICKENSON, ANDREW. *The Rome II Regulation: The Law Applicable to Non-contractual Obligations* (Oxford: Oxford University Press, 2008).

HAY, PETER. "Unjust Enrichment in the Conflict of Laws: A Comparative View of German Law and the *American Restatement 2d*" (1977) 26 *American Journal of Comparative Law* 1.

LESLIE, ROBERT. "Unjustified Enrichment in the Conflict of Laws" (1998) 2 *Edinburgh Law Review* 233.

PITEL, STEPHEN GA. "Choice of Law for Unjust Enrichment: Rome II and the Common Law" [2008] *Nederlands Internationaal Privaatrecht* 456.

STEVENS, ROBERT. "The Choice of Law Rules of Restitutionary Obligations" in Francis Rose, ed, *Restitution and the Conflict of Laws* (Oxford: Mansfield Press, 1995).

CHAPTER 16

NATURE AND *SITUS* OF PROPERTY

A. DISTINCTION BETWEEN MOVABLE PROPERTY AND IMMOVABLE PROPERTY

For the purposes of private international law, common law courts draw a distinction between movable and immovable property rather than using the distinction, drawn for domestic purposes, between personal property and real property. Thus in *Macdonald v Macdonald*, Lord Tomlin said:

> The English law classifies property as real property or personal property. The terms moveable and immoveable are not technical terms in English law when it is not regarding the law of a foreign country. The Scots law distinguishes between property which is heritable and property which is moveable, and, except to this extent, does not any more than the English law recognize for internal purposes the antithesis between moveable and immoveable. But each system, when brought into contact with a foreign system, does, in accordance with the principles of what is called private international law, recognize the antithesis for the purpose of applying the rule of comity that, in matters of succession, moveables devolve according to the law of the domicile of the deceased and immoveables devolve according to the *lex rei sitae*.[1]

---

1 [1932] SC 79 at 84 (HL).

As this quotation indicates, this distinction is particularly important in the context of succession because of the general choice of law rule that succession to movable property is governed by the law of the deceased's domicile and succession to immovable property is governed by the law of the *situs* of the land.² Occasionally, some judges have suggested that the distinction between real property and personal property should continue to be employed where the conflict is with another jurisdiction that also uses that distinction. In *Re Hoyles*, for example, a case in which the conflict was between England and Ontario, Farwell LJ asserted:

> in both England and Ontario the division is into real and personal property. The division into movable and immovable is only called into operation here when the English courts have to determine rights between domiciled Englishmen and persons domiciled in countries which do not adopt our division into real and personal property. In such cases, out of international comity and in order to arrive at a common basis on which to determine questions between the inhabitants of two countries living under different systems of jurisprudence, our courts recognize and act on a division otherwise unknown to our law into movable and immovable. But when there is no such difficulty there is no ground for attempting any such division.³

There is also some Canadian support for this view,⁴ but it is not widespread.

It is clear that the law of the *situs* is used to characterize an asset as movable or immovable. The leading English decision is *Re Berchtold*.⁵ In that case, a count died intestate domiciled in Hungary. At the time of his death, he was entitled to an interest in English land held on a trust for sale, but not yet sold. The question arose as to whether the deceased's interest in the English land should pass to those entitled under Hungarian law or to those entitled under English law. Despite the fact that English law, under the doctrine of conversion, would regard the count's interest as personal property for domestic purposes, it would view the interest as an immovable for the purpose of the conflict of laws. The court applied the English characterization since England was the *situs* of the property. As a result, those entitled under English law succeeded in their claim. The Saskatchewan Court of King's Bench followed *Re Berchtold* in *Re Burke*.⁶ In that case the court concluded that

---

2   See Chapter 19.
3   [1911] 1 Ch 179 at 185 (CA).
4   *Re Hole*, [1948] 4 DLR 419 (Man KB).
5   [1923] 1 Ch 192.
6   [1928] 1 DLR 318 (Sask KB).

a vendor's interest in land in Saskatchewan, subject to an agreement for sale, was by Saskatchewan law an immovable and hence its devolution on an intestacy was governed by Saskatchewan law despite the fact that the deceased had died domiciled in Washington State.

The decision of the Saskatchewan Court of Appeal in *Hogg v Provincial Tax Commission* furnishes a useful illustration of the applicable principles.[7] The Saskatchewan Provincial Tax Commission was attempting to levy succession duty on the beneficiaries of an estate that consisted of thirty-seven mortgages charged on lands in British Columbia. The deceased had died domiciled in Saskatchewan. The right to levy the duty depended on whether the claim of the beneficiaries to the mortgages was based upon a devolution under the law of Saskatchewan. In turn, that question hinged upon whether the mortgages were to be classified as movables or immovables. If they were movables, they would devolve on the beneficiaries under Saskatchewan law as the law of the deceased's last domicile, whereas if they were immovables they would devolve in accordance with British Columbia law as the *lex situs*.

The court applied British Columbia law as the *lex situs* to characterize the mortgages. On the basis of expert testimony, the court concluded that the mortgages were immovables even though, for domestic purposes, they would be characterized as personal property. Thus, the proper law of succession was British Columbia law as the *lex situs* and the mortgages did not devolve upon the beneficiaries under the law of Saskatchewan for the purposes of Saskatchewan's succession duties. Justice MacKenzie did make the point, however, that when it came time to distribute the assets in accordance with British Columbia law the court would have to take account of the common law distinction between real property and personal property. The mortgages would devolve as personal property rather than as real property. For this proposition, the court followed *Duncan v Lawson*, which concerned the intestate succession to leaseholds in England that belonged to a domiciled Scotsman.[8] The leaseholds were characterized as immovables by English law as the *lex situs*. English law therefore governed succession to them. On the question of distribution, however, the leaseholds went to those entitled to them as personal estate, rather than realty, by English law because English domestic law classified leaseholds as personal property.

Where the *situs* of the property is a Canadian common law jurisdiction, then, as a general proposition, all interests in, and charges over, land are classified as immovables even though, for domestic purposes,

---

7 [1941] 4 DLR 501 (Sask CA) [*Hogg*].
8 (1889), 41 Ch D 394 [*Duncan*].

some would be characterized as personal property. Thus, as we have seen, immovables include leasehold interests in land,[9] a mortgagee's interest in land (including the right to payment of the debt),[10] land that is the subject of a trust for sale,[11] and an unpaid vendor's interest in land.[12] Mineral rights in land are also characterized as immovables.[13] Because certain kinds of property, such as patents and trademarks, are formally registered and valid only for a particular jurisdiction, it can be suggested that these are forms of immovable property. All property that is not characterized as immovable is movable. Thus, movable property includes not just chattels and interests in them but what are described as intangible movables such as debts, negotiable instruments, and shares.

B. *SITUS* OF PROPERTY

The *situs* of property[14] is important from a choice of law perspective.[15] It is also relevant for other purposes such as the administration of estates. Immovables are situated where the land is situated and chattels (tangible movables) are situated where they are physically located.[16] The major difficulty in determining *situs* relates to choses in action (intangible movables) because they have no obvious location. The general rule is said to be that choses in action "generally are situate in the country where they are properly recoverable or can be enforced."[17]

Thus, simple debts are regarded as situated where the debtor resides since that is the place where the creditor typically can enforce payment.[18] Specialties, on the other hand, are held to be situated where the deed is situated,[19] the sealed document itself being regarded as a

---

9 See, for example, *Duncan*, ibid.
10 See, for example, *Hogg*, above note 7.
11 See, for example, *Re Berchtold*, above note 5.
12 See, for example, *Re Burke*, above note 6. Contrast *Re Hole*, above note 4.
13 See, for example, *Minera Aquiline Argentina SA v IMA Exploration Inc* (2007), 68 BCLR (4th) 242 (CA).
14 See Lawrence Collins, ed, *Dicey, Morris and Collins on the Conflict of Laws*, 15th ed (London: Sweet & Maxwell, 2012) at paras 22-024 to 22-056 [*Dicey, Morris and Collins*].
15 See Chapter 17 on immovable property and Chapter 18 on movable property.
16 The *situs* of the property is determined by the law of the forum: see *Royal Bank of Canada v Cow Harbour Construction Ltd*, 2012 ABQB 112 at para 62.
17 *Dicey, Morris and Collins*, above note 14, rule 129(1).
18 *McDiarmid Lumber Ltd v God's Lake First Nation* (2005), 251 DLR (4th) 93 (Man CA), aff'd [2006] 2 SCR 846.
19 *Re Hole*, above note 4.

form of tangible movable. The same is true of negotiable instruments and other securities transferable by delivery, with or without an endorsement. These are situated where the document representing the security is located.[20]

The courts have encountered particular difficulties in isolating the *situs* of shares in a corporation. Part of the problem stems from the fact that the test seems to vary with the purpose for which the *situs* is being established. It also appears that the *lex situs* is sometimes used simply as an expression, like proper law, for the governing law whatever that law might be. Certainly the traditional rule is that shares are situated where the appropriate share register is maintained.[21] The English Court of Appeal considered the question of the *situs* of shares in some detail in *Macmillan Inc v Bishopsgate Investment Trust Plc (No 3)*.[22] Lord Justice Auld applied the traditional rule by indicating that the *situs* of shares would "normally be the country where the register [was] kept, usually but not always the country of incorporation."[23] In contrast, Aldous LJ favoured the place of the company's incorporation.[24] In that regard, he applied the reasoning of the Exchequer Court of Canada in *Braun v The Custodian* where Thorson J had said:

> It is, I think, a sound rule of law that the situs of shares of a company for the purpose of determining a dispute as to their ownership is in the territory of incorporation of the company, for that is where the court has jurisdiction over the company in accordance with the law of its domicile and power to order a rectification of its register, where such rectification may be necessary, and to enforce such order by a personal decree against it.[25]

The third judge, Staughton LJ, did not reach a definitive conclusion. He indicated that the *lex situs* would ordinarily be "the law of the place where the company [was] incorporated" but that there might "be cases where it [was] arguably the law of the place where the share register [was] kept."[26]

In the current global economy there is often no direct relationship between the company issuing the shares and the individual investor or shareholder. Instead, shares and other securities are held by investors

---

20 See, for example, *Provincial Treasurer of Manitoba v Bennett*, [1937] SCR 138.
21 *Brassard v Smith*, [1925] AC 371 (PC).
22 [1996] 1 WLR 387 (CA) [*Macmillan*].
23 *Ibid* at 411.
24 *Ibid* at 421.
25 [1944] Ex CR 30 at 47, aff'd [1944] SCR 339.
26 *Macmillan*, above note 22 at 405.

in an indirect holding system in which there is no direct connection between the investor and the issuer. An investor's rights in shares are held in accounts of financial intermediaries and are transferred as easily as the transfer of money from one bank account to another. In such circumstances, the concept of *situs* is almost meaningless. This question is discussed further in Chapter 18.

FURTHER READINGS

CARRUTHERS, JANEEN. *The Transfer of Property in the Conflict of Laws* (Oxford: Oxford University Press, 2005).

COOK, WALTER WHEELER. *The Logical and Legal Bases of the Conflict of Laws* (Cambridge: Harvard University Press, 1942) ch 11 & 12.

FALCONBRIDGE, JOHN. *Essays on the Conflict of Laws*, 2d ed (Toronto: Canada Law Book, 1954) ch 20.

OOI, MAISIE. *Shares and Other Securities in the Conflict of Laws* (Oxford: Oxford University Press, 2003).

ROGERSON, PIPPA. "The *Situs* of Debts in the Conflict of Laws: Illogical, Unnecessary and Misleading" [1990] *Cambridge Law Journal* 441.

CHAPTER 17

IMMOVABLE PROPERTY

A. JURISDICTION OVER FOREIGN IMMOVABLE PROPERTY

1) The General Rule

The general rule, invariably sourced to the decision of the House of Lords in *British South Africa Co v Companhia de Moçambique* and thus known as the *Moçambique* rule, is that a Canadian court has no jurisdiction to determine title to, or the right to possession of, immovable property situated outside the forum.[1] In *Tezcan v Tezcan*, McLachlin JA expressed the rule in the following manner:

> The general rule is that the courts of a country have no jurisdiction to adjudicate on the right and title to lands not situate within its borders. Only the courts of the jurisdiction in which the lands are situate may adjudicate on the right and title to such lands . . . .[2]

The rationale underlying the rule is that a court should not grant a judgment which it has no power to enforce and which may bring the court into conflict with the authority of a foreign sovereign or the jurisdiction

---

1 [1893] AC 602 (HL) [*Moçambique*]. See also *Lucasfilm Ltd v Ainsworth*, [2011] UKSC 39 at para 55 [*Lucasfilm*].
2 (1987), 20 BCLR (2d) 253 at 256 (CA). For a recent application, see *Moradkhan v Mofidi*, 2013 BCCA 132 at para 52.

of a foreign court.³ It is also clear that a foreign court includes one sitting in another part of Canada and that foreign land therefore includes land situated in another part of Canada. In *Montagne Laramee Developments Inc v Creit Properties Inc*,⁴ which concerned an action in Ontario in respect of land in Quebec, Pitt J indicated that the doctrine in *Morguard Investments Ltd v De Savoye*⁵ had not changed that conclusion. He stated:

> Notwithstanding the comment in *Morguard* . . . *per* La Forest J., that "the obvious intention of the constitution is to create a single country," it is still true that the provinces are all separate legal jurisdictions, and the province of Quebec with its civil code *may* even require more deference in circumstances of this nature.⁶

One interesting question concerns the relationship between this rule and the modern real and substantial connection test for jurisdiction *in personam* first established in *Morguard*. In *Khan Resources Inc v WM Mining Co, LLC* the Ontario Court of Appeal seemed to view the rule more as an important factor to be considered within the real and substantial connection test than as an independent ground for denying jurisdiction.⁷ The court was concerned by the fact that, in accordance with the rule of private international law denying jurisdiction over foreign land, "the unchallenged expert evidence in the record [was] to the effect that [the foreign] court would not recognize an Ontario judgment that purported to deal with [certain foreign] mining interests."⁸ The apparent incorporation of the foreign immovable rule within the *Morguard* test raised the question of whether, over time, the rule would cease to operate independently. This would not have been a welcome development.

The foreign immovable rule applies regardless of the basis on which jurisdiction purports to be taken. Subsuming it under the real and substantial connection test could have caused courts to lose sight of its broader relevance. In addition, incorporating it into the test suggests that it becomes just another factor in the analysis, so that the weight of other factors could have led a court to take jurisdiction in a dispute over a foreign immovable. This would have been contrary to the rule

---

3   *Duke v Andler*, [1932] SCR 734 at 739 [*Duke*], relying upon Arthur Berriedale Keith, ed, *Dicey on the Conflict of Laws*, 4th ed (London: Stevens & Sons, 1927) at 393.
4   (2000), 47 OR (3d) 729 (SCJ).
5   [1990] 3 SCR 1077 [*Morguard*]. See the discussion in Chapter 5.
6   Above note 4 at para 10 [emphasis in original].
7   (2006), 79 OR (3d) 411 at para 10 (CA) [*Khan Resources*]. See also *War Eagle Mining Co v Robo Management Co*, (1995), 13 BCLR (3d) 362 at para 14 (SC); *Precious Metal Capital Corp v Smith* (2008), 297 DLR (4th) 746 (Ont CA) [*Precious Metal*].
8   *Khan Resources*, above note 7 at para 15.

as it currently operates. More recently, the Supreme Court of Canada has in *Club Resorts Ltd v Van Breda* rejected the use of the real and substantial connection test as a direct test for taking jurisdiction, requiring instead the identification of a presumptive connecting factor.⁹ This new approach makes it much less likely that the rule relating to foreign immovable property will become conflated, intentionally or otherwise, with the approach for taking jurisdiction in service *ex juris* cases.

In setting out rules for the taking of jurisdiction, the *Court Jurisdiction and Proceedings Transfer Act* does not mention the foreign immovable rule. While not entirely free from doubt, the rule very likely continues to operate alongside that statutory scheme on the basis that the rule is one of subject matter jurisdiction rather than territorial jurisdiction and so is unaffected by the statute.¹⁰

If registered rights such as patents and trademarks are characterized as immovable property, the *Moçambique* rule would preclude a court from taking jurisdiction over a dispute about the ownership or validity of a foreign patent or trademark.¹¹

2) Tortious Damage to Foreign Immovable Property

More controversially, the foreign immovable rule denies a court's jurisdiction to hear an action for damages for trespass to foreign land even where the court has jurisdiction over the parties. It is in this context that there is the greatest likelihood of change in light of the *Morguard* principle. The starting point for this line of authority is the decision in *Moçambique*.¹² In Canada, the doctrine was soon extended beyond trespass to the tort of negligence.¹³

In *Moçambique*, there was a disputed claim to the title to the foreign land in question. Thus, an argument can be made that the rule should apply only in those circumstances. However, the majority of the New Brunswick Court of Appeal rejected that argument in *Albert*

---

9   2012 SCC 17 [*Club Resorts*]. See the discussion in Chapter 5.
10 For discussion, see Vaughan Black, Stephen GA Pitel, & Michael Sobkin, *Statutory Jurisdiction: An Analysis of the Court Jurisdiction and Proceedings Transfer Act* (Toronto: Carswell, 2012) at 46–48.
11 But not, perhaps, over a dispute about the infringement of a foreign patent or trademark: see *Lucasfilm*, above note 1 at paras 102–11. This would depend on the breadth of the rule, discussed in the next section. For a contrary, broader view, see *Aram Systems Ltd v NovAtel Inc*, 2008 ABQB 441, aff'd 2009 ABCA 262, in which the Alberta courts determined, with minimal analysis of the jurisdiction issue, the validity of an American patent.
12 Above note 1. See also *Lucasfilm*, above note 1 at para 55.
13 *Brereton v Canadian Pacific Railway Co* (1898), 29 OR 57 (HCJ) [*Brereton*].

v *Fraser Companies Ltd*.¹⁴ In that case, both parties were residents of New Brunswick. The plaintiff owned land just across the border in Quebec. She alleged that the defendant had negligently and wrongfully obstructed the flow of water from Quebec to New Brunswick with the result that her Quebec land had been flooded. She sought both damages and an injunction to restrain the defendant's wrongful activity in New Brunswick. On the basis of *Moçambique*, the majority held that the New Brunswick courts had no jurisdiction to entertain either claim even in a case where title to the land was not in dispute between the parties. Chief Justice Baxter said:

> it is ... too late in the day to contend that an action founded on trespass to realty in a foreign country whether the title does or does not come into the question, can be tried here. The Province of Quebec is, of course, for the purpose of this case, a foreign country.¹⁵

In a vigorous dissent, Harrison J made some excellent points. While he agreed that New Brunswick could not directly determine title to, or the right to possession of, land situated in Quebec, the rationale underlying that principle did not apply to an action for damages in tort, at least where title was not genuinely in dispute between the parties. The result of the majority's decision was that the plaintiff would be compelled to bring her action in Quebec and would then require any judgment to be enforced in New Brunswick where the defendant carried on business. Moreover, her claim for an injunction was directed at activities in New Brunswick rather than Quebec and, indeed, could be enforced only by the courts of New Brunswick. The judge also suggested that the *Moçambique* principle was inapplicable to wrongs committed in one Canadian province causing damage to land in another Canadian province. Justice Harrison considered that, when formulating its judgment, the House of Lords had simply not had this special situation in mind.

The House of Lords reconsidered the breadth of the *Moçambique* rule in *Hesperides Hotels Ltd v Muftizade*.¹⁶ The case concerned an action for damages for trespass to two hotels in Cyprus. The plaintiffs were two companies owned and controlled by Greek Cypriots and their claims arose out of the invasion of Northern Cyprus by Turkish forces in 1974. In the Court of Appeal, Lord Denning MR had pointed out that in *Moçambique* there had been a disputed claim of title to foreign land and he had indicated that the rule "should not be extended to cases where

---

14 [1937] 1 DLR 39 (NBSCAD).
15 *Ibid* at 46.
16 [1979] AC 508 (HL) [*Hesperides Hotels*].

no issue as to title [was] raised or [could] genuinely be raised."[17] However, the House of Lords held that there was nothing in *Moçambique* to justify the proposition that the rule enunciated there was restricted to cases of disputed title. The House of Lords also gave short shrift to the plaintiffs' argument that their claim was based on a conspiracy to trespass, rather than on the trespass itself, and that the English courts had jurisdiction because the conspiracy had been hatched in England. In rejecting that argument, Lord Wilberforce adopted the reasoning of Scarman LJ in the Court of Appeal.[18] Lord Justice Scarman had stated:

> the reliance upon the alleged conspiracy as distinct from the alleged trespass which it is intended to effect is wrong in principle. The combination or agreement, which is said to constitute (with overt acts and ensuing damage) the tort of conspiracy, is unlawful only if there be the intention to effect a trespass upon foreign land. Unless that be shown, there is nothing unlawful. And that can be established only if the court is prepared to adjudicate upon the right to possession of the foreign land—which is exactly what the House of Lords said the English courts may not do . . . .[19]

Finally, the House of Lords was not prepared to overrule its previous decision in *Moçambique*. In particular, Lord Wilberforce pointed to the fact that the rule had been accepted in some form in much of the common law world, that the nature of the rule itself, involving possible conflict with foreign jurisdictions, favoured a legislative rather than a judicial solution, and that there had not been such a change of circumstances since *Moçambique* was decided in 1893 as to justify the House of Lords overruling itself.[20] However, the House of Lords was prepared to allow the plaintiffs' action to proceed to the extent that it concerned trespass to the contents of the hotels. The *Moçambique* rule had no application to that claim.

Despite the *Moçambique* rule, there have been isolated decisions where its impact has been ignored. In *Malo and Bertrand v Clement*, for example, an Ontario court held that it had jurisdiction to entertain a claim by former tenants against their former landlord for unspecified

---

17 (sub nom Hesperides Hotels Ltd v Aegean Turkish Holidays Ltd) [1977] 3 WLR 656 at 666 (CA).
18 *Hesperides Hotels*, above note 16 at 535–36.
19 Above note 17 at 675.
20 Above note 16 at 536–37. Recently the United Kingdom Supreme Court has reiterated the rule but also noted legislative and European law developments narrowing its scope in various contexts: *Lucasfilm*, above note 1 at paras 56 and 72–77.

damages arising from the collapse of the building's roof.[21] The court reached this conclusion despite the fact that the premises in question were situated in Quebec and that the defendant denied he was the real owner or lessor of the building at the time of the collapse. In allowing the action to proceed in Ontario, Plaxton J stressed the fact that the action was *in personam* and had been brought against a defendant who both resided and had been personally served in Ontario. He continued:

> It is an action for damages arising out of the relationship of landlord and tenant, and involving the rights and liabilities incident to that relationship, under the law of the Province of Quebec. The claim is one which, if well founded, the Courts of this Province can enforce. They can give an effective judgment.[22]

Moreover, the judge determined that the question of title to land in Quebec arose only incidentally. Without referring specifically to the *Moçambique* rule, he concluded, having regard to "settled principles of private international law as applied in English courts as well as [his] own, that [the Ontario] Court ha[d] jurisdiction to entertain the action and to decide the issues which [had] been raised for determination . . . ."[23]

More recently, in *Godley v Coles* an Ontario court was prepared to question expressly the applicability of *Moçambique*.[24] The plaintiffs were a husband and wife as were the defendants. Each couple owned a condominium in Florida. The plaintiffs brought an action against the defendants in Ontario for damages in tort. The plaintiffs alleged that a leak from the toilet in the defendants' unit had damaged the plaintiffs' condominium and its furnishings. Thus, the plaintiffs' claim related to both movable and immovable property. The defendants relied on *Moçambique* and the early Ontario decision in *Brereton v Canadian Pacific Railway Co*[25] to argue that Ontario had no jurisdiction. However, Carnwath DCJ called into question the application of the *Moçambique* rule "in every situation where an interest in land [was] involved in an action in a foreign jurisdiction, even though the predominant qualities of the action in the foreign jurisdiction relate[d] to an action *in personam*, and where the interest in land [was] of secondary importance."[26] In particular, the judge rejected the application of the principle "to fact situations where

---

21 [1943] 4 DLR 773 (Ont HCJ).
22 *Ibid* at 776.
23 *Ibid*.
24 (1988), 39 CPC (2d) 162 (Ont Dist Ct), aff'd (1988), 40 CPC (2d) xlvi (Ont HCJ) [*Godley*].
25 Above note 13.
26 Above note 24 at 164 (Ont Dist Ct).

title to the property [was] not in issue, but rather damage caused by the negligent acts of another person to immovable property [was] in question."²⁷ He pointed out that, in *Brereton* itself, title to the property was apparently disputed. The decision is a sensible one. The only doubt raised by *Godley* was that the court emphasized that the bulk of the plaintiffs' claim related to damage to movables. As a result, it is not entirely clear whether the reasoning was restricted to cases where the damage to immovables was minimal. It is to be hoped that the *Moçambique* rule will soon be discarded at least insofar as it precludes an action for tortious damage to foreign land. The existence of *in personam* jurisdiction should alone be sufficient, especially as such jurisdiction is sufficient, as the next section shows, in an action for breach of contract. It is worth noting that in *Hesperides Hotels* Lord Fraser cogently observed: "the courts . . . in England . . . have asserted jurisdiction in actions to enforce contracts relating to foreign land . . . . Actions of that sort seem to affect the foreign land itself hardly less than actions for damages for trespass to the land."²⁸

3) Exception Based on a Contract or Equity between the Parties

In *Moçambique*, Lord Herschell LC pointed out that "[w]hilst Courts of Equity have never claimed to act directly upon land situate abroad, they have purported to act upon the conscience of persons living here."²⁹ This jurisdiction dates back at least as far as Lord Hardwicke LC's judgment in *Penn v Lord Baltimore*,³⁰ and is well illustrated by the decision of the New Brunswick Court of Appeal in *Ward v Coffin*.³¹ Justice Hughes adopted the definition of the exception from an earlier edition of Dicey's textbook:³²

> Where the court has jurisdiction to entertain an action against a person . . . the court has jurisdiction to entertain an action against such person respecting an immovable situate out of England (foreign land), on the ground of either—(a) a contract between the parties to the action; or (b) an equity between such parties; with reference to such immovable.³³

---

27 *Ibid* at 165.
28 Above note 16 at 544.
29 Above note 1 at 626.
30 (1750), 27 ER 1132 (Ch).
31 (1972), 27 DLR (3d) 58 (NBSCAD) [*Ward*].
32 *Ibid* at 70.
33 JHC Morris, ed, *Dicey on the Conflict of Laws*, 6th ed (London: Stevens & Sons, 1949) at 145.

He then applied the principle in a case involving a contract to sell land in Quebec. The plaintiff sued for specific performance of the agreement or, in the alternative, for damages for breach of contract. There was no doubt that the New Brunswick court had jurisdiction over the defendant who resided in New Brunswick and had been served there. Justice Hughes affirmed the order for specific performance made by the trial judge. Given the general proposition that the transfers of interests in land were governed by the law of the *situs*,[34] the defendant was required "to convey the properties in accordance with law of the Province of Quebec where the properties [were] situate."[35]

The jurisdiction exemplified in *Ward* was used in *Wincal Properties Ltd v Cal-Alta Holdings Ltd*[36] to allow the mortgagee of foreign land to enforce the mortgagor's personal covenant to pay the debt and in *Kung v Kung*[37] to enforce trust or partnership obligations with respect to foreign land. Matrimonial property disputes have proved a fertile ground for the exercise of this jurisdiction. Thus, in *Macedo v Macedo*[38] the court held that, in pursuance of its *in personam* jurisdiction over the husband, it could order him to sell land registered in his name in Portugal and to share the proceeds with his wife in partial satisfaction of his obligations under Ontario's *Family Law Act*.[39] Equally in *Webster v Webster* the court granted a wife an interim order, pending the resolution of her claims for division of marital property, enjoining her husband from proceeding in Bermuda with an application for partition and sale of the parties' Bermuda land.[40]

The exception was discussed in detail by the Ontario Court of Appeal in *Catania v Giannattasio*.[41] The appellants were the two daughters and the respondent was the son of Eugenio Catania. They were the only children and they lived in Ontario. In 1990, Catania had executed a deed in Ontario whereby he transferred to his daughters a house and land in Italy. He died in 1993. In 1997 his daughters registered the deed in the land registry office in Italy. They intended to sell the Italian properties. In response, the son sought a declaration from the Ontario courts that the deed was void on the ground of mental incapacity. The question was whether the Ontario courts had jurisdiction to determine

---

34 See the discussion of choice of law later in this chapter.
35 Above note 31 at 72.
36 (1983), 43 AR 223 (QB).
37 (1990), 42 BCLR (2d) 145 (CA).
38 (1996), 19 RFL (4th) 65 (Ont Ct Gen Div).
39 RSO 1990, c F.3.
40 (1997), 32 OR (3d) 679 (Gen Div).
41 (1999), 174 DLR (4th) 170 (Ont CA) [*Catania*].

the validity of the deed. The Court of Appeal accepted the general proposition that Canadian courts had no jurisdiction to determine title to or an interest in foreign land. The respondent, however, relied on the exception: "He argues that, although the declaration he seeks affects title to the properties in Italy, he is only asking for what amounts to equitable relief against two Ontario residents."[42] The court recognized the potential availability of the exception. Justice Laskin said:

> a long line of authorities has held that Canadian courts have jurisdiction to enforce rights affecting land in foreign countries if these rights are based on contract, trust or equity and the defendant resides in Canada. In exercising this jurisdiction, Canadian courts are enforcing a personal obligation between the parties. In other words, they are exercising an *in personam* jurisdiction. This *in personam* jurisdiction is an exception to the general rule that Canadian courts have no jurisdiction to decide title to foreign land.[43]

The court indicated that it would assert such *in personam* jurisdiction only if four criteria were met:

> In order to ensure that only effective *in personam* jurisdiction is exercised pursuant to the exception, the courts have insisted on four prerequisites:
> (1) The court must have *in personam* jurisdiction over the defendant. The plaintiff must accordingly be able to serve the defendant with originating process, or the defendant must submit to the jurisdiction of the court.
> (2) There must be some personal obligation running between the parties. The jurisdiction cannot be exercised against strangers to the obligation unless they have become personally affected by it . . . .
>   An equity between the parties may arise in various contexts. In all cases, however, the relationship between the parties must be such that the defendant's conscience would be affected if he insisted on his strict legal rights . . . .
> (3) The jurisdiction cannot be exercised if the local court cannot supervise the execution of the judgment . . . .
> (4) Finally, the court will not exercise jurisdiction if the order would be of no effect in the *situs* . . . . The mere fact, however, that the lex situs would not recognize the personal obligation upon which jurisdiction is based will not be a bar to the granting of the order.[44]

---

42 *Ibid* at para 11.
43 *Ibid* at para 12.
44 *Ibid*. The court drew these conditions from James G McLeod, *The Conflict of Laws* (Calgary: Carswell, 1983) at 323–25. For a recent application of them, see *Wu v Ng*, 2014 ONSC 7126.

The court concluded that the second requirement had not been satisfied and so dismissed the application. The deed created an obligation between the father and his daughters but did not create any obligations between the respondent and the appellants. There were no equities running between the children and thus any dispute over title to the two properties had to be decided by the Italian courts.

More recently, in *Minera Aquiline Argentina SA v IMA Exploration Inc* the British Columbia Court of Appeal rejected the defendants' argument that the *in personam* exception to the foreign immovable rule was "an historic anachronism and contrary to the trend in private international law."[45] Rather, the court suggested that the Supreme Court of Canada's decision in *Pro Swing Inc v Elta Golf Inc*,[46] with its reasoning in favour of the enforcement of foreign non-monetary judgments, indicated the reverse. The court, therefore, had no hesitation in affirming the trial judge's imposition of a constructive trust for a misuse of confidential information over certain mineral claims in Argentina, accompanied by a mandatory injunction ordering the defendants to transfer the claims to the plaintiff.[47] The defendants were subject to the jurisdiction of the British Columbia court because they were corporations resident in the province.

In *Precious Metal Capital Corp v Smith*[48] the court considered the four *Catania* prerequisites in light of the *Morguard* real and substantial connection test for *in personam* jurisdiction. As in *Minera*, the plaintiff sought, among other things, a constructive trust over foreign mining claims and an order that they be transferred to it. Unlike in *Minera* and *Catania*, however, most of the defendants were not Ontario residents and so *Precious Metal* was a case of assumed jurisdiction. The trial judge had engaged in a two-step analysis.[49] First, he had applied the *Catania* criteria to determine whether the Ontario courts had jurisdiction to grant remedies that affected foreign land. Second, he had applied the *Morguard* test and the factors identified in *Muscutt v Courcelles*[50] to determine whether the Ontario courts could assume jurisdiction over the non-resident defendants.

According to the Ontario Court of Appeal, however, "Where an Ontario court is asked to assume jurisdiction over a non-Ontario defendant,

---

45 (2007), 68 BCLR (4th) 242 at para 87 (CA) [*Minera*].
46 [2006] 2 SCR 612 [*Pro Swing*]. See the discussion of this case in Chapter 8, Section B(4).
47 (2006), 58 BCLR (4th) 217 (SC).
48 Above note 7.
49 (2008), 60 CPC (6th) 276 (Ont SCJ).
50 (2002), 60 OR (3d) 20 (CA) [*Muscutt*].

the real and substantial connection inquiry should be the exclusive means used to determine jurisdiction."[51] Justice Doherty determined that the considerations underlying the *Catania* test should be taken into account within the broader real and substantial connection test. He pointed out that the first criterion laid down in *Catania* was that the court have *in personam* jurisdiction over the defendant. Satisfaction of that condition in a case of assumed jurisdiction required the court in any event to engage in "the much broader inquiry mandated by the real and substantial connection" test.[52] Justice Doherty therefore concluded: "The comprehensive approach to the determination of whether an Ontario court should assume jurisdiction outlined in *Muscutt* is fully capable of taking into account the factors relating to the nature of the remedy sought and identified in *Catania*."[53] Despite the reasoning in *Precious Metal*, there is no obvious merit in focusing the entire jurisdictional analysis upon the real and substantial connection test. As noted earlier in the discussion of the general rule, it makes analytical sense to deal with jurisdictional issues raised by foreign immovable property as a discrete topic. The second, third, and fourth *Catania* factors do not fit easily within the framework of the real and substantial connection test. In any event, the *Muscutt* approach to jurisdiction has now been overtaken by *Club Resorts*.[54]

B. RECOGNITION OF FOREIGN JUDGMENTS AFFECTING LAND IN THE FORUM

The converse of the foreign immovable rule is that the courts of a foreign country have no jurisdiction to adjudicate title to, or the right to possession of, land outside that foreign country. The leading decision is *Duke v Andler*.[55] All parties were residents of California. The plaintiffs alleged that the defendants had obtained title to the plaintiffs' land in British Columbia by fraud. They brought proceedings in California. The California court ordered the defendants to re-convey the land to the plaintiffs. The judgment went on to provide that, if the defendants failed to comply with the order, the clerk of the court was empowered to do so on their behalf. The defendants refused and so a purported conveyance was enacted by the clerk. The plaintiffs then brought an

---

51 *Precious Metal*, above note 7 at para 16.
52 *Ibid* at para 20.
53 *Ibid* at para 21.
54 Above note 9.
55 Above note 3.

action in British Columbia for a declaration that, as a result of the judgment or the conveyance or both, they were now owners of the land and were entitled to be registered as such.

The Supreme Court of Canada decided that the California court had no jurisdiction to adjudicate on title to land in British Columbia and therefore the judgment, and the conveyance made pursuant to it, could not be regarded as binding in British Columbia. The court recognized that the California court did have *in personam* jurisdiction over the parties. It had the authority to order the defendants to re-convey the land. The enforcement of that order, however, was a matter for the California court.

It is an interesting question as to whether the Supreme Court of Canada's decision in *Pro Swing*[56] will lead to the potential enforcement of such *in personam* decrees. It is also interesting to speculate as to whether the principle from *Duke* precludes the enforcement of a foreign judgment for damages in tort in respect of damage to land outside the foreign jurisdiction. Will personal jurisdiction over the defendant justify the enforcement of such a judgment even though, at present, a Canadian court probably would not take jurisdiction in such a case?

The scope of the rule in *Duke* was examined by the Saskatchewan Court of Appeal in *Chapman Estate v O'Hara*.[57] The Manitoba courts had personal jurisdiction over the parties with respect to an estate that was being administered in Manitoba. Part of the estate was comprised of farmland in Saskatchewan. One of the deceased's children, John O'Hara, claimed that he was beneficially entitled to the farmland as a result of a trust arrangement between his aunt and his mother. In an action in Manitoba brought by the administrator of the estate against O'Hara as the former executor for an accounting of the rents and profits from the estate, O'Hara asserted his beneficial interest. The Manitoba courts, however, determined that O'Hara was not the beneficial owner, and they declared that the Saskatchewan farmland was indeed an asset of the estate. O'Hara then commenced an action in Saskatchewan against the administrator in which he asserted his entitlement to the farm and filed a certificate of pending litigation against the property, which the Manitoba courts ordered him to remove. He ignored that order. The motions judge concluded that the action was similar in its essential respects to the action between the same parties that had been fully litigated in Manitoba. He therefore ordered O'Hara's Saskatchewan action to be struck out as an abuse of process. Before the

---

56 Above note 46.
57 (1987), 61 Sask R 140 (CA) [*Chapman Estate*].

Court of Appeal, the plaintiff argued that the Saskatchewan courts had exclusive jurisdiction to determine title to Saskatchewan land and that a Manitoba judgment could not conclusively determine title to land in Saskatchewan.

The majority of the court dismissed the appeal, being of the opinion that it would be an abuse of process to allow the action to proceed given that the matter had already been litigated in Manitoba. Justice Wakeling pointed out that the Manitoba courts had only ever acted *in personam*. He said that certain general principles had been established and that the Manitoba courts had not offended them:

(1) It was quite proper for the Manitoba courts to rule as they did on this issue, as an *in personam* judgment to be enforced by whatever coercive power that court has over the parties before it.

(2) The Manitoba court has no power to make an *in rem* pronouncement which would be binding in another jurisdiction. It is apparent that no such attempt has been made in this case.

(3) It is recognized that it is up to the courts in the jurisdiction where the property is situate to deal with the foreign judgment in such fashion as it considers appropriate, and this is necessarily recognized by the court granting the *in personam* judgment. That is, the judgment must be enforced by the coercive methods available to the court in question and not by dependence upon the acceptance of the binding nature of the judgment in the courts in the jurisdiction in which the property is situate.[58]

According to the majority, this was not a case, like *Duke*, in which an action was being brought in Saskatchewan to give the Manitoba judgment some *in rem* effect. The Saskatchewan courts were merely being asked to exercise their discretion not to frustrate the coercive power of the Manitoba courts. Justice Wakeling said:

By having control over the estate and perhaps the parties interested in the estate, the Manitoba courts may well be able to enforce their *in personam* judgment which ... was founded upon a sound jurisdictional base. What the courts of this province have been asked to do is to frustrate that coercive power of the Manitoba courts by permitting a similar action to proceed in this province. I see nothing in *Duke v. Andler* which restricts the exercise of the discretion of the Queen's Bench judge to determine whether such second action constitutes an abuse of process. In fact it so clearly appears to be inappropriate to permit two actions on the same issue, it would take the most per-

---

58 *Ibid* at para 29.

suasive, in fact compelling authority to convince me such a second action should be permitted to proceed. There was such compelling authority in *Duke v. Andler*, for the California court had no acceptable jurisdictional basis in the first place, and it clearly made an order that could not be enforced, or there would not have been need to resort to the British Columbia courts. Neither of these attributes is present in this case, and I therefore have no difficulty in distinguishing this case from that of *Duke v. Andler*.[59]

Despite this valiant attempt to distinguish *Duke*, it is hard to disagree with the dissenting judgment of Sherstobitoff JA. He pointed out that the Manitoba judgment was an *in personam* judgment affecting the conscience of the parties subject to the jurisdiction of the Manitoba courts. It could not stand on a different footing in Saskatchewan as an *in rem* judgment affecting land in Saskatchewan. That would contravene the principle underlying *Duke*. The court could not do indirectly, by striking the claim on discretionary grounds, what it could not do directly, namely, give the Manitoba judgment *in rem* effect.

In *Corlett v Hoelker* the court arguably went a step farther than in *Chapman Estate*.[60] The parties spent five years litigating their divorce in Washington State. The court there awarded Hoelker a condominium in British Columbia. Corlett, in proceedings in British Columbia, sought an order regarding entitlement to the condominium. The British Columbia Court of Appeal held that the issue was *res judicata*, having already been decided by the Washington State court. Corlett had

> attorned to the jurisdiction of the Washington court, fully participated in five years of hard-fought litigation in Washington State and actively sought adjudication of her claims to marital property, including the condominium, within the confines of the Washington action, without pleading or adducing evidence of [British Columbia] law . . . [her] failure to urge either the application of the British Columbia *Family Relations Act* and her failure to ever seek to have the Washington court decline jurisdiction and pursue the ownership of the condominium through the British Columbia proceedings resulted in a determination of the characterization of the condominium as non-marital property, rendering that issue *res judicata*.[61]

It is a precondition for *res judicata* to operate that the foreign decision be recognized in the forum. So the court recognized (though did not, as

---

59   *Ibid* at para 38.
60   2012 BCCA 355.
61   *Ibid* at para 37.

attempted but rejected in *Duke*, enforce) a foreign decision concerning title to immovable property in the forum.[62] This recognition appears to be a step beyond what happened in *Chapman Estate*, since to dismiss local proceedings based on an abuse of process (or, even more so, to stay local proceedings based on litigation elsewhere[63]) does not require formal recognition of the foreign decision. The concerns expressed by Sherstobitoff JA in dissent in *Chapman Estate* apply equally, if not more, to this application of *res judicata*.

C. CHOICE OF LAW

It is a universal principle that all questions relating to the transfer of immovables are governed by the law of the place where the immovable property is situated.[64] The *lex situs* therefore governs a party's capacity[65] to transfer immovables, as well as the formal[66] and essential validity[67] of such transfers. It has been suggested[68] that the transfer of immovables is one area in which the courts would be inclined to invoke the doctrine of *renvoi* so as to apply not necessarily the domestic law of the *situs* but the domestic law of the country that the courts of the *situs* would apply.[69] The theory is that it would be pointless to apply any other law since the courts of the *situs* have ultimate control over the land.

Of course, as we have seen, a court will typically have no jurisdiction to determine title to foreign immovables and so there are few decisions dealing with choice of law in this context. Many of the decisions relating to foreign land therefore concern contracts to transfer the land

---

62 See also *Brown v Miller*, 2008 BCSC 1351 (giving *res judicata* effect to a Florida judgment characterizing and dividing matrimonial property located in British Columbia); *Monteiro v Monteiro*, 2015 BCSC 1543 (indicating that a Portuguese order in respect of land in British Columbia would be enforced).

63 As in *Hormandinger v Bender-Hormandinger*, 2007 BCSC 949. In this case the court stayed its proceedings in favour of litigation in Germany, even though the dispute involved immovable property in British Columbia. A significant reason for this was that both parties were resident in Germany so the court there had *in personam* jurisdiction over them both.

64 See Janeen Carruthers, *The Transfer of Property in the Conflict of Laws* (Oxford: Oxford University Press, 2005).

65 *Landreau v Lachapelle*, [1937] OR 444 (CA).

66 *Adams v Clutterbuck* (1883), 10 QBD 403.

67 *Chatillon v The Canadian Mutual Fire Insurance Co* (1877), 27 UCCP 450.

68 See, for example, Lawrence Collins, ed, *Dicey, Morris and Collins on the Conflict of Laws*, 15th ed (London: Sweet & Maxwell, 2012) at para 4-025 [*Dicey, Morris and Collins*].

69 See Chapter 10, Section E(1).

rather than the transfer itself. The courts must be careful to bear in mind the distinction between contract and conveyance.[70] Insofar as a case concerns a contract with respect to foreign land, the normal contractual choice of law rules should apply.[71] Thus, in *Ward* the question arose as to the formal validity of an agreement to sell land, and the court applied the general proposition that a contract would be formally valid if it complied with the formalities imposed either by the proper law of the contract or by the law of the place where the contract was made.[72] Although there is a presumption that the proper law of a contract with respect to land will be the *lex situs*,[73] this is not always the case.[74] In *British South Africa Co v De Beers Consolidated Mines Ltd*, Cozens-Hardy MR had this to say about the effect of the application of the proper law governing a contract to grant a mortgage over foreign land:

> [A]n English contract to give a mortgage on foreign land, although the mortgage has to be perfected according to the *lex situs*, is a contract to give a mortgage which—*inter partes*—is to be treated as an English mortgage and subject to such rights of redemption and such equities as the law of England regards as necessarily incident to a mortgage.[75]

FURTHER READINGS

COOK, WALTER WHEELER. *The Logical and Legal Basis of the Conflict of Laws* (Cambridge: Harvard University Press, 1942) ch 10.

CURRIE, BRAINERD. "Full Faith and Credit to Foreign Land Decrees" (1954) 21 *University of Chicago Law Review* 620.

EDINGER, ELIZABETH. "Is *Duke v. Andler* Still Good Law in Common Law Canada?" (2011) 51 *Canadian Business Law Journal* 52.

FALCONBRIDGE, JOHN. *Essays on the Conflict of Laws*, 2d ed (Toronto: Canada Law Book, 1954) ch 29.

---

70 See the discussion in *Ward*, above note 31 at 71–72. See also *Dicey, Morris and Collins*, above note 68 at para 23E-080.
71 In *Bank of Africa v Cohen*, [1909] 2 Ch 129 (CA), however, the English Court of Appeal seemed to ignore the fact that a contract was involved by holding that a person's capacity to make a contract with regard to an immovable was governed by the *lex situs*.
72 Above note 31.
73 *Ibid*.
74 See, for example, *Re Smith, Lawrence v Kitson*, [1916] 2 Ch 206.
75 [1910] 2 Ch 502 at 515 (CA), rev'd on different grounds, [1912] AC 52 (HL).

GELOWITZ, MARK. "*Bomac* and *O'Hara*: Abuse and Abdication" (1989) 53 *Saskatchewan Law Review* 163.

LEE, STEPHEN. "Title to Foreign Real Property in Transnational Money Claims" (1995) 32 *Columbia Journal of Transnational Law* 607.

PRIBETIC, ANTONIN. "Staking Claims against Foreign Defendants in Canada: Choice of Law and Jurisdictional Issues Arising from the *In Personam* Exception to the *Moçambique* Rule for Foreign Immovables" (2009) 35 *Advocates' Quarterly* 230.

WASS, JACK. "The Court's *In Personam* Jurisdiction in Cases Involving Foreign Land" (2014) 63 *International and Comparative Law Quarterly* 103.

WEINTRAUB, RUSSELL. "An Inquiry into the Utility of '*Situs*' as a Concept in Conflicts Analysis" (1966) 52 *Cornell Law Quarterly* 1.

WELLING, BRUCE, & EA HEAKES. "Torts and Foreign Immovables: Jurisdiction in Conflict of Laws" (1979) 18 *University of Western Ontario Law Review* 295.

CHAPTER 18

MOVABLE PROPERTY

A. INTRODUCTION

Chapters 16 and 17 explained the nature of property in the conflict of laws and rules for immovable property. This chapter covers rules for movable property, sometimes referred to as "movables." For movable property there are no special rules about jurisdiction and recognition and enforcement. The central issue is choice of law, to determine what law governs the issue of ownership of movable property. This issue arises in many different contexts, including the finding of property, gifts, transfers pursuant to contract, and disposition on death. The last of these contexts is considered separately in Chapter 19. The focus of this chapter is on *inter vivos* transfers—transfers made when the transferor is alive—of movable property.

When property is transferred under a contract, the contract will often be silent on issues of ownership, particularly the question of when ownership of the property passes between the parties. The contract could contain express language on this issue but most contracts do not. So in those cases, the law of contract will govern many aspects of the transfer but the law of movable property will govern the issue of ownership. Some commentators have suggested that this separation of issues is unhelpful because it could lead to different but highly related aspects of a single transfer being governed by different, and potentially conflicting, applicable laws. Although the common law separates contract and property issues, in a wholly domestic case one would expect those to work together, complementing each other, to produce an result. That interaction could be very different if, to resolve the contract issues use one legal system and the property issues use a different legal system. As a result, these commentators would prefer property issues to be resolved under the law applicable to the contract. Of course, even if that approach were adopted, choice of law rules for movable property would still be needed for non-contractual transfers and disputes involving third parties to a contract.

The law distinguishes between two types of movable property. The first type is tangible movable property. This covers chattels: things that have a physical existence. Leading examples are raw materials such as timber and oil and finished products such as vehicles and computers. The second type is intangible movable property. This covers choses in action: forms of property that do not have physical existence. Leading examples are debts and shares in a corporation.

B. TANGIBLE MOVABLE PROPERTY

Ownership of, or title to, tangible movable property is governed by the *lex situs*: the law of the place where the movables are at the relevant time. In a leading case, *Cammell v Sewell*, wooden boards were being shipped from Russia to consignees in England.[1] The ship was driven aground in Norway. The consignees claimed the loss from their insurers in England. The ship's captain sold the boards to a Mr Clausen, who sold them to buyers in England. When the boards arrived in England, they were sold and a dispute arose as to who was entitled to the proceeds: the buyers or the insurers of the consignees. There was no contract between the disputing parties. The insurers claimed they took over the consignee's rights when they paid out under the insurance policy. They argued that English law should apply to the issue of ownership, as the place where the boards ended up, and that, under that law, the sale to Mr Clausen was invalid. The court rejected that argument, holding that the law of the place where the boards were located at the time of the sale to Mr Clausen, Norway, should apply, and under that law the sale was legal. The *lex situs* was to be applied even though the boards came into Norway fortuitously and did not remain there. More recently, in *Kuwait Airways Corporation v Iraqi Airways Company* Lord Nicholls stated that "the transfer of title to tangible movable property normally

---

1   (1860), 157 ER 1371 (Exch Ch) [*Cammell*]. See also *Air Foyle Ltd v Center Capital Ltd*, [2003] 2 Lloyd's Rep 753 (HC).

depends on the *lex situs*: the law of the country where the movable was situated at the time of the transfer."[2]

Several reasons can be advanced for using the *lex situs*. First, a rigid rule identifying a specific place helps to establish the scope of the transferee's necessary due diligence. The recipient of movable property can take steps to ensure that the transfer is legal under that particular law and thereby know he or she has obtained good title. Second, the rule promotes transactional security for the recipient. Movable property can be easily transported across borders and so could be moved to a place where the earlier transfer was not valid. Focusing on the location of the property at the time of transfer avoids the risk that such a subsequent move would undo the recipient's ownership. Third, in ownership disputes between two innocent parties, like *Cammell*, the *lex situs* rule tends to prefer the interests of a subsequent purchaser rather than those of an earlier owner. Where both parties are innocent, in that they have not acted wrongfully, this is to some degree a policy choice. Favouring subsequent purchasers arguably better promotes the overall flow of commerce than favouring the earlier owner. Having fewer restrictions on the transfer of movable property reduces transaction costs.

1) Retention of Title Clauses

In *Century Credit Corporation v Richard*, Moses sold Foldes a car.[3] Both parties were resident in Quebec and the car was located there. Because Foldes did not pay the full purchase price, the sale contract provided that Moses remained the owner of the car until that price was paid. Foldes subsequently brought the car to Ontario and sold it to Hamilton Car Refinishers (HCR). In the resulting ligation the central question was whether HCR obtained title to the car or whether it was still owned by Moses. The court had to consider two distinct approaches to the issue. Under the first, it would use the *lex situs* at the time of the second sale to determine all issues. Ontario law would have to determine whether Moses or Foldes owned the car and then whether title passed to HCR. Under the second, the court would use the *lex situs* at the time of the first sale to determine ownership as between Moses and Foldes,

---

2   [2002] 2 AC 883 at para 13 (HL). See also para 161, Lord Hope. See also *Iran v The Barakat Galleries Limited*, [2007] EWCA Civ 1374 at para 132; *Royal Bank of Canada v Cow Harbour Construction Ltd*, 2012 ABQB 112 at para 63; *Dash 224, LLC v Vector Aerospace Engine Services-Atlantic Inc*, 2015 PESC 27 at paras 25–26.

3   [1962] OR 815 (CA) [*Century Credit*]. See also *Price Mobile Homes Centres, Inc v National Trailer Convoy of Canada Ltd* (1974), 44 DLR (3d) 443 (Man QB).

and then the *lex situs* at the time of the second sale to determine HCR's ownership. These two approaches could produce different results if the law of Quebec and Ontario treated reservation of title clauses differently, such that after the first sale under Quebec law Moses remained the owner but under Ontario law Foldes became the owner.

The Court of Appeal specifically rejected the first approach and adopted the second. The analysis had to proceed chronologically through each sale using the relevant *lex situs* for each.[4] The court held that on the first sale, the reservation of title to Moses was valid under Quebec law and so Moses remained the owner. However, in considering the sale to HCR, using Ontario law as the *lex situs*, Ontario's statute law allowed an innocent purchaser such as HCR to obtain title notwithstanding a reservation of title. Moses's claim as owner therefore failed.

A common concern, relevant in *Century Credit*, is whether security interests such as those arising under a conditional sale have been registered in the jurisdiction. Typically, in a wholly domestic case, to take priority over a subsequent purchaser the seller in the conditional sale transaction must register, under a statutory scheme, the security interest in the movable property. This registration provides notice to any subsequent purchaser and so protects the seller's title. In a cross-border case like *Century Credit*, the conditional seller does not contemplate the chattel being taken out of the jurisdiction and so has not registered his or her interest in other provinces or countries. Security interests are now generally regulated under modern provincial statutes such as Ontario's *Personal Property Security Act*.[5] These typically contain specific provisions, which can be quite technical, dealing with choice of law issues relating to the creation and effect of a security interest and with situations in which property is brought into or taken out of the province.[6] The provisions distinguish between different types of property. For example, for "goods," which are defined to include most tangible

---

4   *Century Credit*, above note 3 at 817. The analysis in this case was misunderstood in *Maden v Long* (1982), 41 BCLR 6 (SC), where the court thought the Court of Appeal had applied Ontario law throughout. Its statement that "[a]lmost invariably the authorities apply the law in the country or province where the goods actually are at the time of litigation" (at 10) cannot be regarded as correct.
5   RSO 1990, c P.10.
6   *Ibid* at ss 5–8. For more detail on the Ontario provisions, see Richard McLaren, *The 2015–16 Annotated Ontario Personal Property Security Act* (Toronto: Carswell, 2015) at 101–39. For more detail on the similar provisions in other provincial statutes, see Richard McLaren, *Secured Transactions in Personal Property in Canada*, 3d ed (Toronto: Carswell, 2013) (loose-leaf) ch 8. See also the analysis in Ronald CC Cuming, Catherine Walsh, & Roderick J Wood, *Personal Property Security Law*, 2d ed (Toronto: Irwin Law, 2012) at 180–239.

movables, issues of validity, perfection (a term of art under the statute), and the effect of perfection are governed by the law of the place where the goods are at the time the security interest in them attaches (another term of art). In contrast, for several types of intangible movables these same issues are governed by the law of the place where the debtor is located at the time of attachment.

2) Exceptions

Over time, the common law has developed several exceptions to the general *lex situs* rule. Five of them are summarized in *Winkworth v Christie, Manson and Woods Ltd*.[7]

First, if movable property is in transit, and its location is casual or unknown, then the proper law of the transfer should be used rather than the *lex situs*. For example, a seller might own a container of redwood that is currently en route by train from California to Ontario. If he or she sells the redwood to a buyer in Ontario, the court would not attempt to identify, if it could be done, which state the container was in at the precise time of the transaction. Rather, a proper law approach would be used. There is little authority for this exception but it is clear that some alternative to the *lex situs* must be available for transfers where the location of the property is unknown. It is not clear whether the proper law of the transfer is simply the law of the contract, if there is one, or an objective determination of the law that is to govern the issue of ownership.

The second exception mentioned in *Winkworth* is for cases where a party claiming title has not acted bona fide. However, this is of doubtful authority and likely is not an exception.

The third exception is for cases when the court declines to apply the *lex situs* because it is contrary to the public policy of the forum. In *Winkworth*, the court indicates that the *lex situs* would have to be "outrageous" or "wholly contrary to justice and morality" to trigger this exception.[8] This requirement is consistent with the narrow view of public policy discussed in Chapter 3. Of course, public policy can operate as an exception to many choice of law rules, so it is somewhat unusual to list it separately in this particular context.[9]

---

7   [1980] Ch 496 [*Winkworth*].
8   *Ibid* at 510.
9   In the context of movable property, one of the key public policy concerns is the protection by the state of items of significant cultural heritage. See Pippa Rogerson, *Collier's Conflict of Laws*, 4th ed (Cambridge: Cambridge University Press, 2013) at 393.

The fourth exception is for any rules of the forum that are mandated by statute to apply to the issue of ownership. A Canadian example is not easy to identify.

Fifth, there are special rules for situations of insolvency and bankruptcy.

In *Winkworth*, works of art were stolen in England from their owner, taken to Italy, and sold to an Italian. The buyer then sent the works of art to England to be sold at auction. The original owner sued the buyer, alleging that he remained the owner of the artwork. Under the *lex situs* rule, Italian law would apply to the question of whether the buyer obtained ownership of the artwork, and Italian law gave the buyer good title. The original owner, attempting to have English law applied, argued that the court should consider the artwork to have been in England throughout. The artwork was initially in England, was removed from that jurisdiction without permission, and had returned there. The court rejected this argument: it was too much of a fiction and could give rise to considerable uncertainty. The original owner also argued, in the alternative, that the case came within an exception to the *lex situs* rule. However, he was forced to accept that the Italian law in question did not come within the public policy exception and none of the other four exceptions applied. He advocated a further exception, to apply specifically in cases where movable property was removed from the jurisdiction without consent and then returned to that same jurisdiction. The court refused to create such an exception, largely due to the reasons, discussed above, underlying the *lex situs* rule: the need for security of title and the importance of commercial convenience.[10]

3) A Role for *Renvoi*?

In *Iran v Berend*, at issue was ownership of a fragment of a limestone relief from the fifth century BCE.[11] The defendant had purchased the relief in 1974 at auction in New York and it had been delivered to her in France later that year. In 2005 she had it brought to England to be sold at auction. Before the auction, the state of Iran sued the defendant, claiming that it owned the relief. Both parties accepted that the general choice of law rule for movable property would apply French law to the question of whether the defendant obtained title in 1974. However, the state of Iran argued that the court should apply the doctrine of *renvoi*, discussed in Chapter 10, and apply not French law but rather the law

---

10   *Winkworth*, above note 7 at 512. See *In Re Anziani*, [1930] 1 Ch 407 at 420.
11   [2007] 2 All ER (Comm) 132.

that a French court would apply. It argued that a French court would apply, as an exception to using the *lex situs*, the law of the state of origin—Iran—for cultural or artistic property. The court noted that there was some support for using *renvoi*,[12] but held that both the need for a consistent and certain rule and the weight of authority were against it.[13] As a result the court applied the domestic law of France. Under that law, the defendant had obtained title in 1974. At least one commentator disagrees strongly with this conclusion and thinks that *renvoi* should be applied in this area.[14] However, as explained in Chapter 10, it is difficult to see how the benefits of the doctrine can outweigh the difficulties.[15]

C. INTANGIBLE MOVABLE PROPERTY

Intangible movable property lacks physical form and is often created by contract. A debt is a simple example, created by a contract between creditor and debtor. Intangible movables are also frequently transferred by contract, for example when a creditor assigns a debt to a third party. As with tangible movables, it is important to separate contract issues and property issues.[16] Many issues with a debt and an assignment are contractual and will be governed by the applicable law of the contract. For example, the question of whether an intangible movable can be assigned at all is governed by the proper law of the intangible movable.[17] In the case of a debt this would be the law applicable to the contract creating the debt. However, the issue of who owns the debt is a property

---

12 See *Winkworth*, above note 7 at 514; *Glencore International AG v Metro Trading International Inc*, [2001] 1 Lloyd's Rep 284 at para 41.
13 See, in the context of intangible movables, *Macmillan Inc v Bishopsgate Investment Trust Plc (No 3)*, [1995] 3 All ER 747 at 776–77 (Ch D), aff'd [1996] 1 All ER 585 (CA) [*Macmillan*].
14 Adrian Briggs, *The Conflict of Laws*, 3d ed (Oxford: Oxford University Press, 2013) at 24 and 304.
15 Another English case rejecting *renvoi* in this area is *Blue Sky One Ltd v Mahan Air; PK Airfinance US Inc v Blue Sky Two Ltd*, [2010] EWHC 631 at paras 172–85 (Comm). See Rogerson, above note 9 at 396.
16 In *Republic de Guatemala v Nunez*, [1927] 1 KB 669 (CA), an assignment of a bank account from a father to his son was held to be invalid. At issue was the assignee's capacity and the formal validity of the assignment. While the assignment was a gift, the court, consistent with the choice of law rules for contract, applied the law of the place where the assignment occurred, which was also the law of the parties' domicile. The assignment itself being invalid, the court did not have to consider any issues of title to intangible movable property.
17 *Trendtex Trading Corp v Credit Suisse*, [1980] QB 629 (CA), aff'd [1982] AC 679 (HL).

issue and the applicable law is determined using the choice of law rule for intangible movables.

It is difficult to state the choice of law rule for intangible movable property with precision because the authorities are sparse and inconclusive. The two leading alternatives for the applicable law are the *lex situs* of the intangible movable or the law under which the intangible movable was created. The former rule is the most well-established and has the benefit of parallelism with the choice of law rules for immovable property and tangible movable property.[18]

1) Determining the Location

A crucial issue with a *lex situs* rule is identifying the location of intangible movable property.[19] A debt, for example, is considered to be located in the place where the creditor can recover it using litigation; in other words, where the debtor can be sued. This is generally the place where the debtor resides.[20] However, if the debtor has multiple residences, or is a corporation with branches in different jurisdictions, this rule will not suffice. In such cases, when a single residence of the debtor cannot be identified, the *situs* is the place where the debt would be paid in the ordinary course.[21] The common law distinguishes between ordinary debts and specialty debts, and these are rules for the former. A specialty debt is treated like a negotiable instrument, discussed below.[22]

Under this rule, the debtor can change the location of the debt by changing his or her residence. This variability raises concern about using the *lex situs*. In contrast, the law under which the debt was created is fixed. Nevertheless, it is arguably easier for a third party considering accepting an assignment of the debt from the creditor to ascertain the debtor's residence than to determine the proper law of the debt. So if one aim of the rule is to allow third parties to better identify the applicable law as part of their due diligence before entering into the assignment transaction, the *lex situs* may better serve this purpose.

For another type of intangible movable, negotiable instruments, the rule looks to the place where the negotiable instrument — meaning

---

18 For more detail, see Catherine Walsh, "Movables" in Stephen GA Pitel, et al, *Private International Law in Common Law Canada: Cases, Text and Materials*, 4th ed (Toronto: Emond, 2016) at 828–40.
19 See also the discussion in Chapter 16.
20 *Williams v Canada*, [1992] 1 SCR 877 at 889–90; *Canada v National Indian Brotherhood*, [1979] 1 FC 103 at 109 (TD); *New York Life Insurance Co v Public Trustee*, [1924] 2 Ch 101 at 119.
21 *Jabbour v Custodian of Absentee's Property of State of Israel*, [1954] 1 WLR 139.
22 See *Inter-Leasing Inc v Ontario (Minister of Revenue)*, 2014 ONCA 575 at paras 73–74.

the physical piece of paper—is located.²³ This covers property such as bank drafts, cheques, and bonds transferable by delivery alone. The rule is modelled on the one for tangible movables. However, given the ease of moving these instruments across borders, using the *lex situs* can be challenged as artificial.

Shares in a corporation also pose difficulties using a *lex situs* rule. The approach is not to look for the place where any physical share certificates are located. Historically the rule looked to the place where the register of shares was located.²⁴ In private corporations, each transfer of shares is recorded in the corporation's share register. Often, this register is maintained at the corporation's head office. Some commentators have proposed that instead of a *lex situs* rule, the choice of law rule for shares should be to apply the law under which the interest in the corporation is created, which will be the law of incorporation. If a corporation maintains its head office in the jurisdiction of incorporation, which is often the case, the two rules produce the same result.

However, in some contexts technological developments have strained this approach beyond the breaking point. In the modern economy, many people buy shares in a public corporation—and other similar intangible movables such as units in a trust or fund—without ever having those shares formally registered in the books of the corporation. The shares are acquired through vast indirect holding systems and held in electronic accounts. In such transactions, it is highly questionable whether the old approach to determining the *situs* of the intangible movable is of any relevance.²⁵ In *Re Bloom Estate*, the court had to determine, not for choice of law purposes but rather to calculate probate fees, the *situs* of publicly traded shares held in an electronic account.²⁶ The court noted that

> [n]ot only did the deceased, Bessie Bloom, not have physical possession of the share certificates, in her case no share certificates existed: the securities were in non-certificated form. Moreover, her holdings were not recorded on the books of the issuing companies; rather, she

---

23 *Embiricos v Anglo-Austrian Bank*, [1904] 2 KB 870, aff'd [1905] 1 KB 677. This chapter is concerned with the property issues involved in negotiable instruments. For more on other issues relating to negotiable instruments and the conflict of laws, see Janet Walker, *Castel & Walker: Canadian Conflict of Laws*, 6th ed (Markham, ON: LexisNexis Canada, 2005) (loose-leaf) ch 33; *Bills of Exchange Act*, RSC 1985, c B-4, ss 159–63.
24 See *Macmillan*, above note 13.
25 See the issues raised by the *Hague Convention on the Law Applicable to Certain Rights in Respect of Securities Held with an Intermediary* (concluded 5 July 2006). As of 2015 only Switzerland and Mauritius had ratified this convention.
26 (2004), 27 BCLR (4th) 176 (SC).

held her securities through the now common, indirect multi-tiered holding system.[27]

The court refused to follow the earlier rules based on the place of a corporation's share register. It held that the place where the deceased's interest was recorded was at the securities department of the financial intermediary, The Bank of Nova Scotia Trust Company, which was located in Toronto. The *situs* was therefore held to be Ontario.

In 2006 Alberta and Ontario each enacted a statute to address modern issues in the transfer of securities,[28] and almost all other provinces enacted similar legislation within the next few years. The new statute modernizes the law governing the property rights involved when securities are bought, sold, or used as collateral. The statute contains detailed provisions on choice of law, including new rules for dealings with "securities intermediaries," which include clearing agencies and brokers, banks, and trust companies that maintain securities accounts for customers.[29] In very general terms, for indirectly held securities the applicable law is not that of the corporation that issued the securities or of the place where the corporation keeps its register; rather, it is the law stipulated by the customer and the intermediary or,[30] if there is no such stipulation, the law of the place where the intermediary maintains the office that handles the customer's account.

2) Priorities

An issue that can arise is which of two assignees of an intangible movable, such as a debt, has the better title to the property. A common fact pattern involves an unscrupulous creditor and two innocent assignees. The creditor first sells the debt to one assignee and then, without disclosure of that transaction, again sells the debt to a second assignee. Each legal system will have priority rules for how to handle a domestic case like this. The domestic system could have a first-in-time rule, so

---

27 *Ibid* at para 49.
28 *Securities Transfer Act*, SA 2006, c S-4.5; *Securities Transfer Act, 2006*, SO 2006, c 8. See Robert Scavone, "Stronger Than Fictions: Canada Rethinks the Law of Securities Transfers in the Indirect Holding System" (2007) 45 *Canadian Business Law Journal* 67; Erik Spink, "The *Securities Transfer Act*—Fitting New Concepts in Canadian Law" (2007) 45 *Canadian Business Law Journal* 167; Walsh, above note 18 at 835–39.
29 See, for example, *Securities Transfer Act, 2006*, above note 28, ss 44–46.
30 The stipulation can take one of the following forms: a particular jurisdiction for purposes of the statute, a particular governing law, or a particular location where the account is maintained: *ibid*, s 45(2).

the earlier assignment prevails. Or it could have a first-to-notify rule, so the first assignee to notify the debtor of the assignment prevails.

Where more than one legal system is potentially involved, the issues become more complex. Which legal system should determine which assignee has the better title? It should be clear that here we could not use the law governing the assignment, since each of the two assignments could have a different applicable law. The leading approach, consistent with the general rule throughout this chapter, is to use the *lex situs* of the intangible movable. However, one problem with this approach is that the *situs* of the property could change between the time of the first assignment and the time of the second assignment. In the case of a debt, the debtor could move. If this happened, looking to the *lex situs* does not produce a single answer. The other option available for priority disputes is to apply the proper law of the intangible movable: the law under which it was created.[31] This option at least does provide a single answer.

FURTHER READINGS

BABE, JENNIFER. "Canadian P.P.S.A. Conflict of Laws Rules" (1996) 13 *National Insolvency Review* 3.

BENJAMIN, JOANNA. *Interests in Securities: A Proprietary Law Analysis of the International Securities Markets* (Oxford: Oxford University Press, 2000).

BRIDGE, MICHAEL. "The Proprietary Aspects of Assignment and Choice of Law" (2009) 125 *Law Quarterly Review* 671.

CARRUTHERS, JANEEN. *The Transfer of Property in the Conflict of Laws* (Oxford: Oxford University Press, 2005).

FAWCETT, JAMES, & PAUL TORREMANS. *Intellectual Property and Private International Law* (Oxford: Clarendon Press, 1998).

FORSYTH, CHRISTOPHER. "Certainty versus Uniformity: *Renvoi* in the Context of Movable Property" (2010) 6 *Journal of Private International Law* 637.

GOODE, ROY. "The Assignment of Pure Intangibles in the Conflict of Laws" [2015] *Lloyd's Maritime and Commercial Law Quarterly* 289.

---

31 See *Kelly v Selwyn*, [1905] 2 Ch 117. See also the argument made in James Fawcett & Janeen Carruthers, *Cheshire, North & Fawcett Private International Law*, 14th ed (Oxford: Oxford University Press, 2008) at 1227–29.

HARTLEY, TREVOR C. "Choice of Law Regarding the Voluntary Assignment of Contractual Obligations under the Rome I Regulation" (2011) 60 *International and Comparative Law Quarterly* 29.

MOSHINSKY, MARK. "The Assignment of Debts in the Conflict of Laws" (1992) 109 *Law Quarterly Review* 591.

OOI, MAISIE. "Intermediated Securities: The Choice of a Choice of Law Rule" in Louise Gullifer & Jennifer Payne, eds, *Intermediated Securities: Legal Problems and Practical Issues* (Oxford: Hart, 2010) ch 9.

OOI, MAISIE. *Shares and Other Securities in the Conflict of Laws* (Oxford: Oxford University Press, 2003).

PERKINS, JOANNA. "A Question of Priorities: Choice of Law and Proprietary Aspects of the Assignment of Debts" (2008) 2 *Law and Financial Markets Review* 238.

ROGERS, JAMES STEVEN. "Conflict of Laws for Transactions in Securities Held through Intermediaries" (2006) 39 *Cornell International Law Journal* 285.

ROGERSON, PIPPA. "The *Situs* of Debts in the Conflict of Laws: Illogical, Unnecessary and Misleading" [1990] *Cambridge Law Journal* 441.

WALSH, CATHERINE. "Receivables Financing and the Conflict of Laws: The UNCITRAL Draft Convention on the Assignment of Receivables in International Trade" (2001) 106 *Dickinson Law Review* 159.

CHAPTER 19

SUCCESSION

A. INTRODUCTION

In a broad sense, the topic of succession covers two areas: the administration of the estate and the distribution of the deceased person's property to those beneficially entitled, whether under a will or on intestacy. In a narrow sense, succession refers only to the second of these areas, distribution, and is separate from estate administration. This chapter covers both administration and distribution. It will generally use succession in the narrow sense (as a synonym for distribution).

In common law jurisdictions no one is entitled to deal with the property of a deceased person without a grant of representation from the courts. Such a grant will be in one of three forms: (1) a grant of probate to those appointed in the will as executors; (2) a grant of administration with will annexed where no executors have been appointed by the will or where the named executors have died or renounced; and (3) a grant of administration where the deceased has left no will. Once appointed or recognized by the courts, the personal representative is under a duty to gather in the deceased's assets, to pay off the estate's debts, and to distribute any surplus to those beneficially entitled. In this process, the courts distinguish between matters of administration and matters of distribution. The law governing the administration is the law of the country that appointed the personal representative. The law governing the distribution is, in general, the law of the last domicile of the deceased in the case of movable property and the law of the *situs* in the case of immovable property.

B. ADMINISTRATION OF ESTATES

1) Local Grants of Representation

Traditionally, the presence of local assets was required for a local grant of representation. The courts were, therefore, called on to locate assets for the purpose of the administration of an estate. It was easy to locate tangible property but the court had to develop rules for the *situs* of intangible property in this context.[1] Legislation, however, has broadened the courts' jurisdiction. In the United Kingdom, this expansion occurred by virtue of section 2 of the *Administration of Justice Act 1932*.[2] Equally, provincial statutes now allow for grants of representation even though the deceased left no assets in the province. Ontario's *Estates Act*, for example, provides that an application for a grant of representation shall be made to the court of the district in which the deceased had a fixed place of abode at the time of death.[3] If the deceased had no fixed place of abode in Ontario at the time of death then the application should be made in a district where the deceased left property.[4] The statute also states that, in any other case, an application may be made to the court of any district.[5] Normally, there would be no point in applying for a grant of representation where the deceased did not reside in and left no property in the province. It has been suggested that one such case would be where the deceased died domiciled in the province.[6] In Alberta, it is specifically provided that when the deceased neither died resident nor left property in the province, the court may stay the proceedings.[7]

An estate cannot be administered as a whole. There must be separate administrations of an estate in each jurisdiction in which the deceased left assets. Thus, a provincial grant of representation is effective only in respect of property of the deceased situated in that province. The common law draws a distinction between the principal administra-

---

1   See, generally, Chapter 16.
2   (UK), 22 & 23 Geo 5, c 55.
3   RSO 1990, c E.21, s 7(1).
4   *Ibid*, s 7(2).
5   *Ibid*, s 7(3).
6   Janet Walker, *Castel & Walker: Canadian Conflict of Laws*, 6th ed (Markham, ON: Butterworths, 2005) (loose-leaf) at para 26.2.a.
7   *Estate Administration Act*, SA 2014, c E-12.5, s 2(2).

tion, which takes place in the country of the deceased's domicile, and ancillary administrations, which take place in all other jurisdictions where the deceased left property. In an attempt to coordinate the administration of an entire estate, local courts will typically grant representation to the person who has been appointed, or who is entitled to be appointed, in the country in which the deceased died domiciled, but they retain the discretion not to do so.[8] It should be noted, however, that in some provinces, such as Ontario,[9] a grant of administration, as opposed to probate, cannot be made to a non-resident.[10]

Coordination is further achieved by provincial legislative provisions for the resealing of certain foreign grants made by reciprocating states, typically grants from the other provinces, the United Kingdom, and sometimes other Commonwealth countries.[11] The procedure is simpler since it saves the applicant from having to produce all the documentation required in an application for an original grant of representation.[12] Once resealed, the foreign grant has the same effect as a local grant.

The *Hague Convention Concerning the International Administration of the Estates of Deceased Persons*, which is designed to facilitate the administration of estates that cut across national boundaries, came into force in 1973.[13] The convention provides for a contracting state to issue an international certificate designating the person entitled to administer the "movable estate" of a deceased person and indicating that person's powers. The certificate is to be issued in the state of the deceased's last habitual residence and to be recognized, within certain parameters, by other contracting states. Canada has neither signed nor ratified the convention.

A local grant of representation vests in the personal representative all property, movable or immovable, situated in the province that was vested in the deceased at the time of death.[14]

2) The Law Governing the Administration of an Estate

It is clear that the administration of an estate is governed exclusively by the law of the country from which the personal representative derived

---

8   *Re Kaime Estate* (1938), 53 BCR 190 (SC).
9   *Estates Act*, above note 3, s 5.
10 This provision does not apply to the resealing of a foreign grant, discussed below.
11 See, for example, *Estate Administration Act*, above note 7, s 18; *Estates Act*, above note 3, s 52.
12 See Walker, above note 6 at para 26.3.a.
13 11 ILM 1277 (1972).
14 See, for example, *Estates Administration Act*, RSO 1990, c E.22, s 2. There are exceptions, such as jointly owned property subject to a right of survivorship.

his or her authority. Thus, a provincial personal representative must administer an estate according to the law of the province from which he or she obtained the grant, whether the administration is principal or ancillary. Once the personal representative has collected the assets of the deceased, he or she must pay all the legitimate debts of the estate. As indicated in *Re Kloebe*, all questions as to the admissibility and priority of debts are matters of administration.[15] It is also clear that foreign creditors are to be treated in the same way as local creditors, regardless of whether the local administration is principal or ancillary.[16] In *Re Scatcherd*, the estate was insolvent.[17] The assets situated in Ontario were sufficient to pay the Ontario creditors in full but the assets abroad were insufficient to satisfy the claims of the foreign creditors. The question before the court was whether the Ontario creditors had to be paid in full with the balance remitted to the domiciliary representative for distribution among the foreign creditors. Justice Middleton held based on *Re Kloebe* that all creditors, whether domestic or foreign, had the right to be paid without preference. In *Re Kloebe*, Pearson J expressed a possible qualification to that proposition. He said:

> No doubt in a case in which [foreign] assets were distributed so as to give [foreign] creditors, as such, priority, in distributing the English assets the court would be astute to equalize the payments, and take care that no [foreign] creditors should come in and receive anything till the English creditors had been paid a proportionate amount. But subject to that, which is for the purpose of doing what is equal and just to all the creditors, I know of no law under which the English creditors are to be preferred to foreigners. On the other hand the rule is they are all to be treated equally, subject to what priorities the law may give them, from whatever part of the world they come . . . .[18]

If the local administration is ancillary then the locally appointed representative is normally required to hand over any surplus assets to the principal or domiciliary representative for distribution to the beneficiaries. In *Re Bradley*, for example, an intestate died domiciled in Iowa leaving property in Alberta.[19] Administration was granted in Iowa in ignorance of the Alberta assets. The defendant obtained a grant of administration in Alberta without knowing of the Iowa administrator. After completion of administration of the Iowa estate, the existence of the Alberta assets

---

15 (1884), 28 Ch D 175.
16 *Ibid*.
17 (1918), 15 OWN 222 (HC).
18 Above note 15 at 177–78.
19 [1941] 4 DLR 309 (Alta SC).

became known. The plaintiff obtained a fresh grant of administration in Iowa and applied in Alberta for an order requiring the Alberta administrator to hand over the surplus assets.[20] The court held that he was entitled to the order based upon the following principle from *Re Achillopoulos*:[21]

> Where a testator domiciled abroad has died ... the Court is free in proper circumstances to authorize the administrator to hand over the surplus of the assets in this country to the executors of the law of the domicil .... It seems to me that all that the Court has to do is to satisfy itself that the principal is the person who under the law of the domicil is bound to perform the functions which are imposed by our law upon an executor or administrator.[22]

The courts, however, have discretion to restrain the local representative from handing over the surplus assets to the principal representative. They may exercise this discretion where those assets would be applied in a manner that is contrary to local law. The most notorious exercise of this power occurred in *Re Lorillard*.[23] A testator died domiciled in New York leaving assets and creditors in both England and New York. Administration proceedings were being conducted in both countries. The English creditors were satisfied out of the English assets. The New York assets were exhausted, leaving certain unpaid creditors in New York. In the normal course of events, the surplus English assets would have been transferred to the domiciliary representative. That party, however, would have used those assets to pay off the remaining New York creditors who were statute-barred by English law. The court exercised its discretion to restrain the remission of the English assets to New York. Those creditors had not claimed in the English proceedings because they knew that their claims were barred by English law. The court ordered the English representative to distribute the surplus directly to the beneficiaries under the will who were residing in England. The decision has been criticized as the strange exercise of "judicial discretion to enrich beneficiaries at the expense of creditors who were entitled to payment in the place of the

---

20 The ability of the foreign domiciliary personal representative to seek an order for the transfer of surplus assets is an exception to the general rule, discussed in the next section, that a foreign personal representative has no standing to sue in a local court: see Lawrence Collins, ed, *Dicey, Morris and Collins on the Conflict of Laws*, 15th ed (London: Sweet & Maxwell, 2012) at para 26R-036 [*Dicey, Morris and Collins*].
21 [1928] Ch 433.
22 *Ibid* at 444–45, Tomlin J.
23 [1922] 2 Ch 638 (CA). See also *In the Estate of Weiss*, [1962] P 136.

principal administration."[24] The critics point out that if the beneficiaries had resided in New York or in any other country where statutes of limitation were not classified as procedural, they would have been bound to disgorge what they had received to the creditors.[25] It should be noted that in Canada, since *Tolofson v Jensen*,[26] limitation periods are now characterized as substantive.

To be contrasted with *Re Lorillard* is the briefly reported decision of *Re Donnelly*.[27] Principal administration of an estate took place in Pennsylvania with ancillary administration in Ontario. Justice Middleton held that, as soon as the Ontario creditors had been paid, the local administrator held the surplus solely for the principal administrator. Once the Ontario creditors had been paid, the Ontario representative had no interest in the disposal of the surplus that would be remitted to the principal administrator. Foreign creditors would then look to the foreign representative for payment. Thus, the implication was that local administrators should not concern themselves with how the principal administrator might dispose of the surplus assets even if that disposal would involve the payment to creditors who would be barred from claiming by Ontario law.

A less controversial exercise of the judicial discretion is illustrated by *Re Ritchie*.[28] Ritchie died intestate domiciled in Ohio. He left a large estate there but he also left movable and immovable property in Ontario. Thus, the principal administration was conducted in Ohio and ancillary administration occurred in Ontario. By the law of Ohio, the entire estate went to the widow but by Ontario law the deceased's sister was entitled to a portion of the estate. One question was whether the Ontario administrator should pay over the surplus to the principal administrator. By Ontario's conflicts rules, the distribution of the estate was governed by the law of Ohio with the exception of immovables in Ontario, which were governed by Ontario law. The court ordered the Ontario administrator to pay over to the Ohio administrator that property in Ontario that was governed by Ohio law, namely the movables. It further directed, however, that the Ontario administrator should distribute the Ontario immovables directly to the beneficiaries. The court thus solved any difficulty that might have arisen should it have been discovered that the Ohio administrator would not have distributed the

---

24 James Fawcett & Janeen Carruthers, *Cheshire, North & Fawcett Private International Law*, 14th ed (Oxford: Oxford University Press, 2008) at 1259.
25 *Ibid*.
26 [1994] 3 SCR 1022. See Chapter 11, Section C.
27 (1911), 2 OWN 1388 (HCJ).
28 [1942] 3 DLR 330 (Ont HCJ).

Ontario immovables in accordance with the Ontario law of intestate succession.

Sometimes it can be difficult to determine where administration ends and succession (beneficial distribution) begins. In *Re Wilks*, for example, the English court held that the power granted by English law to postpone the sale of personal property in the interests of beneficiaries who were minors was a rule of administration.[29] Hence, English administrators could exercise that power in respect of company shares situated in England despite the fact that an administrator appointed by the courts of the deceased's domicile, Ontario, would be required to realize the shares. Similarly in *Re Kehr* an intestate died domiciled in Germany leaving property in England.[30] He was survived by a wife and an infant son. The court held that the English administrator had the power, under English legislation, to appoint trustees of the son's property with authority to make payments out of that property for the son's maintenance and advancement. These were matters of administration and therefore governed by English law rather than German law.

Both *Re Wilks* and *Re Kehr* were considered in *Kelemen v Alberta (Public Trustee)*.[31] Julianne Jagos, a Calgary resident, died. By her will, her grandniece in Romania was entitled to money that was in the hands of the Public Trustee of Alberta. The will provided that until the beneficiary reached the age of majority the funds would be held in trust. The grandniece was then sixteen years old. Her mother sought the trust funds on the basis that she was the beneficiary's guardian and trustee under Romanian law. The issue was whether Alberta or Romanian law should be applied to interpret and implement the testamentary trust. If Alberta law applied, then the beneficiary would not reach the age of majority until she was eighteen and the funds could not be transferred by the Public Trustee until that time. By Romanian law, there was an argument that the age of majority was fourteen or, alternatively, that the Public Trustee was required to hand over the funds to the beneficiary's mother as her guardian under Romanian law.

According to the court, the issue could potentially be characterized as one relating to the administration of an estate or the succession to an estate or the administration of a trust. Chief Justice Wachowich held that the issue was one of trust administration. For that conclusion, he relied upon the endorsement in *Re Pemberton*[32] of the argument by the minor's

---

29   [1935] 1 Ch 645.
30   [1952] 1 Ch 26.
31   (2007), 413 AR 305 (QB) [*Kelemen*].
32   (1966), 59 DLR (2d) 44 at 50 (BCSC).

lawyer in *Re Kehr*.[33] The lawyer had contended that once "mechanical" administration had been completed, the administrators became trustees for an infant's share of the estate and therefore all further issues concerned the administration of that trust.[34] In consequence, the Alberta court applied the choice of law rules contained in the 1985 *Hague Convention on the Law Applicable to Trusts and on Their Recognition*[35] that had been implemented in Alberta.[36] On the basis of that convention, Wachowich CJ applied Alberta law. Thus, the trust assets were not releasable until the beneficiary reached eighteen, the age of majority under Alberta law.

3) Foreign Personal Representatives

A foreign personal representative has no official presence in the forum and thus no authority to deal with the deceased's assets there unless he or she obtains a grant of representation from the local courts or has his or her foreign grant resealed. Thus, as a general proposition, a foreign representative can neither sue nor be sued in the forum in the capacity of the deceased's representative.

a) Actions by Foreign Personal Representatives

Foreign personal representatives have no right to recover the deceased's property in the forum. That fact means that they cannot sue in the forum to recover debts owing to the deceased without a local grant since a debt owed by a debtor living in the forum constitutes estate property situated in the forum.[37] Foreign representatives, however, are entitled to assert their title to estate property without a local grant where they have reduced that property into their possession abroad. Importantly, this principle has been extended to intangibles such as negotiable instruments and simple debts.

Negotiable instruments are regarded more as chattels than as debts, and thus their *situs* is the place where the document is situated. A personal representative can, therefore, reduce them into possession by taking hold of the documents. This principle was illustrated in *Crosby v Prescott*.[38] The plaintiff brought an action in Manitoba on certain promissory notes made by the defendant to the order of the deceased,

---

33   Above note 30.
34   *Ibid* at 27.
35   23 ILM 1388 (1984). See Chapter 20.
36   Part 1 of the *International Conventions Implementation Act*, RSA 2000, c I-6.
37   See Chapter 16.
38   (1922), 32 Man R 108 (CA), aff'd [1923] SCR 446.

a resident of Massachusetts. The plaintiff had been appointed as the deceased's administrator in Massachusetts. The defendant argued that the plaintiff had no standing to sue because he had not obtained a local grant of representation. The court held that the plaintiff could sue in Manitoba without the necessity of a further grant. Negotiable instruments were in the nature of chattels and could be sufficiently reduced into possession by means of the paper. Thus, the plaintiff had reduced the notes into his possession in Massachusetts by taking hold of them. He was in fact suing as the holder of the notes, and no grant was required from the Manitoba courts. The courts also made it clear that the principle was not confined to bearer instruments but included the order instruments at issue in the case itself.

In contrast to negotiable instruments, simple contract debts are reduced into possession by the recovery of a judgment against the debtor. Thus, a foreign personal representative is entitled to sue in the forum on a judgment that he or she has obtained abroad in an action against a debtor of the estate without the need for a further grant of representation. In *Peterson v Bezold* the plaintiff was an Idaho executor.[39] He had obtained a judgment in that capacity in Idaho and sued on it in Alberta without obtaining an Alberta grant. The defendant sought to strike out the claim because the plaintiff had no Alberta appointment. The court denied that motion. The plaintiff had reduced the debt into his possession by recovering the judgment in Idaho and therefore an action could be brought on that judgment in Alberta.

b) Actions against Foreign Personal Representatives

The general rule is that a foreign personal representative cannot be sued in the forum in his or her representative capacity. Thus, in *Patterson v Hambleton* the defendants were appointed in New York as the executors of the estate of the deceased.[40] They did not seek to obtain a grant in Ontario because the deceased had left no assets there. The plaintiff sued the defendants in Ontario on a contract made and breached by the deceased in that province. The court held that no action lay against the defendants because they had not taken out probate in Ontario.

In *Nova, An Alberta Corporation v Grove*, the Alberta Court of Appeal followed *Patterson* and applied the same principle to a tort case.[41] The question was whether the plaintiff was entitled to serve *ex juris* the Texas executor of the estate of Julia Grove. She had been a member of a partnership that had allegedly committed a tort in Alberta through

---

39 [1971] 2 WWR 156 (Alta SCAD).
40 [1933] OWN 247 (HCJ) [*Patterson*].
41 (1982), 39 AR 409 (CA) [*Nova*].

negligent manufacturing or design. There was no doubt that any tort had been committed in Alberta. There was also no doubt that, if Grove had been alive, she could have been sued personally. It was also clear that the action against her survived her death. Nevertheless, the majority held that service *ex juris* should not be allowed on the Texas executor. A foreign personal representative had no presence in Alberta and was not subject to the jurisdiction of the Alberta courts. The Texas executor was, therefore, subject only to the jurisdiction of Texas because that was where he had obtained his grant.

There was a vigorous dissent in *Nova* by Laycraft JA. He was influenced by the fact that Alberta was clearly the appropriate place for the action. He decided that the litigation did not constitute an administration action and the rule barring claims against foreign personal representatives was restricted to administration actions. The majority, however, held that any action in which the plaintiff claimed money from an estate was in essence an administration action.

In its turn, the *Nova* principle was applied by the Alberta Court of Appeal in *Canadian Commercial Bank v Belkin*.[42] In that case, the defendant had died after being served but before trial, so the question was whether the action could be continued against a foreign (British Columbia) personal representative. The court refused to distinguish *Nova* on that basis. The *Nova* principle still applied. The court also rejected the theory that *Nova* was inapplicable to other provinces. British Columbia was a foreign country for conflict of laws purposes.

A foreign personal representative who intermeddles with the deceased's assets in the forum without a local grant may incur liability as an executor *de son tort*,[43] as indeed may anybody who interferes in the estate without the requisite grant.[44]

---

42 (1990), 107 AR 232 (CA). In *Hill v Hill*, 2010 ABQB 528 at paras 23–25, the judge followed both this decision and *Nova*, above note 41. However, she stated that if not bound by these precedents, she would have instead followed the dissenting approach in *Nova* and allowed the foreign personal representatives to be sued. The litigation had been started against the deceased before he had died.
43 *Charron v Montreal Trust Co*, [1958] OR 597 (CA); *Re Pemberton*, above note 32; *Nova*, above note 41; *Canadian Commercial Bank v Belkin*, above note 42.
44 *New York Breweries Co Ltd v Attorney-General*, [1899] AC 62 (HL).

C. SUCCESSION (BENEFICIAL DISTRIBUTION)

1) Jurisdiction

Canadian courts have jurisdiction to determine succession to an estate whenever they have jurisdiction to administer that estate within the rules already discussed. The court must, of course, have exercised its jurisdiction to administer the estate through the appointment of a personal representative. Typically, such an appointment will be made where there are local assets. In exercising jurisdiction, however, the courts do not necessarily limit their determinations to local assets but may deal with the estate as a whole. Indeed, as an exception to the general rule,[45] they will even determine title to foreign immovables.[46] Recently in *R Griggs Group Ltd v Evans*, the court expressed the applicable principle and its rationale in the following manner:

> There is another way in which our courts may make orders which affect ownership of foreign land. It often happens that an Englishman dies having made a will disposing of his property both in this country and abroad, including land. In those circumstances our courts may be called upon to administer the estate and, in so doing, to adjudicate upon this question: who succeeds to the title to the foreign land? Two famous examples concern Admiral Lord Nelson (land in Sicily) and the Duke of Wellington (land in Spain): *Earl Nelson v Lord Bridport* (1846) 8 Beav. 547 and *In re Duke of Wellington* [1948] Ch 118. . . . A man may die leaving property in many countries, and it would not be sensible to compel his executors to institute a diversity of proceedings.[47]

Although there are few cases, it appears that the modern doctrine of *forum non conveniens* will be applied to determine the most appropriate jurisdiction to deal with a dispute as to the beneficial distribution of an estate. There is merit in having the validity of a will, for example, determined in one set of proceedings so as to avoid the danger of inconsistent decisions. In *Gillespie v Grant*, the testator left movables in British Columbia and movables and immovables in Alberta, and the estate was being administered in both provinces.[48] Issues were raised as to the testator's testamentary capacity and dependants' relief. Proceedings had

---

45 See Chapter 17, Section A.
46 See, for example, *Re Duke of Wellington*, [1948] Ch 118 (CA). See *Dicey, Morris and Collins*, above note 20 at para 23-052; Fawcett & Carruthers, above note 24 at 486.
47 [2005] Ch 153 at para 70.
48 (1992), 4 Alta LR (3d) 122 (Surr Ct) [*Gillespie*].

been launched in both provinces. The Alberta court determined that the initial question to be resolved was the testator's domicile at death.[49] The court then concluded, in accordance with general *forum non conveniens* principles, that Alberta was the appropriate forum to deal with the issue of domicile. Justice Mason recognized, however, that a further dispute as to the appropriate forum might arise once the testator's domicile had been determined. If British Columbia were found to be the testator's domicile, then British Columbia law would apply to the distribution of the movables though Alberta law would still apply to the immovables. If, on the other hand, Alberta were found to be the testator's domicile, then there would be no realistic *forum non conveniens* issue. Alberta law would govern distribution of the entire estate and thus would be the obvious forum.

2) Recognition of Foreign Decisions

The courts of the deceased's last domicile have jurisdiction to determine succession to all of the deceased's movables wherever situated. The decision of those courts will then be recognized elsewhere. In *Senkiw v Muzyka*, for example, Kost Senkiw died intestate domiciled in Wisconsin and left movables in that state.[50] The Wisconsin administrator experienced difficulties in locating the deceased's relatives. He eventually found a brother living in Saskatchewan. From him, the administrator learned that the deceased had three other brothers and one sister. He could not, however, locate them. He applied to the Wisconsin court for final settlement of the estate. The court issued a judgment whereby it declared that the deceased had been survived by his brother in Saskatchewan and that the other siblings, not having been heard from since 1937, had predeceased Senkiw. The court ordered that the surviving brother should receive the net estate and that the administrator should be discharged. Soon afterwards the brother in Saskatchewan died, leaving his entire estate to his wife and children. Senkiw's four other siblings were then found to be still alive. They claimed that they were entitled to a share of Senkiw's estate. The executors of the Saskatchewan brother's estate pleaded the Wisconsin judgment as a defence. The Saskatchewan Court of Appeal held that there had been a final determination of en-

---

49 In fact, as the court admitted, testamentary capacity with respect to movables is probably governed by the testator's domicile at the time of making the will (see Section C(3)(b)(iii), below in this chapter) though there was no evidence that his domicile had changed between that time and the time of his death.
50 (1969), 4 DLR (3d) 708 (Sask CA), aff'd (1970), 12 DLR (3d) 544 (SCC). See also *Jones v Smith* (1925), 56 OLR 550 (CA).

titlement to Senkiw's estate and that the Wisconsin judgment was binding in Saskatchewan because Wisconsin was Senkiw's domicile at the time of his death. Chief Justice Culliton quoted with approval what is now rule 147 of *Dicey, Morris and Collins*:

> The courts of a foreign country have jurisdiction to determine the succession to all movables wherever situated of a testator or intestate dying domiciled in such country. Such determination will be followed in [the forum].[51]

It is also arguable that foreign courts have jurisdiction to determine the succession to all of the deceased's property which was situated in the foreign country at the time of the judgment irrespective of the deceased's domicile at death.[52] The basis for this principle is that local provincial courts are prepared to assume jurisdiction to determine the succession to property situated in the province. It will be interesting to see whether, in the future, the recognition of foreign determinations as to succession will be based on an application of the real and substantial connection test from *Morguard Investments Ltd v De Savoye*.[53] One potential problem with an extension of the *Morguard* principle in such a manner would be the increased likelihood of conflicting decisions in the area of succession. While it is true that under the present law courts may disagree, for example, as to where a deceased died domiciled, multiple courts may well have a real and substantial connection to a dispute through links with the deceased, the beneficiaries, or the estate property. Although, as we have observed, common law courts are apparently prepared to determine title to foreign immovables in succession proceedings, it is generally assumed that local courts will not recognize foreign determinations with respect to immovables outside the foreign jurisdiction.[54]

3) Choice of Law

For choice of law purposes, common law courts distinguish between intestate and testamentary succession. More importantly and controversially, they also distinguish between succession to movables and succession

---

51   *Dicey, Morris and Collins*, above note 20 at para 27R-004, quoted in *Senkiw v Muzyka*, above note 50 at 712.
52   *Ibid* at paras 27R-007 to 27-008. Walker, above note 6 at para 27.1.b, would confine this principle to immovables.
53   [1990] 3 SCR 1077 [*Morguard*].
54   *Duke v Andler*, [1932] SCR 734; but see *Chapman Estate v O'Hara* (1987), 61 Sask R 140 (CA); Elizabeth Edinger, "Is *Duke v. Andler* Still Good Law in Common Law Canada?" (2011) 51 *Canadian Business Law Journal* 52. See Chapter 17, Section B.

to immovables, with the former governed in general by the law of the deceased's last domicile and the latter governed in general by the law of the *situs* of the immovable property. The result is that a will, for example, may be valid with respect to movables but invalid with respect to immovables or vice versa. This doctrine is known as the principle of scission and is to be contrasted with the principle of unity of succession. The latter principle was espoused by the 1988 *Hague Convention on the Law Applicable to Succession to the Estates of Deceased Persons*.[55] It applies the same rules to succession, both intestate and testamentary, to movables and immovables. In most circumstances the law to be applied is the law of the deceased's last habitual residence. The convention, however, is not in force anywhere in Canada.

a) Intestate Succession

Intestate succession to movables is governed by the law of the deceased's domicile at death and intestate succession to immovables is governed by the law of the *situs*. Thus, if a person dies intestate domiciled in Alberta leaving a cottage in British Columbia, the movables, as well as any Alberta land, will be distributed in accordance with Alberta law but the cottage will go to those entitled by British Columbia law. This is a strange result. It is difficult to see that the *situs* of immovable property has any interest in the determination of who should be entitled to succeed on intestacy. It is the personal law of the deceased, traditionally the law of the last domicile, which has the real interest in determining which parties should share in the estate and in what proportions. That interest is unaffected by the fact that immovable property is involved.[56] A similar division is not made for the purposes of domestic law where there is one system of intestate succession for all kinds of property. The principle of scission also potentially leads to the cumulation of preferential shares under the intestacy legislation of the domicile and of every jurisdiction, other than the domicile, where immovable property is situated.[57]

---

55 28 ILM 146 (1989). See Walker, above note 6 at para 27.6. See also, in the European Union context, the European Succession Regulation: EC, *Commission Regulation (EU) No 650/2012 of 4 July 2012 on jurisdiction, applicable law, recognition and enforcement of decisions and acceptance and enforcement of authentic instruments in matters of succession and on the creation of a European Certificate of Succession*, [2012] OJ, L 201/107 [Brussels IV]. The European Union's predominantly common law countries, the United Kingdom and Ireland, have not opted into this regulation.

56 See the discussion of this question in JHC Morris, "Intestate Succession to Land in the Conflict of Laws" (1969) 85 *Law Quarterly Review* 339.

57 See, for example, *Re Rea*, [1902] 1 IR 451 (Ch D); *Re Collens*, [1986] Ch 505.

Problems like these have led the authors of *Dicey, Morris and Collins* to argue that all issues of intestate succession should be referred to a single law, the law of the deceased's last domicile.[58] Some Canadian lower courts have attempted to modify the traditional rules. In *Re Thom Estate*, the deceased died intestate domiciled in Saskatchewan.[59] He left land and movables in Saskatchewan and land in Manitoba. He was survived by his widow and three children. By Saskatchewan law, the widow was entitled on intestacy to a preferential share of $40,000 plus, in these circumstances, one third of the residue of the estate. By Manitoba law, the widow was entitled to a preferential share of $50,000 plus one half of the residue of the estate. It appeared that the widow had received in Saskatchewan her preferential share of $40,000 and one third of the residue from the Saskatchewan assets. She then claimed $50,000 from the Manitoba land plus one half of the remainder in accordance with Manitoba law as the *lex situs*.

The court was clearly troubled by the prospect of allowing the widow to cumulate preferential shares. Justice Oliphant's solution was to award the widow the higher preferential share. He therefore allowed the widow $10,000 from the Manitoba land so as to top up the $40,000 received in Saskatchewan to the higher preferential share available in Manitoba. He also granted the widow one half of the residue from the Manitoba land in accordance with the law of the *situs*. The children had argued that the court should apply a unified rule of succession favouring Saskatchewan law as the law of the deceased's domicile at death. On that basis, the widow would receive simply one third of the value of the Manitoba land. Justice Oliphant rejected that argument on the misplaced ground that it would entail an application of *renvoi*. He said:

> If I accept the children's position, I would, in effect, be sitting as a court in Saskatchewan, applying the law of that province. This is what is known as the doctrine of *renvoi*. While English courts have applied the doctrine, courts in Canada have not been favourably disposed to do the same. I cannot accede to the children's submission.[60]

---

58 *Dicey, Morris and Collins*, above note 20 at para 27-018.
59 (1987), 50 Man R (2d) 187 (QB) [*Thom*]. See the annotation by Vaughan Black (1987) 27 *Estates and Trusts Reports* 185.
60 *Thom*, above note 59 at para 31. Justice Oliphant would simply be applying Saskatchewan's domestic law on intestate succession and not Saskatchewan's conflicts rules. On *renvoi* see Chapter 10, Section E(1).

The approach taken in *Thom* drew the support of Kinsman J in *Re Vak Estate*.[61] As in *Thom*, the court rejected the traditional "double-dipping" approach of cases like *Re Rea*.[62] It also rejected the idea that it should apply a unified approach whereby the deceased's personal law would govern the intestate succession to all property, both movable and immovable. Instead, Kinsman J approved of the theory advanced in *Thom* that the surviving spouse should be able to take advantage of the higher preferential share. The court, therefore, set out the following rule:

> The assets irrespective of whether they are movables or immovables, should be assembled under the administrator's umbrella, and after setting aside the highest preferential share permitted under the respective jurisdictions where the assets are located, the residue of the estate be divided by the applicable law of the deceased's usual or habitual place of residence.
>
> This will serve to avoid time-consuming and expensive estate litigation which occurs in this and other jurisdictions where residents of Manitoba have elaborate summer homes on Lake of the Woods, Florida condominiums, as well as a transitory population in Canada whose places of employment and assets are scattered throughout North America and elsewhere.
>
> It will also avoid inequitable "double dipping" on the part of the surviving spouse, which in smaller estates could well result in the children being disentitled to any share of their deceased parents' estate.[63]

The proposed rule raises serious questions. First, the decision seems to go further than *Thom* in the sense that, once the spouse has received the highest preferential share available, the residue of the estate is distributed in accordance with the deceased's personal law whether the property is movable or immovable. Second, the court regarded the relevant personal law as the law of the deceased's last habitual residence rather than the law of the domicile, apparently on the ground that the concept of domicile was outmoded. Third, the court stated that the surviving spouse should receive the highest preferential share allowed by the law of any jurisdiction where assets were located. There was no express requirement that substantial assets must have been located in that jurisdiction. The contrast with *Thom* should again be noted. Under *Thom*, it is a question of awarding the highest preferential share among places where the deceased left land and the place where the deceased died domiciled.

---

61 (1994), 20 OR (3d) 378 (Gen Div). See the annotation by Vaughan Black (1994) 4 *Estates and Trusts Reports* (2d) 2.
62 Above note 57.
63 *Re Vak Estate*, above note 61 at 384.

b) Testamentary Succession

i) Formal Validity of a Will

At common law, all issues relating to the formal validity of a will of immovables were referred to the law of the *situs* and the formal validity of a will of movables was referred to the testator's domicile at the time of death. The latter rule in particular caused problems as wills were struck down on what were perceived as technicalities, which frustrated the intentions of testators. These difficulties came to a head in *Bremer v Freeman* in which the court refused to admit to probate the will of a British subject who had died domiciled in France.[64] The will was formally valid by English law but invalid by French law. This decision led to the passage of the *Wills Act, 1861* in England which, for the first time, allowed British subjects to use the form of making a will prescribed by the law of different jurisdictions.[65] Some courts also injected flexibility into the law by using the doctrine of single *renvoi* in an attempt to validate wills. Thus, there were decisions indicating that a will would be valid if it complied either with the form prescribed by the law of the testator's last domicile or with the form prescribed by some law chosen by the conflicts rules of the law of the last domicile.[66]

Modern provincial legislation now allows testators to use the form of several different countries, at least as far as movables are concerned. Alberta's *Wills and Succession Act* is representative of the legislation in place in several provinces.[67] Sections 41(2) and 41(3), respectively, restate the traditional common law choice of law rules using the law of the *situs* in the case of land and the law of the deceased's last domicile in the case of movable property. Section 42 then allows for other laws to be examined to uphold the formal validity of a will with respect to movables, namely the law of the place where the will was made, the law of the place where the testator was domiciled when the will was made, and the law of the testator's domicile of origin. In all three cases, the reference is to the law in force at the time of the will's execution.

The legislation in some other provinces is even more generous. Ontario's *Succession Law Reform Act* is the most far-reaching.[68] Sections 36(1) and 36(2) restate the common law rules pointing to the law of the *situs* and the law of the last domicile. It should be noted, however, that the legislation expressly excludes any possibility of applying *renvoi* by

---

64 (1857), 14 ER 508.
65 (UK) 24 & 25 Vict, c 114. This statute is often referred to as Lord Kingsdown's Act.
66 *Collier v Rivaz* (1841), 2 Curt 855, 163 ER 608. See also *Ross v Ross* (1894), 25 SCR 307.
67 SA 2010, c W-12.2.
68 RSO 1990, c S.26.

referring throughout to the "internal law" of the chosen jurisdiction.[69] The statute further provides:

> 37(1) As regards the manner and formalities of making a will of an interest in movables or in land, a will is valid and admissible to probate if at the time of its making it complied with the internal law of the place where,
> (a) the will was made;
> (b) the testator was then domiciled;
> (c) the testator then had his or her habitual residence; or
> (d) the testator then was a national if there was in that place one body of law governing the wills of nationals.
>
> (2) As regards the manner and formalities of making a will of an interest in movables or in land, the following are properly made,
> (a) a will made on board a vessel or aircraft of any description, if the making of the will conformed to the internal law in force in the place with which, having regard to its registration, if any, and other relevant circumstances, the vessel or aircraft may be taken to have been most closely connected;
> (b) a will so far as it revokes a will which under sections 34 to 42 would be treated as properly made or revokes a provision which under those sections would be treated as comprised in a properly made will, if the making of the later will conformed to any law by reference to which the revoked will or provision would be treated as properly made....

Of special note is the fact that this broadening of the laws to which reference can be made to uphold the formal validity of a will extends to both movables and land. Section 41(2) of the statute states:

> In determining . . . whether or not the making of a will conforms to a particular law, regard shall be had to the formal requirements of that law at the time the will was made, but account shall be taken of an alteration of law affecting wills made at that time if the alteration enables the will to be treated as properly made.

Thus, the statute makes it clear that the relevant time for determining the content of the applicable law is the time of the will's execution but that retrospective changes in that law will be applied if they validate the will.[70]

---

69 The internal law of a place is described in the *Succession Law Reform Act*, ibid, s 34(c), as excluding the choice of law rules of that place.

70 For the common law position on the effect of changes in the law of the last domicile made after the testator's death, see *Lynch v Provisional Government of Paraguay* (1871), LR 2 P & D 268, which is discussed in the next section.

Finally, many provinces have adopted the *Convention Providing a Uniform Law on the Form of an International Will*[71] whereby a will is formally valid when made in the form of an international will as set out in the annex to the convention.[72]

ii) Essential or Intrinsic Validity of a Will
The common law was clear that the essential or intrinsic validity of a will of movables was governed by the law of the last domicile and the essential validity of a will of immovables was governed by the law of the *situs*. Those common law choice of law rules have been codified in wills legislation.[73] There is English authority supporting the application of the foreign court theory of *renvoi* in this context.[74] It seems unlikely that Canadian courts would apply that doctrine, except perhaps in relation to land governed by the law of the *situs*. In some provinces *renvoi* is expressly excluded.[75]

Essential validity deals with questions such as whether gifts to witnesses or relatives of witnesses are valid and whether the testator must leave a certain portion of the estate to a surviving spouse or children. *Re Groos* is a good illustration.[76] The deceased, while domiciled in the Netherlands, made a will there appointing her intended husband, also domiciled in the Netherlands, the heir of her estate with reservations only for the legitimate portion to which her descendants were entitled. The parties married in the Netherlands but they subsequently acquired a domicile in England where the wife died. The court held that English law, as the law of the deceased's domicile at death, governed the essential validity of her will with respect to movables. By Dutch law, three quarters of her movables constituted the legitimate portion for her surviving children. By English law, there was no "legitimate portion" for the children; her husband was entitled to everything. The court held that the entire movable estate went to the husband under the will by virtue of English law. Justice Sargant explained:

---

71 Can TS 1978 No 34.
72 See, for example, *Wills and Succession Act*, above note 67, ss 46–57; *Succession Law Reform Act*, above note 68, ss 42–43.
73 See, for example, *Wills and Succession Act*, above note 67, s 41(2) (immovables) and s 41(3) (movables); *Succession Law Reform Act*, above note 68, s 36(1) (immovables) and s 36(2) (movables).
74 See, for example, *Re Annesley*, [1926] Ch 692; *Re Ross*, [1930] 1 Ch 377.
75 See, for example, *Succession Law Reform Act*, above note 68, which refers to the "internal law" of the last domicile or of the *situs*.
76 [1915] 1 Ch 572.

The legitimate portion having been swept away by reason of the change of domicil, the result is, not that the meaning of the will is in any way altered, but that the area of the property over which the will takes effect is enlarged and the whole of the testatrix's residue instead of one-fourth share only goes to the husband.[77]

Other issues of essential validity are whether a gift violates the rule against perpetuities or whether a charitable gift is valid. These questions arose in the Supreme Court of Canada's decision in *Jewish National Fund Inc v Royal Trust Co*.[78] By his will, a testator who died domiciled in British Columbia created a trust of his movables in British Columbia. The property was to be used by the trustees of the Jewish National Fund in New York for the purchase of lands available in Palestine, the United States, or any British Dominion for the establishment of Jewish colonies. The trust was invalid by British Columbia law as infringing the rule against perpetuities since it did not qualify as a valid charitable trust. The majority applied the general rule that the essential validity of a gift of movables was governed by the testator's last domicile. Thus, the trust was invalid and there was intestacy with respect to the property that was the subject of the gift. The majority, however, did recognize a possible exception to the general rule where the trust was valid by the law of the *situs* of the lands directed to be purchased. In this case, the majority held that the place of administration of the trust would be the country where land was purchased and managed. The land could be purchased in various countries but the content of the laws of those countries had not been proven. They were, therefore, presumed to be the same as British Columbia law by which the trust was void. It was argued that the trust was to be administered in New York because that was where the trustees resided. By New York law, the trust was valid. The majority, however, determined that the residence of the trustees was irrelevant. The trust was not to be administered only in New York. Justice Cartwright concluded:

> It seems to me that a trust of movables void under the law of the testator's domicile and under that of many other countries in which the trustees are authorized to carry it out cannot be rendered valid by the circumstance that the trustees are permitted, but not required, to carry it out in a country in which it would be regarded as valid.[79]

---

77   Ibid at 577.
78   [1965] SCR 784.
79   Ibid at 790.

In a vigorous dissent, Judson and Spence JJ held that the governing law was that of the law of the place of administration of the trust rather than the law of the testator's last domicile. The British Columbia executorship had ended. The residue was handed over to New York trustees on clearly defined trusts that were recognized as valid by the law of New York. It was a New York trust to be administered in New York according to New York law. The matter was of no further concern to the courts of the domicile. There is much to be said for the minority view though it remains a difficult question to determine when the conflict of laws rules governing trusts should be applied in preference to those governing wills. Trusts, including testamentary trusts, are now governed in most provinces by the *Hague Convention on the Law Applicable to Trusts and on Their Recognition*.[80] There is still the need, however, to distinguish between questions relating to the validity of a will and questions relating to the validity of a trust and this process is not necessarily straightforward. An important provision from this perspective is article 4, which states that the convention does not apply to "preliminary issues relating to the validity of wills or of other acts by virtue of which assets are transferred to the trustee."

Lynch v Provisional Government of Paraguay is authority for the proposition that, in applying the law of the last domicile to determine the essential validity of a will of movables, that law should be applied as it stood at the time of death and not as it might have changed.[81] The will of a deceased Paraguayan ruler was presented for probate in England. Its validity was challenged on the ground that, after his death, a law had been passed in Paraguay that declared invalid any testamentary dispositions made by the ruler and that vested his property, wherever situated, in the state of Paraguay. The court applied Paraguayan law as it stood at the time of death and held that the will had not been invalidated by the subsequent legislation. In the case of immovable property, however, it appears that the law of the *situs* should be applied as it stands at the time of the proceedings.[82]

iii) Personal Capacity to Make and to Take under a Will

Personal capacity to make a will covers questions such as whether a minor or a person suffering from mental incapacity can make a valid will. There is very little authority on the question of what law governs a person's capacity. With respect to movables, there is support for using

---

80 Above note 35. See Chapter 20.
81 Above note 70.
82 *Nelson v Bridport* (1845), 8 Beav 537, 50 ER 207.

the law of the testator's domicile.[83] It is unclear, however, whether it is the testator's domicile at the time of making the will or at the time of death that governs. Most commentators favour the application of the law of the testator's domicile at the time of the will's execution.[84] With respect to immovables, the general principle would suggest that the law of the *situs* should apply and there is old authority to that effect.[85]

It appears that a beneficiary has capacity to take a gift of movables under a will if he or she has capacity either by the law of the testator's domicile at death or by the law of the beneficiary's own domicile.[86] Presumably capacity to receive a gift of immovable property is governed by the law of the *situs*.[87]

iv) Construction of a Will

In *Re Bessette*, Hope J stated the general rule with regard to the construction or interpretation of a will: "A will of moveables is to be construed in accordance with that system of law intended by the testator, which is presumed to be the law of his domicile at the date of execution, unless a contrary intention appears from the will."[88] Many of the authorities cited for this proposition in fact state a presumptive rule in favour of the deceased's domicile at death, though the testator's domicile had not changed from the time of the will's execution.[89] There is authority for the proposition that the same rule governs the interpretation of a will of immovables.[90] The law of the *situs* is not dominant in this context. The rule also has the inferential support of wills legislation. Section 39 of Ontario's *Succession Law Reform Act*, for example, provides that nothing "precludes resort to the law of the place where the testator was domiciled at the time of making a will in aid of its construction as regards an interest in land or an interest in movables."[91] Equally, section

---

83   *In the Estate of Fuld (No 3)*, [1968] P 675; *Gillespie*, above note 48.
84   See, for example, Walker, above note 6 at para 27.4.a; *Dicey, Morris and Collins*, above note 20 at paras 27R-023 to 27-025; Fawcett & Carruthers, above note 24 at 1265–66.
85   *Macdonald v Macdonell* (1864), 2 UCE & A 341 (Upper Canada CA). See also *Zilberman Estate v Davis* (1980), 4 Man R (2d) 336 at paras 31–32 (Surr Ct), aff'd (1980) 4 Man R (2d) 325 (CA).
86   *Re Hellmann's Will* (1863), LR 2 Eq 363.
87   See Walker, above note 6 at para 27.4.a.
88   [1942] 3 DLR 207 at 208 (Ont HCJ). See *Curati v Perdoni*, [2012] EWCA Civ 1381 at para 16.
89   See, for example, *Re Cunnington*, [1924] 1 Ch 68; *Re Wilkison*, [1934] OR 6 (HCJ).
90   See, for example, *Re Fulford Estate* (1996), 146 Nfld & PEIR 248 (PEISCTD).
91   Above note 68. See also *Wills and Succession Act*, above note 67, s 44.

38 states that a "change of domicile of the testator occurring after a will is made does not . . . alter its construction."[92]

It is worth noting that the topic of interpretation is potentially broad. It includes, for example, how the law fills gaps in dispositions that have come about when the testator has failed to foresee and guard against certain eventualities. Thus, in Re Cunnington the testator gave the residue of his estate to be divided among ten named legatees.[93] Two of those legatees had predeceased the testator. By French law, the law of the testator's domicile, the shares of those two legatees would be divided among the remaining eight. By English law, there would be intestacy with respect to those two shares.

It is not easy to determine when the *prima facie* rule will be excluded on the basis of a contrary intention. In Re Cunnington, for example, Eve J determined that French law as the law of the domicile governed the construction of the will despite the following facts: the will was made in England in English form, the will used English terminology, the legatees resided in England, and the property was situated in England.[94]

In Re Fergusson's Will a domiciled Englishman bequeathed a legacy to his niece domiciled in Germany.[95] The will further provided that, if his niece predeceased him, then the legacy was to be divided among her "next of kin." The court held that the meaning of "next of kin" was an issue of construction to be ascertained in accordance with English law.[96] Some commentators have argued that in Fergusson German law should have been applied because the deceased legatee died domiciled in that country.[97] It is sometimes difficult to determine whether the question raised is one of interpretation or one of status. In Fergusson, for example, the argument was made unsuccessfully that the question there was one of status. In Re MacDonald, the Supreme Court of Canada held that the law governing the construction of a will determined whether "issue" included both legitimate and illegitimate children but that the law governing status determined the question of legitimacy.[98] In Re Gage, the Supreme Court of Canada held that it was a matter of construction, rather than status, as to whether "children" included adopted children.[99]

---

92 See also *Wills and Succession Act*, ibid, s 43.
93 Above note 89.
94 Ibid. Contrast *Re Wilkison*, above note 89.
95 [1902] 1 Ch 483 [*Fergusson*].
96 See also *Re Bessette*, above note 88, where the court had to divine the meaning of "heirs" of foreign legatees.
97 See, for example, *Dicey, Morris and Collins*, above note 20 at para 27-064.
98 [1964] SCR 317.
99 [1962] SCR 241.

If a will creates a testamentary trust, disputes can raise issues of characterization as between the construction of a will or trust or the administration of an estate or trust: there are thus four potentially applicable choice of law rules.[100]

v) Revocation of a Will

It is fairly standard for domestic purposes that a will can be revoked by (1) another will, or a writing declaring an intention to revoke, made in accordance with the wills legislation; (2) the destruction of the will by the testator with the intention of revoking it; and (3) the subsequent marriage of the testator unless the will was expressly made in contemplation of marriage.[101] Some provinces have also enacted a provision like the following one in Ontario whereby a gift to a spouse is revoked by a subsequent divorce or annulment:

> 17(1) Subject to subsection (2), a will is not revoked by presumption of an intention to revoke it on the ground of a change in circumstances.
>
> (2) Except when a contrary intention appears by the will, where, after the testator makes a will, his or her marriage is terminated by a judgment absolute of divorce or is declared a nullity,
>
> (a) a devise or bequest of a beneficial interest in property to his or her former spouse; . . .
>
> [is] revoked and the will shall be construed as if the former spouse had predeceased the testator.[102]

It is clear that whether a will has been revoked by a later will or other testamentary instrument is dependent upon that later will being valid.[103] In *Re Busslinger Estate*, for example, a testator, while domiciled in Alberta, made a will disposing of his Alberta property, both movable and immovable, which complied with the formalities of Alberta's wills legislation.[104] The testator later acquired a domicile in Switzerland where he made a second will. This will purported to revoke his prior will and to dispose otherwise of his Alberta estate. The Swiss will complied with Swiss formalities but not with Alberta's. The court held that the Swiss will was valid with respect to the Alberta movables because it complied with the law of the testator's domicile at death, but invalid

---

100 See, for example, *Kelemen*, above note 31.
101 See, for example, Saskatchewan's *The Wills Act, 1996*, SS 1996, c W-14.1, ss 16–17. In partial contrast, see *Wills and Succession Act*, above note 67, s 21(2), which provides that a subsequent marriage after 1 February 2012 does not revoke a will.
102 *Succession Law Reform Act*, above note 68, s 17.
103 In this regard, note s 37(2)(b) of Ontario's *Succession Law Reform Act*, ibid.
104 (1952), 6 WWR (NS) 408 (Alta Dist Ct).

with respect to the Alberta land because it did not comply with the law of the *situs*. The Alberta will had, therefore, been revoked as regards the movables that were distributed in accordance with the Swiss will but was still in effect insofar as it dealt with the Alberta land. The court followed the earlier Ontario decision of *Re Howard* in which the material facts were the same.[105] There, the court was clearly unhappy with the state of the law. It aired the possibility that even though the later will could not dispose of the land in the forum, the revocation clause could still apply because it was contained in a will that complied with the law of the deceased's last domicile. On that basis, the deceased would have died intestate with respect to the land and the court would not have been giving effect to a will that the deceased had clearly intended to revoke. Ultimately, however, the court held that the revocation clause was not effective and the land went in accordance with the first will. Where the second will contains no express revocation clause, it is a question of construction as to whether the later will was intended to revoke the earlier one and as to the scope of any such revocation.

There is no authority on what law governs whether a will has been revoked by its destruction. One option is to use the law of the testator's domicile in the case of movables and the law of the *situs* in the case of land.[106] Another is to apply the law of the testator's domicile at the time of the alleged act of revocation to both movables and immovables.[107]

Davies v Davies considered the question of what law should govern whether a will has been revoked by a subsequent marriage.[108] Justice Stuart followed the reasoning of the English Court of Appeal in *Re Martin* and held that the question was properly characterized as one of matrimonial law rather than testamentary law.[109] On that basis, he concluded that the law to be applied was the law of the testator's domicile at the time of the marriage rather than the testator's domicile at death. Moreover, he held that the same logic applied to immovables as well as movables: "If the rule as to revocation of a will by marriage is part of the matrimonial law and not of the testamentary law, it is difficult to see why or how there can be any distinction in this respect between moveables, and immoveables."[110]

---

105 (1923), 54 OLR 109 (HC).
106 Walker, above note 6 at para 27.4.h. This could involve the testator's domicile at death or domicile at the time of the alleged revocation.
107 Dicey, Morris and Collins, above note 20 at paras 27R-086 to 27-088.
108 (1915), 24 DLR 737 (Alta SCTD) [*Davies*].
109 [1900] P 211 (CA).
110 *Davies*, above note 108 at 740. *Davies* was approved and followed in *Allison Estate v Allison* (1998), 56 BCLR (3d) 1 (SC).

To similar effect is *Davies v Collins*, in which the testator was dying in hospital when he entered into an *in extremis* marriage.[111] Such a marriage was valid under the law where he was (Trinidad) but not under the law of his domicile at the time (Nova Scotia). Under both laws marriage revoked an earlier will, but the law of Trinidad had an exception to this for *in extremis* marriages. The beneficiary under the prior will argued it would be inconsistent for the court to treat the marriage as valid but not give effect to the Trinidad exception for such marriages. The Court of Appeal disagreed. It followed the rule that the effect on a will of a subsequent marriage is determined by the law of the testator's domicile at the time of the marriage. It stated: "The choice of domicile at the time of marriage best avoids the eccentric succession difference between Trinidad and Nova Scotia arising from a marriage *in extremis* . . . accepting the validity of the Trinidadian marriage should not oblige this Court to recognize succession consequences unknown to Nova Scotia law and inimical to Dr. Davies' presumed intention."[112] The court also held that the rule should apply to both movable and immovable property rather than using the *lex situs* for the latter.[113]

Page Estate v Sachs[114] is the one case to address revocation because of a subsequent divorce within section 17 of Ontario's *Succession Law Reform Act*.[115] The testator died domiciled in Quebec in 1986. He left a will, made in 1968, naming his wife as the sole beneficiary of all his property. The testator and his wife were divorced in 1974. The testator never remarried, never made a new will, and never revoked his 1968 will even though he was asked whether he wanted to do so. The question before the court concerned succession to Ontario land. By Quebec law, the gift to the testator's former wife remained effective. By Ontario law, the devise was revoked by the divorce. The court applied Ontario law as the law of the *situs* and concluded that the former wife was not entitled to the Ontario land. It intimated that, if it were a question of succession to movables, then it would have looked at the testator's domicile at death. There was no consideration of whether some analogy could be drawn with cases like *Davies* so as to treat the issue as one of matrimonial law. Interestingly, the court applied Ontario's legislative provision retroactively in the sense that the precursor to what is now section 17 of Ontario's *Succession Law Reform Act* had not been enacted until some three years after the divorce.

---

111 2011 NSCA 79.
112 *Ibid* at para 29.
113 *Ibid* at paras 18–19 and 31.
114 (1990), 72 OR (2d) 409 (HCJ), aff'd (1993), 12 OR (3d) 371 (CA).
115 Above note 68.

vi) Doctrine of Election

The doctrine of election has been described as a rule of equity whereby "any person who accepts a benefit under a will is taken to have accepted the whole tenor of the will and must renounce any right that is inconsistent with any provision of the will."[116] In the context of private international law, the question of election typically arises because of the principle of scission and the differing rules governing the validity of wills of movables and wills of immovables. Thus, a person domiciled in Alberta may leave by will land in Costa Rica to a friend but by the same will leave movables to his or her spouse and sole heir. By Costa Rican law, the law of the *situs* of the land, the gift is invalid and the spouse would take the land on intestacy. In that situation, the spouse may be called upon to elect whether to take the land on intestacy or the movables under the will.

In *Re Allen's Estate*, Cohen J held that whether a beneficiary was to be put to his or her election was an issue of construction of the will to be determined by the law governing interpretation.[117] The generally accepted view, however, is that expressed by Younger J in *Re Ogilvie* who held in effect that the doctrine went to the essential validity of a will. He said: "[T]he question whether in any particular case ... a case of election is or is not raised depends upon the domicile of the testator at death—for it is the law of that domicile which governs it."[118] Before any question of election can arise, the court must be satisfied on the interpretation of the will that the testator intended to dispose in the will of the property in question even though the will was not valid in that regard. Moreover, in common law jurisdictions, there is a presumption that where a person uses general words of disposition, that person intended to dispose only of such property that was capable of passing under the will. These principles were illustrated in *Granot v Hersen*.[119] The testator died domiciled in Ontario, leaving property in Ontario and a condominium in Switzerland. He left a large bequest to his son from his Ontario property and the residue of his estate to his daughter. By Swiss law, the law of the *situs* of the condominium, rights

---

116 *Granot v Hersen* (1999), 43 OR (3d) 421 at para 8 (CA) [*Granot*], quoting Thomas Feeney, *The Canadian Law of Wills*, 3d ed (Toronto: Butterworths, 1987) at 214.
117 [1945] 2 All ER 264 (Ch D).
118 [1918] 1 Ch 492 at 498. See also *Re Mengel's Will Trusts*, [1962] Ch 791 at 800. If instead Alberta land were devised to the heir of the foreign land and foreign land were devised away from that heir, then it is assumed that Alberta law as the law of the *situs* would govern whether the heir must elect: see *Dicey, Morris and Collins*, above note 20 at para 27-081; Fawcett & Carruthers, above note 24 at 1283.
119 Above note 116.

of forced heirship gave the son a quarter interest in that immovable. The question was whether the son was required to choose between his entitlement under the will and his entitlement under Swiss law. The trial judge held that the doctrine of election applied.[120] She had no doubt that the testator intended that the Swiss condominium pass under his will to his daughter because the will explicitly covered all of the deceased's property, wherever situated. However, the Court of Appeal overturned that decision because there was insufficient evidence that the gift of the residue to the daughter was intended to include the son's interest in the condominium. It applied the presumption referred to above. The property in question had to be described specifically or by necessary implication.[121] General language was insufficient. Justice Doherty stated that the daughter "could only point to general language in the will to demonstrate the testator's intention to devise property which, by the application of foreign law, belonged to another who was also a beneficiary under the will."[122]

c) Dependants' Relief Legislation

All provinces have enacted legislation granting the courts a discretion to provide support from an estate to dependants of a deceased when adequate provision has not been made by a will or, often, on intestacy.[123] In most jurisdictions, the discretion is one to order such provision as the judge considers "adequate."[124] In some, like British Columbia, the discretion is a broader one to order any provision that the courts think is "adequate, just and equitable in the circumstances."[125] Under the legislation, the court may provide support in various ways ranging from the payment of a lump sum to the transfer of specific property.

Unlike the legislation in England,[126] the power to award relief in Canada is not restricted to those dying domiciled in the province. Indeed, the legislation contains no explicit conflict of laws provisions. There is authority for the proposition, however, that the statutes affect the disposing power of testators and so that they relate to the essential validity of wills. Therefore, in accordance with general principle, they apply to

---

120 (1998), 21 ETR (2d) 153 (Ont Ct Gen Div).
121 The court relied, in particular, upon the old English case of *Maxwell v Maxwell* (1852), 51 ER 717 (Ch Rolls Ct), aff'd (1852), 42 ER 1048 (HL).
122 *Granot*, above note 116 at para 22.
123 See, for example, *Wills and Succession Act*, above note 67, ss 87–108; *Succession Law Reform Act*, above note 68, ss 57–79.
124 See, for example, *Wills and Succession Act*, above note 67, s 88(1); *Succession Law Reform Act*, above note 68, s 58(1).
125 *Wills, Estates and Succession Act*, SBC 2009, c 13, s 60.
126 *Inheritance (Provision for Family and Dependants) Act 1975* (UK), 1975, c 63, s 1(1).

immovables situated within the province and to all movables when the deceased died domiciled in the province.[127] Thus, in *Re Corlet Estate* a widow residing in Alberta applied for relief under dependants' relief legislation.[128] The court held that although her husband had been resident in Alberta, he had died domiciled outside the province. Since the entire estate consisted of movables, the statute was inapplicable.

There are interesting questions that have not been discussed in the cases. For example, in determining whether to make an order for provision and what sort of order to make, must the court determine whether adequate provision has been made as a whole for the dependants rather than just whether adequate provision has been made from the assets governed by the forum's conflict of laws rules?[129] If the former interpretation is correct, could a local court, in respect of a person dying domiciled abroad, transfer, for example, to the dependants the entire value of local land to take account of the fact that inadequate provision has been made for the dependants out of the entire estate? In what circumstances would a local court recognize the order of a foreign jurisdiction where the deceased died domiciled with respect to movables in the forum? Would a local court ever be prepared to apply the dependants' relief legislation of the country where the deceased died domiciled?

d) Claims of Foreign Countries

A foreign country may make a claim in respect of a local estate in two ways. First, it may want to collect taxes, such as unpaid income taxes or succession duties. We have earlier discussed the general rule against the enforcement of the revenue laws of foreign countries.[130] The decision of the Alberta Court of Appeal in *Stringam v Dubois* dealt with such a

---

127 *Re Rattenbury Estate* (1936), 51 BCR 321 (SC); *Re Butchart*, [1932] NZLR 125 (CA); *Ostrander v Houston* (1915), 8 Sask LR 132 (SC En Banc); *Taylor v Farrugia*, 2009 NSWSC 801 [*Taylor*]. See John Falconbridge, *Essays on the Conflict of Laws*, 2d ed (Toronto: Canada Law Book, 1954) ch 35.
128 [1942] 2 WWR 93 (Alta SC).
129 Falconbridge, above note 127 at 661, was of the view that the court should be allowed to take account of all assets of the estate in order to determine whether a dependant had been sufficiently provided for and whether, and to what extent, to exercise its discretionary power. Such has been the view of the Australian courts. In *Taylor*, above note 127, for example, the deceased couple had died domiciled in Malta and so the court had jurisdiction based solely upon immovables of the estate being situated in New South Wales. The court indicated (at para 26) that, in deciding whether adequate provision had been made and what order should be granted affecting that immovable property in New South Wales, it was entitled to take account of all of the assets of the estate, wherever situated.
130 See Chapter 3, Section D.

claim.[131] A woman died domiciled in Arizona. She owned a farm in Alberta that she left to her niece. Her executor sought the sale of the farm to satisfy a claim by the United States for estate taxes. The court denied the executor's motion on the ground that it would give indirect effect to a foreign government's tax claim. It ordered the farm to be transferred to the niece.

Second, a foreign country may claim a deceased's property on intestacy where there are no surviving next of kin. If the foreign country claims by way of succession, then its claim will prevail if its law is the governing law. If, however, the foreign country claims the property as *bona vacantia* by way of some prerogative right, then its claim will fail because it will not be given extraterritorial effect so as to lead to the forfeiture of property situated outside the boundaries of the foreign country. The nature of the foreign country's claim has been regarded as a question of characterization.[132] The leading decision is *Re Maldonado's Estate*.[133] The deceased died intestate with no next of kin domiciled in Spain but leaving movables in England. By Spanish law, the state inherited the estate as the ultimate heir. Spain therefore claimed the movables in England on the ground that it was the true heir of the deceased by Spanish law and Spanish law governed succession to movables as the law of the deceased's last domicile. In response, the English Crown claimed the estate in England on the ground that Spain's claim was a disguised claim to *bona vacantia* and could have no effect outside the territorial confines of Spain. The court characterized the Spanish rule making the state the ultimate heir as a rule of succession. Therefore, the Spanish rule applied given that Spanish law governed succession. According to the court, it was illogical to say that Spanish law governed succession but that English law should decide who could be regarded as a successor. The case has been criticized for paying too much deference to the foreign law's characterization of its claim and as perhaps inviting self-serving characterizations by foreign countries.

FURTHER READINGS

BALE, GORDON. "The Demise of Lord Kingsdown's Act" (1964) 29 *Saskatchewan Bar Review* 179.

---

131 (1992), 135 AR 64 (CA).
132 See Chapter 10, Section D.
133 [1954] P 223 (CA). See also *Re Hole*, [1948] 4 DLR 419 (Man KB).

CASSWELL, DONALD. "The Conflict of Laws Rules Governing the Formal Validity of Wills: Past Developments and Suggested Reform" (1977) 15 *Osgoode Hall Law Journal* 165.

GRAHL-MADSEN, ATLE. "Conflict between the Principle of Unitary Succession and the System of Scission" (1979) 28 *International and Comparative Law Quarterly* 598.

HARRIS, JONATHAN. *The Hague Trusts Convention: Scope, Application and Preliminary Issues* (Oxford: Hart, 2002).

LIPSTEIN, KURT. "Private International Law—*Bona Vacantia* and *Ultimus Heres*" [1954] *Cambridge Law Journal* 22.

MILLER, J GARETH. "Family Provision on Death—The International Dimension" (1990) 39 *International and Comparative Law Quarterly* 261.

MILLER, J GARETH. *International Aspects of Succession* (Aldershot, UK: Ashgate, 2000).

O'SULLIVAN, MARGARET. "The Role of Domicile and *Situs* in Succession Matters" (1996) 15 *Estates and Trusts Journal* 236.

SCOLES, EUGENE. "The Hague Convention on Succession" (1994) 42 *American Journal of Comparative Law* 85.

CHAPTER 20

TRUSTS

A. INTRODUCTION

In general terms, a trust is an equitable obligation under which a trustee holds property for the benefit of a beneficiary. The three main types of trusts are express, constructive, and resulting. The second and third of these types tend to arise by operation of law and can be seen as part of the law of remedies. Accordingly, the law applicable to constructive and resulting trusts is usually the law under which they are held to exist—in other words, the law applicable to the substantive obligation giving rise to the trust. In contrast, express trusts arise as a result of intentional acts taken by a person to create the trust. They are not remedies, arising in response to some situation: they are legal arrangements usually based on consent. This chapter considers the law applicable to express trusts. An express trust can be either a testamentary trust, created by a testator or testatrix on death using a will, or an *inter vivos* trust, created by a settlor during his or her life.

The Hague Conference on Private International Law has been active in the area of choice of law for trusts. In 1985 it drafted the *Convention on the Law Applicable to Trusts and on Their Recognition* and the convention came into force in 1992.[1] The convention has been ratified

---

1 23 ILM 1388 (1984) [*Hague Convention*]. See the Explanatory Report on the convention by Alfred von Overbeck at 25 ILM 593 (1986). A very useful resource on the convention is Jonathan Harris, *The Hague Trusts Convention: Scope, Application and Preliminary Issues* (Oxford: Hart, 2002).

by fewer than twenty countries including Australia, Canada, and the United Kingdom. The Uniform Law Conference of Canada drafted a model statute, the *International Trusts Act*, for provinces to use in implementing the convention. Eight of the nine common law provinces have done so, with Ontario being the only exception.

B. THE *HAGUE CONVENTION*

1) Provincial Implementation

Each of the eight provincial implementation statutes had to address one possible extension and three possible reservations from the provisions of the convention. Under article 3, the convention applies only to trusts created voluntarily and evidenced in writing. However, all of the eight provinces have, in their implementation statute, provided that the convention also applies to trusts created by judicial decision.[2] This provision extends the convention's rules to resulting and constructive trusts. As noted above, these trusts are usually governed by the substantive law that leads to their creation. It is not clear to what extent, if any, the convention's rules produce different results in resulting and constructive trust cases.

Few of the provinces enacted the reservations. The first possible reservation allows a country to remove the ability of a court to override the applicable law and instead apply the rules of another country—not the forum—that are mandatory even in international situations.[3] Only Alberta enacted this reservation.[4] The second possible reservation allows a country to apply the convention's provisions on recognizing a trust governed by a foreign law only to trusts governed by the law of another contracting state under the convention, so as to insist on a degree of reciprocity.[5] No province enacted this reservation. The third possible reservation allows a country to prevent the convention's rules from operating retroactively.[6] Alberta, Saskatchewan, Manitoba, and New Brunswick enacted this reservation.[7]

---

2   See, for example, *International Trusts Act*, RSBC 1996, c 237, s 3(1); *International Trusts Act*, RSNL 1990, c I-17, s 5(1); *International Trusts Act*, RSPEI 1988, c I-7, s 3(1).
3   *Hague Convention*, above note 1, art 16.
4   *International Conventions Implementation Act*, RSA 2000, c I-6, s 1(4).
5   *Hague Convention*, above note 1, art 21.
6   *Ibid*, art 22.
7   *International Conventions Implementation Act*, above note 4, s 1(5); *The Trusts Convention Implementation Act*, SS 1994, c T-23.1, s 4; *The International Trusts Act*,

The *Hague Convention* does not require that its provisions are applied where the conflict of laws issue arises between two units of a federal state,[8] and acting on this, the implementing statute in Alberta, New Brunswick, and Nova Scotia expressly provides that the convention does not apply in interprovincial cases.[9] Instead, the common law rules would apply.[10] In the other five provinces that have implemented the convention, its provisions are not excluded for interprovincial cases and the expectation is that accordingly they would be applied.

2) Scope

The *Hague Convention*'s twin purposes are to identify the law applicable to a trust and to provide for the recognition of a trust validly created under its applicable law.[11] There is no such thing as a trust in the domestic legal system in many countries. As a result, the convention has to bridge the divide between countries familiar with trusts and countries that do not have them. This is the central reason the convention specifically addresses recognition of trusts. It is also why it contains a description of what it means when it refers to a trust: "the term 'trust' refers to the legal relationships created—*inter vivos* or on death—by a person, the settlor, when assets have been placed under the control of a trustee for the benefit of a beneficiary or for a specified purpose."[12] The convention applies to both testamentary and *inter vivos* trusts, but only to trusts created voluntarily and evidenced in writing.[13] This means that it does not apply to certain trusts that arise by operation of law, such as a statutory trust over assets in favour of the state. It also means that it does not cover a purely oral trust. In those situations, the applicable choice of law rules have to be found elsewhere, typically in the common law.[14] In addition, the *Hague Convention* does not apply to preliminary

---

CCSM c T165, s 3; *International Trusts Act*, RSNB 2011, c 178, s 5 [*International Trusts Act* (NB)].

8   Above note 1, art 24.
9   *International Conventions Implementation Act*, above note 4, s 1(2); *International Trusts Act* (NB), above note 7, s 2; *International Trusts Act*, SNS 2005, c 41, s 3(2).
10 Although for New Brunswick, see the *Conflict of Laws Rules for Trusts Act*, SNB 2012, c 102, discussed below.
11 Above note 1, art 1.
12 Ibid, art 2.
13 Ibid, art 3.
14 In the United Kingdom, the statute implementing the *Hague Convention* extends it beyond art 3 to apply to "any other trusts of property arising under the law of any part of the United Kingdom": *Recognition of Trusts Act 1987* (UK), 1987, c 14, s 1(2). But this extension is quite limited, since it does not cover oral or statutory trusts governed by some other law.

issues relating to the validity of wills or of other acts through which assets are transferred to the trustee.[15]

Article 5 contains an important limitation to the scope of the convention. If the law applicable to a trust, identified using the convention's choice of law rules, does not provide for trusts or for the type of trust in issue, then the convention does not apply. For example, if the convention indicates that Romanian law applies to a trust but there is no Romanian law of trusts, the convention ceases to be relevant.

One of the more difficult concerns relating to trusts is characterization, because there is often debate about whether a particular issue is one of trust law, governed by the law applicable to the trust, or instead falls into some other area of law such as succession or transfer of property, which has its own choice of law rules. Article 8 addresses this concern by enumerating various issues that are intended to be characterized as relating to trusts and so governed by the applicable law identified by the *Hague Convention*. These issues include the appointment, resignation, and removal of trustees; the rights, duties, and powers of trustees, including the right to deal with trust assets; the variation or termination of the trust; and the distribution of the trust assets.

3) Choice of Law Rules

The *Hague Convention*'s choice of law rules for trusts are similar to the common law's choice of law rules for contract.[16] Under article 6, a trust is governed by the law chosen to govern it by the person creating the trust. This choice can be either express—through a choice of law clause in the trust instrument—or implied.[17] For an implied choice, the court considers the language of the trust instrument "interpreted, if necessary, in the light of the circumstances of the case."[18] As in the area of contract law, the primacy given to express and implied choices

---

15 Above note 1, art 4. Some of the literature uses the colourful metaphor of the "rocket" (the trust) and the "rocket launcher" (the preliminary matters necessary for creation of the trust), with the *Hague Convention* governing the former but not the latter: see, for example, Harris, above note 1 at 1 and 151–57.
16 See Chapter 14.
17 Article 6 was applied to an express choice in *Royal Trust Corporation of Canada v AS(W)S* (2004), 35 Alta LR (4th) 32 (QB). In contrast, in *Kelemen v Alberta (Public Trustee)* (2007), 71 Alta LR (4th) 366 (QB) [*Kelemen*], the court held that on the evidence the testatrix had not made an express or implied choice. On identifying an implied choice, see also *Re Barton (Deceased)*, [2002] WTLR 469 at para 36 (Ch).
18 For a detailed review of the English cases on implied choice, see Harris, above note 1 at 198–211.

furthers the interests of party autonomy. However, if the chosen law does not provide for trusts or for the type of trust in issue, then the choice is ineffective.

Article 7 provides that in the absence of choice or on an ineffective choice, "a trust shall be governed by the law with which it is most closely connected." The article sets out an open-ended list of four factors that "in particular" are to be assessed in identifying the most closely connected law: (1) the place, designated by the creator of the trust, where the trust is to be administered; (2) the location of the assets subject to the trust; (3) the trustee's place of residence or business; and (4) the objects of the trust and the place where they are to be fulfilled.[19] Justice Braidwood, dissenting in *Rowland v Vancouver College Ltd*, applied article 7 to conclude that

> the St. Thomas More Trust is a purpose trust. Its object is to operate a Roman Catholic High School for the benefit of the parishes of the Roman Catholic Archdiocese of Vancouver in the vicinity of the present location of the St. Thomas More Collegiate. There is no other territory able to claim so close a connection with the St. Thomas More Trust.[20]

In *Kelemen v Alberta (Public Trustee)* the court analyzed the article 7 factors and concluded that the trust was governed by Alberta law.[21] While the beneficiary of the trust was a resident of Romania, the trust assets were located in Alberta and, while the testatrix did not indicate where the trust was to be administered, all the potential trustees were resident in Alberta. In addition to the listed factors, the court also gave weight to the fact that the testatrix died domiciled in Alberta.

The *Hague Convention* allows for the doctrine of *depeçage*, discussed in Chapter 14, so that one part of a trust can have a different applicable law than the rest.[22] This is most likely to arise in relation to the administration of the trust, such that administration issues could be governed by the law of New York while the balance of the trust is governed by the law of England. The convention expressly excludes the doctrine of *renvoi*, discussed in Chapter 10.[23]

Situations can arise in which the parties to the trust desire to change the applicable law. A trust instrument may contain an express English choice of law clause but the parties now want the trust to be

---

19 For more detail, see Harris, *ibid* at 215–32.
20 (2001), 94 BCLR (3d) 249 at para 169 (CA).
21 Above note 17 at paras 40–50.
22 Above note 1, art 9.
23 *Ibid*, art 17.

governed by Alberta law. Article 10 provides that the applicable law is to determine whether the law applicable to all or any part of the trust can be replaced by a different applicable law. So in the above example, it would be up to English law as to whether this is possible. Article 10 applies beyond express and implied choices as to the applicable law, so that the applicable law as determined objectively under article 7 determines whether the applicable law can subsequently be changed, either to a chosen law or, in the case where circumstances change after the trust's creation, a different objectively determined law.[24]

The convention provides for several exceptions to using the applicable law. First, the applicable law need not be applied if doing so would be "manifestly incompatible with public policy."[25] Second, any laws of the forum that are mandatory, in that they must be applied even in international situations, can be applied.[26] Third, any mandatory laws of another country having a "sufficiently close connection" to the dispute can also be applied.[27] In addition to these exceptions, the convention also addresses possible conflicts between its choice of law rules for trusts and related choice of law rules in areas such as succession, marriage, and the transfer of movable and immovable property. Article 15 provides that the *Hague Convention* "does not prevent the application of provisions of the law designated by the conflicts rules of the forum, in so far as those provisions cannot be derogated from by voluntary act" relating to these other areas of law. The focus here, as with the three exceptions, is on mandatory rules. An example of such a rule is one which mandates, on death, that a certain percentage of the available assets must pass to a surviving spouse.

4) Recognition

The recognition of trusts is addressed in articles 11 through 14. Under article 11 a trust that is validly created under the applicable law identified by the *Hague Convention*'s choice of law rules "shall be recognized" as a trust. This provision seems quite unnecessary in a common law system,[28] but is quite important for those contracting states whose domestic law does not contain trusts. It commits those states to giving

---

24 For more on changing the applicable law, see Harris, above note 1 at 297–310.
25 Above note 1, art 18.
26 *Ibid*, art 16.
27 *Ibid*. As discussed above, this part of art 16 can be excluded by a country implementing the *Hague Convention* and it has been excluded by Alberta: see *International Conventions Implementation Act*, above note 4.
28 Harris calls this provision "self-evident": Harris, above note 1 at 311.

effect to the trust. Article 11 outlines at some length the minimum elements that such recognition must include, such as separation of the trust assets from the trustee's personal assets and the ability of the trustee to sue and be sued in his or her capacity as trustee.

Article 13 contains a specific basis on which a state can choose to refuse to recognize a trust. It provides that

> [n]o State shall be bound to recognize a trust the significant elements of which, except for the choice of the applicable law, the place of administration and the habitual residence of the trustee, are more closely connected with States which do not have the institution of the trust or the category of trust involved.

A concern of countries whose legal systems do not contain trusts is that mandatory recognition of certain trusts could lead to trusts in effect becoming part of their domestic law. For example, a settlor in France could purport to create a trust over French assets and have the trust expressly governed by New York law and use a trustee based in New York. If such a trust had to be recognized in France, this would create considerable scope for French residents to create almost entirely local trusts, even though trusts are not part of the domestic law. Article 13 therefore guards against this.[29] In addition, the articles discussed above in the context of choice of law dealing with mandatory rules and with public policy apply equally as possible defences to recognition of a trust.

C. PROVINCIAL STATUTES

British Columbia and New Brunswick have enacted separate statutes dealing with choice of law for trusts.[30] The statutes have quite a restricted scope, in that they apply only when the *Hague Convention* does not apply and when the law governing the trust as determined under the statute is that of a province or territory of Canada.[31] The circularity in the latter restriction is somewhat bewildering, although in fairness the convention uses a similar approach.[32] This means that if the statute's rules lead to the application of English law the statute does not apply, presumably leaving the issue to the common law.

---

29 See the discussion in Harris, *ibid* at 341–46.
30 *Conflict of Laws Rules for Trusts Act*, RSBC 1996, c 65 [*CLRTA* (BC)]; *Conflict of Laws Rules for Trusts Act*, SNB 2012, c 102 [*CLRTA* (NB)].
31 *CLRTA* (BC), above note 30, s 2(1); *CLRTA* (NB), *ibid*, s 30(1).
32 *Hague Convention*, above note 1, art 5. The applicable law has to be ascertained under the convention to determine if the convention applies.

The choice of law rules in these statutes are largely identical to those in the convention. If there is an express or implied choice of law, that is the applicable law unless the law chosen does not provide for the type of trust involved. In the absence of choice, a trust is governed by the law with which it is most closely connected.[33]

It is not entirely clear why New Brunswick expressly excluded the convention from interprovincial cases and then adopted largely the same rules in a separate statute. Along the same lines, the need for the British Columbia statute is not immediately obvious given that British Columbia did not exclude the *Hague Convention* from interprovincial cases.[34]

D. COMMON LAW

There are few modern judicial decisions that clearly set out the common law's choice of law rules for trusts. As a result, it is likely that even in cases in Ontario, and in cases outside the scope of the convention (and, in British Columbia and New Brunswick, outside the scope of the separate provincial statute), the clearer rules spelled out in the convention will influence the results reached at common law.

The older cases have sometimes drawn distinctions between testamentary trusts and *inter vivos* trusts. They have also distinguished between trusts of movable property and trusts of immovable property. However, as a general rule, a trust is governed by the law intended by its creator, whether express or implied.[35] In the absence of any intention it is sometimes claimed that a trust is valid if it complies with either the law of its creator's domicile or the law of the place of administration of the trust. Such an approach gives a court considerable flexibility in upholding trusts but it is not overly helpful when a single applicable law must be identified. A better approach is to use the law of the country to which the trust is most closely connected.[36] As under

---

33 *CLRTA* (BC), above note 30, s 3; *CLRTA* (NB), above note 30, s 5.
34 See the discussion about the implementation of the *Hague Convention* in Section B(1), above in this chapter.
35 For testamentary trusts, see *Attorney-General v Campbell* (1872), LR 5 HL 524; *Re Lord Cable*, [1977] 1 WLR 7 at 20. For *inter vivos* trusts, see *Augustus v Permanent Trustee Co (Canberra) Ltd* (1971), 124 CLR 245; *Chellaram v Chellaram*, [1985] Ch 409 [*Chellaram*].
36 See *Chellaram*, ibid.

the convention, the common law allows for *depeçage* so that a severable part of a trust can have a different applicable law.[37]

Some of the difficulties with formulating a common law rule are illustrated in *Jewish National Fund Inc v Royal Trust Co*.[38] A person domiciled and resident in British Columbia died and in his will he purported to use his movable property to create a trust. The trustees were residents of New York and the object of the trust was to purchase land in one or more stipulated countries for the establishment of Jewish settlements. The question arose as to whether the trust was governed by the law of British Columbia as the law of his domicile, the law of New York as the law of the place of the trust's administration, or the law of wherever the land might be purchased as the law of place where the trust was carried out. It was clear that under British Columbia law the trust was invalid for lack of a charitable purpose but it might have been valid under New York law. The Supreme Court of Canada accepted that both the law of the domicile and the law of the place of administration were relevant and that if the trust were valid under either then that would suffice.[39] But while the dissent held that the place of administration was New York, where the trustees were resident,[40] the majority held that the place of administration was the place where any lands would be purchased and that the residence of the trustees was irrelevant. Because lands could be purchased in countries under whose law the trust was also invalid, the majority held that the trust was invalid.

This decision illustrates two important and perhaps controversial points. The first is the historical importance of the domicile of the creator of the trust. Indeed, courts have been prepared to imply that a trust's creator intended the law of his or her domicile to govern the trust.[41] In contrast, under the *Hague Convention* domicile is significantly less important to identifying the applicable law. The second point illustrated is the potential role of the law of the *situs* of immovable property. While the convention does not distinguish between types of trust assets, the common law has sometimes held that the law of the location of immovable property governs any trust of that property.[42]

---

37 For example, the issue of administration can have a different applicable law than the issue of validity: see *Branco v Veira* (1995), 8 ETR (2d) 49 (Ont Ct Gen Div); *Webster-Tweel v Royal Trust Corp of Canada*, 2010 ABQB 139 at paras 69–71.
38 [1965] SCR 784.
39 *Ibid* at 789–90.
40 *Ibid* at 797.
41 *Re Lord Cable*, above note 35.
42 See the discussion in Chapter 17. This poses obvious difficulties for a trust of immovable property in more than one country.

In *Webster-Tweel v Royal Trust Corp of Canada* the parties agreed that the trusts in issue were governed by the law of Quebec. However, the dispute was not about the validity of the trusts but rather their administration. The court therefore had to identify the applicable law for the administration of the trusts. It held that this was the law "the settlor intended, and absent evidence of intention, the inquiry turns to where the administration of the trust is most closely connected."[43] It acknowledged that intention could be implied rather than explicit and it set out a lengthy list of factors to consider in the absence of intention. Key factors are the location of the assets subject to the trust and the residence or place of business of the trustees. The importance of these factors will vary from case to case, since in some situations there will be assets in different places, or the trustees will be in different places, or both.[44]

FURTHER READINGS

CHONG, ADELINE. "The Common Law Choice of Law Rules for Resulting and Constructive Trusts" (2005) 54 *International and Comparative Law Quarterly* 855.

DELANY, VTH. "Charitable Trusts and the Conflict of Laws" (1961) 10 *International and Comparative Law Quarterly* 385.

GAILLARD, EMMANUEL, & DONALD TRAUTMAN. "Trusts in Non-trust Countries: Conflict of Laws and the Hague Convention on Trusts" (1987) 35 *American Journal of Comparative Law* 307.

GROZINGER, K THOMAS. "Conflict of Laws and Trusts of Movables in Canada: Determining the Applicable Law for Essential Validity and Administration" (2004) 23 *Estates, Trusts and Pensions Journal* 301.

HAYTON, DAVID. "'Trusts' in Private International Law" (2013) 366 *Recueil des Cours* 9.

---

43 Above note 37 at para 76. This approach is quite similar to the analysis under the *Hague Convention*, to which the court referred.
44 The court considered that the law of the administration of a trust could change over time: *ibid* at paras 91 and 99. For example, a trust might involve Manitoba assets and trustees when initially created but over time those assets could be sold and those trustees could cease to act. The trust could subsequently hold Alberta assets and be administered by Alberta trustees. See Donovan WM Waters & K Thomas Grozinger, "Can the Law Governing the Administration of a Trust Be Changed in the Absence of an Express Enabling Power in the Trust Instrument?" (2015) 34 *Estates, Trusts and Pensions Journal* 295.

HAYTON, DAVID. "The *Hague Convention on the Law Applicable to Trusts and on Their Recognition*" (1987) 36 *International and Comparative Law Quarterly* 260.

SCHOENBLUM, JEFFREY. "The *Hague Convention on Trusts*: Much Ado about Very Little" (1994) 3 *Journal of International Tax, Trust and Corporate Planning* 5.

STEVENS, ROBERT. "Resulting Trusts in the Conflict of Laws" in Peter Birks & Francis Rose, eds, *Restitution and Equity—Volume One: Resulting Trusts and Equitable Compensation* (London: Mansfield Press, 2000).

VIRGO, GRAHAM. "Interest, Constructive Trusts and the Conflict of Laws" [2000] *Restitution Law Review* 122.

WALLACE, ANNE. "Choice of Law for Trusts in Australia and the United Kingdom" (1987) 36 *International and Comparative Law Quarterly* 454.

WHITE, RW. "Equitable Obligations in Private International Law: The Choice of Law" (1986) 11 *Sydney Law Review* 92.

CHAPTER 21

MARRIAGE

A. CONSTITUTIONAL FRAMEWORK

The Canadian Constitution divides legislative power over marriage between the federal and provincial governments. Thus, section 91(26) of the *Constitution Act, 1867* grants to the Parliament of Canada authority over "Marriage and Divorce," whereas section 92(13) grants the provinces general legislative authority over "Property and Civil Rights in the Province" and section 92(12) confers on the provinces jurisdiction over "The Solemnization of Marriage in the Province."[1] In *Hill v Hill*, Hyndman JA determined that, as a result of the division of powers, the federal government had "the exclusive right to legislate as to who [should] or [should] not be capable of marrying," while the provincial legislatures were free to decide "what the individual rights of the parties [should] be within the Province after marriage."[2] Equally, the Privy Council made it clear in *Re The Marriage Law of Canada* that the Canadian Parliament did not have exclusive jurisdiction over all questions relating to the validity of marriages.[3] Section 92(12) enabled provincial legislatures "to enact conditions as to solemnization which [might] affect the validity of the contract [of marriage]."[4] In *Kerr v Kerr*, the Supreme Court of Canada held that solemnization of marriage within

---

1   (UK), 30 & 31 Vict, c 3, reprinted in RSC 1985, App II, No 5.
2   [1929] 2 DLR 735 at 741 (Alta SCAD).
3   (1912), 7 DLR 629 (PC).
4   *Ibid* at 636.

401

section 92(12) "include[d] not only the essential ceremony by which the marriage [was] effected, but also parental consent where such consent [was] required by law."[5] Thus, provincial legislatures were competent "to make the preliminaries, leading up to the marriage ceremony, conditions precedent to the solemnization of the marriage" and "to declare that in the event of these conditions precedent not being complied with no valid marriage ha[d] taken place."[6] The division of legislative power over marriage means that both international and interprovincial conflict of laws issues can arise in this context.

B. FORMAL VALIDITY

1) General

In *Brook v Brook*, for the purposes of the conflict of laws, the House of Lords drew the distinction between the formal validity of a marriage and its essential validity, a similar distinction to that drawn in the Canadian Constitution.[7] It made it clear that the forms of entering into the contract of marriage were to be regulated by the law of the place where the marriage was celebrated. In *Berthiaume v Dastous* the parties, who were both domiciled in Quebec, went through a ceremony of marriage in France in accordance with the form of the Roman Catholic Church.[8] However, there was no civil ceremony as required by French law. The Privy Council held that the marriage was void because of its failure to comply with the law of the place of celebration. Viscount Dunedin expressed the applicable principle:

> If there is one question better settled than any other in international law, it is that as regards marriage—putting aside the question of capacity—*locus regit actum*. If a marriage is good by the laws of the country where it is effected, it is good all the world over, no matter whether the proceeding or ceremony which constituted marriage according to the law of the place would or would not constitute marriage in the country of the domicile of one or other of the spouses. If the so-called marriage is no marriage in the place where it is celebrated, there is no marriage anywhere, although the ceremony or

---

5   [1934] 2 DLR 369 at 375 (SCC), Lamont J. See also *Alberta (Attorney-General) v Underwood*, [1934] SCR 635.
6   *Kerr v Kerr*, above note 5.
7   (1861), 9 HL Cas 193 [*Brook*].
8   [1930] AC 79 (PC).

proceeding if conducted in the place of the parties' domicile would be considered a good marriage.⁹

There is some support for the view that the doctrine of *renvoi* applies to the formal validity of a marriage. On that basis, a marriage would be valid if it complied either with the formalities imposed by the domestic law of the place of celebration or with those imposed by the domestic law identified by the choice of law rules of the law of the place of celebration. Thus in *Taczanowska v Taczanowski* two Polish nationals were married in Italy in a form that did not comply with Italian domestic law.¹⁰ Evidence indicated, however, that the Italian courts would have looked to Polish law to govern the formal validity of the marriage because of the parties' nationality. In fact, Polish law would also have invalidated the marriage, but the inference was clear that the marriage would have been regarded as valid if it had complied with Polish law.

The fact that the law of the place of celebration governs the formalities of marriage means that a marriage will be recognized as valid even if no formalities have been followed provided that no formalities are required by the law of the place of celebration. In *Forbes v Forbes* there was doubt as to whether the judge, who had performed a ceremony of marriage in Michigan, had been validly appointed as such in that state.¹¹ The law of Michigan, however, recognized the validity of a common law marriage where there was an agreement to marry followed by a period of cohabitation with the reputation of being husband and wife. The court held that the parties had been validly married. Justice Latchford held:

> it is undoubted that there was an agreement to marry, followed by cohabitation, within the State of Michigan at various times between 1878 and 1892; and, upon evidence that is undisputed, such agreement and cohabitation constituted a valid marriage according to the laws of Michigan.¹²

In *Lee v Chung* the issue arose as to whether the parties were validly married.¹³ They were Koreans who met while living in Ontario. They did not obtain a marriage licence or go through a marriage ceremony. However, they had reported, and thus registered, their marriage with the Korean consulate in Toronto. Under Korean law, they were validly married by virtue of having registered the marriage. The court held

---

9   Ibid at 83. See also *Sahibalzubaidi v Bahjat*, 2011 ONSC 4075 at para 32 [*Sahibalzubaidi*].
10 [1957] P 301 (CA) [*Taczanowska*].
11 (1912), 3 DLR 243 (Ont HCJ).
12 *Ibid* at 246.
13 2014 BCSC 1157.

that "by going to the Korean Consulate and making the report, Mr. Chung and Ms. Lee intended that they would be married 'in Korea' and therefore be validly married under Korean law . . . in effect, the parties' marriage took place in Korea (the *lex loci celebrationis*) and is governed by Korean law."[14] This reasoning is difficult to accept: the better view on these facts is that the place of the marriage was Ontario.

2) Proxy Marriages

In *Apt v Apt* the English Court of Appeal characterized the question of the validity of a proxy marriage as one relating to form and so to be governed by the law of the place of celebration.[15] Lord Justice Cohen reasoned that "the method of giving consent as distinct from the fact of consent is essentially a matter for the *lex loci celebrationis*, and does not raise a question of capacity, or, as counsel preferred to call it, essential validity."[16] The court upheld a proxy marriage, celebrated in Argentina and valid by Argentinian law, despite the fact that the wife was domiciled in England, whose law did not recognize proxy marriages. The Canadian courts applied *Apt* in *Frustaglio v Barbuto*.[17]

3) Parental Consent

Lord Hardwicke's *Marriage Act 1753* introduced in England the requirement of parental consent for the marriage of minors.[18] The statute, however, did not extend to Scotland. The courts held that couples could evade the requirements of the statute by marrying just over the border in Scotland,[19] giving rise to what became known as "Gretna Green" marriages. In *Brook* the House of Lords justified the validity of such marriages on the ground that the statute regulated only "the formalities by which the ceremony of marriage [should] be celebrated" and did "not touch the essentials of the contract."[20] Thus, it became established that the English requirement of parental consent was a matter of form.

Somewhat controversially, the English courts extended this reasoning to foreign requirements of parental consent without a more nuanced assessment of the specific requirement. The most notorious example

---

14 Ibid at paras 60–61.
15 [1948] P 83 (CA) [*Apt*].
16 Ibid at 88.
17 [1960] OWN 551 (HCJ).
18 (UK), 26 Geo 2, c 33.
19 See, for example, *Compton v Bearcroft* (1769), 161 ER 799.
20 Above note 7 at 215, Lord Campbell LC.

was *Ogden v Ogden*.[21] There was a marriage in England between a domiciled Englishwoman and a domiciled Frenchman aged nineteen. The Frenchman did not have parental consent as required by French law. Article 148 of the *Civil Code* provided: "The son who has not attained the full age of twenty-five years . . . cannot contract marriage without the consent of [his] father and mother . . . ."[22] The Court of Appeal concluded that the marriage was valid since it was valid by English law. The French law did not apply because the case raised a question of the formal validity of the marriage which was governed by English law as the law of the place of celebration. The judgment has been heavily criticized for its characterization of the requirement of parental consent in the abstract.[23] The court never examined in detail the wording of the particular provision in the French *Civil Code* which imposed the requirement of parental consent. Thus, Sir Gorell Barnes P asserted:

> [W]e are concerned in this case only with the question of a disability imposed by foreign law upon one of the parties to the marriage in respect only of want of parental consent, and compliance with certain formalities required by such foreign law.[24]

Nevertheless, Canadian courts have consistently regarded requirements for parental consent as relating to the formalities of marriage. In *Solomon v Walters*,[25] for example, a British Columbia court annulled a marriage celebrated in Nevada between two Canadian residents because the petitioner had not obtained parental consent in accordance with Nevada law. Conversely, in *Reed v Reed* the parties, who were domiciled in British Columbia, went through a ceremony of marriage in Washington State in order to avoid parental disapproval.[26] The plaintiff, a minor, required parental consent by British Columbia law but not by Washington law. The court held that there was no basis for annulling the marriage on that ground. County Court Judge Harvey said:

> The matter of parental consent is considered to be part of the ceremony of marriage and not a matter affecting the personal capacity of the parties to enter into a contract of marriage. Hence the absence of

---

21 [1908] P 46 (CA) [*Ogden*].
22 *Ibid* at 50.
23 See, for example, John D Falconbridge, *Essays on the Conflict of Laws*, 2d ed (Toronto: Canada Law Book, 1954) at 74–86.
24 *Ogden*, above note 21 at 61.
25 (1956), 3 DLR (2d) 78 (BCSC). See also *Hunt v Hunt* (1958), 14 DLR (2d) 243 (Ont HCJ).
26 (1969), 6 DLR (3d) 617 (BCSC) [*Reed*].

parental consent is governed not by the laws of British Columbia but by those of Washington.[27]

4) Exceptions to the Law of the Place of Celebration

There are various situations in which some law other than that of the place of celebration can be examined so as to validate a marriage with respect to form.[28] Most of these exceptions are of little practical significance. For example, it appears that where there is insuperable difficulty in using the local form, a marriage will be formally valid if it is celebrated in accordance with the traditional requirements of English common law. It appears also that a marriage celebrated in a country under belligerent occupation in accordance with that traditional common law will be formally valid where one of the parties (or perhaps just the husband) was a member of the occupying forces.[29] In the Canadian context, the most important exception is contained in the *Civil Code of Quebec*.[30] Article 3088 provides for several options to uphold the formal validity of a marriage:

> With respect to [a marriage's] formal validity, it is governed by the law of the place of its solemnization or by the law of the State of domicile or of nationality of one of the spouses.

C. ESSENTIAL VALIDITY: CAPACITY TO MARRY

1) General

The essential validity of a marriage concerns the legal capacity of the parties to marry. Arguably, it includes any potential impediment to a valid marriage other than a lack of form. In this book we use this heading to cover a marriage's potential invalidity on the basis of the relationship between the parties, lack of age, a previous marriage, lack of consent, and gender. We discuss invalidity on the ground of physical incapacity as a discrete topic only because those choice of law rules are still unsettled.[31]

---

27 *Ibid* at 618–19.
28 See Janet Walker, *Castel & Walker: Canadian Conflict of Laws*, 6th ed (Markham, ON: Butterworths, 2005) (loose-leaf) at para 16.3; Lawrence Collins, ed, *Dicey, Morris and Collins on the Conflict of Laws*, 15th ed (London: Sweet & Maxwell, 2012) at paras 17-022 to 17-038 [*Dicey, Morris and Collins*].
29 *Taczanowska*, above note 10.
30 CQLR c C-1991.
31 See Section E, below in this chapter.

In *Brook* the House of Lords made it clear that the essential validity of a marriage was governed not by the law of the place of celebration but by the law of the domicile.³² In that case, a man underwent a ceremony of marriage in Denmark with his deceased wife's sister. Both parties were domiciled in England and returned there after the ceremony. The marriage was void by English law because the parties fell within the prohibited degrees of affinity but was valid by Danish law. The House of Lords applied English law as the law of the domicile and determined that the marriage was void. There was some uncertainty, however, as to whether the court applied English law as the law of the parties' antenuptial domicile or as the law of the intended matrimonial domicile. Lord Chancellor Campbell said that "the essentials of the [marriage] contract depend upon the *lex domicilii*, the law of the country in which the parties are domiciled at the time of the marriage, and in which the matrimonial residence is contemplated."³³

The ambiguity inherent in cases such as *Brook* led to a famous rift between Dicey and Cheshire. Dicey favoured the dual domicile test, whereby each party had to have capacity according to the law of his or her antenuptial domicile.³⁴ In contrast, Cheshire preferred the application of the law of the intended matrimonial home. That rule can be stated as follows:

> The basic presumption is that capacity to marry is governed by the law of the husband's domicile at the time of the marriage, for normally it is in the country of that domicile that the parties intend to establish their permanent home. This presumption, however, is rebutted if it can be inferred that the parties at the time of the marriage intended to establish their home in a certain country and that they did in fact establish it there within a reasonable time.³⁵

Although the weight of authority supports the dual domicile test,³⁶ Canadian courts have not entirely abandoned reference to the intended matrimonial home. In *Feiner v Demkowicz*,³⁷ for example, an aunt and her nephew went through a form of marriage in Poland. The court held that the law of Poland governed the parties' capacity to marry since it

---

32   Above note 7.
33   *Ibid* at 207.
34   See *Dicey, Morris and Collins*, above note 28 at paras 17-057 to 17-070.
35   James Fawcett & Janeen Carruthers, *Cheshire, North & Fawcett Private International Law*, 14th ed (Oxford: Oxford University Press, 2008) at 896.
36   See, for example, *Azam v Jan*, 2013 ABQB 301 at para 53 [*Azam*]; *Nafie v Badawy*, 2015 ABCA 36 at para 44 [*Nafie*].
37   (1973), 2 OR (2d) 121 (HCJ).

was the prenuptial domicile of both parties. In the absence of evidence of Polish law, the court applied Canadian law and determined that the marriage was void as having been contracted within the prohibited degrees of consanguinity. Justice Van Camp, however, also pointed out that the application of Canadian law was justified on the ground that Canada was the parties' intended matrimonial home. The Federal Court of Appeal later applied the intended matrimonial home test to the essential validity of a marriage in *Canada (Minister of Employment and Immigration) v Narwal*.[38]

The relationship between the two tests is important. As phrased, they are not simply two alternative bases on which a marriage can be found valid, such that if one test is not met the marriage can still be found valid under the other. Rather, the intended matrimonial home test applies only "if it can be inferred that the parties at the time of the marriage intended to establish their home in a certain country and that they did in fact establish it there within a reasonable time." When the test does apply, it would seem that only the law of the intended matrimonial home governs and the law indicated by the dual domicile test is irrelevant.

As will be discussed below, both the general rule and its application to the particular aspects of essential validity are subject to possible displacement by the law of the place where the marriage is performed. Under new provisions in the *Civil Marriage Act*, this is especially important for marriages celebrated in Canada in which at least one of the spouses is not domiciled in Canada.

2) Prohibited Degrees of Consanguinity and Affinity

The federal *Marriage (Prohibited Degrees) Act* provides:

> 2(1) Subject to subsection (2), persons related by consanguinity, affinity or adoption are not prohibited from marrying each other by reason only of their relationship.
>
> (2) No person shall marry another person if they are related lineally, or as brother or sister or half-brother or half-sister, including by adoption.
>
> 3(1) Subject to subsection (2), a marriage between persons related by consanguinity, affinity or adoption is not invalid by reason only of their relationship.
>
> (2) A marriage between persons who are related in the manner described in subsection 2(2) is void.

---

38 [1990] 2 FC 385 (CA).

4 This Act contains all of the prohibitions in law in Canada against marriage by reason of the parties being related.[39]

One author has suggested that the effect of the statute has been to eliminate "the application of foreign law to questions of the capacity to marry and the validity of marriages by reason of consanguinity."[40] She reasons:

> A marriage, wherever celebrated, between persons related in any of [the] ways [set out in the Act] is void, but a marriage between persons related in any other way is not invalid by reason only of their relationship, nor are persons related in any other way prohibited from marrying in Canada.[41]

The statute, however, does not explicitly address conflict of laws issues. It is, therefore, a possibility that a Canadian court would not recognize a marriage between, for example, an aunt and her nephew that was prohibited by the law of the parties' antenuptial domicile even though it would not contravene the *Marriage (Prohibited Degrees) Act*. Equally, a marriage that did contravene the statute could potentially be upheld in Canada if it were valid by the parties' antenuptial domicile. Of course, the recognition of any capacity or incapacity inconsistent with the statute could potentially raise issues of public policy.[42]

3) Lack of Age

The federal *Civil Marriage Act* provides that "No person who is under the age of 16 years may contract marriage."[43] At common law, the minimum age of consent was fourteen for males and twelve for females.[44] Provincial legislation, enacted under provincial authority over the solemnization of marriage, also addresses the minimum age for marriage. For example, Ontario law provides that no person shall issue a marriage licence to a minor or solemnize the marriage of a minor except where the minor is at least sixteen years of age and has the requisite parental consent.[45] The Alberta legislation is in similar terms except

---

39 SC 1990, c 46.
40 See Walker, above note 28 at para 16.5.
41 *Ibid*.
42 See Section C(8), below in this chapter.
43 SC 2005, c 33, s 2.2.
44 Ontario Law Reform Commission, *Report on Family Law, Part II, Marriage* (Toronto: Department of Justice, 1970) at 36–38.
45 *Marriage Act*, RSO 1990, c M.3, s 5(2).

that the marriage of a female under the age of sixteen may lawfully take place where she is pregnant or a mother.[46]

The one case to consider the invalidity of a marriage on the basis of lack of age is *Pugh v Pugh*.[47] A domiciled Englishman went through a ceremony of marriage in Austria with a girl, aged fifteen, who had a domicile of origin in Hungary and perhaps a domicile of dependency in Austria. By Hungarian law, the marriage was voidable but could no longer be avoided. By Austrian law, the marriage was valid. However, English law would hold the marriage void. Section 1 of the *Age of Marriage Act 1929* provided that "[a] marriage between two persons either of whom is under the age of sixteen shall be void."[48] The court held that by English law as the law of the husband's antenuptial domicile, he had no capacity to marry a person under the age of sixteen and therefore the marriage was void. The conclusion was strange in that the marriage was declared void despite the fact that the husband was of full age by the law of his domicile and the wife was of full age by the law of her domicile. The court based its decision very much on the precise wording of the English statute.[49] The case does raise the question, however, of whether, as a general proposition, each party must be of full age by his or her own law and also by the law of the other party.

4) Previous Marriage

Where the alleged incapacity is that one of the parties is already married, there is authority for the view that the question is resolved by the general dual domicile test. Thus, in *Padolecchia v Padolecchia* Simon P cited what is now rule 74 of *Dicey, Morris and Collins*,[50] namely "[e]ach party must be capable of marrying by the law of his or her respective antenuptial domicile."[51] Indeed, he indicated, by analogy with *Pugh*,[52] that a marriage would be invalid if either party were regarded as already married by the law of the antenuptial domicile of either party:

> [S]ince nobody who is still married can validly contract a marriage in a monogamous country, nor can anybody validly contract marriage

---

46 *Marriage Act*, RSA 2000, c M-5, s 17(2).
47 [1951] P 482 [*Pugh*].
48 (UK), 19 & 20 Geo 5, c 36.
49 See also *A Local Authority v X & Anor (Children)*, [2013] EWHC 3274 at paras 8–9 (Fam).
50 Above note 28. The current wording is: "As a general rule, capacity to marry is governed by the law of each party's antenuptial domicile."
51 [1968] P 314 at 336 [*Padolecchia*].
52 Above note 47.

in a monogamous country with a person who is already married, if either party is already married by either's personal law, the marriage is invalid . . . .[53]

The courts have encountered difficulties both when a person has remarried following a divorce or annulment of the first marriage that would not be recognized in the forum and when the remarriage follows a divorce or annulment that would be recognized in the forum.

a) Remarriage after Invalid Divorce or Annulment

Normally the solution in this situation is obvious. If the foreign decree is not recognized in the forum, neither spouse has the capacity to remarry. Problems arise, however, where the law governing the parties' capacity would recognize the decree even though the law of the forum would not. *Schwebel v Ungar*[54] provides an illustration. A Jewish husband and wife who were domiciled in Hungary decided to settle in Israel. On route, the husband divorced his wife in Italy by Jewish *get*. That divorce was not recognized in Italy or in Hungary, their domicile at the time, but it was recognized in Israel. The couple then acquired a domicile of choice in Israel. While still domiciled in Israel, the woman married her second husband in Toronto. He later petitioned for nullity on the ground of bigamy. The Supreme Court of Canada, affirming the judgment of the Ontario Court of Appeal, dismissed the petition. The courts held that the woman had capacity to remarry in Ontario because, according to the law of her antenuptial domicile, Israeli law, she had the status of a single woman, the divorce from her first husband being recognized in Israel.[55]

The decision is interesting because, under the traditional common law rules for the recognition of foreign divorce decrees in existence at the time, the extra-judicial divorce was not recognizable in Ontario: it would not have been recognized by the parties' domicile at the time when the divorce was obtained.[56] On that basis, the case raised the problem of the incidental question[57] and illustrated the application of the conflict of laws rules of the law governing the main question (capacity to marry) to govern the incidental question (the recognition of a foreign divorce). Neither the Ontario Court of Appeal nor the Supreme Court of Canada, however, analyzed the case in terms of the incidental question and neither court addressed in any direct way that conceptual

---

53 *Padolecchia*, above note 51 at 336.
54 [1964] 1 OR 430 (CA), aff'd [1965] SCR 148 [*Schwebel*].
55 *Ibid* at 154 (SCC) and at 441 (CA).
56 *Ibid* at 154–55 (SCC).
57 See Chapter 10, Section E(2).

conundrum. The decision did have the effect of validating the Ontario marriage but the approach taken in *Schwebel* could certainly lead to difficulties. If, for example, the woman had acquired a domicile of choice in Canada, she would not have been capable of validly marrying there. The same would have been true of her first husband if he had later moved to Canada, even though the wife had validly married in Ontario.

There is another interpretation of *Schwebel* that is tied very much to the particular facts and that removes the incidental question. Passages in both judgments suggest that a divorce will be recognized in a Canadian court if it would be recognized by a domicile that the parties acquire subsequent to the divorce.[58] The scope of any such rule, however, is highly uncertain. It is unclear, for example, whether it is sufficient that the law of any subsequent domicile would recognize the divorce or whether it must be the law of the domicile first acquired after the divorce. If the parties in *Schwebel* had moved from Israel to another country that would not recognize the divorce, would a Canadian court still recognize the decree under this rule?

b) Remarriage after Valid Divorce or Annulment

Normally, of course, in this scenario there would be no impediment to the remarriage. Again, however, the problem of the incidental question can arise. It did so in *R v Brentwood Superintendent Registrar of Marriages*.[59] In that case an Italian man divorced his first wife in Switzerland where they were both domiciled. Despite the fact that the divorce would be recognized in England, the court held that the man could not remarry in England. His capacity to marry was governed by Swiss law as the law of his antenuptial domicile. By Swiss law, capacity to marry was governed by the law of his nationality and Italian law would not recognize the divorce.[60] Section 7 of the *Recognition of Divorces and Legal Separations Act 1971*[61] was enacted to reverse *Brentwood*. It provided that where a foreign divorce was entitled to recognition under the statute, "neither spouse [should] be precluded from marrying in the United Kingdom on the ground that the validity of the decree would not be recognized in any other country."

This particular piece of legislative reform had two major gaps: it did not extend to foreign nullity decrees and it did not cover remar-

---

58 *Schwebel*, above note 54 at 154 (SCC) and at 442 (CA).
59 [1968] 2 QB 956 (Div Ct) [*Brentwood*].
60 The decision also seems to be an example of the application of *renvoi* to the issue of capacity to marry: see Fawcett & Carruthers, above note 35 at 73.
61 (UK), 1971, c 53, as amended by the *Domicile and Matrimonial Proceedings Act 1973* (UK), 1973, c 45.

riages outside the United Kingdom. Both of these limitations were later removed in 1986.[62] Even before that time, however, the English courts had closed the legislative gaps by taking the step of recognizing a party's capacity to remarry where a dissolution or annulment of the first marriage was entitled to recognition in England. In *Perrini v Perrini*,[63] for example, the court was called upon to determine the validity of an English marriage. The wife argued that the marriage was void on the ground that her husband was already married at the time of the English ceremony. The husband relied upon a New Jersey decree annulling his first marriage. English law would have recognized the nullity decree. However, the husband was domiciled in Italy at the time of the English marriage and Italian law would not have recognized the nullity decree and, therefore, according to that law, the husband would not have had capacity to enter the English marriage. The court concluded that the English marriage was valid despite the incapacity existing under the husband's domiciliary law. Baker P reasoned:

> Once the New Jersey decree is recognised here the fact that [the husband] could not marry in Italy, the country of his domicile, on April 8, 1967, [the date of the English marriage] is, in my opinion, no bar to his marrying in England where by the New Jersey decree he was free to marry. No incapacity existed in English law.[64]

Equally, the English Court of Appeal in *Lawrence v Lawrence* upheld a remarriage celebrated outside England on the ground that the wife's prior divorce would be recognized in England despite the fact that it would not have been recognized by the law of her antenuptial domicile.[65] It is unclear what Canadian courts would do in similar circumstances. At the very least, one would assume that a Canadian court would affirm a party's capacity to marry based upon a prior Canadian decree of divorce or nullity whatever the position taken by the law of that party's antenuptial domicile.

---

62 The *Family Law Act 1986* (UK), 1986, c 55, s 50, now provides:

> Where, in any part of the United Kingdom (a) a divorce or annulment has been granted by a court of civil jurisdiction, or (b) the validity of a divorce or annulment is recognised by virtue of this Part, the fact that the divorce or annulment would not be recognised elsewhere shall not preclude either party to the marriage from re-marrying in that part of the United Kingdom or cause the re-marriage of either party (wherever the re-marriage takes place) to be treated as invalid in that part.

63 [1979] Fam 84.
64 *Ibid* at 92.
65 [1985] Fam 106 at 134 (CA).

5) Lack of Consent

There is a dearth of authority as to what law determines whether one of the parties has consented to marry the other. In *Szechter v Szechter* Simon P approved of an earlier version of rule 75 of *Dicey, Morris and Collins* which stated that "No marriage is valid if by the law of either party's domicile one party does not consent to marry the other."[66] On this phrasing, each party would have to have consented under both the law of his or her own domicile and the law of the other party's domicile. However, rule 75 now states "No marriage is (*semble*) valid if by the law of either party's domicile he or she does not consent to marry the other."[67] On this wording, where each party is domiciled in a different country at the time of the marriage, the courts should refer solely to the law of the antenuptial domicile of the party who allegedly did not consent.[68]

6) Same-Sex Marriages

Same-sex marriages are lawful in Canada. Section 2 of the *Civil Marriage Act* states that "Marriage, for civil purposes, is the lawful union of two persons to the exclusion of all others."[69] Although there is no authority on the point, a party's capacity to enter into a same-sex marriage is presumably governed by the dual domicile test in accordance with the general rule.

7) Relevance of the Law of the Place of Celebration

There are still some questions, at common law and now under the *Civil Marriage Act*, as to whether the law of the place of celebration is ever relevant to the essential validity of a marriage. Based on *Sottomayor v De Barros (No 2)*[70] and *Ogden*,[71] *Dicey, Morris and Collins* propounds the following:

---

66 [1971] 2 WLR 170 at 177 (PDA).
67 Above note 28.
68 *Ibid* at para 17-123, approving of the position taken in Fawcett & Carruthers, above note 35 at 973–76: "It seems adequate to analyse the issue of consent as a personal issue to be referred to the law governing capacity, without requiring a wife to have consented not only according to her own law but also according to her husband's, or vice versa." See *Davison v Sweeney*, 2005 BCSC 757 at para 23 [*Davison*]; *Grewal v Kaur*, 2011 ONSC 1812 at paras 75–80.
69 Above note 43. See also s 4. See *Reference re Same-Sex Marriage*, [2004] 3 SCR 698.
70 (1879), 5 PD 94.
71 Above note 21.

The validity of a marriage celebrated in England [the forum] between persons of whom the one has an English, and the other a foreign, domicile is not affected by any incapacity which, though existing under the law of such foreign domicile, does not exist under the law of England [the forum].[72]

There is no Canadian jurisprudence directly supporting this proposition. The *Civil Marriage Act* has been amended recently to provide that

> [a] marriage that is performed in Canada and that would be valid in Canada if the spouses were domiciled in Canada is valid for the purposes of Canadian law even though either or both of the spouses do not, at the time of the marriage, have the capacity to enter into it under the law of their respective state of domicile.[73]

This provision adopts, for marriages celebrated in Canada, a special choice of law rule for essential validity of the marriage. Its core practical thrust—discerned, in part, from the statute's lengthy preamble—is to allow same-sex couples domiciled elsewhere to validly marry in Canada.

The wording raises some questions. One question is how it interacts with the intended matrimonial home test, discussed above. If a court held the view that the essential validity of marriage was, in the circumstances, governed by the law of the intended matrimonial home, treating the parties as if they were domiciled in Canada might not change the analysis under that test. In other words, the provision appears to assume that the court will use the dual domicile test, despite conflicting decisions on that point. Another question is the meaning of "for the purposes of Canadian law." Would the meaning of section 5(1) change if these limiting words were removed? A third question is whether there is any conflict between the provision, which refers to domicile, and the heading preceding the provision, which refers to non-residents. As explained in Chapter 2, domicile and residence are different legal concepts. To date no cases have considered this provision.

Dicey, Morris and Collins also suggests that a marriage celebrated in the forum may not be valid if either of the parties is under an incapacity to marry the other by virtue of the domestic law of the forum.[74] Likewise, another leading treatise asserts that probably "all marriages celebrated in England must comply with English law, not only as to

---

72 Above note 28, r 74, exception 4. See the commentary at paras 17-108 to 17-110.
73 Above note 43, s 5(1). Additional provisions address the extent to which this rule operates retroactively.
74 *Dicey, Morris and Collins*, above note 28, r 74, exception 3. See the commentary at paras 17-100 to 17-106.

formal validity but also as to matters of essential validity."[75] On the other hand, the Supreme Court of Canada's decision in *Schwebel* is arguably inconsistent with that proposition.[76] In *Reed* the British Columbia Supreme Court made it clear that the place of celebration, when it is not the forum, is irrelevant.[77] Thus, a marriage celebrated in the state of Washington between first cousins was held valid despite the fact that it was void by Washington law. The parties were domiciled in British Columbia and there was no impediment by that law. County Court Judge Harvey concluded:

> As the parties to this action were domiciled in British Columbia at the time of their marriage and intended to and did remain so domiciled, and as they had capacity to marry under the laws of this Province notwithstanding that they were first cousins, their marriage in the State of Washington, conforming as it did with the formal requirements of that jurisdiction, is a valid marriage.[78]

8) Public Policy

In *Cheni v Cheni*, Simon P indicated that exceptionally an English court might "refuse to recognise and give effect to a capacity or incapacity to marry by the law of the domicile on the ground that to give it recognition and effect would be unconscionable in the circumstances in question."[79] Presumably the same possibility exists in Canadian law,[80] though it should be equally exceptional and thus used only rarely.[81]

D. SUBSEQUENT VALIDATION OF A MARRIAGE

Sometimes the courts have to address problems raised by the fact that a marriage, initially void by the applicable law, has subsequently been validated by that same law. The parties, however, may have moved since the time of their marriage and the question arises as to whether the retrospective change in the law has altered their status. This type

---

75 Fawcett & Carruthers, above note 35 at 907.
76 Above note 54.
77 Above note 26.
78 *Ibid* at 621.
79 [1965] P 85 at 98 [*Cheni*]. See also *KC v City of Westminster Social & Community Services Dept*, [2008] EWCA Civ 198 at paras 31–32 and 101.
80 See Walker, above note 28 at para 16.5.
81 See Chapter 3.

of problem involves the time element[82] in the conflict of laws. There are no easy answers.

The leading decision is *Starkowski v Attorney-General*.[83] A couple, domiciled in Poland, went through a religious ceremony of marriage in Austria in May 1945. At that time, the marriage was void by Austrian law because there had been no civil ceremony. In June 1945, a law was passed in Austria that retrospectively validated the marriage upon registration. Through the neglect of the priest, the marriage was not registered until July 1949. Before that time, the couple had acquired a domicile in England and had separated. In 1950, the wife married another man in England where they were both domiciled. The House of Lords held that the first marriage was valid and therefore that the second was void. It concluded that there was no difficulty in applying the law of the place of celebration as it stood at the time of the present proceedings to govern the formal validity of the marriage. The court did, however, leave open two questions. First, what would have been the situation if an English court had previously annulled the Austrian marriage? Presumably in those circumstances the retrospective Austrian legislation would have come too late to have had any effect. Second, what would have been the result if the wife had entered the English marriage before the registration of the Austrian marriage? In those circumstances, the validation of the first marriage would have had the effect of retrospectively invalidating the second. Lord Tucker at least suggested that the relevant date should be the date of the second ceremony and thus, inferentially, that the second marriage would have remained valid.[84]

In *Ambrose v Ambrose,* in 1935 a woman married in Washington State a man who was domiciled in British Columbia.[85] At that time, the wife had only an interlocutory divorce decree from her first husband from the California courts. That decree was not made final until 1939. The woman and her second husband lived together in British Columbia until 1956 when they separated. In 1958, the wife obtained an order, under legislation passed in 1956, from the California courts backdating her final divorce decree to 1931. In response to her second husband's petition for nullity in British Columbia, the woman, on the basis of

---

82 See Chapter 10, Section E(3). See FA Mann, "The Time Element in the Conflict of Laws" (1954) 31 *British Yearbook of International Law* 217; JK Grodecki, "Conflicts of Laws in Time" (1959) 35 *British Yearbook of International Law* 58; JHC Morris, "The Time Factor in the Conflict of Laws" (1966) 15 *International and Comparative Law Quarterly* 422.
83 [1954] AC 155 (HL) [*Starkowski*].
84 *Ibid* at 175.
85 (1960), 25 DLR (2d) 1 (BCCA) [*Ambrose*].

Starkowski, argued that by virtue of California law, the law governing her capacity to marry as the law of her antenuptial domicile in 1935, she had acquired retrospectively the capacity to marry her second husband because California now recognized the divorce from her first husband as effective from 1931. The British Columbia Court of Appeal rejected her argument and granted her second husband's nullity petition.

The court in *Ambrose* distinguished *Starkowski* in two ways. First, *Starkowski* dealt with the question of the formal validity of a marriage. That issue was governed by the law of the place of celebration and Austrian law still retained effective control over that issue because the place of celebration was a constant connecting factor. *Ambrose*, however, concerned the issue of capacity to marry that was governed by the law of the antenuptial domicile, California law, but effective control over the issue of the woman's capacity was lost once she had acquired a domicile outside California. That occurred in 1939 when the California divorce was made final and her domicile no longer depended upon that of her first husband. At the time of the retrospective California order, the woman was domiciled in British Columbia. That order therefore had no effect on her marital status.

Second, in *Starkowski* the validation of the first marriage preceded the second ceremony, whereas in *Ambrose* the validation of the divorce came after the second marriage. According to the Court of Appeal, the question raised in *Ambrose* was the one left open in *Starkowski*. The court resolved it by holding that the validity of the second marriage had to be determined by the state of the law as it stood at the time of the second marriage. But the question left open in *Starkowski* was not exactly the same as the one in *Ambrose*. In *Starkowski*, the issue was whether retrospective legislation would be allowed to invalidate a marriage that had taken place before the legislation was enacted. In *Ambrose*, it was whether retrospective legislation would be allowed to validate a marriage that had taken place in the interim.

E. PHYSICAL INCAPACITY

There is a lack of authority addressing the question of what law determines whether a marriage is invalid on the ground of the inability of one of the parties to consummate it. There have been some English cases dealing with nullity petitions on the basis of a wilful refusal to consummate, which is not a ground for annulment in Canada.[86] No clear rule

---

86 On nullity generally, see Chapter 23.

emerges. Part of the problem is that a refusal to consummate is a postnuptial event. The most important decision is probably *Ponticelli v Ponticelli*, in which Sachs J favoured the application of English law as the law of the husband's domicile or the law of the forum rather than Italian law, which was the law of the place of celebration and the law of the wife's antenuptial domicile.[87] *Dicey, Morris and Collins* favours the law of the forum or the law of the petitioner's domicile at the time of the marriage.[88] It points out that in *Ponticelli* the petitioner was in fact the husband.

The one Canadian case to consider the question in any depth is *Sangha v Mander*, in which the court canvassed the English cases but rejected them.[89] It favoured the application of either the antenuptial domicile of the impotent person or the intended matrimonial domicile. On the facts of the case it was not necessary to choose between the two alternatives. Lord Justice Huddart said:

> There is much to be said in support of both. The former may be more rational, given that the issue of impotence is best characterized as one of capacity, that the trend of legislative enactment is toward independent post-nuptial domiciles, and that it is best supported by the limited jurisprudence. A matrimonial domicile may be a practical alternative.[90]

F. POLYGAMOUS MARRIAGES

Traditionally polygamous marriages, whether actual or potential, have caused problems for common law courts, which have treated them with hostility. In *Hyde v Hyde*, the court refused to dissolve a potentially polygamous marriage.[91] Lord Penzance famously defined marriage "as understood in Christendom . . . as the voluntary union for life of one man and one woman to the exclusion of all others."[92] He determined that English matrimonial law was "adapted to the Christian marriage and it [was] wholly inapplicable to polygamy."[93] Over the years, judicial suspicion has eased substantially and there have also been some sporadic legislative changes.

---

87 [1958] P 204 [*Ponticelli*].
88 Above note 28 at paras 18-037 to 18-044.
89 [1985] 6 WWR 250 (BCSC).
90 *Ibid* at 257. See also *Davison*, above note 68 at paras 31–32; *Sahibalzubaidi*, above note 9 at paras 45–46.
91 (1866), LR 1 P & D 130 [*Hyde*].
92 *Ibid* at 133.
93 *Ibid* at 135.

The nature of a marriage as monogamous or polygamous is governed by the law of the place of celebration.[94] Thus in *Lee v Lau*, Cairns J said that "the nature and incidents of the union [were] ascertained according to the local law."[95] He held, however, that it was for the law of the forum to characterize the marriage ultimately as monogamous or polygamous based upon its nature and incidents. Canadian domestic law does not recognize polygamous marriages. This proposition is confirmed by section 2 of the *Civil Marriage Act*.[96] It follows that any marriage celebrated in Canada in accordance with provincial and federal law must be monogamous. English authorities have made it clear that a marriage which, at its inception, was potentially polygamous may be converted into a monogamous marriage by subsequent events, such as a change of religion,[97] a change in the law of the place of celebration that subsequently prohibits polygamy,[98] or a change in the domicile of the parties to a country whose law prohibits polygamy.[99] These decisions were endorsed by Cory J in his influential decision in *Re Hassan and Hassan*.[100] An Egyptian husband and wife were parties to a potentially polygamous marriage celebrated in Egypt. The court held that the marriage was converted into a monogamous marriage after the couple immigrated to Canada and acquired a domicile of choice in Ontario. As a result, the principle in *Hyde*[101] did not prevent the wife from being considered a wife pursuant to the provisions of the *Deserted Wives' and Children's Maintenance Act*,[102] nor did it preclude the courts from taking jurisdiction to hear the wife's application for matrimonial relief pursuant to that statute.

It is unclear which law governs a party's capacity to contract a polygamous marriage. General principle suggests that this question should be governed by the dual domicile test.[103] On that basis, it has been said that "a polygamous marriage is void if entered into outside Canada when at the time of the marriage either party was domiciled in Canada."[104]

---

94 See *Dicey, Morris and Collins*, above note 28 at paras 17-144 to 17-146; *Kaur v Ginder* (1958), 13 DLR (2d) 465 (BCSC) [*Kaur*].
95 [1967] P. 14 at 20.
96 Above note 43. See also s 2.3.
97 *Cheni*, above note 79 at 90–91.
98 *Parkasho v Singh*, [1968] P 233.
99 *Ali v Ali*, [1968] P 564.
100 (1976), 69 DLR (3d) 224 (Ont HCJ). See also *Nafie*, above note 36 at paras 42–47; *Azam v Jan*, 2012 ABCA 197 at para 17.
101 Above note 91.
102 RSO 1970, c 128.
103 See Albert Venn Dicey & JHC Morris, *Dicey and Morris on the Conflict of Laws*, 9th ed (London: Stevens & Sons, 1973) at 288–89.
104 Walker, above note 28 at para 16.6. See *Azam*, above note 36 at paras 53–56.

There is, however, some authority favouring the law of the intended matrimonial domicile.[105] There is even Canadian authority favouring the application of the law of the place of celebration.[106]

Although *Hyde* indicates that parties to a polygamous marriage are not entitled to matrimonial relief, the courts have tried to give effect as far as possible to valid polygamous marriages. Thus in *Shahnaz v Rizwan*, Winn J relied on an earlier edition of Dicey's textbook[107] for the proposition that a polygamous marriage, valid both as regards form and capacity, would be recognized as a valid marriage in the forum unless there was some strong reason to the contrary.[108] It has already been seen that a potentially polygamous, but *de facto* monogamous, marriage may be converted into a monogamous marriage by virtue of altered circumstances, such as a change of domicile.[109] There is also authority to the effect that a polygamous marriage constitutes a bar to a subsequent monogamous marriage.[110] Equally, children of such marriages are legitimate[111] and there is no bar to succession by children and spouses of such marriages.[112]

In some provinces, legislation has specifically recognized polygamous marriages. Section 1(2) of Ontario's *Family Law Act* provides:

> In the definition of "spouse", a reference to marriage includes a marriage that is actually or potentially polygamous, if it was celebrated in a jurisdiction whose system of law recognizes it as valid.[113]

Recently the Alberta Court of Appeal has been critical of *Hyde*. In *Azam v Jan* the court, without resolving the issue, forcefully developed the argument that a Canadian court could grant a divorce of an active polygamous marriage.[114] In light of the developments noted above, giving at least some effect to such marriages, the court considered the *Hyde* rule outdated. It stated:

> There is no modern, persuasive or binding authority that holds that relief cannot be given in these circumstances. Cases like *Hyde*, with

---

105 *Radwan v Radwan (No 2)*, [1973] Fam 35.
106 *Kaur*, above note 94. See the rejection of this decision by Fawcett & Carruthers, above note 35 at 927.
107 Albert Venn Dicey & JHC Morris, *Dicey and Morris on the Conflict of Laws*, 7th ed (London: Stevens & Sons, 1958), r 37.
108 [1965] 1 QB 390 at 397 (Div Ct).
109 See, for example, *Re Hassan and Hassan*, above note 100.
110 *Baindail v Baindail*, [1946] P 122 (CA); *Kaur*, above note 94.
111 *Re Tse and Minister of Employment and Immigration*, [1983] 2 FC 308 (CA).
112 See Fawcett & Carruthers, above note 35 at 933.
113 RSO 1990, c F.3. A similar provision is in the *Succession Law Reform Act*, RSO 1990, c S.26, s 1(2).
114 Above note 100.

its overtly Christian foundation, were decided in a different social context and in an age when the pedigree of people was critical to the passage of large estates and hereditary titles. That law seems out of place in our highly mobile and multicultural society . . . . Taking jurisdiction to grant a divorce of an actively polygamous marriage does not logically compel the recognition of polygamous marriages entered into in Canada or other jurisdictions in which they are illegal, nor mandate the expansion of Canadian immigration law or policy to admit parties to such marriages as immigrants to Canada . . . . Whether cases like *Hyde* . . . should continue to reflect the law of Canada is very much an open issue.[115]

Acting on this view, the Alberta Court of Queen's Bench rejected the approach in *Hyde* and indicated a willingness to grant matrimonial relief in respect of a foreign polygamous marriage.[116]

G. CIVIL UNIONS

Some provinces have created by legislation the formal institution of a civil union and have, to a large degree, assimilated the effect of such unions with that of marriages. In Nova Scotia, for example, Part II of the *Vital Statistics Act* establishes the concept of the registered domestic partnership: "two individuals who are cohabitating or intend to cohabit in a conjugal relationship may make a domestic-partner declaration."[117] The statute further provides that a person, in order to make such a declaration, must be ordinarily resident in Nova Scotia or the owner of real property in the province.[118] Upon registration, domestic partners have the same rights and obligations as spouses for the purpose of various provincial statutes, such as those dealing with support, succession, and matrimonial property.[119] Over time, conflict of laws issues with respect to such domestic partnerships and foreign civil unions of a similar character will have to be resolved by the courts.

The most far-reaching reforms have been enacted in Quebec. In 2002,[120] new articles were added to the *Civil Code of Quebec*[121] providing for the creation of civil unions and for their assimilation with marriages. At

---

115 *Ibid* at paras 21–24.
116 *Azam*, above note 36 at paras 39–44.
117 RSNS 1989, c 494, s 53(1).
118 *Ibid*, s 53(4).
119 *Ibid*, s 54(2).
120 SQ 2002, c 6.
121 Above note 30, arts 521.1 to 521.19 and 3090.1 to 3090.3.

the same time, amendments were made to various provisions in the *Civil Code* dealing with private international law.[122] Some of the new articles contained explicit choice of law provisions. Thus, article 3090.1 states:

> Civil union is governed with respect to its essential and formal validity by the law of the place of its solemnization.
>
> That law also applies to the effects of civil union, except those binding all spouses regardless of their regime, which are subject to the law of the State of their domicile.

In other provinces, *de facto* civil unions have been recognized for certain purposes such as support.[123]

In *Hincks v Gallardo* the Ontario courts treated a same-sex civil partnership entered into under United Kingdom legislation as amounting to a marriage under the *Civil Marriage Act*.[124] The motions judge noted that "where the parties were denied the choice to marry in the place where the union was celebrated I would perpetuate impermissible discrimination if I failed to recognize their civil partnership as a marriage."[125] In contrast, where the parties did have the choice to marry, such as in Nova Scotia, their choice to instead enter into a civil union would be respected as distinct from a marriage.[126]

FURTHER READINGS

BAILEY, MARTHA. "Same-Sex Relationships across Borders" (2004) 49 *McGill Law Journal* 1005.

BAILEY, MARTHA ET AL. "Expanding Recognition of Foreign Polygamous Marriages: Policy Implications for Canada" in Angela Campbell et al, *Polygamy in Canada: Legal and Social Implications for Women and Children: A Collection of Policy and Research Reports* (Ottawa: Status of Women Canada, 2005) 1-56.

BARTHOLOMEW, GW. "Recognition of Polygamous Marriages in Canada" (1961) 10 *International and Comparative Law Quarterly* 305.

BLACK, VAUGHAN. "Choice of Law and Territorial Jurisdiction of Courts in Family Matters" (2013) 32 *Canadian Family Law Quarterly* 53.

---

122 *Ibid*, arts 3122–23, 3144–45, 3154, and 3167.
123 See, for example, Ontario's *Family Law Act*, above note 113, s 29; Ontario's *Succession Law Reform Act*, above note 113, s 57.
124 Above note 43.
125 2013 ONSC 129 at para 84, aff'd 2014 ONCA 494.
126 *Ibid* at paras 45–46 (SC) and para 31 (CA).

BORNHEIM, JAN JAKOB. "Same-Sex Marriages in Canadian Private International Law" (2013) 51 *Alberta Law Review* 77.

CARRUTHERS, JANEEN. "Party Autonomy in the Legal Regulation of Adult Relationships: What Place for Party Choice in Private International Law?" (2012) 61 *International and Comparative Law Quarterly* 881.

COLLIER, JOHN. "Conflict of Laws—Foreign Divorces and Capacity to Marry—Judiciary and Jurists" [1985] *Cambridge Law Journal* 378.

FENTIMAN, RICHARD. "The Validity of Marriage and the Proper Law" [1985] *Cambridge Law Journal* 256.

GLENN, H PATRICK. "Capacity to Marry in the Conflict of Laws: Some Variations on a Theme" (1977) 4 *Dalhousie Law Journal* 157.

JAFFEY, AJE. "The Essential Validity of Marriage in the English Conflict of Laws" (1978) 41 *Modern Law Review* 38.

KAUFMAN, AMY. "Polygamous Marriages in Canada" (2005) 21 *Canadian Journal of Family Law* 315.

LIBBERT, LJ. "Marriage—Conflict of Laws—Validity of Polygamous Marriage of Person Domiciled in British Columbia" (1959) 37 *Canadian Bar Review* 357.

LYSYK, KEN. "Conflict of Laws—Status—Capacity to Marry—Recognition of Prior Foreign Divorce—The Incidental Question" (1965) 43 *Canadian Bar Review* 363.

MADDAUGH, PETER. "Validity of Marriage and the Conflict of Laws: A Critique of the Present Anglo-American Position" (1973) 23 *University of Toronto Law Journal* 117.

NG, LILY. "Covenant Marriage and the Conflict of Laws" (2007) 44 *Alberta Law Review* 815.

PRYLES, MICHAEL. "The Time Factor in Private International Law" (1980) 6 *Monash University Law Review* 225.

SHAKARGY, SHARON. "Marriage by the State or Married to the State? On Choice of Law in Marriage and Divorce" (2013) 9 *Journal of Private International Law* 499.

SWAN, JOHN. "A New Approach to Marriage and Divorce in the Conflict of Laws" (1974) 24 *University of Toronto Law Journal* 17.

WADE, JA. "Capacity to Marry: Choice of Law Rules and Polygamous Marriages" (1973) 22 *International and Comparative Law Quarterly* 571.

CHAPTER 22

DIVORCE

A. JURISDICTION TO GRANT A DIVORCE

1) Existence of Jurisdiction

By section 91(26) of the *Constitution Act, 1867*, the Parliament of Canada has exclusive legislative jurisdiction over divorce.[1] The federal *Divorce Act* establishes the jurisdiction of provincial superior courts to entertain petitions for divorce.[2] It states in section 3(1): "A court in a province has jurisdiction to hear and determine a divorce proceeding if either spouse has been ordinarily resident in the province for at least one year immediately preceding the commencement of the proceeding." The concept of ordinary residence was discussed earlier in this book.[3] The leading authority in the divorce context is *MacPherson v MacPherson*,[4] in which the Ontario Court of Appeal interpreted the corresponding provision in the previous *Divorce Act*.[5] The question was whether the petitioning wife had been ordinarily resident in Ontario for at least one year immediately preceding the presentation of her petition in July 1974. The wife was born in Ontario and had resided there

---

1   (UK), 30 & 31 Vict, c 3, reprinted in RSC 1985, App II, No 5.
2   RSC 1985 (2nd Supp), c 3.
3   See Chapter 2.
4   (1976), 13 OR (2d) 233 (CA) [*MacPherson*]. See also *Quigley v Willmore* (2008), 264 NSR (2d) 293 (CA); *Armoyan v Armoyan*, 2013 NSCA 99 at para 214 [*Armoyan*].
5   RSC 1970, c D-8, s 5(1).

until her marriage in Nova Scotia at the end of 1968. The parties moved to Ontario in the spring of 1969 where they lived until September 1973. At that time, they and their three children moved back to Nova Scotia where they established a home. Apart from a four-week visit by the wife to Ontario in November and December 1973, the family lived in Nova Scotia until April 1974 when the wife returned to Ontario. The husband continued to live in Nova Scotia. The wife asserted that she had not intended to establish a permanent residence in Nova Scotia when she moved there in September 1973.

The court held that the wife had not complied with the jurisdictional requirement that she be ordinarily resident in Ontario for a period of at least one year immediately preceding the presentation of the petition. In defining ordinary residence for the purpose of divorce jurisdiction, Evans JA relied upon the important tax case of *Thomson v Minister of National Revenue* in which Rand J had described ordinary residence as "residence in the course of the customary mode of life of the person concerned" and had said that it was to be "contrasted with special or occasional or casual residence."[6] Justice Evans drew support from several earlier decisions, including *Hardy v Hardy*.[7] There, the court held that a member of the Armed Forces who was born and had lived in Ontario continuously until he joined the army and who had returned on leave to his parents' Ontario home had remained ordinarily resident in Ontario despite his being moved by the army from place to place outside Ontario. Justice Evans approved of the test of ordinary residence applied by Houlden J in *Hardy*: "Where did this petitioner regularly, normally or customarily live in the year preceding the filing of the petition? . . . 'Where was his real home in that period?'"[8] He stated that "the arrival of a person in a new locality with the intention of making a home in that locality for an indefinite period ma[de] that person ordinarily resident in that community."[9] Unlike domicile, however, intention was not all-important. Thus, the wife's stated intention of returning to live in Ontario did not detract from her ordinary residence in Nova Scotia, which she acquired when she left Ontario to reside with her husband in Nova Scotia. She did not re-establish an ordinary residence in Ontario until she moved back in April 1974 and that was less than a year before the presentation of her petition.[10]

---

6   [1946] SCR 209 at 224.
7   [1969] 2 OR 875 (HCJ) [*Hardy*]. See also *Marsellus v Marsellus* (1970), 13 DLR (3d) 383 (BCSC).
8   *Hardy*, above note 7 at 877, cited in *MacPherson*, above note 4 at 237.
9   *MacPherson, ibid* at 239.
10 Similarly, in *Nafie v Badawy*, 2015 ABCA 36, the majority held that the motions judge had placed too much emphasis on Ms Nafie's stated intention (paras 57–63)

In *Hinter v Hinter*, Epstein J followed the reasoning in *MacPherson*.[11] The question was whether the wife had been ordinarily resident in Ontario for one year preceding the filing of her petition in March 1996. Although the matrimonial home was in Ontario, the wife had lived in the couple's condominium in Florida since November 1995. She had not placed any time limit upon her stay in Florida. Thus, the court concluded that, when she left for Florida, she did so with the intention of making her home there for an indefinite period. She had exclusive possession of the Florida condominium and had established a personal relationship with another man there. She had not even returned to Toronto when she learned that the matrimonial home had been stripped of its contents. Accordingly, the court held that she had established her ordinary residence in Florida because that was where she regularly, normally, and customarily lived. Therefore, the Ontario courts had no jurisdiction to entertain her divorce petition.

The courts have held that there is no constitutional right to a divorce so as to allow a court to reduce or eliminate the requirements of section 3(1) of the *Divorce Act*. Justice Archambault held in *Garchinski v Garchinski* that the "right to petition for divorce [was] created by statute and [could] only be exercised within the confines of the statute."[12] In *Thurber v Thurber*,[13] a wife argued unsuccessfully that the ordinary residence requirement in section 3(1) of the *Divorce Act* violated sections 6 (the mobility right) and 7 (the right to life, liberty, and security of the person) of the *Canadian Charter of Rights and Freedoms*.[14] In *Winmill v Winmill*, the Federal Court of Appeal made it clear that, if the petitioner could not satisfy the jurisdictional requirements of the *Divorce Act* because neither party had been ordinarily resident in a province for the requisite one-year period, then no Canadian court, including the Federal Court, could assume jurisdiction.[15]

Ordinary residence is a question of fact. It is therefore not dependent upon "citizenship, domicile or even immigration status."[16] A person does not lose his or her ordinary residence in a province "until there is

---

and that the objective facts indicated she had ceased to be ordinarily resident in Alberta while living in Saudi Arabia (paras 77–80). See also *Wang v Lin*, 2013 ONCA 33 at paras 40–44.

11   (1996), 23 RFL (4th) 401 (Ont Ct Gen Div). See also *Molson v Molson* (1998), 38 RFL (4th) 385 (Alta QB); *Tower v Tower* (2008), 52 RFL (6th) 455 (Ont SCJ).
12   [2002] SJ No 465 at para 25 (QB).
13   (2002), 322 AR 242 (QB).
14   Part I of the *Constitution Act, 1982*, being Schedule B of the *Canada Act 1982* (UK), 1982, c 11.
15   [1974] 1 FC 686 (CA).
16   *Jenkins v Jenkins* (2000), 8 RFL (5th) 96 at para 15 (Ont SCJ).

an intention to give up that residence and then to live in another province."[17] Such a conclusion was reached in *Wrixon v Wrixon* despite the petitioner's assertion to the contrary.[18] She had resided in Alberta for more than twenty years. However, she filed her petition for divorce in the province only two months after returning from an eighteen-month stay in Hawaii. She argued that she had not lost her ordinary residence in Alberta during that period. She testified that her stay in Hawaii was just an "extended vacation." The court held that the evidence negated her claim. Justice Purvis pointed out that while she was in Hawaii she had "acquired fixed addresses at several locations" and had been "gainfully employed for at least part of the time."[19] It therefore could not be said that, in the twelve months immediately preceding the filing of the petition, she, in the settled routine of her life, regularly, normally, or customarily lived in Alberta.

Given that the *Divorce Act* is a federal statute and so applies uniformly across all provinces, it is open to question why section 3(1) is phrased so as to require the year of ordinary residence to have been in one particular province rather than in Canada as a whole.[20]

The *Divorce Act* defines "spouse" in section 2(1) as "either of two persons who are married to each other." It has been argued that a party to a foreign polygamous marriage does not fit within this definition and thus cannot rely on the statute to seek a divorce. This view has been rejected, and the statute applied, in at least one polygamous marriage case.[21]

The *Civil Marriage Act* has recently been amended to include a special jurisdictional basis, independent of the *Divorce Act*, to grant a divorce to spouses who are not resident in Canada.[22] The practical concern the provisions address is that, for example, a non-resident same-sex couple might marry in Canada and then be unable to obtain a divorce from the courts where they reside because that jurisdiction does not recognize the marriage as valid.[23] Accordingly, section 7(1) provides that the court of the province where the marriage was performed may, on application, grant a divorce if three conditions are met: (1) the marriage

---

17 *Cadot v Cadot* (1981), 49 NSR (2d) 202 at 206 (SC).
18 (1982), 42 AR 198 (QB).
19 *Ibid* at 199.
20 See Vaughan Black, "Choice of Law and Territorial Jurisdiction of Courts in Family Matters" (2013) 32 *Canadian Family Law Quarterly* 53 at 62.
21 *Azam v Jan*, 2012 ABCA 197 at para 20, applied in subsequent proceedings in *Azam v Jan*, 2013 ABQB 301. For additional analysis of the courts' ability to deal with foreign polygamous marriages, see Chapter 21, Section F.
22 SC 2005, c 33.
23 See Brenda Cossman, "Exporting Same-Sex Marriage, Importing Same-Sex Divorce" (2013) 32 *Canadian Family Law Quarterly* 1.

has broken down (such that the spouses have lived separate and apart for at least one year); (2) neither spouse resides in Canada at the time of the application; and (3) each spouse resides, and has done so for at least one year immediately prior to the application, in a jurisdiction where a divorce cannot be granted because that jurisdiction does not recognize the marriage as valid. Additional provisions address the process to be followed for such an application and the effect of the divorce.

2) Exercise of Jurisdiction: Parallel Proceedings

Where divorce proceedings between the same spouses are commenced in more than one jurisdiction, questions may arise as to where the matter should be resolved. In the case of parallel proceedings within Canada, the *Divorce Act* mandates the solution.[24] Section 3(2) provides that, where divorce proceedings between the same parties are pending in two courts that would otherwise have jurisdiction under the statute and were commenced on different days and the first proceeding is not discontinued within thirty days of its commencement, then the court in which the proceeding was commenced first has exclusive jurisdiction to entertain the divorce proceeding. If the two divorce proceedings were commenced on the same day and neither is discontinued within thirty days of commencement, then, by virtue of section 3(3), the Federal Court has exclusive jurisdiction to entertain the divorce proceeding between the spouses and the divorce proceeding must be transferred to that court.

In addition, section 6(1) of the *Divorce Act* provides that, where a divorce proceeding involves a contested claim to the custody of, or access to, a child of the marriage, then the court entertaining that proceeding may transfer the divorce proceeding to a court in the province to which the child is most substantially connected. According to section 6(4), the court in the province to which the proceeding is transferred then has exclusive jurisdiction to hear and determine that proceeding.

The *Divorce Act*, however, is silent in relation to parallel divorce proceedings in a Canadian province and a foreign country. In those circumstances, the Canadian court may be faced with an application to stay its own proceeding or to issue an anti-suit injunction to prevent one of the spouses from commencing or continuing a divorce proceeding abroad. The applicable principles are those addressed in Chapter 6 on *forum non conveniens* and Chapter 7 on anti-suit injunctions.

---

24 Above note 2.

One of the earliest cases to discuss the applicable principles both in the context of a stay and in the context of an anti-suit injunction is the decision of the Manitoba Court of Appeal in *Kornberg v Kornberg*.[25] The case illustrates the point that sometimes neither remedy will be appropriate. The parties were married in Manitoba and lived there until their separation in 1987. After the separation, the husband moved to Minnesota. The wife commenced an action in Minnesota for divorce and division of assets. The husband subsequently started a similar action in Manitoba. He then sought an injunction restraining the wife from continuing the Minnesota action while she in turn moved to stay the Manitoba proceeding.

The Manitoba Court of Appeal observed that no special principles applied in matrimonial proceedings. In determining, therefore, that the husband was not entitled to an anti-suit injunction to restrain the Minnesota proceeding, the court applied the test from the leading decision of the day, *Société Nationale Industrielle Aérospatiale v Lee Kui Jak*.[26] Justice Philp stressed that the dominant issue between the parties was not the divorce per se but the discovery, valuation, and disposition of their substantial commercial assets. In that context, the husband had not discharged the burden of establishing that the continuation of the proceeding in Minnesota would cause him injustice. There were ample connections with Minnesota given that that was where the husband permanently resided and that there were real estate holdings in that state and elsewhere in the United States.

When it came to the wife's motion for a stay of the Manitoba action, the court relied upon the leading English decision of *Spiliada Maritime Corp v Cansulex Ltd*.[27] Justice Philp held that the wife had failed to establish that Minnesota was clearly and distinctly more appropriate than Manitoba for the trial of the action and thus the stay was refused. The court pointed out that where both sets of proceedings were within Canada, the *Divorce Act*, by section 3(2), employed "a 'first out of the starting gates' test."[28] In the international context, however, that was "only one of many factors, and not the dominant one . . . to be considered on an application for a stay or an anti-suit injunction where proceedings are

---

25 (1990), 76 DLR (4th) 379 (Man CA) [*Kornberg*].
26 [1987] AC 871 (PC). This decision was highly influential in the Supreme Court of Canada's judgment in *Amchem Products Inc v British Columbia (Workers' Compensation Board)*, [1993] 1 SCR 897 [*Amchem*].
27 [1987] AC 460 (HL). This case was also influential in Sopinka J's judgment in *Amchem*, above note 26, and in his elaboration of a Canadian doctrine of *forum non conveniens*.
28 *Kornberg*, above note 25 at 388.

continuing in a foreign jurisdiction."[29] Later cases also support the view that *forum non conveniens* issues will be treated no differently in divorce proceedings than in any other kind of proceeding. The courts will apply the same basic principles to determine whether a stay should be granted in light of the precise issues in dispute between the parties. In *Nicholas v Nicholas*, for example, the husband instituted divorce proceedings in Trinidad while the wife did so in Ontario.[30] The lower court stayed the Ontario proceeding at the behest of the husband and so the question before the Court of Appeal was whether Trinidad was indeed the appropriate jurisdiction for resolving the divorce action. The parties had been married in Trinidad in 1969. They had moved to Ontario in 1980 for the sole purpose of having their children educated in Canada. They maintained a home in Ontario but they spent extensive periods of time each year in Trinidad. The husband ran substantial business activities from Trinidad and was not a Canadian resident. All but the youngest child had completed their education and moved back to Trinidad. The Court of Appeal determined that the lower court was correct in concluding that Trinidad was the appropriate jurisdiction. It applied the test from *Amchem Products Inc v British Columbia (Workers' Compensation Board)*.[31] It pointed out that the dispute was about money and property and that custody was not an issue.[32] Those circumstances established Trinidad as the *forum conveniens* because virtually all the disputed assets were located in Trinidad. Moreover, there was no evidence that the wife would suffer any juridical disadvantage from litigating in Trinidad.

Cases subsequent to *Kornberg* have exhibited a similar reluctance to grant an anti-suit injunction to prevent a divorce action from proceeding abroad. It has become clear that the test to be applied is the general test from *Amchem*.[33] In *Harris v Murray*, for example, the Alberta court applied that test to deny a wife's motion to restrain her husband from continuing his divorce action in Indonesia.[34] The Indonesian court had not assumed jurisdiction in a manner that contravened Canadian principles of *forum non conveniens*. Additionally, there was no merit in the wife's claim that a divorce decree from Indonesia would foreclose, or

---

29 *Ibid.* See also *Gyuzeleva v Angelov*, 2012 ONSC 6628 at para 16.
30 (1996), 139 DLR (4th) 652 (Ont CA). See also *LGV v LAP*, 2016 NBCA 23.
31 Above note 26.
32 Contrast with *Alexiou v Alexiou* (1996), 41 Alta LR (3d) 90 (QB), where custody was a major issue in the dispute. The Alberta court declined jurisdiction in favour of Greece largely because there were various witnesses there, such as relations, friends of the family, and teachers, who could give evidence on what was in the best interests of the children.
33 Above note 26. See also *Armoyan*, above note 4 at paras 192–204.
34 (1995), 28 Alta LR (3d) 377 (QB).

even substantially impair, her claims in Alberta for spousal support and a division of matrimonial property.

The nature of an ongoing dispute over the proper forum for divorce proceedings will change if a foreign court grants a divorce which, in accordance with the principles discussed later in this chapter, is recognized in the forum. For example, in *Armoyan v Armoyan* divorce proceedings had been initiated in both Florida and Nova Scotia.[35] While the Nova Scotia courts were considering a motion to stay its proceedings, the Florida court granted a divorce. The Nova Scotia court accordingly stayed its proceedings for dissolution of the marriage.[36]

B. CHOICE OF LAW

Traditionally, divorce has not presented a choice of law problem. At common law, jurisdiction was based on the domicile of the parties.[37] Where a court had jurisdiction, it would apply the law of the forum without question. The present *Divorce Act*[38] contains no choice of law provisions. To date, Canadian courts have continued to apply Canadian law to determine whether a divorce should be granted. Given, however, that jurisdiction is no longer based on domicile, the law which has traditionally governed parties' status, but on one party's ordinary residence in the province for one year, there is the theoretical possibility that the courts may apply the substantive grounds of divorce of some law other than Canadian law.[39]

C. RECOGNITION OF FOREIGN DIVORCE DECREES

Section 13 of the *Divorce Act* provides that a divorce granted under the statute "has legal effect throughout Canada." Thus the issue of the

---

35 Above note 4.
36 *Ibid* at paras 247 and 377.
37 *Le Mesurier v Le Mesurier*, [1895] AC 517 (PC) [*Le Mesurier*].
38 Above note 2.
39 See Janet Walker, *Castel & Walker: Canadian Conflict of Laws*, 6th ed (Markham, ON: Butterworths, 2005) (loose-leaf) at para 17.1.d. See also the discussion of the choice of law question in James Fawcett & Janeen Carruthers, *Cheshire, North & Fawcett Private International Law*, 14th ed (Oxford: Oxford University Press, 2008) at 966–70; Black, above note 20 at 73.

recognition of foreign decrees does not arise among the provinces. It is relevant only where some foreign country has granted a divorce.

1) Statutory Grounds for Recognition

Section 22 of the *Divorce Act* provides:

> (1) A divorce granted, on or after the coming into force of this Act [June 1, 1986], pursuant to a law of a country or subdivision of a country other than Canada by a tribunal or other authority having jurisdiction to do so shall be recognized for all purposes of determining the marital status in Canada of any person, if either former spouse was ordinarily resident in that country or subdivision for at least one year immediately preceding the commencement of proceedings for the divorce.
>
> (2) A divorce granted, after July 1, 1968, pursuant to a law of a country or subdivision of a country other than Canada by a tribunal or other authority having jurisdiction to do so, on the basis of the domicile of the wife in that country or subdivision determined as if she were unmarried and, if she was a minor, as if she had attained the age of majority, shall be recognized for all purposes of determining the marital status in Canada of any person.
>
> (3) Nothing in this section abrogates or derogates from any other rule of law respecting the recognition of divorces granted otherwise than under this Act.

Section 22(1) recognizes foreign decrees that mirror the basis for Canadian divorce jurisdiction under the statute. It is not, however, retroactive and applies only to foreign divorce decrees granted after the coming into force of the *Divorce Act*. It should be noted that it is irrelevant whether the foreign tribunal took jurisdiction on the basis of one party's ordinary residence for one year or on some other basis. Section 22(2) preserves the statutory ground for the recognition of foreign divorces first enacted by section 6(2) of the 1968 *Divorce Act*.[40] Despite the wording, which suggests that the foreign tribunal must have taken jurisdiction on the basis that the wife was domiciled in the foreign country, it appears that it is sufficient merely that the wife was domiciled there according to Canadian law.[41] Equally, there appears to be no requirement that the wife be the petitioner in the foreign divorce proceedings.[42]

---

40 SC 1967–68, c 24 [1968 *Divorce Act*].
41 *La Carte v La Carte* (1975), 60 DLR (3d) 507 (BCSC) [*La Carte*].
42 *Szabo v Szabo* (1980), 15 RFL (2d) 13 (Ont UFC).

Section 22(3) retains the common law rules for the recognition of foreign divorces. These are discussed in the next section of this chapter. The general effect of section 22, therefore, is to make the rules for the recognition of foreign divorces considerably broader than the rules governing the jurisdiction of the Canadian courts. As earlier explained, under section 3(1) the jurisdiction of Canadian courts is confined to situations where one of the spouses has been ordinarily resident in the province for at least one year immediately preceding the commencement of proceedings.

Finally, note should be made of the unique situation in Quebec. Article 3167 of the *Civil Code of Quebec*[43] provides for a broader recognition of foreign divorces than set out in sections 22(1) and (2) of the *Divorce Act*. It allows for recognition

> if one of the spouses had his or her domicile in the State where the decision was rendered, or had his or her residence in that State for at least one year before the institution of the proceedings, if the spouses are nationals of that State or if the decision has been recognized in any of those States.[44]

2) Common Law Grounds for Recognition

In *Orabi v El Qaoud*,[45] the Nova Scotia Court of Appeal summarized the common law bases for the recognition of foreign divorce decrees by adopting[46] the following extract from *Payne on Divorce*:

> Canadian courts will recognize a foreign divorce: (i) where jurisdiction was assumed on the basis of the domicile of the spouses; (ii) where the foreign divorce, though granted on a non-domiciliary jurisdictional basis, is recognized by the law of the domicile of the parties; (iii) where the foreign jurisdictional rule corresponds to the Canadian jurisdictional rule in divorce proceedings; (iv) where the circumstances in the foreign jurisdiction would have conferred jurisdiction on a Canadian court had they occurred in Canada; (v) where either the petitioner or respondent had a real and substantial connection with the foreign jurisdiction wherein the divorce was granted; and (vi) where the foreign divorce is recognized in another foreign

---

43 CQLR c C-1991.
44 See Walker, above note 39 at para 17.2.a for a discussion of the constitutionality of this provision.
45 (2005), 12 RFL (6th) 296 (NSCA) [*Orabi*].
46 *Ibid* at para 14. See also *Quigley v Willmore* (2008), 272 NSR (2d) 61 at para 16 (SC).

jurisdiction with which the petitioner or respondent has a real and substantial connection.⁴⁷

The authorities can be divided into three groups: those dealing with recognition based on domicile, those dealing with recognition based on reciprocity, and those dealing with recognition based on a real and substantial connection.

a) Domicile

The original common law rule was that a decree granted in the country where the spouses were domiciled, and only such a decree, would be recognized as validly dissolving the marriage. The spouses' common domicile had exclusive jurisdiction to entertain divorce proceedings. This proposition became known as the rule in *Le Mesurier*.⁴⁸

The rule was very hard on the wife because, at that time, her domicile was dependent upon that of her husband. Thus, the wife was required to seek a divorce in the jurisdiction where her husband was currently domiciled. In effect, the rule in *Le Mesurier* was that a divorce granted by the courts of the husband's domicile would be recognized as valid. Indeed, the court expressed the rule in this way in *Szabo v Szabo* when it recognized a divorce from Yugoslavia on the basis of *Le Mesurier* because the respondent husband was domiciled there at the time of the proceedings.⁴⁹ Arguably, therefore, the *Le Mesurier* rule can apply where the parties have separate domiciles and the divorce is granted in the husband's domicile. After all, divorces granted by the courts of the wife's domicile are covered by section 22(2) of the *Divorce Act*.

In *Armitage v Attorney General*, the English courts extended the *Le Mesurier* rule and held that a foreign divorce would be recognized, even though not granted by the courts of the parties' domicile, if it would be recognized by the courts of the parties' domicile at the time of the divorce as validly dissolving the marriage.⁵⁰ Canadian courts have followed *Armitage*,⁵¹ though it can be questioned whether the rule can withstand scrutiny under the doctrine developed in *Morguard Investments Ltd v De Savoye*.⁵² Presumably, where the spouses do not have a common domicile, the divorce would have to be recognized by each

---

47 Julien D Payne, *Payne on Divorce*, 4th ed (Scarborough, ON: Carswell, 1996) at 111. See also Walker, above note 39 at para 17.2.a.
48 See above note 37.
49 Above note 42.
50 [1906] P 135 [*Armitage*].
51 See, for example, *Walker v Walker*, [1950] 4 DLR 253 (BCCA).
52 [1990] 3 SCR 1077 [*Morguard*].

party's domicile. Additionally, in *Schwebel v Ungar*,[53] the Supreme Court of Canada appeared to extend the *Armitage* principle to hold that a divorce will be recognized in Canada if it would be recognized by a domicile that the parties acquire immediately after their divorce.[54]

b) Reciprocity

In *Travers v Holley*, the English Court of Appeal decided that a foreign divorce decree would be recognized if the foreign court took jurisdiction in circumstances in which an English court could have taken jurisdiction and if the bases for jurisdiction in the two countries were substantially similar.[55] Canadian courts have adopted this approach.[56] Later, starting with *Robinson-Scott v Robinson-Scott*, the English courts determined that there was no longer any need for there to be a substantial similarity between the basis for jurisdiction in the foreign country and the basis on which jurisdiction could have been taken in England.[57] All that was important was that an English court could have taken jurisdiction to dissolve the marriage had the facts occurred in England. Again, the Canadian courts have followed suit.[58]

Although, to a large extent, the reciprocity principle is embodied in sections 22(1) and (2) of the *Divorce Act*,[59] one significant difference lies in the fact that *Travers v Holley* can operate retrospectively.[60] Thus a foreign decree granted in the country where one of the spouses had been ordinarily resident for one year preceding the commencement of proceedings could apparently be recognized in Canada even though the divorce had been granted prior to 1 June 1986.

c) Real and Substantial Connection

In *Indyka v Indyka* the House of Lords determined that a foreign divorce could be recognized where there was a real and substantial connection

---

53 [1965] SCR 148 [*Schwebel*]. See the discussion of this case in Chapter 21, Section C(4)(a).
54 *Ibid* at 154. See also the decision of the Ontario Court of Appeal: *Schwebel v Ungar*, [1964] OR 430 at 442 (CA).
55 [1953] P 246 (CA).
56 See, for example, *Allarie v Director of Vital Statistics* (1963), 41 DLR (2d) 553 (Alta SC); *Januszkiewicz v Januszkiewicz* (1965), 55 DLR (2d) 727 (Man QB).
57 [1958] P 71 [*Robinson-Scott*].
58 See, in the context of foreign nullity decrees, *Gwyn v Mellen* (1979), 15 BCLR 78 (CA). See also *La Carte*, above note 41, and the court's interpretation of s 6(2) of the 1968 *Divorce Act*, above note 40, in accordance with the reasoning in *Robinson-Scott*, above note 57.
59 Above note 2.
60 See *Indyka v Indyka*, [1969] 1 AC 33 (HL) [*Indyka*]; *Bevington v Hewitson* (1974), 4 OR (2d) 226 (HCJ).

between the petitioner and the foreign jurisdiction.⁶¹ The Canadian courts soon applied *Indyka*.⁶² They also followed the English extension of the principle from the petitioner to the respondent,⁶³ so that the rule can now be stated as follows: "a foreign divorce will be recognized where there exists some real and substantial connection between the petitioner or the respondent and the granting jurisdiction."⁶⁴ In determining the existence of such a connection, the courts will examine diverse factors such as "residence, employment, nationality, citizenship and holding of property."⁶⁵ In *Morguard*,⁶⁶ the Supreme Court of Canada clearly approved of the approach taken in *Indyka* and used it as one of the bases of its new doctrine of *in personam* jurisdiction.⁶⁷

In *Edward v Edward Estate*, the Saskatchewan Court of Appeal, after a lengthy discussion of the question, made it clear that judicial changes to the common law were, in general, to be applied retrospectively and that courts should not engage in prospective overruling.⁶⁸ Chief Justice Bayda stated:

> the most cogent reason for rejecting this technique is the necessity for our courts to maintain their independent, neutral and non-legislative role. The practice of giving prospective effect to law is endemic to legislatures. By deciding an existing case under the old rule but warning that future cases will be decided under a new rule now being announced, a court is really usurping the function of the legislature.⁶⁹

In accordance with this position, the court applied *Indyka* to recognize a California divorce granted to a husband from his second wife in 1953 and, consequently, the validity of that husband's marriage to his third wife two years later.

Undoubtedly the broad statutory grounds for the recognition of foreign divorces in section 22 of the *Divorce Act* have reduced significantly the judicial need to rely on the common law rules. Nevertheless, the preservation of those rules by section 22(3) is still important, with the result that the jurisdiction of foreign courts may more readily be recognized than the jurisdiction of Canadian courts. In *Wlodarczyk v Spriggs*, for example, the Saskatchewan court recognized an Australian divorce

---

61 *Ibid*.
62 *Kish v Director of Vital Statistics* (1973), 35 DLR (3d) 530 (Alta SC).
63 *Mayfield v Mayfield*, [1969] P 119.
64 *Bate v Bate* (1978), 1 RFL (2d) 298 at 304 (Ont HCJ).
65 *Ibid* at 311. See, for example, *Martinez v Basail*, 2010 ONSC 2038 at para 11.
66 Above note 52.
67 *Ibid* at 1104.
68 (1987), 57 Sask R 67 (CA).
69 *Ibid* at para 30.

based on *Indyka* despite the fact that the husband had lived with his wife in Saskatchewan for some seventeen years and had resided in Australia for only four months before commencing divorce proceedings.[70] Despite his failure to satisfy section 22(1) of the *Divorce Act*, the court concluded that Australia nevertheless had a real and substantial connection with the husband. He was an Australian citizen, had lived in Australia for fifteen years and had married in Australia, and, after the marital breakdown, had moved back to Australia and taken up employment there.[71]

The English courts extended the *Indyka* principle so as to recognize a divorce that, although not granted in such a jurisdiction, would be recognized in a jurisdiction with a real and substantial connection to the petitioner or, presumably, the respondent.[72] Despite some academic support for this position,[73] there is some doubt as to whether it represents Canadian law. There are, however, Canadian cases where the principle appears to be accepted as correct.[74]

D. EXTRA-JUDICIAL DIVORCES

Some religious laws, such as the Jewish *get* or Muslim *talaq*, allow one of the parties (typically the husband) to divorce the other by a unilateral act without the need to resort to judicial proceedings. Under Jewish law, it appears that the divorce must be formalized before a rabbinical court. Under Muslim law, in some countries the "bare" *talaq* is sufficient. In others, there are further procedures to be followed. In Pakistan, for example, the *Muslim Family Laws Ordinance 1961* requires the husband to notify the authorities and his wife so that reconciliation proceedings can be attempted and the *talaq* is not effective until ninety days have elapsed from the time when notice was given.[75]

---

70 (2000), 200 Sask R 129 (QB).
71 See also *RNS v KS*, 2013 BCCA 406 [*RNS*]. Interestingly, in that case the court recognized the decision of a state court, the Family Court of Western Australia, on the basis of a real and substantial connection to Australia without requiring that such a connection be shown with the specific state. It did so on the basis that the divorce was under Australian federal legislation: see para 28.
72 See *Mather v Mahoney*, [1968] 1 WLR 1773 (PDA); *Messina v Smith*, [1971] P 322.
73 Payne, above note 47 at 111.
74 See, for example, *Rowland v Rowland* (1973), 2 OR (2d) 161 (HCJ).
75 See the discussion of this legislation in several cases such as *Qureshi v Qureshi*, [1972] Fam 173 [*Qureshi*]; *Amin v Canada (Minister of Citizenship and Immigration)*, [2008] 4 FCR 531 (Fed Ct) [*Amin*].

There have been few Canadian cases dealing with the recognition of extra-judicial divorces. One question is whether they fall within sections 22(1) and (2) of the *Divorce Act*.⁷⁶ Arguably they do not because they have not been granted by some "other authority having jurisdiction" to grant a divorce. There was some consideration of this question in *Amin v Canada (Minister of Citizenship and Immigration)*.⁷⁷ In order to sponsor his second wife as a permanent resident of Canada, the applicant had to prove that his first marriage had been validly dissolved. Prior to his second marriage in 2002, the applicant had divorced his first wife by Muslim *talaq* in Pakistan in 1993. That *talaq*, however, did not become effective under Pakistan's *Muslim Family Laws Ordinance 1961* until 2005, well after the second marriage. The court concluded that the applicant had failed to establish the legal validity in Pakistan of his 1993 religious divorce. In any event, the court determined that the bare Muslim *talaq* was "nothing more than a unilateral declaration of divorce made by the husband, usually in the presence of witnesses, and sometimes recorded in a private divorce deed."⁷⁸ As such, the 1993 *talaq* did not meet the requirements of section 22(1). The court added that the intent of the section was "to require that some form of adjudicative or official oversight be present before Canada [would] recognize a foreign divorce."⁷⁹ Such a requirement would be fulfilled by the process established by the *Muslim Family Laws Ordinance 1961* but not by the bare *talaq*.

The language of section 22(3) of the *Divorce Act*, which preserves the common law rules for the recognition of divorces, is clearly broad enough to include extra-judicial divorces. The problem is that the existing rules are far from clear. *Schwebel v Ungar*⁸⁰ is the one Canadian case where the courts did recognize an extra-judicial divorce. A couple, domiciled in Hungary, travelled to Israel with the intention of settling there. On their way, they obtained a Jewish bill of divorcement in Italy in conformity with rabbinical law by appearing, in the presence of witnesses, before a rabbi at which time the husband delivered a *get* to his wife. Both the Supreme Court of Canada and the Ontario Court of Appeal made it clear that the divorce would be recognized in Canada if it would be recognized by the parties' domicile at the time of the divorce. Hungarian law, however, would not have recognized the divorce. Despite that fact, the courts apparently determined that it was sufficient that the divorce was "recognized in Israel where the [parties]

---

76   Above note 2.
77   Above note 75.
78   *Ibid* at para 19.
79   *Ibid* at para 20.
80   Above notes 53 and 54.

established a domicile of choice within three weeks of it having been granted."[81]

Schwebel suggests that the common law rules for the recognition of foreign judicial divorces will be adapted to the case of extra-judicial divorces. The Ontario Court of Appeal, for example, relied upon both *Le Mesurier* and the *Armitage* principle.[82] In *Amin*,[83] the court seemed to accept that the real and substantial connection test from *Indyka* could equally be applied to extra-judicial divorces. On that basis, a Canadian court could recognize the validity of an extra-judicial divorce where it would be recognized by the law of a jurisdiction with a real and substantial connection to one of the parties. As we have seen, however, the court determined on the facts that the marriage had not been effectively dissolved by the bare *talaq*.

The court in *Amin* also made the point that an overarching difficulty with recognizing extra-judicial divorces was the need for there to be due process and fairness.[84] Justice Barnes stated that the foreign divorce must be "a divorce obtained by a process that [was] consistent with Canadian notions of fairness and in harmony with Canadian public policy."[85] It was not enough merely to satisfy the real and substantial connection test because that was "not a test by which the legal frailties of a foreign, extrajudicial divorce [would] be overcome."[86]

In the English case of *Qureshi v Qureshi*, the issue arose as to whether an extra-judicial divorce obtained in England could be recognized as valid.[87] In 1966, the parties, who were Muslims, were married at an English registry office. That marriage was followed by a Muslim ceremony. The parties continued to reside in England after their marriage. In April 1967, the husband sent a letter to his wife whereby he divorced her in compliance with the Islamic law of *talaq*. That letter was followed by a hearing at the London office of the High Commissioner for Pakistan to explore the possibilities of reconciliation in accordance with Pakistan's *Muslim Family Laws Ordinance 1961*. Following that hearing, the divorce was pronounced absolute on 1 August 1967. The court determined that, during his residence in England, the husband retained his domicile of choice in Pakistan. Simon P held that the marriage had been validly dissolved either in April or in August 1967 because the divorce complied

---

81 Above note 53 at 154–55.
82 Above notes 37 and 50 respectively.
83 Above note 75.
84 See Section E, below in this chapter.
85 *Amin*, above note 75 at para 25.
86 *Ibid*.
87 Above note 75.

with the law of Pakistan, the parties' domicile. The fact that the divorce had occurred in the forum and was outside local matrimonial law was no barrier to its recognition. Simon P stated:

> I respectfully agree with the view expressed in *Dicey and Morris, The Conflict of Laws*, 8th ed. (1967) at pp. 319–320: "In spite of earlier dicta to the contrary, it is now clear that English courts will recognize non-judicial divorces obtained by mutual agreement between the spouses or unilaterally by one party to the marriage in accordance with a religious law (e.g., a Jewish *ghet* or a Mohammedan *talak*), provided the parties are domiciled in a country (e.g., Israel or Egypt) the territorial laws of which permit such a method. The recognition of such divorces is perfectly consistent with the status theory of divorce and with the paramount importance of domicile in questions of status. If the cause for divorce is immaterial so ought the method to be. It is immaterial that the religious divorce takes place in England, provided of course that the parties are not domiciled in England."[88]

It is unclear whether Canadian courts would follow the approach taken in *Qureshi* or whether, in order to secure a divorce in Canada, a party must comply with the requirements of the *Divorce Act*.[89] The decision of *Canada (Minister of Citizenship and Immigration) v Hazimeh* suggests that an extra-judicial divorce obtained in Canada will not be entitled to recognition.[90] The question, again for immigration purposes, was whether the respondent's divorce from her first husband should be recognized in Canada. The respondent was originally from Lebanon. In August 1992, she had married Ali Hammoud in Lebanon. She moved to Canada in October 1993 on Hammoud's sponsorship. On 5 November 1993, she underwent a *talaq* divorce in Ontario before a representative of the Supreme Shiite Islamic Council. At that time, the respondent was not eligible to obtain a legal divorce in Ontario. On 13 May 1999, she registered the divorce with the Jaafari Religious Court of Saida in Lebanon. The registration document indicated the divorce date to be 5 November 1993. The primary issue was whether the respondent's divorce could be recognized pursuant to section 22(1) of the *Divorce Act*. The court held that it could not because it did not constitute a divorce granted pursuant to a law other than Canadian law. It was not a foreign divorce for the purpose of that section. There was no evidence that the *talaq* divorce, which had taken place in Canada, had become

---

88 *Ibid* at 199.
89 See the discussion in James McLeod, *The Conflict of Laws* (Calgary: Carswell, 1983) at 689–93.
90 [2009] FCJ No 482 (Fed Ct).

a Lebanese divorce. Indeed, as far as Lebanese law was concerned, the divorce had taken place in Canada and Lebanon was simply recognizing it for the purpose of its own law. Justice Russell held that it "remain[ed] a *talaq* divorce that [had taken] place in Canada and ha[d] been registered and recognized in Lebanon. That *talaq* divorce, recognized by Lebanon, [was] not a divorce that Canada recognize[d]."[91]

The respondent also argued that her divorce should be recognized on common law principles because, under *Indyka*,[92] both parties had a real and substantial connection to Lebanon at the time of the divorce. In the final analysis, the court did not pursue this argument. Nevertheless, it clearly intimated that only the Ontario superior courts had jurisdiction to grant divorces in Ontario and that a *talaq* divorce obtained in Ontario under Sharia law was a legal nullity despite its recognition by the law of a country with a real and substantial connection to the parties. It has been argued that "no divorce granted within Canada [should] be valid or recognizable unless it is granted under the divorce legislation in effect from time to time."[93]

E. DEFENCES TO THE RECOGNITION OF FOREIGN DIVORCE DECREES

The courts do not generally concern themselves with the merits of foreign divorce decrees. As Dickson J observed in *Powell v Cockburn*, "the substantive grounds upon which the decree is granted have never been of concern to the recognizing Court."[94] Where a foreign court of competent jurisdiction within the principles just discussed has granted a divorce decree, then that decree is in general conclusive on the merits: Canadian "standards and divorce principles are irrelevant if the foreign court had jurisdiction to deal with the matter."[95] To investigate the merits afresh is to encroach upon the jurisdiction of the foreign court.[96] Nevertheless, there are defences to the recognition of foreign divorce decrees, though the grounds of impeachment "are, properly, few in number."[97] Justice Fichaud summarized the available defences

---

91 *Ibid* at para 63.
92 Above note 60.
93 McLeod, above note 89 at 692.
94 [1977] 2 SCR 218 at 228 [*Powell*].
95 *Dashtarai v Shahrestani*, [2006] OJ No 5367 at para 24 (SCJ) [*Dashtarai*].
96 *Pitre v Nguyen*, [2007] BCJ No 1708 at para 17 (SC) [*Pitre*].
97 *Powell*, above note 94 at 234.

in *Orabi* by adopting the following passage from an earlier edition of *Castel & Walker*:[98]

> Although the foreign court that granted the decree may be jurisdictionally competent in the eyes of Canadian law, recognition will be refused if the respondent did not receive notice of the proceeding, especially if fraud was present. The jurisdiction of the foreign court must not be established "through any flimsy residential means" and the petitioner must not have resorted to the foreign court for any fraudulent and improper reasons such as solely "for the purpose of obtaining a divorce." The foreign decree must not be contrary to Canadian public policy. Denial of natural justice may also be a reason for refusing recognition.[99]

In *Bavin v Bavin* the respondent did not receive notice of a divorce action through fraud.[100] A husband obtained a divorce decree in Mexico. In those proceedings, he had fraudulently represented to the court that he did not know of his wife's whereabouts. He had repeated this representation at the trial. As a result of the husband's perjury, the Mexican court made an order for substituted service by means of publication in two Mexican newspapers. The wife never heard of the divorce until after it had been granted. The Ontario courts held that they would not recognize the Mexican divorce despite the fact that Mexico had jurisdiction based on the husband's domicile in that country.

Bavin involved both fraud and a denial of natural justice in the sense that the wife received no notice of the proceedings and therefore had no opportunity to participate in them. Fraud and the denial of natural justice are in fact separate and independent defences and do not have to be combined to justify the refusal to recognize a foreign decree. The leading case on fraud is the decision of the Supreme Court of Canada in *Powell*.[101] The court refused to recognize a Michigan divorce decree on the ground that it had been obtained by fraud. Justice Dickson drew a distinction between fraud relating to the jurisdiction of the foreign court and fraud relating to the merits of the action. He expressly refrained from dealing with a court's competence to look into fraud going to the merits, though he did indicate that, "for reasons of comity and practical difficulties, in the past [the courts had] refused to

---

98 Above note 45 at para 17.
99 Jean-Gabriel Castel & Janet Walker, *Canadian Conflict of Laws*, 5th ed (Markham, ON: Butterworths, 2002) at para 17.2.c. See now Walker, above note 39 at para 17.2.c; *Zhang v Lin*, 2010 ABQB 420 at para 47.
100 [1939] 2 DLR 278 (Ont SC), aff'd on this point [1939] 3 DLR 328 (Ont CA) [*Bavin*].
101 Above note 94.

inquire into"[102] fraud as to the merits. The courts could, however, refuse to recognize a foreign decree where the fraud concerned jurisdiction. Justice Dickson said that the "aim of the Courts, in refusing recognition because of fraud, [was] to prevent abuse of the judicial process" and that, in so doing "the Courts [were] enforcing the public policy of the forum." He concluded: "The weight of authority seems to recognize, however, that if the granting State takes jurisdiction on the basis of facts which, if the truth were known, would not give it jurisdiction the decree may be set aside."[103] In the case itself, the husband had falsely represented to the Michigan court that he had been a resident of the state for one year, which was a necessary condition of the court's jurisdiction. It is noteworthy that in *Beals v Saldanha*, the leading decision on the enforcement of *in personam* judgments,[104] the Supreme Court of Canada expressly endorsed the reasoning in *Powell*.[105] Recent cases have affirmed the approach in *Powell* and have stressed that "[i]f fraud is alleged, it must go to jurisdiction and not simply the merits of the case."[106]

In *Orabi*, a foreign divorce decree was refused recognition because of a violation of natural justice.[107] The husband obtained an *ex parte* divorce from a Shariite Council in Jordan in October 2002. The Nova Scotia Court of Appeal agreed with the trial judge that the Jordanian tribunal lacked jurisdiction to dissolve the marriage. It also held that it should deny recognition because of a contravention of the rules of natural justice. Justice Fichaud explained:

> Mr. El Qaoud knew where Ms. Orabi resided. Yet Mr. El Qaoud did not serve Ms. Orabi with notice of the divorce proceeding. This was not a case where the respondent was difficult to locate, avoiding service, or subject to an order for substituted service. The Jordanian tribunal granted the divorce apparently without requiring any proof that Ms. Orabi had been served with notice. In December, 2002, Ms. Orabi received her couriered divorce decree, issued by a tribunal before which there was no role for her participation in a country to which she had no connection, after a proceeding of which she received no notice . . . . This violates the principles of natural justice.[108]

---

102 *Ibid* at 234.
103 *Ibid*.
104 [2003] 3 SCR 416. See Chapter 8.
105 *Ibid* at para 49.
106 *Pitre*, above note 96 at para 15. See also *Dashtarai*, above note 95 at paras 9–11.
107 Above note 45.
108 *Ibid* at para 18.

A Canadian court could also refuse to recognize a foreign divorce decree if it contravened Canadian public policy. In *Indyka*, Lord Pearce stated that a foreign divorce should be refused recognition where it could "be said not to be genuine according to [the forum's] notions of divorce."[109] Justice Barnes relied upon that statement in *Amin* to conclude that a bare *talaq* was not recognizable in Canada: "In the result, I do not agree that the apparently unilateral, extrajudicial declaration of divorce made by Mr. Amin in Pakistan in 1993 is a form of divorce which meets Canadian notions of genuine divorce and it cannot be recognized here."[110] In *Re Meyer*, the court indicated that a foreign divorce decree could be regarded as a sham where the stated grounds on which the decree was sought were untrue.[111] The principal aspect of that decision, however, was the determination that a foreign divorce decree was not entitled to recognition where the petitioner had acted under duress. The case involved a German divorce decree of 1934. The wife, to ensure her survival and that of her daughter, had been compelled to divorce her Jewish husband who had fled Germany to avoid Nazi persecution. Justice Bagnall expressed the applicable principle in the following manner:

> [T]his court will declare a foreign decree of divorce invalid if the will of the party seeking the decree was overborne by a genuine and reasonably held fear caused by present and continuing danger to life, limb or liberty arising from external circumstances for which that party was not responsible.[112]

There are two questionable English decisions in which the courts refused to recognize foreign nullity decrees on the ground that they contravened English views of substantial justice.[113] In each case, the court refused to recognize a foreign decree annulling an English marriage on the ground that there had been no religious ceremony in accordance with the husband's Roman Catholic faith. The decisions are perhaps better explicable as illustrations of the defence of public policy. They can be criticized, however, for the judicial willingness to investigate the underlying merits of the foreign proceedings. The indications are that they will be regarded as special cases. In *Re Meyer*, for example, the

---

109 Above note 60 at 88.
110 Above note 75 at para 23. Contrast *Qureshi*, above note 75.
111 [1971] P 298.
112 *Ibid* at 307.
113 *Gray v Formosa*, [1963] P 259 (CA); *Lepre v Lepre*, [1965] P 52. See the discussion of these authorities in Chapter 23, Section E. The courts derived this defence from *dicta* in *Pemberton v Hughes*, [1899] 1 Ch 781 at 790 (CA).

court equated substantive justice with a broad view of natural justice and stressed that a violation of natural justice should relate to the proceedings and not to the merits.[114] Justice Bagnall emphasized that the court had no "general discretion . . . to substitute its own view of the merits of a foreign decree for the view of the court of competent jurisdiction,"[115] though he did leave open "the difficult question of what conclusion [to] reach if a foreign decree were expressed to be solely on racial or religious grounds."[116]

In *Zhang v Lin* the court explicitly refused to recognize a Texas divorce on public policy grounds. Its concern was not with the divorce itself but with corollary support proceedings. It held that "the clear differences in treatment of child and spousal support between Texas law and Canadian law justify Canada's non-recognition of a Texas divorce in the circumstances here."[117] There is room to debate whether this is an overly broad view of the public policy defence.[118] It should be noted that this analysis was in the context of an application by Ms Zhang for a declaration that the Texas divorce was not recognized in Canada and that Mr Lin did not appear in response. So the point may not have been fully canvassed. Moreover, the perceived basis for the court's concern, namely its inability to order support in the face of a foreign divorce, may have been incorrect.[119]

F. THE EFFECT OF AN INVALID FOREIGN DIVORCE: THE DOCTRINE OF PRECLUSION

The question arises as to whether a spouse who has obtained an invalid divorce should be allowed to rely on the invalidity of that divorce so as to be able to claim benefits from the other spouse or perhaps even to deny obligations to a subsequent spouse. The leading decision is that of the Supreme Court of Canada in *Downton v Royal Trust Co.*[120] A husband separated from his wife. The parties were both domiciled and resident in Newfoundland and they reached a separation agreement by

---

114 Above note 111 at 308.
115 *Ibid* at 309.
116 *Ibid* at 310.
117 Above note 99 at paras 67–71. See also *Marzara v Marzara*, 2011 BCSC 408 at paras 64–79.
118 See Gerald B Robertson, "Public Policy and Recognition of Foreign Divorces: *Zhang v Lin* and *Marzara v Marzara*" (2012) 49 Alberta Law Review 745 at 748.
119 See the explanation in *RNS*, above note 71 at paras 30 and 34–47. See Chapter 25.
120 [1973] SCR 437 [*Downton*].

which the husband undertook to support his wife and children. Five years later the husband went to Nevada to obtain a divorce. He resided in Nevada for a short period of time, just long enough to satisfy Nevada's jurisdictional requirements. The husband's lawyer wrote to the wife asking her to sign a power of attorney authorizing an appearance in the action on her behalf. The power specified that the terms of the separation agreement would be incorporated into the decree with the consent of the court. The wife executed the power of attorney and a decree which incorporated the terms of the agreement was pronounced. The husband married his second wife on the same day and they returned to live in Newfoundland. The husband died in 1969. In his will, he left the residue of his estate to his second wife. The first wife claimed a portion of the estate pursuant to Newfoundland's family relief legislation. In order to recover, she had to establish that she was the husband's widow. Although the Nevada divorce decree would not be recognized in Newfoundland, the estate argued that the first wife was estopped from relying upon her status as the deceased's widow by virtue of her participation in the Nevada divorce proceedings.

The Supreme Court of Canada recognized a doctrine of preclusion as being potentially applicable in cases like the one before it. Justice Laskin explained the operation of the doctrine in the following way:

> My canvass of typical cases which have reached Canadian Courts indicates that the only claim to consistency that they exhibit is the application of a preclusion doctrine against a spouse who, having obtained a decree of divorce or nullity from a foreign Court incompetent to give it, seeks thereafter to assert that incompetence in order to gain a pecuniary advantage against his or her spouse or the estate of the spouse. The doctrine has an ethical basis: a refusal to permit a person to insist, to his or her pecuniary advantage, on a relationship which that person has previously deliberately sought to terminate.[121]

He therefore supported

> the application of a preclusion doctrine against a spouse who has ignored the jurisdictional requirements for a valid dissolution and who would none the less insist to his or her own pecuniary advantage that the law be applied strictly in his or her favour in disregard of an attempted dissolution which is invalid.[122]

---

121 *Ibid* at 450.
122 *Ibid* at 451.

The court pointed out that the ethical basis for the doctrine was lost where both spouses had participated in the invalid foreign divorce unless there was "an alleviating explanation for the submission to the jurisdiction of an incompetent foreign Court."[123] Justice Laskin concluded that the first wife had submitted to the jurisdiction of Nevada purely to protect her existing benefits to which she was entitled by virtue of the separation agreement. This was not a case where she had obtained benefits as a result of the foreign decree and was now trying to invalidate that decree in order to claim against her husband's estate. Nor had she relied on that decree by, for example, remarrying. There was, therefore, no reason to preclude her from applying for family relief. He agreed that it was difficult to formulate a precise rule in this context. He therefore favoured the flexible approach taken in the American *Restatement*: "A person may be precluded from attacking the validity of a foreign divorce if, under the circumstances, it would be inequitable for him to do so."[124] The court did, however, stress that the doctrine of preclusion could not alter marital status per se. Thus, a spouse would not be denied the right to seek a divorce merely because he or she had previously invoked the jurisdiction of an incompetent court.[125] Equally, a person will not be estopped from impugning the jurisdiction of a foreign court to grant a divorce in a nullity action brought in Canada in respect of a subsequent marriage.[126] Similarly, O'Sullivan JA in *Holub v Holub* held that a man who had obtained an invalid foreign divorce and remarried would be able to defend a divorce action by his second wife on the ground that his second marriage was bigamous.[127]

In *Downton*, Laskin J also left unclear the question of whether estoppel could ever be raised in an action by a third party, such as the second spouse, against the person who obtained an invalid divorce.[128] The second spouse might seek to claim against the estate of the person who obtained the invalid decree and the estate might defend on the basis that the plaintiff was not the spouse of the deceased. Subsequently, in *Knight v Knight*, an Ontario trial court applied the doctrine in favour of a third party.[129] The parties had been married in 1959 in Pennsylvania. Thirty years later, they separated. The wife claimed for

---

123 *Ibid* at 450.
124 *Ibid* at 451, quoting American Law Institute, *Restatement of the Law (Second), Conflict of Laws*, 2d (St Paul, MN: American Law Institute, 1971) at § 74.
125 *Downton*, above note 120 at 451.
126 *Seagull v Seagull* (1974), 6 OR (2d) 467 (CA).
127 (1976), 71 DLR (3d) 698 (Man CA). Justice O'Sullivan was in dissent but not on this point because the majority did not have to deal with the preclusion doctrine.
128 Above note 120 at 448.
129 (1995), 16 RFL (4th) 48 (Ont Ct Gen Div).

support and division of family assets. The husband attempted to avoid his obligations by challenging the plaintiff's marital status. He argued that the marriage was invalid because, prior to the marriage, he had obtained in Mexico an invalid divorce from his first wife. The court held that the husband was estopped from denying the validity of his second marriage.

In *Fromovitz v Fromovitz*, the court held that the doctrine of preclusion only estopped a party to an invalid decree from relying upon that invalidity.[130] The plaintiff obtained a Mexican divorce in order to marry the defendant. Both parties knew that a marriage in Ontario, where they lived, would be invalid because of the invalidity of the divorce decree. They therefore went through a ceremony of marriage in New Jersey in the belief that it would be recognized in Ontario. The marriage began to deteriorate and the plaintiff sought an order for alimony based on the defendant's cruelty. The court held that the defendant was entitled to defend that action on the ground that the New Jersey marriage was invalid because of the invalidity of the Mexican divorce. Not being a party to that divorce, the defendant was not precluded from setting up its invalidity despite the fact that he had counselled the plaintiff to obtain the divorce and had offered to pay for it. In any event, the court concluded that it was not inequitable for him to impugn the divorce in an action by the plaintiff because she herself had obtained the decree. The equities were at least equally balanced.

G. DISSOLUTION OF CIVIL UNIONS

Chapter 21 examined the creation of civil unions with particular reference to legislation in Nova Scotia and Quebec. Section 55 of Nova Scotia's *Vital Statistics Act* provides the circumstances in which a domestic partnership will be terminated.[131] The statute, however, contains no conflict of laws provisions. The same is not true of Quebec's law on civil unions. Under article 3144 of the *Civil Code*, Quebec has jurisdiction to dissolve a civil union "if the domicile or place of residence of one of the spouses or the place of solemnization of their . . . civil union is in Quebec."[132] Under article 3090.2, the dissolution of a civil union is governed by the law of the spouses' domicile or by the law of its place of solemnization and the effects of the dissolution are

---

130 (1977), 16 OR (2d) 751 (HCJ).
131 RSNS 1989, c 494, Part II.
132 Above note 43.

subject to the law governing the dissolution. Article 3090.3 provides that where the spouses are domiciled in different countries, the applicable law is the law of their common residence or, failing that, the law of their last common residence or, failing that, the law of the place of solemnization or the law of the forum. Finally, article 3167 deals with the recognition of foreign dissolutions of civil unions. It provides that the jurisdiction of a foreign authority is recognized only where the foreign country recognizes the institution of civil unions. If it does, then the jurisdiction of foreign courts is the same as with respect to divorce.

FURTHER READINGS

BLOM, JOOST. "Divorce in the Canadian Conflict of Laws: Two Recent Developments" (1973) 11 *Canadian Yearbook of International Law* 193.

BLOM, JOOST. "The Recognition of Foreign Divorces in British Columbia" (1976) 34 *The Advocate* 95.

COLLIER, JOHN. "Recognition and Non-recognition of Foreign Divorces: Public Policy and Judicial Discretion" [1978] *Cambridge Law Journal* 45.

GLENN, H PATRICK. "On Blackstone, California Divorces and the Retrospectivity of the Common and Civil Laws: *Edward v. Edward*" (1989) 34 *McGill Law Journal* 186.

MACKINNON, STUART. "Conflict of Laws—Recent Divorce Recognition Cases in England and Canada" (1970) 48 *Canadian Bar Review* 716.

MCLEOD, JAMES. "Conflict of Laws—Nullity—Recognition of Foreign Divorce—Common Law Principles—*Divorce Act*—Intertemporal Conflict" (1976) 54 *Canadian Bar Review* 169.

MENDES DA COSTA, D. "Some Comments on the Conflict of Laws Provisions of the *Divorce Act, 1968*" (1968) 46 *Canadian Bar Review* 252.

NORTH, PETER. "Reform, but Not Revolution: Divorce" (1990) 220 *Recueil des Cours* 97.

SHAKARGY, SHARON. "Marriage by the State or Married to the State? On Choice of Law in Marriage and Divorce" (2013) 9 *Journal of Private International Law* 499.

CHAPTER 23

NULLITY

A. VOID AND VOIDABLE MARRIAGES

The law distinguishes between void and voidable marriages. In *De Reneville v De Reneville*, Lord Greene MR explained the distinction in the following manner:

> a void marriage is one that will be regarded by every court in any case in which the existence of the marriage is in issue as never having taken place and can be so treated by both parties to it without the necessity of any decree annulling it: a voidable marriage is one that will be regarded by every court as a valid subsisting marriage until a decree annulling it has been pronounced by a court of competent jurisdiction.[1]

In the past, the distinction was of particular consequence in the determination of the domicile of the parties. At common law, in the case of a voidable marriage, a married woman's domicile was dependent upon that of her husband. A void marriage, on the other hand, was regarded as a complete nullity and thus a woman was free to acquire a domicile separate from that of her supposed husband.[2] Since the abolition of a married woman's domicile of dependency,[3] the importance of the distinction has lessened substantially. Any remaining significance is

---

1   [1948] P 100 at 111 (CA) [*De Reneville*].
2   *Savelieff v Glouchkoff* (1964), 45 DLR (2d) 520 (BCCA) [*Savelieff*].
3   See Chapter 2.

restricted to nullity jurisdiction and the recognition of foreign nullity decrees based on the place of celebration of the marriage.[4]

There is still considerable doubt as to what law determines whether a particular marriage is void or voidable. In some English cases, the law of the forum has been applied without question.[5] It seems more logical for the character of a marriage to be determined by the law that governs its validity or invalidity under the relevant choice of law rule. This possibility was first envisaged by the English Court of Appeal in *De Reneville* in the context of domestic jurisdiction.[6] In that case the wife, who had an English domicile of origin, was petitioning in England for the annulment of her marriage to a domiciled Frenchman on the alternative grounds of impotence or wilful refusal to consummate. The marriage had been celebrated in France and the husband was resident and domiciled in France at the time of the proceedings. The English courts could take jurisdiction only if the wife was domiciled in England and that depended upon the marriage being void: otherwise she had a French domicile of dependency. Lord Greene MR held that French law should determine the character of the marriage for the following reasons:

> In my opinion, the question whether the marriage is void or merely voidable is for French law to answer. My reasons are as follows: The validity of a marriage so far as regards the observance of formalities is a matter for the *lex loci celebrationis*. But this is not a case of forms. It is a case of essential validity. By what law is that to be decided? In my opinion by the law of France, either because that is the law of the husband's domicile at the date of the marriage or (preferably, in my view) because at that date it was the law of the matrimonial domicile in reference to which the parties may have been supposed to enter into the bonds of marriage.[7]

Since French law had not been pleaded, it was assumed to be the same as English law by which the marriage was voidable. The court therefore declined to take jurisdiction.

Lord Greene MR clearly believed that the character of a marriage as void or voidable must be determined by the law indicated by the appropriate choice of law rule for determining the effect of an alleged defect on the validity of a marriage. One problem with *De Reneville* lies in the fact that the law chosen by the court to govern all issues of essential validity of a marriage, namely the husband's domicile at the time of

---

4   See Sections B(3) and D(2)(b), below in this chapter.
5   See, for example, *Ross-Smith v Ross-Smith*, [1963] AC 280 (HL) [*Ross-Smith*].
6   Above note 1.
7   *Ibid* at 114.

marriage or the law of the intended matrimonial home, is not generally supported. The typically accepted proposition is that each party must have capacity to marry the other by the law of his or her antenuptial domicile, though it must be admitted that the law governing physical incapacity is less clear.[8]

Canadian authorities support the approach taken in *De Reneville*. In *Solomon v Walters*, for example, a wife petitioned in British Columbia for nullity of a marriage celebrated in Nevada on the grounds that her parents had not consented to the marriage.[9] Her husband was domiciled in British Columbia. Without citing *De Reneville*, the judge applied the law of Nevada as the law of the place of celebration because the particular defect—the lack of parental consent—related to the required formalities of the marriage. By Nevada law, the marriage was voidable and therefore the spouses had a common domicile in British Columbia that conferred jurisdiction on the British Columbia courts.

Of course, the *De Reneville* approach does have its drawbacks. It is essential, for example, that reference be made to a single law to determine whether a marriage is void or voidable. However, the dual domicile test for determining capacity to marry contemplates a potential reference to two laws. The difficult question of characterization would be irrelevant if no distinction were drawn between void and voidable marriages for the purposes of nullity jurisdiction or the recognition of foreign nullity decrees.

B. JURISDICTION TO GRANT A NULLITY DECREE

The rules governing the jurisdiction of the courts in nullity petitions are based on the common law. They represent something of a confused jumble and are in need of rationalization. Many of the earlier cases are also unsatisfactory because of the common law proposition that, in the case of a voidable marriage, the wife took the domicile of her husband. In light of the real and substantial connection test laid down by the Supreme Court of Canada in *Morguard Investments Ltd v De Savoye* in the context of *in personam* jurisdiction,[10] the question arises as to whether some of the existing grounds for jurisdiction will survive and whether

---

8   See Chapter 21, Sections C and E.
9   (1956), 3 DLR (2d) 78 (BCSC). See also *Savelieff*, above note 2; *Feiner v Demkowicz* (1973), 2 OR (2d) 121 (HCJ) [*Feiner*].
10 [1990] 3 SCR 1077 [*Morguard*]. See the discussion of the *Morguard* doctrine in Chapter 5.

the existence of a real and substantial connection will now suffice for jurisdictional purposes.

1) Domicile

In the area of domicile, the distinction between void and voidable marriages was historically important. If the allegation was that the marriage was void, the court could take jurisdiction if the petitioner was domiciled in the forum. In contrast, if the allegation was that the marriage was voidable, the court required that both parties be domiciled in the forum.[11]

There is clear authority to the effect that the courts of the parties' common domicile have jurisdiction to annul a marriage.[12] In *Inverclyde v Inverclyde*, Bateson J drew a distinction between void and voidable marriages.[13] He saw a decree annulling a voidable marriage as being indistinguishable from a decree of divorce because in both cases there was a valid marriage in existence unless and until a decree was granted by a court of competent jurisdiction. Since at that time the courts of the parties' domicile had the exclusive jurisdiction to grant a divorce, Bateson J concluded that the courts of the parties' domicile had the exclusive jurisdiction to annul a voidable marriage. Initially, *Inverclyde* received a favourable response in Canada and was applied in both Ontario[14] and Manitoba.[15] It was later overruled in England.[16] In *Re Capon* the Ontario Court of Appeal suggested, *obiter dicta*, that the common domicile did indeed have the exclusive jurisdiction to annul a voidable marriage.[17] That observation, however, was based on the common law rule that the parties, in a voidable marriage, would have a common domicile whereas the same would not automatically be true in the case of a void marriage. Thus, it would be impossible to grant exclusive jurisdiction to the courts of the common domicile in the case of a void marriage. Given the abolition of the married woman's domicile of dependency, however, there is no possible rationale for retaining the *Inverclyde* rule.

---

11 See the analysis in *Feiner*, above note 9.
12 *Re Capon* (1965), 49 DLR (2d) 675 at 684 (Ont CA); *Stuart v Stuart* (1983), 34 RFL (2d) 104 (Ont HCJ); *Fulton v Fulton* (1984), 28 Man R (2d) 251 (QB); *Ward v Ward* (1985), 66 NBR (2d) 44 (QB) [*Ward*].
13 [1931] P 29 [*Inverclyde*].
14 *Fleming v Fleming*, [1934] OR 588 (HCJ).
15 *Diachuk v Diachuk* (1941), 49 Man R 102 (KB).
16 *Ramsay-Fairfax v Ramsay-Fairfax*, [1956] P 115 (CA) [*Ramsay-Fairfax*].
17 Above note 12 at 683–84.

There was a line of Canadian authority denying jurisdiction over voidable marriages based on the domicile of the petitioner alone.[18] More recent cases, however, have accepted the domicile of the petitioner as sufficient to confer jurisdiction.[19] The effect of this development removes the distinction between void and voidable marriages: the basis for jurisdiction is the same in each situation. Moreover, since the domicile of the petitioner is now a sufficient basis for jurisdiction, there is every reason to believe that the domicile of the respondent should equally be enough. There is certainly *obiter dicta* in Canadian cases to that effect.[20]

2) Residence

In *Ramsay-Fairfax* v *Ramsay-Fairfax* the English Court of Appeal held that the residence of both parties within the jurisdiction at the commencement of the nullity proceedings was a sufficient basis for jurisdiction whether the marriage was void or voidable.[21] There were various Canadian authorities supporting this view in the case of a void marriage.[22] It is now clear, however, that the Canadian courts also no longer draw any distinction between void and voidable marriages in this regard and have applied the principle from *Ramsay-Fairfax*.[23] Thus, the common residence of the parties is a sufficient jurisdictional basis for the annulment of a voidable marriage.[24]

---

18   Hutchings v Hutchings (1930), 39 Man R 66 (CA); Manella v Manella, [1942] OR 630 (CA) [*Manella*]; Shaw v Shaw (1945), 62 BCR 52 (CA) [*Shaw*]; Gower v Starrett, [1948] 2 DLR 853 (BCSC) [*Gower*].
19   Bevand v Bevand, [1955] 1 DLR 854 (NS Div & Mat Causes Ct) [*Bevand*]; Khan v Khan (1959), 21 DLR (2d) 171 (BCSC) [*Khan*]; Savelieff, above note 2, distinguishing Shaw, above note 18, and overruling Gower, above note 18; Re Capon, above note 12, not following Manella, above note 18; Feiner, above note 9; Grewal v Sohal (2004), 246 DLR (4th) 743 (BCSC); Davison v Sweeney (2005), 42 BCLR (4th) 69 (SC).
20   Bevand, above note 19 at 856; Khan, above note 19 at 174; Grewal v Kaur, 2011 ONSC 1812 at para 55; Sarmiento v Villarico, 2014 BCSC 455 at para 31. In Drake v MacLaren, [1929] 3 DLR 159 (Alta SC), the court assumed jurisdiction where the respondent was domiciled in the province. The judgment, however, did not discuss the question of jurisdiction and did not indicate the domicile of the petitioner.
21   Above note 16.
22   See, for example, Adelman v Adelman, [1948] 1 WWR 1071 (Alta SC) [*Adelman*]; Khan, above note 19.
23   Shaw, above note 18; Gower, above note 18.
24   Sangha v Mander (1985), 65 BCLR 265 (SC).

While the Court of Appeal in *Ramsay-Fairfax* spoke in terms of the common residence of the parties, it justified its reliance on residence solely on the ground that the ecclesiastical courts had based their jurisdiction upon residence.[25] Lord Justice Denning pointed out that, to the ecclesiastical courts, the residence of the respondent alone was all important.[26] In Canada, there is clear authority for the view that the courts have jurisdiction to annul a void marriage on the basis of the respondent's residence alone[27] and strong indications that the same position holds true of a voidable marriage.[28] It appears, however, that the residence of the petitioner alone is an insufficient ground for nullity jurisdiction.[29]

3) Place of Celebration of the Marriage

Domestic jurisdiction based on the place of celebration of the marriage derives from *Simonin v Mallac*.[30] The court took jurisdiction over a marriage celebrated in England between two French domiciliaries. Sir Cresswell Cresswell said: "the parties, by professing to enter into a contract in England, mutually gave to each other the right to have the force and effect of that contract determined by an English tribunal."[31] *Simonin* came under intense scrutiny by the House of Lords in *Ross-Smith*.[32] Even though a substantial majority of the judges were of the opinion that *Simonin* could not be justified on the grounds stated by Sir Cresswell Cresswell or on historical grounds, the court decided not to overrule *Simonin* but to confine its reach to marriages alleged to be void, as apparently the case in *Simonin* itself, rather than merely voidable. This conclusion was particularly anomalous because four of the six Law Lords were in favour of drawing no distinction between void and voidable marriages for this purpose. The position in Canada is not entirely free from doubt. There are two early Saskatchewan cases where the courts of the place of celebration took jurisdiction to annul a voidable marriage.[33]

---

25 The Court of Appeal pointed out that jurisdiction in nullity cases derived from s 22 of the *Matrimonial Causes Act 1857* (UK), 20 & 21 Vict, c 85, which provided that the courts should proceed and give relief in nullity cases on the basis of principles developed from the ecclesiastical courts.
26 Above note 16 at 133.
27 *Adelman*, above note 22; *Khan*, above note 19.
28 *Shaw*, above note 18; *Gower*, above note 18; *Ward*, above note 12.
29 *Shaw*, above note 18. It is also clear from *Gwyn v Mellen* (1979), 15 BCLR 78 (CA) [*Gwyn*], a case dealing with the recognition of foreign nullity decrees, that the residence of the petitioner is not a basis for jurisdiction.
30 (1860), 2 Sw & Tr 67, 164 ER 917 [*Simonin*].
31 *Ibid* at 920 (ER).
32 Above note 5.
33 *G v G* (1928), 22 Sask LR 376 (KB); *Reid v Francis* (1929), 24 Sask LR 1 (CA).

The same was true in Nova Scotia in *Steele v Steele*,[34] in which the court relied upon the judgment of the Court of Appeal in *Ross-Smith*.[35] On the other hand, in *D v D*, Lerner J applied the House of Lords' decision in *Ross-Smith* and refused jurisdiction over a voidable marriage celebrated in Ontario.[36] Moreover, in *Gwyn v Mellen*, the British Columbia Court of Appeal assumed that the courts could take jurisdiction over a void, as opposed to a voidable, marriage celebrated in the province.[37]

In contrast to the common law position, the jurisdiction of the Quebec courts to annul a marriage, and indeed a civil union,[38] is clearly set out in the *Civil Code*.[39] Article 3144 provides:

> Quebec authorities have jurisdiction in matters of nullity of marriage or dissolution or nullity of civil unions if the domicile or place of residence of one of the spouses or the place of solemnization of their marriage or civil union is in Quebec.

C. CHOICE OF LAW

In determining whether to annul a marriage, the courts apply the law governing the validity of the marriage as determined by the choice of law rules already discussed in Chapter 21. There, we noted that, as a general proposition, the law of the place of celebration governs the formal validity of a marriage while the antenuptial domicile of each party governs its essential validity. In that chapter, consider in particular the discussion of lack of consent and of physical incapacity.[40] These are common bases for seeking to annul a marriage.

D. RECOGNITION OF FOREIGN NULLITY DECREES

A foreign nullity decree will be recognized as binding in Canada when it has been granted by a court of competent jurisdiction. The various bases for a foreign court's jurisdiction are discussed in this section.

---

34 (1963), 43 DLR (2d) 57 (NS Div & Mat Causes Ct).
35 [1961] 1 All ER 255 (CA).
36 [1973] 3 OR 82 (HCJ).
37 Above note 29.
38 See Chapter 21, Section G.
39 CQLR c C-1991.
40 See Chapter 21, Section C(5) and Section E, respectively.

1) Domicile

a) Decree Granted by the Courts of the Parties' Common Domicile

In *Gwyn* the British Columbia Court of Appeal accepted the proposition formulated in the then-current edition of Dicey's textbook[41] that a foreign nullity decree would be recognized if both parties were domiciled in the foreign country at the commencement of the proceedings.[42] The leading authority is the decision of the House of Lords in *Salvesen v Administrator of Austrian Property* in which a German nullity decree was recognized on the ground that Germany was the common domicile of the parties at the time of the nullity proceedings.[43] The court drew an analogy with divorce and held that a nullity decree, just as much as a divorce decree, was a judgment *in rem* affecting the status of the parties. At that time, the courts of the parties' domicile were recognized as having the jurisdiction to determine conclusively the parties' status by granting a divorce decree.[44] Therefore, those courts equally had jurisdiction to grant a nullity decree.

b) Decree Granted by the Courts of the Domicile of One Party

In *Re Capon* the Ontario Court of Appeal recognized a decree granted in Nevada in respect of a void marriage where only the petitioning wife was domiciled in that state.[45] The decision left open two unresolved questions. The first was whether a decree granted by the courts of the domicile of the respondent alone would be recognized in Canada. *Re Capon* suggested that it would. Thus, there is *obiter dicta* to the effect that there could be "no valid reason for withholding recognition from a decree . . . made by the forum of the country in which only one of the parties [was] domiciled."[46]

The second question was whether the *Re Capon* principle was restricted only to void marriages. At the time that *Re Capon* was decided, it was only in the case of a void marriage that a wife was free to acquire an independent domicile. Given the abolition of the married woman's domicile of dependency, there seems no reason not to extend the principle to any situation where each party is domiciled in a different country. Certainly, the court stressed the problems that would arise if recognition were limited to decrees granted by the courts of the

---

41 Albert Venn Dicey & JHC Morris, *Dicey and Morris on the Conflict of Laws*, 9th ed (London: Stevens & Sons, 1973), r 50(1).
42 Above note 29 at 84.
43 [1927] AC 641 (HL).
44 *Le Mesurier v Le Mesurier*, [1895] AC 517 (PC).
45 Above note 12.
46 *Ibid* at 687.

common domicile. Justice Schroeder said that such a restriction would lead to the "deplorable condition in which one of the parties would be regarded as married in one country and unmarried in another."[47] This reasoning clearly applies to any situation where the parties have different domiciles, whether the marriage is void or voidable.

c) **Decree Recognized by the Courts of the Parties' Domicile**
There is English authority for the proposition that a foreign nullity decree will be recognized in England if it would be recognized by the courts of the country where, at the time of the proceedings, the parties were domiciled.[48] There is *obiter dicta* in Canada to similar effect.[49] If the parties do not have a common domicile, presumably the same result would ensue if the foreign decree would be recognized by each party's domicile.

2) Reciprocity

The Ontario Court of Appeal in *Re Capon*[50] justified its recognition of a nullity decree granted by the courts of the petitioner's domicile on the basis of the reciprocity principle that had first been applied to foreign divorce decrees by the English Court of Appeal in *Travers v Holley*.[51] The British Columbia Court of Appeal in *Gwyn* also supported the application of *Travers* in the nullity context.[52] Briefly stated, the principle is that a foreign decree will be recognized by a Canadian court if the Canadian court, placed in the geographical location of the foreign court, could have taken jurisdiction to grant the decree on the facts of the case. There is no need for the basis upon which the foreign court assumed jurisdiction to be the same as, or substantially similar to, the basis upon which the Canadian court could have taken jurisdiction under its own law. All that is important is that the Canadian court could have assumed jurisdiction under its own rules if it had been in the position of the foreign court.[53]

a) **Residence**
We have already observed that nullity jurisdiction can be based on the common residence of the parties and probably on the residence of the

---

47   Ibid.
48   *Abate v Abate*, [1961] P 29.
49   *Gwyn*, above note 29 at 85.
50   Above note 12.
51   [1953] P 246 (CA) [*Travers*]. See Chapter 22, Section C(2)(b).
52   Above note 29.
53   *Ibid* at 92, relying upon the decision in the divorce context of *Robinson-Scott v Robinson-Scott*, [1958] P 71.

respondent alone.[54] On the basis of reciprocity, a foreign decree should therefore be recognized where the parties, or at least the respondent, were resident in the foreign country at the time of the commencement of the proceedings. In *Merker v Merker*, Simon P recognized a foreign decree granted by the courts of the common residence of the parties and justified his conclusion on the basis of the reciprocity principle.[55] Equally, the British Columbia Court of Appeal in *Gwyn* accepted that the common residence of the parties was a ground for recognition.[56] It is also clear from *Gwyn* that the residence of the petitioner is an insufficient basis for recognition. In that case the English court apparently had taken jurisdiction on that ground but there was no indication that the principle of reciprocity would merit the recognition of the English decree for that reason.

b) Place of Celebration of the Marriage

In *Gwyn* the court held that reciprocity would justify the recognition of the annulment of a void marriage by the courts of the place of celebration of that marriage. Justice MacDonald gave the following reasons for his conclusion:

> British Columbia will take jurisdiction in an action to annul a void marriage if the marriage was celebrated in British Columbia .... So on the facts of this case, if the geographical jurisdiction had been reversed, British Columbia would have taken jurisdiction on the basis of being the place of celebration of the marriage alleged to be void. England took jurisdiction on the basis of the residence of the wife, and, in 1977, would not have taken jurisdiction on the basis of being the place of celebration of the marriage. However, in my opinion, the principle of recognition based on reciprocity is founded on the concept that both the domestic Court and the foreign Court would have exercised the jurisdiction that the foreign Court in fact exercised to decide the question that it decided. It is not a part of the reciprocity principle that the jurisdiction must be assumed by each of the Courts for the same reason .... In my judgment, the weight of authority is such that, on the basis of the reciprocity principle, our Courts should recognize the nullity decree pronounced in this case in England ....[57]

We have already observed that it is still an open question as to whether the courts of the place of celebration of the marriage can exercise juris-

---

54 See Section B(2), above in this chapter.
55 [1963] P 283 at 297.
56 Above note 29 at 84.
57 *Ibid* at 92.

diction over a voidable marriage. Equally, on the basis of reciprocity, it remains to be seen whether the annulment of a voidable marriage by the courts of the place of its celebration will be recognized.

3) Real and Substantial Connection

As explained in Chapter 22,[58] since the House of Lords' decision in *Indyka v Indyka*,[59] a "foreign divorce [has been] recognized where there exists some real and substantial connection between the petitioner or the respondent and the granting jurisdiction."[60] The English courts have applied this broad doctrine to foreign nullity decrees.[61] The Canadian courts took the same step in *Gwyn*.[62] As an alternative ground for decision, the court held that an English nullity decree should be recognized on the ground that a real and substantial connection existed between England and the petitioning wife. She had been a resident of England, without interruption, from a time before the marriage until the date of the institution of the nullity proceedings.

Of course, the decision in *Indyka* was an important influence in the development of the real and substantial connection requirement imposed in *Morguard*.[63] It is still an open question as to whether the courts will apply the *Morguard* doctrine in the context of the recognition of a foreign nullity decree when *Morguard* itself dealt with *in personam* jurisdiction and judgments. If the courts do apply *Morguard*, then the question arises as to whether some of the traditional grounds of recognition will be able to withstand scrutiny under that doctrine.

The civil law position in Quebec represents something of a combination of reciprocity (the "mirror principle") and the *Indyka* doctrine. Thus, article 3164 of the *Civil Code* provides:

> The jurisdiction of foreign authorities is established in accordance with the rules on jurisdiction applicable to Quebec authorities under Title Three [International Jurisdiction of Quebec Authorities] of this Book [Private International Law], to the extent that the dispute is substantially connected with the country whose authority is seised of the case.[64]

---

58 See Chapter 22, Section C(2)(c).
59 [1969] 1 AC 33 (HL).
60 *Bate v Bate* (1978), 1 RFL (2d) 298 at 304 (Ont HCJ), Boland J.
61 *Law v Gustin*, [1976] Fam 155; *Perrini v Perrini*, [1979] Fam 84.
62 Above note 29.
63 Above note 10.
64 Above note 39.

E. DEFENCES TO THE RECOGNITION OF FOREIGN NULLITY DECREES

As a general proposition, a foreign nullity decree granted by a court of competent jurisdiction within the rules discussed is conclusive on the merits. As with the case of the enforcement of foreign judgments in *personam*,[65] however, there are certain limited defences to the recognition of foreign nullity decrees. Thus, a foreign nullity decree will not be recognized if it was obtained by fraud.[66] In *Powell v Cockburn*, the Supreme Court of Canada refused to recognize a Michigan divorce decree on the ground that it had been obtained by fraud.[67] The court held that the fraud must relate to the jurisdiction of the foreign court and not simply to the merits of the action. Presumably, the principle in *Powell* is just as applicable to foreign nullity decrees.[68]

Equally, a foreign nullity decree will not be recognized if it is contrary to public policy[69] or was obtained in contravention of the principles of natural justice.[70] In the controversial decision of *Gray v Formosa*, the English Court of Appeal extended the traditional boundaries of natural justice by holding that a Maltese decree annulling an English marriage on the ground that it had not been conducted in a Roman Catholic church in accordance with the husband's religion should be denied recognition because it offended English notions of substantial justice.[71] The case represented a marked departure from prior authority where the courts had concentrated on some procedural impropriety in the foreign proceedings. In effect, the court delved into the underlying merits of the proceedings in Malta. In giving the primary judgment, Lord Denning MR focused on *obiter dicta* of Lindley MR in *Pemberton v Hughes* to the effect that a court could refuse to recognize a foreign decree if it contravened English views of substantial justice.[72] In *Re*

---

65 See Chapter 8, Section C.
66 *Lepre v Lepre*, [1965] P 52 at 63 [*Lepre*].
67 [1977] 2 SCR 218 [*Powell*]. See Chapter 22, Section E.
68 In *Beals v Saldanha*, [2003] 3 SCR 416, the leading decision on the enforcement of foreign *in personam* judgments, the Supreme Court of Canada endorsed the reasoning in *Powell*, *ibid* at para 49, and described fraud going to jurisdiction as "extrinsic" fraud and distinguished it from fraud going to the merits or "intrinsic" fraud.
69 *Vervaeke v Smith*, [1983] 1 AC 145 (HL).
70 *Lepre*, above note 66 at 63.
71 [1963] P 259 (CA) [*Gray*]. *Gray* was followed with obvious reluctance by Simon P in *Lepre*, above note 66.
72 [1899] 1 Ch 781 at 790 (CA).

Meyer, however, Bagnall J questioned the Court of Appeal's reliance on those *dicta*.[73] He said:

> That case [*Pemberton v. Hughes*] appears to me to be authority for the proposition that if this court is to refuse to recognise the validity of a foreign decree pronounced by a court of competent jurisdiction because of a violation of natural justice, the violation must relate to the proceedings themselves and not to the merits.[74]

Justice Bagnall appeared to be in favour of restricting *Gray* to its particular facts by stating that the "crux of the decision"[75] was accurately described by Simon P in *Lepre v Lepre*: "it was an intolerable injustice that a system of law should seek to impose extraterritorially, as a condition of the validity of a marriage, that it should take place according to the tenets of a particular faith."[76]

FURTHER READINGS

KENNEDY, GILBERT. "Recognition of Foreign Divorce and Nullity Decrees" (1957) 35 *Canadian Bar Review* 628.

LATEY, WILLIAM. "Basis of Jurisdiction in Nullity of Marriage" (1962) 78 *Law Quarterly Review* 417.

LYSYK, KEN. "Conflict of Laws—Nullity Proceedings—Jurisdiction Based on Petitioner's Domicile—Application of the Distinction between Void and Voidable Marriages to the Jurisdictional Problem—Unity of Domicile" (1965) 43 *Canadian Bar Review* 107.

LYSYK, KEN. "Jurisdiction and Recognition of Foreign Decrees in Nullity Suits" (1964) 29 *Saskatchewan Bar Review* 143.

RAFFERTY, NICHOLAS. "Recognition of Foreign Nullity Decrees" (1981) 46 *Saskatchewan Law Review* 73.

SMITH, RAYMOND. "The Recognition of Foreign Nullity Decrees" (1980) 96 *Law Quarterly Review* 380.

---

73   [1971] P 298.
74   *Ibid* at 308.
75   *Ibid* at 309.
76   Above note 66 at 64.

CHAPTER 24

CHILDREN

A. INTRODUCTION

Legal issues relating to children can involve private international law issues in cases where the factual situation has connections to more than one jurisdiction. In Canada, domestic family law considers that the "best interests of the child" are of paramount importance.[1] In cross-border cases, it is possible for those interests to be in conflict with the notion of comity.[2] This chapter focuses on three specific issues: custody of children,[3] abduction of children across borders, and adoption.

As will be discussed, several aspects of the law relating to children in the conflict of laws are governed by international conventions that have been adopted in Canada. A broader range of issues is addressed in the *Hague Convention on Jurisdiction, Applicable Law, Recognition, Enforcement and Co-operation in Respect of Parental Responsibility and Measures for the Protection of Children*,[4] which entered into force in 2002. However Canada has not yet signed or ratified this convention.

---

1   See, for example, *Young v Young*, [1993] 4 SCR 3; *Gordon v Goertz*, [1996] 2 SCR 27.
2   See Peter M North, "Reform, but Not Revolution: Children" (1990) 220 *Recueil des Cours* 127. See also *Gunsay v Gunsay* (1999), 70 BCLR (3d) 104 at para 27 (CA) [*Gunsay*].
3   For more detail on this topic, see Berend Hovius, "Territorial Jurisdiction and Civil Enforcement Issues in Interprovincial Custody and Access Disputes in Canadian Common Law Provinces" (2002) 20 *Canadian Family Law Quarterly* 155.
4   35 ILM 1391 (1996).

B. CUSTODY

1) Jurisdiction

If a custody order is sought alongside a divorce, the proceeding comes within the federal *Divorce Act*'s definition of a "divorce proceeding."[5] Jurisdiction over divorce proceedings is discussed in Chapter 22. The *Divorce Act* also deals with "corollary relief proceedings," which include a proceeding in which a custody order is sought.[6] The provincial superior courts have jurisdiction to grant a custody order if either former spouse is "ordinarily resident" in the province when the proceedings are commenced or if both former spouses accept the court's jurisdiction.[7] These are also the jurisdictional requirements for a proceeding seeking to vary a custody order.[8] However, somewhat at odds with the statutory language, appellate courts have held that in each of these situations, there must have first been a Canadian divorce for the court to have jurisdiction under the statute.[9] If an application for custody is made in a divorce proceeding in circumstances where the custody application is opposed and the child is more closely connected with a province other than the one seized of the divorce proceeding, the divorce proceeding may be transferred to that other province.[10]

While divorce is a matter of federal law, each province has enacted statutes that deal with custody.[11] For example, the Ontario *Children's Law Reform Act* allows a parent or any other person to apply for a custody order.[12] There are three ways the court can have jurisdiction to hear such an application. First, the child is habitually resident in Ontario at

---

5   RSC 1985 (2nd Supp), c 3, s 2(1).
6   *Ibid*.
7   *Ibid*, s 4(1). Parallel proceedings for the same corollary relief are avoided through the operation of ss 4(2) & (3).
8   *Ibid*, s 5(1). Parallel proceedings for the same variation order are avoided through the operation of ss 5(2) & (3).
9   *Leonard v Booker* (2007), 321 NBR (2d) 340 (CA); *V(LR) v V(AA)* (2006), 52 BCLR (4th) 112 (CA); *Rothgiesser v Rothgiesser* (2000), 46 OR (3d) 577 at paras 58–59 (CA). For further discussion of this issue in the context of support orders, see Chapter 25.
10 Above note 5, s 6(1). Corollary relief proceedings and proceedings for a variation order that, in each case, do not involve custody can similarly be transferred if a custody order or variation of a custody order is sought: ss 6(2) & (3).
11 The provincial power to do so was confirmed in *Reference re Family Relations Act (BC)*, [1982] 1 SCR 62.
12 RSO 1990, c C.12, s 21 [*CLRA* (Ont)].

the time of the application.[13] Second, the child is physically present in Ontario at the time of the application and several other conditions are met, such as there being substantial evidence of what is in the child's best interests available in Ontario and a real and substantial connection between the child and Ontario.[14] Third, the child is physically present in Ontario and would suffer "serious harm" by remaining with, or being returned to, the current custodian or by being removed from Ontario.[15] The court can decline to exercise jurisdiction in respect of custody on the basis that it is more appropriate for another province or country to exercise jurisdiction.[16] In addition, if divorce proceedings are started, they take priority: any application concerning custody under the provincial statute is stayed unless the court orders otherwise.[17] The British Columbia *Family Law Act* adopts the same approach to jurisdiction over "parenting time" and "parental responsibilities."[18]

The overlap of federal and provincial legislation on custody has led to some constitutional debates about jurisdiction. One key issue was whether a custody order under the *Divorce Act* could be varied by an order under provincial legislation. In *Williams v Hillier* the Alberta Court of Appeal held that "in enacting the *Divorce Act*, Parliament did not purport to assert jurisdiction in the provincial fields of adoption or child welfare or guardianship. I do not see, therefore, that any issue of paramountcy arises where the court is dealing with those provincial topics."[19] This approach has been followed in subsequent cases.[20]

---

13 *Ibid*, s 22(1)(a). "Habitually resident" is defined in s 22(2), and that definition is narrower than that used by the common law: see *Dovigi v Razi*, 2012 ONCA 361 at para 18. Of note, some decisions have held that under this definition a child can concurrently have more than one habitual residence: see *Riley v Wildhaber*, 2011 ONSC 3456 at para 42 (Div Ct).

14 CLRA (Ont), above note 12, s 22(1)(b). Courts have consistently required that each of the listed conditions is satisfied, as noted in *Magee v Morrison*, [1993] OJ No 1912 at para 18 (Gen Div); *Brooks v Brooks* (1998), 41 OR (3d) 191 at 211 (CA) [*Brooks*]; *HE v MM*, 2015 ONCA 813 at para 90, rev'g 2014 ONSC 7409 at para 96.

15 CLRA (Ont), above note 12, s 23. In *Gunsay*, above note 2, the British Columbia Court of Appeal relied on expert testimony from two psychologists in finding that returning the child to her father would cause her to suffer serious harm.

16 CLRA (Ont), above note 12, s 25. In *KN v SQ*, 2013 BCSC 1433, the courts of British Columbia and Alberta held a joint hearing to determine where the custody dispute should be resolved.

17 CLRA (Ont), above note 12, s 27.

18 *Family Law Act*, SBC 2011, c 25, s 74 [*FLA* (BC)]. The statute uses these terms instead of "custody."

19 (1981), 17 Alta LR (2d) 139 at 151 (CA). See also *Re Clarke & Hutchings* (1976), 71 DLR (3d) 356 (Nfld CA); *Dugay v Dugay* (1978), 8 RFL (2d) 208 (Ont Prov Ct).

20 See, for example, *Kunkel v Kunkel* (1994), 111 DLR (4th) 457 at 474–75 (Alta CA).

The jurisdictional overlap also has an impact on which courts can hear custody disputes. Divorce, as a federal area of competence, is required to be handled in the superior court of the province. Custody issues addressed as corollary relief in divorce proceedings similarly are heard in that court. Custody issues that are not linked to divorce proceedings can be handled by provincial inferior courts.[21]

The legislation in some provinces gives the court the jurisdiction to make an interim custody order in certain circumstances. Such an order is designed to work in tandem with a custody order made elsewhere. In British Columbia and Ontario, this jurisdiction is quite broad and includes situations where a child has been wrongfully removed to, or is wrongfully detained in, the province.[22] This jurisdiction is commonly used in cases of international child abduction, discussed later in this chapter.

As has been explained, jurisdiction over custody is heavily regulated by statute. However, it is possible that a custody issue could arise that does not fall within the specific statutory provisions, particularly in a province with a less elaborate legislative framework.[23] In such a case, the primary jurisdictional basis at common law is that the child is ordinarily resident in the province.[24] It is also possible to take jurisdiction on the basis that the child is present in the province and that making a custody order is in his or her best interests.[25] In an exceptional case, the court might be able to exercise *parens patriae* jurisdiction, based on the notion that the state must protect those who are unable to protect themselves, as a basis for a custody order.[26]

2) Choice of Law

For custody, as for several other aspects of family law, there is no independent choice of law analysis. The jurisdictional rules aim to ensure

---

21 See the *FLA* (BC), above note 18, s 193; *CLRA* (Ont), above note 12, s 18(1).
22 *FLA* (BC), above note 18, s 77; *CLRA* (Ont), above note 12, s 40. See *Baker v Arthurs* (1994), 124 Nfld & PEIR 69 (Nfld CA).
23 See *Martodam v Martodam*, [2007] AJ No 179 at para 32 (QB).
24 See *Re Ritchie and Ritchie* (1974), 5 OR (2d) 520 (CA); *Sturkenboom v Davies* (1993), 11 Alta LR (3d) 147 (QB). For a classic statement of the meaning of ordinary residence, see *Re P(GE) (an infant)*, [1965] Ch 568 (CA). The Ontario courts have held that the Ontario statutory test cannot be supplemented by a common law analysis of jurisdiction: *Wang v Lin*, 2013 ONCA 33 at para 51.
25 See *Grewal v Grewal* (1982), 29 RFL (2d) 23 (Sask QB).
26 See *Yassin v Loubani* (2006), 69 BCLR (4th) 36 (CA), drawing on *Hope v Hope* (1854), 43 ER 534; see also *HE v MM*, above note 14 at para 26. Section 69 of the *CLRA* (Ont), above note 12, explicitly preserves the superior court's *parens patriae* jurisdiction.

that the custody issue is heard by an appropriate court, which, in turn, applies the law of the forum. In this area the court is more concerned with its own sense of what custody order is in the child's best interests than with considerations arising under another law such as that of the child's domicile.

3) Recognition and Enforcement

Section 20(2) of the *Divorce Act* provides that a custody order or a variation order involving custody made under the statute has legal effect throughout Canada. The order may be (1) registered in any court in a province and enforced as an order of that court or (2) enforced in any other manner provided by the laws of the province, including its laws respecting reciprocal enforcement between the province and a jurisdiction outside Canada.[27]

The provinces have adopted legislation to govern the recognition and enforcement of foreign custody orders.[28] The legislation is not standard throughout the provinces. Although the legislation is based on the same principles, the statutes are worded differently. Some statutes contain provisions that outline the purposes and objectives of either their custody legislation as a whole or specifically their legislation about the recognition and enforcement of custody orders.[29] These objectives are frequently referred to by the courts.[30]

In both British Columbia and Ontario the court is required to recognize a custody order made by an "extraprovincial tribunal," defined as a court or tribunal outside the province that has jurisdiction to make custody orders.[31] This requirement is subject to five conditions or exceptions, depending on the wording of the specific statute. Four of these are best considered as defences to recognition and are discussed below. The fifth relates more directly to the foreign court's jurisdiction and so should be addressed here. The court is not required to recognize an extraprovincial tribunal's order if that tribunal, were it a court in the province, would not have had jurisdiction under the provincial

---

27 Above note 5, s 20(3). This includes the Federal Court: *Young v Hubbert*, [1988] 1 FC 354 (TD).
28 For example, the *CLRA* (Ont), above note 12, ss 40–45; *Extra-provincial Enforcement of Custody Orders Act*, RSA 2000, c E-14 [*EECOA* (Alta)]; *FLA* (BC), above note 18, ss 72–79.
29 *CLRA* (Ont), above note 12, s 19; *FLA* (BC), above note 18, s 73.
30 See, for example, *Brooks*, above note 14 at 207–8.
31 *FLA* (BC), above note 18, ss 72(1) and 75(1); *CLRA* (Ont), above note 12, ss 18(1) and 41(1). See *Gillespie v Gillespie* (1992), 10 OR (3d) 641 at 649–50 (CA) [*Gillespie*].

statute to make the order.³² As outlined above, this requires jurisdiction based on the child's habitual residence or the child's presence and, among other things, a real and substantial connection.

In several provinces a foreign custody order will be recognized if at the time the order was made the child had a real and substantial connection with the jurisdiction.³³ The Nova Scotia legislation is much more limited, as it will enforce a foreign custody order only if the order is made in a "reciprocating state" as identified in the regulations.³⁴

Once a foreign custody order is recognized, the provincial statutes typically provide that it can be enforced as if it were a domestic order.³⁵ The statutes also contain provisions to address the possibility of conflicting custody orders. For example, an Ontario court asked to recognize conflicting foreign custody orders is to recognize and enforce the order that the court considers is in the best interests of the child.³⁶

4) Defences

In Ontario, the provincial legislation sets out four reasons why a court can refuse to recognize a foreign custody order; in British Columbia, the provincial legislation frames these as criteria for recognition. These reasons are: (1) the respondent was not given reasonable notice of the proceeding in which the order was made; (2) the respondent was not given an opportunity to be heard by the foreign tribunal; (3) the law of the place where the order was made does not require the tribunal to consider the best interests of the child; and (4) the order is contrary to the province's public policy.³⁷ In a province where these defences are not set out in the legislation, there is a strong argument that they can be raised as a matter of common law.

In *Ndegwa v Ndegwa* the court held that the opportunity to be heard meant "knowing the case to be met and having the opportunity to address

---

32 *FLA* (BC), above note 18, s 75(1)(a); *CLRA* (Ont), above note 12, s 41(1)(e).
33 See, for example, *Child Custody Enforcement Act*, CCSM c C360, s 3; *EECOA* (Alta), above note 28, s 2(1).
34 *Reciprocal Enforcement of Custody Orders Act*, RSNS 1989, c 387, s 3. The only such states are eight of the nine other common law provinces (not Newfoundland and Labrador).
35 See, for example, *CLRA* (Ont), above note 12, ss 41(2) and (4); see also *FLA* (BC), above note 18, s 75(2).
36 See, for example, *CLRA* (Ont), above note 12, s 41(3); *FLA* (BC), above note 18, s 75(3). This section does not address a conflict between an order of the forum and a foreign order. On that conflict, see *Miller v Miller* (1999), 121 OAC 300 at para 17 (CA), where the court held the forum order takes priority.
37 *FLA* (BC), above note 18, s 75(1); *CLRA* (Ont), above note 12, s 41(1).

the factual and legal issues of the case."[38] In that case the court refused to recognize a Kenyan custody order due to both lack of notice and a lack of opportunity to be heard.

5) Varying and Superseding Foreign Custody Orders

Under the *Divorce Act*, a provincial superior court can, on an application by either or both former spouses or any other person, make an order varying a custody order. The court must be satisfied that the child's condition, needs, or situation has changed and must take into account the best interests of the child.[39] Under this power, the court can vary a custody order made under the *Divorce Act* by a court in another province.[40]

Provincial legislation allows the court to vary a recognized foreign custody order in two main situations. The first arises when there has been a material change in circumstances since the foreign order was made. The second arises when the child is at risk of serious harm under the foreign order.[41]

In British Columbia and Ontario the court can supersede a foreign custody order if (1) there has been a material change in circumstances that affects the child's best interests and (2) the child has a sufficient degree of connection to the forum. This connection requires either that the child is habitually resident in the forum or can satisfy all five of the following conditions: (1) the child is present in the forum, (2) the child no longer has a real and substantial connection to the foreign forum, (3) substantial evidence of the child's best interests is available in the forum, (4) the child has a real and substantial connection to the forum, and (5) the balance of convenience favours the forum court superseding the order.[42] What will amount to a material change in circumstances is highly fact-specific. In *Gillespie v Gillespie* the court held that the mere relocation of children away from their habitual residence was insufficient.[43] In *Semogas v Semogas* the fact that the child was now habitually resident in the forum and was fearful of visiting her father outside Ontario was held to be a material change.[44]

---

38   (2001), 20 RFL (5th) 118 at para 15 (Ont SCJ).
39   *Divorce Act*, above note 5, ss 17(1) and (5). See also s 20(4).
40   See *Brooks*, above note 14 at 215.
41   See, for example, EECOA (Alta), above note 28, ss 3 & 4.
42   FLA (BC), above note 18, s 76(1)(b); CLRA (Ont), above note 12, s 42(1). See *Brooks*, above note 14 at 211–12.
43   Above note 31 at 650.
44   [1991] OJ No 678 (Gen Div).

In these same two provinces, the court can also supersede a foreign custody order if satisfied that the child would suffer serious harm by remaining in, or being returned to, the custody of the current custody holder or by being removed from the province.[45] Expert psychological evidence can play an important role in establishing serious harm.[46] General evidence, such as allegations of a higher rate of crime and violence in a foreign country, is much less likely to establish serious harm.[47]

C. INTERNATIONAL CHILD ABDUCTION

Canada is a contracting state under the *Hague Convention on the Civil Aspects of International Child Abduction*,[48] and the convention is in force in all provinces.[49] The objectives of the convention are to protect children from the harmful effects of their wrongful removal or retention, to establish procedures to ensure their prompt return to their habitual residence, and to secure protection for rights of access. If a child is not voluntarily returned, a court in a contracting state has jurisdiction to determine whether that child has been wrongfully removed or retained. The terms of the convention apply only between contracting states and do not apply to jurisdictional issues within a country.[50] About eighty countries are signatories to the convention.[51]

---

45 *CLRA* (Ont), above note 12, s 43; *FLA* (BC), above note 18, s 76(1)(a).
46 Though, of course, such evidence is not determinative and can be conflicting: see, for example, *Solnik v Solnik* (1983), 41 OR (2d) 427 (UFC), aff'd (1983), 44 OR (2d) 684 (CA).
47 *de Medeiros v de Medeiros* (1992), 39 RFL (3d) 274 at para 41 (Ont Ct Gen Div); *Martinez v Martinez-Jarquin*, [1990] OJ No 1385 (Prov Ct).
48 19 ILM 1501 (1980) [*Hague Convention*]. For a recent comprehensive analysis from a Canadian perspective, see Nicholas Bala & Mary Jo Maur, "The Hague Convention on Child Abduction: A Canadian Primer" (2014) 33 *Canadian Family Law Quarterly* 267.
49 See, for example, *CLRA* (Ont), above note 12, s 46; *International Child Abduction Act*, RSA 2000, c I-4; *FLA* (BC), above note 18, s 80.
50 *Brouillard v Racine* (2002), 33 RFL (5th) 48 (Ont SCJ). For a sense of the analysis outside the convention context, see *Shortridge-Tsuchiya v Tsuchiya*, 2010 BCCA 61.
51 Jurisprudence on the convention's provisions from other contracting states, especially the United States and the United Kingdom, is frequently considered by Canadian courts. Accordingly, for a review of the central English cases, see James Fawcett & Janeen Carruthers, *Cheshire, North & Fawcett Private International Law*, 14th ed (Oxford: Oxford University Press, 2008) at 1104–17. See also the database of convention jurisprudence, online: www.incadat.com.

The Supreme Court of Canada explained the aim of the convention in *VW v DS*.[52] It held that the convention

> is ultimately intended to deter the abduction of children by depriving fugitive parents of any possibility of having their custody of the children recognized in the country of refuge and thereby legitimizing the situation for which they are responsible. To that end, the [convention] favours the restoration of the status quo as soon as possible after the removal of the child by enabling one party to force the other to submit to the jurisdiction of the court of the child's habitual place of residence for the purpose of arguing the merits of any custody issue.[53]

In *Aulwes v Mai* Cromwell JA for the Nova Scotia Court of Appeal observed that "[t]he watchwords of the Convention . . . are deterrence of international child abduction, rapid return of the child, restoration of the status quo and deference, in so far as determining the child's best interests is concerned, to the courts of the place of habitual residence."[54]

1) Scope

The convention applies only to children under sixteen who were habitually resident in a contracting state immediately before the breach of custody or access rights.[55] The convention does not define "habitually resident." In *Chan v Chow* the British Columbia Court of Appeal held that this is a question of fact to be decided by reference to all the circumstances of the case.[56] It held that a habitual residence is established by residing in a place for an appreciable period of time with a settled intention and that a child's habitual residence is tied to the habitual residence of his or her custodian.[57] The court also considered the definition of "settled intention," noting that this concept requires that the child's reasons for living in a particular place have a sufficient degree of continuity.[58] These concepts have a specific meaning under the con-

---

52 [1996] 2 SCR 108 [*VW*].
53 *Ibid* at para 36. See also *Thomson v Thomson*, [1994] 3 SCR 551 at 559 [*Thomson*].
54 (2002), 209 NSR (2d) 248 at para 31 (CA) [*Aulwes*].
55 *Hague Convention*, above note 48, art 4.
56 (2001), 90 BCLR (3d) 222 (CA) [*Chan*].
57 *Ibid* at para 32. The court approved of the definition in *Re J (A Minor) (Abduction: Custody Rights)*, [1990] 2 AC 562 at 578 (HL). See also *Korutowska-Wooff v Wooff* (2004), 188 OAC 376 (CA); *O'Brien v O'Brien*, [2008] OJ No 3977 (SCJ); *Proia v Proia* (2003), 340 AR 363 (QB) [*Proia*]; *Anamur v Anamur*, [2009] OJ No 5576 (SCJ); *Ellis v Wentzell-Ellis*, 2010 ONCA 347 at para 22 [*Ellis*].
58 *Chan*, above note 56 at paras 33–35. See also *R v Barnet London Borough Council, Ex Parte Shah*, [1983] 2 AC 309 at 344 (HL).

vention and accordingly other definitions of them, such as those found in provincial family law legislation, cannot be applied in this context.[59]

In *Wilson v Huntley*,[60] the parents had joint custody and the child lived with each parent—the mother in the United Kingdom and the father in Canada—for six months of each year. After his period concluded, the father refused to return the child to her mother. The mother applied under the convention but the father argued that the child's habitual residence was Canada. This argument was in part based on the traditional notion that a person can have only one habitual residence. However, on these facts, the court was prepared to find that the child had "consecutive habitual residences alternating between those of her parents."[61] Yet the court went on to hold that "[b]ecause the child can only have one habitual residence at a time, when [the child] was retained in Canada, the United Kingdom remained only her next intended habitual residence . . . both at the moment and immediately prior to the retention, the child was habitually resident in Canada."[62]

2) Protection Provided

The convention protects children from wrongful removal or retention. Article 3 provides that the removal or retention of a child is wrongful where it breaches rights of custody under the law of the state in which the child was habitually resident. At the time of the removal or retention, these rights of custody either must be being exercised or would have been exercised but for the removal or retention.

The meaning of habitual residence was discussed above. The term "rights of custody" is defined by article 5(a) as rights relating to the care of the person of the child and, in particular, the right to determine the child's place of residence. The nature of the custody rights of the party seeking an order for the return of a child must be determined in accordance with the law of the habitual residence of the child.[63] In the face of conflicting expert evidence of foreign law, evidence from a foreign state's central authority as to the interpretation of its own custody

---

59 *Chan*, above note 56 at paras 35–42. Two recent United Kingdom decisions on the meaning of habitual residence in the context of the convention are *AR v RN*, [2015] UKSC 35, and *In Re LC (Children)*, [2014] UKSC 1.
60 (2005), 13 RFL (6th) 435 (Ont SCJ).
61 *Ibid* at para 34.
62 *Ibid* at paras 57–58.
63 For further analysis of this issue, see Kisch Beevers & Javier Perez Milla, "Child Abduction: Convention 'Rights of Custody'—Who Decides? An Anglo-Spanish Perspective" (2007) 3 *Journal of Private International Law* 201.

and access laws can be persuasive.⁶⁴ The court considers whether there has been a breach of custody rights at the time of the child's removal or retention rather than at the time of the application. The notion of custody is to be given a "large and liberal" interpretation.⁶⁵ Under the language of article 3, rights of custody can be held by a person, an institution, or another body. This includes a court seized with an application for custody.⁶⁶

Canadian courts have held that when one parent interferes with a joint custody relationship by removing a child from the jurisdiction, he or she has breached the other parent's custody rights.⁶⁷ In *Spini v Spini*, the court determined that a prior custody order is not required if the law of the habitual residence of the child provides each parent with rights of custody.⁶⁸ Many cases have considered the meaning of "rights of custody" in the context of the convention.⁶⁹ A key issue is whether a parent who does not have custody but whose consent is required before the custodial parent can change the child's habitual residence—often under what is called a "non-removal clause"—is protected. In some countries this has been held to constitute a right of custody,⁷⁰ but the prevailing view in Canadian courts, while not free of debate, is that this falls short.⁷¹

3) Process

The central operative provision of the *Hague Convention* is article 12. It provides that where a child has been wrongfully removed or retained, as defined in article 3, and where less than a year has elapsed from the date of the wrongful removal or retention, the court of the contracting state where the child now is shall order the return of the child forthwith.

---

64 *Finizio v Scoppio-Finizio* (1999), 46 OR (3d) 226 (CA) [*Finizio*]. Note also that under art 14 of the *Hague Convention*, above note 48, the court is allowed to take direct notice of the law of the state of habitual residence, which is an exception to how the content of foreign law is usually ascertained: see Chapter 12.

65 *VW*, above note 52 at para 33. On "inchoate rights of custody," see *In the matter of K (A Child) (Northern Ireland)*, [2014] UKSC 29.

66 *Thomson*, above note 53.

67 *Morris v Poole*, [1995] 6 WWR 166 (NWTSC); *Chan*, above note 56; *C(DM) v W(DL)*, (2001) 155 BCAC 235 (CA).

68 (1994), 157 NBR (2d) 1 (QB).

69 See, for example, *Thorne v Dryden-Hall* (1997), 35 BCLR (3d) 174 (CA), aff'g [1995] BCJ No 2009 (SC) and (1995), 18 RFL (4th) 15 (SC) [*Thorne*]; *Espiritu v Bielza* (2007), 39 RFL (6th) 218 (Ont Ct J).

70 See *Re D (A Child) (Abduction: Rights of Custody)*, [2007] 1 AC 619 (HL); *Abbott v Abbott*, 130 S Ct 1983 (2010); Martha Bailey, "*Abbott v. Abbott*: Do *Ne Exeat* Provisions Create Rights of Custody?" (2010) 29 *Canadian Family Law Quarterly* 171.

71 See *Thomson*, above note 53 at 589–90. See, however, *Thorne*, above note 69.

If more than a year has elapsed, that court shall also order the return of the child unless the child is now settled in his or her new environment.

Article 8 of the convention outlines the procedure to apply for a child's return. Any person, institution, or other body may apply either to the central authority of the child's habitual residence or to the central authority of any other contracting state for assistance in securing the return of the child.[72] Under article 9, a central authority that believes the child is in another contracting state is required to transmit the application to the central authority in that state.

The convention does not specifically address the commencing of legal proceedings to obtain a court order for return of a child. The central authority where the child is must take all appropriate measures to secure the "voluntary" return of the child,[73] but it is not directed to start proceedings. However, in implementing the convention the legislation authorizes an application to a court to pursue a right or an obligation under the convention.[74] In practice this allows the parent seeking return of the child to commence proceedings. An application under the convention is a summary procedure, designed to proceed swiftly. Affidavit evidence is generally used and a party is not entitled to a full trial. In ordering a child's return, courts can impose undertakings on parties to deal with the transition period between the order and the time when any outstanding issues are addressed by the courts of the country of habitual residence.[75] In situations in which competing custody disputes are proceeding in different countries, it is possible for courts to develop creative solutions, such as court-to-court communications and joint hearings, to help better resolve the issues.[76]

4) Grounds for Refusing to Order a Child's Return

Notwithstanding the core obligation in article 12 to order a child's return, the *Hague Convention* addresses several situations in which a court is not required to make such an order even though the child has been wrongfully removed or retained. All of these grounds are discretionary.

---

72 Each contracting state must designate a central authority (art 6), which is to co-operate with the central authority in other states to secure the prompt return of children and achieve the objectives of the convention (art 7). The federal government and the provinces have appointed central authorities.
73 *Hague Convention*, above note 48, art 10.
74 See, for example, *CLRA* (Ont), above note 12, s 46(5). See also *Hague Convention*, above note 48, art 29.
75 *Cannock v Fleguel*, 2008 ONCA 758 at paras 13 and 27.
76 See, for example, *Hoole v Hoole*, 2008 BCSC 1248.

One of the grounds is found in the language of article 12 itself. If a year or more has elapsed between the removal or retention and the commencement of legal proceedings and if it can be demonstrated that the child is now settled into his or her new environment, the court is not required to order his or her return.[77] In *Szalas v Szabo*, the court held that a child could "settle into" a new environment much more quickly than the length of time necessary to acquire a habitual residence and that the strong mental commitment required for a "settled intention" was not required.[78] However, in *New Brunswick (Attorney General) v Majeau-Prasad* the court held that this concept had to be interpreted narrowly. In that case the court held that a young child who had lived in Moncton for seventeen months, started attending daycare, and made new friends had not settled into a new environment.[79] This issue requires difficult balancing: if this condition is triggered too easily it can upset the fundamental aims of the convention, but if it is too difficult to trigger then considerable disruption could result for the child.[80] The assessment of the child's circumstances is done as of the time of the hearing rather than the earlier time of application for return.[81]

In *Aulwes* the Nova Scotia Court of Appeal analyzed this issue at length.[82] The court noted that both the child's present circumstances and the ways that the underlying purposes of the convention could be furthered had to be considered. On the latter issue, the court considered whether a return order would (1) effect a prompt return, (2) restore the status quo, (3) deter other parents from similar conduct, and (4) allow the courts of the child's habitual residence to resolve the issue of custody. The passage of time frustrated the first two purposes but not the third and the fourth. On the former, the court found that while factors of "place, home, school, friends and activities" favoured not making an order, the fact that the mother was illegally in Canada made it very difficult to consider the child settled into that environment.[83]

Even if the child is found to be settled into the new environment, there is some question as to whether the court can nonetheless order

---

77 Courts should be wary in cases where the abductor's conduct, through concealment or delay, has contributed to this passage of time: see *Abib v Abib*, 2010 ONSC 5869 at para 22, aff'd 2010 ONCA 827, and, in England, *Cannon v Cannon*, [2005] 1 FLR 169 at para 50 (CA).
78 (1995), 16 RFL (4th) 168 at para 56 (Ont Prov Div).
79 (2000), 229 NBR (2d) 296 (QB).
80 *Aulwes*, above note 54 at para 61.
81 *Kubera v Kubera*, 2010 BCCA 118 at paras 49–69 [*Kubera*].
82 Above note 54 at paras 69–85. See also the analysis in *Francis v Maharaj*, 2014 ONCJ 285.
83 *Aulwes*, above note 54 at paras 85–88.

his or her return. At least one appellate decision, without resolving the issue, has suggested not.[84]

As a second ground, a court is not required to order the return of a child where the applicant was not actually exercising the custody rights or had consented to or subsequently acquiesced in the removal or retention.[85] In *Zimmerhansl v Zimmerhansl* the court held that a failure to exercise custody rights must be demonstrated by a clear and unequivocal abandonment of the child.[86] Similarly, there must be clear and unequivocal evidence of consent or acquiescence.[87]

Third, under article 13(b) a court is not required to order the return of a child where there is a grave risk that the return would expose the child to physical or psychological harm or otherwise place the child in an intolerable situation.[88] In *Thomson v Thomson* the Supreme Court of Canada held, in interpreting this provision, that the threshold for harm was a high one, such that the harm would have to amount to an intolerable situation.[89] The harm must be substantial and more than what would normally be expected in removing a child from one parent. As a general rule, the court should take the approach that the courts of the child's habitual residence will be able to safeguard against harm. Article 13(b) is commonly used where one parent alleges that the other has physically harmed either the parent or the child. In *Pollastro v Pollastro* the court observed that "returning a child to a violent environment places that child in an *inherently* intolerable situation."[90] In *Kovacs v Kovacs* the court refused to order a child returned to the custody of a fugitive from the law with a substantial criminal record, determining that this would be an intolerable situation for the child.[91] Courts have also considered the possibility that a parent would hide the returned

---

84 *Kubera*, above note 81 at para 103. See also *JL v British Columbia (Director of the Child, Family and Community Service Act)*, 2010 BCSC 1234 at paras 63–64.
85 *Hague Convention*, above note 48, art 13(a).
86 (2001), 289 AR 165 at para 28 (QB) [*Zimmerhansl*]. See also *Medina v Pallett*, 2010 BCSC 259 at paras 29–30.
87 *Zimmerhansl*, above note 86 at para 33; *Proia*, above note 57 at para 59.
88 For more detail on this provision, see Peter Ripley, "A Defence of the Established Approach to the Grave Risk Exception in the Hague Child Abduction Convention" (2008) 4 *Journal of Private International Law* 443.
89 Above note 53 at 596; *Hoskins v Boyd* (1997), 34 BCLR (3d) 121 at para 11 (CA); *Jabbaz v Mouammar* (2003), 171 OAC 102 at paras 22–23 (CA); *Ellis*, above note 57 at paras 37–50.
90 (1999), 43 OR (3d) 485 at 496 (CA) [emphasis in original]. In *Finizio*, above note 64 at para 32, the Court of Appeal for Ontario held that a single assault by the husband against the wife during an eight-year marriage did not rise to this level. See also *Sampley v Sampley*, 2015 BCCA 113.
91 (2002), 59 OR (3d) 671 (SCJ) [*Kovacs*].

child as creating such a situation.⁹² If a child has been found to be a Convention refugee,⁹³ this gives rise to a presumption that return would expose him or her to the risk of harm.⁹⁴

Fourth, article 13 also provides that the court need not order a child returned if the child objects to being returned and has attained an age and degree of maturity such that it is appropriate to consider his or her views. The court takes care to ensure that the child's stated wishes are independent of those of his or her parents.⁹⁵ The court's assessment of a child's maturity is heavily dependent on the specific facts of the case.⁹⁶ In *Aulwes*, the Nova Scotia Court of Appeal noted that this part of article 13 gave the child "a voice, not a veto."⁹⁷ The child did not want to return because of fear of possible abuse by her father, but the court ordered the child's return. It held that her views were not sufficiently independent of those of her mother. It also cautioned against allowing a child's fear of abuse to lower the threshold under article 13(b), discussed above. The court had already concluded that that return would not place the child in an intolerable situation.

Finally, the *Hague Convention* also includes a public policy provision. Under article 20, the return of a child may be refused where it is contrary to the jurisdiction's fundamental principles relating to the protection of human rights and fundamental freedoms.

5) Rights of Access

The Supreme Court of Canada explained the relative importance of custody and access in *Thomson*. It stated that

> the primary object of the Convention is the enforcement of custody rights. . . . Such rights of custody are given effect through proceedings for the return of the child under Article 12.
>
> By contrast, the Convention leaves the enforcement of access rights to the administrative channels of central authorities designated by the state parties to the Convention.⁹⁸

---

92   See *Chan*, above note 56 at paras 63–66.
93   See *Immigration and Refugee Protection Act*, SC 2001, c 27, s 96. See also s 115(1).
94   *Issasi v Rosenzweig*, 2011 ONCA 302, additional reasons at 2011 ONCA 417 at paras 74, 78, and 87 [*Issasi*].
95   See *Thorne*, above note 69 at para 25 (SC). See also *Beatty v Schatz*, [2009] BCJ No 1557 (CA).
96   See, for example, the analysis in *T(TN) v T(J)* (2001), 288 AR 362 (QB); *Wubben v Lang-Ernst*, [2000] BCJ No 2662 (SC); *GAGR v TDW*, 2013 BCSC 586.
97   Above note 54 at para 53. See also *Re M*, [2008] 1 All ER 1157 (HL).
98   Above note 53 at 579–80.

Article 5 provides that rights of access include the right to take a child to a place other than his or her habitual residence for a limited period of time. Under article 21, a person can apply to a central authority to organize or secure rights of access. The application process is similar to that concerning rights of custody. The central authority is required to attempt to remove obstacles to the exercise of access rights. Doing so can include commencing proceedings. However, because article 3 of the convention defines wrongful removal or retention in terms of rights of custody and not rights of access, the strong protection provided to rights of custody under article 12 does not apply to rights of access.[99] As a result, a parent with rights of access only will not be able to obtain an order for the return of the child.[100]

6) Interplay between the *Hague Convention* and Legislation

The convention provides a regime for the return of children who have been wrongfully removed or retained. One issue that has arisen is whether provincial legislation can be used in conjunction with the convention.[101] In *Thomson*, the judge hearing the application had both ordered the child returned to Scotland under the convention and granted the mother, resident in the province, interim custody under the relevant provincial statute.[102] However, the Supreme Court of Canada indicated that the convention and the provincial statute were two separate regimes that were to be applied independently.[103] The court stated that it was not helpful to have simultaneous applications under each of the convention and the statute. Where this does occur, the convention takes priority and no order should be made under the statute. Two judges dissented in *Thomson* on this point. They held that the convention should be read in conjunction with provincial statutory schemes, and where there is no conflict the court could use the legislation to make transitory orders such as the one for interim custody.[104]

---

99 See *VW*, above note 52 at paras 21 and 31.
100 As illustrated in *VW*, *ibid*.
101 See Vaughan Black, "Statutory Confusion in International Child Custody Disputes" (1993) 9 *Canadian Family Law Quarterly* 279.
102 Above note 53 at 570–71. The statute is the *Child Custody Enforcement Act*, CCSM c C360.
103 *Thomson*, above note 53 at 603–4. The court's comments on this point were *obiter dicta* because the interim custody order had already expired.
104 *Ibid* at 618–23.

In *Kovacs*, a mother brought her son to Ontario from Hungary and both made a refugee claim.[105] The father sought a return order under the convention and the mother argued the court did not have the authority to order the son's return while his refugee claim was pending. The court refused to delay the convention proceedings. It engaged in a detailed interpretation of the federal *Immigration Act*,[106] finding that it was not inconsistent with the convention. The court held that the federal statute did not give the child a right to remain in Canada that took priority over the provisions of the convention. The court was particularly concerned that the length of refugee proceedings in Canada was incompatible with the convention's goal of prompt return of children to their habitual residence.[107]

D. ADOPTION

Each province has enacted a legislative scheme to deal with the adoption of children. For example, in Ontario the *Child and Family Services Act* covers adoption in Part VII.[108] These schemes allow the provincial courts to make adoption orders. From a conflict of laws perspective, two important issues are the scope of the court's jurisdiction to make such orders and the law the court is to apply.

1) Jurisdiction

It is typical for the provincial legislation to require some connection to the forum before the court has the power to make an adoption order. The Ontario scheme requires that both the child being adopted and the person applying for the adoption order must be residents of Ontario.[109] If two people apply jointly for the order, both must be Ontario residents. In *Re Rai* the Court of Appeal for Ontario stated that residence is to be determined by looking at factors such as time, object, intention, and continuity.[110] The court also stated that the purpose of the requirement of residence "will have been met if there is a reasonable connection between the child and Ontario, and if the child has lived here for sufficient time to enable an effective investigation to be made

---

105 Above note 91.
106 RSC 1985, c I-2 (since repealed).
107 *Kovacs*, above note 91 at para 75. See also the analysis in *Issasi*, above note 94.
108 RSO 1990, c C.11.
109 *Ibid*, s 146(5). See also the *Adoption Act*, CCSM c A2, ss 10–11.
110 (1980), 27 OR (2d) 425 at 429 (CA).

into the suitability of the adopting parents and whether the proposed adoption order would be in the best interests of the child."[111] In *TIL v JLF*, the Manitoba Court of Appeal held that an inquiry into a person's residence did not require analysis of the concepts of domicile or habitual residence.[112]

The jurisdiction requirements vary somewhat between provinces. In British Columbia, the sole or both joint applicants must be residents.[113] The same is the case in Saskatchewan, but subject to the court's power to waive the residency requirement if it is the best interests of the child to do so.[114] In Newfoundland and Labrador the sole or both applicants must be resident in the province and the child must have resided with the applicant or applicants, as the case may be, for at least six months.[115] The scope is broader in Nova Scotia, where the applicant must be either resident or domiciled in the province or the child must be born, resident, or domiciled in the province or be a child in care.[116] So the requirement can be satisfied by either the applicant or the child. In Alberta, the applicant must maintain his or her usual residence in Alberta or have done so at the time of receiving custody of the child.[117] In addition, the child must be a Canadian citizen or have been "lawfully admitted to Canada for permanent residence."[118]

2) Choice of Law

The statutory schemes on adoption do not address the law to be applied. In practice, the courts apply the law of the forum to determine whether to grant the adoption order.

3) Intercountry Adoptions

The adoption of a child from another country raises some significant issues. Canada is a contracting state under the *Hague Convention on Protection of Children and Cooperation in Respect of Intercountry Adoption*.[119] The convention has the force of law in each of the provinces and

---

111 *Ibid* at 430. See also *Re MNS*, 2012 ONSC 1596.
112 (2001), 153 Man R (2d) 241 at paras 22–25 (CA).
113 *Adoption Act*, RSBC 1996, c 5, s 29(3) [*Adoption Act* (BC)].
114 *The Adoption Act, 1998*, SS 1998, c A-5.2, ss 16(3) and (5).
115 *Adoption Act, 2013*, SNL 2013, c A-3.1, s 27.
116 *Children and Family Services Act*, SNS 1990, c 5, s 72(1).
117 *Child, Youth and Family Enhancement Act*, RSA 2000, c C-12, s 62(1).
118 *Ibid*, s 62(3).
119 32 ILM 1134 (1993) [*Intercountry Adoption Convention*].

territories.[120] In any conflict between a province's general law on adoption and the provisions in the convention or its implementing statute, the latter take priority.[121] The objectives of the convention are to establish safeguards to ensure that intercountry adoptions take place in the best interests of the child, to take steps to prevent the abduction of or traffic in children, and to secure the recognition of adoptions made in accordance with the convention.[122] Each contracting state designates a central authority, whose purpose is to co-operate with other central authorities to achieve the convention's objectives.[123]

The scope of the convention is explained in article 2. It applies where a child habitually resident in a contracting state (the "state of origin") has been, is being, or is to be moved to another contracting state (the "receiving state") either (1) after having been adopted in the state of origin by a habitual resident of the receiving state or (2) for the purposes of being adopted by a habitual resident of the receiving state in either the receiving state or the state of origin. The convention covers only adoptions that create a permanent parent–child relationship.

If an adoption falls within the scope of the convention, articles 4 and 5 set out detailed requirements that must be satisfied in the state of origin and the receiving state before the adoption can take place. One of these requirements is that the competent authorities in the state of origin must determine that an intercountry adoption is in the child's best interests.

The convention also contains detailed procedural requirements for intercountry adoption.[124] Under article 14, persons habitually resident in a contracting state who wish to adopt a child habitually resident in another contracting state must apply to their local central authority. The authority prepares a report on their eligibility and suitability and provides it to the central authority in the state of origin.[125] In turn, the central authority in the state of origin prepares a report on the child and

---

120 See, for example, the *Intercountry Adoption Act, 1998*, SO 1998, c 29; *Intercountry Adoption (Hague Convention) Act*, CCSM c A3; *Adoption Act* (BC), above note 113, s 51.
121 See, for example, the *Intercountry Adoption Act, 1998*, above note 120, ss 3(2) and 23.
122 *Intercountry Adoption Convention*, above note 119, art 1. One key concern is to prevent improper payments and rewards in intercountry adoptions.
123 *Intercountry Adoption Convention*, ibid, arts 6 & 7. The federal government and each of the provinces have designated a central authority.
124 These can be mirrored or expanded in the provincial legislation implementing the convention: see, for example, the *Intercountry Adoption Act, 1998*, above note 120, s 5.
125 *Intercountry Adoption Convention*, above note 119, art 15.

provides it to the central authority in the receiving state.[126] Article 17 sets out conditions that must be met before the state of origin can transfer the child to the receiving state. One of these is that the central authorities in each of the two states must agree that the adoption may proceed.[127]

Few cases have considered the convention. In *Re G* a judge of the Ontario Court of Justice stated that "intercountry adoptions are limited to adoptions finalized in the child's country of origin."[128] This comment misinterprets Ontario's legislation, under which an intercountry adoption includes one meeting the definition in article 2, discussed above, which is significantly broader.[129] The state of origin in that case was India, which is a contracting state, so the convention should have been applied.

Because the convention applies only to contracting states, some provinces have adopted an expanded definition of an intercountry adoption to provide further safeguards outside convention cases. In Ontario, the legislation defines an intercountry adoption as either an adoption caught by the convention or an adoption by an Ontario resident of a child habitually resident outside Canada that is "finalized in the child's country of origin,"[130] which would seem to mean the state of his or her habitual residence.[131] It can be more challenging, outside the convention context, to assess the validity of the adoption.

4) Recognition of Foreign Adoptions

Provincial adoption legislation generally provides that an adoption under the laws of another jurisdiction has the same effect in the province as would an adoption under the province's law.[132] Most provinces do not impose any threshold conditions on the foreign adoption. However, the legislation in Nova Scotia requires that at the time of the foreign adoption either the child was born, domiciled, or resident in the other

---

126 *Ibid*, art 16.
127 For an example, in the immigration context, in which the state of origin's agreement was not established, see *Singh v Canada (Minister of Citizenship and Immigration)*, [2014] IADD No 131 at paras 40–42.
128 (2008), 56 RFL (6th) 232 at para 10 (Ont Ct J).
129 See the *Intercountry Adoption Act, 1998*, above note 120, s 1(1).
130 *Ibid*. See also the approach in the *Adoption Act* (BC), above note 113, ss 48–49.
131 *Intercountry Adoption Act, 1998*, above note 120, s 1(2).
132 See, for example, the *Child and Family Services Act*, above note 108, s 159; *Adoption Act* (BC), above note 113, s 47; *Child, Youth and Family Enhancement Act*, above note 117, s 73. For a case predating this statutory provision and thus using the common law, see *Re Jensen Estates* (1963), 40 DLR (2d) 469 (BCSC). See also *Re AP* (2002), 30 RFL (5th) 377 at para 5 (Ont Ct J).

jurisdiction or the adopting parent was domiciled or resident there.¹³³ In practice this threshold should be quite easy to satisfy. In addition, some provinces use language that requires that the foreign adoption will be recognized only if it is similar in effect to a domestic adoption. This can allow a court to refuse to recognize an adoption, for example, that does not create a parent–child relationship.¹³⁴ In ME v Alberta (Minister of Human Services) the issue was whether a "kafala" obtained in the Republic of Sudan was equivalent to an adoption order. The difficulty was that the kafala did not terminate the prior parent–child relationship. However, the court held that because its effect was to create a new and permanent parent–child relationship, it should be treated as an adoption order for purposes of recognition under the provincial statute.¹³⁵

An adoption in one jurisdiction can have an impact on rights in another jurisdiction.¹³⁶ In Williams v Hillier the parties obtained a divorce in Alberta.¹³⁷ The court awarded the mother custody of their two children and the father reasonable access. The mother remarried and the couple adopted the children in Manitoba. The father subsequently applied, in Alberta, to fix dates for access to the children. The mother argued that the Manitoba adoption should be recognized in Alberta and that it put an end to the father's rights of access. The Manitoba Court of Appeal agreed.

Foreign adoptions that are contrary to the public policy of a province will not be recognized. In Wende v Victoria (County) Official Administrator, an eighty-two-year-old man had adopted a forty-three-year-old woman in 1951 in Germany.¹³⁸ At that time the couple was, and had been for many years, living as husband and wife. It was then common in Germany to use adoption as a means to legalize a life partnership between an aristocrat and a person without noble birth. The court held that only in rare cases would it refuse to recognize a foreign adoption. However, the primary purpose of this adoption was to allow the couple to live as a married couple. This was so foreign to the public policy of British Columbia that recognition was refused.¹³⁹ An important consideration in the analysis of public policy is whether the foreign adoption was intended to create a parent–child relationship.

---

133 *Children and Family Services Act*, above note 116, s 86.
134 See the discussion in *Wende v Victoria (County) Official Administrator* (1998), 48 BCLR (3d) 219 at paras 29–31 (SC).
135 2015 ABQB 251.
136 See, for example, *Oliphant v Oliphant Estate* (1990), 84 Sask R 44 (QB).
137 Above note 19.
138 Above note 134.
139 *Ibid* at para 37. See also *Re Raghbeer* (1977), 3 RFL (2d) 42 at 44 (Ont Co Ct).

Under the *Intercountry Adoption Convention*, discussed above, a contracting state is required to recognize an adoption certified by the competent authority of a contracting state as having been made in accordance with the convention. The certificate must indicate the date on which the state of origin and the receiving state consented to the adoption.[140] However, recognition of an adoption may be refused if the adoption is manifestly contrary to the state's public policy, taking into account the best interests of the child.[141]

FURTHER READINGS

ANTON, AE. "The Hague Convention on International Child Abduction" (1981) 30 *International and Comparative Law Quarterly* 537.

BAILEY, MARTHA. "Canada's Implementation of the 1980 *Hague Convention on the Civil Aspects of International Child Abduction*" (2000) 33 *New York University Journal of International Law and Politics* 17.

BEAUMONT, PAUL, & PETER MCELEAVY. *The Hague Convention on International Child Abduction* (Oxford: Oxford University Press, 1999).

BLACK, VAUGHAN. "GATT for Kids: New Rules for Intercountry Adoption of Children" (1994) 11 *Canadian Family Law Quarterly* 253.

BROWNE, NOAH. "Relevance and Fairness: Protecting the Rights of Domestic-Violence Victims and Left-Behind Fathers under the *Hague Convention on International Child Abduction*" (2011) 60 *Duke Law Journal* 1193.

FARQUHAR, KEITH. "The *Hague Convention on International Child Abduction* Comes to Canada" (1983) 4 *Canadian Journal of Family Law* 5.

KENNEDY, GILBERT. "Adoption in the Conflict of Laws" (1956) 34 *Canadian Bar Review* 507.

KRUGER, THALIA. *International Child Abduction: The Inadequacies of the Law* (Oxford: Oxford University Press, 2011).

O'HALLORAN, KERRY. *The Politics of Adoption: International Perspectives on Law, Policy and Practice*, 3d ed (Dordrecht: Springer, 2015) ch 5 and 9.

RAINS, ROBERT, ED. *The 1980 Hague Abduction Convention: Comparative Aspects* (London: Wildy, Simmonds and Hill, 2014).

---

140 *Intercountry Adoption Convention*, above note 119, art 23(1).
141 *Ibid*, art 24.

SCHUZ, RHONA. *The Hague Child Abduction Convention: A Critical Analysis* (Oxford: Hart, 2013).

SCHUZ, RHONA. "The Hague Child Abduction Convention: Family Law and Private International Law" (1995) 44 *International and Comparative Law Quarterly* 771.

SILBERMAN, LINDA J. "Cooperative Efforts in Private International Law on Behalf of Children: The Hague Children's Conventions" (2006) 323 *Recueil des Cours* 261.

CHAPTER 25

SUPPORT OBLIGATIONS

A. INTRODUCTION

In Canada jurisdiction over family law, and specifically over spousal and child support, is divided between the federal and provincial governments. Under the *Constitution Act, 1867* the federal Parliament has jurisdiction to enact laws on marriage and divorce and this includes the jurisdiction to make laws that enable the granting and variation of support orders when the orders arise from divorce proceedings.[1] The provincial jurisdiction over property and civil rights gives the provincial legislatures the jurisdiction to enact laws about support obligations for separated but not divorced partners, unmarried cohabitants, and children of parents who are not married. The provinces also have jurisdiction over the enforcement of support orders. This division between federal and provincial jurisdiction over support orders adds an extra layer of complexity when considering conflict of laws issues such as jurisdiction, choice of law, and enforcement.

B. JURISDICTION UNDER THE *DIVORCE ACT*

The federal *Divorce Act* provides for the making of both spousal support and child support orders.[2] If a support order is sought alongside a

---

1 (UK), 30 & 31 Vict, c 3, s 91(26).
2 RSC 1985 (2nd Supp), c 3, ss 15.1 & 15.2.

divorce, the proceeding comes within the statute's definition of a "divorce proceeding."[3] Jurisdiction over divorce proceedings is discussed in Chapter 22. Support orders are also available under the *Divorce Act* as corollary relief separate from, but in conjunction with, a Canadian divorce. Section 2(1) defines a "corollary relief proceeding" as "a proceeding in a court in which either or both former spouses seek a child support order, a spousal support order or a custody order." Section 4(1) provides that the superior court of a province has jurisdiction to hear and determine corollary relief proceedings if either former spouse is ordinarily resident in the province or if both former spouses accept the jurisdiction of the court. The corollary relief proceedings need not be heard by the court of the province in which the divorce was granted.[4] A potential conflict of jurisdiction, possible if the former spouses are ordinarily resident in different provinces, is resolved in sections 4(2) and (3).[5] The *Divorce Act* also gives the provincial superior courts the jurisdiction to vary, rescind, or suspend any child or spousal support order if either former spouse is ordinarily resident in the province or if both spouses accept the jurisdiction of the court.[6]

1) Ordinary Residence

For the purposes of the *Divorce Act* a person is "ordinarily resident" in a Canadian province when his or her customary residence is in that province.[7] Residence is not dependent on citizenship or immigration status.[8] In *MacPherson v MacPherson* the Ontario Court of Appeal held that the arrival of a person in a new locality with the intention of making a home there for an indefinite period of time was sufficient to establish ordinary residence.[9] Similarly in *Cadot v Cadot* the court held that ordinary residence ended when there was an intention to leave and to reside in a different jurisdiction.[10] There is no statutorily mandated minimum time for which an individual must have been ordinarily resident in a

---

3   *Ibid*, s 2(1).
4   See *Arsenault v Arsenault* (2006), 242 NSR (2d) 340 (CA) [*Arsenault*].
5   See, for example, *Santos v Santos*, 2010 BCSC 331.
6   Above note 2, s 5(1), and see ss 2(1) and 17(1). Specific provisions relate to variation of support orders in cross-border situations: see ss 17.1 and 18–19; see also *Chree v Chree*, 2015 ONSC 6480 [*Chree*].
7   See the discussion in Chapter 2 and Chapter 22.
8   *Murphy v Wulkowicz*, [2003] NSJ No 324 (SC); *Jenkins v Jenkins* (2000), 8 RFL (5th) 96 (Ont SCJ).
9   (1976), 13 OR (2d) 233 (CA).
10 (1981), 49 NSR (2d) 202 (SCTD).

province in order to apply for corollary relief. The analysis of ordinary residence is highly fact-specific.[11]

2) Support Orders and Foreign Divorces

The *Divorce Act* does not authorize a Canadian court to grant corollary relief in respect of a foreign divorce.[12] In *V(LR) v V(AA)* the British Columbia Court of Appeal outlined the historical evolution of the jurisdictional rules in the *Divorce Act*, noting that prior to amendments made in 1993, it granted jurisdiction to the court to determine corollary relief only where the court itself had granted the divorce.[13] The broader provisions of the current section 4, which give the court jurisdiction where either spouse is ordinarily resident in a province or where both spouses accept the jurisdiction of the court, had led some commentators to suggest that the amendment was sufficiently broad to enable a foreign divorcee to institute support proceedings under section 15 if he or she was now ordinarily resident in Canada.[14] However, the British Columbia Court of Appeal held that there was nothing in the statute to lead to the conclusion that Parliament intended to give jurisdiction to a Canadian court to grant corollary relief with respect to a foreign divorce.[15] Just as Canadian courts do not have jurisdiction to grant corollary relief in respect of a foreign divorce, they also are not authorized to vary the corollary relief granted by a foreign court in conjunction with the foreign divorce.[16] This is so even where both parties reside in the province and have consented to the court's jurisdiction.[17]

This situation likely reflects the constitutional limitations on the authority that the federal Parliament has over support obligations. In *Rothgiesser v Rothgiesser* the Ontario Court of Appeal held that "any attempt to

---

11 See, for example, *Quigley v Willmore*, 2008 NSCA 33 at para 21; *Nafie v Badawy*, 2015 ABCA 36.
12 *Wlodarczyk v Spriggs* (2000), 200 Sask R 129 (UFC); *Jahangiri-Mavaneh v Taheri-Zengekani* (2003), 66 OR (3d) 272 (SCJ), rev'd on other grounds (2005), 14 RFL (6th) 9 (Ont CA); *V(LR) v V(AA)* (2006), 52 BCLR (4th) 112 (CA) [*V(LR)*]; *Stefanou v Stefanou*, 2012 ONSC 7265 at paras 162–70. These cases cast doubt on the correctness of the approach taken in *OM v AK — Droit de la famille 3148* (SOQUIJ) (2000), 9 RFL (5th) 111 (Que SC).
13 *Ibid*. See also *Arsenault*, above note 4.
14 See Julien Payne, *Payne on Divorce*, 4th ed (Scarborough: Carswell, 1996) at 17.
15 *V(LR)*, above note 12 at para 59.
16 *Rothgiesser v Rothgiesser* (2000), 46 OR (3d) 577 (CA); *Okmayansky v Okmayansky* (2007), 86 OR (3d) 587 (CA); *Trotter v Trotter* (1992), 90 DLR (4th) 554 (Ont Ct Gen Div).
17 *Leonard v Booker* (2007), 321 NBR (2d) 340 (CA).

deal with support obligations in the absence of a Canadian divorce would encroach on provincial jurisdiction (s. 92, 'Property and Civil Rights').[18] Although the British Columbia Court of Appeal in V(LR) did not specifically rule on the constitutional question, it also conceded that "much can be said for the proposition that such an enactment would be invading provincial jurisdiction over 'property and civil rights in the Province.'"[19]

Although a court cannot address support obligations under the *Divorce Act* if the divorce was granted in a foreign jurisdiction, support can be available to a foreign divorcee who is now resident in Canada. To obtain it, he or she must rely on the provincial jurisdiction over support.[20]

C. PROVINCIAL JURISDICTION

In most provinces, both federally and provincially appointed judges may adjudicate spousal and child support claims that arise independently of divorce. Separated spouses who are not divorced may seek support under provincial legislation. This legislation also applies to unmarried cohabiting partners of the opposite or same sex and to children of unmarried parents. Spouses divorced outside Canada and spouses divorced inside Canada who do not seek a support order as part of the divorce proceedings or as a corollary relief proceeding under the *Divorce Act* can also use the provincial legislation.

The provincial statutes that provide for spousal support vary widely in the specifics of the support provisions.[21] However, none impose any particular jurisdictional requirements. For example, the Ontario *Family Law Act* simply provides that "[a] court may, on application, order a person to provide support."[22] There is no domicile or residency requirement. The same is also true for applications to vary support orders.[23]

This broad jurisdiction must be exercised consistently with the more general principles of adjudicatory jurisdiction discussed in Chapter 5. In

---

18 Above note 16 at para 59.
19 Above note 12 at para 60.
20 See *RNS v KS*, 2013 BCCA 406 at paras 34–42.
21 See, for example, the *Family Law Act*, SBC 2011, c 25 [*FLA* (BC)]; *Family Law Act*, RSO 1990, c F.3 [*FLA* (Ont)]; *The Family Maintenance Act, 1997*, SS 1997, c F-6.2.
22 *FLA* (Ont), above note 21, s 33(1). See also *FLA* (BC), above note 21, ss 149 and 165. Provisions in the family law rules in some provinces that require a case to be started in the municipality where a party resides (see, for example, *Family Law Rules*, O Reg 114/99, r 5(1)) should not in themselves be seen as imposing a residency requirement.
23 See, for example, *FLA* (Ont), above note 21, s 37; *FLA* (BC), above note 21, ss 152 and 167.

other words, jurisdiction must be established under the province's general statute on jurisdiction, if it has one, or be founded on presence, submission, or a real and substantial connection to the province.[24] In the wake of *Club Resorts Ltd v Van Breda*, courts would seem to need to identify a presumptive connecting factor for the latter basis.[25] However, some decisions continue to refer only to a real and substantial connection.[26] Particular presumptive connecting factors will continue to be developed by the courts for the family law context.[27] This broad jurisdiction also means that the doctrine of *forum non conveniens*, discussed in Chapter 6, is often relevant since the respondent can allege that another jurisdiction is better suited to resolve the issue of support. The general approach to this doctrine is routinely applied to family law disputes including those about support.[28]

For spousal support, the *Divorce Act* gives the court jurisdiction only to grant lump sum or periodic payments.[29] On the other hand, most provincial support statutes confer broader powers on the courts with respect to the types of orders that can be granted.[30] Relief under provincial statutes can include lump sum and periodic payments but also transfers or settlements of property, possession of the matrimonial home, security for support payments, and designation of a spouse as a beneficiary under a life insurance policy or pension plan. For child support, there is greater uniformity in the available remedies as between federal and provincial law.

If there is a valid foreign support order, it cannot be avoided by commencing new proceedings for support under the provincial legislation.[31] The proper approach is to apply to vary the foreign order. In some situations this may be possible in the local forum. The most common situation is under the interjurisdictional support order scheme, discussed below.[32] In addition, if variation of not only child support but

---

24 See, for example, *Jasen v Karassik* (2009), 95 OR (3d) 430 at para 16 (CA) [*Jasen*]; *AG v LS* (2006), 397 AR 296 at para 15 (CA); *Kasprzyk v Burks* (2005), 15 RFL (6th) 221 at para 13 (Ont SCJ).
25 2012 SCC 17. See the discussion in Chapter 5.
26 See *Navarro v Parrish*, 2014 ONCA 856 [*Navarro*].
27 See, for example, *Ghaeinizadeh v Ku De Ta Capital Inc*, 2013 ONCA 2 at para 15; *Knowles v Lindstrom*, 2014 ONCA 116 [*Knowles*]; *Wang v Lin*, 2013 ONCA 33 at para 47.
28 See, for example, *Follwell v Holmes*, [2006] OJ No 4387 at paras 26–27 (SCJ); *Stefanou v Stefanou*, [2009] OJ No 852 (CA), rev'g (2008), 50 RFL (6th) 345 (Ont SCJ); *Sun v Guilfoile*, 2011 ONSC 1685 [*Sun*].
29 Above note 2, s 15(1).
30 See, for example, *FLA* (Ont), above note 21, s 34(1); *FLA* (BC), above note 21, s 170.
31 See, for example, *Sun*, above note 28 at paras 39–55; *Kaur v Guraya*, 2011 ONSC 2853 at paras 20–22 [*Kaur*].
32 See, for example, *Besha v Lisanework*, 2010 BCCA 580 at paras 23–25.

also child custody is sought, it appears that the court may be willing to vary the support order.[33] Outside these situations, the variation must be sought in the foreign forum.

While there is broad jurisdiction to make and vary support orders under provincial family law legislation, there is one important qualification. As discussed in the next section, specific statutes have been enacted to address cross-border cases involving support obligations. These statutes raise the issue of whether they are complete codes in this area so that when they apply they must be used rather than other, more general family law statutes. If they are complete codes, this restricts, for example, the ability of an applicant to seek support in a province through direct proceedings there with the intention of enforcing the resulting order in another province. The province's court will refuse to allow such a proceeding and will instead insist that the statutory process be followed.

The cases on this issue are not uniform. Earlier courts had proceeded as though these statutes were not an exclusive regime.[34] Since then some courts have held that the statutes provide a comprehensive and exclusive scheme for dealing with interjurisdictional support orders.[35] In *Jasen v Karassik*, the Ontario Superior Court held that these specific statutes must be used when they apply and recourse cannot be had instead to the more general provisions discussed above.[36] However, this decision was overturned by the Court of Appeal. It held that a resident of Ontario may bring an application for support or variation of a support agreement under either the province's general family law legislation or the interjurisdictional support legislation, for two reasons.[37] First, not only did the latter not indicate that resort to the former was precluded, it expressly preserved the continued availability of remedies under other legislation. Second, applicants should not be precluded from seeking remedies in their own domestic courts. This has become the dominant view.

In contrast, there are British Columbia decisions that appear to hold that the interjurisdictional support legislation is a complete code and

---

33 Variation of custody orders is discussed in Chapter 24. See *Kaur*, above note 31 at paras 20–26; *Gavriluke v Mainard*, 2012 ONSC 6928 at paras 32–33, aff'd 2013 ONSC 2337 (Div Ct). In these cases the court has made a new support order and insisted on an undertaking that enforcement of the original order will not be attempted. This approach was doubted in *Mittoo v Nanda*, 2015 ONCJ 401.
34 *Humphries v Rokoss*, [2004] OJ No 4658 (Ct J); *Bouchard v Ouellet* (2005), 15 RFL (6th) 77 (Ont Ct J).
35 *V(LR)*, above note 12 at para 62.
36 *Jasen v Karassik* (2008), 92 OR (3d) 283 (SCJ).
37 *Jasen*, above note 24 at para 56. See also *Navarro*, above note 26; and *Krushelinski v Wehner*, 2015 SKQB 195.

that the more general provincial family law legislation cannot be used to obtain a support order.[38] But in these cases the court did not have jurisdiction, on the facts, under the more general legislation, leaving the interjurisdictional support legislation as the only option available.

1) Interjurisdictional Support Orders Statutes

In response to many difficulties with respect to jurisdiction, choice of law, and enforcement of interjurisdictional child and spousal support orders, in 2001 Canadian provinces began implementing a uniform and simplified regime to streamline the making and enforcement of interprovincial and foreign support orders. This legislation is almost uniformly titled the *Interjurisdictional Support Orders Act* and is nearly identical in each common law province.[39] Under the interjurisdictional support order (ISO) statutes, the regulations contain a list of reciprocating jurisdictions. In addition to all other Canadian provinces and territories, the reciprocating jurisdictions for most provinces include the United States, Australia, the United Kingdom, several other European countries, and some countries from other parts of the world.[40]

The purpose of the ISO regime is to avoid making people travel to another jurisdiction to obtain, enforce, or defend against support orders while at the same time ensuring that each party is provided with an adequate opportunity to present his or her case. Under the previous legislation in this area, two hearings were required: one in the jurisdiction of the individual seeking the support and the other, the "confirmation hearing," in the jurisdiction of the payor. A key element of the new ISO regime removes the need for a two-stage hearing process. Now, a court in the originating jurisdiction does not hold a hearing: only the court in the receiving jurisdiction does so.

a) Claimant in the Province

A claimant who is ordinarily resident in a province can start a proceeding in that province aiming to obtain a support order in respect of a person ordinarily resident in a reciprocating jurisdiction.[41] Under this process, the support order is made by the court in the reciprocating jurisdiction. The application is submitted to the province's designated

---

38 See the analysis in *Cockerham v Hanc*, 2014 BCSC 2432 at paras 78–93.
39 See, for example, the *Interjurisdictional Support Orders Act*, SBC 2002, c 29 [*ISOA* (BC)]; *Interjurisdictional Support Orders Act*, SA 2002, c I-3.5; *Interjurisdictional Support Orders Act, 2002*, SO 2002, c 13 [*ISOA* (Ont)].
40 See, for example, *Reciprocating Jurisdictions*, O Reg 53/03.
41 See, for example, *ISOA* (Ont), above note 39, s 5(1).

authority.⁴² This is an administrative process and does not require starting court proceedings. The support application must include the claimant's name and address, a copy of the statutory or other legal authority on which the application is based if it is not the law of the jurisdiction in which the respondent resides, the particulars of the support being claimed, and an affidavit. The affidavit must set out the respondent's name and identifying or locating information, the respondent's financial circumstances, the name of each person for whom support is claimed and the birthdates of children for whom support is claimed, details of the claimant's or child's financial circumstances, and evidence that establishes entitlement to and the amount of support.⁴³

The designated authority then forwards the application to the designated authority in the reciprocating jurisdiction, where its courts follow their own procedures and make an order as to the claimant's entitlement to and quantum of support.⁴⁴ Although the ISO statutes no longer require a preliminary order to be made in the originating jurisdiction, if the reciprocating jurisdiction requires one, the court in the province may, taking into account the legal authority on which the application is based, make such a provisional order without notice to the respondent and forward that order to the reciprocating court.⁴⁵

b) **Respondent in the Province**

A claimant residing in a reciprocating jurisdiction who wishes to obtain support from a person ordinarily resident in a province starts the process by following the appropriate procedure in the jurisdiction where the claimant resides. This can involve either obtaining a provisional support order from the local court or filing an application with a designated authority. When the designated authority of a province receives a support application from a reciprocating jurisdiction it is required to verify that the respondent is resident in the province. If he or she is, the designated authority sends the application to the court. If the authority has information that the respondent resides in another province, it transfers the application to that province. If the authority is unable to locate the respondent, it returns the application to the originating jurisdiction.⁴⁶

---

42 See, for example, *ibid*, s 6(1).
43 See, for example, *ibid*, ss 5(2) & (3).
44 See, for example, *ibid*, ss 6(2)(b) and (4).
45 See, for example, *ibid*, s 7. It appears that the law to be applied in making such a provisional order is the law of the forum: see *Lei v Kwan*, 2010 MBCA 108.
46 See, for example, *ISOA* (Ont), above note 39, s 9.

If the application is sent to the court, the clerk of the court serves the respondent with the application and notice to appear.[47] The court holds a hearing and decides the application based on the information received in the initial application, information submitted by the respondent, and any additional information that the court requests from the claimant.[48] The court may make a support order, adjourn the hearing with or without an interim support order, or refuse to make a support order.[49] The court may make an order in the absence of the respondent.[50] Any order made by the court is provided to the province's designated authority which in turn transmits the order back to the designated authority in the originating jurisdiction.[51] The transmission process does not make the order one by the courts of the originating jurisdiction: it remains an order of the province.

c) **Variation Orders**

The ISO statutes also provide a mechanism to vary existing support orders made in another jurisdiction. The mechanism is very similar to the process by which people either inside or outside a province obtain their initial support order. A person ordinarily resident in a province who wants a support order concerning a respondent ordinarily resident in a reciprocating jurisdiction varied by that jurisdiction can apply to the designated authority in the province.[52] The application is then processed much like an initial application for support. If the respondent no longer resides in a reciprocating jurisdiction, an applicant ordinarily resident in a province can instead apply directly to the court of the province to vary the order as long as the respondent is given notice of the application.[53] A person ordinarily resident in a reciprocating jurisdiction who wants a support order concerning a respondent ordinarily resident in a province varied by that province starts the process under the law of the reciprocating jurisdiction and, like an initial application, it is transmitted to the province's designated authority for processing in much the same way as an initial application.[54]

Despite the interjurisdictional process, orders under the ISO statutes remain the orders of the courts of the jurisdictions that issued

---

47 See, for example, *ibid*, s 10.
48 See, for example, *ibid*, s 11.
49 See, for example, *ibid*, s 14.
50 See, for example, *ibid*, s 15.
51 See, for example, *ibid*, ss 15(2) and 16.
52 See, for example, *ibid*, ss 27–28.
53 See, for example, *ibid*, s 29.
54 See, for example, *ibid*, ss 32–38.

them. They do not automatically have any effect in another jurisdiction. However, the statutes also provide for registration of support orders in order to aid enforcement. This is discussed later in this chapter. For present purposes, it is important to note that if a foreign support order has been registered in a province, it can then be varied by that province's courts. For this to happen, one of three conditions must be met: (1) both parties accept the court's jurisdiction, (2) both parties are ordinarily resident in the province, or (3) the respondent is ordinarily resident in the province and the applicant registered the support order under the ISO statute or its predecessor.[55] If this requirement can be met, it is probably easier for the applicant to have the local court vary the order than to use the interjurisdictional variation process outlined above. If this requirement cannot be met, it would seem open to the applicant to use that process. The fact that the foreign order has been registered would not seem to preclude doing so.[56]

The process for varying support orders under the ISO statutes does not apply to support orders made under the federal *Divorce Act*.[57] That statute has its own process for variation orders for situations in which the former spouses are in different provinces.[58]

D. CHOICE OF LAW

Under the common law, the law of the forum is generally applied to resolve issues of spousal and child support.[59] However, it is open to a party to argue that the issue should be resolved by another, more closely connected system of law. In *Kearney v Willis* the court considered choice of law separately from the issue of jurisdiction.[60] It applied the law of the forum, not automatically but because the child for whom support was sought had been born and raised there. It did not apply the law of the place where the respondent resided.

---

55 See, for example, *ibid*, s 39.
56 See, for example, *ibid*, s 24, which seems to contemplate a court in a reciprocating jurisdiction varying a support order that had been registered in a province.
57 See, for example, *CAE v MD*, 2011 NBCA 17 at paras 15 and 21; *Chree*, above note 6 at para 11.
58 Above note 2, ss 17–19.
59 In *Van de Perre v Edwards* (2004), 26 BCLR (4th) 380 (SC), the court, in making a support order, applied the law of the forum. It expressly indicated (at para 13) that it would, in its reasons, set out the forum law at length so that a foreign court asked to enforce the order would appreciate the basis on which the order was made.
60 (2001), 15 RFL (5th) 96 (Nfld UFC). See also *Knowles*, above note 27 at para 48.

The ISO statutes contain their own specific choice of law provisions. On an application for child support from a reciprocating jurisdiction, to determine entitlement to support the court must first apply the law of the jurisdiction where the child ordinarily resides. However, if the child is not entitled to support under that law, the court must instead apply the law of the forum. The amount of child support is determined by the law of the forum.[61] On an application from a reciprocating jurisdiction to vary a province's child support order, the same approach is used for the issue of entitlement. However, the amount of support is determined by applying the law of the jurisdiction where the payor ordinarily resides.[62]

On an application for spousal support from a reciprocating jurisdiction, to determine entitlement to support the court must first apply the law of the forum. However, if the applicant is not entitled to support under that law, the court must instead apply the law of the jurisdiction in which the parties last maintained a common habitual residence. The amount of spousal support is determined by the law of the forum.[63] On an application from a reciprocating jurisdiction to vary a province's spousal support order, entitlement to support is determined under the law of the forum. However, if the applicant is not entitled to support under that law, the court must instead apply the law of the jurisdiction where the applicant ordinarily resides. Furthermore, if there is no entitlement under that law, the court must then apply the law of the jurisdiction in which the parties last maintained a common habitual residence. The amount of spousal support is determined by the law of the forum.[64]

To assist the court in applying foreign law, the ISO statutes provide that courts are mandated to take judicial notice of the law of a reciprocating jurisdiction and to apply it where required. An enactment of a reciprocating jurisdiction can be pleaded and proven simply by producing a copy received from that jurisdiction.[65]

E. RECOGNITION AND ENFORCEMENT

1) Statutory Provisions

Section 20(2) of the *Divorce Act* provides that a support order or a variation order involving support made under the statute has legal effect

---

61 See, for example, *ISOA* (Ont), above note 39, s 13.
62 See, for example, *ibid*, s 35.
63 See, for example, *ibid*, s 13.
64 See, for example, *ibid*, s 35.
65 See, for example, *ibid*, s 47. This is in contrast to the general approach to pleading and proving foreign law discussed in Chapter 12.

throughout Canada. The order may be (1) registered in any court in a province and enforced as an order of that court or (2) enforced in any other manner provided by the laws of the province, including its laws respecting reciprocal enforcement between the province and a jurisdiction outside Canada.[66]

The provincial ISO statutes also address recognition and enforcement. If a person has a support order from a reciprocating jurisdiction, he or she can send a copy of that order to the designated authority in the province where the support payor ordinarily resides. On receipt, it is registered as an order of the court of that province and has the same effect as if it were an order made by that court.[67] Such an order can then be filed with the local support order enforcement authorities. If the foreign support order is from outside Canada, the designated authority notifies the respondent of the registration and he or she has thirty days to apply to have the registration set aside.[68] An order may be set aside on one of three grounds: (1) the respondent did not have proper notice or reasonable opportunity to be heard in the proceeding in which the foreign order was made, (2) the foreign order is contrary to public policy, and (3) the court that made the foreign order did not have jurisdiction to make the order.[69] As to the third of these, the statute provides that the foreign court has jurisdiction if both parties to the order ordinarily reside in the reciprocating jurisdiction or one of the parties is not ordinarily resident there but is subject to the jurisdiction of the court that made the order.[70]

Several cases have found that the respondent was not given notice or did not have a reasonable opportunity to be heard in the foreign court.[71] In some of these, the respondent did not participate in the foreign proceedings because of the prohibitive cost or difficulty of doing so.[72]

The public policy ground was considered in *Waszczyn v Waszczyn*, which concerned a support order issued by a Polish court.[73] While the court noted the need for caution in invoking this ground,[74] it nonethe-

---

66 Above note 2, s 20(3). This includes the Federal Court: *Young v Hubbert*, [1988] 1 FC 354 (TD).
67 See, for example, *ISOA* (Ont), above note 39, ss 17–19.
68 See, for example, *ibid*, ss 19(3) and 20.
69 See, for example, *ibid*, s 20(4)(b).
70 See, for example, *ibid*, s 20(6).
71 *Gal v Lukasiewcz*, [2008] OJ No 5358 (Ct J); *Nowosielska v Nowosielski*, [2004] OJ No 4702 (Ct J); *Szostek v Szostek*, 2011 ONCJ 663.
72 *Ziemianczyk v Ziemianczyk*, [2008] OJ No 1479 at paras 6–8 (Ct J) [*Ziemianczyk*]; *Waszczyn v Waszczyn* (2007), 45 RFL (6th) 441 at paras 8–10 (Ont Ct J).
73 *Ibid* at paras 11–13.
74 See *EK v DK* (2005), 43 BCLR (4th) 272 (CA).

less found that the order was against public policy. There was compelling evidence that the mother had fraudulently amended the child's birth certificate to represent to the Polish court that the respondent was the child's father, but he was not. In *Leger v Schultz* a German support order was set aside as against public policy because it was eighteen years old and enforcement was only being sought in order to seek revenge against the respondent.[75] In some recent cases, support awards that were significantly higher than what would have been awarded under the law of the forum in similar circumstances were held to violate the forum's public policy.[76]

In *Vargo v Saskatchewan (Family Justice Services Branch)* the issue was whether a registered North Dakota support order ought to be set aside for lack of jurisdiction.[77] The onus was on the respondent to establish a lack of jurisdiction and he failed to do so. Under North Dakota law there were several bases on which a court could assume jurisdiction over a non-resident for family law purposes. The fact that the North Dakota court had not specifically indicated the basis for its jurisdiction did not mean the judgment could not be registered.

If a registered order is set aside on any of the above grounds, the foreign order must then be dealt with under the ISO statute as if it were an application made by a person from outside the province for either an original support order or a variation order.[78]

2) At Common Law

As explained in Chapter 8, at common law a foreign judgment had to be a final order for a fixed sum of money before it could be enforced. Under this approach, orders for support are therefore not enforceable. They are not final, because they are subject to variation based on the changing means and needs of the parties. They are not for a fixed sum, because they provide for a series of periodic payments. Admittedly Canadian courts have consistently enforced foreign judgments for arrears of support since they are considered final and are for a fixed amount.[79] But this provides little real assistance, since a plaintiff would

---

75 (2006), 28 RFL (6th) 160 (Ont Ct J).
76 See, for example, *Hastings v Deakin*, 2014 ONCJ 618; *Ziemianczyk*, above note 72; *MWG v KAA*, 2012 NBQB 402.
77 (2006), 280 Sask R 28 (QB).
78 See, for example, ISOA (BC), above note 39, s 20; ISOA (Ont), above note 39, s 21. See *JCH v MBH* (2006), 27 RFL (6th) 218 (BC Prov Ct).
79 *Swaizie v Swaizie* (1899), 31 OR 324 (Div Ct); *Burchell v Burchell*, [1926] 2 DLR 595 (Ont HCJ); *Lear v Lear* (1974), 5 OR (2d) 572 (CA). See, however, *Small v Zacher* (1975), 8 OR (2d) 372 (HCJ).

have to allow arrears of unpaid support to build up before being able to sue and obtain an enforceable judgment. Reciprocal enforcement legislation, discussed above, was developed to address the common law's difficulties with enforcement.

Although the ISO statutes provide a mechanism for enforcing support orders from reciprocating jurisdictions,[80] the principles of the common law still apply to other jurisdictions throughout the world. This means support recipients face considerable difficulties enforcing support orders from non-reciprocating jurisdictions, such that the only viable solution may be to sue for support in the jurisdiction where the other party resides. As suggested in Chapter 8, Canadian courts are continuing to develop the common law on the enforcement of foreign judgments, so that in the future it may be possible to enforce a foreign support order.

FURTHER READINGS

BALA, NICHOLAS J, THOMAS OLDHAM, & ALISON PERRY. "Regulating Cross-Border Child Support within Federated Systems: The United States, Canada and the European Union" (2005) 15 *Transnational Law & Contemporary Problems* 87.

RAMANATHAN, SEETHA. "The *Interjurisdictional Support Orders Act* and the Concept of Judicial Notice" (2003) 27 *Advocates' Quarterly* 205.

WALSWORTH, LYNN. "Interprovincial Enforcement of Maintenance Orders: New Principles, New Approaches" (1997) 20 *Dalhousie Law Journal* 197.

---

80 As discussed in Section C(1), above in this chapter, if this mechanism is mandatory in situations covered by these statutes, enforcement will not be available at common law. If it is not, there is more scope to use the common law.

CHAPTER 26

MATRIMONIAL PROPERTY

A. INTRODUCTION

Most legal systems have laws that address the division of the property of spouses on the dissolution of their marriage. For example, after a lengthy marriage, most of the property—all immovable property and all significant movable property—might be owned by one of the spouses. When the marriage ends, it is unfair for that person to retain all of that property. Accordingly, some division of the spouses' matrimonial property is necessary. If they cannot resolve the division themselves, court proceedings will be required.

Similar issues can arise on the dissolution of a common law relationship. Absent specific statutory provisions,[1] a claim to property division in this context is treated by the common law as an unjust enrichment claim. Such claims are examined in Chapter 15.[2]

While it is common to refer to this process as a division of matrimonial property, it is unusual in practice for the court to make an order that specific items of property are owned, going forward, by one spouse or the other. The property is not divided in that way. The typical order simply requires the spouse owning more of the matrimonial property

---

1 See, for example, *The Family Property Act*, CCSM c F25, s 2.1.
2 See, for example, *Christopher v Zimmerman*, 2000 BCCA 532; *Knowles v Lindstrom*, 2014 ONCA 116.

to pay the amount of money to the other spouse required to equalize or share the property's value between them.

B. JURISDICTION

A court can have jurisdiction over a matrimonial property dispute under the general rules of jurisdiction or under a specific provincial statute. A court might also have jurisdiction under the *Divorce Act*.[3]

In the absence of a more specific basis for jurisdiction, the general rules apply. Those rules are set out in detail in Chapter 5. A key issue, discussed in that chapter, is the extent to which the general rules might be developed in the family law context. In particular, under the approach in *Club Resorts Ltd v Van Breda*,[4] either at common law or under a province's *Court Jurisdiction and Proceedings Transfer Act*,[5] courts will need to formulate presumptive connecting factors for matrimonial property disputes.

Some provinces have specific provisions on jurisdiction. For example, under the Alberta *Matrimonial Property Act* a spouse can apply for an order dividing matrimonial property only if (1) the habitual residence of both spouses, whether living together or apart, is in Alberta; (2) the last joint habitual residence of the spouses was in Alberta; or (3) the habitual residence of both spouses at the time of marriage was in Alberta and they have not since established a joint habitual residence.[6] A specific provision such as this one is not an alternative to the general rules on jurisdiction; rather, it overrides them.[7]

A different kind of provision on jurisdiction is found in the British Columbia *Family Law Act*.[8] Section 106 applies only if an order respecting

---

3   RSC 1985, c 3 (2nd Supp).
4   2012 SCC 17.
5   See, for example, *The Court Jurisdiction and Proceedings Transfer Act*, SS 1997, c C-41.1.
6   RSA 2000, c M-8, s 3(1). See also *The Family Property Act*, above note 1, ss 2(1) and 2.1(1). These provisions were interpreted in *Adderson v Adderson* (1987), 51 Alta LR (2d) 193 (CA); and *Wolch v Wolch* (1980), 19 RFL (2d) 307 (Man QB), var'd (1981), 20 RFL (2d) 325 (Man CA) [*Wolch*]. See also *Marital Property Act*, SNB 2012, c 107, s 44.
7   *Wolch*, above note 6. For the contrary view, see Janet Walker, *Castel & Walker: Canadian Conflict of Laws*, 6th ed (Markham, ON: LexisNexis Butterworths, 2005) (loose-leaf) at para 25.2.b: "When the statutory jurisdiction threshold is not met, it should still be possible for the courts . . . to take jurisdiction under general jurisdiction rules."
8   SBC 2011, c 25. The key provisions of this statute came into force in 2013.

property division may be made in more than one jurisdiction. If so, one of the specified bases for jurisdiction must be satisfied before the court can make such an order. The bases are quite broad: for example, one is either spouse being habitually resident in the province and another is a real and substantial connection between the province and the facts on which the proceeding is based. Such a connection is presumed if, *inter alia*, there is property at issue located in the province.[9]

As explained in earlier chapters, the *Divorce Act* provides a court with jurisdiction not only over the divorce but also over corollary relief proceedings. These are defined as proceedings for support or custody, so they do not include matrimonial property division.[10] There is some debate about whether a court with jurisdiction to grant a divorce, as explained in Chapter 22, can also divide matrimonial property. In *Hunter v Hunter* the court had divorce jurisdiction but held it did not have jurisdiction over the property division,[11] and in *Theriault v Theriault* the court had divorce jurisdiction but separately analyzed whether it had jurisdiction over the matrimonial property division claim under the general rules.[12] But it has been argued that, in the interests of procedural efficiency, a court with divorce jurisdiction should be viewed as having jurisdiction to divide matrimonial property.[13] In some provinces, such as Alberta, this is expressly provided for by legislation.[14] This issue could be resolved by a court concluding, under the general rules set out in Chapter 5, that one year's ordinary residence in the province by either spouse prior to the proceedings constitutes a presumptive connecting factor for a matrimonial property division claim.

Because matrimonial property can include immovable property, the issue of jurisdiction over foreign immovable property arises in this context. This issue is discussed in Chapter 17. As noted there, as a general rule a court will not make an order in respect of foreign immovable property.[15] However, the court can rely on the exception to this rule for cases in which it has *in personam* jurisdiction over the defendant such that its order in respect of the division of foreign immovable property can be effectively enforced locally.[16] It can also indirectly address

---

9   See, for example, *Monteiro v Monteiro*, 2015 BCSC 1543.
10 Above note 3, s 2(1).
11 2005 SKCA 76.
12 2014 SKQB 373.
13 Vaughan Black, "Choice of Law and Territorial Jurisdiction of Courts in Family Law Matters" (2013) 32 *Canadian Family Law Quarterly* 53 at 64.
14 *Matrimonial Property Act*, above note 6, s 3(2).
15 *British South Africa Co v Companhia de Moçambique*, [1893] AC 602 (HL); *Duke v Andler*, [1932] SCR 734.
16 See, for example, *Macedo v Macedo* (1996), 19 RFL (4th) 65 (Ont Ct Gen Div).

foreign immovable property by taking its value into account when making an order either requiring the transfer of other assets such as immovable property in the province or requiring the payment of money.[17] Both of these issues are explicitly addressed in some of the provincial legislation.[18]

C. CHOICE OF LAW

1) At Common Law

Understandably, the choice of law rules for the division of matrimonial property have historically reflected a tension between those for contract and those for property.[19] Possible applicable laws include the law governing the marriage, the personal law of the parties at the time of its dissolution, and the law of the place where property is located. In *Devos v Devos* the Ontario Court of Appeal suggested a contractual approach, looking to the law that governed the marriage.[20] In contrast, in *Palmer v Palmer* the Saskatchewan Court of Appeal held, in a dispute between spouses resident in Manitoba, that Saskatchewan law applied to a property division claim related to immovable property in that province.[21] It did not apply the law of the marriage or the personal law of either spouse.

In *Tezcan v Tezcan* the parties were both Turkish citizens who had married and divorced in Turkey.[22] They owned real property in British Columbia but most of their assets were in Turkey. Ms Tezcan sued in British Columbia seeking property division. The British Columbia

---

17 See, for example, *Laurence v Laurence* (1991), 56 BCLR (2d) 254 (CA); *Tezcan v Tezcan* (1992), 62 BCLR (2d) 344 (CA) [*Tezcan*]; *Hlynski v Hlynski* (1999), 180 Sask R 1 (CA).
18 See, for example, *Family Law Act*, above note 8, s 109. This provision was considered in *Slavenova v Ranguelov*, 2015 BCSC 79.
19 See Black, above note 13 at 74–75.
20 [1970] 2 OR 323 (CA) [*Devos*], relying on *De Nicols v Curlier*, [1900] AC 21 (HL). In some cases, the court suggests that there is an implied marriage contract between the spouses under which they agree to divide property on dissolution in accordance with the law of the marriage. The notion of an implied contract has been criticized (see Bruce Welling, "Conflict of Laws Issues Arising from Matrimonial Property Statutes in Canada" (1993) 9 *Canadian Family Law Quarterly* 225 at 239–40) and has not been relied on in the recent jurisprudence. In the absence of an express contract, the court should objectively identify the law to govern the property division claim.
21 (1979), 2 Sask R 112 (CA).
22 Above note 17.

Court of Appeal analyzed whether this was a matrimonial or a property claim, concluding that it was the latter. As a result, the *lex situs* governed the claim to division of immovable property in the province. The court rejected a contractual approach which would have applied Turkish law. It could be argued that this conclusion is based on a particular aspect of British Columbia's legislation on matrimonial property division. The court noted that

> [t]he rights which arise by operation of the *Family Relations Act* [now the *Family Law Act*] are not simply matrimonial rights between the parties *inter se*. Part 3 of the Act differs from other similar Canadian enactments which create only a payment obligation between spouses and do not, as does the British Columbia statute, create interests in real property. Upon dissolution of the marriage the Act operates to vest a proprietary interest in land in the non-titled spouse which would be recognized in the land titles system and affect title in respect of all persons.[23]

This does strengthen the rationale for a property law approach, but it should not be understood as the determinative consideration. Even absent this particular legislation it is open for a court to adopt a property law approach. Indeed, in *Tezcan* the court does so even before noting the effect of the province's legislation.

On a property approach, it is clear that the *lex situs* governs division of immovable property. The law governing division of movable property is less clear. Options include the law of the spouses' first common domicile, the law of their last common domicile, or the law with which the marriage has its closest connection. In *Tezcan* the court stated that claims to movable property are governed by the law of the matrimonial domicile,[24] which would seem to mean the domicile of the parties at the time of the dissolution since the matrimonial domicile can change over the course of a marriage.

There are problems with both the contract and the property approaches. The property approach suffers from many of the shortcomings seen in the succession context, discussed in Chapter 19, including using different choice of law rules for immovable and movable property. The contract approach can lead to the application of a law not reasonably contemplated by the parties. Spouses might marry in one country, under its law, and then live their lives and acquire their property in another country. When the marriage ends and division issues arise,

---

23   *Ibid* at 353–54.
24   *Ibid* at 352.

arguably it would violate reasonable expectations to resolve them by the law of the first country rather than the second.

As a result of these difficulties, most provinces have reformed the choice of law rules for matrimonial property by legislation. Saskatchewan is the only province still using the common law rules, although British Columbia did so until 2013. It is an open question as to whether the common law rules might, by judicial evolution, be reformed along similar lines.

2) Statutory Rules

In most provinces, statutes have changed the choice of law analysis in one of two ways. In those provinces that have enacted specific provisions on jurisdiction for matrimonial property disputes, discussed above, the court has applied the law of the forum if it has jurisdiction without engaging in a separate choice of law analysis.[25]

In other provinces, the legislation contains specific choice of law provisions. While the provisions differ somewhat, in general the choice of law rule adopted is to use the law of the last common habitual residence of the parties. In Ontario, for example, the statute provides that the "property rights of spouses arising out of the marital relationship are governed by the internal law of the place where both spouses had their last common habitual residence or, if there is no place where the spouses had a common habitual residence, by the law of Ontario."[26] The meaning of habitual residence is explained in Chapter 2. Use of the last common habitual residence as the connecting factor for matrimonial property has been well received. There is more scope, however, to criticize use of the law of the forum in cases in which the parties did not have a common habitual residence. Some other system of law may have a stronger connection to the marriage and so a better claim to govern the distribution of matrimonial property.

In British Columbia the choice of law rule adopted in the *Family Law Act* is more detailed. It gives priority to an initial "regime of community of property," which is a defined term. It provides that

> if the spouses' first common habitual residence during the relationship between the spouses was in a jurisdiction in which a regime of

---

25 See Walker, above note 7 at para 25.2.b.
26 *Family Law Act*, RSO 1990, c F.3, s 15. The *Matrimonial Property Act*, RSNS 1989, c 275, s 22, is very similar but does not include reference to the "internal" law. It has been held that this omission allows a court to apply the doctrine of *renvoi*, discussed in Chapter 10: *Vladi v Vladi* (1987), 79 NSR (2d) 356 (SCTD).

community of property applies, property owned or acquired and debt owing or acquired during the relationship between the spouses that is property or debt to which the regime of community of property applies must be divided at the end of the relationship between the spouses according to that regime of community of property.[27]

Otherwise, the applicable law is that of the jurisdiction in which the spouses had their most recent common habitual residence, subject to two exceptions. First, if that jurisdiction is outside Canada and is not the jurisdiction most closely associated with the relationship between the spouses, the law of the jurisdiction that is most closely associated with the relationship between the spouses applies. Second, if the spouses did not have a common habitual residence, the law of the jurisdiction in which the spouse applying for an order was most recently habitually resident governs.[28] The British Columbia rule is based on a model statute, the *Jurisdiction and Choice of Law Rules in Domestic Property Proceedings Act*, proposed in 1997 by the Uniform Law Conference of Canada.

3) Marriage Contracts

Spouses can contract, in advance, about the division of their property on the dissolution of the marriage. Such agreements are typically called marriage contracts, though the term "prenuptial agreement" is also used. In *Devos* the Ontario Court of Appeal confirmed that it "is settled in English law that where there is a marriage contract, the terms of the contract govern the mutual rights of husband and wife in respect of the property affected by the contract which may be then possessed or afterwards acquired."[29] This is also acknowledged in the provincial statutes. For example, the British Columbia legislation provides that "if spouses make an agreement respecting the division of property or debt, the substantive rights of the spouses . . . are determined by the agreement."[30] However, under some provincial statutes the court retains the power to override the contract and divide the property in some other way.[31]

If the contract does not address the issue of matrimonial property division, it plays no role. For example, in *Assinck v Assinck* the court

---

27 Above note 8, ss 108(1) and (5).
28 *Ibid*, ss 108(6) and 107. See *Parker v Mitchell*, 2016 BCSC 723 at paras 30–40.
29 Above note 20 at 330.
30 *Family Law Act*, above note 8, s 108(3). However, under s 108(4) the enforcement of such an agreement is subject to any restriction that the proper law of the relationship places on the spouses' ability to determine the division of property or debt by agreement.
31 *Ibid*, s 93.

held that the contract between the spouses did not address the economic consequences to flow from the dissolution of the marriage and as a result it could not override the legislative scheme.[32]

As noted in *Devos*, the "marriage contract will be construed with reference to the proper law of the contract."[33] This approach is preserved in the provincial legislation. For example, in Ontario the *Family Law Act* provides that the "manner and formalities of making a domestic contract and its essential validity and effect are governed by the proper law of the contract," subject to some exceptions.[34]

The notion of the proper law of the contract is explained in Chapter 14. If the parties have expressly chosen a governing law, that choice is given effect as the proper law.[35] In the absence of an express choice, historically the courts started from the presumption that the contract was governed by the husband's domicile at the time of marriage.[36] This presumption has increasingly been treated as quite easy to rebut, and in *Sangi v Sangi* the court rejected it as outdated.[37] The court considered that it could start with the law of the matrimonial domicile at the time of the marriage if, considered separately, each spouse had the same domicile as the other. It appeared both spouses had been domiciled in Iran. Despite this, the court's central concern was to identify the system of law with the closest and most real connection to the contract, which, on the facts, it found was Iran.

As discussed in Chapter 14, not all issues will necessarily be governed by the proper law of the contract. One such issue is the capacity to enter into a marriage contract. In *Charron v Montreal Trust Co* the court considered the issue of capacity to enter into a separation agreement, made by the parties after twelve years of marriage.[38] It held that the issue was to be determined by the proper law of the contract. However, in passing it noted that for marriage and "marriage settlements" capacity was generally governed by the law of the party's domicile.[39]

---

32 [1998] OJ No 875 (Gen Div). See also *Webster v Webster Estate* (2006), 28 RFL (6th) 79 (Ont SCJ).
33 Above note 20 at 330. See also *Vien Estate v Vien Estate* (1988), 64 OR (2d) 230 (CA).
34 Above note 26, s 58.
35 *Re Jutras*, [1932] 2 WWR 533 at 536 (Sask CA). See, for example, *Friedl v Friedl*, 2009 BCCA 314, in which the contract provided that it was governed by German law.
36 *Devos*, above note 20 at 330.
37 2011 BCSC 523 at paras 204–20.
38 [1958] OR 597 (CA).
39 *Ibid* at 603.

Another issue is the contract's formal validity. If a province's legislation sets out formal validity requirements for a marriage contract,[40] there is an issue as to whether they apply regardless of the contract's applicable law. One of the most stringent requirements is in the Alberta statute. It provides that a marriage contract is enforceable only if each spouse has separately acknowledged, in writing and before an independent lawyer, that he or she is aware of the nature and the effect of the agreement, is aware of the possible future claims to property the spouse may have under the statute and intends to give up these claims to the extent necessary to give effect to the agreement, and is executing the agreement voluntarily.[41] There is little objection to applying these requirements to a marriage contract that is governed by Alberta law, but it is more controversial to apply them to a marriage contract governed by a different system of law. Spouses might make a marriage contract in California, formally valid under California law, and then move to Alberta and reside there for many years. On the dissolution of the marriage, it would be odd to hold, in Alberta proceedings, that the contract cannot be enforced.

In some cases, courts have faced the threshold issue of whether a particular arrangement under a foreign legal system is to be treated as a marriage contract or is something different. In *Amlani v Hirani*, as part of an Islamic wedding ceremony, Mr Amlani agreed to pay a sum of money to Ms Hirani by way of "Maher."[42] The British Columbia Supreme Court had to determine whether to treat this as a marriage contract governing property division on the dissolution of the marriage. The contract did not specify when the amount was to be paid. Mr Amlani's evidence was that the Maher "is a traditional custom of Muslim law that was intended to provide financial compensation for a wife and children in the event of a marriage break-up."[43] The court accepted this evidence and treated the Maher as a marriage contract.

D. RECOGNITION AND ENFORCEMENT

Unlike custody or support orders, there are no special common law or statutory rules dealing with the recognition and enforcement of a matrimonial property division order. Such orders are recognized and enforced in accordance with the general rules set out in Chapter 8.

---

40   See, for example, *Family Law Act*, above note 26, s 55.
41   *Matrimonial Property Act*, above note 6, s 38.
42   2000 BCSC 1653. See also *Ghaznavi v Kashif-Ul-Haque*, 2011 ONSC 4062.
43   *Ibid* at para 28.

FURTHER READINGS

BLACK, VAUGHAN. "*Tezcan v. Tezcan*: Choice of Law in Matrimonial Property" (1993) 9 *Canadian Family Law Quarterly* 293.

BRITISH COLUMBIA LAW INSTITUTE. *The Need for Uniform Jurisdiction and Choice of Law Rules in Domestic Property Proceedings* (Vancouver: British Columbia Law Institute, 1998).

JAMAL, FAREEN L. "Enforcing Mahr in Canadian Courts" (2013) 32 *Canadian Family Law Quarterly* 97.

MCLEOD, JAMES G. "The Judicial Approach to Matrimonial Property Disputes and the Conflict of Laws" (1993) 9 *Canadian Family Law Quarterly* 203.

MCLEOD, JAMES G ET AL. *Matrimonial Property Law in Canada* (Toronto: Thomson Reuters Canada, 1993) (loose-leaf).

RAFFERTY, NICHOLAS. "Matrimonial Property and the Conflict of Laws" (1982) 20 *University of Western Ontario Law Review* 177.

TABLE OF CASES

2106701 Ontario Inc v 2288450 Ontario Limited, 2016 ONSC 2673 288
2249659 Ontario Ltd v Sparkasse Siegen, 2013 ONCA 354 .... 70, 96, 131
243930 Alberta Ltd v Wickham (1990), 75 OR (2d) 289,
    73 DLR (4th) 474, [1990] OJ No 1781 (CA) 237–41
405431 Ontario Ltd v Midas Canada Inc, 2010 ONCA 478 226
472900 BC Ltd v Thrifty Canada, Ltd (1998), 168 DLR (4th) 602,
    57 BCLR (3d) 332, [1998] BCJ No 2944 (CA) 123

A Local Authority v X & Anor (Children), [2013] EWHC 3274 (Fam) 410
Aamco Transmissions Inc v Kunz (1991), 97 Sask R 5,
    [1991] SJ No 404 (CA) 212
Abate v Abate, [1961] P 29 459
Abbott v Abbott, 130 S Ct 1983 (2010) 474
Abbott-Smith v Governors of University of Toronto (1964),
    45 DLR (2d) 672, 49 MPR 329, [1964] NSJ No 13 (SC) 88
Abdula v Canadian Solar Inc, 2015 ONSC 53 109
Abela v Baadarani, [2013] UKSC 44 54
Abib v Abib, 2010 ONSC 5869, aff'd 2010 ONCA 827 476
Aboulof v Oppenheimer (1882), 10 QBD 295 188
Achillopoulos, Re, [1928] Ch 433 363
Acme Video Inc v Hedges (1993), 12 OR (3d) 160, [1993] OJ No 585 (CA) 204
ACTIV Financial Systems, Inc v Orbixa Management Services, Inc,
    2011 ONSC 7286 .... 212, 214
Adams v Cape Industries Plc, [1990] Ch 433 (CA) 64, 170
Adams v Clutterbuck (1883), 10 QBD 403 344
Adderson v Adderson (1987), 77 AR 256, 51 Alta LR (2d) 193,
    [1987] AJ No 252 (CA) 25, 502

Adelman v Adelman, [1948] 1 WWR 1071, [1948] AJ No 35 (SC) 455–56
Aetna Financial Services Ltd v Feigelman, [1985] 1 SCR 2,
    15 DLR (4th) 161, [1985] SCJ No 161 167
Afonina v Jansson, 2015 BCSC 10 239
AG Armeno Mines and Minerals Inc v PT Pukuafu Indah (2000),
    190 DLR (4th) 173, 77 BCLR (3d) 1, 2000 BCCA 405 101–2
AG v LS (2006), 397 AR 296, 275 DLR (4th) 338, 2006 ABCA 311 491
Aggeliki Charis Compania Martima SA v Pagnan SpA,
    The Angelic Grace, [1995] 1 Lloyd's Rep 87 (CA) 160
Agro Co of Canada Ltd v The "Regal Scout" (1983),
    148 DLR (3d) 412, [1983] FCJ No 424 (TD) 32–33, 289
Air Foyle Ltd v Center Capital Ltd (2002), [2003] 2 Lloyd's Rep 753,
    [2002] EWHC 2535 (Comm) 348
Airbus Industrie GIE v Patel (1998), [1999] 1 AC 119,
    [1998] 2 WLR 686, [1998] 2 All ER 257 (HL) 146, 152, 156
Airia Brands v Air Canada, 2015 ONSC 5332 109
AK Investment CJSC v Kyrgyz Mobile Tel Ltd, [2011] UKPC 7 137
Al Habtoor v Fotheringham, [2001] 1 FLR 951 (CA) 24
Albert v Fraser Companies Ltd, [1937] 1 DLR 39, 11 MPR 209,
    [1937] NBJ No 2 (SCAD) 70
Alberta (Attorney-General) v Underwood, [1934] SCR 635,
    [1934] 4 DLR 167, [1934] SCJ No 43 402
Albionex (Overseas) Ltd v Conagra Ltd, 2011 MBCA 95 48
Aldo Group Inc v Moneris Solutions Corp, 2013 ONCA 725 132
Aleong v Aleong, 2013 BCSC 1428 .... 80, 95
Alexiou v Alexiou (1996), 188 AR 149, 41 Alta LR (3d) 90,
    [1996] AJ No 696 (QB) 431
Ali v Ali, [1968] P 564 420
Allard v Charbonneau, [1953] 2 DLR 442, [1953] OWN 381,
    [1953] OJ No 57 (CA) 241
Allarie v Director of Vital Statistics (1963), 41 DLR (2d) 553,
    44 WWR 568 (Alta SC) 436
Allen v Hay (1922), 64 SCR 76, 69 DLR 193, [1922] SCJ No 28 259
Allen's Estate, Re, [1945] 2 All ER 264 (Ch D) 385
Allison Estate v Allison (1998), 56 BCLR (3d) 1, 23 ETR (2d) 237,
    [1998] BCJ No 2274 (SC) 383
Amaca Pty Ltd v Bernard George Frost, [2006] NSWCA 173 278
Ambrose v Ambrose, (1960), 25 DLR (2d) 1, 32 WWR 433,
    [1960] BCJ No 113 (CA) 417–18
Amchem Products Inc v British Columbia (Workers' Compensation
    Board) (1989), 42 BCLR (2d) 77, 65 DLR (4th) 567, [1989]
    BCJ No 2216 (SC), aff'd (1990), 75 DLR (4th) 1, 50 BCLR
    (2d) 218, [1990] BCJ No 2331 (CA), rev'd [1993] 1 SCR 897,
    102 DLR (4th) 96, [1993] SCJ No 34 .... 116, 120, 122–23, 135, 145–46,
    148–55, 157, 160–61, 430–31

Amin Rasheed Shipping Corp v Kuwait Insurance Co (1983),
   [1984] AC 50, [1983] 2 All ER 884, [1983] 3 WLR 241 (HL) 286–87, 292
Amin v Canada (Minister of Citizenship and Immigration),
   [2008] 4 FCR 531, 322 FTR 293, 2008 FC 168 .... 438–41, 445
Amlani v Hirani, 2000 BCSC 1653 509
Amoco Cadiz, The, 954 F2d 1279 (7th Cir 1992) 47
Amosin v "The Mercury Bell," [1986] 3 FC 454, 27 DLR (4th) 641,
   [1986] FCJ No 1044 (CA) 257–58
Amtim Capital Inc v Appliance Recycling Centers of America,
   2014 ONCA 62 196
Anamur v Anamur, [2009] OJ No 5576 (SCJ) 472
Anand v Rumpal, 2014 ONSC 7560 .... 252, 271
Anderson v Nobel's Explosives Co (1906), 12 OLR 644,
   [1906] OJ No 165 (Div Ct) 87
Andrews v Grand & Toy Alberta Ltd, [1978] 2 SCR 229,
   83 DLR (3d) 452, [1978] SCJ No 6 239
Annesley, Re, [1926] Ch 692 .... 20, 230, 377
Anziani, In Re, [1930] 1 Ch 407 352
AP, Re (2002), 30 RFL (5th) 377, [2002] OJ No 2373 (Ct J) 483
Apt v Apt, [1948] P 83 (CA) 404
AR v RN, [2015] UKSC 35 473
Arab Monetary Fund v Hashim, [1996] 1 Lloyd's Rep 589 (CA),
   rev'g [1993] 1 Lloyd's Rep 543 (QB) 308–10, 320
Aram Systems Ltd v NovAtel Inc, 2008 ABQB 441, aff'd 2009 ABCA 262 332
Armitage v Attorney General, [1906] P 135 .... 435–36, 440
Armoyan v Armoyan, 2013 NSCA 99 .... 24, 152, 163, 425, 431–32
Armstrong v Armstrong, [1971] 3 OR 544, 21 DLR (3d) 140,
   [1971] OJ No 1672 (HCJ) 11
Arsenault v Arsenault (2006), 242 NSR (2d) 340, 265 DLR (4th) 1,
   2006 NSCA 38 488–89
Ash v Lloyd's Corporation (1992), 9 OR (3d) 755, 60 OAC 241,
   [1992] OJ No 3986 (CA) 128
Ashad v Deutsche Lufthansa Aktiengesellschaft (cob Lufthansa
   German Airlines), [2009] OJ No 4979, 2009 CanLII 64820 (SCJ) 70
Assinck v Assinck, [1998] OJ No 875 (Gen Div) 507–8
Attorney General for the United Kingdom v Wellington
   Newspapers Ltd, [1988] 1 NZLR 129 (CA) 40
Attorney General of Canada v RJ Reynolds Tobacco Holdings, Inc,
   268 F3d 103 (2d Cir 2001) 38
Attorney-General (United Kingdom) v Heinemann Publishers
   Australia Pty Ltd (1988), 165 CLR 30 (HCA) 39–40
Attorney-General of New Zealand v Ortiz, [1984] 1 AC 1 (CA) 34–35, 37, 40
Attorney-General v Campbell (1872), LR 5 HL 524 397
Auckland Corp v Alliance Assurance Co Ltd, [1937] AC 587 (PC) 294
Aucoin v Murray, 2013 NSSC 37 241

Augustus v Permanent Trustee Co (Canberra) Ltd (1971),
124 CLR 245, [1971] ALR 661, 45 ALJR 365 397
Aulwes v Mai (2002), 209 NSR (2d) 248, 33 RFL (5th) 1,
2002 NSCA 127 .... 472, 476, 478
Australian Broadcasting Corp v Waterhouse (1991), 25 NSWLR 519 (CA) 280
Avanti Management & Consulting Ltd v Argex Mining Inc,
2012 ONSC 4395 .... 93, 122
Avenue Properties Ltd v First City Development Corp (1986),
32 DLR (4th) 40, 7 BCLR (2d) 45, [1986] BCJ No 843 (CA) 299
Axis Management Inc v Alsager (2000), 197 Sask R 234, [2000]
SJ No 535, 2000 SKQB 382 27
Azam v Jan, 2012 ABCA 197 .... 420–21, 428
Azam v Jan, 2013 ABQB 301 .... 407, 420, 422, 428

Babcock v Jackson, 191 NE2d 279 (NY 1963) 233–34, 267
Baindail v Baindail, [1946] P 122 (CA) 421
Baker v Arthurs (1994), 124 Nfld & PEIR 69, [1994] NJ No 343 (CA) 467
Banco Atlantico SA v British Bank of the Middle East, [1990]
2 Lloyd's Rep 504 138
Bank of Africa v Cohen, [1909] 2 Ch 129 (CA) 345
Bank of Mongolia v Taskin, 2011 ONSC 6083, aff'd 2012 ONCA 220 195
Baring Brothers v Cunninghame District Council, [1997]
CLC 108 (Scotland Court of Session: Outer House) 317
Barrick Gold Corp v Goldcorp Inc, 2011 ONSC 3725 .... 238, 269, 312–13
Barrick Gold Corp v Lopehandia (2004), 71 OR (3d) 416,
49 CPC (5th) 1, [2004] OJ No 2329 (CA) 91–92, 186
Barros Mattos Junior v Macdaniels Ltd, [2005] EWHC 1323 (Ch D) 310
Barton (Deceased), Re, [2002] WTLR 469 (Ch) 393
Batavia Times Publishing Co v Davis (1977), 18 OR (2d) 252,
82 DLR (3d) 247, [1977] OJ No 1736 (HCJ) 173
Batavia Times Publishing Co v Davis (1978), 20 OR (2d) 437,
88 DLR (3d) 144, [1978] OJ No 3450 (HCJ) 47, 49
Bate v Bate (1978), 1 RFL (2d) 298, [1978] OJ No 113 (HCJ) 437, 461
Bavin v Bavin, [1939] 2 DLR 278, [1939] OWN 149 (SC), aff'd
[1939] OR 385, [1939] 3 DLR 328, [1939] OJ No 482 (CA) 443
Beals v Saldanha, [2003] 3 SCR 416, 234 DLR (4th) 1,
2003 SCC 72 .... 32, 60, 73, 168–69, 174–76, 187, 188–90, 193–95, 444, 462
Beals v Saldhana (1998), 42 OR (3d) 127, 27 CPC (4th) 144, [1998]
OJ No 4519 (SCJ) 187
Beatty v Beatty, [1924] 1 KB 807 179
Beatty v Schatz (2009), 98 BCLR (4th) 81, 69 RFL (6th) 107,
[2009] BCJ No 1557 (CA) 478
Bell v Kennedy (1868), LR 1 Sc & Div 307 (HL) 13
Bell'O International LCC v Flooring and Lumber Co, [2001]
OTC 362, 11 CPC (5th) 327, [2001] OJ No 1871 (SCJ) 153–55
Berchtold, Re, [1923] 1 Ch 192 .... 325, 327

Berezovsky v Michaels, [2000] 1 WLR 1004 (HL) 281
Berthiaume v Dastous, [1930] AC 79, [1930] 1 DLR 849,
    47 BR 533 (PC) 402–3
Besha v Lisanework, 2010 BCCA 580 491
Bessette, Re, [1942] 3 DLR 207, [1942] OWN 278 (HCJ) 380–81
Bevand v Bevand, [1955] 1 DLR 854, 35 MPR 244
    (NS Div & Mat Causes Ct) 455
Bevington v Hewitson (1974), 4 OR (2d) 226, 47 DLR (3d) 510,
    [1974] OJ No 1943 (HCJ) 436–37
Bezan v Vander Hooft, 2004 ABCA 44... 268
Bieberstein v Kirchberger, 2012 ONSC 6524 225
Bienstock v Adenyo Inc, 2014 ONSC 4997, aff'd 2015 ONCA 310 .... 40, 184
Blaha v Canada (Minister of Citizenship & Immigration), [1971]
    FC 521, [1971] FCJ No 43 (CA) 21
Blazek v Blazek, 2010 BCCA 188 115
Blizzard Entertainment, Inc v Simpson, 2012 ONSC 4312 184
Block Bros Realty Ltd v Mollard (1981), 122 DLR (3d) 323,
    27 BCLR 17, [1981] BCJ No 4 (CA) 237
Bloom Estate, Re (2004), 27 BCLR (4th) 176, 5 ETR (3d) 1, 2004 BCSC 70 355
Blue Sky One Ltd v Mahan Air; PK Airfinance US Inc v
    Blue Sky Two Ltd, [2010] EWHC 631 353
Boardwalk Regency Corp v Maalouf (1992), 6 OR (3d) 737,
    88 DLR (4th) 612, [1992] OJ No 26 (CA) 30–31, 191
Bodley Head Ltd v Flegon, [1972] 1 WLR 680... 297
Bonbright v Bonbright (1901), 1 OLR 629, [1901] OJ No 117 (HCJ)................... 16
Bonython v Commonwealth of Australia, [1951] AC 201 (PC) 286
Borgstrom v Korean Air Lines Co (2007), 241 BCAC 279,
    70 BCLR (4th) 206, 2007 BCCA 263 68–69
Bouch v Penny (Litigation Guardian of) (2009), 281 NSR (2d) 238,
    310 DLR (4th) 433, [2009] NSJ No 339 (CA), aff'g (2008),
    305 DLR (4th) 412, 272 NSR (2d) 259, 2008 NSSC 378 .... 76–78, 120, 122
Bouchard v Ouellet (2005), 15 RFL (6th) 77, [2005] OJ No 2852,
    2005 ONCJ 335... 492
Boulanger v Johnson & Johnson Corp (2003), 64 OR (3d) 208,
    32 CPC (5th) 203, [2003] OJ No 1374 (Div Ct) 250, 255
Bouzari v Bahremani, [2011] OJ No 5009 (SCJ) 110
Bouzari v Bahremani, 2015 ONCA 275.. 110
Boys v Chaplin (1969), [1971] AC 356, [1969] 3 WLR 322,
    [1969] 2 All ER 1085 (HL)... 238, 263–65, 276
Bradley, Re, [1941] 4 DLR 309, [1941] 3 WWR 173, [1941]
    AJ No 53 (SC).. 362
Braintech, Inc v Kostiuk (1999), 120 BCAC 1, 63 BCLR (3d) 156,
    [1999] BCJ No 622 (CA)...176
Branco v American Home Assurance Co, 2015 SKCA 71 .... 31–32, 292
Branco v Veira (1995), 8 ETR (2d) 49, [1995] OJ No 1071 (Gen Div) 398
Brassard v Smith, [1925] AC 371 (PC) 328

Braun v The Custodian, [1944] Ex CR 30, [1944] 3 DLR 412,
[1944] Ex CJ No 3, aff'd [1944] SCR 339, [1944] 4 DLR 209,
[1944] SCJ No 35 328
Breeden v Black, 2012 SCC 19 .... 90, 124, 136–37, 281
Breen v Breen (1929), 38 Man R 409, [1930] 1 DLR 1006, [1930]
1 WWR 30 (CA) 16
Bremer v Freeman (1857), 10 Moo PC 306, 14 ER 508 375
Brereton v Canadian Pacific Railway Co (1898), 29 OR 57,
[1898] OJ No 69 (HCJ) 332, 335–36
British Airways Board v Laker Airways Ltd (1984), [1985] AC 58,
[1984] 3 WLR 413, [1984] 3 All ER 39 (HL) 146
British Columbia v Imperial Tobacco Canada Ltd (2006),
56 BCLR (4th) 263, 31 CPC (6th) 243, 2006 BCCA 398 76
British South Africa Co v Companhia de Moçambique, [1893] AC 602,
[1891–94] All ER Rep 640 (HL) 330, 332–36, 503
British South Africa Co v De Beers Consolidated Mines Ltd,
[1910] 2 Ch 502 (CA), rev'd [1912] AC 52 (HL) 345
Britton v O'Callaghan (2002), 62 OR (3d) 95, 219 DLR (4th) 300,
[2002] OJ No 3857 (CA) 272
Brodin v A/R Seljan, [1973] SC 213 279
Brook v Brook (1861), 9 HL Cas 193 .... 402, 404, 407
Brooks v Brooks (1998), 41 OR (3d) 191, 163 DLR (4th) 715,
[1998] OJ No 3186 (CA) 466, 468, 470
Brouillard v Racine, [2002] OTC 836, 33 RFL (5th) 48, [2002]
OJ No 4215 (SCJ) 471
Brown v Mar Taino SA, 2015 NSSC 348 85
Brown v Miller, 2008 BCSC 1351 344
Brown v Pulley, 2015 ONCJ 186 258
Bryant Press Ltd v Acme Fast Freight Inc, [1951] OWN 665 (HCJ) 252
Buchanan v Rucker (1808), 9 East 192 168
Bumper Development Corp Ltd v Commissioner of Police of the
Metropolis, [1991] 4 All ER 638 (CA) 246, 251, 259
Burchell v Burchell, [1926] 2 DLR 595, 58 OLR 515, [1926]
OJ No 125 (HCJ) 499
Burke, Re (1927), [1928] 1 DLR 318, [1927] 3 WWR 718,
22 Sask LR 142 (KB) 325, 327
Bushell v T & N Plc (1992), 67 BCLR (2d) 330, 9 CPC (3d) 59,
[1992] BCJ No 1120 (CA) 121
Busslinger Estate, Re (1952), 6 WWR (NS) 408, [1952] AJ No 29 (Dist Ct) 382
Butchart, Re, [1932] NZLR 125 (CA) 387

C(DM) v W(DL) (2001), 155 BCAC 235, 15 RFL (5th) 35, 2001 BCCA 285 474
Cabaniss v Cabaniss, 2010 BCCA 348 189
Cadot v Cadot (1981), 49 NSR (2d) 202, 130 DLR (3d) 166, [1981]
NSJ No 522 (SCTD) 428, 488
CAE v MD, 2011 NBCA 17 496

Cammell v Sewell (1860), 157 ER 1371 (Exch Ch) 348–49
Canada (Deputy Minister of National Revenue, Customs and Excise —
    MNR) v White (1995), 92 FTR 285, [1995] FCJ No 378 (TD) 15
Canada (Minister of Citizenship and Immigration) v Hazimeh (2009),
    344 FTR 160, 78 Imm LR (3d) 232, [2009] FCJ No 482 441
Canada (Minister of Citizenship and Immigration) v Naveen,
    2013 FC 972 22
Canada (Minister of Employment and Immigration) v Narwal,
    [1990] 2 FC 385, 111 NR 316, [1990] FCJ No 317 (CA) 408
Canada v National Indian Brotherhood (1978), [1979] 1 FC 103,
    92 DLR (3d) 333, [1978] FCJ No 82 (TD) 354
Canadian Commercial Bank v Belkin (1990), 107 AR 232,
    75 Alta LR (2d) 40, [1990] AJ No 507 (CA) 368
Canadian Imperial Bank of Commerce v Glasford, 2015 ONSC 197,
    aff'd 2015 ONCA 523 155
Canadian International Marketing Distributing Ltd v Nitsuko Ltd
    (1990), 68 DLR (4th) 318, 56 BCLR (2d) 130, [1990] BCJ No 569 (CA) 56
Canadian National Steamships Co v Watson (1938), [1939] SCR 11,
    [1939] 1 DLR 273, [1938] SCJ No 53 .... 256, 272
Cannock v Fleguel, 2008 ONCA 758 475
Cannon v Cannon, [2005] 1 FLR 169 (CA) 476
Capon, Re (1965), 49 DLR (2d) 675, 49 DLR (2d) 675, [1965]
    OJ No 684 (CA) 454–55, 458
Cariello v Perrella, 2013 ONSC 7605 19
Carom v Bre-X Minerals Ltd (1999), 44 OR (3d) 173,
    35 CPC (4th) 43, [1999] OJ No 1662 (SCJ) 198
Carrick Estates Ltd and Young, Re (1987), 43 DLR (4th) 161,
    24 CPC (2d) 70, [1987] SJ No 551 (CA) 170
Carron Iron Co Proprietors v Maclaren (1855), 5 HLC 415 148
Castanho v Brown and Root (UK) Ltd, [1981] AC 557 (HL) 147
Castillo v Castillo, [2005] 3 SCR 870, 260 DLR (4th) 439,
    2005 SCC 83 .... 243–44, 283
Catania v Giannattasio (1999), 174 DLR (4th) 170,
    28 CPC (4th) 207, [1999] OJ No 1197 (CA) 337–40
Cavell Insurance Co, Re (2006), 80 OR (3d) 500, 30 CPC (6th) 1,
    [2006] OJ No 1998 (CA), aff'g (2004), 6 CBR (5th) 11,
    11 CPC (6th) 239, [2004] OJ No 5166 (SCJ) 167
Central Guaranty Trust Co v Deluca (1994), [1995] NWTR 200,
    34 CPC (3d) 293, [1994] NWTJ No 78 (SC) 202–3
Central Sun Mining Inc v Vector Engineering Inc, 2012 ONSC 7331,
    rev'd 2013 ONCA 601 .... 85, 89, 97
Century Credit Corporation v Richard, [1962] OR 815,
    34 DLR (2d) 291, [1962] OJ No 603 (CA) 349–50
Cesario v Gondek, 2012 ONSC 4563 100–1
Chan v Chow (2001), 199 DLR (4th) 478, 90 BCLR (3d) 222,
    2001 BCCA 276 .... 472–74, 478

Chapman Estate v O'Hara (1987), [1988] 2 WWR 275, 61 Sask R 140,
 [1987] SJ No 874 (CA) 195, 341, 343–44, 371
Charron v Montreal Trust Co, [1958] OR 597, 15 DLR (2d) 240,
 [1958] OJ No 640 (CA) 297, 368, 508
Chateau des Charmes Wines Ltd v Sabate, USA, Inc, [2005]
 OTC 936, [2005] OJ No 4604 (SCJ) 129
Chatillon v The Canadian Mutual Fire Insurance Co (1877), 27 UCCP 450.... 344
Chellaram v Chellaram, [1985] Ch 409 397
Chen v Canada (Minister of Citizenship and Immigration) (2001),
 213 FTR 137, 17 Imm LR (3d) 222, 2001 FCT 1229 23
Cheni v Cheni, [1965] P 85 .... 416, 420
Cherry v Thompson (1872), LR 7 QB 573 85
Chevron Corp v Yaiguaje, 2015 SCC 42 .... 54, 60, 62, 92–93, 165–66, 169
Chien, Re (1992), 51 FTR 317, [1992] FCJ No 104 (TD) 22
Chree v Chree, 2015 ONSC 6480 .... 488, 496
Christmas v Fort McKay First Nation, 2014 ONSC 373 84
Christopher v Zimmerman, 2000 BCCA 532 .... 311, 501
Cirque du Soleil Inc v Volvo Group Canada Inc, 2015 ONSC 2698 246
Clancy v Beach, [1994] 7 WWR 332, 92 BCLR (2d) 82,
 [1994] BCJ No 280 (SC) 192
Clark v Clark, 107 NH 351, 222 A2d 205 (1966) 233–34
Clarke & Hutchings, Re (1976), 9 Nfld & PEIR 438, 71 DLR (3d) 356,
 [1976] NJ No 3 (CA) 466
Claxton Engineering Services Ltd v TXM Olaj-Es Gazkutato KTF,
 [2011] EWHC 345 (Comm) 160
Cleveland Museum of Art v Capricorn Art International SA, [1990]
 2 Lloyd's Rep 166 132
Clinton v Ford (1982), 37 OR (2d) 448, 137 DLR (3d) 281, [1982]
 OJ No 3336 (CA) 172, 173
Club Resorts Ltd v Van Breda, 2012 SCC 17, aff'g
 (sub nom Van Breda v Village Resorts Ltd),
 2010 ONCA 84 .... 57–59, 62, 64–65, 73, 76, 78–82, 84, 86, 90, 93,
  94–101, 109–10, 114, 116, 120, 122, 136–37, 176, 200, 332, 340, 491, 502
Coast Lines Ltd v Hudig and Veder Chartering NV, [1972] 2 QB 34 (CA) 292
Cockerham v Hanc, 2014 BCSC 2432 493
Cohn, Re, [1945] Ch 5 .... 225, 226
Coldmatic Refrigeration of Canada Ltd v Leveltek Processing LLC (2004),
 70 OR (3d) 758, [2004] OTC 298, [2004] OJ No 1396 (SCJ), aff'd
 (2005), 75 OR (3d) 638, 5 CPC (6th) 258, [2005] OJ No 160 (CA) 67
Collavino Inc v Yemen (Tihama Development Authority),
 2007 ABQB 212 247
Collens, Re, [1986] Ch 505 372
Collier v Rivaz (1841), 2 Curt 855, 163 ER 608 375
Columbia Pictures Industries Inc v Wang, 2007 SKCA 133 83
Commission de la Construction du Québec v Access Rigging
 Services Inc, 2010 ONSC 5897 197

Compagnie Tunisienne de Navigation SA v Compagnie D'Armement
    Maritime SA, [1971] AC 572 (HL) 290
Compania Maritima Villa Nova SA v Northern Sales Co (1991),
    [1992] 1 FC 550, 137 NR 20, [1991] FCJ No 1163 (CA), aff'g
    (1989), 29 FTR 136, [1989] FCJ No 526 (TD) 208–9
Compania Naviera Micro SA v Shipley International Inc (The Parouth),
    [1982] 2 Lloyd's Rep 351 (CA) 295
Compton v Bearcroft (1769), 161 ER 799 (Court of Delegates) 404
Connelly v RTZ Corporation plc, [1998] AC 854 (HL) 136
Continental Casualty Co v Symons Estate, 2015 ONSC 6394 167
Cook v 1293037 Alberta Ltd (cob Traveller's Cloud 9), 2015 ONSC 7989 111
Corlet Estate, Re, [1942] 3 DLR 72, [1942] 2 WWR 93 (Alta SC) 387
Corlett v Hoelker, 2012 BCCA 355 343
Corporate Bank and Trust Co v Toronto Dominion Bank, [1987]
    OJ No 418 (HCJ) 52
Court v Debaie, 2012 ABQB 640 .... 90, 124
Coutu v Gauthier (Estate) (2006), 296 NBR (2d) 34, 264 DLR
    (4th) 319, 2006 NBCA 16 .... 76, 120–21
Cox v Ergo Versicherung AG (formerly known as Victoria), [2014]
    UKSC 22 238
Craig Broadcast Systems Inc v Magid (Frank N) Associates Inc (1998),
    123 Man R (2d) 252, 15 CPC (4th) 95, [1998] MJ No 25 (CA) 121
Crosby v Prescott (1922), 68 DLR 250, [1922] 2 WWR 737,
    32 Man R 108 (CA), aff'd [1923] SCR 446, [1923] 2 DLR 937,
    [1923] SCJ No 12 366
Cruse v Chittum, [1974] 2 All ER 940 (QB Fam D) 25
Cunningham v Hamilton (1997), 209 AR 123, [1997] AJ No 1076 (CA) 137
Cunnington, Re, [1924] 1 Ch 68 380–81
Curati v Perdoni, [2012] EWCA Civ 1381 380
Currie v McDonald's Restaurants of Canada Ltd (2005),
    74 OR (3d) 321, 7 CPC (6th) 60, [2005] OJ No 506 (CA) 199–200
Custodian v Blucher, [1927] SCR 420, [1927] 3 DLR 40, [1927] SCJ No 33 47

D (A Child) (Abduction: Rights of Custody), Re (2006), [2007]
    1 AC 619, [2006] UKHL 51 474
D v D, [1973] 3 OR 82, 36 DLR (3d) 17, [1973] OJ No 1990 (HCJ) 457
Dalimpex Ltd v Janicki (2003), 64 OR (3d) 737, 35 CPC (5th) 55,
    [2003] OJ No 2094 (CA) 131, 142, 212
Dalmia Dairy Industries Ltd v National Bank of Pakistan, [1978]
    2 Lloyd's LR 223 (CA) 214
Danyluk v Ainsworth Technologies Inc, [2001] 2 SCR 460,
    2001 SCC 44 196
Dash 224, LLC v Vector Aerospace Engine Services-Atlantic Inc,
    2015 PESC 27 .... 30, 36, 191, 349
Dashtarai v Shahrestani, [2006] OJ No 5367 (SCJ) 32, 442, 444
Davies v Collins, 2011 NSCA 79 .... 218, 384

Davies v Davies (1915), 24 DLR 737, 8 WWR 803, [1915]
  AJ No 79 (SCTD) 383–84
Davison v Sweeney (2005), 255 DLR (4th) 757, 42 BCLR (4th) 69,
  2005 BCSC 757 .... 414, 419, 455
de Medeiros v de Medeiros (1992), 39 RFL (3d) 274, [1992]
  OJ No 3865 (Gen Div) 471
De Nicols v Curlier, [1900] AC 21 (HL) 504
De Reneville v De Reneville, [1948] P 100 (CA) 451, 452–53
Dell Computer Corp v Union des consommateurs, [2007]
  2 SCR 801, 284 DLR (4th) 577, 2007 SCC 34 142
Depo Traffic Facilities (Kunshan) Co v Vikeda International Logistics
  and Automotive Supply Ltd, 2015 ONSC 999 213
Despina R, The, [1977] 3 WLR 617 (CA) 50
Deuruneft Deutsche-Russische Mineralol Handelsgesellschaft mbH v
  Bullen (2003), 349 AR 221, 21 Alta LR (4th) 349, 2003 ABQB 743 76
Deutsche Schachtbau-und Tiefbohrgesellschaft mbH v Shell
  International Petroleum Co Ltd, [1990] 1 AC 295 (HL) 210
Devon Canada Corp v PE-Pittsfield, LLC (cob as Pittsfield
  Generating Co, LP) (2008), 446 AR 62, 63 CPC (6th) 127,
  [2008] AJ No 1263 (CA) 246
Devos v Devos, [1970] 2 OR 323, 10 DLR (3d) 603,
  1970 CanLII 486 (CA) 504, 507–8
Di Ferdinando v Simon, Smits & Co Ltd, [1920] 3 KB 409 (CA) 46
Diachuk v Diachuk, [1941] 2 DLR 607, [1941] 2 WWR 599,
  49 Man R 102 (KB) 454
Dingwall v Foster, 2014 ABCA 89 .... 37, 180
Dipalma v Smart (1995), 176 AR 326, 35 Alta LR (3d) 119, [1995]
  AJ No 1027 (QB), rev'd (1996), 190 AR 142, 43 Alta LR (3d) 161,
  [1996] AJ No 752 (QB) 242
Donaldson International Livestock Ltd v Znamensky Selekcionno-Gibridny
  Center LLC (2008), 305 DLR (4th) 432 (Ont CA) 142
Donnelly, Re (1911), 2 OWN 1388, 19 OWR 708, [1911] OJ No 634 (HCJ) 364
Donohue v Armco Inc (2001), [2002] 1 All ER 749, [2001] UKHL 64 158
Douez v Facebook, Inc, 2015 BCCA 279, leave to appeal to
  SCC granted, [2015] SCCA No 367 .... 125, 130
Dovigi v Razi, 2012 ONCA 361 466
Dow Jones & Company Inc v Gutnick (2002), 210 CLR 575,
  [2002] HCA 56 .... 90, 280
Downton v Royal Trust Co (1972), [1973] SCR 437, 34 DLR (3d) 403,
  [1972] SCJ No 94 446–48
Drake v MacLaren, [1929] 3 DLR 159 (Alta SC) 455
Dreco Energy Services Ltd v Wenzel Downhole Tools Ltd (2008),
  443 AR 116, [2008] AJ No 758, 2008 ABQB 419, aff'd (2008),
  440 AR 351, 2 Alta LR (5th) 120, 2008 ABCA 395 101
Dugay v Dugay (1978), 8 RFL (2d) 208, [1978] OJ No 1963 (Prov Ct) 466
Duke of Wellington, Re, [1948] Ch 118 (CA) 369

Duke v Andler, [1932] SCR 734, [1932] 4 DLR 529, [1932]
  SCJ No 55..195, 331, 340–45, 371, 503
Duncan v Lawson (1889), 41 Ch D 394 326–27

Eastern Power Ltd v Azienda Communale Energia (1999),
  178 DLR (4th) 409, 39 CPC (4th) 160, [1999] OJ No 3275 (CA) 123
Eco-Tec Inc v Lu, 2015 ONCA 818 122
Ed Miller Sales & Rentals Ltd v Caterpillar Tractor Co (1988),
  90 AR 323, 22 CPR (3d) 290, [1988] AJ No 810 (CA) 42
Éditions Écosociété Inc v Banro Corp, 2012 SCC 18.......................... 90, 268, 281
Edward Jones v Raymond James Ltd, 2013 ONSC 4640 ....84, 98
Edward v Edward Estate (1987), 39 DLR (4th) 654, 57 Sask R 67,
  [1987] SJ No 42 (CA) 437
Egbert v Short, [1907] 2 Ch 205... 115
EK Motors v Volkswagen Canada Ltd (1972), [1973]
  1 WWR 466, [1972] SJ No 324 (CA) 70
EK v DK (2005), 257 DLR (4th) 549, 43 BCLR (4th) 272, 2005 BCCA 425 498
Eleftheria, The (1969), [1969] 2 All ER 641, [1970] P 94.................................. 128
Elga Laboratories Ltd v Soroko Inc (2002), 61 OR (3d) 324,
  27 CPC (5th) 293, [2002] OJ No 3492 (SCJ)....................................... 154–55
Ellis v Wentzell-Ellis, 2010 ONCA 347...472, 477
Emanuel v Symon, [1908] 1 KB 302 (CA), rev'g [1907] 1 KB 235 .... 168, 171
Embiricos v Anglo-Austrian Bank, [1904] 2 KB 870, aff'd [1905]
  1 KB 677 (CA) 355
Empresa Minera Los Quenuales SA v Vena Resources Inc,
  2015 ONSC 4408 212
Entores Ltd v Miles Far East Corp, [1955] 2 All ER 493 (CA) 85
Equustek Solutions Inc v Google Inc, 2014 BCSC 1063, aff'd
  2015 BCCA 265, leave to appeal to SCC granted, [2015] SCCA No 355 65
Espiritu v Bielza (2007), 39 RFL (6th) 218, [2007] OJ No 1587,
  2007 ONCJ 175 474
Etler v Kertesz, [1960] OR 672, 26 DLR (2d) 209, [1960]
  OJ No 568 (CA) 286, 292, 300
Europcar Italia SpA v Alba Tours International Inc (1997),
  23 OTC 376, [1997] OJ No 133 (Gen Div)... 212
Excalibur Special Opportunities LP v Schwartz Levitsky Feldman LLP,
  2014 ONSC 4118, aff'd 2015 ONSC 1634 (Div Ct)................................... 105
Expedition Helicopters Inc v Honeywell Inc, 2010 ONCA 351...................... 129
Export Packers Co v SPI International Transportation, 2012 ONCA 481 .....82, 91
Ezer v Yorkton Securities Inc (2005), 207 BCAC 65, [2005] BCJ No 30,
  2005 BCCA 22 68

Fairfield v Low (1990), 71 OR (2d) 599, 44 CPC (2d) 65, [1990]
  OJ No 58 (HCJ)... 128
Fédération des producteurs acéricoles du Québec v SK Export Inc,
  2015 NBCA 30 168

Feiner v Demkowicz (1973), 2 OR (2d) 121, 42 DLR (3d) 165,
[1973] OJ No 2241 (HCJ) 407, 453–55
Ferguson v Arctic Transportation Ltd (1998), 147 FTR 96, [1998]
FCJ No 634 (TD) 278
Fergusson's Will, Re, [1902] 1 Ch 483 381
Fewer v Sayisi Dene Education Authority, 2011 NLCA 17 .... 76, 111
FH v McDougall, [2008] 3 SCR 41, 297 DLR (4th) 193, 2008 SCC 53 11
Finizio v Scoppio-Finizio (1999), 46 OR (3d) 226,
179 DLR (4th) 15, [1999] OJ No 3579 (CA) 474, 477
Fiona Trust & Holding Corp v Privalov, [2010] EWHC 3199 (Comm) 311
First National Bank of Houston v Houston E & C, Inc, [1990]
5 WWR 719, 47 BCLR (2d) 347, [1990] BCJ No 1559 (CA) 171–72
Fleming v Fleming, [1934] OR 588, [1934] 4 DLR 90, [1934]
OJ No 277 (HCJ) 454
Folias, The, [1979] AC 685 (HL) 50–51
Follwell v Holmes, [2006] OJ No 4387 (SCJ) 491
Food Services of America Inc (cob Amerifresh) v Pan Pacific Specialties
Ltd (1997), 32 BCLR (3d) 225, [1997] BCJ No 1921 (SC) 213
Foote Estate, Re [2009] AJ No 1250, 2009 ABQB 654 .... 10–11, 13, 16–17, 20
Forbes v Forbes (1912), 3 DLR 243, 3 OWN 557 (HCJ) 403
Forbes v Simmons (1914), 20 DLR 100, [1914] AJ No 70 (SC) 170
Foresight Shipping Co v Union of India, 2004 FC 1501 253
Forsythe v Westfall, 2015 ONCA 810 91
Foster v Driscoll, [1929] 1 KB 470.. 301
Four Embarcadero Venture Center v Mr Greenjeans Corp (1988),
64 OR (2d) 746, 26 CPC (2d) 248, [1988] OJ No 210 (HCJ) 167
Francis v Maharaj, 2014 ONCJ 285 476
Fraser v 4358376 Canada Inc (cob Itravel 2000 and Travelzest PLC),
2014 ONCA 553 68
Friedl v Friedl, 2009 BCCA 314 508
Frischke v Royal Bank of Canada (1977), 17 OR (2d) 388,
80 DLR (3d) 393, [1977] OJ No 2411 (CA) 42
Fromovitz v Fromovitz (1977), 16 OR (2d) 751, 79 DLR (3d) 148,
[1977] OJ No 2345 (HCJ) 449
Frustaglio v Barbuto, [1960] OWN 551 (HCJ) 404
Frymer v Brettschneider (1994), 19 OR (3d) 60, 115 DLR (4th) 744,
[1994] OJ No 1411 (CA) 121–22
Fuld (No 3), In the Estate of, [1968] P 675 .... 11, 13, 380
Fulford Estate, Re (1996), 146 Nfld & PEIR 248, 14 ETR (2d) 225,
[1996] PEIJ No 102 (SCTD) 380
Fulton v Fulton (1984), 28 Man R (2d) 251, [1984] MJ No 389 (QB) 454

G v G (1928), 22 Sask LR 376 (KB)... 456
G, Re (2008), 56 RFL (6th) 232, [2008] OJ No 1906, 2008 ONCJ 227 483
Gage, Re, [1962] SCR 241, 31 DLR (2d) 662, [1962] SCJ No 7 381
GAGR v TDW, 2013 BCSC 586.. 478

Gajraj v DeBernardo (2002), 60 OR (3d) 68, 213 DLR (4th) 651,
  [2002] OJ No 2130 (CA) 73
Gal v Lukasiewcz, [2008] OJ No 5358, 2008 ONCJ 676 498
Garchinski v Garchinski, [2002] SJ No 465, 2002 SKQB 323 427
Garland v Consumers' Gas Co, [2004] 1 SCR 629, 237 DLR (4th) 385,
  2004 SCC 25 305
Gasque v Commissioners of Inland Revenue, [1940] 2 KB 80 27
Gatineau Power Co v Crown Life Insurance Co, [1945] SCR 655,
  [1945] 4 DLR 1, [1945] SCJ No 32 47
Gavriluke v Mainard, 2012 ONSC 6928, aff'd 2013 ONSC 2337 (Div Ct) 492
Gemstar Canada Inc v George A Fuller Co, [2009] OJ No 4878 (SCJ) 136
General Motors Acceptance Corp of Canada v Town and
  Country Chrysler Ltd (2007), 88 OR (3d) 666, 288 DLR
  (4th) 74, 2007 ONCA 904 251
General Refractories Co of Canada v Venturedyne, [2002]
  OTC 10, [2002] OJ No 54 (SCJ) 48, 51
Gentra Canada Investments Inc v Lehndorff United Properties
  (Canada) (1995), 173 AR 161, 31 Alta LR (3d) 322, [1995]
  AJ No 706 (QB), aff'd (1995), 174 AR 193, 34 Alta LR (3d) 360,
  [1995] AJ No 944 (CA) 157–58
George Monro Ltd v American Cyanamid & Chemical Corp,
  [1944] 1 KB 432 (CA) 87
Ghaeinizadeh v Ku De Ta Capital Inc, 2013 ONCA 2 .... 95, 491
Ghana Gold Corp, Re, 2013 ONSC 3284 100
Ghaznavi v Kashif-Ul-Haque, 2011 ONSC 4062 509
Gillespie Management Corp v Terrace Properties (1989), 62 DLR
  (4th) 221, 39 BCLR (2d) 337, [1989] BCJ No 1768 (CA) 301
Gillespie v Gillespie (1992), 10 OR (3d) 641, 96 DLR (4th) 731,
  [1992] OJ No 2138 (CA) 468, 470
Gillespie v Grant (1992), 132 AR 288, 4 Alta LR (3d) 122,
  [1992] AJ No 723 (Surr Ct) 13, 20, 369, 380
Girsberger v Kresz (2000), 47 OR (3d) 145, [2000] OJ No 266 (SCJ),
  aff'd (2002), 50 OR (3d) 157, 1 CPC (5th) 250, [2000] OJ No 266 (CA) ... 196
Glencore International AG v Metro Trading International Inc,
  [2001] 1 Lloyd's Rep 284 353
Godard v Gray (1870), LR 6 QB 139 187
Godley v Coles (1988), 39 CPC (2d) 162, [1988] OJ No 2808
  (Dist Ct), aff'd (1988), 40 CPC (2d) xlvi (Ont HCJ) 335–36
Gold v Reinblatt (1928), [1929] SCR 74, [1929] 1 DLR 959,
  [1928] SCJ No 78 253
Golden Acres Ltd v Queensland Estates Pty Ltd, [1969]
  Qd R 378 (SC), aff'd (sub nom Freehold Land
  Investments Ltd v Queensland Estates Pty Ltd)
  (1970), 123 CLR 418, [1970] HCA 31 289
Goldhar v Haaretz.com, 2015 ONSC 1128, aff'd 2016 ONCA 515 .... 98, 281
Gordon v Goertz, [1996] 2 SCR 27, 134 DLR (4th) 321, [1996] SCJ No 52 464

Government of India, Ministry of Finance (Revenue Division) v
  Taylor, [1955] AC 491, [1955] 1 All ER 542 (HL) 37
Gower v Starrett, [1948] 2 DLR 853, [1948] 1 WWR 529,
  [1948] BCJ No 90 (SC) 455–56
Granot v Hersen (1998), 21 ETR (2d) 153, [1998] OJ No 922
  (Gen Div), var'd (1999), 43 OR (3d) 421, 173 DLR (4th) 227,
  [1999] OJ No 1302 (CA) 385–86
Gray v Formosa, [1963] P 259 (CA) 445, 462–63
Gray v Kerslake (1957), [1958] SCR 3, 11 DLR (2d) 225, [1957] SCJ No 62 257
GreCon Dimter Inc v JR Normand Inc, [2005] 2 SCR 401,
  255 DLR (4th) 257, 2005 SCC 46 120
Greenshields Inc v Johnston (1981), 28 AR 1, 119 DLR (3d) 714,
  [1981] AJ No 946 (QB), aff'd (1981), 35 AR 487, 131 DLR (3d) 234,
  [1981] AJ No 695 (CA) 297
Grewal v Grewal (1982), 29 RFL (2d) 23, [1982] SJ No 1166 (QB) 467
Grewal v Kaur, 2011 ONSC 1812 .... 414, 455
Grewal v Sohal (2004), 246 DLR (4th) 743, 12 RFL (6th) 55,
  2004 BCSC 1549 455
Griffin v Dell Canada Inc, 2010 ONCA 29 142
Grimes v Cloutier (1989), 69 OR (2d) 641, 61 DLR (4th) 505,
  [1989] OJ No 1458 (CA) 265, 268
Groos, Re, [1915] 1 Ch 572 377–78
Guarantee Co of North America v Mercedes-Benz Canada Inc
  (2005), 83 OR (3d) 316, 33 MVR (5th) 147, [2005]
  OJ No 6149 (SCJ), aff'd (2006), 86 OR (3d) 479,
  34 MVR (5th) 21, [2006] OJ No 2358 (CA) 258
Gulevich v Miller, 2015 ABCA 411 89
Gulf Canada Resources Ltd v Arochem International Ltd (1992),
  66 BCLR (2d) 113, 43 CPR (3d) 390, [1992] BCJ No 500 (CA) 142
Gunn v Gunn (1956), 2 DLR (2d) 351, 18 WWR 85, [1956] SJ No 41 (CA) 16
Gunsay v Gunsay (1999), 70 BCLR (3d) 104, 2 RFL (5th) 90,
  1999 BCCA 454 .... 464, 466
Gurniak v Nordquist, [2003] 2 SCR 652, 232 DLR (4th) 635, 2003 SCC 59 272
Gwyn v Mellen (1979), 15 BCLR 78, 13 RFL (2d) 298, [1979]
  BCJ No 10 (CA) 436, 456–61
Gyuzeleva v Angelov, 2012 ONSC 6628 431

Haig v Canada (Chief Electoral Officer), [1993] 2 SCR 995,
  105 DLR (4th) 577, [1993] SCJ No 84 21
Halley, The (1868), LR 2 PC 193 262
Hamlyn & Co v Talisker Distillery, [1984] AC 202 (HL) 291
Hanlan v Sernesky (1998), 38 OR (3d) 479, 108 OAC 261, [1998]
  OJ No 1236 (CA) 270
Harding v Wealands, [2006] 3 WLR 83, [2006] UKHL 32 238–39
Hardy v Hardy, [1969] 2 OR 875, 7 DLR (3d) 307, [1969]
  OJ No 1414 (HCJ) 426

Harrington v Dow Corning Corp (2000), 193 DLR (4th) 67,
    82 BCLR (3d) 1, 2000 BCCA 605, aff'g (1996), 22 BCLR
    (3d) 97, 48 CPC (3d) 28, [1996] BCJ No 734 (SC).................. 105–6, 108, 198
Harris v Murray (1995), 168 AR 271, 28 Alta LR (3d) 377, [1995]
    AJ No 347 (QB) 431
Harris v Taylor, [1915] 2 KB 580 (CA) 172
Harrods v Dow Jones & Co Inc, [2003] EWHC 1162 (QB) 90
Harry, Re (1998), 144 FTR 141, [1998] FCJ No 189 (TD) 23
Hassan and Hassan, Re (1976), 12 OR (2d) 432, 69 DLR (3d) 224,
    [1976] OJ No 2131 (HCJ) 420–21
Hastings v Deakin, 2014 ONCJ 618 499
Haugesund Kommune v Depfa ACS Bank, [2010] EWCA Civ 579 298
Haut v Haut (1978), 20 OR (2d) 126, 86 DLR (3d) 757, [1978]
    OJ No 3402 (HCJ) 11
HE v MM, 2015 ONCA 813, rev'g 2014 ONSC 7409 466–67
Hellens v Densmore, [1957] SCR 768, 10 DLR (2d) 561, [1957] SCJ No 53...... 257
Hellmann's Will, Re (1863), LR 2 Eq 363... 380
Henderson v Henderson, [1967] P 77... 11
Hendsbee v Khuber (1995), 148 NSR (2d) 270, 47 CPC (3d) 258,
    [1995] NSJ No 543 (SC) 242
Henry v Geoprosco International Ltd, [1975] 3 WLR 620, [1975]
    2 All ER 702 (CA) 69, 172
Herceg Novi v Ming Galaxy, [1998] 4 All ER 238 (CA) 136
Hesperides Hotels Ltd v Muftizade, [1979] AC 508 (HL), rev'g
    (sub nom Hesperides Hotels Ltd v Aegean Turkish Holidays Ltd)
    [1977] 3 WLR 656 (CA)... 333–34, 336
Highland Crusader Offshore Partners LP v Deutsche Bank AG,
    [2009] EWCA Civ 725... 160
Hill v Church of Scientology, [1995] 2 SCR 1130, 126 DLR (4th) 129,
    [1995] SCJ No 64 19
Hill v Hill, [1929] 2 DLR 735, [1929] 2 WWR 41, [1929]
    AJ No 27 (SCAD) 401
Hill v Hill, 2010 ABQB 528... 368
Hilton v Guyot, 159 US 113 (1875) 218
Hincks v Gallardo, 2013 ONSC 129, aff'd 2014 ONCA 494 423
Hinter v Hinter (1996), 8 OTC 185, 23 RFL (4th) 401, [1996]
    OJ No 2601 (Gen Div) 427
Hipperson v Newbury District Electoral Registration Officer, [1985]
    QB 1060 (CA) 21
Hlynski v Hlynski (1999), 176 DLR (4th) 132, 180 Sask R 1,
    1999 CanLII 2761 (CA) 504
Hogg v Provincial Tax Commission, [1941] 4 DLR 501, [1941]
    3 WWR 605 (Sask CA) 228, 326–27
Hollandia, The, [1983] 1 AC 565 (HL) 33
Hollowcore Inc v Visocchi, 2014 ONSC 6802 48
Holman v Johnson (1775), 1 Cowp 341, 98 ER 1120 (KB) 37, 179, 220

Holt Cargo Systems Inc v ABC Containerline NV (Trustees of),
    [2001] 3 SCR 907, 207 DLR (4th) 577, 2001 SCC 90 254
Holub v Holub (1976), 71 DLR (3d) 698, [1976] 5 WWR 527,
    [1976] MJ No 73 (CA) 448
Hoole v Hoole, 2008 BCSC 1248 475
Hope v Hope (1854), 43 ER 534 467
Hormandinger v Bender-Hormandinger, 2007 BCSC 949 344
Hoskins v Boyd (1997), 90 BCAC 111, 34 BCLR (3d) 121, [1997]
    BCJ No 958 (CA) 477
Household Fire & Carriage Accident Insurance Company v Grant
    (1879), 4 Ex D 216 (CA) 286
Howard, Re (1923), [1924] 1 DLR 1062, 54 OLR 109, [1923] OJ No 19 (HC) 383
Hoyles, Re, [1911] 1 Ch 179 (CA) 325
HSBC Bank of Canada v Hocking, [2006] RJQ 804, [2006]
    QJ No 507, 2006 QCCS 330, aff'd [2008] RJQ 1189,
    [2008] JQ no 3423, 2008 QCCA 800 200
Huang v Canada (Minister of Citizenship and Immigration),
    2013 FC 576 23
Hudon v Geos Language Corp (1997), 34 OR (3d) 14,
    10 CPC (4th) 92, [1997] OJ No 2245 (Div Ct) 146, 152–55
Hudye Farms Inc v Canadian Wheat Board, 2011 SKCA 137 129
Humphries v Rokoss, [2004] OJ No 4658, 2004 ONCJ 277 492
Hunt v Hunt (1958), 14 DLR (2d) 243, [1958] OWN 332 (HCJ) 405
Hunt v T&N plc, [1993] 4 SCR 289, 109 DLR (4th) 16,
    [1993] SCJ No 125 .... 42, 55, 57, 72–73, 107, 175, 178, 251, 254, 256
Hunter v Hunter, 2005 SKCA 76 503
Huntington v Attrill, [1893] AC 150 (PC) 34, 179–80
Hurst v Societe Nationale de L'Amiante (2008), 93 OR (3d) 338,
    297 DLR (4th) 543, 2008 ONCA 573 136
Hutchings v Hutchings (1930), 39 Man R 66 (CA) 455
Hyde v Hyde (1866), LR 1 P & D 130 .... 419, 421–22

Ibrahim v Robinson, 2015 ONCA 21 111
Ichi Canada Ltd v Yamauchi Rubber Industry Co (1983),
    144 DLR (3d) 533, 43 BCLR 215, [1983] BCJ No 2266 (CA) 89
Ikimi v Ikimi, [2001] 3 WLR 672, [2001] EWCA Civ 873 25
Impala Warehousing and Logistics (Shanghai) Co Ltd v Wanxiang
    Resources (Singapore) PTE Ltd, [2015] EWHC 811 (Comm) 158
Imperial Life Assurance Co of Canada v Colmenares, [1967] SCR 443,
    62 DLR (2d) 138, [1967] SCJ No 30 291–92
In Re LC (Children), [2014] UKSC 1 473
In the Estate of Weiss, [1962] P 136 363
In the matter of K (A Child) (Northern Ireland), [2014] UKSC 29 474
Incorporated Broadcasters Ltd v Canwest Global Communications
    Corp (2003), 63 OR (3d) 431, 223 DLR (4th) 627,
    [2003] OJ No 560 (CA) 61

India v Bumper Development Corp (1995), 29 Alta LR (3d) 194,
    36 CPC (3d) 249, [1995] AJ No 380 (QB), aff'd 4
    December 1995 (Alta CA) 246
Indyka v Indyka, [1969] 1 AC 33 (HL) 436–38, 440, 442, 445, 461
Infineon Technologies AG v Option Consommateurs, 2013 SCC 59 82
Ingenium Technologies Corp v McGraw-Hill Companies, Inc (2005),
    49 BCLR (4th) 120, 13 CPC (6th) 234, 2005 BCCA 358 134
Inter Metal Group Ltd v Worslade Trading Ltd, [1998] 2 IR 1 (SC) 118
Inter-Leasing Inc v Ontario (Minister of Revenue), 2014 ONCA 575 354
International Association of Science and Technology for Development v
    Hamza (1995), 162 AR 349, 28 Alta LR (3d) 125, [1995]
    AJ No 87 (CA) 245–46
International Power and Engineering Consultants Ltd v Clark (1963),
    41 DLR (2d) 260, [1963] BCJ No 168 (SC), aff'd (1964),
    43 DLR (2d) 394, 46 WWR 310, [1964] BCJ No 127 (CA) 86
Inukshuk Wireless Partnership v 4253311 Canada Inc, 2013 ONSC 5631 85
Invar Manufacturing, a Division of Linamar Holdings Inc v Giuliani,
    a Division of IGM USA Inc (2008), 235 OAC 202, [2008]
    OJ No 1303, 2008 ONCA 256 134
Inverclyde v Inverclyde, [1931] P 29 454
Iran v Berend, [2007] 2 All ER (Comm) 132 (QB) 352
Iran v The Barakat Galleries Limited (2007), [2008] 1 All ER 1177,
    [2007] EWCA Civ 1374 .... 35–36, 40, 349
Iran Vojdan, The, [1984] 2 Lloyd's Rep 380 (QB) 290
IRC v Bullock, [1976] 1 WLR 1178 14
Issasi v Rosenzweig, 2011 ONCA 302, additional reasons
    2011 ONCA 417 .... 478, 480
iTV Games Inc, Re (2001), 18 BLR (3d) 312, 29 CBR (4th) 85,
    2001 BCSC 1391, leave to appeal denied (2002),
    21 BLR (3d) 258, 31 CBR (4th) 279, 2002 BCCA 38 31

J (A Minor) (Abduction: Custody Rights), Re, [1990] 2 AC 562 (HL) 472
Jabbaz v Mouammar (2003), 171 OAC 102, 38 RFL (5th) 103,
    [2003] OJ No 1616 (CA) 477
Jabbour v Custodian of Absentee's Property of State of Israel,
    [1954] 1 WLR 139 354
Jablonowski v Jablonowski, [1972] 3 OR 410, 8 RFL 36, [1972]
    OJ No 1869 (HCJ) 15
Jahangiri-Mavaneh v Taheri-Zengekani (2003), 66 OR (3d) 272,
    39 RFL (5th) 103, [2003] OJ No 3018 (SCJ), rev'd (2005),
    14 RFL (6th) 9, [2005] OJ No 2055 (CA) 489
James Bay Resources Ltd v Mak Mera Nigeria Ltd, 2015 ONCA 781 137
James C Bennett Holdings Ltd v EMD Management Ltd (1991),
    74 Man R (2d) 92, 47 CPC (2d) 13, [1991] MJ No 244 (QB) 203
Januszkiewicz v Januszkiewicz (1965), 55 DLR (2d) 727,
    55 WWR 73, [1965] MJ No 76 (QB) 436

Jasen v Karassik (2009), 95 OR (3d) 430, 306 DLR (4th) 723,
    2009 ONCA 245, rev'g (2008), 92 OR (3d) 283, 295 DLR (4th) 703,
    [2008] OJ No 3031 (SCJ) 491–92
JCH v MBH (2006), 27 RFL (6th) 218, [2006] BCJ No 580, 2006 BCPC 76 499
Jenkins v Jenkins (2000), 8 RFL (5th) 96, [2000] OJ No 1631 (SCJ) 427, 488
Jenner v Sun Oil Co Ltd, [1952] OR 240, [1952] 2 DLR 526,
    [1952] OJ No 535 (HCJ) 89–90
Jensen Estates, Re (1963), 40 DLR (2d) 469, 42 WWR 513,
    [1963] BCJ No 136 (SC) 483
Jewish National Fund Inc v Royal Trust Co, [1965] SCR 784,
    53 DLR (2d) 577, [1965] SCJ No 50 .... 378, 398
JL v British Columbia (Director of the Child, Family and Community
    Service Act), 2010 BCSC 1234 477
John Pfeiffer Pty Ltd v Rogerson (2000), 203 CLR 503 (HCA) 239, 277
Jones v Kansa General Insurance Co (1992), 10 OR (3d) 56,
    57 OAC 213, [1992] OJ No 1597 (CA) 50
Jones v Smith, [1925] 2 DLR 790, 56 OLR 550, [1925]
    OJ No 165 (CA) 370
Jordan v Schatz (2000), 189 DLR (4th) 62, 77 BCLR (3d) 134,
    2000 BCCA 409 56
Josephson (Litigation guardian of) v Balfour Recreation Commission,
    2010 BCSC 603 110–11

Kaime Estate, Re (1938), 53 BCR 190, [1938] 4 DLR 806, [1938]
    BCJ No 33 (SC) 361
Kanto Yakin Kogyo Kabushiki-Kaisha v Can-Eng Manufacturing Ltd
    (1992), 7 OR (3d) 779, 4 BLR (2d) 108, [1992] OJ No 198 (Gen Div),
    aff'd (1995), 22 OR (3d) 576, [1995] OJ No 971 (CA) 212
Kasprzyk v Burks, [2005] OTC 67, 15 RFL (6th) 221, [2005]
    OJ No 289 (SCJ) 491
Kaur v Ginder (1958), 13 DLR (2d) 465, 25 WWR 532, [1958]
    BCJ No 123 (SC) 420–21
Kaur v Guraya, 2011 ONSC 2853 491–92
Kaverit Steel and Crane Ltd v Kone Corp (1992), 120 AR 346,
    85 Alta LR (2d) 287, [1992] AJ No 40 (CA) 131
Kaynes v BP, Plc, 2014 ONCA 580 .... 89, 122, 135
KC v City of Westminster Social & Community Services Dept,
    [2008] EWCA Civ 198 416
Kearney v Willis (2001), 15 RFL (5th) 96, [2001] NJ No 99 (UFC) 496
Kehr, Re, [1952] 1 Ch 26 365–66
Kelemen v Alberta (Public Trustee) (2007), 413 AR 305,
    71 Alta LR (4th) 366, 2007 ABQB 56 .... 365, 382, 393–94
Kellogg Brown & Root Inc v Aerotech Herman Nelson Inc,
    2004 MBCA 63 48
Kelly v Selwyn, [1905] 2 Ch 117 357
Kerr v Baranow, 2011 SCC 10 305

Kerr v Kerr (1933), [1934] SCR 72, [1934] 2 DLR 369,
  [1933] SCJ No 66 401–2
Khalij Commercial Bank Ltd v Woods (1985), 50 OR (2d) 446,
  17 DLR (4th) 358, [1985] OJ No 2500 (HCJ) 238
Khan Resources Inc v Atomredmetzoloto JSC, 2013 ONCA 189 103
Khan Resources Inc v WM Mining Co, LLC (2006), 79 OR (3d) 411,
  208 OAC 204, [2006] OJ No 845 (CA) 331
Khan v Khan (1959), 21 DLR (2d) 171, 29 WWR 181, [1959]
  BCJ No 129 (SC) 455–56
Kilderry Holdings Ltd v Canpower International BV, 2013 BCCA 82 80
Kilpatrick v Kilpatrick, [1929] 3 WWR 463, 42 BCR 88, [1929]
  BCJ No 15 (SC) 17
Kim v Toronto (City), 2013 ONSC 6831 239
Kinch v Pyle, [2004] OTC 1117, 8 CPC (6th) 66, [2004] OJ No 5232 (SCJ) 67
King v Drabinsky (2008), 91 OR (3d) 616, 58 CPC (6th) 223,
  2008 ONCA 566 191
Kish v Director of Vital Statistics (1973), 35 DLR (3d) 530, [1973]
  2 WWR 678, [1973] AJ No 151 (SC) 437
Kleinwort Benson Ltd v Glasgow City Council, [1999] 1 AC 153 (HL) 315
Kloebe, Re (1884), 28 Ch D 175 362
KN v SQ, 2013 BCSC 1433 466
Knight v Knight (1995), 16 RFL (4th) 48, [1995] OJ No 3242 (Gen Div) 448
Knowles v Lindstrom, 2014 ONCA 116 .... 24, 83, 311, 491, 496, 501
Kollaras v Olympic Airways SA (1999), 100 OTC 241, [1999]
  OJ No 1447 (SCJ), aff'd (2000), 132 OAC 67, [2000] OJ No 1104 (CA) 259
Komer, Re, [1925] 2 DLR 86, 27 OWN 467, [1925] OJ No 533 (SC) 254
Koo, Re (1992), [1993] 1 FC 286, 59 FTR 27, [1992] FCJ No 1107 (TD) 22
Kornberg v Kornberg (1990), 76 DLR (4th) 379, 47 CPC (2d) 58,
  [1990] MJ No 659 (CA) 430–31
Korutowska-Wooff v Wooff (2004), 242 DLR (4th) 385,
  188 OAC 376, [2004] OJ No 3256 (CA) 472
Kovacs v Kovacs (2002), 59 OR (3d) 671, 212 DLR (4th) 711,
  [2002] OJ No 3074 (SCJ) 477, 480
Kroetsch v Domnik Industries Ltd (1985), 60 AR 69, [1985]
  AJ No 857 (QB) 62, 65
Krushelinski v Wehner, 2015 SKQB 195 492
Kubera v Kubera, 2010 BCCA 118 476–77
Kuehne + Nagel Ltd v Agrimax Ltd, 2010 FC 1303 48
Kung v Kung (1990), 42 BCLR (2d) 145, [1990] BCJ No 5 (CA) 337
Kunkel v Kunkel (1994), 111 DLR (4th) 457, 2 RFL (4th) 1,
  [1994] AJ No 82 (CA) 466
Kuwait Airways Corporation v Iraqi Airways Company, [2002]
  2 AC 883 (HL) 32, 348–49

La Carte v La Carte (1975), 60 DLR (3d) 507, 23 RFL 112,
  [1975] BCJ No 843 (SC) 433, 436

Laane v Estonian State Cargo & Passenger Steamship Line,
  [1949] SCR 530, [1949] 2 DLR 641, [1949] SCJ No 24 36
Laasch v Turenne, 2012 ABCA 32 197
Lailey v International Student Volunteers, Inc, 2008 BCSC 1344 99
Lamborghini (Canada) Inc v Automobili Lamborghini SPA, [1996]
  JQ No 4175 (CA) 110
Landmark Sport Group Atlantic Ltd v Karpov (1995),
  142 NSR (2d) 280, 39 CPC (3d) 162, [1995] NSJ No 304 (SC) 121
Landreau v Lachapelle, [1937] OR 444, [1937] 2 DLR 504,
  [1937] OJ No 282 (CA) 344
Lau v Li (2001), 53 OR (3d) 727, [2001] OTC 248, [2001] OJ No 1389
  (SCJ), application for leave dismissed, [2001] OJ No 5437 (SCJ) 267
Laurence v Laurence (1991), 56 BCLR (2d) 254, 33 RFL (3d) 27,
  1991 CanLII 1705 (CA) 504
Law v Gustin, [1976] Fam 155 461
Lawrence v Lawrence, [1985] Fam 106 (CA) 413
Lax v Lax (2004), 70 OR (3d) 520, 50 CPC (5th) 266, [2004]
  OJ No 1700 (CA) 196
Laxton v Jurem Anstalt, 2011 BCCA 212 97
Le Mesurier v Le Mesurier, [1895] AC 517 (PC) 432, 435, 440, 458
Lear v Lear, [1973] 3 OR 935, 38 DLR (3d) 655, [1973] OJ No 2114
  (HCJ), rev'd (1974), 5 OR (2d) 572, 51 DLR (3d) 56, [1974]
  OJ No 2100 (CA) 259, 499
Lee v Chung, 2014 BCSC 1157 403–4
Lee v Lau, [1967] P 14 420
Leger v Schultz (2006), 28 RFL (6th) 160, [2006] OJ No 131,
  2006 ONCJ 103 499
Lei v Kwan, 2010 MBCA 108 494
Lemmex v Bernard (2000), 51 OR (3d) 164, [2000] OJ No 4350 (Div Ct) 120
Lemmex v Bernard (2002), 60 OR (3d) 54, 213 DLR (4th) 627,
  [2002] OJ No 2131 (CA) 73
Leonard v Booker (2007), 321 NBR (2d) 340, 286 DLR (4th) 451,
  2007 NBCA 71 .... 465, 489
Lepine v Canada Post Corp, [2009] 1 SCR 549, 67 CPC (6th) 201,
  2009 SCC 16, aff'g [2007] RJQ 1920, [2007] QJ No 8498,
  2007 QCCA 1092, aff'g [2005] JQ no 9806 (CS) 200
Lepre v Lepre, [1965] P 52 .... 445, 462–63
Leufkens v Alba Tours International Inc (2002), 60 OR (3d) 84,
  213 DLR (4th) 614, [2002] OJ No 2129 (CA) 73
Lewis v King, [2004] EWCA Civ 1329 90
LGV v LAP, 2016 NBCA 23 431
Li v MacNutt & Dumont, 2015 NSSC 53 80
Libman v The Queen, [1985] 2 SCR 178, 21 DLR (4th) 174,
  [1985] SCJ No 56 34
Libyan Arab Foreign Bank v Bankers Trust Co, [1989] QB 728 293
Lilydale Cooperative Ltd v Meyn Canada Inc, 2015 ONCA 281 292

Lincoln-General Insurance Co v Insurance Corp of British Columbia,
[2001] OTC 366, 27 CCLI (3d) 127, [2001] OJ No 1903 (SCJ),
aff'd (2002), 163 OAC 188, [2002] OJ No 2059 (CA) 160–61
Litecubes, LLC v Northern Light Products Inc (cob Glowproducts.com),
2009 BCSC 427 49
Littauer Glove Corp v FW Millington (1920) Ltd (1928),
44 TLR 746 (KB) 63
Livesley v E Clements Horst Co (1924), [1924] SCR 605, [1925]
1 DLR 159, [1924] SCJ No 40 .... 196, 219
Lixo Investments Ltd v Gowling, Lafleur, Henderson, 2013 ONSC 4862,
aff'd 2014 ONCA 114 94
Loat v Howarth, 2011 ONCA 509 .... 125, 128
Lor v Lor (1978), 25 NSR (2d) 243, 5 RFL (2d) 138, [1978]
NSJ No 502 (SCAD) 21
Lord Advocate v Jaffrey, [1921] 1 AC 146 (HL) 18
Lord Cable, Re (1976), [1976] 3 All ER 417, [1977] 1 WLR 7 397–98
Lord v Colvin, (1859), 62 ER 141 14
Lorillard, Re, [1922] 2 Ch 638 (CA) 363–64
Loucks v Standard Oil Co of New York, 120 NE 198 (NY 1918) 30
Lubbe v Cape plc, [2000] 1 WLR 1545 (HL) 139
Lucasfilm Ltd v Ainsworth, [2011] UKSC 39 .... 330, 332, 334
Lynch v Provisional Government of Paraguay (1871),
LR 2 P & D 268 .... 231, 376, 379

M, Re (2007), [2007] 3 WLR 975, [2008] 1 All ER 1157, [2007] UKHL 55 478
Macdonald v Macdonald, [1932] SC 79 (HL) 324
Macdonald v Macdonell (1864), 2 UCE & A 341 (Upper Canada CA) 380
MacDonald, Re, [1964] SCR 317, 44 DLR (2d) 208, [1964] SCJ No 13 381
Macedo v Macedo (1996), 19 RFL (4th) 65, [1996] OJ No 435
(Gen Div) 337, 503
Machado v Fontes, [1897] 2 QB 231 (CA) 262–63, 265
Mackender v Feldia AG, [1967] 2 QB 590 (CA) 294–96
Macmillan Inc v Bishopsgate Investment Trust Plc (No 3), [1995]
3 All ER 747 (Ch D), aff'd (1995), [1996] 1 WLR 387,
[1996] 1 All ER 585 (CA) 220, 223, 224–25, 310, 328, 353, 355
MacPherson v MacPherson (1976), 13 OR (2d) 233,
70 DLR (3d) 564, [1976] OJ No 2195 (CA) 425, 426–27, 488
Macrae v Macrae, [1949] 2 All ER 34 (CA) 25
MacShannon v Rockware Glass Ltd, [1978] AC 795 (HL) 115–16
Maden v Long (1982), [1983] 1 WWR 649, 41 BCLR 6,
[1982] BCJ No 93 (SC) 350
Magee v Morrison, [1993] OJ No 1912 (Gen Div) 466
Magic Sportswear Corp v OT Africa Line Ltd (2006),
[2007] 2 FCR 733, 273 DLR (4th) 302, 2006 FCA 284 159–60
Maharanee of Baroda v Wildenstein, [1972] 2 WLR 1077, [1972]
2 All ER 689 (CA) 59–60

Mainguy v Mainguy (1984), 42 CPC 84, [1984] OJ No 859 (HCJ) 15–16
Maldonado's Estate, Re, [1954] P 223 (CA) 226, 228, 388
Malo and Bertrand v Clement, [1943] 4 DLR 773, [1943] OWN 555,
  [1943] OJ No 510 (HCJ) 334–35
Manella v Manella, [1942] OR 630, [1942] 4 DLR 712, [1942]
  OJ No 470 (CA) 19, 455
Mantini v Smith Lyons LLP (2003), 64 OR (3d) 505, 228 DLR
  (4th) 214, [2003] OJ No 1831 (CA) 131
Mark v Mark (2005), [2006] 1 AC 98, [2005] 3 All ER 912, [2005]
  UKHL 42 .... 11, 15, 21
Marriage Law of Canada, Re The (1912), 7 DLR 629, [1912] AC 880,
  [1912] JCJ No 4 (PC) 401
Marsellus v Marsellus (1970), 13 DLR (3d) 383, 75 WWR 746,
  [1970] BCJ No 241 (SC) 25, 426
Martin v Perrie, [1986] 1 SCR 41, 24 DLR (4th) 1, [1986] SCJ No 1 241
Martin, Re, [1900] P 211 (CA) 383
Martinez v Basail, 2010 ONSC 2038 437
Martinez v Martinez-Jarquin, [1990] OJ No 1385 (Prov Ct) 471
Martinez-Caro v Canada (Minister of Citizenship and Immigration),
  2011 FC 640 23
Martodam v Martodam, [2007] AJ No 179, 2007 ABQB 100 467
Marzara v Marzara, 2011 BCSC 408 .... 32, 446
Mather v Mahoney, [1968] 1 WLR 1773 (PDA) 438
Matrix Integrated Solutions Ltd v Naccarato (2009), 97 OR (3d) 693,
  75 CPC (6th) 17, [2009] OJ No 3187 (CA) 132
Maxwell v Maxwell (1852), 51 ER 717 (Ch Rolls Ct), aff'd (1852),
  42 ER 1048 (HL) 386
Mayfield v Mayfield, [1969] P 119 437
Mbasogo v Logo Ltd (2006), [2007] 2 WLR 1062, [2006] EWCA Civ 1370 40
McCain Foods Ltd v Agricultural Publishing Co (1979), 26 OR
  (2d) 758, 14 CPC 168, [1979] OJ No 1182 (CA) 69
McCutcheon v The Cash Store Inc (2006), 80 OR (3d) 644,
  27 CPC (6th) 293, [2006] OJ No 1860 (SCJ) 107–8, 200
McDiarmid Lumber Ltd v God's Lake First Nation (2005),
  251 DLR (4th) 93, 192 Man R (2d) 82, 2005 MBCA 22,
  aff'd [2006] 2 SCR 846, 274 DLR (4th) 577, 2006 SCC 58 327
McLean v Pettigrew (1944), [1945] SCR 62, [1945] 2 DLR 65,
  [1944] SCJ No 49 .... 262, 264–65, 270
McMillan v McMillan, 2012 BCSC 32 155
ME v Alberta (Minister of Human Services), 2015 ABQB 251 484
Medina v Pallett, 2010 BCSC 259 477
Meeking v Cash Store Inc, 2013 MBCA 81 .... 109, 200
Mercedes Benz AG v Lieduck, [1996] 1 AC 284 (PC) 92
Merker v Merker, [1963] P 283 460
Messina v Smith, [1971] P 322 438
Mester v Kummu (1957), 11 DLR (2d) 217, [1957] OWN 534 (HCJ) 24

Metcalfe v Yamaha Motor Powered Products Co, 2012 ABCA 240 103
Meyer, Re, [1971] P 298 .... 445, 462–63
Microcell Communications Inc v Frey, 2011 SKCA 136............................ 129–30
Midland Bank plc v Laker Airways Ltd, [1986] QB 689 (CA) 146
Mid-Ohio Imported Car Co v Tri-K Investments Ltd (1995), 129 DLR
    (4th) 181, 13 BCLR (3d) 41, [1995] BCJ No 2199 (CA)............. 68–69, 172–73
Mignacca v Merck Frosst Canada Ltd (2009), 95 OR (3d) 269,
    71 CPC (6th) 350, [2009] OJ No 821 (Div Ct) 134
Miliangos v George Frank (Textiles) Ltd, [1976] AC 443 (HL) 46–49
Miller v Miller (1999), 121 OAC 300, 1 RFL (5th) 391, [1999]
    OJ No 2250 (CA) 469
Milliken v Pratt, 125 Mass 374, 28 Am Rep 241 (1878)........................... 232, 234
Minera Aquiline Argentina SA v IMA Exploration Inc (2006),
    58 BCLR (4th) 217, 32 CPC (6th) 31, 2006 BCSC 1102,
    aff'd (2007), 68 BCLR (4th) 242, 43 CPC (6th) 45,
    2007 BCCA 319.. 311–13, 327, 339
Mining Technologies International, Inc v Krako Inc, 2012 ONCA 847............. 97
Misyura v Walton, 2012 ONSC 5397 81
Mitchell v Jeckovich, 2013 ONSC 7494 111
Mittoo v Nanda, 2015 ONCJ 401.. 492
MJ Jones Inc v Kingsway General Insurance Co (2004),
    72 OR (3d) 68, [2004] OJ No 3286 (CA)..67
MJ Jones Inc v Kingsway General Insurance Co, [2003] OJ No 4409
    (SCJ), aff'd (2004), 185 OAC 113, [2004] OJ No 1087 (CA) 67
Molson Coors Brewing Co v Miller Brewing Co (2006),
    83 OR (3d) 331, 37 CPC (6th) 394, [2006] OJ No 4236 (SCJ)............ 126, 134
Molson v Molson (1998), 222 AR 130, 38 RFL (4th) 385,
    1998 ABQB 476 .... 25, 427
Momentous.ca Corp v Canadian American Association of
    Professional Baseball Ltd, 2012 SCC 9............................... 70, 123, 130–31
Montagne Laramee Developments Inc v Creit Properties Inc
    (2000), 47 OR (3d) 729, 45 CPC (4th) 345, [2000]
    OJ No 959 (SCJ)... 331
Monte Cristo Investments LLC v Hydroslotter Corp, 2011 ONSC 6011,
    aff'd 2012 ONCA 213 189
Monteiro v Monteiro, 2015 BCSC 1543.. 344, 503
Monteiro v Toronto Dominion Bank (2008), 89 OR (3d) 565,
    234 OAC 156, 2008 ONCA 137... 163
Montreal Trust Co v Stanrock Uranium Mines Ltd (1965), [1966]
    1 OR 258, 53 DLR (2d) 594, [1965] OJ No 1170 (HCJ)............................ 293
Mooney v Orr (1994), [1995] 1 WWR 517, 98 BCLR (2d) 318,
    [1994] BCJ No 2322 (SC).. 7
Moore v Mercator Enterprises Ltd (1978), 31 NSR (2d) 327,
    90 DLR (3d) 590, [1978] NSJ No 705 (SC)... 64, 170
Moore v Mitchell, 30 F2d 600 (2d Cir 1929) 33
Moradkhan v Mofidi, 2013 BCCA 132 330

Moran v Pyle National (Canada) Ltd (1973), [1975] 1 SCR 393,
    43 DLR (3d) 239, [1973] SCJ No 149..86–89, 269
Morgardshammar AB v HR Radomski & Co Ltd (1983),
    145 DLR (3d) 111, [1983] OJ No 3342 (HCJ), aff'd (1984),
    5 DLR (4th) 576, [1984] OJ No 3477 (CA).......................................256
Morguard Investments Ltd v De Savoye, [1990] 3 SCR 1077,
    76 DLR (4th) 256, [1990] SCJ No 135.........................37, 39, 42, 55–60, 71–75,
    77–78, 81–82, 93, 104, 107, 109, 111, 117, 166, 168–69, 173–79, 181, 186–87,
    197, 203–4, 218, 250, 283, 331–32, 339, 371, 435, 437, 453, 461
Morris v Poole, [1995] 6 WWR 166, [1995] NWTJ No 47 (SC).........................474
Moses v Shore Boat Builders Ltd (1993), 83 BCLR (2d) 177,
    19 CPC (3d) 219, [1993] BCJ No 1910 (CA)......................................175
Murphy v Wulkowicz, [2003] NSJ No 324, 2003 NSSC 181..............................488
Murray Estate, Re (1921), 31 Man R 362 (KB)..18
Muscutt v Courcelles (2002), 60 OR (3d) 20, 213 DLR
    (4th) 577, 26 CPC (5th) 206, [2002] OJ No 2128
    (CA).................................57, 71, 73, 75– 81, 97, 120, 123, 175–77, 339–40
MWG v KAA, 2012 NBQB 402..499

Na v Renfrew Security Bank & Trust (Offshore) Ltd (2003),
    16 BCLR (4th) 345, 35 CPC (5th) 381, 2003 BCSC 1204 62
Nackawic Mechanical Ltd (cob SDI Aviation) v Ward, 2015 NBCA 1 ....171, 179
Nafie v Badawy, 2015 ABCA 36...24, 407, 420, 426, 489
Nagra v Malhotra, 2012 ONSC 4497..97, 124
Nalcor Energy—Oil and Gas Inc v Husky Oil Operations Ltd,
    2016 NLTD(G) 5 131
National Trust Company Ltd v Ebro Irrigation and Power Company Ltd,
    [1954] OR 463, [1954] 3 DLR 326, [1954] OJ No 545 (HCJ).................26–27
Navarro v Parrish, 2014 ONCA 856..491–92
Ndegwa v Ndegwa (2001), 20 RFL (5th) 118, [2001] OTC 525,
    [2001] OJ No 2849 (SCJ)..469–70
Neilson v Overseas Projects Corporation of Victoria Ltd (2005),
    223 CLR 331, 221 ALR 213, [2005] HCA 54.........................229, 258, 277–78
Nelson v Bridport (1845), 8 Beav 527, 50 ER 207 379
Nelson v Nelson, [1925] 3 DLR 22 (Alta SC)...........................12, 14, 20
New Brunswick (Attorney General) v Majeau-Prasad (2000),
    229 NBR (2d) 296, 10 RFL (5th) 389, [2000] NBJ No 363 (QB)..................476
New York Breweries Co Ltd v Attorney-General, [1899] AC 62 (HL)...............368
New York Life Insurance Co v Public Trustee, [1924] 2 Ch 101 354
Newfoundland and Labrador (Attorney General) v Rothmans Inc,
    2013 NLTD(G) 180 102
Nicholas v Nicholas (1996), 139 DLR (4th) 652, 94 OAC 21,
    [1996] OJ No 3543 (CA) 431
Nicholls v Brisbane Slipways and Engineering P/L, [2003] QSC 193 278
Nike Infomatic Systems Ltd v Avac Systems Ltd (1979), 105 DLR
    (3d) 455, 16 BCLR 139, [1979] BCJ No 1277 (SC) 289

Noël et Associés, SENCRL v Sincennes, 2012 ONSC 3770 164
Norske Atlas Ins Co v London General Ins Co (1927), 28 Ll LR 104 (KB) 214
Nouvion v Freeman (1889), 15 App Cas 1 (HL) 164, 167
Nova, An Alberta Corporation v Grove (1982), 39 AR 409,
 31 CPC 219, [1982] AJ No 1011 (CA) 101–2, 367–68
Nowosielska v Nowosielski, [2004] OJ No 4702, 2004 ONCJ 282 498
Noyes v Cardinal Couriers Ltd (1993), 109 Sask R 108,
 13 CPC (3d) 144, [1993] SJ No 155 (CA) 178
NV Kwik Hoo Tong Handel Maatschappij v James Finlay & Co Ltd,
 [1927] AC 604 (HL) 291
Nystrom v Tarnava (1996), 191 AR 325, 44 Alta LR (3d) 355, [1996]
 AJ No 1243 (QB) 255

O'Brien and Canadian Pacific Railway Co, Re (1972), 25 DLR (3d) 230,
 [1972] 3 WWR 456, [1972] SJ No 331 (CA) 291
O'Brien v Canada (Attorney General) (2002), 201 NSR (2d) 338,
 210 DLR (4th) 668, 2002 NSCA 21 78
O'Brien v O'Brien (2008), 59 RFL (6th) 389, [2008] OJ No 3977 (SCJ) 472
O'Brien v Simard, 2006 BCSC 814, leave to appeal refused
 (2006), 230 BCAC 120, [2006] BCJ No 2130, 2006 BCCA 410 .... 68, 115
Oakley v Barry (1998), 166 NSR (2d) 282, 158 DLR (4th) 679,
 [1998] NSJ No 122 (CA) 57, 78
Oakwell Engineering Ltd v Enernorth Industries Inc (2006),
 81 OR (3d) 288, 30 CPC (6th) 253, [2006] OJ No 2289 (CA) 190
Obégi Chemicals LLC v Kilani, 2011 ONSC 1636 92
Occidental Chemical Corp v Sovereign General Insurance Co (1997),
 32 OR (3d) 277, [1997] OJ No 6294 (Gen Div) 123
Ogden v Ogden, [1908] P 46 (CA) 405, 414
Ogilvie, Re, [1918] 1 Ch 492 385
OJSC Oil Company Yugraneft v Abramovich, [2008] EWHC 2613
 (Comm) 310
OJSC TNK-BP Holding v Beppler & Jacobson Ltd, [2012]
 EWHC 3286 (Ch) 311, 322
Okmayansky v Okmayansky (2007), 86 OR (3d) 587, 284 DLR
 (4th) 152, 2007 ONCA 427 489
Old North State Brewing Co v Newlands Services Inc (1997),
 47 BCLR (3d) 254, [1997] BCJ No 2484 (SC), aff'd (1998),
 58 BCLR (3d) 144, 41 BLR (2d) 191, [1998]
 BCJ No 2474 (CA) 49, 175, 186, 192, 194
Oliphant v Oliphant Estate (1990), 84 Sask R 44, 38 ETR 133,
 [1990] SJ No 238 (QB) 484
OM v AK — Droit de la famille 3148 (SOQUIJ), [2000] RJQ 2339,
 9 RFL (5th) 111, [2000] QJ No 3224 (SC) 489
Ontario (Attorney General) v Rothmans Inc, 2013 ONCA 353 .... 89, 97, 102
Ontario Stone Corp v RE Law Crushed Stone Ltd, [1964] 1 OR 303,
 [1964] OJ No 685 (HCJ) 252

Ontario v Mar-Dive Corp (1996), 141 DLR (4th) 577, 20 OTC 81,
  [1996] OJ No 4471 (Gen Div) 176
OPO v MLA, [2014] EWCA Civ 1277, rev'd (sub nom Rhodes v OPO)
  [2015] UKSC 32 258
Oppenheimer v Cattermole, [1976] AC 249 (HL) 31, 191
Oppenheimer v Louis Rosenthal & Co AG, [1937] 1 All ER 23 138
Orabi v El Qaoud (2005), 12 RFL (6th) 296, [2005] NSJ No 76,
  2005 NSCA 28 .... 434, 443–44
Original Cakerie Ltd v Renaud, 2013 BCSC 755 80
Ostrander v Houston (1915), 8 Sask LR 132, [1915] SJ No 19 (SC En Banc) 387
Ostroski v Global Upholstery, [1995] OJ No 4211 (Gen Div) 269
Osvath-Latkoczy v Osvath-Latkoczy, [1959] SCR 751,
  19 DLR (2d) 495, [1959] SCJ No 55 .... 13, 14
OT Africa Line Ltd v Magic Sportswear Corp, [2005]
  2 Lloyd's Rep 170, [2005] EWCA Civ 710 .... 151–52, 159
Oulton Agencies Inc v Knolloffice Inc (1988), 69 Nfld & PEIR 65,
  30 CPC (2d) 12, [1988] PEIJ No 10 (SCAD) 128
Owens Bank Ltd v Bracco, [1992] 2 AC 443 (HL) 188

P(GE) (an infant), Re, [1965] Ch 568 (CA) 467
Page Estate v Sachs (1990), 72 OR (2d) 409, 37 ETR 226, [1990]
  OJ No 478 (HCJ), aff'd (1993), 12 OR (3d) 371,
  99 DLR (4th) 209, [1993] OJ No 269 (CA) 384
Palmer v Palmer (1979), 2 Sask R 112, [1980] 2 WWR 557,
  1979 CanLII 2280 (CA) 504
Papadogiorgakis, Re, [1978] 2 FC 208, 88 DLR (3d) 243,
  [1978] FCJ No 31 (TD) 22
Paraie v Cangemi, 2012 ONSC 6341 98–99
Parkasho v Singh (1967), [1967] 1 All ER 737, [1968] P 233 420
Parker v Mitchell, 2016 BCSC 723 507
Patel v Kanbay International Inc (2008), 93 OR (3d) 588,
  244 OAC 61, [2008] OJ No 5256 (CA) 142
Patterson v Hambleton, [1933] OWN 247, [1933] OJ No 69 (HCJ) 367
Pattni v Ali, 2006 UKPC 51 54
Paulsson v Cooper, 2011 ONCA 150 90
Pavilion Financial Corp v Highview Financial Holdings Inc, 2013 MBQB 95 84
Pei v Bank Bumiputra Malaysia Berhad (1998), 41 OR (3d) 39,
  21 CPC (4th) 289, [1998] OJ No 2645 (Gen Div) 138
Pemberton v Hughes, [1899] 1 Ch 781 (CA) 445, 462–63
Pemberton, Re (1966), 59 DLR (2d) 44, 57 WWR 552, [1966]
  BCJ No 132 (SC) 365, 368
Penn v Lord Baltimore (1750), 1 Ves Sen 444, 27 ER 1132 (Ch) 336
Perrini v Perrini, [1979] Fam 84 .... 413, 461
Peter v Beblow, [1993] 1 SCR 980, 101 DLR (4th) 621, [1993] SCJ No 36 311
Peterson v Bezold (1970), 17 DLR (3d) 471, [1971] 2 WWR 156,
  [1970] AJ No 170 (SCAD) 367

Pettkus v Becker, [1980] 2 SCR 834, 117 DLR (3d) 257, [1980]
  SCJ No 103 .... 249–50, 254, 305, 311
Phillips v Eyre (1870), LR 6 QB 1 (Ex Ct) 262, 266
Phillips v Ford Motor Co of Canada, [1971] 2 OR 637,
  18 DLR (3d) 641, [1971] OJ No 1564 (CA) 251
Pitre v Nguyen, [2007] BCJ No 1708, 2007 BCSC 1161 .... 442, 444
Poje v Attorney General for British Columbia, [1953] 1 SCR 516,
  [1953] 2 DLR 785, [1953] SCJ No 25 184
Pollastro v Pollastro (1999), 43 OR (3d) 485, 171 DLR (4th) 32,
  [1999] OJ No 911 (CA) 477
Ponticelli v Ponticelli, [1958] P 204 419
Pope & Talbot Ltd, Re, [2009] BCJ No 2248, 2009 BCSC 1552 .... 290, 293
Pourghasemi, Re (1993), 62 FTR 122, 19 Imm LR (2d) 259,
  [1993] FCJ No 232 (TD) 22–23
Powell v Cockburn (1976), [1977] 2 SCR 218, 68 DLR (3d) 700,
  [1976] SCJ No 66 .... 442–44, 462
Precious Metal Capital Corp v Smith (2008), 92 OR (3d) 701,
  297 DLR (4th) 746, 2008 ONCA 577, aff'g (2008),
  60 CPC (6th) 276, [2008] OJ No 1236 (SCJ) 132, 331, 339–40
Prefontaine Estate v Frizzle (1990), 71 OR (2d) 385,
  40 CPC (2d) 161, [1990] OJ No 75 (CA) 265
Premium Nafta Products Limited v Fili Shipping Company Limited,
  [2007] UKHL 40 131
Preymann v Ayus Technology Corp, 2012 BCCA 30 130
Price Mobile Homes Centres, Inc v National Trailer Convoy of Canada
  Ltd (1974), 44 DLR (3d) 443, [1974] MJ No 115 (QB) 349
Prince v ACE Aviation Holdings Inc, 2014 ONCA 285 .... 37, 62, 137
Pro Swing Inc v Elta Golf Inc, [2006] 2 SCR 612, 273 DLR (4th) 663,
  2006 SCC 52 .... 34, 157, 167, 181–87, 339, 341
Proia v Proia (2003), 340 AR 363, 41 RFL (5th) 371, 2003 ABQB 576 .... 472, 477
Provincial Treasurer of Manitoba v Bennett, [1937] SCR 138,
  [1937] 2 DLR 1, [1937] SCJ No 5 328
Prudential Insurance Company of America v O'Grady,
  396 P2d 246 (Ariz 1964) 234
PT ATPK Resources TBK (Indonesia) v Diversified Energy and
  Resource Corporation (appeal by Hopaco Properties Ltd),
  2014 ONCA 466, aff'g 2013 ONSC 5913 .... 184, 197
Pugh v Pugh, [1951] P 482 410
Purple Echo Productions Inc v KCTS Television (2008),
  76 BCLR (4th) 21, 52 CPC (6th) 15, 2008 BCCA 85 102

Quadrangle Holdings Ltd v Coady, 2015 NSCA 13 225
Quigley v Willmore (2008), 264 NSR (2d) 293, 50 RFL (6th) 1,
  2008 NSCA 33 .... 24, 425, 489
Quigley v Willmore (2008), 272 NSR (2d) 61, [2008] NSJ No 552,
  2008 NSSC 353 434

Qureshi v Qureshi, [1972] Fam 173 .... 438, 440–41, 445

R (Abduction: Habitual Residence), Re (2003), [2004] 1 FLR 216,
 [2003] EWHC 1968 (Fam) 24
R Griggs Group Ltd v Evans, [2005] Ch 153 369
R v Anderson (1868), LR 1 CCR 161 272
R v Barnet London Borough Council, Ex Parte Shah, [1983]
 2 AC 309 (HL) 24–25, 472
R v Brentwood Superintendent Registrar of Marriages, [1968]
 2 QB 956 (Div Ct) 412
R v Klassen (2008), 240 CCC (3d) 328, 63 CR (6th) 373,
 [2008] BCJ No 2485 (SC) 34
R v R (Divorce: Jurisdiction: Domicile), [2006] 1 FLR 389 11
Radwan v Radwan (No 2), [1973] Fam 35 421
Raghbeer, Re (1977), 3 RFL (2d) 42, [1977] OJ No 1698 (Co Ct) 484
Rai, Re (1980), 27 OR (2d) 425, 106 DLR (3d) 718, [1980]
 OJ No 3513 (CA) 480–81
Ralli Bros v Compania Naviera Sota y Aznar, [1920] 2 KB 287 (CA) 301
Ramsay v Liverpool Royal Infirmary, [1930] AC 588 (HL) 16
Ramsay-Fairfax v Ramsay-Fairfax, [1956] P 115 (CA) 454–56
Rastell v Draper (1605), 80 ER 55 (KB) 46
Rattenbury Estate, Re, [1936] 2 WWR 554, 51 BCR 321, [1936]
 BCJ No 43 (SC) 387
Re Friction Division Products, Inc v El Du Pont de Nemours &
 Co Inc (No 2) (1986), 56 OR (2d) 722, 32 DLR (4th) 105,
 [1986] OJ No 1029 (HCJ) 6
Re Hole, [1948] 4 DLR 419, 56 Man R 295, [1948]
 MJ No 60 (KB) 325, 327, 388
Re Jutras, [1932] 2 WWR 533, [1932] SJ No 50, 1932 CanLII 241 (CA) 508
Re Lambert, [2001] OTC 514, 26 CBR (4th) 235, [2001]
 OJ No 2776 (SCJ) 31, 191
Re Matol Botanical International Ltd, [2001] RJQ 2333, [2001]
 QJ No 4195 (CS) 39, 180
Re Mengel's Will Trusts, [1962] Ch 791 385
Re MNS, 2012 ONSC 1596 481
Rea, Re, [1902] 1 IR 451 (Ch D) 372, 374
Red Sea Insurance Co Ltd v Bouygues SA, [1995] 1 AC 190 (PC) 264
Reed v Reed (1969), 6 DLR (3d) 617, 69 WWR 327, [1969]
 BCJ No 433 (SC) 405–6, 416
Reference re Family Relations Act (BC), [1982] 1 SCR 62,
 131 DLR (3d) 257, [1982] SCJ No 112 465
Reference re Same-Sex Marriage, [2004] 3 SCR 698,
 246 DLR (4th) 193, 2004 SCC 79 414
Regas Ltd v Plotkins, [1961] SCR 566, 29 DLR (2d) 282, [1961]
 SCJ No 34 245
Regazzoni v KC Sethia (1944) Ltd, [1958] AC 301 (HL) 301

Regie Nationale des Usines Renault SA v Zhang (2002),
  210 CLR 491 (HCA) 277
Reid v Francis, [1929] 4 DLR 311, 24 Sask LR 1 (CA) 456
Republic de Guatemala v Nunez, [1927] 1 KB 669 (CA) 353
Research in Motion Ltd v Visto Corp (2008), 93 OR (3d) 593,
  68 CPR (4th) 321, [2008] OJ No 3671 (SCJ) 63
Rhodes v Shorter (1981), 27 BCLR 60, 20 CPC 25, [1981]
  BCJ No 1713 (CA) 85
Richardson International, Ltd v Mys Chikhacheva (The),
  2002 FCA 97 291
Right Business Ltd v Affluent Public Ltd, 2011 BCSC 783,
  aff'd 2012 BCCA 375 137
Riley v Wildhaber, 2011 ONSC 3456 (Div Ct) 466
Ritchie and Ritchie, Re (1974), 5 OR (2d) 520, 20 RFL 225, [1974]
  OJ No 2093 (CA) 467
Ritchie, Re, [1942] OR 426, [1942] 3 DLR 330, [1942] OJ No 453 (HCJ) 364
RNS v KS, 2013 BCCA 406 .... 438, 446, 490
Robb Evans v European Bank Limited, [2004] NSWCA 82 40–41
Robertson v Thomson Corp (1999), 43 OR (3d) 161, 30 CPC (4th) 182,
  [1999] OJ No 280 (Gen Div) 198
Robinson v Bland (1760), 2 Burr 1077 286
Robinson-Scott v Robinson-Scott, [1958] P 71 .... 436, 459
Ross v Ross (1894), 25 SCR 307, [1894] SCJ No 72 .... 230, 375
Ross, Re, [1930] 1 Ch 377 377
Ross-Smith v Ross-Smith, [1961] 1 All ER 255 (CA), rev'd
  [1963] AC 280 (HL) 452, 456–57
Rothgiesser v Rothgiesser (2000), 46 OR (3d) 577,
  183 DLR (4th) 310, [2000] OJ No 33 (CA) 70, 465, 489
Rowland v Rowland (1973), 2 OR (2d) 161, 42 DLR (3d) 205,
  [1973] OJ No 2246 (HCJ) 438
Rowland v Vancouver College Ltd (2001), 205 DLR (4th) 193,
  94 BCLR (3d) 249, 2001 BCCA 527 394
Roy v North American Leisure Group Inc (2004), 73 OR (3d) 561,
  3 CPC (6th) 387, [2004] OJ No 4767 (CA) 271, 287–88
Royal and Sun Alliance Insurance Co of Canada v Wainoco Oil &
  Gas Co (2004), 364 AR 151, 50 CPC (5th) 371, 2004 ABQB 643,
  aff'd (2005), 367 AR 177, 11 CPC (6th) 319, 2005 ABCA 198 76
Royal Bank of Canada v Cow Harbour Construction Ltd,
  2012 ABQB 112 .... 327, 349
Royal Bank of Canada v DCM Erectors Inc, 2013 ONSC 2864 93
Royal Exchange Assurance Corp v Sjoforsakrings Aktiebologet Vega,
  [1902] 2 KB 384 (CA) 291
Royal Trust Corporation of Canada v AS(W)S (2004), 365 AR 385,
  35 Alta LR (4th) 32, 2004 ABQB 284 393
Rubin v Eurofinance SA; New Cap Reinsurance Corporation
  (In Liquidation) v AE Grant, [2012] UKSC 46 .... 168, 177

Rutledge v The United States Savings and Loan Co (1906),
    37 SCR 546, [1906] SCJ No 31 196

Sahibalzubaidi v Bahjat, 2011 ONSC 4075 .... 403, 419
Salvesen v Administrator of Austrian Property, [1927] AC 641 (HL) 458
Sampley v Sampley, 2015 BCCA 113 477
Sandy Frank Film Syndication Inc v CFQC Broadcasting Ltd,
    [1983] 4 WWR 360, 23 Sask R 241, [1983] SJ No 278 (CA) 49
Sangha v Mander, [1985] 6 WWR 250, 65 BCLR 265, [1985]
    BCJ No 2688 (SC) 419, 455
Sangi v Sangi, 2011 BCSC 523 508
Santa Marina Shipping Co SA v Lunham & Moore Ltd (1978),
    18 OR (2d) 315, 82 DLR (3d) 295, [1978] OJ No 3225 (HCJ) 62
Santos v Santos, 2010 BCSC 331 488
Sarabia v The "Oceanic Mindoro" (1996), 26 BCLR (3d) 143,
    4 CPC (4th) 11, [1996] BCJ No 2154 (CA) 129
Sarmiento v Villarico, 2014 BCSC 455 455
Savelieff v Glouchkoff (1964), 45 DLR (2d) 520, 48 WWR 335,
    [1964] BCJ No 163 (CA) 451, 453, 455
Sayers v International Drilling Co NV, [1971] 1 WLR 1176, [1971]
    3 All ER 163 (CA) 279
Scatcherd, Re (1918), 15 OWN 222, [1918] OJ No 320 (HC) 362
Schibsby v Westenholz (1870), LR 6 QB 155 164
Schreiber v Mulroney (2007), 88 OR (3d) 605, 288 DLR (4th) 661,
    [2007] OJ No 4997 (SCJ) 102
Schreter v Gasmac Inc (1992), 7 OR (3d) 608, 6 BLR (2d) 71,
    [1992] OJ No 257 (Gen Div) 212
Schwebel v Ungar (1963), [1964] 1 OR 430,
    42 DLR (2d) 622, [1963] OJ No 846 (CA),
    aff'd (1964), [1965] SCR 148, 48 DLR (2d) 644,
    [1964] SCJ No 57 .... 16, 230, 411–12, 416, 436, 439–40
Scott v Hale, [2009] BCJ No 327, 2009 BCSC 228 .... 53, 58
SDI Simulation Group Inc v Chameleon Technologies Inc (1994),
    34 CPC (3d) 346, [1994] OJ No 2195 (Gen Div) 123
Seagull v Seagull (1974), 6 OR (2d) 467, 53 DLR (3d) 230,
    [1974] OJ No 2193 (CA) 448
Sears Canada Inc v C & S Interior Designs Ltd, 2012 ABQB 573 93
Sefel Geophysical Ltd, Re (1988), [1989] 1 WWR 251,
    62 Alta LR (2d) 193, [1988] AJ No 917 (QB) 39, 180
Seidel v TELUS Communications Inc, 2011 SCC 15 143
Semogas v Semogas, [1991] OJ No 678 (Gen Div) 470
Senkiw v Muzyka (1969), 4 DLR (3d) 708, 68 WWR 515,
    [1969] SJ No 277 (CA), aff'd (1970), 12 DLR (3d) 544,
    72 WWR 314, [1970] SCJ No 112 370–71
Shah v LG Chem Ltd, 2015 ONSC 2628 102
Shahnaz v Rizwan, [1965] 1 QB 390 (Div Ct) 421

Sharn Importing Ltd v Babchuk (1971), 21 DLR (3d) 349, [1971]
  4 WWR 517, [1971] BCJ No 477 (SC) 286
Sharpe v Crispin (1869), 1 LR P & D 611 19
Shaw v Shaw (1945), [1946] 1 DLR 168, 62 BCR 52, [1945]
  BCJ No 6 (CA) 455–56
Shekhdar v K & M Engineering & Consulting Corp, [2006] OJ No 2120
  (CA), rev'g (2004), 71 OR (3d) 475, [2004] OJ No 2548 (SCJ) 71
SHN Grundstuecksverwaltungsgesellschaft MBH & Co Seniorenresidenz
  Hoppegarten—Neuenhagen KG v Hanne, 2014 ABCA 168 189
Shortridge-Tsuchiya v Tsuchiya, 2010 BCCA 61 471
Showlag v Mansour, [1995] 1 AC 431 (PC) 195
Silver v IMAX Corp (2009), 86 CPC (6th) 273, 2009 CanLII 72334
  (Ont SCJ) 198
Silver v IMAX Corp, 2013 ONSC 1667 199
Simonin v Mallac (1860), 2 Sw & Tr 67, 164 ER 917 456
Sims v Bower (1993), 138 NBR (2d) 302, 108 DLR (4th) 677,
  [1993] NBJ No 576 (CA) 178
Sincies Chiementin SpA (Trustee of) v King, 2012 ONCA 653 177
Sinclair v Cracker Barrel Old Country Store Inc (2002), 60 OR (3d) 76,
  213 DLR (4th) 643, [2002] OJ No 2127 (CA) 73
Singer Sewing Machine Co of Canada Ltd, Re (2000), 259 AR 364,
  [2000] 5 WWR 598, [2000] AJ No 212 (QB) 176
Singh v Canada (Minister of Citizenship and Immigration),
  [2014] IADD No 131 483
Sirdar Gurdyal Singh v Rajah of Faridkote, [1894] AC 670 (PC) 170
Siskina, The, [1977] 3 All ER 803 (HL) 92
Skyway Canada Ltd v Clara Industrial Services Ltd (2005),
  47 CLR (3d) 311, [2005] OJ No 4887 (SCJ) 129
Slavenova v Ranguelov, 2015 BCSC 79 504
Slegers v Sullivan (2009), 84 CPC (6th) 156, 2009 CanLII 66376 (Ont SCJ) ... 252
Small v Zacher (1975), 8 OR (2d) 372, [1975] OJ No 2295 (HCJ) 499
Smallman v Smallman Estate (1991), 35 CCEL 146, 41 ETR 86,
  [1991] OJ No 1718 (Gen Div) 11
Smith, Lawrence v Kitson, Re, [1916] 2 Ch 206 345
Sociedade-de-fomento Industrial Private Ltd v Pakistan Steel Mills Corp
  (Private) Ltd, 2014 BCCA 205 209
Société Nationale Industrielle Aérospatiale v Lee Kui Jak, [1987]
  AC 871 (PC) 147–48, 150–51, 160, 430
Society of Lloyd's v Meinzer (2001), 55 OR (3d) 688,
  210 DLR (4th) 519, [2001] OJ No 3403 (CA) 30–31, 191
Soleh Boneh International Ltd v Government of the Republic of
  Uganda, [1993] 2 Lloyd's LR 208 (CA) 212
Solehdin v Stern Estate, 2014 BCCA 482 202
Soleimany v Soleimany (1998), [1999] QB 785, [1998] EWCA Civ 285 210
Solnik v Solnik (1983), 41 OR (2d) 427, [1983] OJ No 2998 (UFC),
  aff'd (1983), 44 OR (2d) 684, [1983] OJ No 3284 (CA) 471

Solomon v Walters (1956), 3 DLR (2d) 78, 18 WWR 257, [1956]
  BCJ No 133 (SC) 405, 453
Somers v Fournier (2002), 60 OR (3d) 225, 214 DLR (4th) 611,
  [2002] OJ No 2543 (CA) 239–40, 271
Somji v Somji (2001), 292 AR 337, 21 RFL (5th) 223, 2001 ABQB 665 138
Sorochan v Sorochan, [1986] 2 SCR 38, 29 DLR (4th) 1,
  [1986] SCJ No 46 311
Sottomayor v De Barros (No 2) (1879), 5 PD 94 414
South Pacific Import, Inc v Ho, 2009 BCCA 163 .... 179, 195
Spar Aerospace Ltd v American Mobile Satellite Corp, [2002]
  4 SCR 205, 220 DLR (4th) 54, 2002 SCC 78 .... 72–73, 81, 117
Speers Estate v Reader's Digest Association (Canada) ULC (2009),
  73 CPC (6th) 281, 2009 CanLII 28404, [2009] OJ No 2332 (SCJ) 158
Spencer v The Queen, [1985] 2 SCR 278, 21 DLR (4th) 756,
  [1985] SCJ No 60 42
Spiliada Maritime Corp v Cansulex Ltd (1986), [1987] AC 460,
  [1986] 3 WLR 972, 3 All ER 843
  (HL) 59, 115–16, 123, 126–27, 135, 139, 430
Spini v Spini (1994), 157 NBR (2d) 1, [1994] NBJ No 567 (QB) 474
St Pierre v South American Stores Ltd, [1936] 1 KB 382 (CA) 115
Stanton v Gudbranson (1999), 45 RFL (4th) 85, [1999] BCJ No 896 (SC) 188
Stanway v Wyeth Pharmaceuticals Inc, [2009] BCJ No 2538,
  2009 BCCA 592 78
Star Reefers Pool Inc v JFC Group Co Ltd, [2012] EWCA Civ 14 .... 147, 158
Star Shipping AS v China National Foreign Trade
  Transportation Corp, [1993] 2 Lloyd's Rep 445 (CA) 290–91
Starkowski v Attorney-General, [1954] AC 155 (HL) 231, 417–18
State Bank of India v Navaratna, [2006] OTC 285, [2006]
  OJ No 1125 (SCJ) 190
State of Norway's Application (Nos 1 & 2), Re, [1990] 1 AC 723 (HL) 33
Steele v Steele (1963), 43 DLR (2d) 57, 1 RFL (Rep) 429
  (NS Div & Mat Causes Ct) 457
Stefanou v Stefanou (2009), 306 DLR (4th) 526, 62 RFL (6th) 315,
  [2009] OJ No 852 (CA), rev'g (2008), 50 RFL (6th) 345,
  [2008] OJ No 531 (SCJ) 491
Stefanou v Stefanou, 2012 ONSC 7265 489
Stephen v Stephen (1961), 51 MPR 65 (NBCA) 13
Stephens v Falchi, [1938] SCR 354, [1938] 3 DLR 590, [1938] SCJ No 15 220
Stevens v Head (1993), 176 CLR 433 (HCA) 239
Stevenson Estate v Siewert, 2001 ABCA 180 48
Stewart v Stewart (1997), 30 BCLR (3d) 233, 7 CPC (4th) 221,
  [1997] BCJ No 636 (CA) 242
Stichting Shell Pensioenfonds v Krys, [2014] UKPC 41 148
Stolp & Co v WB Browne & Co, [1930] 4 DLR 703 (Ont HCJ) 212
Stott v Merit Investment Corp (1988), 63 OR (2d) 545,
  48 DLR (4th) 288, [1988] OJ No 134 (CA) 49

Stringam v Dubois (1992), 135 AR 64, 48 ETR 248, [1992]
AJ No 1075 (CA) 38, 387–88
Stuart Budd & Sons Ltd v IFS Vehicle Distributors ULC,
2014 ONCA 546 67
Stuart v Stuart (1983), 34 RFL (2d) 104, [1983] OJ No 363 (HCJ) 454
Stubbs v ATS International BV, 2010 ONCA 879 130
Sturkenboom v Davies (1993), 142 AR 144, 11 Alta LR (3d) 147,
[1993] AJ No 516 (QB) 467
Stylianou v Toyoshima, [2013] EWHC 2188 (QB) 276
Subway Franchise Systems of Canada Ltd v Laich, 2011 SKQB 249 213
Sullivan v Four Seasons Hotels Ltd (cob Four Seasons Hotels &
Resorts), 2013 ONSC 4622 93
Sun v Guilfoile, 2011 ONSC 1685 491
Sutcliffe v Sotvedt, 2015 NSSC 194 188
Swaizie v Swaizie (1899), 31 OR 324, [1899] OJ No 110 (Div Ct) 499
Szabo v Szabo (1980), 15 RFL (2d) 13, [1980] OJ No 1700 (UFC) 433, 435
Szalas v Szabo (1995), 16 RFL (4th) 168, [1995] OJ No 1918
(Prov Div) 476
Szalatnay-Stacho v Fink (1946), [1947] 1 KB 1, [1946] 2 All ER 231,
62 TLR 573 (CA) 90, 280
Szechter v Szechter, [1971] 2 WLR 170 (PDA) 414
Szostek v Szostek, 2011 ONCJ 663 498

T(TN) v T(J) (2001), 288 AR 362, [2001] AJ No 559 (QB) 478
Taczanowska v Taczanowski, [1957] P 301 (CA) 403, 406
Tadros v Barratt, [2014] EWHC 2860 (Ch) 147
Tamminga v Tamminga, 2014 ONCA 478 91
Taylor v Farrugia, 2009 NSWSC 801 387
TDI Hospitality Management Consultants Inc v Browne, [1994]
9 WWR 153, 28 CPC (3d) 232, [1994] MJ No 448 (CA) 204
Teck Cominco Metals Ltd v Lloyd's Underwriters, [2009] 1 SCR 321,
303 DLR (4th) 385, 2009 SCC 11, aff'g (2007),
279 DLR (4th) 257, 67 BCLR (4th) 101,
2007 BCCA 249 .... 119, 124, 130, 133–34
Texaco Melbourne, The, [1994] 1 Lloyd's Law Rep 473 (HL) 46
Tezcan v Tezcan (1987), 20 BCLR (2d) 253, 24 CPC (2d) 13,
[1987] BCJ No 2450 (CA) 330
Tezcan v Tezcan (1992), 62 BCLR (2d) 344, 38 RFL (3d) 142,
1992 CanLII 1075 (CA) 504–5
Theriault v Theriault, 2014 SKQB 373 503
Thom Estate, Re (1987), 40 DLR (4th) 184, 50 Man R (2d) 187,
[1987] MJ No 665 (QB) 373–74
Thomson v Minister of National Revenue, [1946] SCR 209,
[1946] 1 DLR 689, [1946] SCJ No 5 .... 22–24, 426
Thomson v Thomson, [1994] 3 SCR 551, 119 DLR (4th) 253,
[1994] SCJ No 6 .... 472, 474, 477–79

Thorne v Dryden-Hall (1997), 35 BCLR (3d) 174, 28 RFL (4th) 297,
[1997] BCJ No 1243 (CA), aff'g [1995] BCJ No 2009 (SC) and
(1995), 18 RFL (4th) 15 (SC) 474, 478
Thurber v Thurber (2002), 322 AR 242, [2002] AJ No 992, 2002 ABQB 727 427
TIL v JLF (2001), 197 DLR (4th) 721, 153 Man R (2d) 241, 2001 MBCA 22 481
Timberwest Forest Ltd v Gearbulk Pool Ltd, 2001 BCSC 882,
aff'd 2003 BCCA 39 296
Tipperary Developments Pty Ltd v The State of Western Australia,
[2009] WASCA 126 237
Tolofson v Jensen, [1994] 3 SCR 1022, 120 DLR (4th) 289,
[1994] SCJ No 110 .... 120, 241–44, 250, 265–72, 279, 281–83, 364
Tomkinson v First Pennsylvania Banking and Trust Co, [1961]
AC 1007 (HL) 286
Tower v Tower (2008), 52 RFL (6th) 455, [2008] OJ No 1668 (SCJ) 427
Tracy v The Iranian Ministry of Information and Security,
2016 ONSC 3759 .... 194, 202
Trade Fortune Inc v Amalgamated Mill Supplies Ltd (1994),
89 BCLR (2d) 132, 24 CPC (3d) 362, [1994] BCJ No 427 (SC) 213
Transat Tours Canada Inc v Tescor, SA de CV, 2007 SCC 20 92
Travers v Holley, [1953] P 246 (CA) 436, 459
Trendtex Trading Corp v Credit Suisse, [1980] QB 629 (CA),
aff'd [1982] AC 679 (HL) 353
Trepca Mines Ltd, Re, [1960] 3 All ER 304 (CA) 168
Triathlon Leasing Inc v Juniberry Corp (1995), 157 NBR (2d) 217,
[1995] NBJ No 36 (CA) 258
Trillium Motor World Ltd v General Motors of Canada Ltd, 2013 ONSC 2289,
aff'd 2014 ONCA 497, aff'd (sub nom Lapointe Rosenstein Marchand
Melançon LLP v Cassels Brock & Blackwell LLP) 2016 SCC 30 .... 85, 91
Trillium Motor World Ltd v General Motors of Canada Ltd,
2015 ONSC 3824 226
Trotter v Trotter (1992), 90 DLR (4th) 554, 40 RFL (3d) 68,
[1992] OJ No 733 (Gen Div) 489
Trottier v Rajotte (1939), [1940] SCR 203, [1940] 1 DLR 433,
[1939] SCJ No 41 .... 12, 15
Tse and Minister of Employment and Immigration, Re, [1983]
2 FC 308, 144 DLR (3d) 155, [1983] FCJ No 51 (CA) 421
Tucows.com Co v Lojas Renner SA, 2011 ONCA 548 83
Turner v Bell Mobility Inc, 2014 ABQB 36 82
Tyoga Investments Ltd v Service Alimentaire Desco Inc,
2015 ONSC 3810, aff'd 2016 ONCA 15 84

Udny v Udny (1869), LR 1 Sc & Div 441 (HL) 10–12, 17
Uniforêt Pâte Port-Cartier Inc v Zerotech Technologies Inc, [1998]
9 WWR 688, 50 BCLR (3d) 359, [1998] BCJ No 192 (SC) 180
UniNet Technologies Ltd v Communication Services Inc (2005),
38 BCLR (4th) 366, 9 CPC (6th) 337, 2005 BCCA 114 .... 76, 102

United Nurses of Alberta v Alberta (Attorney General), [1992]
    1 SCR 901, 89 DLR (4th) 609, [1992] SCJ No 37.................................184–85
United Railways of the Havana and Regla Warehouses Ltd, Re,
    [1961] AC 1007 (HL) 46–48
United States of America v Harden, [1963] SCR 366, 41 DLR (2d) 721,
    [1963] SCJ No 38 37
United States of America v Inkley, [1989] QB 255... 35
United States of America v Ivey (1995), 26 OR (3d) 533,
    130 DLR (4th) 674, [1995] OJ No 3579 (Gen Div), aff'd
    (1996), 30 OR (3d) 370, 139 DLR (4th) 570, [1996]
    OJ No 3360 (CA) 34–35, 40, 175, 179–80, 189
United States of America v Levy (1999), 45 OR (3d) 129,
    [1999] OJ No 1204 (Gen Div)...40
United States of America v Levy (2002), 1 CPC (6th) 386,
    [2002] OJ No 2298 (SCJ), aff'd [2003] OJ No 56 (CA)..............................191
United States of America v Mgbolu, 2015 ONSC 1273................................... 256
United States of America v Yemec (2009), 97 OR (3d) 409, [2009]
    OJ No 3546 (SCJ) rev'd 2010 ONCA 414...................................... 35, 183, 188
United States Securities and Exchange Commission v
    Manterfield, [2009] EWCA Civ 27.. 36
United States v Friedland (1996), 13 CPC (4th) 296 (BCSC).............................92
United States v Monsanto Co, 858 F2d 160 (4th Cir 1988)............................... 35
University of Calgary v Colorado School of Mines (1995),
    179 AR 81, 43 CPC (3d) 189, [1995] AJ No 1026 (QB).............................247
Upper Ottawa Improvement Co v Hydro-Electric Power Commission of
    Ontario, [1961] SCR 486, 28 DLR (2d) 276, [1961] SCJ No 26 255
Urquhart Estate, Re (1990), 74 OR (2d) 42, 50 CCLI 304, [1990]
    OJ No 1203 (HCJ), aff'd (1991), 3 OR (3d) 699, 6 CCLI (2d) 167,
    [1991] OJ No 1027 (Div Ct) 13
Ust-Kamenogorsk Hydropower Plant JSC v AES Ust-Kamenogorsk
    Hydropower Plant LLP, [2013] UKSC 35... 160

V(LR) v V(AA) (2006), 52 BCLR (4th) 112, 43 RFL (6th) 59,
    2006 BCCA 63 ....465, 489–90
Vak Estate, Re (1994), 20 OR (3d) 378, 117 DLR (4th) 122, [1994]
    OJ No 1704 (Gen Div) 374
Van Breda v Village Resorts Ltd, [2010] OJ No 402,
    2010 ONCA 84... 110
Van Damme v Gelber, 2012 ONSC 6277, aff'd 2013 ONCA 388......... 167, 171, 184
Van de Perre v Edwards (2004), 26 BCLR (4th) 380, 19 RFL (6th) 442,
    2004 BCSC 537.. 496
Vanston v Scott, 2014 SKQB 64 12
Vargo v Saskatchewan (Family Justice Services Branch) (2006),
    280 Sask R 28, [2006] SJ No 350, 2006 SKQB 253 499
Veritas Investment Research Corp v Indiabulls Real Estate Ltd,
    2015 ONSC 6040 154

Vervaeke v Smith, [1983] 1 AC 145 (HL) 195, 462
Vien Estate v Vien Estate (1988), 64 OR (2d) 230, 49 DLR (4th) 558,
    1988 CanLII 4690 (CA) 508
Viroforce Systems Inc v R&D Capital Inc, 2011 BCCA 260 129
Vishva Ajay, The, [1989] 2 Lloyd's Rep 558... 136
Vita Food Products Inc v Unus Shipping Co, [1939] AC 277,
    [1939] 2 DLR 1, [1939] 1 WWR 433 (PC)..................................... 287–89, 302
Vitapharm Canada Ltd v F Hoffmann-La Roche Ltd, [2002] OTC 57,
    20 CPC (5th) 351, [2002] OJ No 298 (SCJ), appeal quashed (2002),
    163 OAC 189, 23 CPC (5th) 230, [2002] OJ No 2010 (CA) 104–5
Vladi v Vladi (1987), 79 NSR (2d) 356, 39 DLR (4th) 563,
    [1987] NSJ No 204 (SC)... 230, 506
Vogler v Szendroi (2007), 255 NSR (2d) 190, 42 CPC (6th) 222,
    2007 NSSC 154, rev'd (2008), 263 NSR (2d) 172,
    50 CPC (6th) 264, [2008] NSJ No 71 (CA) 237, 244
Volkswagen Canada Inc v Auto Haus Frohlich Ltd (1985), 65 AR 271,
    41 Alta LR (2d) 5, [1985] AJ No 719 (CA)... 70
Voth v Manildra Flour Mills Pty Ltd (1990), 171 CLR 538 (HCA)................... 118
VTB Capital Plc v Nutritek International Corp, [2013] UKSC 5 .... 101, 116, 126
VW v DS, [1996] 2 SCR 108, 134 DLR (4th) 481,
    [1996] SCJ No 53 .... 472, 474, 479

Waggoner v Waggoner (1956), 20 WWR 74, [1956] AJ No 22 (SC) 13
Walker v Walker, [1950] 4 DLR 253, [1950] 2 WWR 411 (BCCA).................... 435
Wang v Lin, 2013 ONCA 33 ....95, 427, 467, 491
War Eagle Mining Co v Robo Management Co (1995), 13 BCLR (3d) 362,
    44 CPC (3d) 118, [1995] BCJ No 2142 (SC) 331
Ward v Canada (Attorney General) (2007), 220 Man R (2d) 224,
    46 CPC (6th) 67, 2007 MBCA 123 .... 61–62, 103
Ward v Coffin (1972), 4 NBR (2d) 481, 27 DLR (3d) 58, [1972]
    NBJ No 67 (SCAD)...336–37, 345
Ward v Ward (1985), 66 NBR (2d) 44, [1985] NBJ No 296 (QB).............. 454, 456
Waszczyn v Waszczyn (2007), 45 RFL (6th) 441, [2007]
    OJ No 4307, 2007 ONCJ 512 498
Webster v Webster (1997), 32 OR (3d) 679, 28 OTC 81, [1997]
    OJ No 1422 (Gen Div).. 337
Webster v Webster Estate (2006), 28 RFL (6th) 79, 25 ETR (3d) 141,
    2006 CanLII 22941 (Ont SCJ) 508
Webster-Tweel v Royal Trust Corp of Canada, 2010 ABQB 139 398–99
Weir v Lohr (1967), 65 DLR (2d) 717, 62 WWR 99, [1967]
    MJ No 61 (QB) 39, 179
Weiss Estate v State Life Insurance Co, [1935] SCR 461, [1935]
    4 DLR 5, [1935] SCJ No 17... 50
Wende v Victoria (Country) Official Administrator (1998),
    48 BCLR (3d) 219, 37 RFL (4th) 172, [1998]
    BCJ No 570 (SC) 484

Wescott v Alsco Products of Canada Ltd (1960), 26 DLR (2d) 281,
   45 MPR 394, [1960] NJ No 3 (CA) 70
West Van Inc v Daisley, 2014 ONCA 232 111
Westacre Investments Ltd v Jugoimport-SPDR Holding Co Ltd,
   [2000] QB 288 (CA) 210
Westec Aerospace Inc v Raytheon Aircraft Co (1999),
   67 BCLR (3d) 278, 34 CPC (4th) 1, 1999 BCCA 243 .... 132–33, 136
Wheeler v 1000128 Alberta Ltd (2008), 431 AR 209,
   87 Alta LR (4th) 138, 2008 ABQB 70, aff'd (sub nom
   Wheeler v China Natural Petroleum Corp) (2008),
   433 AR 234, 92 Alta LR (4th) 19, 2008 ABCA 228 76
Whiten v Pilot Insurance Co, [2002] 1 SCR 595, 209 DLR (4th) 257,
   2002 SCC 18 192
Whitworth Street Estates (Manchester) Ltd v James Miller &
   Partners Ltd, [1970] AC 583 (HL) 293
Wilkison, Re (1933), [1934] OR 6, [1934] 1 DLR 544, [1933]
   OJ No 391 (HCJ) 380–81
Wilks, Re, [1935] 1 Ch 645 365
Williams v Canada, [1992] 1 SCR 877, 90 DLR (4th) 129,
   [1992] SCJ No 36 354
Williams v Hillier (1981), 33 AR 613, 17 Alta LR (2d) 139, [1981]
   AJ No 478 (CA) 466, 484
Williams v Jones (1845), 13 M & W 628 164
Wilmot v Shaw (1881), 14 NSR 343 (CA) 285
Wilson v Huntley, [2005] OTC 311, 13 RFL (6th) 435, [2005]
   OJ No 1664 (SCJ) 473
Wilson v Riu, 2012 ONSC 6840 .... 94, 98
Wilson v Servier Canada Inc (2000), 50 OR (3d) 219, 49 CPC
   (4th) 233, [2000] OJ No 3392 (SCJ) 106–8, 198
Wilton v Wilton, [1946] OR 117, [1946] 2 DLR 397, [1946] OJ No 576 (HCJ) 13
Wincal Properties Ltd v Cal-Alta Holdings Ltd (1983),
   43 AR 223, [1983] 3 WWR 57, [1983] AJ No 559 (QB) 337
Winkworth v Christie, Manson and Woods Ltd, [1980] Ch 496,
   [1980] 1 All ER 1121 351–53
Winmill v Winmill, [1974] 1 FC 686, 47 DLR (3d) 597, [1974]
   FCJ No 86 (CA) 427
Winrow v Hemphill, [2014] EWHC 3164 (QB) 276
Winvan Paving Ltd v Gencor Industries Inc, 2015 BCSC 233 129
Wlodarczyk v Spriggs (2000), 200 Sask R 129, 12 RFL (5th) 241,
   2000 SKQB 468 .... 437–38, 489
Wolch v Wolch (1980), 19 RFL (2d) 307, [1980] MJ No 275 (QB),
   var'd (1981), 20 RFL (2d) 325, [1981] MJ No 87 (CA) 502
Wong v Lee (2002), 58 OR (3d) 398, 211 DLR (4th) 69, [2002]
   OJ No 885 (CA) 270
Wong v Wei, [1999] 10 WWR 296, 65 BCLR (3d) 222, [1999]
   BCJ No 768 (SC) 238

Woolcock v Bushert (2004), 246 DLR (4th) 139, 3 CPC (6th) 25,
[2004] OJ No 4498 (CA) 131
Wrixon v Wrixon (1982), 42 AR 198, [1982] 6 WWR 476, [1982]
AJ No 933 (QB) 428
Wu v Ng, 2014 ONSC 7126... 338
Wubben v Lang-Ernst, [2000] BCJ No 2662, 2000 BCSC 1546 478

Yassin v Loubani (2006), 232 BCAC 203, 69 BCLR (4th) 36,
2006 BCCA 509 467
Yew Bon Tew v Kanderaan Bas Mara, [1983] 1 AC 553 (PC).............................241
Yordanes v Bank of Nova Scotia (2006), 78 OR (3d) 590,
23 CPC (6th) 7, [2006] OJ No 280 (SCJ)... 252
Young v Hubbert (1987), [1988] 1 FC 354, 8 RFL (3d) 453,
[1987] FCJ No 602 (TD) 468, 498
Young v Tyco International of Canada Ltd (2008), 92 OR (3d) 161,
300 DLR (4th) 385, 2008 ONCA 709 118
Young v Young (1959), 67 Man R 108, 21 DLR (2d) 616, [1959]
MJ No 65 (CA)... 15
Young v Young, [1993] 4 SCR 3, 108 DLR (4th) 193, [1993] SCJ No 112 464
Yugraneft Corp v Rexx Management Corp, 2010 SCC 19 214–15

Zehring v Zehring (1965), 55 DLR (2d) 283, 55 WWR 90
(Man QB) 11
Zhang v Lin, 2010 ABQB 420 .... 32, 443, 446
ZI Pompey Industrie v ECU-Line NV, [2003] 1 SCR 450,
224 DLR (4th) 577, 2003 SCC 27 .... 70, 127–28, 130, 159–60
Ziemianczyk v Ziemianczyk, [2008] OJ No 1479,
2008 ONCJ 172..498–99
Zilberman Estate v Davis (1980), 4 Man R (2d) 336, 6 ETR 187,
[1980] MJ No 54 (Surr Ct), aff'd (1980) 4 Man R (2d) 325,
7 ETR 207, [1980] MJ No 53 (CA)... 380
Zimmerhansl v Zimmerhansl (2001), 289 AR 165, 20 RFL (5th) 218,
2001 ABQB 589 477
Zivnostenska Banka National Corp v Frankman, [1950] AC 57 (HL)...............301

INDEX

Actions *in personam*, 53–56, 58–59, 66, 71, 146, 149, 186, 331, 335–44, 437, 461–62, 503
Actions *in rem*, 54, 342, 343, 458
Administration of estates
    choice of law, 361–66
    distinguished from succession, 359, 365–66
    jurisdiction, 360–61
    personal representatives, 360–61, 366–68
        actions by and against, 366–68
    resealing of grants, 361, 366
Administration of trusts, 382, 394, 398–99
Adoption
    choice of law, 481
    intercountry, 481
        Hague Convention, 481–83
    jurisdiction, 480–81
    recognition of orders, 483–85
Animus manendi, 13–15
Animus non revertendi, 16–17
Anti-suit injunctions
    arbitration clauses, and, 158–61
    comity, and, 156–57, 159
    English law, 147–48
    interaction with *forum non conveniens*, 145, 147, 148–54
    interprovincial, 157–58
    jurisdiction, 149, 155–57
    jurisdiction clauses, and, 158–61
    test for granting, 152–58
Arbitration. *See also* Recognition and enforcement
    anti-suit injunctions, and, 158–61
    stay of proceedings, 141–43
Assignment, 353–54, 356–57

Blocking statutes, 41–42
Bona vacantia, 388
Brussels Regulation, 119

Capacity
    contract, 297–98
    marriage, 406–16
    marriage contract, 508
    succession, 379–80
Characterization
    causes of action, of, 223–24
    enlightened *lex fori*, 227
    general approach, 222–23
    immovable property, 227
    issues, of, 223–25
    legal rules, of, 225
    limitation periods, 241–44
    movable property, 227

parties, 245–47
pleadings, and, 223
procedure, as, 225, 236–37
remedies, 237–41
stages of, 225–28
substance, as, 225, 236–37
unjust enrichment, 224, 306–7, 501
using *lex causae*, 227–28
using *lex fori*, 227–28

Child abduction
  Hague Convention
    interaction with provincial statutes, 479–80
    process, 474–75
    provincial implementation, 471
    refusal to order return, 475–78
    rights of access, 478–479
    rights of custody, 473–74
    scope, 472–73

Children. *See also* Adoption; Child abduction; Custody; Support
  domicile, 17–18
  legitimacy and illegitimacy, 11, 17, 381, 421

Choice of law. *See also* separate entries by subject area
  characterization, 222–28
  connecting factors, 221–22, 224, 232
  exclusion of foreign laws, 29–30
  incidental question, 230–31
  process
    alternative, 231–34
    traditional, 221–22
  rationale, 217–20
  renvoi, 229–30
  theories, 217–20
  time, 231

Civil Code of Quebec. See Quebec Civil Code

Civil unions. *See* Marriage

Class actions
  arbitration, and, 142–43
  jurisdiction
    defendants, over, 103–5
    non-resident plaintiffs, over, 105–9
  recognition and enforcement of judgments, 198–201

Comity, 29–30, 39, 42, 75, 132, 136–37, 176, 181, 218

Connecting factors. *See* Choice of law

Constitution
  blocking statues, and, 42
  choice of law, and, 244, 282–83
  custody, and, 466
  divorce, and, 425
  forum of necessity, 111
  influence of, 7
  jurisdiction, and, 55–56, 72, 79, 166
  marriage, and, 401–2
  penal law exclusion, and, 37
  recognition and enforcement, 174, 178
  support, and, 487–90

Contract
  absence of choice, 291–93
  capacity, 297–98
  characteristic performance, 303
  closest and most real connection, 286, 291–93
  connecting factors, 292–93
  construction, 294
  depeçage, 293, 302
  essential validity, 294
  express choice, 287–90
    limits on, 288–90
  formal validity, 296–97
  formation, 294–96
  frustration, 294, 311–14
  illegality, 300–2
  immovable property, and, 336–40
  implied choice, 290–91
  interaction with tort, 278–79
  interaction with unjust enrichment, 315–18
  jurisdiction, 83–86
  mandatory rules, 298–300
  place of contracting, 84–85, 285–86
  place of performance, 84, 291–93, 300–2
  policy considerations, 285
  proper law, 285–93, 295
  putative proper law, 288, 294–96, 297–98
  renvoi, 287
  Rome I Regulation, 302–3

Corporations
  capacity to sue, 245
  carrying on business, 62–66, 170, 203
  domicile of, 26–27
  law governing, 26–27, 245–47
  presence, 62–66, 170–71

registration requirements, 62–66
residence of, 26–27
Country
meaning of, 3–4
Court Jurisdiction and Proceedings Transfer Act. See Jurisdiction; Stay of proceedings
Cultural property, 35–36, 40–41, 351–53
Currency
breach-date rule, 46–47
conversion date, 50–52
judgment, of, 45–50
loss, of, 50–52
statutory provisions, 48–50
Custody. *See also* Child abduction
choice of law, 467–68
corollary relief, 465, 467
enforcement of orders, 468–69
defences, 469–70
jurisdiction, 465–67
recognition of orders, 468–69
statutory provisions, 465–67
stay of proceedings, 465–66
variation of orders, 470–71

Damages. *See also* Remedies
characterization, 239–41
public policy and, 191–95
Debts, 31, 96, 191, 232, 327, 353–54, 356–57, 366, 367, 507
Depeçage, 293, 302, 394, 398
Divorce
anti-suit injunction, 429–32
choice of law, 432
civil unions, 449–50
domicile, 435–36
jurisdiction, 425–32
ordinary residence, 425–29
polygamous marriage, 428
preclusion, 446–49
real and substantial connection, 436–38
recognition of foreign decree
common law, at, 434–38
defences, 442–46
extra-judicial, 438–42
statutory provisions, 433–34
same-sex marriage, 428–29
statutory provisions, 425, 429, 433–34
stay of proceedings, 429–30

Domicile
abandonment or loss of, 16–17
acquisition of, 13–14
change of, 11, 15, 380, 421
choice, of
illegality, 15
intention, 13–15
residence, 15–16
choice of law, 20
compulsion, 13
corporations, 26–27
criticisms, 12, 17, 20
dependency, of, 17–19
divorce, 435–36
marriage, 11
married women, 18–19
mentally incapable persons, 19
minors, 17–18
nullity, 454–55, 458–59
origin, of, 10–13
revival of, 12, 16
statutory reforms, 11, 17–18

Enforcement. *See* Recognition and enforcement
Estates. *See* Succession
Evidence. *See* Proof of foreign law
Exchange rates, 45–46
Exclusion of foreign law. *See also* Other public law; Penal law; Public policy; Revenue law
effect of, 29–30
Extraterritoriality, 34, 42, 55, 163, 186, 244, 266, 388

Family law. *See* separate entries by subject area
Foreign arbitral awards. *See* Recognition and enforcement
Foreign judgments. *See* Recognition and enforcement
Foreign law. *See* Pleading of foreign law; Proof of foreign law
Formal validity
contract, 296–97
marriage, 402–6
succession, 375–77
Forum of necessity. *See* Jurisdiction
Forum non conveniens
appropriate remedy for, 121

criticisms of, 118–19
factors considered
   applicable law, 126
   expertise, 126–27
   juridical advantages, 135–37
   jurisdiction clauses, 127–32
   parallel proceedings, 118, 132–35
   physical connections, 125–26
framework for analysis, 124–25
history of, 115–16
onus of proof, 121–22
rationale for, 117–19
relation to taking jurisdiction, 56–58, 119–21
role of conditions and undertakings, 138–39
statutory provisions, 116, 119, 122–24, 129–30
Forum selection. *See* Jurisdiction clauses
Forum shopping
  currency of awards, and, 47, 50
  renvoi, and, 229–30
  substance-procedure distinction, and, 236, 238
Fraud
  defence to recognition and enforcement, 188–89, 204, 442–44, 462

Governmental interests. *See* Interest analysis
Grants
  representation, of, 360–61
  resealing, 361, 366

Habitual residence, 25–26

Illegitimacy. *See* Legitimacy
Immovable property
  characterization, 228, 324–27
  choice of law, 344–45
  contracts, and, 336–40
  jurisdiction, 82–83, 330–40
  lex situs, 344–45
  location of, 327
  matrimonial property, 503–6
  recognition and enforcement of judgments, 340–44
  renvoi, 344
  succession to, 359, 372, 374, 375, 377, 380

torts, and, 332–36
Incapacity. *See* Capacity
Incidental question, 230–31, 411
Injunctions. *See also* Anti-suit injunctions
  jurisdiction, 91–92
  recognition and enforcement, 167, 181–84
Interest analysis, 232–34, 264, 283, 323
Intestate succession
  choice of law, 372–74
  immovable property, 372–74
  movable property, 372–74
  preferential share, 372–74

Judicial notice, 251, 254–55, 497
Jurisdiction. *See also* Presumptive connecting factors; Real and substantial connection
  administration of estates, 83
  assumed, 54–55, 71–80
  class actions, 103–9
  consent. *See* Submission
  constitutional issues, 55–56
  contracts, 83–86
  concurrent claims, 99–101
  custody, 465–67
  damage in the forum, 61–62, 74–75, 76, 82
  defamation, 89–90, 91, 186
  divorce, 425–32
  enforcement of judgments, 92, 165–66
  forum of necessity, 109–11
  immovable property, 82–83, 330–36
    exceptions to general rule, 336–40
  injunctions, 91–92
  interaction with *forum non conveniens*, 56–58, 119–21
  marriage, 401–2
  matrimonial property division, 502–4
  movable property, 82–83
  necessary or proper party, 82
  nullity, 453–57
  presence
    corporations, 62–66
    individuals, 59–62
    partnerships, 66
    separate from assumed jurisdiction, 60–62
    transitory, 59, 61, 62
  service *ex juris*

Index 553

Hague Convention, 102–3
  leave requirements, 54, 69
  process and manner of, 101–3
  statutory provisions, 58–59, 62, 65–66,
    82–86, 92–94, 96, 99, 109–11
  subject matter, 4, 53, 58–59, 70,
    130–31, 332
  submission, 66–71
    challenges to jurisdiction, and,
      66–70, 101
    contract, by, 69
    separate from assumed jurisdiction, 70–71
  succession, 369–70
  support, 487–96
  torts, 86–91
  trusts, 83
  unjust enrichment, 86
Jurisdiction clauses, 69–70
  anti-suit injunctions, and, 158–61
  relationship to *forum non conveniens*,
    127–32
  scope, 131–32
  stay of proceedings, and, 127–32
Justice
  choice of law theory, 220

Land. *See* Immovable property
Legitimacy
  domicile, and, 11, 17–18
  succession, and, 381, 421
Limitation periods
  characterization, 241–44
  enforcement, and, 196–97, 214–15
  statutory provisions, 243–44
Lis alibi pendens. See Parallel proceedings
Local law theory, 219

Maintenance. *See* Support
Mandatory rules, 298–300
Marriage
  capacity, 406–16
  choice of law, 402–23
  civil unions, 422–23
  consanguinity and affinity, 408–9
  constitutional issues, 401–2
  consummation, 418–19
  domicile, 407–8, 410–13, 419–22
  effect of prior, 410–13
  essential validity, 406–8

formal validity, 402–6
intended matrimonial home, 407–8, 453
minors, 409–10
parental consent, 404–6
place of celebration, 406, 414–15
polygamous, 419–22, 428
proxy, 404
public policy, 416
remarriage, 410–13
renvoi, 403, 412
same-sex, 414, 415, 428–29
statutory provisions, 408–9, 414,
  420–22
subsequent validation, 416–18
Marriage contracts. *See* Matrimonial
  property
Married women
  domicile, 18–19
Matrimonial causes. *See* Divorce; Nullity
Matrimonial property
  choice of law
    common law rules, 504–6
    marriage contracts, for, 507–9
    statutory rules, 506–7
  jurisdiction to divide, 502–4
  recognition and enforcement of foreign orders, 509
Mentally incapable persons
  domicile, 19
Methods of choice of law, 221–22, 231–34
Minors. *See* Children
Model Law on International Commercial
  Arbitration, 142–43, 210–13, 214
Money. *See* Currency
Mortgages, 83, 227–28, 326–27, 337, 345
Movable property. *See also* Debts, Securities
  assignment, 353–54, 356–57
  contracts, and, 347–48
  cultural, 35–36, 40–41, 351–53
  debts, 327–28
  defined, 347–48
  exceptions to *lex situs*, 351–52
  intangible, 353–56
  jurisdiction, 82–83
  lex situs, 348–50
  location of, 353–56
  matrimonial, 503–6
  negotiable instruments, 328, 354–55
  priorities, 350–51, 356–57

renvoi, 352–53
retention of title clauses, 349–51
succession to, 228, 325, 359, 371–72, 374, 375, 377, 379–80
tangible, 367–68

Natural justice
defence to recognition and enforcement, 189–91, 442–43
Negative declaration, 132–33, 195–96
Negotiable instruments, 328, 354–55, 366–67
New York Convention, 208–10, 214
Nullity
choice of law, 457
jurisdiction
domicile, 454–55
place of celebration, 456–57
residence, 455–56
recognition of decree
defences, 462–63
domicile, 458–59
real and substantial connection, 461
reciprocity, 459
void and voidable marriages, 451–53

Ordinary residence
defined, 23–25
divorce, and, 425–28, 488–89
Other public law
meaning of, 39–41
Ownership
immovable property, of, 330–32
movable property, of, 348–52
renvoi, 352–53

Parallel proceedings, 118–19, 133–34, 149, 195, 429–32, 465
Parties
autonomy of, 131, 159–60, 276, 285–86, 296, 302, 394
characterization, 245
expectations of, 49, 131, 233, 285–86, 290, 292, 314, 316
necessary or proper, 82, 104
Patents, 327, 332
Penal law
meaning of, 33–37
non-enforcement of judgment, 34–37, 179–80, 185

Personal law, 9–12, 20, 26, 314, 319, 372–74, 504
Personal property. *See* Movable property
Personal representative, 359, 361–62, 366–68, 369
Pleading of foreign law, 252
Polygamous marriage. *See* Marriage
Presence
jurisdiction, 54, 59–66
Presumption of similarity. *See* Proof of foreign law
Presumptive connecting factors
carrying on business, 93–94
claims on foreign judgments, 92–93, 165–66
class actions, 109, 200
contract claims, 83–86
creation of new factors, 79, 81
domicile, 93–94
family law, 94–95, 491, 502
generally, 80–81
injunctions, 91–92
other factors, 96
property claims, 82–83
rebuttal of, 96–99
rejected factors, 82
residence, 93–94
tort claims, 79, 86–91
unjust enrichment claims, 86
Priorities, 350–51, 356–57, 362
Procedure. *See* Characterization; Substance-procedure distinction
Proceedings transfer, 141
Proof of foreign law
expert evidence, 251, 253, 259
failure to prove, 256–59
foreign law as fact, 251
judicial notice, 254–55
methods, 253–55
presumption of similarity, 256–58
validity of foreign law, 255–56
Proper law
contract, 221, 285–93, 295
marriage contract, 508
movable property, 351, 357
tort, 264, 267, 270, 273, 275
unjust enrichment, 307–9, 314, 319–20, 323
Property. *See* Immovable property; Movable property

Proximity, 220, 233, 263, 266, 314, 322
Public policy
　adoption, and, 484–85
　child abduction, and, 478
　contracts contrary to, 289, 299–301
　defence to recognition and enforcement, 32, 191–95, 210, 212–13, 469, 498–99
　divorce, and, 440, 443–45
　jurisdiction agreements and, 32–33
　marriage, and, 409, 416
　meaning of, 30–33
　multiple damages and, 194–95
　nullity, and, 462
　punitive damages and, 192–94
　role of public international law, 31–32
　support, and, 498–99

Quebec *Civil Code*, 72, 81, 200, 406, 422–23, 434, 449, 457, 461

Real and substantial connection
　analysis of, 59–62, 70, 72–81, 106–9
　criticisms of, 177–78
　divorce, and, 436–38, 442
　jurisdiction, 72–79
　　approach under statutory provisions, 77–78, 80–82
　　interaction with presence and submission, 60–62, 70–71, 168–69
　　interaction with service *ex juris*, 71–72, 80–85, 101
　　Muscutt approach, 73–77
　　Morguard principle, 55–56, 71–73, 168–69
　nullity, and, 461
　recognition and enforcement of judgments, 173–77
Real property. *See* Immovable property
Reciprocity, 218, 436, 459–61
Recognition and enforcement
　arbitral awards
　　common law, at 213–14
　　defences, 209–10, 212–13, 214
　　limitation periods, 214–15
　　Model Law on International Commercial Arbitration, 210–13
　　New York Convention, 208–210
　　distinction between, 163

foreign adoptions, of, 483–85
judgments
　class actions, 198–200
　contempt orders, 184–85
　custody, 468–69
　divorce decrees, 432–42
　finality requirement, 167–68
　fraud defence, 188–89
　immovable property, 340–44
　jurisdiction, 92–93, 165–66
　limitation periods, 196–97
　matrimonial property, 509
　monetary, 179–80
　natural justice defence, 189–91
　negative declarations, 195–96
　non-monetary, 181–86
　nullity decrees, 457–61
　presence, 170–71
　process, 164
　public policy defence, 191–95
　real and substantial connection, 173–77
　scope of defences, 187–88
　statutory provisions, 178–79
　submission, 171–73
　succession, 370–71
　support orders, 497–500
registration
　defences, 203–4
　process, 202–3
　scope, 201–2
　statutory provisions, 201–4
trusts, of, 395–96
Registration. *See* Recognition and enforcement
Remedies
　characterization, 237–41
Renvoi
　arguments for, 229–30
　contract, and, 287
　criticism of, 229–30
　immovable property, and, 344
　marriage, and, 403, 412
　matrimonial property, and, 506
　meaning, 229
　movable property, and, 352–53
　succession, and, 373–75, 377
　tort, and, 277–78
　trusts, and, 394
Residence

contrasted with domicile, 20–21
corporations, 26–27
custody, 465–66, 470
divorce, 425–29, 432
habitual, 25–26, 465–66, 470, 472–73
meaning of, 21–26
nullity, 455–56
ordinary, 23–25, 425–29, 467
physical presence, 23
reform, 26
role of context, 21
test for citizenship, 21–23
Res judicata, 163, 196, 199, 343–44
Restitution. *See* Unjust enrichment
Revenue law
    meaning of, 37–39
    non-enforcement of judgment, 37–39, 179–80
Rome I Regulation, 302–3
Rome II Regulation, 275–76, 307, 321–22
Rule selection, 232–34

Same-sex marriage. *See* Marriage
Securities, 224, 310, 328–29, 355–56, 365
Security interests, 224, 228, 350–51
Service *ex juris*. *See also* Jurisdiction
    grounds, 71–73, 80–96
    process and manner of, 101–3
Shares. *See* Securities
Sources of conflict of laws rules, 7
Sovereign immunity, 247
Stay of proceedings. *See also Forum non conveniens*; Jurisdiction clauses
    arbitration, and, 141–43
    custody, and, 465–66
    divorce, and, 429–32
Submission
    jurisdiction, 54, 66–71
    recognition and enforcement of judgments, 171–73
Substance-procedure distinction. *See also* Characterization
    limitation periods, 241–44
    remedies, 237–41
Succession. *See also* Administration of estates; Intestate succession
    choice of law
        capacity, 379–80
        construction, 380–82
        election, 385–86

        essential validity, 377–79
        formal validity, 375–77
        revocation, 382–84
    claims of foreign countries, 387–88
    dependents' relief legislation, 386–87
    immovable property, 359, 372, 374, 375, 377, 380
    jurisdiction, 369–70
    movable property, 359, 371–72, 374, 375, 377, 379–80
    recognition and enforcement of judgments, 370–71
    renvoi, 373–75, 377
Support
    choice of law, 496–97
    interjurisdictional
        process, 493–95
        provincial statutes, 493–96
        variation orders, 495–96
    jurisdiction
        corollary relief, 488
        federal, 487–90
        provincial, 487, 490–96
    recognition and enforcement of orders
        common law, at, 499–500
        statutory provisions, 497–99

Taxation. *See* Revenue law
Territorial sovereignty, 33–34, 37–38, 40, 162–63, 217–19, 330
Theories of choice of law, 217–20
Time
    choice of law, and, 231
Tort
    airborne torts, 271–72
    constitutional considerations, 282–83
    criticism of rule, 267
    defamation, 268, 275, 279–82
        single publication rule, 279
    double actionability, 262–63, 264–65
    exceptions to general rule, 263–64, 270–71
    exemption clauses, 279
    general rule, 266
    historical development
        Australia, 277–78
        England, 261–64, 273–76
    immovable property, and, 332–36
    interaction with contract, 278–79

international torts, 266, 270–71
interprovincial torts, 266
jurisdiction, 86–91
lex fori, 262
lex loci delicti, 261, 266–71
maritime torts, 271–72
most significant relationship, 263–64
proper law, 264, 267, 270, 273–75
renvoi, 277–78
Rome II Regulation, 275–76
scope of the rule, 267–71
Transfer of proceedings, 141
Trademarks, 327, 332
Trusts
administration of, 382, 394, 398–99
common law, at, 397–99
constructive, 390–91
Hague Convention
choice of law, 393–95
provincial implementation, 391–92
recognition, 395–96
scope, 392–93

jurisdiction, 83
mandatory rules, 395
resulting, 390
statutory provisions, 396–97

Unjust enrichment
characterization as, 224, 306–7, 501
considerations in formulating rule, 314–15
English common law, 307–11
frustrated contracts, 313–14
jurisdiction, 86
place of enrichment, 318–19
proper law, 307–9, 314, 319–20, 323
related contract, 315–18
Rome II Regulation, 321–22

Vested rights theory, 218–19, 261–62, 266, 285, 318

Wills. *See* Succession

ABOUT THE AUTHORS

Stephen GA Pitel (BA Carleton University, LLB Dalhousie University, LLM and PhD University of Cambridge) is a professor at the Faculty of Law of Western University. He has co-authored, edited, or co-edited sixteen books including *Emerging Issues in Tort Law* (2007), *Statutory Jurisdiction: An Analysis of the Court Jurisdiction and Proceedings Transfer Act* (2012), and *Tort Law: Challenging Orthodoxy* (2013). He is the general editor of *Private International Law in Common Law Canada: Cases, Text and Materials* (4th ed, 2016). His teaching and research are focused on international commercial litigation, civil procedure, torts, unjust enrichment, and legal ethics. He has published many articles on the conflict of laws and on legal ethics. He has received several teaching awards including the Ontario Confederation of University Faculty Associations Teaching Award, the Edward G Pleva Award for Excellence in Teaching, and the Bank of Nova Scotia, University of Western Ontario Alumni Association and University Students' Council Award of Excellence in Undergraduate Teaching.

Nicholas S Rafferty obtained an undergraduate and a master's degree in law from the University of Cambridge and a further master's degree from the University of Illinois. He began teaching at the University of Manitoba in 1975. He is currently an Emeritus Professor of Law at the University of Calgary, where he taught from 1977 to 2015. He is also a member of the Law Society of Alberta. His teaching and research interests included conflict of laws, contracts, and torts. He has written extensively in those and other areas. He was the general editor of *Private International Law in Common Law Canada: Cases, Text and Materials* (3d ed, 2010). He has received several awards for teaching and scholarship, including the University of Calgary President's Circle Award for Achievement in Teaching Excellence in 2000 and the Distinguished Service Award from the Law Society of Alberta and the Canadian Bar Association for distinguished service in legal scholarship in 2007.